This is a monumental work. . . . It is the greatest of its kind in our age, and stands true to the Holy Word. You have used to great advantage your specialized training in geophysics to give the best presentation of biblical chronology and the associated history of anything that I have seen. Your charts really help in tying together the divided kingdom history and many other portions of the Bible that are difficult to follow. It is particularly helpful to those of us who believe in the infallibility of the Scriptures but are not knowledgeable enough to support it as you have. I greatly admire your work.
– *Dr. Thomas G. Barnes, first president of Creation Research Society*

I'm working now on the historical books for the BE series, and your *Chronology of the Old Testament* sits at my right hand. . . . It is invaluable. I have several other chronologies, . . . but your charts are the most helpful and the supporting evidence the most sensible. . . . You amaze me with your scholarly accomplishments.
– *Dr. Warren Wiersbe, author & former pastor of Moody Church, Chicago*

Dr. Floyd Nolen Jones has faced every Old Testament chronology problem "squarely and given straightforward God-honoring biblical answers to all of them."
– *Larry Pierce, editor,* Annals of the World

The CHRONOLOGY of the OLD TESTAMENT

FLOYD NOLEN JONES, Th.D., Ph.D.

16th Edition
A Major Revision, Reformatted with Additional Appendices

Master Books
A Division of New Leaf Publishing Group

About the CD and the Charts

The CD included with this book contains the several charts that are discussed in the book. The CD is formatted for use with Adobe Acrobat software.* The CD should work automatically when you place the CD in your computer's disk drive or go to START; RUN; then type "D:autorun.exe". This book will explain each of the charts and how the dates were determined. If you would like to purchase full-size prints of the charts, please refer to the information on page 325.

* If you do not currently have Acrobat, then locate the folder labeled "Installers" on the CD. Choose the appropriate version for your computer system and double click to install. If your system is not listed, then you may download a free version of Acrobat Reader at www.Adobe.com. After you have installed the software, you will need to restart your computer.

Chronology of the Old Testament: A Return to the Basics

First Printing: 1993
Master Books Edition
First Printing: March 2005
Second Printing: October 2005
Third Printing: May 2007

ISBN 10: 0-89051-416-X
ISBN 13: 978-0-89051-416-0
Library of Congress Control Number: 2004106969

Charts typeset by Mark Handly
All Scripture is from the Authorized (KJV) Version of the Bible unless otherwise noted.

Printed in the United States of America
Please visit our website for other great titles: www.masterbooks.net

For information regarding author interviews,
please contact the publicity department at (870) 438-5288.

ACKNOWLEDGMENTS

I am gratefully indebted to Dr. Alfred Cawston (d. 3/21/91), founder of two Bible colleges in India and former dean and past president of Continental Bible College in Brussels, Belgium, as well as Jack Park, former president and teacher at Sterling Bible Institute in Kansas and now president of Jesus' Missions Society in Huntsville, Texas. These Bible scholars painstakingly reviewed every Scripture reference and decision in the preparation of the biblical time charts herewith submitted.

My thanks also to: Mark Handley who put my crude charts into AutoCAD format giving us broad computer capabilities, Paul Raybern and Barry Adkins for placing their vast computer skills at my every beckoning, Larry Pierce of Winterbourne, Ontario, Canada and Pete Moore of Houston, Texas whose insightful input and calendar expertise helped bring the work into final form, my daughter Jennifer and friend Shirley Howard for their exhausting efforts – especially on the index, Julie Gates who tirelessly assisted and proofed most of the data, words fail – the Lord himself shall bless and reward her for her kindness, competence and patience, and particularly to my wife Shirley, who for two years prior to the purchase of a drafting table put up with a dining room table constantly covered with charts and who lovingly understood my preoccupation with this project. Her proofing and insights along the way were truly a labor of love; her price is "far above rubies."

Finally, to James Ussher (1581–1656), learned Archbishop of Armagh – the highest position in the Irish Anglican Church – scholar and historian of the first rank. Entering Trinity College at 13, he prepared a detailed work on Hebrew chronology in Latin at 15 and received a master's degree when 18. At 19 he engaged in controversy the Jesuit scholar Henry Fitzsimons. Overthrowing him, none could thereafter match him in debate. An expert in Semitic languages and history, at 20 he was ordained. At 26, he earned a doctorate and became Professor of Divinity at Dublin. So great was his repute of tolerance, sincerity and amassed learning (characterized by John Selden as "miraculous") that, despite the fact he had been critical of the rebellion against Charles the First, Oliver Cromwell greatly esteemed Ussher and awarded him a magnificent state funeral in Westminster Abbey. His epitaph reads: "Among scholars he was the most saintly, among saints the most scholarly."

Over a five-year period of research and writing, Ussher integrated biblical and secular world history (about 15 percent of the text is from Scripture) into a continuous account. While so engaged, he derived 4004 BC as the year of Creation. For nearly three centuries (until the mid-1900s when the satanic three-pronged attack against the Word of God in the areas of evolution, textual criticism and Bible chronology was launched) his dates were almost universally accepted. This assault has resulted in clouding the minds of the human race against the veracity and accuracy of the Holy Writ and, subsequently, to God's claims on the lives of all mankind.

Knowing little of Bishop Ussher until midway into my own investigations, my efforts often yielded results reflecting, or nearly so, those he made in his *Annals of the World* over 300 years ago. As admiration for his dedication and skill grew, inquiry into his life soon followed. Today, Ussher is oft maligned by men not worthy of his glance whose mindset is confident that modern scientific dating methods have punctured and totally invalidated his findings. However, those who know the trade secrets and the nuances concerning the differing radiometric dating techniques, be they radiocarbon, potassium-argon, uranium-lead, etc., are neither impressed nor intimated by such pretensions. We are aware that the numerous scientifically invalid philosophical assumptions imposed upon the mathematics force the answers to balloon to enormous proportions in order to obtain sufficient time to justify the apparent feasibility of the untestable, unfalsifiable hypothesis of evolution. Moreover, the evolution hypothesis violates probability laws and numerous scientific laws in differing disciplines.

Having thoroughly perused *Annals*, it can only be concluded that those who deprecate this unrivaled piece of classical scholarship either have not so examined or lack the ability to perceive that which they have before them. Having now studied the works of over 40 other scholars in this field, this author affirms that for him, Ussher is and will remain the unrivaled "prince" of chronologists.

PREFACE

This dissertation addresses the conflict between the presuppositions and methodologies utilized by the modern school of biblical chronology whose procedure rests on the Assyrian Eponym Canon, the royal inscriptions of the Assyrians and Babylonians and the Ptolemaic Canon as being absolute and accurate as opposed to the traditional biblically oriented school which regards the Holy Scripture as the factual source against which all other material must be weighed.

The propositions advanced are: (1) There is academic justification that the chronology of the biblical record can be fully substantiated with internal formulae documentation independent of religious overtones; and (2) This internal structure has been preserved in a specific rendering of the biblical record, namely, the Hebrew Masoretic Text and the Greek *Textus Receptus* (the only current English translation being the King James Bible). In support of these propositions, standard objections, i.e., "generation gaps," "scribal errors," etc. will be met with forthright solutions and alternatives based upon the internal data, not by "emendations," "restorations," or "corrections" of the Text.

The "kings of the divided monarchy" portion of the Hebrew record, long considered the "Gordian knot" of sacred chronology, is the major focus of this endeavor. Commonly purported as the most difficult and error prone period, it is actually capable of straightforward solution by use of the aforementioned internal composition. Moreover, an improvement on a previous technique by devising a specific "triangulation" formula has been introduced, applied, and illustrated on the accompanying charts. This being done, the justified conclusion is substantiated that the dates as preserved in the King James Bible are reliable and demonstrable. Such must be seen to strongly argue that the biblical text is a factual account of the actual history of the Hebrew people, that it is both accurate and self-consistent — complete and self-sufficient.

A critical examination of the period of the disruption naturally entails an investigation of the heretofore mentioned secular material in order to properly establish synchronisms if and when they exist. It will be shown that most of the conflict reported to exist between the Hebrew Text and that of the Assyrian Annals, etc. is the result of misunderstanding, misreporting, misrepresenting, misapplication and/or the taking of unjustified liberties in the emendations and restorations by the translators of the Assyrian records. Some of the work of these scholars and their associates, referred to collectively under the title of the "Assyrian Academy" within this study, is thereby called into question by the author.

Moreover, Dr. Edwin R. Thiele, long recognized as their leading proponent in the field of biblical chronology, while claiming to have defended the reliability of the Hebrew Text, will be shown to have again and again applied these often mishandled Assyrian data in violation of the clear Hebrew history. In so doing, he created problems with and greatly undermined the integrity of the Hebrew Text. Dr. Thiele shall be refuted.

A more exacting solution to the chronology of the judges is included herein. In addition, a solution to the 483-year Daniel 9:25 prophecy based upon a modification to the previous work of Ussher which he founded largely upon the writings of the great Greek historian of the fifth century BC, Thucydides of Athens, is offered as decisive and final.

Finally, those comparing earlier editions prior to AD 2003 will occasionally find Gregorian dates that have changed by one day. This is because the calendar conversion program originally used (designed by the Harvard Center for Astrophysics which employs the ephemeris in Jean Meeus' *Astronomical Formulae for Calculators*) lacked written documentation. As the program was seemingly intuitive, calculations were merely performed and posted. However, the documented upgraded version revealed that, as some of the calculations fall between the six-hour overlap, the Hebrew dates had to be confirmed by taking the Gregorian date first generated and inputting it again to obtain the final results (also for Julian Period dates). Occurring only rarely within the text, this slight adjustment is mainly confined to Chart 4 and the Course of Abijah discussion (pp. 212, 213, 222, and 223).

INTRODUCTION

Is it important for the Christian to have a reliable text as the basis for his faith and conduct? Moreover, should not the text preserved and passed down throughout the centuries to today's generation be academically defendable? As the biblical text contains much information of a chronological and mathematical nature, a careful and thorough investigation of this data accompanied by detailed charts should serve as a decisive test as to its reliability and trustworthiness. Conversely, the failure of such a study could be seen as a falsification of the divine inspiration/preservation doctrine of the Sacred Writ, long held by the conservative wing of Christianity.

Toward that end, a standard chronology of the Old Testament has been constructed utilizing diagrams, charts and other forms of graphic representation which addresses this complex subject in a scriptural and scholarly yet easy to understand manner. Beginning with the Creation recorded in the first two chapters of Genesis, the continuous unbroken line of dated events embedded within the Holy Scriptures is logically followed as it spans across 40 centuries to the Crucifixion and Resurrection of the Lord Jesus Christ. It will be demonstrated that every chronological statement contained in the Sacred Writ is consistent with all other chronological statements contained therein.

Moreover, if the text, composed as it is by many human authors over a span of many centuries, yields itself to such analysis wherewith all the chronological data may be arranged without violation, contradiction or conflict into a harmonious systematic framework, faith should be all the more solidly founded. Such a framework would tend to substantiate and establish: (1) a Divine intellect undergirding both the Old and New Testaments; (2) the fact of the GOD of the Bible; (3) the divine inspiration of Scripture; and (4) faith in GOD through and in His Word. These in turn should then act in concert pointing to and certifying the deity of Christ Jesus and His gospel. Indeed, if we can thus correctly interpret the history of the past by means of such a systematic framework, it should enhance our understanding of the present as well as greatly encourage our confidence in the great chronological predictions of Scripture with regard to the future.

In order to exhaustively investigate the subject at hand, it is necessary to determine and examine the original text, formulate an approach and pattern for scientific analysis, and come to logical conclusions. The ability to so do would set the Holy writings of the Christian faith in bold relief, totally above and apart from those of other world religions. Neither Islam's *Koran,* the pantheistic *Vedas, Upanishads* and *Bhagavad-Gita* of the Hindus, the *Eightfold Path* of Buddhism, nor the *Analects* of Confucius, etc. possesses any revelatory text that would allow similar formalistic scrutiny. Thus these humanistic cults and their devotees must be viewed in stark contrast to the Christian faith and its disciples as they are not able to academically defend their texts or the authority of these writings.

It is the firm conviction and considered conclusion of this author that it is important to have a reliable written authority. Furthermore, a "triangulation" formula procedure is developed and introduced which sustains and precisely verifies the academic status of the Word of God over the controversial period of the divided monarchy. Moreover, after extensive examination regarding all chronological data and related statements contained therein, the justifiable conclusion of this research is that the text of the Holy Writ can be academically defended.

TABLE OF CONTENTS

ABBREVIATIONS

ABC	Assyrian, Babylonian Chronicles
AD	*Anno Dei* (Year of God)
AH	*Anno Hominis* (Year of Man)
AM	*Anno Mundi* (Year of World)
ANET	Ancient Near East Text
ARAB	Ancient Records of Assyria and Babylon
ARI	Assyrian Royal Inscriptions
AUC	*Anno Urbis Conditae* – from the foundation of Rome
AV	Authorized King James Version (1611)
BC	Before the Birth of Christ
BM	British Museum
ISBE	International Standard Bible Encyclopedia
JP	Julian Period or astronomical calendar
KJB	King James Bible
Loeb	Loeb Classical Library, Cambridge, MA: Harvard University Press
LXX	Septuagint
NAS	New American Standard Version
NIV	New International Version
NK	Northern Kingdom, the 10 Tribe Kingdom of Israel formed by Jeroboam
NT	New Testament
OT	Old Testament
Oly.	Olympiad
SK	Southern Kingdom, the Kingdom of Judah – David's dynasty
YOR	Years of Rome (same as A.U.C.)

✳ ✳ ✳

c.	*circa* ("about/approximately")
ch., chs.	chapter(s)
comp.	compiled by
cont.	continued/contents
cp.	compare
ed., eds.	edition(s)/editor(s)
e.g.	*exempli gratia* ("for example")
et al.	*et alii* ("and others")
etc.	*et cetera* ("and so forth")
ff.	and the following (verses, pages, etc.)
fl.	*Floruit* ("flourished," used when birth and death dates are not known)
fn.	footnote
gen. ed.	general editor
ibid.	*ibidem* ("in the same place")
i.e.	*id est* ("that is")
ms., mss.	manuscript(s)
n.d.	no date
n.p.	no place; no publisher
op. cit.	*opere citato* ("in the work previously cited")
p., pp.	page(s)
rev.	revision/ revised/revised/reviewed by
rpt.	reprint/ reprinted
sec., secs.	section(s)
sup.	supplement
trans.	translated by/ translator/ translation
UP	University Press
viz.	*videlicet* ("namely")
vol., vols.	volume(s)
vs., vv.	verse(s)

ILLUSTRATIONS, DIAGRAMS ETC.

Genesis	Event	Yrs.	AM Age of Earth	Genesis	Event	Yrs.	AM Age of Earth
Ch. 1	Creation	0	0	7:6	The Flood when Noah was 600[1]		1656
5:3	Seth born when Adam was	130	130	11:10	Arphaxad born when Shem was	100	1658
5:6	Enos born when Seth was	105	235	11:12	Salah born when Arphaxad was	35	1693
5:9	Cainan born when Enos was	90	325	11:14	Eber born when Salah was	30	1723
5:12	Mahalaleel born when Cainan was	70	395	11:16	Peleg born when Eber was	34	1757
5:15	Jared born when Mahalaleel was	65	460	11:18	Reu born when Peleg was	30	1787
5:18	Enoch born when Jared was	162	622	11:20	Serug born when Reu was	32	1819
5:21	Methuselah born when Enoch was	65	687	11:22	Nahor born when Serug was	30	1849
5:25	Lamech born when Methuselah was	187	874	11:24	Terah born when Nahor was	29	1878
5:28	Noah born when Lamech was	182	1056	11:26	Abraham born when Terah was	130	2008
11:10	Shem born when Noah was	502	1558	12:4	Abraham enters Canaan, age 75	75	2083

Scripture has several large time spans that enable us to begin at 2083 AM & quickly obtain a BC date for Creation.[2]

Scripture	EVENT	Years	AM Age of Earth
Gen. 12:4	Abraham enters Canaan and begins sojourn, age 75	75	2083
Gen 12:10; Exo 12:40; Gal 3:17	From when Abraham left Haran to enter Canaan until the Exodus from Egypt (to the very day)	430	2513
1 Kings 6:1	Exodus to start of Temple, 479 years (in the 480th year which is 479 years plus 16 days — p. 52, fn. 2)	479	2992
1 Kings 11:42; 6:1, 37–38	Start of Temple to division of the Kingdom. Solomon reigned 40 yrs, Temple begun *in* his fourth year	37	3029
Ezek 4:4–6	Division of kingdom to destruction of Jerusalem *in* the 390th year (inclusively numbered = 389[+])	389	3418

The Kingdom of Judah fell to Babylon in 586 BC.[3] Hence the date of the Creation is 586 + 3418 = 4004 BC.

---

[1] The year 1656 is obtained by adding the 600th year of Noah, during which the Flood took place, to 1056 — the year he was born as found at Genesis 5:28 on this same chart.

[2] A most important chronological key is to be found in the fact that Ish-bosheth, Saul's son, was 40 years old when he began to reign (2 Sam. 2:10) over the kingdom of Israel. Since Ish-bosheth is not listed among the sons of Saul at the beginning of his father's reign (1 Sam.14:49) but is included in the much later written complete list in 1 Chron. 8:33, he must have been born after Saul became king. Thus, Saul must have reigned at least 40 years.

With no other information upon which to draw, a chronologist working before New Testament time would be forced to so deduce and accept that length of reign for Saul and hope that it fit. There would have been no justification for arbitrarily taking any number greater than 40. From Acts 13:21 we know that it would have tallied, and done so on his very first attempt. Thus, the Acts verse must now be seen as confirmatory (and vice versa!).

The principle to be seen from this is that the Hebrews had access to all the information necessary for them to trace their own history from the Old Testament, and thus no New Testament information was or is necessary whatsoever to construct the chronology from Creation to the time of Christ. The O.T. is a complete self-contained revelation in all such matters. Furthermore, this is why the 480 years from the Exodus to the start of the Temple in the 4th year of Solomon's sole reign must be taken as the factual chronological key for that period and the Acts 13:17–22 passage understood and interpreted accordingly – and not the reverse as so many would have it. Indeed, we affirm that the 300-year statement of Judges 11:26 absolutely confirms 1 Kings 6:1 and its 480-year declaration.

[3] This study has meticulously and precisely derived the date of the fall of Jerusalem as 586 BC (also see Charts 5 and 5c). The years 588 and 587 also receive able support by careful men. Ussher, Browne, and more recently E. W. Faulstich held to 588, whereas H. F. Clinton, Sir Robert Anderson, W. F. Albright, and D. J. Wiseman championed 587 BC. Daniel was carried to Babylon in the 3rd year of Jehoiakim (606 BC) by Nebuchadnezzar who was then general of the army as well as crown prince. This event began the 70-year servitude for Babylon (Jer. 29.10; Dan 1:1).

ESTABLISHING THE CORRECT FOUNDATION

A. BASIC CONSIDERATIONS

Chronology is the science of dividing time into regular intervals and assigning dates to historic events in their proper order. Without it, we would find it impossible to understand the sequence of historical events, biblical or non-biblical. As chronology is the very foundation on which history rests and the skeletal framework giving it structure and shape, the events of history can only be meaningful and properly understood as long as they are kept in their proper time sequence. If the time sequence becomes altered, the interpretation of the events becomes distorted and no longer dependable. The basic unit of time in chronology is the year.

Thus, two basic concepts are involved in the process of all chronological endeavors. The first entails *anachronisms*. An anachronism is the placing of a person or thing outside its proper time frame. The result would be the creation of an erroneous historical setting. Conversely, a *synchronism* is the proper chronological account of persons or events in history. The goal of the chronologist is to achieve synchronism and remove the anachronisms that have been placed in history by others. As historical events happened at precise moments of time, the chronologist must exert great care in not creating history while he is endeavoring to recover history. He must fit the events into their exact proper time sequence.

Although biblical chronology has been studied for centuries, its importance has waned in the past century. Originally such studies were conducted by men who were committed to the position that the Sacred Writ was to be taken as an accurate, factual and historical record containing its own chronological agenda. With the emergence of rationalism and the modern development of the theory of evolution, humanistic scholars began to challenge the chronological framework of the Bible.

These "progressives" were not willing to reject all of the historical data contained within the God-given Hebrew record, but they did reject most of the chronological data. The result has been to separate history from Bible chronology. Eventually it was proclaimed by nearly all scholars, Christian as well as secular, that a chronology for the Hebrew kings was hopeless, and biblical chronology was generally unreliable. Yet without the framework and foundation of chronology, biblical history lies in ruins. What is at the heart of this departure?

B. TWO DISTINCT WORLD VIEWS

It is a natural consequence that one's environment, paternal upbringing, formal education and life's experiences shape his world view. Although many variations and dissimilarities exist at an individual level, amazingly there are but two such outlooks or systems of belief.

1. MAN-CENTERED WORLD VIEW

The first is a humanistic account which places man's destiny squarely upon the shoulder of the individual. Many "denominations" with widely differing doctrines exist within the boundaries of this world view. Of course, this is equally true of the second or God-centered system of belief.

Adherents of this outlook generally believe that each person must look deep within himself for the answers to life's questions and problems in order to find his true "self" and the meaning of his existence. They hold that man is innately good, is able to solve all of life's problems and although the sources of his problems are mainly external to himself, they have adversely affected his thinking about himself thus leading him to wrong actions. The solution to man's problems is to reorient his thinking so that he recognizes and accepts his inner goodness, which supposedly will cause him to act according to his true self.

Basically, the followers of this position view matter as being eternal and the universe as well as all life as ever evolving to higher degrees of order. Man especially is generally viewed as being the highest of the "animals," having evolved to his present form through the energizing by some outside force such as a random lightning bolt upon nonliving chemicals in a primeval ocean. This humanistic explanation sees man as continuing his evolutionary

process, ever raising his state of consciousness as he approaches a state of godhood.

According to the mainstream of those who share this belief, there are no absolutes, hence truth is relative. Consequently "sin" is mainly considered to be ignorance, low self-esteem or negative thinking rather than as an affront to the deity. Positive mind sets, meditation on personal worth and education are believed by its disciples to be the vehicles through which man will finally overcome all that plagues him. Achieving a higher state of consciousness will at last allow such "gods" to eliminate fears, doubts, interpersonal conflicts, wars, etc. which have resulted from negativism and a lack of education.

If, as these devotees suppose, all of reality is the result of blind random chance evolution occurring in ever existing matter, there is little need for any external Creator God. Such a concept is generally tolerated as long as that god (he, she or it) does not become too personal, but those nearest the pinnacle feel that these vestiges of flawed thinking will also soon disappear as the process continues. The same may be said to be true of the concept of Satan. There is little room or need for an external deity in a scenario that views man as being or becoming one with some god or the universe, needing only either a moment of "enlighten-ment" where he realizes the truth and reality of this or attaining such status in the ongoing upward spiral of the thought process via the aforementioned higher state of consciousness achieved by "meditation" and/or higher educa-tion.

2. GOD-CENTERED WORLD VIEW

The other world view is that there is a Creator who is not merely a "force" for good but rather an all-powerful, purposeful, and personal God. His power is attested to by the declaration that by His wisdom and immeasurable understand-ing, He spoke the entire universe, the earth and all its various complicated forms of living things into being in but six literal days.

Moreover, man is biblically portrayed as having been taken from the lowly dust of the earth and majestically yet lovingly fashioned by the very hands of the Living God into a noble creature, conformed in the image of his Maker. Thus man was separate and distinct from the animals.

The earth and all that lived therein were placed under the care and dominion of this first man, Adam. This placing depicted that although man was princely made, endowed and a unique self, he was innately a dependent creature. That is, he was to acknowledge his total dependence upon the Father God who had formed him, breathed the breath of "lives" into his being, and given him authority and domain. Thus the answers and needs that would arise during the course of life were not to be found "deep within" himself, but rather external to and outside the self-life.

The first man rebelled against his Maker, choosing instead to obey a literal fallen (sinning) angel named Satan. This act of rebellion (sin) incurred various judgments against Adam, the earth and its creatures which the Creator had placed under his dominion. The severity of this verdict was intended not only as righteous judgment but to speak in testimony as to the incredible degree of holiness of the LORD God himself. That is, if the only righteous judgment for but one act of sin against the person of the Creator was pain, suffering, affliction, struggle, sickness, death, and even eternal conscious punishment for the fallen angels and unrepentant men in a literal place called hell, such would attest in the clearest manner possible as to the degree of holiness and purity that had been offended.

Work, which had been easy, became difficult, and all that had been placed by God under the man's authority would now resist Him. Although His holy and just nature demanded that sin be dealt with in the severest measures, God demonstrated that His grace, compassion and love remained upon mankind.

Sin had caused Adam and Eve to forget that they were and would always be dependent creatures, needing God to do something about the terrible predicament in which they had placed themselves. But God took the initiative and by slaying animals, He established for all time that the "wages of sin is death" and that without the shedding of blood there could be no remission (forgiveness) of sin. Until Adam's sin, all the animals and man had eaten herbs, fruit and plants (Genesis 1:29–30); thus originally there was no "struggle for survival" or "survival of the fittest."

ISAIAH 9

The promise of "the seed of the woman" (Genesis 3:15) was given making clear that the blood of animals could merely temporarily "cover" sin; but the actual debt incurred by sin would need be paid by something of far, far greater value. Mankind's purchase and redemption would have to come at the ultimate price, as his sin had incurred the ultimate judgment. God, not man, would rectify man's dilemma.

Precisely four thousand years later God incarnate came as the babe of Bethlehem, born of the Virgin Mary. Jesus the Christ came to Earth, lived a sinless life, and voluntarily shed His blood on the cross legally purchasing back all that Adam had lost. Thus as Adam's offspring, all mankind has obtained as a free gift the legal right to forgiveness and eternal life with the Father. This inheritance becomes one's possession when he chooses to receive God's only provision for sin. This is not merely a mental approbation, but a commitment of one's life to the Lord Jesus believing that He is the Creator/Savior come in the flesh, that He died for man's sins and rose again on the third day.[1] This God has revealed himself to man through His Creation, the deposit of the Holy Scriptures, and the finished blood atonement along with the bodily resurrection of Christ Jesus.

3. THE AUTHOR'S WORLD VIEW

Whereas the first world view is man-centered and the second God-centered, the line between is clearly drawn. A natural consequence is that each person must choose which he will embrace. This choice colors all the thought processes carrying along with it frames of reference with regard to every area and field of human endeavor. These various frames of reference force all people to approach situations, problems, and projects with presuppositions. Thus research regarding biblically related themes is almost never carried out with cold, objective scientific methods. The researcher's presuppositions are brought to the task with him.

The current author is no exception. Until his thirty-sixth year, the humanistic uniformitarian-evolutionary beliefs held sway over his life. However, he now candidly acknowledges to hold the God-centered world view, believing God has kept to this day His promises to preserve inerrant the text of the Scriptures which He directed man-ward. He is likewise firmly committed not only to special Creation of the universe, earth, and man but to all the other supernatural and miraculous events as recorded in Scripture.

Although the findings presented in this thesis are in a very real sense a chronology for the biblicist, they should be equally of interest to all as it is unceasingly being reported that such cannot be constructed due to the many "errors, emendations, contradictions, etc." present within the biblical text. With great difficulty the author has come to appreciate the value of scientific integrity with respect to the subjects herein addressed and thus has empathy for those with the contrary view.

As the term biblicist may be unfamiliar to some and since it will appear throughout this paper, a clarification as to the sense the expression is meant to convey when used herein is deemed necessary. By biblicist, this author does not merely refer to a fundamentalist or a biblical scholar as many dictionaries so define. By it, much more is intended. The word connotes one who, while taking both the immediate and the remote context into account, interprets and believes the Bible literally.

This necessitates that the person so designated has chosen to believe God's many promises that, despite all textual criticism objections to the contrary, He would forever preserve His infallible Word. Moreover, the meaning intended to be conveyed by this Word carries with it the concept that such a person trusts

---

[1] "For unto us a child is born, unto us a son is given: and the government shall be upon his shoulder: and his name shall be called Wonderful, Counsellor, The mighty God, The everlasting Father, The Prince of Peace." (Isaiah 9:6)

"In the beginning was the Word, and the Word was with God, and the Word was God. The same was in the beginning with God. All things were made by him; and without him was not any thing made that was made." (John 1:1–3)

"And the Word was made flesh, and dwelt among us, (and we beheld his glory, the glory as of the only begotten of the Father,) full of grace and truth." (John 1:14)

"And without controversy great is the mystery of godliness: God was manifest in the flesh, justified in the Spirit, seen of angels, preached unto the Gentiles, believed on in the world, received up into glory." (I Timothy 3:16)

that the Authorized Bible (Hebrew Masoretic and Greek *Textus Receptus*)[1] in his hand is a fulfillment of those promises. Sadly, even among the pastors and seminary professors, most of today's conservative evangelical Christians do not qualify to bear this appellation which many in the not too distant past bore, counting the cost while enduring the shame.

4. SUMMARY OF WORLD VIEWS

Tragically, the vast majority of contemporary university professors and various media personalities are representatives of the first world view. In striving to inculcate their beliefs in others, their opinions are primarily the only ones receiving a hearing. The second view, if allowed a voice at all, is nearly always presented in a patronizing atmosphere or one of open ridicule.

Unfortunately, the umbrella under which each group encamps is quite broad. Thus specifics must be dealt with in the most sweeping generalities despite a common "glue" that binds each devotee to one distinct camp or the other. The reason this is said to be "unfortunate" is that due to man's fallen condition, issues often

become unclear within a resulting sea of gray rather than the sharp distinct black or white which the Word of God draws.

Of course there are "progressives" and "free thinkers" attempting to dwell between these extremes, picking and choosing at will ideas and beliefs from each camp but never fully understanding the claims and agendas of either or both; hence they constantly live surrounded by self-contradictory views and compromise, a condition of which they are generally unaware. These inconsistencies are able to exist and continue undetected because either man rarely thinks through his untested opinions to a logical conclusion or his reason becomes flawed.

C. THE EFFECT ON BIBLE CHRONOLOGY

As stated previously, this conflict over world views overshadows all areas of human endeavor. Many educators embracing the humanistic world view are using chronology in making a major negative impact in disciplines other than those directly related to theology. A large segment of the attacks against the Bible, hence against the LORD and the followers of the Lord Jesus Christ, are based on errors in chronology. This is why Bible chronology is so important.

For example, it has become widely accepted and commonplace for college text books on history, especially in the study of western civilizations, to move forward the dates of historical events and persons from those dates indicated by the Sacred Writ. By advancing the period in which Moses and Abraham lived by approximately 200 years, the illusion is created and taught that Moses learned about God from the Egyptians and Abraham from the Babylonians rather than from God's having personally revealed himself to them. Once these dates are moved forward and compared to archaeological findings, it appears that the Egyptians and Babylonians had certain concepts about God before learning about them from Moses and Abraham; yet, the very opposite is true.

A highly touted widely disseminated college text[2] has a section titled "The Hebrew Religious

---

[1] John W. Burgon, *The Revision Revised* (Paradise, PA: Conservative Classics, 1883). D.O. Fuller, ed., *Which Bible?* (Grand Rapids, MI: Intl. Pub., 1970). Edward F. Hills, *The King James Version Defended*, 4th ed. (Des Moines, IO: Christian Research Press, 1984). Edward F. Hills, *Believing Bible Study*, 2nd ed. (IO: 1977). Theodore P. Letis, ed., *The Majority Text* (Grand Rapids, MI: Institute for Biblical Textual Studies, 1987). Theodore P. Letis, *Edward Freer Hill's Contribution to the Revival of the Ecclesiastical Text*, unpub. M.T.S. Thesis (Emory U, 1987). Jack A. Moorman, comp., *Forever Settled* (NJ: B.F.T., 1985). Jack A. Moorman, *When The KJV Departs From The "Majority" Text* (NJ: B.F.T., 1988). Wilbur N. Pickering, *The Identity of the New Testament Text* (Nashville, TN: Thomas Nelson, 1977). Jasper James Ray, *God Wrote Only One Bible* (Junction City, OR: Eye Opener Pub., 1980). Harry A. Sturz, *The Byzantine Text-Type And New Testament Textual Criticism* (Nashville, TN: Thomas Nelson, 1972). Jakob Van Bruggen, *The Ancient Text of the New Testament* (Winnipeg, Manitoba, Canada: Premier Printing, 1976). F.E. Wallace, *A Review of the New Versions* (Ft. Worth, TX: Noble Patterson, 1973). B.F. Westcott and F.J.A. Hort, *Introduction to the New Testament in the Original Greek* (NY: Harper, 1882). Benjamin C. Wilkinson, *Our Authorized Bible Vindicated* (England and U.S.A., 1930). Floyd Nolen Jones, *Which Version is The Bible?*, 17th ed., rev. (The Woodlands, TX: KingsWord Press, 1999). Floyd Nolen Jones, *The Septuagint: A Critical Analysis*, 6th ed., rev. and enl. (The Woodlands, TX: KingsWord Press, 2000).

[2] Edward McNall Burns, *Western Civilizations* (New York: W.W. Norton & Co., Inc., 1963), pp. 100–120.

Evolution" which teaches that the Hebrews originally worshiped animals and their concept of God *evolved* over time into that of anthropomorphic gods, Moses finally bringing them to serve but one "god" as their national deity. Whereas the Bible reveals that there were many Jews who worshiped animals, etc., such acts were in direct disobedience to the revelation of God which He had already given from the time of Adam. Indeed, they were always punished for worshiping idols, animals and other gods.

Moreover, these conflicting world views and their effect on the field of Bible chronology have given rise to two distinct schools or academies.[1] Each approaches the undertaking with different mind sets, goals and thereby different methodologies.

1. THE ASSYRIAN SCHOOL

The modern school of biblical chronology has attempted to establish its chronology by examining the biblical record for a synchronistic point of contact between Israel and the Assyrian, Babylonian or Egyptian records. Assuming the chronologies of these kingdoms to be established, at least at the points of contact, the foreign kingdom's date is assigned at the synchronous encounter to the scriptural event. However, such procedure is founded on the fallacious presupposition and attending methodology that the Assyrian Eponym Canon, the royal inscriptions of the Assyrian and Babylonian records and eclipse identification

with a subsequent date assignment, are sources of absolute and accurate chronology.

Acceptance of these assumptions has been due to the aura of precision given by astronomical "fixes" such as the solar eclipse found in the eponym of Bur-Sagale and the astronomical calculations compiled by the second-century-AD astronomer Claudius Ptolemy (Ptolemaeus). As this faction favors the Assyrian data above all other during the period of the Hebrew divided monarchy, using it to "establish" both the Hebrew and the Egyptian chronology of the XXII Dynasty as well as the earlier adjoining portion of the XXI Dynasty, it will be hereafter referred to as the "Assyrian School" or "Academy."

2. THE BIBLICIST SCHOOL

The second is the traditional biblically oriented school which regards the Holy Scriptures as the factual source against which all other material must be weighed. The goal of the members of this school is to construct a "standard" chronology of the Bible from the chronological data embedded within the Hebrew Masoretic Text of the Old Testament, independent of any outside sources. In the past, James Ussher has been its leading proponent. Hereafter the adherents of this position will be acknowledged as being biblicist or of that school.

D. METHODOLOGY

As to the aforementioned Assyrian Eponym Canon, the royal inscriptions of the Assyrian and Babylonian records, the solar eclipse of Bur-Sagale and the astronomical calculations and eclipse identifications of Claudius Ptolemy, the present study carefully examined these and other profane data (the author's having come under the discipline of astronomy at the university). Where conflict in synchronization arose between biblical data based on its own internal evidence and extra biblical sources, solutions were sought but never at the expense of Scripture. At every point, the integrity, veracity and accuracy of the Word of God were maintained. If synchronization were not possible under those conditions, the secular was rejected as inaccurate. If it conformed, it was incorporated. All too often, the profane material has been found to be a staff of a bruised reed which has been leaned upon and

---

[1] Eugene W. Faulstich, *History, Harmony and the Hebrew Kings* (Spencer, Iowa: Chronology Books, Inc., 1986), pp. 8–9. Recently Faulstich has championed that which he perceives as a distinctly third approach. He asserts that he relies on "the original Hebrew principles of biblical chronology based on the Hebrew calendar and its cyclical phenomena ... (Sabbath days, Sabbath and Jubilee years) and the cycle of the twenty-four sections of the Levitical priesthood established by David ..." Faulstich believes his system is a truly biblical one as it "both takes the text seriously and assigns priority to the historical data of the Hebrew record" allowing "the Bible itself to be its own interpreter of chronological data." Such is truly a noble and worthy goal; however after establishing the chronology of the Hebrew kings, he then places the Assyrian and Babylonian histories in parallel, and when conflicting with secular history, "new interpretations are sought and found." During the early phases of his research he stated that the Assyrian data had ensnared Edwin R. Thiele and he warned others to beware of that pitfall. Unfortunately, as time passed he became partially lured into the same snare (continued page 17).

broken, piercing those who would so incline (2 Kings 18:21; Isa. 36:6).

It must be seen that the Bible, even taken merely as a history book, is still the most remarkably unique book at man's disposal because it provides a system of mathematical "checks and balances" which maintains accuracy in chronology via synchronism. Consequently, the study of Bible chronology, especially if approached from a believing frame of reference, is a most powerful apologetic tool and weapon in the defense of the written Word. As a faith builder, it is second only to the study of Scripture itself. Many "discrepancies" and paradoxes (apparent errors) simply vanish when the data is charted on paper. Thus, this undertaking is an attempt to recover the credibility which has been lost over time to the gainsayers.

This research was greatly facilitated and enhanced by the aid of a "state of the art" IBM computer supported by an array of potent peripherals. Three large Bible programs were utilized as well as a calendar conversion-new moon conjunction program designed by the Harvard Center for Astrophysics. As the biblical months were regulated by the new moon, the latter was especially beneficial. The ephemeris generator for this software was developed from Jean Meeus' *Astronomical Formulae for Calculators*. This is the standard formula used by astronomers today.

E. ARCHBISHOP JAMES USSHER

As mentioned in the Acknowledgments (page iii), the findings of this enterprise often yielded results reflecting, or nearly so, those made by Ussher. Having compiled a list of all Scriptures relevant to the task at hand, mathematical decisions and computations were made, especially utilizing the larger chronological numbers recorded in the text, thereby formulating a skeletal outline for the project. The outline from this initial effort now appears as Chart 1 (also see p. xiii). As the numbers were summed none were recognized as significant until the final calculation, that of the date of Creation. That number was 4004 BC and it leaped, as it were, from the page – being immediately recognized as that which the now oft maligned yet learned Anglican Archbishop of

Ireland, James Ussher, had determined over three hundred years earlier.

The resultant scheme presented herewith is an altogether independent work even though the results have turned out to largely be a confirmation of Ussher's chronology. This is especially true with regard to the overall skeletal outline although many of the details differ. These disparities are most noticeable in the period of the judges; still, for practical purposes, these charts generally depict Ussher's conclusions.

Amazingly then two men, whose lives were separated by a time span of more that 300 years, independently derived from the Scriptures the very same year of Creation. This unlikely circumstance could only have occurred by both using the same verses and reaching the selfsame conclusions as to their application. As the mindset and frame of reference of the current author is that the Scriptures are the infallible deposit of the Creator's revelation breathed man-ward and every verse germane to the question should be honored (in context), none being altered or swept away as being an "unfortunate scribal error," the mindset that Ussher brought to the task is, to a large degree, now manifest.

Whereas Ussher conceded that both the Old and New Testaments contained copyists' errors[1], a compromise for which he is to be blamed, to his credit he did not allow this to justify his altering a single verse of the Masoretic Text in constructing his chronology system. As demonstrated herein, he could not otherwise have derived the dates recorded in his classic work *Annalium Pars Prior* (1650) and *Pars Posterior* (1654), which were combined in 1659 into the *"Annales Veteris et Novi Testamenti."* Two years after Ussher's death, an English translation (with additions) of his original Latin was published in 1658 at London as the *Annals of the World to the Beginning of the Emperor Vespasian's Reign*. Bishop William Lloyd of Worcester slightly revised Ussher's dates and interjected many of his own in places where Ussher offered none in his 1701 *Holy*

---

[1] John Owen, "Of the Integrity and Purity of the Hebrew and Greek Text of the Scriptures," *The Works of John Owen*, vol. XVI, ed. William H. Goold (Edinburgh: Banner of Truth 1968), p. 302.

Bible with Chronological Dates and Index. Accordingly "Lloyd's Bible" was the first with dates in the margins.[1]

Thus, though this work is "independent," the task was approached, as Sir Isaac Newton aptly penned, standing "on the shoulders of those giants who went before us."[2] Before us lay the sum total of centuries of research, prayer and wisdom.

F. THE TRIDENT

In its quest for "more dependable data," most modern scholarship has gravitated down and away from the data-rich, uninterrupted Hebrew testimony to that of other nations neighboring the Holy Land, especially that of the Assyrians. Thus, we see Satan effectively using his "trident" to cloud the issues and facts in his ongoing war for the minds and allegiance of the fallen sons of Adam.

The first prong, that of textual criticism, successfully cripples one's confidence in the actual wording of the Scriptures as it causes the individual to succumb to the temptation of not trusting God to keep His promises to preserve His Word. The pale of doubt, once established and overhanging the matter, needs only the passing of time and a few scriptural paradoxes to come to the attention of the unaware, and they soon lose faith that God's Word is accurate.

The trident's central spike is that of evolution. Its place is at the center of the entire controversy. This is the barb that pierces the unsuspecting, even as young teens, often ensnaring and confusing their minds for life. This prong is central, assaulting as it does the Word of God at its very inception by calling into question the most basic tenets of Scripture. Once hooked by this spike, gone for the most part is trust in an instantaneous special creation by God, a literal Adam and Eve, the fall of man, and his subsequent need for a Redeemer. The first eleven chapters of Genesis,

the seed bed for all the doctrines that follow in the remainder of Scripture, become little more than a fable or parable. The rudimentary truth of fallen man's proclivity toward evil and of eventual judgment against impenitence, as demonstrated by the worldwide Flood, is lost in the battle for the hearts and souls of those for whom the ultimate sacrifice has been made.

The nature, power and character of the Living God so clearly set forth in these and the ensuing chapters of Genesis, as well as in the rest of the Decalogue, become blurred and faith is shipwrecked in the fog of doubt and confusion. The beached casualties now find the meticulously recorded names and ages of the patriarchs, as well as the fact of and reasons for the Deluge, incompatible and as irreconcilable with the so-called "proven facts" of science. The nature myth of pre-Adamic brutish "cavemen" evolving over time into modern man becomes seen as intellectual and scholarly in this bewildered state. This is especially so in light of the accompanying implication: if God made man in His image, does this mean God himself is an illiterate brutish subhuman? Hardly! The teaching of Scripture is clear that man was created a noble creature, separate and distinct from all the animals.

Strangely, the understanding for many becomes confounded to the extent that both scenarios for origins are accepted as equally viable and the Christian becomes spiritually immobilized. Few of these theistic evolutionists become fervent witnesses for Christ Jesus, having already compromised the fundamentals. But there is no room here for Hegelian Dialectic philosophy. True logic dictates that two opposing statements cannot both be true, nor can two totally contradicting views of origins.

The third prong is the primary subject under consideration, that of biblical chronology. It should be evident that as the teaching of evolution entails as an integral part of its doctrine the concept of time (hence chronology), all those who have succumbed to its influence will of necessity tend to skeptically assess biblical chronology. However it is precisely at this very point that the Sacred Text can be demonstrated academically verifiable. The sharp contrast between the two views thus crescendos here and forces the focus of all

---

[1] After my 6th edition, a reference was encountered stating that Ussher's dates had been inserted by an unknown authority in a 1703 London printing of the AV, [Jack Finegan, *Handbook of Biblical Chronology,* (Princeton: 1964), p. 191].

[2] Sir Isaac Newton, *Observations on Daniel and the Apocalypse of St. John,* (London: 1733). Newton is quoting Bernard of Clairvaux.

parties on the dramatic significance of the subject and the ramifications that accompany the individual's decision regarding it.

In light of the preceding, it should be obvious that because of the different world views with their accompanying frames of reference, Bible chronology cannot be discussed or considered by most as an independent subject. Their pre-suppositions would tend to cause them to suppose the matter of no consequence. After all, if one has been led to believe that the earth has been scientifically established beyond all reasonable doubt as being billions of years old rather than the approximate 6,000 attested to by the Scriptures, the issue is completely closed from his perspective. Of what interest or value could that person ever place in Bible chronology? Yet astronomer Dr. John Eddy admits:[1]

> There is no evidence based solely on solar observations that the Sun is 4.5–5 x 10^9 years old. I suspect that the Sun is 4.5 billion years old. However, given some new and unexpected results to the contrary, and some time for frantic recalculation and theoretical readjustment, I suspect that we could live with Bishop Ussher's value for the age of the Earth and Sun. I don't think we have much in the way of observational evidence in astronomy to conflict with that.

Moreover, if the individual has accepted as irrefutable fact that the Scriptures are full of scribal errors, emendations, corruptions, etc., no matter how painstakingly prepared, any chronology would be deemed of little worth and certainly not deserving of the time necessary to evaluate it. Those who have fallen under this spell would tend to give the matter even less consideration. Due to the fact that the vast majority of educators and members of various news media have already succumbed to these beliefs, the world view of the populace in general is rapidly falling in line, brainwashed by the unending torrent of misinformation, half-truths and lies.[2] The evolutionary aspect of the

trident brings up another phase of the problem that requires elucidation at this point.

G. HISTORY

The natural relationship that exists between history and chronology has been alluded to on the first page of this dissertation. However a clarification as to what is meant by the word "history" must be made before continuing. It must be understood that real history requires an intelligent observer present to record the events, persons, dates, etc. Yet, even this essential prerequisite is not sufficient. The recorder or alert witness must be without bias for, rather than a factual account, a distortion will be created. Without such an observer, regardless of the amount of research or facts brought to bear upon a given subject, that which follows will be laced with conjecture and prejudice.

Napoleon grasped this, at least in part, when he skeptically observed: "What is history but a fable agreed upon?"[3] Accordingly, historical geology is not history. If the earth were 4.6 billion years old and if, as we are being told, life has been here hundreds of millions of years, yet man has only occupied the planet for "merely" two or three million years, then there was no intelligent historian present to record the presumed events. This is why originally such speculations were designated as "prehistoric," i.e., *before* history.

It is also imperative to understand that historical geology is neither "historical" nor "science" for it fails to meet their basic prerequisites. True science is based on "what you can see." The first statement in the Scientific Method declares that we begin with

---

1 John A. Eddy, Ph.D. (astrogeophysics) (a solar astronomer at Boulder, Colo.) *Geotimes*, vol. 23, (September, 1978), p. 18.

2 See Henry M. Morris, *Scientific Creationism,* (San Diego, CA: Master Books, 1974); John C. Whitcomb, Jr. and Henry M. Morris, *The Genesis Flood,* (San Diego, CA: Baker Book House, 1972); Harold S. Slusher, *Critique of Radiometric Dating,* (San Diego, CA: Master Books,

1973); Harold S. Slusher, *The Origin of the Universe,* (San Diego, CA: Master Books, 1978); Duane T. Gish, *Evolution, the Fossils Say No!,* (San Diego, CA: Master Books, 1972); Robert V. Gentry, *Creation's Tiny Mystery,* (San Diego, CA: Master Books, 1986); Henry M. Morris, *The Scientific Case for Creation,* (San Diego, CA: Master Books, 1977); Gerald E. Aardsma, *Radiocarbon and the Genesis Flood,* (San Diego, CA: Master Books, 1991); Thomas G. Barnes, *Origin and Destiny of the Earth's Magnetic Field,* (San Diego, CA: Master Books, 1973); Malcom Bowden, *Ape-Men: Fact or Fallacy?* (Kent, ENG: Sovereign Pub., 1977).

3 Napoleon Bonaparte, *Instant Quotation Dictionary,* compiled by D.O. Bolander, (Mundelein, IL: Career Institute Inc., 1969), p. 138.

an "observed phenomenon." This stringent limitation which excludes GOD from the arena of science also excludes evolution as both are beyond the realm of human observation. This is especially true of the "punctuated" version of evolution, and places the problem beyond and outside the realm of science.

As by definition science deals with observed phenomena, it becomes obvious that the true realm of science is that of the present (or near present) and not that of the distant past. Despite all their protestations to the contrary, no matter how much intellect, technology, etc., uniformitarian evolutionists may bring to bear on the question of origins, by their own time-honored definition, such is not science.[1]

It is readily acknowledged that men have the right to embrace any opinion they desire. However, if these beliefs are founded upon no more than conjecture, speculation, and assumption, they must be seen as stripped of their cloak of respectability – no longer able to masquerade under the guise of history and/or science. Having been exposed for what they truly represent, the question arises: If such views are neither history nor science, what are they? Left naked save for a monk's habit to enshroud them, they stand exposed as merely philosophical "belief" systems. Today's society has a name for such systems. That name, hated among those who cleave to the dogmas of historical geology and uniformitarianism, is "religion."

The truth that must be honestly faced and acknowledged by all is that both the biblicist and the evolutionist are going through life practicing their faith. The problem is that only one side has been forthright enough to recognize and concede this as being the true assessment of fact. The other has long been self-deceived. Consequently, we are justified in contending and proclaiming that "real" history began, not billions, but only about six thousand years ago.

H. THE TEXT

At this point, it is deemed obligatory to comment concerning the text used to produce these biblical time lines. Besides the Hebrew Masoretic Text, two other sources are found in the literature which must be considered with regard to the true foundational base upon which to draw in obtaining the biblical chronological data. These are the Samaritan Pentateuch (not the Samaritan Version) and the Septuagint (often cited as LXX). As the numerical data involving the lives of the patriarchs differs greatly between these three,[2] a crucial decision must be faced at the very onset.

1. THE SAMARITAN PENTATEUCH

The Samaritan Pentateuch is not a version; it is the Hebrew Text written in Samaritan or old pointed Hebrew script and is preserved in the Sanctuary of the Samaritan Community at Nablous (Shechem). It was quoted by Jerome and Eusebius in the third and fourth centuries AD as well as other so-called church fathers, and was published in AD 1632.

There are discrepancies between the Samaritan Pentateuch and that of the Hebrew. For example, the editor(s) who produced this ancient document from the older Hebrew Text apparently felt that the antediluvians were not likely to have lived 150 years or so without begetting any sons. Accordingly, the ages in which several of these patriarchs fathered, as well as the total length of their lives, has been reduced by a century such that the span from the Creation to the Deluge is 349 years shorter than recorded in the Hebrew Text.

---

[1] Over a 14-year professional career during which he held varying positions of responsibility as Paleontologist, Geophysicist, District Geophysicist, Geophysical Manager, and Regional Geophysicist with Texaco and Tenneco respectively, the author is qualified to make such a judgment. Shortly before resigning from his scientific career in 1974 to pursue biblical studies, he was selected to attend Division Manager School. Attaining the Ph.D. as well as a Th.D., Dr. Jones has garnered majors in the disciplines of geology, chemistry, mathematics, theology, and education from six different institutions of higher learning. A magna cum laude graduate and an ex-evolutionist, he also possesses a minor in physics. and is an ordained Minister (SBC). Having authored a definitive analytical red-letter harmony of the Gospels, he has also published several books on textual criticism in defense of the traditional biblical text. Twice serving as adjunct professor at Continental Bible College in Brussels, Belgium, Dr. Jones is currently engaged in ongoing biblical research and the teaching of God's infallible Word.

[2] McClintock and Strong, *Cyclopedia of Biblical Theological and Ecclesiastical Literature,* vol. II, (Grand Rapids, MI: Baker Book House, 1867), p. 298.

Contrariwise, the interval from the Flood to Abraham's departure from Haran into the land of Canaan is 490 years longer in the Samaritan Pentateuch than the values recorded in the Masoretic Hebrew Text. Moreover, the Samaritan text differs in matters of varying significance from the Masoretic Text in about 6,000 places.

Although the text itself is believed by many to go back as far as the time of the 9th century BC Moabite Stone (or at least to the time of Hezekiah in the 8th century BC), most of the Samaritan scrolls containing the whole or a part of the Pentateuch are supposed not to be older than the 10th century AD.[1] In 1815, the text came under the careful scrutiny of the great Hebrew scholar Gesenius. He concluded, as does the present author, that it was a vulgar text with many corruptions, hence far inferior to the Masoretic Text with little critical value. In AD 1867, McClintock and Strong succinctly summed the Samaritan Pentateuch's status:[2]

> This last (the Samaritan Pentateuch), however, need not come into consideration, since it is well understood that the Samaritan text, here (Genesis 5 and 10) as well as elsewhere, is merely fabricated from the Greek; and those who treat it as an independent authority only show themselves ignorant of the results of criticism on the subject.

2. THE SEPTUAGINT

Of far greater significance has been the influence of the other aforementioned document, the Greek Old Testament known as the Septuagint. A significant number of chronologists have fallen into error by using for their foundation the material contained in the Septuagint rather than the Hebrew Masoretic Text. This mistake is calamitous.

The author is not unfamiliar with the nuances associated with the LXX having produced a definitive work relevant to its content.[3] Not

wishing to press the matter unduly, some exposition is unavoidable for the text selected by a chronologist contains the raw data used in the construction of not only his chronology but the history as well.

That which the chronologist brings to the task by way of his own view of the Sacred Writ is all important as to the materials chosen and the final outcome. If he has not dealt in faith that God has kept His many promises to preserve His Word, he may well gravitate to the accepted position in vogue today among scholastic, text critical, and seminary circles. That position is that the Scriptures have been corrupted over time and are currently in the process of being "restored" to their original pristine form by text critics — rather than that God has always "providentially preserved" them within and by the believing Church throughout history.

Until this matter is settled in favor of "preservation," the worker will always have a "tentative" Bible. The "restorationist" will always be wondering if some new archaeological discovery or Greek/Hebrew grammatical nuance will not alter his raw data, and he will be left with maximum uncertainty as to the precision of his final product.

By stark contrast, that person who simply puts his/her faith in God's promise to *preserve* His Word (Jer. 1:12; Psa. 12:6–7; Isa. 40:8; Mark 13:31) concludes that God has done so and that it is to be found where He originally deposited it, namely, in the Hebrew Masoretic Text. It is likewise faithfully preserved in the English translation of the 1611 King James Bible. This person is left with *maximum certainty*, with peace of heart and peace of mind. Such is a true biblicist.

The LXX is a very old translation of the Hebrew Scriptures into Hellenistic Greek. Presumably, it was an "authorized" Greek translation of the Old Testament prepared in Alexandria Egypt around 285–250 BC. The enterprise is said to have been accomplished by 72 Jewish scholars at the request of Ptolemy II Philadelphus or possibly begun during the reign of his father, Ptolemy Soter.

The history of the origin of the Septuagint is embellished with many diverse fables, hence its actual derivation is still being debated. As to

---

[1] J.I. Munro, *The Samaritan Pentateuch and Modern Criticism*, (London: J. Nisbet & Co., 1911).

[2] McClintock and Strong, *Cyclopedia of Biblical Theological and Ecclesiastical Literature, op. cit.,* vol. II, p. 299.

[3] Floyd Nolen Jones, *The Septuagint: A Critical Analysis,* 6th ed., rev. and enl., (The Woodlands, TX: KingsWord Press, 2000).

hard provable facts, little is known. However, one thing has become clear – it was not administered by Jews from Israel. It was generated by Jews, or those acquainted with the Hebrew tongue, who were of Egypt. This is demonstrated beyond all doubt by the presence of many words and conspicuous expressions that are unmistakably Alexandrian.[1]

Moreover, all text critics feel that the LXX contains readings that have been lost or corrupted in the Hebrew Scriptures. Subsequently, these men hold that the Septuagint may be used in determined places to "correct and restore these adulterated readings."[2] But is such veneration justified?

a. Discordant Ages of the Patriarchs in the LXX

One point where the LXX and the Hebrew Text differ in the Pentateuch is with regard to the ages of the antediluvian patriarchs relevant to the birth of their sons.[3] Six of the first ten of these patriarchs fathered exactly 100 years later in the LXX than in the Hebrew Old Testament. The total span of these differences is 586 years – the LXX being greater than that of the Hebrew Text. The importance of this discrepancy can hardly be overstated as in calculating and reckoning the chronology of the Old Testament, the numbers recorded in Scripture are our only guide. That the variations in the Septuagint are due to contrivance or design, and not due to accident, is plain from the systematic way in which the alterations have been made.

It is simple to demonstrate which list is correct. The majority of LXX manuscripts give 167 as the age of Methuselah at the birth of his son,

Lamech (the Hebrew reads 187, Gen. 5:25). However, if Methuselah were 167 at the birth of Lamech, Lamech 188 at the birth of Noah, and Noah 600 at the Flood (as recorded in the LXX), Methuselah would have been 955 at the date of the Flood. Since he lived to be 969 (the life span given in both) the LXX becomes entangled in the absurdity of making Methuselah survive the Flood by 14 years!

Yet Genesis 7–10 and 2 Pet. 3:20 are adamant in proclaiming that only Noah, his three sons and their wives (that is, only eight souls) survived the Deluge. Discordances of a similar nature and magnitude are found with regard to the postdiluvian patriarchs except that here the life spans also differ, often by more than 100 years.

The patriarchal chronology of the LXX can be explained from the Hebrew on the principle that the translators of the former desired to lengthen the chronology and to graduate the length of the lives of those who lived after the Flood so as to make the shortening of the life spans gradual and continuous, instead of sudden and abrupt. This fit into their philosophic concept of gradual and uniform change (pre "uniformitarianism"), a philosophy that embraced the basic precepts of evolution.

That is, they were primeval evolutionists. Thus the dramatic life span changes, which manifested the historic results of the sudden catastrophic transformations upon the earth and all life due to the worldwide Deluge, were altered to eliminate such positive evidence which was contrary to their religious and philosophic beliefs.

The constructor of the scheme lengthens the chronology of the patriarchs after the Flood unto Abraham's leaving Haran by 720 years. He also graduates the length of the lives of the patriarchs throughout the entire register, both those before and after the Flood.

The curious result is that with the three exceptions of Enoch, Cainan (whose life exceeds that of his father by only five years) and Reu (whose age at death is the same as that of his father), every one of the patriarchs from Adam to Abraham is made to die a few years younger than his father. Could anything be more manifestly artificial?

---

[1] *Septuagint*, "Introduction," (Grand Rapids, MI: Zondervan Edition, 1974), p. ii.

[2] Upon noting differences in the figures in the Hebrew, Septuagint, and Samaritan texts, Eusebius of Caesarea (Pamphili, *circa* AD 260–340, the so-called "Father of Church History") decided that the extant Hebrew text contained mistakes and that the LXX had been translated from more ancient and accurate copies of the Hebrew. He therefore preferred the Septuagint (the LXX text used by Eusebius differed somewhat from that available today) as did his predecessor, Julius Africanus; see Jack Finegan, *Handbook of Biblical Chronology*, (Princeton: 1964), pp. 156 and 141.

[3] Martin Anstey, *The Romance of Bible Chronology*, (London: Marshall Bros., 1913), pp. 73–76. See his diagrams for a more detailed analysis.

b. Discordant Lengths of Kings' Reigns in the LXX

Significant discrepancies are also found with regard to various lengths of reign of several kings during the period of the divided monarchy. The Greek variants came into being because the translator either failed to understand the meaning of the Hebrew or, as was the usual occurrence, from an effort to "correct" the supposed errors.

Discrepancies between the LXX and the Hebrew Scriptures regarding the various kings may be readily appraised below:

1 KINGS	HEBREW TEXT	SEPTUAGINT
15:9 Asa	20th of Jeroboam	24th of Jeroboam
16:8 Elah	26th of Asa	20th of Asa
16:15 Zimri	27th of Asa	not given
16:29 Ahab	38th of Asa	2nd of Jehoshaphat
22:41 Jehosha.	4th of Ahab	11th of Omri

2 KINGS		
1:17 Joram	2nd of Jehoram	18th of Jehoshaphat
8:16 Jehoram	8 years of reign	40 years of reign

A careful investigation of these variations reveals that they are not the result of scribal errors, but constitute *editorial changes* made with the object of correcting what were considered as "errors" in the original Hebrew Text. In no instance is a Greek variation an improvement over the Hebrew. The fallacious nature of the Greek innovations may be proved by the wide divergence of the patterns of reign that they call for from the years of contemporary chronology.

For example, the Hebrew Text of 1 Kings 22:41 states that Jehoshaphat ascended to the throne of Judah in the fourth year of the reign of Ahab of the Kingdom of Israel. The Septuagint gives the same data here, but the Greek has another account of Jehoshaphat's reign at 1 Kings 16:28 (III Kings by LXX reckoning) which places the accession of Jehoshaphat in the 11th year of Omri of Israel – some four years earlier.

In addition, 1 Kings 16:29 of the Hebrew Bible records that Ahab ascended to the throne of Israel in the 38th year of Asa, King of Judah, whereas the Greek gives Ahab's accession as the 2nd year of Jehoshaphat *which is five years later* (see Chart 5 and 5c).

The question naturally arises in the mind of the text critic, "Did the Greek text precede the Hebrew text, or the Hebrew precede the Greek?" James D. Shenkel "affirmed" in his 1964 doctoral dissertation that the Greek was the early and correct pattern for the Hebrew rulers and that the Hebrew regnal data arose as variants from an original Greek pattern.[1] Such is representative of current critical thinking with regard to the LXX as being preferred over the Hebrew Scripture.

Conclusive proof that the current Hebrew Text was in existence before the Greek is found at 1 Kings 16:28 where the Greek places an additional account of Jehoshaphat. That verse is the concluding statement concerning the reign of King Omri. The narrative relating to the next monarch should begin with verse 29. In both the Greek and the Hebrew, verse 29 is where the account of Ahab commences. But in order to permit the account of Ahab to begin there and yet have the account of Jehoshaphat precede that of Ahab, the Greek has attached the entire account of Jehoshaphat as an appendage to the account of Omri's reign.

The account of Jehoshaphat (1 Kings 22:41–50) takes up ten verses. If the Greek text had been in existence before the Hebrew Text, the account of Jehoshaphat would have been given at 1 Kings 16:29–38, and it would then have been followed by the account of Ahab. There would have been no second account of Jehoshaphat after the account of Ahab at 1 Kings 22:41.[2]

Obviously, the Greek editor was endeavoring to follow the arrangement of chapters and verses found in the Hebrew. The Hebrew is perfectly consistent in the matter of sequence, with Ahab following Omri and Jehoshaphat following Ahab. However the Greek is conspicuously inconsistent. It depicts Jehoshaphat following Ahab at 1 Kings 22:41–50, but preceding him at 1 Kings 16:28.

---

[1] James D. Shenkel, *Chronology and Recensional Development in the Greek Text of Kings,* (Cambridge, MA: Harvard University Press, 1968), pp. 22, 110–111.

[2] Edwin R. Thiele, *The Mysterious Numbers of the Hebrew Kings,* Revised (*Grand Rapids, MI:* Zondervan, 1983), pp. 90–94. See the more detailed explanation of this problem which is well taken even though Thiele's "dual dating" concept violates Scripture and is thoroughly erroneous.

The problem arose when the Greek editor could not understand how a reign of 12 years for Omri that began in the 31st year of Asa could terminate in the 38th year of Asa with Ahab's coming to the throne at that time. But the data does not represent an error; rather it is merely a paradox, an *apparent* error. This apparent error in the Hebrew Scripture left him on the horns of a dilemma. So the Greek editor attempted to "correct" the "contradiction" by beginning the 12 years of Omri's dominion in the 31st year of Asa's reign (the year Omri became ruler over all Israel upon the death of his rival, Tibni) not in the 27th year of Asa as 1 Kings 16:8–18 demands (the year Omri began to rule over only part of the kingdom of Israel).

As Asa reigned 41 years, the first part of Omri's dominion would, in such case, parallel the last part of Asa's and the final years of Omri would parallel the first years of Jehoshaphat. Under this contrivance, Jehoshaphat would come to the throne in the 11th year of Omri in accordance with the Greek version of 1 Kings 16:28, and Ahab would begin to reign in the 2nd year of Jehoshaphat in accordance with the Greek version of 1 Kings 16:29.

The foregoing unmistakably discloses that the Hebrew was the original account, not the Greek. Thus, the Greek arrangement reveals itself to be a late artificial contrivance brought into being in an attempt to correct something that was actually accurate but appeared wrong to the reviser.

We add that though his work contains about eight discordances with the Hebrew Masoretic Text (seven of which are very small), none of Josephus' variations is the same as any found in the Septuagint. We submit this indicates that:

1. Josephus did not consider the LXX reliable, or
2. The LXX did not exist in his day!

Either is devastating to the position to which the LXX has somehow ascended in the minds of most scholars. Even a cursory comparison between the Septuagint and the Hebrew Masoretic Text (as translated in the King James Bible) clearly reveals that the LXX as it is today is highly inaccurate and deficient as a translation. To attempt to reconstruct the Hebrew Text (as many connected with the modern versions are trying to do) from such a loose, deficient and unacceptable translation would be analogous to trying to reconstruct the Greek New Testament Text from the paraphrased *Living Bible*.

c. Irrefutable Internal Evidence

From a Bible honoring frame of reference, there is strong internal evidence that challenges the authenticity of the existence of a pre-Christian era Septuagint or, more precisely, if such an entity had existed Jesus and His apostles did not use it. That is, there are various references in the New Testament which clearly demonstrate that the Lord Jesus referred to the Hebrew Old Testament rather than to the Greek LXX or any other version.[1]

(1) Mat. 5:17,18   Think not that I am come to destroy the law or the prophets: I am not come to destroy, but to fulfill. For verily I say unto you, Till heaven and earth pass, one jot or one tittle shall in no wise pass from the law, till all be fulfilled.

The reference to the "law or the prophets" is a reference to the two major portions of the tripartite Hebrew Canon, (the third is called the Writings)! Yet more to the point, our Lord's reference to "jot" and "tittle" *could only refer to the Hebrew* and *not the Greek Old Testament!* The Greek alphabet has neither jot nor tittle. Only the Hebrew alphabet contains "jots" (the letter "yod," i.e., י which is about one-third normal height of the other Hebrew letters) and "tittles" (the minute "horns" or extensions seen on the letters ד, ר, ב, פ, etc.).

(2) Mat. 7:12   ... law and the prophets

(3) Mat. 11:13   ... all the prophets and the law

(4) Mat. 22:40   ... all the law and the prophets

(5) Luke 24:27,44   And beginning at Moses and all the prophets, He expounded unto them in all the Scriptures the things concerning himself ... These are the words which I spake unto you, while I was yet with you, that all things must be fulfilled, which were written in the law of Moses, and in the prophets, and in the psalms, concerning me.

---

[1] D.A. Waite, *ASV, NASV, and NIV Departures From Traditional Hebrew and Greek Texts*, (Collingswood, NJ: Bible For Today Press, #986, 1981), pp. A-xiv and xv. Credit for nearly all the insights in this section rightly belongs to Dr. Waite.

Here is a very clear indication of the threefold division of the Hebrew Canon into Law, Prophets and Psalms (which appears first in order in the Writings).

The Septuagint, interspersed as it is with the books of the Apocrypha[1], does not have this threefold division – *thus Christ was not using it!*

> (6) Luke 4:16–21 ... He went into the Synagogue on the Sabbath day, and stood up for to read. And there was delivered unto Him the book of the prophet Esaias (Isaiah).

Since the language used by the Jews in their synagogues was Hebrew, we can be certain that the scroll which was delivered to Him was written in Hebrew.[2] Even today the Jews read and use Hebrew in their synagogues as it is their one and only "holy language" – the language in which their Scriptures were originally written. The Lord Jesus Christ showed great respect for the Old Testament Word and upheld it completely.

> (7) Mat. 23:35 ... That upon you may come all the righteous blood . . . of righteous Abel unto the blood of Zacharias son of Barachias, whom ye slew between the temple and the altar.

By this reference, the Lord intended to charge the scribes and Pharisees with the blood of all the righteous people shed in the entire Old Testament. One may inquire, but how can one know that this is His intent? Abel is found in Genesis 4 which is the first book in the Hebrew Bible, whereas Zacharias is found in 2 Chron. 4:20–22. If one examines a Hebrew Bible, he finds that 2 Chronicles is the very last book within that volume (i.e. it is the last book in the

third section, the Writings). Thus, "Abel unto Zacharias"[3] is but another way of saying "from beginning to end."

If, on the other hand, one looks at the Septuagint edition, such as that published by the American Bible Society, 1949, Third Edition, edited by Alfred Rahlfs, he finds that it ends with Daniel followed by Bel and the Dragon! This is clear proof that our Savior referred to and used the Hebrew and not the Greek Old Testament. It is submitted that the Apostles would have followed their Master's lead in this.

d. Final Considerations

Nevertheless, despite the mythological nature concerning the origin and history of the LXX, one cannot be certain that a Greek Old Testament did not exist before the time of Christ.[4] What we do know is that if it did, little if anything is known about it. What is abundantly clear is that if such an entity existed, it does not necessarily follow that it read anything like the LXX preserved for us

---

1 The books of the Apocrypha are mainly the product of the last three centuries BC, a time during which written prophecy had ceased. They were accepted as part of the sacred literature by the Alexandrian Jews and, with the exception of the Second Book of Esdras, are found interspersed throughout the ancient copies of the Septuagint. The godly Jews under Ezra rejected the Apocrypha as having been inspired by the LORD when they formed the Old Testament canon. Josephus (c. AD 100) confirms that these books were not considered as "divine" in his day. He informs us that the canon was closed c. 425 BC [*Against Apion*, I, 8] (continued p. 18).

2 Thomas Hartwell Horne, *An Introduction to the Critical Study and Knowledge of the Holy Scriptures,* vol. II, 9th ed., (London: Spottiswoode and Shaw, 1846), fn., p. 291. Many others could be cited. The matter is not controvertible.

3 Most scholarship is in agreement with this identification of the Zacharias cited here in Mat. 23:35 as being that of the priest in 2 Chron. 24. However, the reference could be to the prophet Zechariah (cp. Zechariah 1:1). If this be the correct interpretation, the Lord Jesus is still making the same charge, but in this instance it would be understood to be in terms of *"time"* rather than "position" in Scripture. That is, that Abel was the first martyr recorded in the Holy Writ of the OT and the prophet Zechariah the last therein (i.e., that Malachi was not martyred). As Zechariah's death is not mentioned in the book of Zechariah, this would constitute a NT revelation as to his end which would have heretofore been known among the Jews via oral attestation. In such case, Zechariah would be included among those mentioned in Hebrews 11:36–38.

4 In addressing the question as to whether there had been a pre-Christian era Septuagint and whether the Apostles actually cited Scripture from it, Terence Brown (who was for some years Secretary of the Trinitarian Bible Society of London, England and a scholar in his own right) took a Bible-honoring frame of reference (quoted from Moorman's, *Forever Settled, op. cit.*, page 16). Brown comments: ."... if we observe the manner in which the Apostles refer to the Old Testament Scripture, we see a striking indication of the inspiration under which they themselves wrote. When they referred to the Septuagint, they were doing so under the supernatural guidance of the Holy Spirit, the Divine Author of the original revelation. Their authority is therefore higher than that of a translator." This would have been even more true since there is not the slightest indication that God had called for the undertaking or in any way sanctioned the translation in question (continued p. 18).

today. That is, the one at our disposal represents a very corrupted form of the LXX of their day. This is especially true if in fact the Apostles and the early church made extensive use of it as we are so often assured by nearly all theologians, for it flagrantly contradicts the Hebrew.

Moreover, Jesus' testimony as to the degree of the accuracy of the preserved copies from the time of Moses to His own day is irrefutable testimony as to God's faithfulness to sustain the Holy Writ exactly as He promised. Faith demands that He has continued to keep these many promises to our day; hence the Hebrew Text is as pure as when given. This is likewise true of the New Testament. Thus the need of the Church for any ancient Greek translation, either pre or early AD, is wholly without merit.

The reader should, in all fairness, be apprised of the fact that very nearly all references in the literature which allude to the Septuagint actually pertain to only two manuscripts, *Vaticanus* B and *Sinaiticus Aleph*. This is especially true of *Vaticanus*.[1] These two uncial MSS[2] also contain Bel and the Dragon, Tobit, Judith, etc. Thus, the Septuagint which we utilize in practical outworking, the LXX which is cited almost 90 percent of the time, *is* actually the LXX that was *written* more than 250 years *after* the completion of the New Testament canon.

Moreover, the Septuagint manuscripts exhibit considerable significant differences among themselves and disagree with the Hebrew Masoretic Text in many places. Both cannot be correct. As the Hebrew Masoretic Text is the inerrant, infallible Word of God, the Septuagint should be seen as spurious and rejected. The crux of the matter is not whether we have extant ancient Greek witnesses to the Old Testament Text, but rather, do they represent an accurate BC translation of the original Hebrew Text? It is generally asserted that the LXX was the "Bible" actually used by the Lord Jesus and the Apostles and that Christ Jesus and the Apostles quoted from the *Greek* version at times in preference to the Hebrew Bible. However one cannot even be certain that the LXX which is extant today (c. AD 350) represents a faithful reproduction of the c. 260 BC original, if such a translation ever existed before the time of Christ.

The irrefutable fact is that the divine oracles of the Old Testament were given to the Jews and the Jews only to both write and preserve (Rom. 3:1–3), *never* to the Greeks.[3] It is therefore the *Hebrew* writing that is the true infallible Word of the Living God.

The devastating and unanswerable question for the supporters of today's LXX is: if the Savior, the apostles and the early church used the Septuagint for their Bible, why would the true believers have ever left it and why did they return to the Hebrew Text? The answer is obvious — they would never have done so. Furthermore, why are not the early translations simply rife with readings from the LXX, moreover nearly word for word the same? Since these early works are not so constructed, it follows that if the translators of these early versions did use a Greek Old Testament, it was certainly not the one containing the many perverted readings which we have today.

It is deplorable enough that a witness so corrupt, depraved, and morally impaired as the LXX has been allowed a place in the witness box as to the true text of the Old Testament by text critics and other scholars. Far worse and

---

[1] Jones, *The Septuagint: A Critical Analysis, op. cit.,* pp. 51–52.

[2] These MSS (B and *Aleph*) are probably two of the 50 copies of the Bible (or at least first generation copies of these 50) which Constantine commissioned Eusebius to prepare and place in the major churches throughout the empire.

See Frederick Nolan, *An Inquiry into the Integrity of the Greek Vulgate or Received Text of the New Testament,* (London: F.C. and J. Rivington Pub., 1815), pp. 25–42, 94, 99; Ira M. Price, *Ancestry of Our English Bible,* 3rd ed., rev., (New York: Harper & Bros., 1956, orig. pub. 1906), p. 79. Also see *Apocrypha,* page 14, fn. 1.

[3] Contrary to nearly all modern scholarship, Luke was *not* a Gentile. The Romans 3:1–2 citation is in itself absolutely conclusive and serves to correct any and all who instruct otherwise: "What advantage then hath the Jew? ... Much every way: chiefly, because that unto them were committed the oracles of God." Luke penned more text than any other NT writer, more than either Paul or John. Were Luke indeed non-Jewish, the Lord not only failed to honor His testimony in Romans 3, He also entrusted more of the NT revelation into the hands of a Gentile than those of His "chosen people" (continued page 18).

much less excusable, they have also made room for it on the bench.

3. THE FAITHFULNESS OF THE HEBREW TEXT

In Old Testament times, the Levitical priests copied and preserved the Living Words of God. Throughout Scripture, all the scribes were of the tribe of Levi (Mal.2:7; Deut. 31:25; Deut. 17:18). This method of preserving the text was extremely successful as our Lord bore witness that not "one jot or tittle" had been altered in the 1,500 years from Moses to His day.

As to the accuracy of the Hebrew Old Testament in our day, Bishop Benjamin Kennicott did a study of 581 manuscripts of the Old Testament which involved 280,000,000 letters. Out of that 280,000,000, there were 900,000 variants. Although seemingly large to the reader, it is only one variant in 316 letters which is only 1/3 of 1 percent. But there is more. Of those 900,000 variants, 750,000 pertain to spelling – whether the letter should be an "i" or "u." This has to do with vowel points for the purpose of pronunciation which were supposedly added c. AD 600 by a group of Jewish scribes known as the Masoretes. Thus we are left with only 150,000 variants in 280,000,000 letters or only one variant in 1580 letters, a degree of accuracy of .0006 (six ten thousandths). Most of those variants are found in only a few manuscripts; in fact, most are from just *one* corrupted copy.

The Dead Sea Scrolls of Isaiah agree with the Hebrew Masoretic Text (the Hebrew OT along with the vowel points to aid in pronunciation). The earliest Masoretic Text which we have is dated c. AD 900. Almost no changes have occurred in the Book of Isaiah. Isaiah 53, for example, contains only *one word* of three letters which is in doubt after nearly eleven hundred years of copying. In a chapter of 166 words, only 17 were different, 10 were spelling and 4 were conjunctions.

Actually, the Masoretic Text is the true text, not the Dead Sea Scrolls, even though the Scrolls are more than a thousand years older. The Dead Sea material was not written by Jews who were given the charge by God to oversee and protect them. They were not of the tribe of Levi. They were Essenes, a Jewish cult of ascetics whose teachings were rife with heresies.

It has been related that both the Septuagint and Samaritan texts show the effects of obvious tampering. Summarizing, the interval from Adam to the Deluge is 349 years (AM 1656–1307) shorter in the Samaritan text as compared to the Hebrew and lengthened in the LXX by 586 (AM 2242–1656). Both texts lengthen the interval from the Flood to Abraham; the Samaritan by 490 years (AM 917–427) and the LXX by 720 (AM 1147–427). Thus, the interval from Creation to Abraham is 1306 years longer in the LXX than in the Hebrew. After analyzing this situation, C.F. Keil concluded that the Hebrew Text was the only reliable account:[1]

> That the principal divergences of both texts from the Hebrew are intentional changes, based upon chronological theories or cycles, is sufficiently evident from their internal character, viz. from the improbability of the statement, that whereas the average duration of life after the flood was about half the length that it was before, the time of life at which the fathers begot their first-born after the flood was as late and, according to the Samaritan text, generally later than it had been before. No such intention is discernible in the numbers of the Hebrew text; consequently every attack upon the historical character of its numerical statements has entirely failed, and no tenable argument can be adduced against their correctness.

Thus for all of the foregoing reasons, the present endeavor deals only with the Hebrew Text of the Old Testament as it has come down to us from the Masoretes. This writer's heretofore stated world view brings him to estimate the origin, history and authority of this Text as *sui generis*, of inestimable value and integrity. All questions relating to the preservation and transmission of the Text are accepted as having been accomplished via providential preservation[2] in fulfillment of God's promises to so do. Exhaustive study into

[1] C.F. Keil, *Commentary On The Old Testament*, trans. by James Martin, (Grand Rapids, MI: Eerdmans Pub. Co., 1976), p. 123.

[2] Edward F. Hills, *The King James Version Defended*, 4th ed., (Des Moines, IO: Christian Research Press, 1984), pp. 106–114, etc. Dr. Hills (d.1981), a Yale Phi Beta Kappa graduate who completed his Th.D. in New Testament text criticism at Harvard, was the first modern textual critic to champion the Reformer's views on the preservation of biblical text known as "providential preservation."

the matter has led to the further conclusion that this preserved Text has best and most faithfully been rendered into English by the AD 1611 King James translators. Thus, it only remains for this author to ascertain and extract from the Holy Text, precisely as it stands, the chronological scheme lying embedded therein, and this is that which follows.

(Faulstich continued from footnote 1, page 5)

Faulstich is convinced that by utilizing the previously mentioned cyclical phenomena in concert with computer derived astronomical calculations and a calendar converter, he has successfully established an "absolute" chronology. He likewise believes that an absolute chronology was impossible in the past as previous workers lacked a computer. Using these methods, Faulstich has produced three extensive works, chronology charts and many periodicals, nearly all of which the present author has perused at length.

To his credit, Faulstich rightly set about to correct the damage Thiele had done to the Hebrew record in *The Mysterious Numbers of the Hebrew Kings* (Grand Rapids, MI: Zondervan, 1983), and *A Chronology of the Hebrew Kings* (Grand Rapids, MI: Zondervan, 1977). Moreover, there is much excellent information to be found in his works and his computer calendar conversion program from which this author has profited. Nevertheless, his work should not be seen as a *third* approach.

The computer-driven cyclical biblical data appears very impressive and convincing; however it is no better than the precise accuracy at which its initial inception date may be determined. That is, exactly which is the first year these various cycles began? Unfortunately when such information cannot be arrived at directly from Scripture, one must resort to assumptions. Assumptions, of course, mar the apparent precision which is implicit with the use of computers. If the first year is incorrect, the computer blindly repeats cycle after cycle each falling at the wrong place.

Attempting to establish the correctness, accuracy and finality of his chronology, Faulstich often states or implies that many of his findings could not have been determined prior to the advent of the computer which allows for so many rapid computations and decisions. In this regard, he bases the identification of the "Artaxerxes" at Ezra 6:14–15 as being Darius I Hystaspis solely upon the retranslating of a Hebrew word in verse 14 from "and" to "even" (see *History, Harmony, The Exile and Return*, 1988, pp. 142–145). Contending that this identification is the key to the correct understanding and unification of the Book(s) of Ezra-Nehemiah (Darius also being the "Artaxerxes" in Nehemiah), elsewhere among his writings he again attributes this determination as having been possible only by utilization of the computer.

However, Martin Anstey made the same identification also resting the entire interpretation on changing "and" to "even" in AD 1913, long before the development of the computer (*The Romance of Bible Chronology*, Vol. I, 1913, pp. 244, 269–270.). Having consulted a Hebraist, such construction admittedly is possible but it is noted that

upon consulting over 20 versions at Ezra 6:14, not one translator or team of translators rendered the "waw" (vau) at the beginning of the Hebrew word for Artaxerxes as "even." The same may be said for the author's four Hebrew interlinear Old Testaments. When so many independent translations are made all designating the Hebrew as "and", can there be any real doubt as to the true interpretation and can such be any more than grasping at straws? Why not insist upon "even" Darius in the same verse as the "waw" is also present there?

Inasmuch as Faulstich often allows the Assyrian data to cloud his judgment whereupon he overrules Scripture, he falls short of his stated goals. Aside from his not infrequent departures from Scripture (i.e., giving Saul but ten years' reign instead of forty, cp. Acts 13:21), the studies suffer from his insistence that a statue found in Nineveh of a seven inch high winged man holding a spotted fallow deer in one arm and a branch of a limb in the other is the representation of the image that Nebuchadnezzar saw in his dream as recorded in the second chapter of the Book of Daniel (Faulstich, *History Harmony and Daniel,* (IO: Chronology Books, Inc., 1988), pp. 44–51).

Faulstich contends that the image bears prophetic and Messianic significance and that it is proportioned to the scale of approximately one hundred years to the inch. In other words, the image's dimensions are arranged such that beginning at the head as the year of Nebuchadnezzar's dream, which he gives as 628 BC, each anatomical part of the man's body is scaled off to fit the chronology of the kingdoms that followed. For example, the third empire in the dream, represented by the brass which extended from the waist to the knees and included the thighs, represents Alexander the Great c. 331 BC and the Grecian Empire. Thus Faulstich finds great significance in the fact that it is about three inches from the top of the statue to the waist. Stating that Greek domination lasted until 161 BC when the Jews made an alliance with Rome (1 Maccabees 8), he converts this 170 years (331 minus 161) to 1.7 inches and notes that this measures to the knees denoting the end of the Greek Empire. He goes on to proportionally scale downward, insisting that the results may be used to foretell the time of John the Baptist, the crucifixion and the dispersion at the hands of Titus in AD 70.

In so doing, he counts as meaningless the import of the 483-year prophecy in Daniel 9:24–27 with its relation to the coming of Messiah preferring the somewhat mystical interpretation relevant to the statue. Moreover, Faulstich's statue manifestly does not fit the description of the dream-image found in the Book of Daniel. In fact, it is the long established well known figure of Nimrod [see Alexander Hislop, *The Two Babylons,* (NJ: Loizeaux Brothers, Inc., 1916) pp. 43–51.].

Faulstich vigorously revived the theory that there were two Belshazzar's, one the son of Nabonidus and another who was the actual son of Nebuchadnezzar (Faulstich, *History Harmony and Daniel,* (IO: Chronology Books, Inc., 1988), pp. 13–17). Faulstich envisions the latter as merely reigning as co-regent during the first three years of Nebuchadnezzar's madness whereupon he is assassinated by his reckoning in 574 BC by the Medes, about 35 years *before* the fall of the city of Babylon. Thus, he curiously maintains and strives at great length to establish that Daniel chapter 5 is not describing the fall

of the city of Babylon. It is felt that the "two Belshazzar" proposal, being readily refutable, is another major flaw in his studies that will, unfortunately, eventually undermine and diminish the credibility of his prodigious undertaking.

* * * * * * * * * * * * *

(Apocrypha continued from fn. 1, page 14) The Apocrypha gradually rose in esteem within the apostate Roman (Western) Church until finally the Council of Trent (AD 1546) affirmed the canonicity of the greater part. In making this decision the Catholic Church sided with the Jews of Alexandria, Egypt in considering the Apocrypha sacred. It was in Alexandria that Mary was revered as the second person of the Trinity by the so-called "Christians." Although Jerome rejected it, the Apocrypha has now been incorporated into his Vulgate by the Roman Catholic Church.

The New Testament contains 263 direct quotes from the Old Testament and 370 allusions to the Old Testament. Though some have claimed for the Apocrypha several vague "allusions" in the New Testament, these are nebulous mirages. Not one time did anyone in the New Testament refer to or quote from the Old Testament Apocrypha [Gleason Archer, *A Survey of Old Testament Introduction*, rev. ed., (Chicago: Moody Press, 1974), p. 75.]. Jesus never referred to the Apocrypha. · Had these books belonged in the Old Testament, why did the Lord not so clarify? The Old Testament had been canonized long before Jesus was born. Yet Origen's fifth column includes the Old Testament Apocrypha. *Vaticanus* B and *Sinaiticus* א include the Apocrypha as part of the text of the Old Testament along with spurious "Apocryphal" books such as "Epistle to Barnabas" and "Shepherd of Hermas" in the New Testament. We are being told that *Vaticanus* is the most accurate Greek text that we have, yet it includes the Apocrypha and Apocryphal books, none of which were canonized.

How does one know that Tobit, for example, is not a God inspired book? In the story, Tobit was blinded by bird dung (2:10); his son, Tobias, went on a journey with an angel who lies about his name (3:17, cp. 5:4, 11–12); the angel instructed Tobias that a fish's gall would heal his blinded father (which it does, 6:8; 11:4–13); and the book teaches that alms and works purge away all sins (12:9). The Word of God, however, teaches that Jesus accomplished that by His once for all finished work in His atoning death and resurrection for the sins and sin of all of Adam's offspring. It affirms that man is saved by God's grace (unmerited favor) through faith in Christ Jesus as a free gift (Eph.2:8), and not by works of righteousness which we have done (Titus 3:5)!

GRACE

The book of Tobit also teaches that demons are to be cast out of a person by the smoke produced by burning the heart and liver of a fish (6:6–7, 16–17; 8:2–3). In the Scriptures, exorcism is produced simply by the power and authority of the Name of Jesus, as is healing. Yet according to Origen, Tobit is "inspired" in the same sense as were the four gospels.

The only books of value among any of those in the Apocrypha are First and Second Maccabees. Although they do not belong to the OT canon, unlike the mythological, spurious Bible contradicting material found in the other extra-biblical books, the data found in Maccabees does seem to be a fairly reliable historical

account of the Seleucid oppression of the Jews and the revolt led by the Maccabean priesthood against that tyranny and persecution (171–37 BC).

Much has been said over the years concerning the fact that the first edition of the King James Bible contained the Apocrypha. It is true that the *publisher* of the 1611 edition did insert the Apocrypha between the Testaments, but it was never included within the Old Testament text as it was so done in the Hexapla, in *Vaticanus*, and *Sinaiticus*. The Apocrypha section from the Cambridge Group of the 1611 translators rendered the entire work into English but for historical purposes only – not as inspired Scripture. The Apocrypha was removed even from the space between the Testaments in the second edition.

* * * * * * * * * * * * *

(Septuagint continued from fn. 4, page 14) Brown continues: "This higher authority would be manifested in three ways. Firstly, where the LXX translators were correct, the Apostles would quote verbally and literally from the Septuagint, and thus remind their readers of the Scriptures with which they were already familiar in that particular form. Secondly, where the LXX is incorrect, the Apostles amend it, and make their quotations according to the Hebrew, translating it anew into Greek, and improving upon the defective rendering. Thirdly, when it was the purpose of the Holy Spirit to point out more clearly in what sense the quotations from the Old Testament Scriptures were to be understood, the Apostles were guided to restate the revealed truth more fully or explicitly. By the hands of the Apostles, the Holy Spirit thus delivers again His own inspired message, in order to make more clear to later generations what had been formerly declared through the prophets in an earlier age. By giving again the old truth in new words, the Holy Ghost infallibly imparted teaching which lay hidden in the Old, but which could only be fully understood by a later generation if given in a different form."

Thus, these type of examples would be seen as the Holy Spirit's own commentary with regard to these OT verses. This last proclamation would also hold to be the true situation and explanation for all of the NT quotes differing from the OT had no pre-Christian LXX existed.

"... From this it is evident that the Holy Spirit exercises independence of all human versions when He guides His Apostles to quote in the New Testament that which He had caused to be written in the Old. The Lord Jesus Christ, being One in Divine power and glory with the Eternal Father and Eternal Spirit, demonstrated the same independence, and exercised the same authority."

Yet as we have already explained, all of this is highly unlikely to be the case as the internal evidence, etc., militates against the early Church's having used the LXX.

* * * * * * * * * * * * *

(Luke not a Gentile cont. from fn. 3, page 15) The contrary evidence foremost in the mind of the scholars, is gleaned from the fourth chapter of Colossians. Here, Paul closes his letter by listing the various people that are with him as he writes (Col.4:7–13), as well as the names of several of those to whom the letter is addressed (Col.4:15–17). Among those whom Paul lists as

being at his side, some are said to be "of the circumcision" (i.e., Jewish, vs. 11). It is generally acknowledged from the syntax and context, etc. (and probably correctly so) that they are the three mentioned immediately before the "circumcision" reference in verse 11: Aristarchus, Marcus, and Jesus called Justus. As Paul mentions Luke (vs. 14) after the "circumcision" allusion (vs. 11), it is deduced that he must not be Jewish. However, this argument has little force. A careful reading of the Colossian passages discloses that verses 7–8 are introducing Tychicus, the letter bearer, to the Church. They also give commendation and new status to his travel companion, Onesimus, whom they have known in the past as a runaway slave who seems to have stolen from Philemon, a wealthy member of their congregation (Philemon 10–21). Clearly then from the context, Aristarchus, Marcus, and Justus are grouped and introduced next, not because they are Jews, but rather because they are the only three with Paul (other than Tychicus whom they now behold) that the church at Colosse does not already know. Their nationality is thereby not given for the purpose of ethnic grouping, but for the purpose of identification and information concerning the three.

The proof of this is straightforward for as we read verses 12–14 it becomes abundantly clear that the Colossians already know Epaphras, Luke, and Demas. This is what they have in common and is the reason for the positioning of their names. Thus, Tychicus and Onesimus are listed together because they are the bearers of Paul's letter to the church; Aristarchus, Marcus, and Justus are grouped together because they are not known by those of Colosse; Epaphras, Luke, and Demas are so placed because, being already known by that local church, they need no introduction. This is the obvious correct and true reason for the arrangement of the names in the fourth chapter of Colossians. Hence, we see there are reasons other than that of merely racial or national background involved as to why Luke was not included among those of the "circumcision." From this it may be seen how imprudent is it to erect a tenet on such trivial, flimsy evidence. Yet this is the *strongest* offered by those who would have us accept that Luke was indeed a Gentile, and that against the clear testimony of Romans 3!

The lame argument that "Luke" (or Lucas, Philemon 24) is a Gentile name and not Jewish is of no force. Not only is it common practice today in countries throughout the world to give children non-ethnic names and even the name of famous people from any place or any time frame (i.e., Blacks naming sons "Washington" or "Roosevelt" and Hispanics naming sons "Jesus"), the Scriptures furnish similar examples. "Alexander" is manifestly a Greek or Macedonian name, yet Acts 19:33–34 mentions an "Alexander" and states that he is a Jew! "Apollos" is unmistakably a Greek designation but Acts 18:24 records that he is Jewish. Moreover, Aristarchus, Marcus, and Justus (the very names given in Colossians 4 and said to be "of the circumcision") are all Gentile designations! Throughout his ministry among the Gentiles, Paul used his Roman name rather than his Hebrew (i.e., Saul) as did Peter (Hebrew name = Simon) In fact, most Jews who lived in the Diaspora used two names: the Jewish was used in the synagogue, and the Gentile in business dealings. Thus, "Luke" could well have been the public or professional (as a Doctor) name of a Jew who lived among the Gentiles. More examples could be furnished but what

need? The mouth of two or more witnesses has spoken; the matter is incontestable and closed.

Their third proof is similar; namely, that Luke's profession as a physician is evidence that he was non-Jewish. Yet on several occasions Christ referred to physicians; hence the practice existed in Israel at that time (Luke 4:23; Mat. 9:12). Thus we have seen that the arguments used to support the opinion that Luke was a Gentile are neither compelling nor well founded.

To the contrary, Romans 3:1–2 straightforwardly states that the chief advantage of being a Jew was that they were the God-chosen national vehicle through which He gave revelation to the human race. Therefore the burden of proof is on those who claim that Luke was somehow an exception to this biblical decree. Yet we have already seen that the evidence from the names listed in Colossians, etc. is far too vague, inconsequential, and inconclusive for us to accept as justification to override the Romans testimony. Moreover the Romans 3:1–2 statement is so clear and unambiguous, a later written Scripture of equal or superior clarity must be found and offered to overwhelm its witness. But the Holy Writ has never indicated that God ever changed His established rule of using only the Hebrews to record His revelation.

Furthermore, Luke was with Paul on his last trip to Jerusalem and seems to have been an eyewitness to Paul's arrest at the Temple as recorded in Acts 21. The crowd was aroused by Jews from Asia who charged, among other things, that Paul had brought Gentiles into the Temple area. Luke records that Paul had not so done, but as these Asian Jews had earlier seen Paul in the city with Trophimus the Ephesian, they had assumed Paul had brought that outsider into the Temple grounds with him. The false accusation aroused the populace into a frenzy which resulted in Paul's arrest at the Temple Mount by several hundred Roman soldiers under the command of Claudius Lysias (21:32, cp. 23:26).

The point is that when the Jews accused Paul of polluting the Temple by bringing Gentiles therein, why did they only allude to Trophimus? Why did they not include Luke who was also with Paul in the streets of Jerusalem (21:15–18, e.g., "we," "us")? The fact that Luke was not mentioned in the accusation is a most convincing indication that he was not a Gentile. Indeed, after joining the second missionary journey at Troas (Acts 16:10, the change here of the personal pronoun "they" in vv. 6–8 to "we" indicates that Luke, the narrator, had joined Paul's company), Luke accompanied Paul on several trips back to Jerusalem at which time they reported on their travels to the apostolic church (here and Acts 18:21), yet the issue was never raised over his being a Gentile. It is therefore concluded Luke was not named in the accusation when Paul was arrested because it was well known that he was a Hebrew, and this should be acknowledged as confirming evidence to our thesis.

As stated initially, it must be concluded that Luke was a Hebrew. The notion that he was a Gentile is based on little more than tradition. The biblical account strongly evinces his Jewishness, and we must always hold to the Scriptures over tradition when the two conflict. The infallible Word of God is the source and fountain for all real wisdom and scholarship.

CHART ONE

A. STANDARD OR AN ABSOLUTE CHRONOLOGY

As previously stated, the purpose of this endeavor is to construct a "standard" chronology for the span covered within the Old Testament. Specifically, the *terminus a quo* is the Creation and the *terminus ad quem* is the crucifixion and resurrection of the Lord Jesus Christ.

It will be noted that the goal is that of a "standard" chronology, not an "absolute" chronology. As Scripture normally records only entire years for a given event and not the days and months, summing the years may yield an inaccurate total because the partial years were not included. After twelve years of examining numerous arguments, date placements, regnal data, ancient inscriptions, royal annals, eclipse calculations, etc., this researcher has concluded that any such assignment is not realistic of any chronology of prolonged duration.[1] Even the serious notion of an absolute chronology stretches credulity and borders on the ludicrous. The critical secular dates at the few points of synchronization have simply never been established.

For example, the 19th year of Nebuchadnezzar in which the City of Jerusalem fell in conjunction with the burning of the Temple has received three "absolute" dates, 588, 587 and 586 BC by various scholars of notable merit. The same may be said for the year in which Nebuchadnezzar ascended the throne of Babylon, the year of Christ's birth, the 15th year of the reign of Tiberius Caesar, and the year of the Crucifixion. It must be remembered that chronology is a branch of historical science; hence, it is constantly subject to revision.

Each expert presents a most authoritative case for his position yet not without some assumptions, however valid they may be deemed, hence some conjecture is always present. The same is true concerning a great many of the historical dates regarding the Empires of Egypt, Babylon, Assyria, Syria, etc. which are germane to such a study. The most convincing is usually the one last examined by the reader. The probability of determining each of these with flawless precision borders on the impossible.

Nonetheless, it is believed that the effort herein presented is as accurate as may be attained, apart from Divine revelation, from the available data and is more than sufficient for the study of the kingdoms whose existence falls within the history of that contained in Scripture. The overall skeletal outline as presented is believed to be within three years of absolute, although the dates of individual events and persons located within the outline during the latter period of the judges may be of greater error. This will be clarified in the detailed explanation of Chart 4.

The final product of this dissertation is a series of chronological charts displaying the dated major events in the Old Testament which can be tested and checked by the user. This is significant because most previous works are either on a scale so minute that they must be accepted or rejected as a whole, or else they are so encumbered with extraneous data relating to other nations with whom the Hebrews came in contact such as Babylon, Egypt, Assyria, etc., as to be hopelessly bewildering to the everyday reader.

The accompanying charts portray that which the Holy Scriptures themselves state. For example, when it is written that a certain king began to reign in a specific year of the rule of another king and that he reigned for so many years, the data is accepted and charted down accordingly. It cannot be overemphasized that the charts themselves are the very heart of the dissertation. That they exist, without the context of a single Scripture having been violated, is proof of our aforementioned proposal (page iv).

Doubtless, the author will seem outrageously naive to most, for the chronology presented

---

[1] One merely has to observe the numerous times qualifying words such as "if," "probably," "perhaps," "it would seem," "suggesting," "we believe," "presumably," "it is possible," etc. in any standard work such as Jack Finegan's, *Handbook of Biblical Chronology*, (Princeton: 1964) to prove to oneself the limitations regarding the accuracy of chronology studies. This is all the more so when different calendars, regnal years, and methods of reckoning regnal year must be considered.

herewith is so out of step with modern thinking. However it should be remembered that many brilliant scholars of the past accepted without hesitation the concept of Creation as being only about 6,000 years ago. To name but a few who held to this "romantic" view includes not only James Ussher, but his contemporary William Shakespeare (1564–1616) – himself a biblical scholar. Another was Sir Isaac Newton (1642–1727),[1] the undisputed greatest scientist and mathematician yet to live. He was also an outstanding biblical chronologist.

Indeed, unlike nearly all today who fancy themselves scientists, Newton and many of his day who cleaved to the scriptural account of Creation and the Deluge were scientists in the true sense. Being well grounded in many different disciplines of scientific investigation and study, they were able to discern when a theory or hypothesis in one field violated well-known, well-established laws and principles in that of another.

Conversely, most moderns specialize to the point that they have no broad scientific base upon which to stand. The result is that while theorizing in their field (e.g., geology, biology) they are oblivious to the fact they are moving against the laws of physics, chemistry and statistics. In so doing they venture farther and farther from reality and fact, all the time deluded that such flights of imagination are science.

Newton defended the chronology of Ussher against those who tried to push back the date of Creation and wrote powerful refutations on atheism while defending the literal six-day Bible Creation account. Moreover, he believed that the worldwide flood of Noah's day accounted for most of the geologic phenomena observed in his day. Newton authored two volumes addressing biblical chronology: *The Observations Upon the Prophecies of Daniel*, and the great work, *The Chronology of Ancient Kingdoms Amended*. These were published posthumously in 1728. In the latter, Newton decimated and overthrew the then accepted current dates of Greek, Latin and Egyptian chronology by demonstrating the impossibility of using any of their chronologies as a stable foundation which could be used as a standard.

The actual fact is that neither geology, paleontology, nor any evolutionist can extract precise dating for the age of the earth and the antiquity of man. As Creation scientists have shown that all radiometric dating, including radiocarbon, is inaccurate, historical records are still the only reliable method of obtaining these dates.[2] It cannot be overemphasized that all the actual historical records agree in substance with the so-called "short chronology" as found in the Bible. Significantly longer chronologies, which are required to support the modern dogma of evolution, are all based on uniformitarian extrapolation and other assumptions associated with particular present physical processes.

As can be demonstrated, all such calculations are founded upon unproven, untestable, and often illogical and unreasonable assumptions;[3] thus they can never be accurate or reliable in obtaining actual historical dates. We proclaim and shall show that the Word of the Living God is the most accurate and trustworthy source. Hence the weight of the scientific data, when properly understood, is firmly in support of a recent creation and the chronology of history which is in accord with the biblical record. Comprehending this, we unashamedly stand beside the promises of God to preserve His Word as inerrant as He originally gave it and beside such men of God from the past whose faith stands forth unto this day.

---

[1] Sir Isaac Newton is the discoverer of the law of universal gravitation, the formulation of the three laws of motion, the binomial theorem, the calculus (a basic tool in the more exact fields of science) and anticipated the great law of the conservation of energy. As an astronomer, Newton constructed the first reflecting telescope. He held the chair of Mathematics at Cambridge for 33 years, represented the university in Parliament and for 24 years was president of the Royal Society (a group of scientists whose names read like "Who's Who"). In 1705 he was knighted and upon his demise in his eighty-fifth year, buried in Westminster Abbey. Newton made a hobby of chronology, becoming its avid student during the last 30 years of his life.

[2] See Harold S. Slusher, *Critique of Radiometric Dating, op. cit.*, pp. 1–43; Henry M. Morris, *The Scientific Case for Creation, op. cit.*, pp. 43–64; Gerald E. Aardsma, *Radiocarbon and the Genesis Flood, op. cit.*, pp. 1–22; and Thomas G. Barnes, *Origin and Destiny of the Earth's Magnetic Field*, (San Diego, CA: Master Books, 1973), pp. 1–64.

[3] *Ibid.*

B. THE SKELETAL OUTLINE

Chart 1 is simple, direct and straightforward. The major problem here lies in the fact that it is at this point that a principal date must be determined, one which will affect all anterior values. The date is that of the fall of the Kingdom of Judah with the subsequent burning of the Temple, destruction of the city of Jerusalem along with its walls and the accompanying deportation (the third) of most of its citizens to Babylon. The Scriptures date this as occurring in the 19th year of the reign of Nebuchadnezzar (cp. Jer. 52:12–14; 32:1; and see page 125).

This is critical from a chronological perspective as it represents one of only three places where firm dated secular historical events overlap the Scriptures, thus forming a connecting bridge between the two. The others are the fourth year of Jehoiakim with Nebuchadnezzar's first which was also the year of the great battle of Carchemish (Jer. 25:1; 46:2), and the 15th year of the reign of Tiberius Caesar with the 30th year of our Lord Jesus, the Christ (Luke 3:1,23). Moreover, it is only at these infrequent bridges that Bible chronology may be assigned and fixed as to a "BC" designation (this study uses Gregorian, not astral or Julian dates, see page 287). All other biblical dates are so assigned by numbering backward and forward from these three anchor points.[1] Thus, if we err at these contact points the mistake will be uniformly disseminated throughout the chronology.

The date of the fall of Jerusalem has been taken as 586 BC (see Appendix N, page 309). About 80 percent of the previous works concur. The years 588 and 587 also receive able support by careful men. For example Ussher, who held to the 588 BC date,[2] was later upheld by Henry Browne.[3] They have recently been joined in

that decision by Eugene W. Faulstich,[4] whereas Henry Fynes Clinton championed 587 BC.[5] Clinton's conclusions were later vigorously upheld by Sir Robert Anderson, who was for many years head of the criminal investigation division of Scotland Yard.[6]

Much later, William F. Albright[7] joined Clinton and Anderson in upholding 587 as the year of Jerusalem's destruction at the hands of Nebuchadnezzar. More recently, this date has received even wider credence and acceptance within academic circles due to the fact that Donald J. Wiseman, formerly of the British Museum and later professor of Assyriology at the University of London, published in its favor.[8] Biblically the latter date has much in its favor and if it were known to be the true date, this writer would neither find it offensive nor an incompatible adjustment with the aforementioned guidelines in establishing a "standard" chronology.

As can readily be seen from the chart, once the BC date of the fall in the 19th year of Nebuchadnezzar's rule has been established, the other major Bible occurrences are "fixed" by measuring from 586 BC. The span from that year to a given biblical event is determined exclusively by using data gleaned directly from the Scriptures themselves, adding them to this 586 BC base until we arrive at a date for the Creation.

The first decisive Scripture is Ezekiel 4:4–5 where the Word of God indicates that the period of time from the division of the monarchy to the final fall of Judah to Babylon is a span of 390 years. Thus, beginning at 586 we number back 390 years arriving at 975 BC (inclusive numbering, hence minus one) to arrive at the

[1] A fourth is the 1st official year of Evil Merodach with the 37th year of Jeconiah's captivity. A "reported" 4 July 568 BC lunar eclipse (Julian, Gregorian = 28 June – Thiele, *Chronology*, 1977, p. 69) and c.30 astral observations in Nebuchadnezzar's 37th year helps solidify this bridge, but more effort is required than for the other three.

[2] James Ussher, *Annals of the World*, revised by Larry & Marion Pierce, (Green Forest, AR: Master Books, 2003), pp. 104–107 (1658 ed., p. 91).

[3] Henry Browne, *Ordo Saeclorum*, (London: John Parker Pub., 1844), pp. 185, 230.

[4] Faulstich, *History, Harmony and the Hebrew Kings, op. cit.*, pp. 77, 218–220.

[5] Henry Fynes Clinton, *Fasti Hellenici, vol. I*, (Oxford, England: 1834), appendix, p. 319.

[6] Sir Robert Anderson, *The Coming Prince*, (Grand Rapids, MI: Kregel Publications, 1882), Appendix I, pp. 230–237.

[7] William F. Albright, "The Chronology of the Divided Monarchy of Israel," *Bulletin of the American Schools of Oriental Research*, 100 (1945), pp. 16–22.

[8] D.J. Wiseman, *Nebuchadressar And Babylon*, (Oxford, England: Oxford University Press, 1983), p. 37.

date of the death of Solomon whereupon the Kingdom divided.

586 + 390 = 976 − 1 = 975 BC (inclusive)

This Ezekiel passage is most significant for it takes the date of the division of the kingdom out of the hands and subjective devising of man, chronologist and archaeologist alike, and sets a fixed God-given mathematical value of 390 years for the interval. This is confirmed by the lengths of the reigns of the kings of Judah from Rehoboam's first year to Zedekiah's 11th. However the justification for this interpretation and its application shall await our discussion of the fifth chart. As it will be seen at that time, this is the basic concept behind the laying out of Chart 5 although the time span is extended to the days of Alexander the Great for clarity and completeness.

From 975 BC, one merely continues back to Adam. The 40-year dominion of Solomon is added to this 975 taking us back to 1015 BC, the year David died and Solomon began his sole reign. To this established date three years must be subtracted in order to arrive at the inception of the Temple construction, Solomon's having begun the work but three years one month and two days from his coronation (1 Ki. 6:1; 2 Chron. 3:1–2). As will be documented later, Solomon's coronation as sole rex would have taken place in the month Abib of the year 1015 BC (Nisan, not Tishri as Edwin R. Thiele maintains; cp. 1 Kings 6:37–38); hence, the first months of his fourth year would fall in the year 1012, not 1011. Before continuing, the reader should prove this for himself by taking a few moments and sketching this.

975 + 40 = 1015 BC − 3 = 1012 BC

From the commencement of the Temple back to the Exodus spans 480 years (1 Kings 6:1). Note that only 479 is actually added, as the work began very early in the 480th year as Ussher also detected:[1]

> When the Israelites are said to go out of Egypt the fifteenth day of the first moneth (Num. 33:3): and Solomon to begin to build the temple, in the 480 year after their departure (1 Kings 6:1), on the second day of the second

month (2 Chron. 3:2), the moneths and dayes which bound each termination of that Period, shew, that 11 moneths and 14 dayes are to be taken away; and not that the whole 480, but only 479 years, and sixteen dayes are to be taken for the space of that Period.

This places the year of the Exodus under Moses' leadership at 1491 BC.

1012 + 479 = 1491 BC

Many theories regarding this "480-year" passage have been proposed. For now, it is merely being set forth demonstrating the method and relative ease with which one may move back through time to the Creation as depicted on the first chart. An appropriate defense is given in the discussion of the fourth chart where it more properly belongs. The resolving of this problem and the disposition of this number is most critical to any biblical chronology.

Having established 1491 as the year of Exodus, a period of 430 years representing the time from that point unto the covenant which God made with Abraham when he entered the land of Canaan must be added. This takes us to 1921 BC, the year Abraham's father, Terah, died and he departed from Haran, entering into the land of promise.

1491 + 430 = 1921 BC

By comparing Genesis 12:4, Exodus 12:40, and Galatians 3:17, the much debated 430-year epoch can be properly understood. Never is it said in these Scripture references that the Jews dwelt in or were slaves in Egypt for 430 years. Rather, they teach that the duration of their sojourn from the time Abraham (Abram) entered the promised land until the giving of the Law three months after the Exodus was that of 430 years.

That is, Exodus 12:40 does not say that the children of Israel sojourned 430 years in Egypt. It does say that the sojourn of that particular branch of Abraham's lineage as traced through Isaac and Jacob, with which we are specifically concerned, was the group which eventually went down to Egypt.

In other words, it is a statement of identification as to which of Abraham's lineages the narrative is dealing as Abraham had numerous other lineages, e.g., that of Ishmael and also

---

[1] Ussher, *Annals, op. cit.,* "The Epistle to the Reader," p. 8 (1658 ed., p. iii).

many offspring from his marriage to Keturah (Genesis 25). The verse is telling us which children of Abraham are being focused upon, not how long they were in Egypt. That the lineage of Isaac was the branch selected by God is indisputable for "in Isaac shall thy seed be called" (Genesis 21:12c, cp. 17:19,21 and Hebrews 11:17–18). All this will be enlarged upon when the third chart is explored; for now only enough is being given to establish the general method and logic in the outline exhibited on the first chart.

To the year 1921 BC we must add the number of years from the Flood to the covenant with Abraham in order to derive the year of the Deluge. A misjudgment is often made at this point leading many investigators into a 60-year error. Although Chart 1 directs the reader to the sixth chart for the derivation of this span, an explanation is deemed appropriate at this point in order to establish the correctness of the logic and methods employed in the preparation of the skeletal outline found on the first chart.

Numerous authorities determine this span as being 367 years instead of 427 because they either fail to notice or accept the data given in Genesis 11 and 12 as being genuine. That is, many authorities have been speared by the trident, consequently they have erroneously concluded that the Scriptures contain errors.

Others fall into this error due to the fact that Genesis 11:26 says that Terah was 70 years old when he began to beget sons. The verse places Abraham (Abram) first in the list of Terah's three sons, hence they assume without further consideration Abraham to be the firstborn. They then total the life spans of the patriarchs in Genesis 11:10-25 obtaining 222 years, add to that 70 for Terah's age when he supposedly fathered Abraham and 75 for Abraham's age when he left Haran and entered Canaan (Gen. 12:4) deriving the sum of 367 years.

The problem with this calculation is that it is based upon a faulty presumption. Albeit Abraham's name is given first, he was not the firstborn son. Logic and proper scientific bearing demand that before coming to final conclusions, one first obtains and considers all data pertinent to a problem. Comparing Genesis 11:32 with 12:4, it may be seen that Abraham was 75 when Terah died at age 205.

From this, the fact is firmly established that Terah was 130 years old (205 − 75 = 130) when Abraham was born. This means that although Terah was 70 when he had his first son, that son could not have been Abraham; it had to have been either Nahor or Haran.

Moreover, that was one of the main reasons why God had to remove Abraham from Ur. As long as he remained there, he would never become the head of the family clan for, by the law of primogeniture, the firstborn son would have so been. Why was Abraham listed first? Because he was the son who received the blessing and the birthright. This is most important to perceive and a biblical precedence had already been given.

When speaking of Noah's sons Shem, Ham and Japheth, Shem's name is always mentioned first because he received the birthright and the blessing (Gen. 9:26; Luke 3:36), hence we find the Messiah coming through his lineage. However, Genesis 9:24–25 speaks of Ham as being the youngest son, 10:21 unmistakably says Japheth was the elder, leaving Shem as the middle son. Likewise Isaac is placed before Ishmael in 1 Chron. 1:28 although Isaac was not the older but the younger of the two. The 427 years is thus obtained:

    222 Total of patriarchs' life spans in Gen. 11:10-25
  + 130 Add Terah's age of 130 when Abram was born
  + 75 Abraham's age when he left Haran (Gen. 12:4)
  = 427 years

At the inception of this research, it was not known by the author that the time from the Flood to the beginning of Abraham's sojourn was such a point of contention. Years after having independently solved the puzzle, it was learned that Ussher was the first to make the correction of Terah's age from 70 years to 130 at the birth of Abraham (*Annals*, p. 22; 1658 ed. page 4), again justifying our admiration for his insight and careful attention.

To obtain the year of the Flood, take the 1921 BC date derived previously as the year of Terah's death when Abraham departed from Haran, entering into the land of promise and beginning the sojourn, and add the preceding 427 years.

    1921 + 427 = 2348 BC (year of the Flood)

Among all who use the Masoretic Text as the basis and foundation for their chronology, there is no dispute over the length of time traversed from the Flood back to the Creation. As shown on the extreme left side of Chart 6, by summing the life spans of the patriarchs listed in the fifth chapter of Genesis, 1656 years are determined as the intervening period. Add this to the previously derived 2348 BC year of the Flood thereby securing the year of Creation as 4004 BC.

$$2348 + 1656 = 4004 \text{ BC}$$

C. DATE OF THE CREATION

The date of Creation as taken from the Scriptures has been calculated by many scholars over the centuries resulting in a significant divergence of solutions. As is true for nearly each of the natural major time segments into which biblical chronology has been divided (i.e., the 430-year sojourn, the 480 years from Exodus to the commencement of the Temple, etc.), the answers fall into two general categories, that of the "long chronology" or the "short chronology."

CHRONOLOGIST	BC YEAR
1. J. Africanus	5501
2. G. Syncellus	5492
3. J. Jackson	5426
4. W. Hales	5411
5. Eusebius	5199
6. M. Scotus	4192
7. L. Condomanus	4141
8. T. Lydiat	4103
9. M. Maestlinus	4079
10. J. Ricciolus	4062
11. J. Salianus	4053
12. H. Spondanus	4051
13. M. Anstey	4042
14. W. Lange	4041
15. E. Reinholt	4021
16. J. Cappellus	4005
17. J. Ussher	4004
18. E. Greswell	4004
19. F. Jones	4004
20. E. Faulstich	4001
21. D. Petavius	3983
22. F. Klassen	3975
23. Becke	3974
24. Krentzeim	3971
25. W. Dolen	3971
26. E. Reusnerus	3970
27. J. Claverius	3968
28. C. Longomontanus	3966
29. P. Melanchthon	3964
30. J. Haynlinus	3963
31. A. Salmeron	3958
32. J. Scaliger	3949
33. M. Beroaldus	3927
34. A. Helwigius	3836

The preceding table[1] portrays the calculated interval from the Creation to the birth of Christ Jesus and depicts an objective sampling of chronologers over the past several hundred years.

As a matter of curiosity and completeness, we add the Indian chronology at 6,174 years for the interval in question (as computed by Gentil), the Babylonian at 6,158 years (computed by Bailly), the Chinese at 6,157 years (Bailly), the Septuagint at 5,508 years (by Abulfaragus) while most of the Jewish writers bring it down to 4,000 and even 3,760.

The scatter effect may seem strange and unaccountable to many, but by now most probably already begin to see some of the rationale leading up to the unevenness in the results.

Julius Africanus, Georgius Syncellus, John Jackson and Dr. William Hales are representative of those who used the Septuagint for the patriarchal generations and other "Long" interval determinations (as that with the Exodus, see discussion on Chart 3).

The "short chronology" is the result of relying upon the Hebrew; the disagreements are the result of differing opinions and interpretations by the individual workers within the Masoretic Text and of some coming to the task with various doctrinal presuppositions to maintain.

Pierre Simon LaPlace (1749-1827), the famous French mathematician and astronomer, found Ussher's 4004 BC (23 October, 6:00 P.M. Julian) Creation data[2] as being most remarkable for it

---

[1] Charles Roger Dundee, *A Collation of The Sacred Scriptures* (1847), p. 20.

[2] Ussher, *Annals, op. cit.,* p. 17 (1658 ed., p. 1). Also see C. O. Dunbar, *Historical Geology,* (New York: John Wiley and Sons, Inc., 1953), p. 21. where, curiously, Dr. Dunbar wrongly states Ussher's date as 9:00 A.M., October 26.

corresponded with an extremely significant astronomical alignment. LaPlace described it as being "one in which the great axis of the earth's orbit coincided with the line of the equinoxes, and consequently when the true and mean equinoxes were united."[1]

Ussher has been greatly disparaged for stating the precise date as being 6:00 P.M., October 23, 4004 BC (Julian calendar, see p. 287). That notwithstanding, it should be affirmed that his calculation was actually not as difficult or out of the realm of probability as one might imagine at first glance. The reason that such a seemingly ridiculous explicit date may be assigned to the Creation is not only biblically sound, it needs but the simplest forthright logic.

Until God told the Jews to change their calendar at the time of the Exodus, the beginning of their year had been in the autumn (Exo. 12:2; 13:4; cp. 9:31 and 23:15). The month which they designate "Tishri" (September-October) had been their first month whereas "Abib" (Hebrew meaning "first ear of ripe grain," March-April) had been their seventh month. The current arrangement of the Jewish calendar, with its civil year beginning in Tishri and its religious calendar beginning in Nisan, is a vestigial reminder finding its roots in this God-given decree.

As many of the Old Testament books were written while the Jews were in Babylonian captivity, these latter books used the Babylonian (Aramaic) word for Abib which is "Nisan." Thus in Scripture, both Nisan and Abib signify the same month. From the historical account of the plagues of Egypt in the cited verses, the departure occurred in early springtime. Thus the Hebrews changed their calendar by calling Abib their first month whereas it had been their seventh and Tishri, formerly their first month, became the seventh.

The question that focuses upon the solution is: before God told the Hebrews to alter their calendar so that their seventh month would become their first month, why had these people of God chosen the fall for the beginning of their year? Logic demands that they were merely continuing that which had been handed down as tradition from generation to generation from the time of Adam.

As proof of such a propensity among these people attention is called to the fact that the first chapter of Genesis records "the evening and the morning were the first day ... the evening and the morning were the second day," etc. In point of fact the Jews still begin their 24-hour-day at evening, having obviously obtained the idea from the Creation account and continued it down through the centuries. Therefore the Creation occurred at eventide (about 6:00 P.M.) near October 1 in 4004 BC.

From similar logic and using the Julian calendar, Ussher selected the first Sunday (the biblical first day of the week) after the autumnal equinox. As Julian leap year rules do not drop three days every 400 years, the seasons drift. This is why Ussher has the autumnal equinox on October 23 for 4004 BC.[2] October 23 is the correct Julian date; however, the modern Gregorian date is September 21. This was Ussher's rationale, and it illustrates the soundness and clarity of his thought.

If the mathematical outline given on Chart 1 is correct, Adam was created out of the dust of the earth on the sixth day, Friday the 28th of October, 4004 BC (Julian). Were Christ Jesus born in 4 BC, as most researchers reckon, His birth took place in the 4,000th year after Adam.

The framework displayed on Chart 1 coincides with Ussher's with but one year's difference here or there. If Chart 1 is incorrect, other charts based upon it will likewise be inaccurate. This is why Chart 1 is so important. However it will be noted that although specific dates may be incorrect, if the first chart contains error, the compartmentalized blocks (or "mathematical fences") of data remain intact, lacking only new beginning and ending points in terms of years.

---

[1] Anstey, *The Romance of Bible Chronology*, op. cit., pp. 48-49. Anstey quotes LaPlace without giving the reference.

[2] Such computations assume that the period of the sun and moon have remained constant since Creation. No allowance was made for the "long day of Joshua," etc., as eclipse studies show that no time was lost. Rather, a miraculous alteration in the normal day occurred so that there was no change in the predictable motion and harmony of the heavenly bodies. As much time was subtracted from the night as was added to the daylight period, thus maintaining the integrity of the 24-hour-day.

That is, the 390-year span of the divided monarchy would remain unaltered save the beginning and ending dates, but the chronological data contained between these boundaries would remain in the same relative positions with regard to each other and the beginning and ending points. Only their numerical values would alter, and those in direct relation to the number of years in which the *terminus a quo* and the *terminus ad quem* might be changed. The same would hold true for the 480, 430, 427, and 1,656-year segments. That is, any errors arising within the compartmentalized segments are not cumulative due to the biblically established length of the sections.[1]

Axiomatically it follows that an error in the *terminus a quo* or *terminus ad quem* of any of the compartmentalized sections will obviously cause the starting and ending dates to be incorrect by the same number of years in those segments which follow. Again a cumulative error will not result as the next compartment is of fixed duration.

From the preceding, observe that since beginning the analysis of Chart 1 the Word of God allows one to trace quickly back to the Creation,[2] usually with a series of rather large leaps which place the inquirer at a significant biblical happening. As the pertinent Scriptures

are given beside the dates, their accuracy and veracity may be readily ascertained except the few cases where the amount of data needed to derive the number of years between the bounding events would clutter the chart.

These dates thus become "biblical anchor points" from which further detailed investigation can begin and end. The data required to confirm these is located and clarified on other charts (Chart 3 for the controversial "430-year" sojourn and Chart 6 for the 427 and 1656 segments) and referenced accordingly on the first chart. This was done in order to keep the initial chart simple and uncluttered whereby the user might "enter into the flow" more readily.

Of course, the initial study actually began at the Creation and dated forward from that miraculous event by adding and assigning AM (*Anno Mundi* = year of the world) or AH (*Anno Hominis* = year of man) numbers to these years.[3] Nevertheless, as described previously, in order to convert these categories into BC designations, the starting point was taken at 586, working backward to Creation.

Note that in order to convert an *Anno Mundi* date to a BC date or vice versa, merely subtract the given year from the year of Creation or 4004. That is, 586 BC is 3418 AM (4004 − 586 = 3418). Another way of saying this is that summing any given years *Anno Mundi* date and its BC designation will always yield 4004 (i.e., 586 + 3418 = 4004).

Normally the other charts were prepared by utilizing the dates contained within the rectangles on Chart 1. For example, Chart 2 was derived by beginning with the year enclosed inside the fourth rectangle, 1921 BC. However, most of the main charts portray the time between two of the circumscribed years as formerly set forth with regard to Chart 5. Chart 3 is also an example of these as it depicts

---

[1] Although the Holy Writ normally notes only entire years and not the days and months of events, it must be seen as most significant that the Holy Spirit has guided the writers of Scripture to diligently add the very day and month involved for the beginning and ending of each of these large compartmentalized blocks in which merely summing of the years would lead to an inaccurate total because the partial years had not been taken into account (e.g., see footnote 2, p. 52).

[2] D.A. Waite, *Biblical Chronology,* (Collingswood, NJ: Bible For Today #9, 1973), page 11. There are two distinct approaches employed in performing biblical chronology. This method is referred to as "retrospective chronology." The technique involves beginning at the end of a historical sequence and working in a logical fashion back in time to some earlier point. Dr. Waite is citing, by permission, from Dr. Charles Fred Lincoln who was his former Dallas Theological Seminary professor between 1948–50. Dr. Lincoln lectured on Bible Chronology and distributed mimeographed notes to his students. Dr. Waite freely acknowledges that he has drawn from these notes in compiling his publication. Also see the *International Standard Bible Encyclopedia,* (ISBE), G. W. Bromiley, ed., (Grand Rapids, MI: Eerdmans Printing Co., 1979), pp. 673–685.

[3] Waite, *Biblical Chronology, op. cit.,* p. 11. This second method of performing biblical chronology is known as "progressive chronology." This technique involves beginning at the Creation and working forward in a logical systematic fashion using the chronological and genealogical data found within the Scriptures to determine the elapsed time to the succeeding events, solve any problems that may be encountered and thereby establish dates for these happenings.

the 430-year span between 1921 BC when Abraham entered Canaan and began the "sojourn" and 1491 BC, the year of the Exodus.

Chart 4 represents the 480 years from the Exodus to the fourth year of Solomon's reign during which the building of the Temple was initiated (1 Kings 6:1). The fifth chart has already been mentioned; however it should be added that an expanded explanation as to the validity of the interpretation and application of the Ezekiel 4:4–5 passages will be given within the detailed account of that graph. Chart 6 is an overall panorama of the whole of Chart 1 with supplementary embellishments.

Thus it becomes abundantly manifest that if we err on the first chart, other departures (anachronisms) will follow. Truly, Chart 1 is the substructure, the skeletal foundation for the entire undertaking. A summary of this entire skeletal outline is also in the compendium on p. xiii.

It should be pointed out that in a very real sense there are but six charts (1–6). A chart bearing an alphanumeric designation such as 3a–3f indicates that either it has been derived from data on Chart 3 and/or was prepared to confirm and substantiate it. Accordingly, Charts 4a and 4b were primarily created for the purpose of verifying our interpretation of the data on Chart 4. It should be noted that these corroborating charts contain in and of themselves a wealth of profitable information related to but apart from its numerically designated chart.

D. THE SECOND CAINAN

As Chart 1 displays the 1,656-year period from the Creation to the Flood and refers to Chart 6 for the derivation, it has been deemed necessary to address a paradox associated with this time interval here rather than waiting to confront it later during the discussion of Chart 6. It is because this problem is of such magnitude in the minds of nearly all who examine biblical chronology that for most any continuing discussion beyond this point is considered totally futile, a waste of time and effort. Thus it and other similar stumbling blocks must be met head on at the beginning, that credibility may be established at the very inception.

The insuperable impasse arises in the third chapter of the Gospel of Luke which contains a genealogy of Christ Jesus (Mary's, "the Seed of the woman"). For most, Luke 3:36 presents a chronological problem of major proportion. The 37th verse records a "Cainan," the son of Enos (vs.38), who fathered Mahalaleel (Maleleel).

This is in perfect agreement with Genesis 5:9–17; however Luke 3:36 goes on to say that Noah's (Noe) son Shem (Sem) fathered Arphaxad who in turn fathered a second Cainan who was the father of Salah (Sala, vs. 35).[1] Yet this part of Christ's genealogy as recorded in the Hebrew Masoretic Text of Genesis 11:1–15 states that Shem begat Arphaxad who begat Salah rather than a second Cainan.

As some of the extant Septuagint manuscripts contain the second Cainan at Genesis 11, many see the problem of dating across the patriarchs and fixing the date of Creation or the Flood as being unattainable for if one generation is missing who knows how many others may also have been lost or left out? First, the LXX has already been dealt with in detail as being spurious and shown that every single altered age was the result of deliberate tampering, not the result of accidental copying errors.

Thus the problem involving the Septuagint is not merely that of an extra name; it is an intentional altering of the chronological data after the fact in order to bring it in line with someone's personal scheme of how the chronology "ought to be" rather than to accept that which has been passed down over the centuries as having been faithfully preserved as promised by the Deity.

Many evangelical gap theorists who place the evolutionary hypothesis above the clear declaration and context of Scripture seize on the testimony of the second Cainan in these LXX manuscripts, asserting that the genealogies of Genesis 5 and 11 are "selective" falling into a pattern of listing the names in an artificially numbered arrangement as each series contains ten individuals, the tenth in each case having

---

[1] The spelling difference of the names of the patriarchs is mainly due to the fact that the translators are going from Hebrew to English in the Genesis account whereas the Luke list is being translated from *Koine* Greek to English.

three sons.[1] For many in the Church these gaps are confirming proof that the genealogies of these two chapters of Genesis are not to be taken literally. "Gappers" see the existence of these so-called gaps as justification for their placing all of evolutionary and geological time in their postulated gap between Genesis 1:1 and 1:2.

However, not only are these LXX manuscripts inconsistent within themselves omitting the second Cainan in the parallel passage 1 Chron. 1:17, the oldest Septuagint manuscripts do not include Cainan in the Genesis 11 listing. In addition, the fact that this second Cainan found in some of the LXX manuscripts has exactly the same dates assigned to him as Salah further attests to its spurious nature and militates against its being an original reading:[2]

> And Arphaxad lived a hundred and thirty five-years, and begot Cainan. And Arphaxad lived after he had begotten Cainan four hundred years, and begot sons and daughters. And Cainan lived a hundred and thirty years and begot Sala: and Cainan lived after he had begotten Sala, three hundred and thirty years, and begot sons and daughters, and died. And Sala lived an hundred and thirty years, and begot Heber. And Sala lived after he had begotten Heber three hundred and thirty years, and begot sons and daughters, and died.

The probability of two successive patriarchs having such identical statistics as given in this LXX reading is unlikely in the extreme.

The importance attached to this problem with respect to its chronological implications cannot be overstated. Even the most conservative Christian scholars and writers fall before the intellectual and spiritual attack it ominously infers. Merrill F. Unger is no exception; writing against the chronological reliability of these chapters, he says:[3]

> The total length of the period from the creation of man to the flood and from the flood to Abraham *is not specified* in Scripture. That the genealogies in Genesis chapters 5 and 11 are most certainly drastically shortened and contain names that are *highly selective* is suggested by the fact that each list contains only ten names, ten from Adam to Noah and ten from Shem to Abraham (author's italics).

Unger is not alone among the fundamentalists failing to perceive Satan's weapon is a trident and not merely a single prong. Even some of the science staff at the very conservative Institute of Creation Research concur in principle with Unger in their assessment of the "Cainan" issue.[4]

---

[1] Oliver R. Blosser, "Historical Reliability of Genesis 1–11," *It's About Time,* (Spencer, Iowa: Chronology-History Research Institute, April–July 1986), Part 1–4, pp. 8–9. Blosser, who has an earned Ph.D. in biblical Hebrew, insists that according to all Hebrew linguists the two Genesis chapters cannot contain gaps. Although this writer does not agree with Dr. Blosser's final conclusion that Luke's gospel did not originally contain the name "Cainan" in verse 36 or that Luke was a Gentile, his scholarly four part treatise contains much good material.

His conclusion that a Christian scribe at a later date deliberately altered the genealogical register at Luke 3:36 (called an interpolation) is absolutely unacceptable, i.e.: that Christians over the years have intentionally altered Scripture. This is the poison that Textual Criticism has introduced into the Church since the days of the infamous Westcott and Hort and continues today through their heirs in the modern Eclectic School of text criticism.

[2] Charles Lee Brenton, ed., *The Septuagint Version of the Old Testament and Apocrypha With an English Translation,* (Grand Rapids, MI: Zondervan Publishing House, 1978), p. 13.

---

[3] Merrill F. Unger, *Introductory Guide To The Old Testament,* (Grand Rapids, MI: Zondervan Pub. House, 1976), p. 193.

[4] See John C. Whitcomb, Jr. and Henry M. Morris, *The Genesis Flood,* (Grand Rapids, MI: Baker Book House, 1972), Appendix 2, pp. 474–489 and Gerald E. Aardsma, *Radiocarbon and the Genesis Flood,* (San Diego, CA: Master Books, 1991), pp. 41–42.

There is no intention here to be derogatory or demeaning concerning the character, commitment or professional ability of these three good and very able Christian scholars/scientists for this writer deeply respects their spirit, skill and work from whom he has learned much. This is especially true of Dr. Henry Morris. Having poured countless hours over many of his Creation science books, articles and commentaries, I not only profoundly admire him as a theologian and fellow scientist, but have heartfelt affection for him as a man and Christian brother. We support him and his efforts both in prayer and financially.

Tragically, Dr. G.E. Aardsma (specialization in radiocarbon dating) has been overtaken by this deception to the extent that he views tree ring chronology (dendrochronology) more accurate and reliable than that found in the Word of the God whom he serves. The tree ring calibration technique has led him to date the Flood at 12,000 BC rather than the biblically derived year 2348 BC, rendering ineffectual the resulting dates in his

Believing that the father-son relationships are not necessarily intended hence successive patriarchs may be grandfathers, great grand-fathers, etc. (often the case in Scripture) John Davis dogmatically affirms: "It (Genesis 5) does not list every antediluvian patriarch, but it does mention the key ones."[1] Having decided that these genealogies are selective and contain gaps, Meredith G. Kline asserts: "The antiquity of the race cannot, then, be determined even approximately from the data of Genesis 5 and 11:10 ff."[2] John W. Klotz well sums all of the previously addressed evaluations in his lucid declaration:[3]

> ..., there is some evidence that these may not be simple father-and-son relationships. We know that abridgment of genealogies is very common in Scripture and may almost be said to be the rule. Time after time we find the term *son* used where clearly the term means *descendant*, not *son*. For instance, in the very first verse of Matthew's Gospel, Christ is called 'the Son of David, the Son of Abraham.' ... The most convincing evidence comes from another genealogy in the Bible itself. Luke, in the third chapter of his Gospel, traces the genealogy of Christ back to Adam. And in that genealogy he mentions a name [Cainan] which is not recorded in the account of Moses in Genesis. ... Clearly this indicates that there is at least one name omitted by Moses in the Genesis account. And if there is one omission, is it possible that there are more?

> It should be noted in passing that Cainan is included in the genealogical table of Genesis 11 in the Septuagint. Here he is said to have had a life span of 565 years. It is possible that the translators of the Septuagint had access to the same genealogical tables that Luke studied and copied and they felt it necessary *to correct the Hebrew text.* ...

> It may be helpful to consider the purpose of the genealogical tables in Genesis. Certainly the purpose was not to give us an exact chronological account of those times, for if that were the case, there would be no omissions. ... It seems rather that God wanted to give us the names of the most important men who lived between Adam and Abraham and wanted to give us a brief account of what occurred in that period. ... We shall have to say that Scripture gives us no exact dates before the time of Abraham. (author's bracket and italics)

Of course, Klotz is undeniably correct in the first paragraph. Often the contextual use of the word "son" is that of a descendant and his Matthew 1:1 citation is an irrefutable and classic example. With these and many other conservatives' having lost confidence in the preservation and faithfulness of the text at this early juncture along with the united voice of all liberals, modernist and infidels, obviously this issue must be dealt with and solved in the strongest measures if the chronology that follows is to be certified and taken seriously even by the Church.

1. SOLUTIONS OF COMPROMISE

Solutions to the conundrum range over a huge gamut and it is here that a distinction between the fundamentalist, conservative, and the biblicist is drawn. The problem is that the definition of fundamentalism and conservatism deteriorated through compromise over the past forty years.

The result is that men who consider themselves as such today would not have been so deemed by their peers half a century ago, thus this dissertation emphasizes the term "biblicist" as being a fundamentalist and/or conservative in the grand old connotation — as one who under no circumstances compromises the Word of God as preserved to this generation.

---

otherwise excellent work. Yet all the while the data has been available to enable him to convert the radiocarbon content (^{14}C to ^{12}C ratio) to an accurate calendrical date by calibrating to the biblical chronology. Any conservative's chronological scheme, regardless of its errors, is at least 100 percent more accurate than that of using tree rings.

The point being made is that of the subtleties and ubiquitousness with which the trident ensnares whereby even men such as these can be overtaken and entangled. While defending the flock of God against the dangers of one of the prongs, they themselves fall under the spell laid by another of the remaining barbs. Moreover, if even these can fall into this well camouflaged pit, into how much danger must the rest be of doing likewise, present author included?

[1] John Davis, *Paradise to Prison: Studies in Genesis,* (Grand Rapids, MI: Baker Book House, 1975), p. 104.

[2] Meredith G. Kline, "Genesis," D. Guthrie, et al., eds., *The New Bible Commentary: Revised,* (Grand Rapids, MI: Eerdmans Pub. Co., 1984).

[3] John W. Klotz, *Genes, Genesis, and Evolution,* (St. Louis, MO: Concordia Pub. House, 1970), pp. 89–91.

For the biblicist, there are no scribal errors, emendations, etc. And neither is this "blind faith"; it is a faith anchored to the Rock of Ages and in the veracity of His promises. Moreover, compromising Christians cannot abide the presence of a man of God who will not yield before any of the "trident's" prongs for his very existence is an indictment against them, condemning their actions.

Many opt for Dr. Oliver R. Blosser's solution, viz. that Luke's gospel did not originally contain the name "Cainan" in verse 36. He concludes that a Christian scribe, rather than the profane or apostates, deliberately altered the genealogical register at a later date (called an "interpolation") i.e., that Christians, over the years have intentionally altered Scripture.

This is the poison that Textual Criticism has injected into the Church since the days of the infamous Westcott and Hort. It continues today through their heirs in the modern Eclectic School of text criticism. Good men of God, though often excellent scholars, are taken unawares and thus pierced by the trident. For the biblicist, regardless of sincerity or scholarship, such an explanation is absolutely unacceptable.

Other proposals are that the second Cainan was first introduced into the Gospel of Luke inadvertently by a copyist and from there into the LXX, or that he was found in some manuscript of the LXX and introduced into the Gospel, spreading from there into all other copies of the LXX.[1]

Martin Anstey favors an answer similar to the latter. Imputing as do nearly all a Gentile origin to Luke and noting that he was writing specifically to a Greek reader (1:3), Anstey feels that he would naturally quote from the Greek version and that the manuscript he quoted from contained the spurious addition of the name of the second Cainan.[2]

However this assumes much; in the first place it supposes that Luke compiled his Gospel as a result of study and reflection rather than writing freely as the Holy Spirit carried him along according to the Scriptures (2 Pet. 1:19–20, etc.).

Secondly, it would certainly appear from most of the explanations above that the LORD was neither doing a very able job of inspiring (2 Tim. 3:16) nor preserving the true Text as He promised on the day poor Luke picked up the wrong copy of the LXX.

Thirdly, where is the proof that merely because Luke is a Gentile name he is in fact non-Jewish[3] and, lastly, what proof other than inference is there that Luke was actually using a Septuagint rather than the Hebrew or even that he was using any text at all?

2. THE BIBLICIST SOLUTION TO CAINAN II

The solution of this impasse, this Gordian of Gordian knots, begs to be told and it shall, but first the obvious. As pointed out previously by several scholars, since each series in Genesis 5 and 11 contains ten individuals, the tenth in each occurrence having three sons, they have assumed such to be an artificial arrangement.

However, this totally ignores the self-evident possibility that these genealogies may have ten names respectively because there are in fact ten generations in each list. What possible intent would God have in giving the interlocking numeric formulas recorded in these chapters if not for their summation for the purpose of dating these events?

Moreover, as Dr. Blosser has well noted,[4] the Word of God provides its own internal safeguards giving cross-checks as to the true condition with regard to the presence or absence of gaps in the fifth chapter of Genesis. The following have been taken from his referenced source.

[1] McClintock and Strong, *Cyclopedia of Biblical Theololgcal and Ecclesiastical Literature, op. cit.,* p. 298. The *Companion Bible* concurs, Appendix 99, p. 145.

Here we note that the Greek scholar Georgius Syncellus (writing c. AD 800) repeatedly criticized both Africanus and Eusebius for omitting the second Cainan in their chronologies: *Historia Chronographia,* (Paris, France), pp. 59, 90, 104, 132, 197, and 395. As the Greek church uses the LXX as its OT, Syncellus did likewise.

[2] Anstey, *The Romance of Bible Chronology, op. cit.,* p. 86.

[3] As to Luke's nationality, see page 15, fn. 3 and pp. 18–19.

[4] Blosser, *Historical Reliability of Genesis. op. cit.,* p. 11.

(1) A comparison of Genesis 2–4; I Corinthians 15:45 and 1 Timothy 2:13 demands that Adam was the first patriarch;

(2) Genesis 4:25 makes unmistakably clear that Seth was born to Adam and Eve (reference to direct parentage) as a replacement for Abel who had been murdered by Cain;

(3) Genesis 4:26 is also an allusion to direct parentage for Enos' birth to Seth and is given in the same context and manner as the previous verse referenced the birth of Seth from Adam;

(4) the Book of Jude verse 14 confirms the position of Enoch in Genesis 5:18–25 as being the seventh from Adam;

(5) Genesis 6:10 and 18; 9:8,18–27; 10:1–32 and 11:10 demand that Shem, Ham and Japheth were Noah's immediate sons and 1 Peter 3:20 along with 2 Pet. 2:5 corroborate that only Noah's family (eight souls) was preserved through the Flood; and

(6) the ten patriarchs listed in this chapter along with Noah's three sons are confirmed by the 1 Chronicles 1:1–4 genealogy in the Hebrew Text.

Once again, these cross-references substantiate beyond any reasonable doubt as to the faithfulness of the genealogy found in the fifth chapter of Genesis.

The solution to this dilemma is twofold. The first and most important aspect deals with the problem that as the name Cainan is not recorded in Genesis, it implies that there is at least one name omitted by Moses in the Genesis account. Indeed, as Klotz remarked, if there is one omission it is possible that there may be an indeterminable number of other missing names from the Genesis register, thus the antiquity of man cannot be determined or even approximated from the data of Genesis 5 and 11. However all such objections are of absolutely no force whatsoever as they overlook the obviously simple and direct answer.

For example, consider the sixth chart around the 1700–1900 AM time frame while examining the data recorded in the eleventh chapter of Genesis. The typical construction includes the age of the "father" at the time of the designated son's birth, the number of years that he lived after the birth of that son (or descendant) and the total years the "father" lived.

Now observe that the interlocking numeric values given to each patriarch in the two chapters under discussion cannot change the time frame! That is, the Scripture precisely lists the age of each patriarch (i.e. Arphaxad = 35 years old) when the next patriarch (i.e. Salah) is born. Thus, even if the next patriarch in the recorded genealogy was a great-grandson rather than a son, this procedure of giving the age of one patriarch when the next is born fixes the two men's lives relative to each other. In so doing, it provides an exact continuous chronology across this time span.

The interval between Adam and Abraham is thus clearly maintained and is obtainable. Furthermore, the possibility of missing names (gaps) in the recorded genealogy would in no way alter the duration of this period. For regardless of the number of names or descendants that might be missing between Arphaxad and Salah (or any other two patriarchs) their lives are mathematically interlocked and a fixed relationship exists; when Salah was born, Arphaxad was thirty-five years old and so on across the entire span in question. Consequently, no time can possibly be missing even though names may so be. Strange as it may seem at first, in this instance the two concepts are mutually exclusive.

The first part of the enigma has been met and answered. Still there remains the question of why the second Cainan was omitted from the Genesis 11 register. It must be frankly admitted that as the Scriptures do not in any way explain the omission, a direct answer has never been offered in the past, neither can one be given at this time. Nevertheless, possible yet logical biblical explanations do exist.

Of course, such explanations must spring from the same foundation and frame of reference elucidated heretofore, namely faith demands that God has kept His many promises to preserve the text of His Word; therefore the condition found in Genesis 11 and Luke 3:36 is both correct and true. The only problem that remains is that of "How can these things be so"? Toward answering this question, consider the following table:

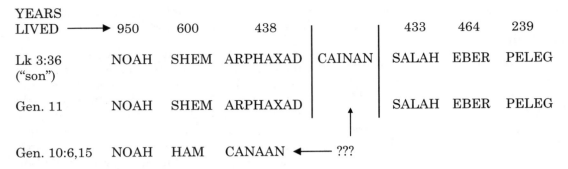

YEARS LIVED ⟶	950	600	438			433	464	239
Lk 3:36 ("son")	NOAH	SHEM	ARPHAXAD	CAINAN		SALAH	EBER	PELEG
Gen. 11	NOAH	SHEM	ARPHAXAD	↑		SALAH	EBER	PELEG
Gen. 10:6,15	NOAH	HAM	CANAAN ⟵ ???					

Cainan and Canaan may be the same person and the spelling difference due in part to Greek in Luke compared to Hebrew in Genesis (LXX = Chanaan, Luke = Kainan). Cainan is the 13th in Jesus' lineage from Adam as is Nimrod in Ham's lineage.

The following scenarios' roots lie embedded in the Law, the first five books of the Old Testament. They are offered as possible yet plausible reasons for the omission of Cainan's name in Genesis 11:

(1) Cainan could be Arphaxad's (Arpachshad) firstborn but did not get the blessing hence his name is not listed in Genesis. Arphaxad died relatively very young. He was the first to do so, hence Salah (Shelah) may have been adopted by Cainan, his older brother, so as to make him the heir (Cainan having no issue or having been so instructed by his father).

(2) Arphaxad dies and Canaan (Cainan?) marries his widow. Salah then became his stepson and/or is subsequently "adopted" and his name altered to indicate his having become part of the chosen lineage; again, so as to become the heir.

(3) Ham dies and Arphaxad marries his widow, adopting Canaan (Cainan?) and alters his name to indicate his changed status in order to place him as the heir. After Arphaxad dies, Canaan, as the older family head, adopts Salah to make him the heir.

(4) Cainan could have married one of Arphaxad's daughters and, being older, become the clan leader, later adopting Salah to make him heir for the same reasons listed in (1).

(5) In this scenario, both Arphaxad and Cainan married young. Cainan dies after conceiving Salah but before his birth. At age 35, Arphaxad then adopts his grandson, Salah

(like Jacob adopted his grandsons, Ephraim and Manasseh) (Mat. 1:1; Heb.7:9–10).[1]

In either (2) or (3) above, Salah (Shelah) could have married Canaan's daughter and then become his heir through adoption. Reflect on the preceding examples and note that in all five cases no time or generation is missing! Of course, all of the five are not of equal merit. The underlying motive behind them all is obviously that of placing Salah as the chosen recipient of the blessing.

Since in Scripture "begot" does not always refer to the next successive generation but rather direct lineage of descent (cp. Mat. 1:1, 8; Heb.7:9–10), it is concluded that one way or another Arphaxad (Arpachshad) was the father of Cainan and he was also the (grand?) father of Salah when he was 35 years old. This resolution is the only way found by this study to honor all the relevant Scriptures. Thus Cainan is probably either (a) a son by adoption and/or a son-in-law, not a direct son — hence he is not listed in Genesis 10:24 or (b) Cainan is not mentioned in Genesis as the blessing passes over him, going directly from Arphaxad to Salah who is almost certainly Cainan's younger brother.

---

[1] Compare Ruth 4:17 which declares that "there is a son born to Naomi," whereas technically she is his step mother-in-law. This depicts that the Bible's usage of many words, especially family terms, is often wider and more generalized. The same is done today when, for example, one may introduce one's son-in-law simply as "my son." Matthew 1:1 is another of many citations that could be given illustrating the same point.

The latter solution is considered to be the most biblically sound and probable answer to the anomaly. Not only would this result in neither time nor generation being absent, there is much precedent for the setting aside of the elder brother. Examples are Cain for Abel, Japheth for Shem, Haran and Nahor for Abraham, Esau for Jacob, Manasseh for Ephraim, Reuben for Judah, Aaron for Moses, etc. However, unlike these examples, the narrative of Cainan's being passed over is not recorded in the Genesis record. Doubtless, it was well known and carried along as part of the Jewish oral tradition much like the names of the Egyptian sorcerers Jannes and Jambres who withstood Moses before Pharaoh (2 Tim. 3:8) until the Holy Spirit had Paul add it to the written record.[1]

Indeed, it is well known that other biblical genealogical registers have names omitted such that Cainan's absence from the Genesis 11 record is not unique. Of course most of these omissions also cause much consternation and loss of faith in the veracity of God's Word, yet as we shall see forthwith, there are logical reasonable theological reasons involved for their exclusion.

Therefore from all that has been said previously, the genealogical lists in Genesis 5 and 11 must be seen to not necessarily reflect the firstborn son from the time aspect but at times may represent the name of the son that received the birthright and the blessing. A possible example of this may exist between Noah's son Shem and Arphaxad (Arpachshad). The register of Shem's sons as given in 1 Chron. 1:17–18 places an "Elam" and "Asshur" before Arphaxad (Arpachshad) who may thus be Shem's third born son and not his first as the Genesis 11:10–13 passages might be taken to

imply. Even if this is the actual case, it is most likely that only a few years would separate the ages of Elam and Arphaxad (Arpachshad); thus the boys' being of the same generation, no time gap would be missing.

As demonstrated heretofore, the father's (ancestor's) name is mathematically interlocked to the chosen descendant; hence no gap of time or generation is possible. In such an event, the positioned number of the patriarch may not represent the actual number of people as much as number of generations or the number of succeeding descendants who so obtained the inheritance. Regardless, it has been demonstrated that no time has been forfeited.

As Dr. Oliver Blosser has adroitly pointed out, Matthew uses the Greek word for "beget" (1:2–17), which is comparable to the Genesis registers; however, Luke employs the repeated expression "Which was the son of" (3:23–38). Indeed, the Hebrew words "father" and "son" do not occur in the Genesis genealogies and most significantly, it is the Genesis accounts only which provide any numeric data containing as they do both birth and death records. Neither Matthew nor Luke offers its readers this information, thus demonstrating that it was not the Holy Spirit's intent to rewrite portions of the Genesis registers. The purpose for the genealogical accounts given through these two evangelists must thus be seen to be different from that of the Genesis record as given to Moses.[2]

The New Testament registers were given to certify the Messianic lineage of Christ Jesus and so establish His credentials and claim to the throne. By going back through Joseph's lineage to Abraham, the father of the Hebrew nation, and thence to David, his son Solomon, and thereafter to all the kings of Judah that proceeded from his loins, Matthew demonstrated that Jesus had the royal right to the long promised throne of Messiah's father David.

Luke also traces the Lord's lineage back to David but through his mother Mary whose issue came not through the kingly pedigree but by way of another of David's sons, Nathan. This was to prove that Jesus also had the

---

[1] Other examples of a similar nature are Matthew 2:23; 27:9 (both say "spoken") and Jude 4. In the latter, Jude the brother of the Lord Jesus is not quoting the noncanonical "Book of Enoch" (1:9) as some pretend. He is giving this revelation exactly as the Holy Spirit is guiding him. The date of the writing of the Book of Enoch is not really known; hence, the unknown author may be merely writing down that which is well known among the Jews via oral tradition. Further, as there is no evidence as to the precise contents of this apocryphal book until many centuries after the time when Jude was written, Jude 4 may well be the source from which the author of "Enoch" copied.

[2] Blosser, *Historical Reliability of Genesis, op. cit.*, p. 6.

natural blood right to David's throne, Joseph being merely the foster or legal father and not his actual parent.[1] Thus Mary is seen to not

only be related to the priestly family of the Levitical tribe (maternally, cp. Luke 1:5 and 1:36), she must also be of the Tribe of Judah, the family of David (paternally, cp. Psa. 132:11; Acts 2:30; Rom.1:3–4; Rev.22:16, etc.).

Yet Luke's Gospel register accomplishes far more than even this. By going back to Adam in Mary's family tree, Christ Jesus is seen to be the "seed of the woman" in fulfillment of Genesis 3:15, the first prophecy promising and foretelling the coming Messiah. This promise of a woman having a "seed" and not an egg was a veiled allusion to the virgin conception as a fertilized egg (a "seed") and is predicted with no mention of a man. Still there is more, for Luke carries the register back to God revealing that not only was God the Creator and Father of Adam, He is the answer to the problem of the "missing" father in Genesis 3:15. God is the real Father of the Messiah, Jesus the Christ.

The various alleged charges notwithstanding, Genesis 5 and 11 present a precise and accurate biblical chronology; neither is there any legitimate reason to doubt the Hebrew Text as it stands. Herbert C. Leupold's appraisal was both lucid and incisive when he admonished: "There is no reason for doubting the correctness of the chronology submitted by the Hebrew Masoretic text. ... The claim that the Scriptures do not give a complete and accurate chronology for the whole period of the Old Testament that they cover is utterly wrong, dangerous and mischievous."[2]

E. GENEALOGICAL GAPS

There are several genealogies within Scripture that indeed do contain gaps as well as several other alleged instances. The omission of six names in the lineage of the high priests between Meraioth and Azariah in Ezra 7:1–5 as compared to 1 Chron. 6:3–15 is an undisputed

---

[1] As Jesus is not actually blood related to Joseph and those of his direct lineage, the judgment against Coniah and his descendants (Jeconiah) recorded in Jeremiah 22:28–30 is avoided. Moreover, the Scriptures teach that the sin nature resulting from the revolt and fall of Adam is imposed on all of his offspring and passes down by inheritance through the father. This nature is not the result of an addition of something to Adam, but rather is the result of a subtraction.

That is, man was created in the image of God as a tripartite being. As such, man is body, soul (intellect, ego, will, emotions, psyche) and spirit (I Thes.5:23). The spirit of man is differentiated from the soul as it is that part of man intended by the Creator through which man may communicate directly to the Deity without seeing or audibly hearing Him. It is a far deeper realm than can be achieved through the avenue of the soul. It is only here that relationship, peace and fellowship with God can be established for the soul.

Man was originally created as primarily a spiritual being. By close fellowship with the Creator, the spirit was intended to dominate his soul whereby the two of them would hold sway over the flesh, keeping it in check and submission and thus maintain a right relationship with the Father. The spirit connection, much like an umbilical cord, served as a constant reminder and demonstrated that man was a dependent creature in continual need of care, leading and supervision. Adam's sin changed all of this as it brought about the immediate death of his spirit. The communication line had been severed whereupon he now feared and hid from the God who had been both Father and friend. Man was no longer in the image of his Maker, three in one. He was only two in one — body and soul. Soul power was not sufficient to keep the lust against the body in check and tragically, for man, it left him pridefully deceived into viewing himself as an independent creature, not requiring any help beyond his own strength and mental abilities.

This condition, man with only soul, body and a "dead" spirit is what the sin nature is all about; with the subtraction of a live spirit, a sin nature is the resulting consequence. Ever since the Fall in the garden, all mankind is born with this condition. This is why the Scriptures declare we must be reborn whereupon rather than Adam being our father and our bearing his nature, God becomes our adopted Father, the spirit comes back to life and man again is a tripartite being, albeit with a damaged soul, able to freely communicate with the Creator. Until this happens by receiving the Lord Christ Jesus as Savior, God is only the individual's Life Giver and Judge, not his Father in the generic sense.

As Mary's egg was supernaturally fertilized (Scripture oft repeats "conceive," i.e. genuine conception, Matthew 1:20; Luke 1:31, 36) sans intercourse by the Holy Spirit (Luke 1:35), Jesus had no father of Adam's lineage; He inherited no sin nature and possessed an un-fallen nature. The entire problem is solved by God through the miracle of the incarnation.

Through the incarnation of the virgin Mary, Jesus inherits the nature of his true Father thus the answer to Job 14:4 is solved: "Man that is born [merely] of a woman is of few days, and full of trouble. Who can bring a clean thing out of an unclean? There is not one." (Job 14:1, 4). The Roman Catholic cult has not been able to scripturally answer this question and has thus invented the anti-biblical myth of Mary's being sinless (immaculate) in an attempt at an answer. [author's italics]

[2] H.C. Leupold, *Exposition of Genesis*, (Columbus, OH: The Wartburg Press, 1942), pp. 237–238.

example of the presence of these gaps. However this is not to be taken as an admission on the part of the author of a scribal error, mutilation, etc. to the text; rather it is being contended that the Ezra list has six names from the central portion omitted deliberately.

The purpose in Ezra was not to give the complete register of the high priests; that had already been done in the sixth chapter of I Chronicles. The seventh chapter of the Book of Ezra begins by introducing the reader to Ezra, a new prominent character who will play a major role in the remainder of that book as well as in the Book of Nehemiah.

In so doing, the Holy Spirit gives us Ezra's lineage portraying him as being of the direct line through the high priests back to Aaron, although Ezra himself did not serve as such, not being the firstborn son. To accomplish this intended purpose, it was not necessary to record his genealogy in its entirety. That was done in the first part of Chronicles which was recorded for the people about the same time as the writing of the Book of Ezra. For the sake of brevity, a condensed register was all that was necessary in order to let the reader know who and what Ezra was; more would have been superfluous.

As this study is not a complete apologetic, it will be limited hereafter by addressing only those genealogical gaps appearing in the first chapter of Matthew's gospel. These particular gaps or "omissions" are well known, and the literature abounds with multitudinous opinions, denigrating comments, and solutions. These must be clarified as they directly affect the literal interpretation of the previously discussed Genesis eleven genealogy.

Excluding them could leave too great a doubt in the minds of many and diminish the positive impression which this work is attempting to set forth and establish. As these gaps appear in the very first chapter of the New Testament and within the genealogy of the Lord Jesus as well, their importance cannot be overly stressed for if the Gospels begin with perceived errors how can one proceed with confidence and faith?

1. MATTHEW 1:8

The difficulty in this so-called "problem" text is that the names of three of the kings of Judah between Jehoram (Joram) and Uzziah (Azariah) are not present. Moreover, Uzziah was not the son as might be inferred from verse 8, but the great-great-grandson of Jehoram (cp. 2 Kings 8:25; 13:1–15:38; 2 Chron. 22–25). The names of Ahaziah, Joash and Amaziah are omitted here, but there are logical as well as reasonable theological grounds involved in their being excluded. An examination of 2 Chron. 22–25 (also 2 Kings 8–15) reveals that the foremost theological reason was idolatry.

Ahaziah heeded the counsel of his mother, wicked Athaliah the daughter of Ahab and Jezebel of Israel, and "walked in the ways of the house of Ahab" (2 Chron. 22:3–4). This "walk" would include not only a continuation of the worship of the golden calves but to placate Jezebel, the Sidonian princess whom he took to wife (1 Ki. 16:31), Ahab had a temple and altar built for Baal, her Phoenician god. Although mentioned as a sin into which the Jews fell victim during the period of the judges (2:13; 6:28–32), this act introduced into Israel for the first time the worship of Baal on a grand scale.

Jezebel's religious influence was so great that at one point it could be said that there were but 7,000 in all Israel who had not bowed the knee to Baal or kissed his image. This form of idolatry remained a snare for the Hebrew people for years to come. Moreover, Jezebel supported at her table no less than 450 prophets of Baal and 400 of Asherah (Astarte ?).

Joash (Jehoash) came to the throne as a mere seven-year-old (2 Chron. 24:1). While a child, the character of his rule depended upon his guardian uncle Jehoiada, the high priest. During the period in which Jehoiada continued to serve as his counselor, a mature Joash raised funds (via the proverbial chest) and brought about major temple repairs. However, like Solomon and Asa before him, toward the end of his life he ceased to follow the Lord with his whole heart. Upon the death of the aged Jehoiada (130 years old), evil advisers led Joash into sin such that both the king and the people began to ignore the house of God and set up Asherim and other idols. God sent prophets to warn them but they were not heeded.

Finally the Lord sent Zechariah, son and successor of Joash's mentor uncle Jehoiada, to call the king and the people to repentance. The ungrateful monarch responded by commanding his death at the hands of the stone-throwing multitude (2 Chron. 24:20–22). Joash's idolatry had brought him to include the murder of the son of the man who had saved his life as an infant from the murdering hands of his grandmother, Athaliah the usurper.

Soon thereafter the Lord sent Hazael, king of Syria, with a small army against Joash (2 Kings 12:17; 2 Chronicles 24:23–24). Hazael's smaller army was used by the Lord as a judgment upon Judah and Joash. Being badly wounded, Joash paid the Syrians a large sum to depart. Shortly afterward, Joash's servants assassinated him while in bed recuperating from his wounds.

Amaziah also started his reign faithfully following the Lord but the pride that often accompanies success brought him low (2 Chron. 25). He fell into worshiping the gods of the Edomites and silenced the prophet God had sent to invoke his repentance with the threat of death. Like Joash, the Lord disciplined Amaziah with military defeat and humiliation, culminating many years later with his assassination.

There is a popular notion among fundamental conservatives that because of the aforementioned idolatry the Jews had come to traditionally omit these three from the Messianic registers. Accordingly, when Matthew, writing especially for the Jews penned his gospel, he merely followed that tradition. All such drivel is categorically rejected as well it should be for it wholly ignores the supernatural aspect as to how the Scriptures were given to man. David's statement from 2 Sam. 23:1–2, written under the inspiration of the Holy Spirit, makes it unmistakably clear how God accomplished this:

> Now these be the last words of David. David the son of Jesse said, and the man who was raised up on high, the anointed of the God of Jacob, and the sweet psalmist of Israel, said, The Spirit of the LORD spake by me, and his word was in my tongue.

There is yet another theological reason contributing to the exclusion of Ahaziah, Joash and Amaziah from Matthew 1:8. They are also excluded due to their relationship with Ahab's and Jezebel's evil and murderous daughter Athaliah (see 2 Kings 8:18, 26; 2 Chron. 21 [esp. vs.6]; 22:2). Jehoshaphat attempted in the energy of the flesh to reunite the Kingdoms of Israel and Judah through the marriage which he arranged with Ahab between his son Jehoram (SK, the Joram of Matthew 1:8) and Athaliah.

It is most significant to note that it is the names of the three kings following this act that are missing. The instigation of such an unholy union by godly King Jehoshaphat was a great compromise. This sin was a snare for his people, the Kingdom of Judah. The issue of the missing names is related to this marriage and the offspring which it produced, but there is an aspect that goes far beyond the Baal worship, etc. which Athaliah brought to Judah.

That which we are focusing upon may be comprehended by asking the simple biblical question: the Messiah, "whose son is he?" (Mat. 22:42). Of course he was to be son of God (Isa. 7:14; 9:6, etc.), but he was also to be the "son of David" after the flesh (2 Sam. 7; Psa. 89:28–45; 110:1; 132:11 cp. Rom.1:3–4; Rev.22:16). That is, Messiah was to be a direct descendant of David and this is at the heart of this theological problem for Ahaziah, the son of Jehoram (Joram) and Athaliah, was as much the "son of Omri" (Ahab's father and founder of that dynasty) as he was the "son of David"! Genetically, Ahaziah was 50 percent of Omri's lineage and 50 percent of David's.

The Scriptures further state that Ahaziah, grandson to Ahab, married Zibiah of Beersheba (2 Kings 12:1) who was the mother of Joash; yet Ahaziah is also said to be a son-in-law of the house of Ahab (2 Kings 8:27). For Ahaziah to be both Ahab's grandson and son-in-law to his house demands that either he married one of Ahab's daughters, one of his own sisters, a half-sister, or a daughter of one of Ahab's sons.

The implication is that Zibiah was a daughter (or granddaughter) of Ahab who had moved to Beersheba prior to her marriage to Ahaziah, Joash's father. The point is that even more of Omri's blood line is being brought to bear on the Messiah's lineage through Zibiah such that Joash is 75 percent of Omri's ancestry and merely 25 percent of David's.

Joash married Jehoaddan of Jerusalem giving birth to Amaziah (2 Chron. 25:1) who subsequently married Jecoliah, also of Jerusalem (2 Chron. 26:3). These two marriages to women of Judah, and very probably of David's lineage, would serve to infuse and reestablish the blood line as that of being predominantly David's. Amaziah and Jecoliah were the parents of Uzziah (Azariah) who would be the first descendant since the marriage of Jehoram (Joram) to Athaliah that it could be clearly maintained that he was a "son of David" without the possible rejoinder being made that he was even more so a "son of Omri."

Moreover, Jehoshaphat's great sin in unequally yoking his family to the golden calf/Baal-worshiping dynasty of Omri was an act of hatred against the clear teachings of God which forbade such actions. As the sins of the parents are visited to the children to the third and fourth generation (Exo. 20:5), attention is called to the fact that Uzziah is the fifth generation from Jehoshaphat, hence the first that can be unmistakably said to be free of the disciplinary vexation from God.

Considering this, can there be any real doubt left that the exclusion of Ahaziah, Joash, and Amaziah from Matthew 1:8 is intentional and for the most part due to the relationship of Omri's ancestry as outlined heretofore?

The Old Testament testifies quite honestly that these three men ruled over the Kingdom of Judah and records their significant deeds, but God has seen fit to let all succeeding generations know how seriously He viewed these acts and the lineage of His only begotten Son by their removal at the introduction of the New Testament, the time of the long awaited Messiah.

2. MATTHEW 1:17

Two further "omission" or gap problems which are looked upon as inaccuracies by the vast majority of scholars are found in the 17th verse of the first chapter of Matthew. The first is that Matthew is deemed by most to be saying that there are three sets of 14 generations listed from verse 2 through verse 16; hence there should be 42 generations or names included in these passages and yet there are only 41. However the conclusion that a generation has

been omitted is due to a faulty perception and is totally unwarranted. Truly, there are but 41 names given. Nevertheless the 17th verse does not say there are 42 names or generations present; it says there are three sets of 14 (see outline on next page).

David is counted twice as he is the connecting link between the patriarchal line and the royal line to Christ Jesus. David is the last patriarch (Acts 2:29) but also the first sovereign king of the Tribe of Judah. Thus we see from the outline of Joseph's genealogy (Mary's husband) that the generations from Abraham to David are 14; from David until the carrying away into Babylon are 14; and from the carrying away into Babylon unto Christ are 14 (see outline, page 42 ff.).

Jeconiah (or Coniah, Jehoiachin, Jechoniah, cp. 2 Kings 25:27; 1 Chron. 3:16; Jer. 22:24–30; 29:1–2; 37:1; 52:31) does not belong in the second group where most place him. The first key in Matthew 1:17 is the word until (or to) "the carrying away into Babylon" which limits the second set of fourteen. The second key in the seventeenth verse is the word from "the carrying away into Babylon." This "from" sets limits on the third set of 14 such that when considering the other restricting passages:

vs.11: and Josiah begat Jeconiah *and his brothers* **about** the time they were carried away to Babylon.

vs.12: and *after* they were brought to Babylon, Jeconiah begat Shealtiel, etc.

it may be clearly resolved that Jeconiah is to be counted only in the third group (cp. 2 Kings 24:8–12, 2 Chron. 36).

Furthermore, as the previously cited outline relates, Josiah is the last of the sovereign kings of David's lineage that sat upon his throne. The point that is being made is that God promised David that his throne and kingdom were to have an enduring and everlasting fulfillment and that the throne of David was a sovereign dominion, not a puppet or vassal of any foreign kingdom (2 Sam. 7; Psalm 89). Whereas it is true that some on the list such as Ahaz, Hezekiah and Manasseh did have periods during their reigns in which they endured subjugation and the paying of tribute to various monarchs of the Assyrian Empire, all enjoyed intervals of sovereign autonomous rule.

SET 1 PATRIARCHS	SET 2 SOVEREIGN KINGS	SET 3 PUPPET-VASSAL STATE
	Only 14 sovereign kings in the tribe of Judah	605 BC – [Babylon] None of Jeconiah's sons sat on the throne
1. Abraham	David (vs. 17)	Jeconiah
2. Isaac	Solomon	Shealtiel
3. Jacob	Rehoboam	Zerubbabel
4. Judah	Abijah	Abiud
5. Perez	Asa	Eliakim
6. Hezron	Jehoshaphat	Azor
7. Ram	Joram	Sadoc
8. Amminadab	Uzziah	Achim
9. Nahshon	Jotham	Eliud
10. Salmon	Ahaz	Eleazar
11. Boaz	Hezekiah	Matthan
12. Obed	Manasseh	Jacob
13. Jesse	Amon	Joseph
14. David the King	Josiah (vs.11) ["About" Babylon]	JESUS (God's Son)

The three deportations to Babylon:

Final siege began Dec. 588 BC

1st - 606 BC	2nd - 597 BC	3rd - 586 BC
(Jehoiakim king)	(Jeconiah king)	(Zedekiah king)

All of Josiah's sons and his grandson, Jeconiah (Mat. 1:11, "Jeconiah and his brethren") were vassals to either Egypt or Babylon and not sovereign rulers; thus they do not belong in Matthew's second set.

It should be clear from the preceding paragraph that the curse God placed upon Jehoiakim, i.e.,

> Therefore thus saith the LORD of Jehoiakim king of Judah; He shall have *none* to sit upon *the throne of David*: and his dead body shall be cast out in the day to the heat, and in the night to the frost (Jer. 36:30, author's italics).

and upon Jeconiah (Coniah = Jehoiachin = Jechoniah)

> 24 As I live, saith the LORD, though Coniah the son of Jehoiakim king of Judah were the signet upon my right hand, yet would I pluck thee thence; 25 And I will give thee into the hand of them that seek thy life, and into the hand of them whose face thou fearest, even

into the hand of Nebuchadrezzar king of Babylon, and into the hand of the Chaldeans. 26 And I will cast thee out, and thy mother that bare thee, into another country, where ye were not born; and there shall ye die. 27 But to the land whereunto they desire to return, thither shall they not return. 28 Is this man Coniah a despised broken idol? is he a vessel wherein is no pleasure? wherefore are they cast out, he *and his seed*, and are cast into a land which they know not? 29 O earth, earth, earth, hear the word of the LORD. 30 Thus saith the LORD, Write ye this man *childless*, a man that shall not prosper in his days: *for no man of his seed shall prosper, sitting upon the throne of David*, and ruling any more in Judah (Jer. 22:24–30, author's italics).

was fulfilled and that no contradiction exists, though many so claim, as Jehoiakim's son Jeconiah (Coniah) did not sit on David's sovereign throne but only upon the vassal throne under King Nebuchadnezzar of Babylon. Also observe that the above verses do not say

Jeconiah was to have no children at all. In fact they speak of his having "seed" and they are listed in 1 Chron. 3:16–18 and Matthew 1:12–13. Rather, Jeremiah 22:30 says to count him childless in the sense that none of his offspring would ever sit on the sovereign throne of his ancestor (father) David. This was fulfilled as his successor on the chattel throne to Nebuchadnezzar was his uncle Zedekiah, not his son Shealtiel (Jer. 37:1).

Lastly, it should be noted that this curse on Jeconiah (Coniah) necessitates a miraculous birth for the Messiah as He must somehow come through the kingly line in order to obtain the royal right to David's throne; yet he cannot be a blood descendant of Jeconiah (Coniah). Again, God solves this and other similarly related incongruities through the miracle of the incarnation.

Another bewildering problem associated with these verses centers around whether Jeconiah (or Jehoiachin) was 8 or 18 years old when he ascended the throne of Judah (1 Chron. 36:9–10; compare 2 Kings 24:15). This matter will be addressed and resolved beyond any reasonable doubt in the chapter covering Chart 5 (page 192 ff.).

3. THE 14 GENERATIONS FROM DAVID TO THE CARRYING AWAY TO BABYLON: MAT. 1:17

For now, the last "gap" problem remaining concerns the undeniable fact that Matthew 1:17 states that there are 14 generations "from David until the carrying away into Babylon." This issue is closely related to the problem of the deletion of Ahaziah, Joash, and Amaziah which has been fully dealt with heretofore. Yet some may still insist that as the books of Kings and Chronicles relate that 17 monarchs ruled over the Kingdom of Judah from David to Josiah, an inaccuracy of some kind must be admitted.

Most scholars negotiate the presumed flaw by insisting that Matthew has arbitrarily arranged three sets of 14 generations in this artificial fashion due to some supposed penchant that he or the Jews in general had for that number or,

for the sake of symmetry, he allegedly omitted three names from the "begets" in the second set (1:8). However, it must be pointed out that technically speaking, there were but 14 actual *generations* between David and Josiah.

1. David
2. Solomon
3. Rehoboam
        ← Abijah (reigned 3 years)
4. Asa
5. Jehoshaphat
6. Jehoram
        ← Ahaziah (reigned 1 year)
7. Joash
8. Amaziah
9. Uzziah
10. Jotham
11. Ahaz
12. Hezekiah
13. Manasseh
        ← Amon (reigned 2 years)
14. Josiah

Although there were seventeen kings, as shown in the outline above, three reigned for such short terms that it may not properly be said that the duration of their governing or its omission is that of a "generation." Moreover, it actually could be misleading to insist that the interval from David to Josiah was that of 17 generations whereas it is that of 17 *monarchies*.

By now it should be evident beyond a reasonable doubt, or at least nearly so, even to the honest skeptic that all such problematic occurrences as discussed in the preceding sections are present in the Holy Writ exactly as they are for God's intended purposes. They must not be regarded as a *faux pas* or inaccuracy as though God somehow became lax in overseeing His Word and in keeping His abundant promises to preserve it as originally given to man. At least they must not be so considered by biblicists. No further effort will be made for the unconvinced implacable cynic; we leave them to God.

Generations of Jesus

Book of Matthew

Mat. 1:1   The book of the generation of Jesus Christ, the son of David, the son of Abraham.

Mat. 1:2
Abraham	(1)	begat
Isaac;	(2)	and Isaac begat
Jacob;	(3)	and Jacob begat
Judas	(4)	and his brethren;

Mat. 1:3   And Judas begat
Phares	(5)	and Zara of Thamar; and Phares begat
Esrom;	(6)	and Esrom begat
Aram;	(7)	

Mat. 1:4   And Aram begat
Aminadab;	(8)	and Aminadab begat
Naasson	(9)	and Naasson begat
Salmon;	(10)	

Mat. 1:5   And Salmon begat
Booz	(11)	of Rachab; and Booz (Boaz) begat
Obed	(12)	of Ruth; and Obed begat
Jesse;	(13)	

Mat. 1:6   And Jesse begat
| David | (14) | (1) the king; and David the king begat |
| Solomon | (15) | (2) of her that had been the wife of Urias; |

Mat. 1:7   And Solomon begat
Roboam;	(16)	(3) and Roboam begat
Abia;	(17)	(4) and Abia begat
Asa;	(18)	(5)

Mat. 1:8   And Asa begat
Josaphat;	(19)	(6) and Josaphat begat
Joram;	(20)	(7) and Joram begat
Ozias;	(21)	(8)

Mat. 1:9   And Ozias begat
Joatham;	(22)	(9) and Joatham begat
Achaz;	(23)	(10) and Achaz begat
Ezekias;	(24)	(11)

Mat. 1:10   And Ezekias begat
Manasses;	(25)	(12) and Manasses begat
Amon;	(26)	(13) and Amon begat
Josias;	(27)	(14)

Mat. 1:11	And Josias begat			
	Jechonias	(28)	<u>(1)</u> and his brethren, about the time	
			they were carried away to Babylon:	

Mat. 1:12	And after they were brought to Babylon,			
	Jechonias begat			
	Salathiel;	(29)	<u>(2)</u> and Salathiel begat	
	Zorobabel;	(30)	<u>(3)</u>	

Mat. 1:13	And Zorobabel begat			
	Abiud;	(31)	<u>(4)</u> and Abiud begat	
	Eliakim;	(32)	<u>(5)</u> and Eliakim begat	
	Azor;	(33)	<u>(6)</u>	

Mat. 1:14	And Azor begat			
	Sadoc;	(34)	<u>(7)</u> and Sadoc begat	
	Achim;	(35)	<u>(8)</u> and Achim begat	
	Eliud;	(36)	<u>(9)</u>	

Mat. 1:15	And Eliud begat			
	Eleazar;	(37)	<u>(10)</u> and Eleazar begat	
	Matthan;	(38)	<u>(11)</u> and Matthan begat	
	Jacob;	(39)	<u>(12)</u>	

Mat. 1:16	And Jacob begat			
	Joseph	(40)	<u>(13)</u> the husband of Mary,	
			of whom was born	
	<u>Jesus,</u>	(41)	<u>(14)</u> who is called Christ.	

Mat. 1:17 So all the generations from Abraham **to David** are fourteen generations; and **from David** until the carrying away into Babylon are fourteen generations; and from the carrying away into Babylon unto Christ are fourteen generations.

	Abraham	to	**David**	= 14
<u>from</u>	**David**	to	**Jechonias**	= 14
	Salathiel	to	**Jesus**	$= 14$
				$= 42$

Note that from Mat. 1:17 David is counted **twice**, once with the **patriarchs** (cp. Acts 2:29!) and again with the **kings**. Thus, there are fourteen generations in each grouping but only forty-one (41) total generations or names listed. This is not a contradiction or an error in God's Word.

Generations of Jesus

Book of Luke

Luke 3:23	And **Jesus**	(1)	himself began to be about thirty years of age, being (as was supposed) the son of
MARY	+ **Joseph,**	(2)	which was the son of
	Heli,	(3)	
Luke 3:24	Which was the son of		
	Matthat,	(4)	which was the son of
	Levi	(5)	which was the son of
	Melchi,	(6)	which was the son of
	Janna,	(7)	which was the son of
	Joseph,	(8)	
Luke 3:25	Which was the son of		
	Mattathias,	(9)	which was the son of
	Amos,	(10)	which was the son of
	Naum,	(11)	which was the son of
	Esli,	(12)	which was the son of
	Nagge,	(13)	
Luke 3:26	Which was the son of		
	Maath	(14)	which was the son of
	Mattathias,	(15)	which was the son of
	Semei,	(16)	which was the son of
	Joseph,	(17)	which was the son of
	Juda,	(18)	
Luke 3:27	Which was the son of		
	Joanna,	(19)	which was the son of
	Rhesa,	(20)	which was the son of
	Zorobabel,	(21)	which was the son of
	Salathiel,	(22)	which was the son of
	Neri,	(23)	
Luke 3:28	Which was the son of		
	Melchi,	(24)	which was the son of
	Addi,	(25)	which was the son of
	Cosam,	(26)	which was the son of
	Elmodam,	(27)	which was the son of
	Er,	(28)	
Luke 3:29	Which was the son of		
	Jose,	(29)	which was the son of
	Eliezer,	(30)	which was the son of
	Jorim,	(31)	which was the son of
	Matthat,	(32)	which was the son of
	Levi,	(33)	
Luke 3:30	Which was the son of		
	Simeon	(34)	which was the son of
	Juda,	(35)	which was the son of
	Joseph,	(36)	which was the son of
	Jonan,	(37)	which was the son of
	Eliakim,	(38)	

Luke 3:31	Which was the son of		
	Melea,	**(39)**	which was the son of
	Menan,	**(40)**	which was the son of
	Mattatha,	**(41)**	which was the son of
	Nathan,	**(42)**	which was the son of
	David,	**(43)**	
Luke 3:32	Which was the son of		
	Jesse,	**(44)**	which was the son of
	Obed,	**(45)**	which was the son of
	Booz,	**(46)**	which was the son of
	Salmon,	**(47)**	which was the son of
	Naasson,	**(48)**	
Luke 3:33	Which was the son of		
	Aminadab,	**(49)**	which was the son of
	Aram,	**(50)**	which was the son of
	Esrom,	**(51)**	which was the son of
	Phares,	**(52)**	which was the son of
	Juda,	**(53)**	
Luke 3:34	Which was the son of		
	Jacob	**(54)**	which was the son of
	Isaac,	**(55)**	which was the son of
	Abraham,	**(56)**	which was the son of
	Thara,	**(57)**	which was the son of
	Nachor,	**(58)**	
Luke 3:35	Which was the son of		
	Saruch,	**(59)**	which was the son of
	Ragau,	**(60)**	which was the son of
	Phalec,	**(61)**	which was the son of
	Heber,	**(62)**	which was the son of
	Sala,	**(63)**	
Luke 3:36	Which was the son of		
	Cainan,	**(64)**	which was the son of
	Arphaxad,	**(65)**	which was the son of
	Sem,	**(66)**	which was the son of
	Noe,	**(67)**	which was the son of
	Lamech,	**(68)**	
Luke 3:37	Which was the son of		
	Mathusala,	**(69)**	which was the son of
	Enoch,	**(70)**	which was the son of
	Jared,	**(71)**	which was the son of
	Maleleel,	**(72)**	which was the son of
	Cainan,	**(73)**	
Luke 3:38	Which was the son of		
	Enos,	**(74)**	which was the son of
	Seth,	**(75)**	which was the son of
	Adam,	**(76)**	which was the son of
	God.	**(77)**	

CHART TWO

This chart serves as an elementary yet instructive example as to how other charts are constructed from the data on Chart 1. As a beginning point for Chart 2, extract from the first the number 1921 BC (AM 2083), the year 75-year-old Abraham (Abram) upon the death of his father left Haran and began his sojourn (Gen. 12:4).

An intermediate result may be gleaned from Genesis 16:3 and 16:16 which state that ten years after his entry into Canaan (1921 BC), Abraham (Abram) who was then 85 (75 + 10) took to wife Hagar, Sarah's (Sarai) Egyptian handmaid. The following year Ishmael was born unto this latter "marriage" in the year 1910 BC.

1921 − 11 = 1910 BC (Ishmael's birth)

Genesis 21:5 says that Abraham was 100 at the birth of his son Isaac, thus Ishmael was 14 years older than Isaac (100 − 86 = 14). As Abraham was 75 upon his entry into the land of Canaan, 25 years had elapsed by Isaac's birth (100 − 75 = 25). Hence to the preestablished 1921 BC anchor point, 25 years is subtracted establishing the year 1896 BC as the year of Isaac's birth:

1921 − 25 = 1896 BC (Isaac's birth)

Isaac was 40 years old when he married Rebekah (Gen. 25:20) so by subtracting this from the year of his birth (1896) the year of their marriage may be fixed as 1856 BC.

1896 − 40 = 1856 BC (Isaac weds Rebekah)

Twenty years afterward, when Isaac was 60 years of age (a "score" = 20), Jacob and his older twin Esau were born (Gen. 25:26). Subtracting 20 from the year of the marriage of Isaac and Rebekah establishes the year 1836 BC as the year of the twins' birth.

1856 − 20 = 1836 BC (Jacob's birth)

Beginning here, Jacob's age when he fled from Esau's wrath can be mathematically determined. Leaving his parents in Beer-sheba (Gen. 28:10), Jacob journeyed to Haran of Padan-aram (Syria, Deut. 26:5; see Gen. 28–29 and cp. Gen. 27:43; 28:2), the place where his

Uncle Laban (brother of his mother Rebekah) dwelt. (Gen. 29:10)

Chart 2 depicts two different methods of determining the shocking circumstance showing Jacob to be 77 years old at the time of his trek. At first glance, this consequence seemed so bizarre that it was deemed necessary to offer a second method of deriving this age in order to validate and confirm the calculation. Having examined over 30 chronologies, commentaries and other scholarly undertakings, all using the Masoretic Text, save one, have obtained the same result.

Based upon certain problems which arise due to having to utilize Jacob's advanced age as a beginning point in computing the dates of other events, the commentary of Adam Clarke offers for consideration a quote from Dr. Kennicott's work whereby both agreed with the conclusions of a certain Mr. Skinner who rejected Jacob's age, deeming it too large. Mr. Skinner suggested that 57, rather than 77, might be better.[1] The importance of this age is paramount in determining the chronology for the remainder of the book of Genesis. Mr. Skinner's hypothesis is the result of deductive reasoning in order to circumvent other related chronological problems which he argues cannot be satisfactorily met if Jacob's age is made to stand at 77 upon his arrival at Padan-aram.

However these conclusions are fallacious and groundless as they are based upon slight flaws of logic involved in handling the other difficulties. Mr. Skinner's solution creates far more havoc than it solves as his proffered "fifty-seven" violates several of the Scriptures listed on Chart 2. No such contriving is necessary; all his perceived paradoxes are satisfactorily resolved by the present research on the accompanying charts that sustain Chart 3 (i.e., 3c–3f).

Biblically, Jacob's age as being 77 when he arrived at Laban's home in Haran is irrefutable and its importance is incalculable in many ways. First, it demonstrates the great significance chronology plays in understanding the events and persons in any given biblical

---

[1] Adam Clarke, *Clarke's Commentary,* vol. I, (Nashville, TN: Abingdon, 1830), pp. 176, 196–199.

narrative. How different the conflict between Esau and Jacob appears when it is realized that this is not a sibling rivalry between twins in their 20's or, at most, their 30's as may otherwise be assumed from a casual reading. No! Rather, after 77 years, they have not resolved their contentions.

Indeed, the story is much more reprehensible than normally perceived. Does not the story of Jacob, Leah and Rachel take on a totally different color when it is realized that Jacob is 77 and certainly much older than his beloved Rachel or even Leah? Many other such surprises which significantly alter the settings and perception of the stories lie concealed within the Holy Writ and only careful proper chronological effort can bring them to light.

Further, the data on this second chart is the foundation which enables us not only to determine the chronological outline of Jacob's entire life, but as a natural by-product data emerges which is invaluable in delineating events in the life of his son Joseph.

Consequently, the information procured here is foundational in the preparation of Chart 3 as well as Charts 3a–3f. This is especially true regarding Charts 3c–3f where Jacob's age as derived here becomes the indispensable basal number from which these charts are constructed. Moreover:

1. the ages of the 12 sons of Jacob and the years of their births,

2. the age of Jacob's daughter Dinah at the time she was raped,

3. the ages of Judah's sons Er and Onan at which God struck them down,

4. and the year of Judah's fornication with his daughter-in-law Tamar, etc.,

are all obtainable only by beginning with the information found on Chart 2, especially with that single fact of Jacob's having been 77 at the time of his arrival to sojourn at Laban's. As a matter of fact, this innocuous chart contains all the basic material for the chronology from Genesis chapters 12 through 50.

CHART THREE

A. THE 430-YEAR SOJOURN

A motif characteristically utilized in the preparation of nearly all of the time/event displays produced in this analysis involves extracting chronological data from a previous chart to assist in preparing the succeeding chart. Thus, the computations at the upper left of Chart 3 have been carried over from Chart 2. For reference, beneath these figures is a condensed version of Chart 1 to assist in sketching the lives of Jacob and Joseph.

Again note that the number of years from the Flood to the Covenant with Abraham is 427 years (222 + 130 + 75), *not* 367 years (222 + 70 + 75) as is often erroneously asserted. This critical determination is forthright and is given at the lower left of Chart 3 as well as on the left of Chart 6. It has already been discussed and defended in the section dealing with the first chart (page 25 ff.).

The purpose of this chart is to create an uncluttered display portraying major events occurring during the 430-year sojourn of the children of Israel (Exo. 12:40; cp. Gal. 3:17). Following our established pattern, from Chart 1 the year Abraham initiated the sojourn (1921 BC; AM 2083) is taken as the beginning point (*terminus a quo*) and the year of the Exodus (1491 BC; AM 2513) as the ending (*terminus ad quem*). The remaining task is to fill the area between these two extremes with pertinent biblical data.

B. EARLY OR LATE EXODUS

Volumes have been written by myriads of investigators as to the date of the Exodus; hence much debate exists concerning the identity of the various pharaohs referred to in the biblical account. Setting aside extreme views the principal positions are whether there was:

(1) an early Exodus (15th century BC) with the entire 430 years spent in Egypt (the "long sojourn" position);

(2) a late date for the Exodus (13th century BC; Rameses II's dynasty), again placing the 430 years as spent in Egypt; and

(3) an early Exodus (15th century BC) with but 215 of the 430 years of sojourn spent in Egypt ("short sojourn" position).

Thus two major questions must be settled in a Scripture-honoring manner. Did the Exodus take place during the 15th or the 13th centuries BC, and was the duration of the sojourn in Egypt 430 years or less?

Although much research continues, it must first be noted that even to this day the period under discussion (c. 1780–1546 BC) is one of great obscurity in Egyptian history. This writer has done not a little investigation into this matter having examined the findings of L. Wood, Hall, J. Davis, M. Unger, J.H. Breasted, Eerdmans, Petrie, H.H. Rowley, Gardner, Harrison, W.F. Albright, Bunsen, J. Free, S. Schults, and Sir J. Gardiner Wilkinson to name but a few.

That notwithstanding, it is not the purpose of this study to attempt to solve the problems of Egyptology and Egyptian chronology relating to the issue at hand. To prepare a correct chronology of the Holy Text, it is neither necessary nor at all essential to know the names of the pharaohs alluded to in the Book of Exodus; otherwise God would have identified them. Rather, this work will be limited to giving biblical answers to the two questions previously set forth.

Regarding the question as to whether the Exodus was a 15th (early date) or 13th century (late date) BC episode, the biblical evidence unmistakably places the event in the 15th. Moreover, those who defend the late date such as Albright and Rowley placing the Exodus at 1290 and 1225 BC respectively, do so by rejecting the 480 years of 1 Kings 6:1, deeming it completely unreliable.

From Chart 1 it may be seen that this study considers the 480-year statement as not only correct, as does Hillel (author of modern Jewish chronology), Ussher, Petavius, Unger, etc., but absolutely essential to accurate and proper biblical chronology. The rejoinder and defense for 1 Kings 6:1 will be found in the discussion of Chart 4.

Briefly, some of the more salient points offered by the 13th century (late date) defenders with rebuttals following are:[1]

1. The 15th century would place Joseph and the arrival of Jacob with his family in Egypt during the reign of the Hyksos (Egyptian for "rulers of foreign lands") period (c. 1730–1580 BC; XV and XVI dynasties). Had the reigning king been Hyksos (Semitic, the so-called "shepherd kings"), the Hebrew shepherds would not have been segregated in Goshen and a point made of the fact that "every shepherd is an abomination to the Egyptians" (Gen. 46:34). Thus the Exodus must be later (13th century).

In reply, it must be set forth that the fact the Hyksos were also Semitic[2] and that Jacob's family was placed in Goshen does not at all demand "segregation" by way of bias as the above argues, at least not to the ruling class. Genesis 46:28–47:11 makes it absolutely clear that when they arrived in Egypt, Jacob sent Judah ahead to Joseph who met them when they stopped in Goshen, allowing their flocks and herds to graze and secure water. It was then that Joseph, knowing that it was the best land for livestock in all of Egypt and that the native Egyptians were highly biased against their method of livelihood, instructed five of his brothers to request that they be allowed to abide in Goshen.

Joseph presented the five brothers to Pharaoh (vv.1–2) who, having seen for themselves that Goshen was a choice location for the nurturing of their animals and having been so directed by Joseph, requested to so remain (vs.4) explaining that they were shepherds. Pharaoh then told Joseph that his family could settle anywhere they chose in all of Egypt and to see to it that they received the best (vs.6).

Moreover, the gist of the verse is that as they had requested to live in Goshen and inasmuch as it was the best of all Egypt for raising livestock, they could certainly have it with the king's blessing. The 11th verse confirms that they were given Goshen because it was the best land in Egypt. The verse stating that shepherds were an abomination refers to the native Egyptians (cp. Genesis 43:32 for same context); it says nothing about the sentiments of the Hyksos toward their fellow Semites.

Of course this natural segregation would undoubtedly be beneficial in assisting the Pharaoh to maintain peace and harmony throughout the realm between the native populace and the sojourning Hebrews. It further explains why the isolation, once initiated, would tend to continue until the time of the Exodus 215 years thereafter and why there was relatively so little intermarriage between the native Egyptians and the Hebrews. Finally, as the Egyptian dates are so uncertain, the possibility remains that some future study could even establish the Hyksos period to not correspond with the time of Joseph; hence the prudent would be wise to guard against overzealous, premature conclusions.

2. Exodus 1:11 supposedly places the Exodus in the late date as Israelites are there said to have been building the treasure city of Rameses (Raamses). These proponents insist that this must be so named in honor of Rameses II of the 19th Dynasty (13th century).

In reply to the preceding claim, first it must be acknowledged that 1 Kings 6:1 is just as explicit for the 15th century (early) date. As shall be shown, the two verses are not at all at variance with one another.

Secondly, the name "Rameses" is referred to in a burial painting from the reign of Amenhotep III of the 18th Dynasty. This would precede the reign of Rameses I by at least sixty years.[3] Moreover, the Scriptures refer to Goshen as "the land of Rameses" in the year Jacob joined his son Joseph in Egypt (Gen. 47:11), nearly 400 years *before* the reign of Rameses I and just over 400 years before the time of Rameses II. Remember, these Roman numeral assignments to the pharaohs do not appear in the Egyptian records. They have been so designated by

---

[1] These arguments, often enlarged upon to the point of monotony and boredom, may be found in many sources. A good brief by Merrill F. Unger may be found in *The New Unger's Bible Dictionary,* (Chicago, IL: Moody Press, 1988), pp. 384–387. Also an excellent contrast between the 15th and 13th century positions in concise outline form has been given by John H. Walton, *Chronological And Background Charts of The Old Testament,* (Grand Rapids, MI: Zondervan, 1978), pp. 29–30.

[2] William F. Albright, *The Old Testament and Modern Study,* (Oxford: 1951), p. 44.

[3] *Liberty Bible Commentary* (Nashville, TN: Thomas Nelson Publishers, 1983), p. 110.

modern scholars, thus there well could have been a famous "Rameses" long before Rameses I as Genesis 47:11 strongly asserts.

In fact, the Scripture in question (Exo. 1:11) informs us that the city of Rameses (older names = Tanis, Zoan or Avaris) was under construction and completed before the birth of Moses (cp. Exo. 2:2–10); thus it was built long before the rule of Rameses II. Besides, this was a treasure storage city, not a capital or palace. Thus, it was hardly befitting to be so named for the purpose of honoring a living king of Egypt but very appropriate for the name of a hero of the past. The entire point is left devoid of all its apparent force when it is brought to light that Amosis, 16th century BC founder of the 18th Dynasty, bore the name "Rameses" (son of Ra = the sun),[1] probably as a throne name.

3. Surface explorations in Transjordan and in the Arabah by Nelson Glueck[2] supposedly indicate that the sedentary Edomite, Moabite and Ammonite Kingdoms did not exist in the 15th century. As Israel had contact with these nations, the Exodus must have occurred later for these kingdoms supposedly could not have resisted them earlier. Only scattered nomads could have resisted them (cp. Num. 20:14,17).

In reply, the finds at the temple at Timna indicate that sedentary civilizations were present in the Negev at least in the early 14th century. In addition, Unger assures us that the archaeological evidence at Lachish and Debir used by Glueck in reaching this conclusion is not sufficiently evident to justify setting aside the whole body of testimony supporting the 15th century date.[3]

---

[1] McClintock and Strong, *Cyclopedia of Biblical Theological and Ecclesiastical Literature, op. cit.,* vol. II, p. 305.

[2] Dr. Nelson Glueck is generally acknowledged as the leading Palestinian archaeologist of our time. With regard to his studies and relevant Scripture he wrote: "As a matter of fact, however, it may be stated categorically that no archaeological discovery has ever controverted a biblical reference. Scores of archaeological findings have been made which confirm in clear outline or in exact detail historical statements in the Bible"; *Rivers in the Desert,* (New York: Farrar, Strauss & Cudahy, 1959), p. 31.

[3] Merrill F. Unger, *Unger's Bible Dictionary,* (Chicago, IL: Moody Press, 1966), pp. 333–334.

4. A layer of ash indicates that the destruction of Lachish, Debir and Bethel occurred in the 13th century.

In reply, the Scriptures say nothing of these three cities being torched at the time of the conquest under Joshua (Josh. 10:29–43). Although it is true that some cities of Canaan were burned such as Heshbon, Jericho, Ai, Hazor, etc., the normal procedure was to leave the cities standing so that the Israelites could immediately move in and "inherit" homes, vineyards, etc. which they had not themselves built.

> And it shall be, when the LORD thy God shall have brought thee into the land which he sware unto thy fathers, to Abraham, to Isaac, and to Jacob, to give thee great and goodly cities, which thou buildedst not, And houses full of all good things, which thou filledst not, and wells digged, which thou diggedst not, vineyards and olive trees, which thou plantedst not; when thou shalt have eaten and be full; (Deut. 6:10–11).

> And I have given you a land for which ye did not labour, and cities which ye built not, and ye dwell in them; of the vineyards and oliveyards which ye planted not do ye eat (Josh. 24:13; cp. Josh. 11:13).

The layer of ash could be due to the later Egyptian incursions of Seti I or Rameses II.

5. Thutmose III was not known as a great builder and therefore does not fit into the historical picture.

In reply, Thutmose III may not be recognized as a "great" builder, but he is known to have had some building projects in the delta region. However, the point is that he may not be the Pharaoh of the great oppression but rather that of the Exodus.

6. The Scriptures do not mention the sorties into Palestine by Seti I or Rameses II, therefore the Hebrews were not yet in the Land of Promise until later in the 13th century.

In reply, as these Egyptian incursions took place during the period of the judges, they may have been carried out against various groups of Canaanites such as Jabin (Judg. 4:2–3) and/or even the Philistines, etc., not conquered by Joshua (Josh. 13:1–6; cp. Judg. 1:19, 21, 27–36; 2:21–23; 3:1–3) and not have involved the Hebrews. One of the forays could have taken

place during one of the periods of servitude, hence the Egyptians would have engaged the armies of that nation holding dominion over the Land of Promise, not Israel, and thus not deemed worthy of mention in the Hebrew history.

7. Pushing the Exodus back to the 15th century means pushing the patriarchs back in time and they cannot be taken back any further.

In reply, first, Walton informs us that there is just as much evidence for placing the patriarchs in the Middle Bronze I as there is for putting them in the Middle Bronze II.[1] However, the real answer to this apparent problem is that although the Exodus is "pushed back to the 15th century" the patriarchs are *not* pushed back into the Middle Bronze I as some fear and others proclaim. This is because the sojourn in Egypt was not the entire 430 years as these two groups of scholars envision.

This has been mentioned during the discussion of Chart 1 and it will presently be enlarged upon in this chapter. For now, it is sufficient to merely counter by replying that the period in Egypt was but half of the 430 or 215 years; thus the patriarchs are not pushed back an additional 215 years as many suppose.

Having forthrightly met the principal objections, the most important positive evidences for the 15th century Exodus must be considered. Again, the chief evidence is the testimony of 1 Kings 6:1 which must not and cannot be set aside. It is the plenary inspired Word of God; no amount of circumstantial evidence to the contrary or even that which is held as viable or factual must be set above its declaration.

The purported Exodus 1:11 counter-Scripture has previously been answered. Nevertheless, it must be seen that a vast difference exists between the utilization and interpretations placed on these two passages. In appealing to the Exodus 1:11 passage in support of the proposed 13th century dating of the Exodus, these proponents are not able to invoke the verse exactly as it reads as full proof of the

correctness of their thesis. Secondary reasoning, i.e. "the building of the treasure city of Rameses *must* have been in honor of Rameses II of the 19th Dynasty of the 13th century BC," must be applied to the verse in order to reach their final conclusion.

By way of contrast, 1 Kings 6:1 requires no such further deductions. It straightforwardly informs us that *in*[2] the 480th year from the Exode, Solomon began to build the Temple. Chart 1 shows the construction to have begun in 1012 BC, thus the Exodus took place in the spring of 1491 BC.

1012 + 479 ("in" the 480th year) = 1491 BC

For the biblicist, this should be sufficient, but there is more.

Jephthah assigns 300 years between the eve of his going to battle against the king of Ammon in the first year of his judgeship and the conquering of the city of Heshbon (Judg. 11:26). Jephthah's statement concerning the controversial 300-year span will be analyzed and defended in the chapter dealing with Chart 4. For now, the Scriptures affirm that the conquest of Heshbon (Num. 21:21–31) took place while Moses was still alive but only several months before the crossing of the Jordan under the command of Joshua.

From Chart 1 the date of Solomon's death and the subsequent division of the Kingdom is given as 975 BC. As Saul, David and Solomon each reigned 40 years, 120 (40 + 40 + 40 = 120) must be added to this in order to come to the year of Saul's coronation, 1095 BC.

975 + 120 = 1095 BC (Saul begins to reign)

From the placing of the names of the various judges and the lengths of their judgeships between Jephthah's day and Saul's, Jephthah's judgeship had to have begun, at the very least, 55 years prior to that of Saul's inauguration. Adding to this the 300 years from Judges 11:26

---

[1] John H. Walton, *Chronological And Background Charts of The Old Testament,* (Grand Rapids, MI: Zondervan, 1978), p. 30.

[2] The Israelites left Egypt on the 15th day of the first month. (Num. 33:3). In the 480th year after the Exodus, in the 2nd month on the 2nd day, Solomon began to build the Temple (1 Kings 6:1). The months and days given for the start and end of the period show that 11 months and 14 days must be taken away. The period is not 480 whole years, but only 479 years and 16 days (2 Chron. 3:2).

demands a 15th century BC Exodus and confirms the 1 Kings 6:1 480-year text.

The mouth of two witnesses has spoken; the matter is biblically forever settled. If the biblical text is to be taken at all literally, the length of time that Scripture assigns to the period of the judges, even with overlapping, cannot be squeezed into the century and a half required by a 13th century Exodus.

Still some may ask whether there is any extra-biblical evidence of the Exodus and subsequent invasion of Canaan under the direction of Joshua at the time of the entry? There is! The Amarna Tablets (c. 1400 BC) discovered in AD 1886 refer to an incursion by the "Habiru" during this very period which J.W. Jack declares is etymologically equatable with the Hebrews.[1]

The Amarna Tablets contain correspondence from Abi-Hiba, ruler of Jerusalem, requesting Egyptian military aid from Pharaoh Akhnaton of the 18th Dynasty against the invading Habiru. Although scholars are divided on the matter (and when have they not so been where anything related to authenticating the biblical account has been involved?), J.W. Jack astutely sets forth the question:[2]

> Who are these invaders of south and central Palestine. ... Who else could they be but the Hebrews of the Exodus, and have we not here the native version of their entry into the land?

Jack's penetrating statement is as fitting and pertinent today as it was the day he penned it. This is especially true in light of the unmistakable pronouncements and clear intimations contained in the Old Testament concerning the time of the Exodus.

Although not as compelling as the preceding, there is also an allusion to Israel in the Egyptian Monuments which is deserving of consideration. The black granite Merneptah Stele (Israel Stele) located in the Cairo Museum relates a triumphal account of Pharaoh

Merneptah, the 13th son and successor of Rameses II, who reigned about 1224–1214 BC.[3]

Speaking of his conquest of Canaan in the spring of his fifth year, Merneptah says:

> Plundered is the Canaan with every evil.
> Carried off is Ascalon;
> Siezed upon is Gezer;
> Yanoam is made as that which does not exist;
> *Israel is laid waste,* his seed is not;
> Hurru (Palestine) has become a widow for Egypt!
> All lands together, they are pacified,
> Everyone who was restless,
> he has been bound by ... King Merneptah.

The current author is persuaded that a proper understanding of this inscription substantiates a 15th century Exodus. The fact that Merneptah refers to Israel by name as a nation bears witness that they have been in the land for an extended period of time prior to this invasion, certainly longer than the days of Merneptah's father, Rameses II.

C. THE LENGTH OF THE SOJOURN IN EGYPT

The length of the stay in Egypt and the span of the oppression during that sojourn is the subject of much controversy among scholars; yet for all that, the biblical solution is very forthright. It merely requires that the researcher bring to the problem the proper frame of reference. This includes an abiding commitment to the fact that he is dealing with material which has been supernaturally given to man, providentially preserved over the centuries and hence is still infallible.

Thus no doubt or allowance for error in the Text will be made and the resulting chronology will reflect the honoring of all Scripture (in context) that bears on the area under study. Anything else is neither the world view of a biblicist nor the work of a biblicist.

Having established 1491 as the year of Exodus from Chart 1 (see Chart 3, lower left), 430 years are added. This represents the time from that point unto the covenant which God made with Abraham when he *entered* the land of Canaan (Gen. 12:4; Exo. 12:40; Gal.3:17). This takes us

[1] J.W. Jack, *The Date of the Exodus*, (Edinburgh: 1925), pp. 119–141.

[2] *Ibid.*, p. 128.

[3] James B. Pritchard, *Ancient Near East Text* [hereafter designated *ANET*], (Princeton: University Press, 1969), pp. 376–378.

to 1921 BC, the year Abraham departed from Haran after the death of his father (Terah) and entered into Canaan.

$$1491 + 430 = 1921 \text{ BC}$$

From Chart 2 (see Chart 3, upper left) we now extract the birth year of Jacob, 1836 BC. As the Scriptures declare that Jacob came to Egypt when he was 130 years old (Gen. 47:1–12; cp. Deut. 26:5; Psa. 105:23), the year 1706 BC is established for the date of that event.

1836 − 130 = 1706 BC (Jacob's arrival in Egypt)

This is most significant as the year 1706 is precisely midway between 1921 BC (Abraham's entry) and 1491 (the Exodus), thus Jacob appeared before Pharaoh 215 (430 divided by 2) years after Abraham entered Canaan and 215 years before the Exodus.

$$1921 - 1706 = 215 \text{ years}$$
$$1706 - 1491 = 215 \text{ years}$$

From a biblical perspective, the matter is incontrovertible and the significance of this happenstance cannot be overstated for it at once set limits as to the length of the sojourn in Egypt and to the time span of the affliction and oppression by the new dynasty of pharaohs. The total time of this sojourn in Egypt has been settled as that of 215 years.[1]

It now remains to examine the matter relative to the interval of the hard oppressive bondage. Recalling that Jacob was born in 1836 BC, we find he died in 1689 BC at age 147 some 12 years after the seven-year famine ended (Gen. 47:28; 49:33; cp. 45:1–6).

1836 − 147 = 1689 BC (Jacob's death)

On Chart 2 it was ascertained that Jacob was 91 when Joseph was born (confirmed on Chart 3d), hence this birth falls in the year 1745 BC.

1836 − 91 = 1745 BC (Joseph's birth)

Joseph lived to be 110 (Gen. 50:26) therefore his death year was 1635 BC, some 54 years after the passing of his father Jacob (Jacob's death year minus Joseph's death year, 1689 − 1635 = 54).

1745 − 110 = 1635 BC (Joseph's death)

---

[1] Josephus corroborates this 215-year conclusion in his *Antiquities of the Jews*, II, 15, 2.

Next, it remains for us to work out the Joseph-Moses connection. As the date of the Exodus has already been secured on Chart 1, this becomes an easy matter. However a digression is necessary at this point in order to establish a chronological technique to which we shall much later have to resort. This is a most convenient place to address it for here it can be readily explained and its merit demonstrated.

The following describes the actual approach used in the preparation of the chronological charts which accompany this dissertation. Although not very difficult, as will be seen, it is generally harder to set forth in writing and also more arduous for the reader to comprehend. This explains why the author has chosen to follow the simpler method as presented in this work.

The patriarchal chronology comes to an end with the death of 110-year-old Joseph at the close of the Book of Genesis. If the chronology begins in the normal fashion by commencing with Adam and numbering the years forward (*Anno Mundi* = AM) the chronologist will have come to a dead end. He can proceed no further for Joseph's age at the birth of Ephraim and/or Manasseh, his sons born to him in Egypt, is not given. A chronological gulf or chasm is found to exist between the end of Genesis and the beginning of Exodus.

Genesis closes with Israel's enjoying favor with the ruling dynasty, but Exodus opens with the rise of a new Pharaoh from a different dynasty who "knew not Joseph," and with Israel in affliction under the Egyptian oppressors. The chronological continuity of the narrative begins afresh with the birth of Moses. The problem becomes one of how this gulf is to be bridged and the number of years between the death of Joseph and birth of Moses determined.

The solution is obtained by utilizing the numerical value of the large time span which begins with Abraham's departure from Haran upon the death of his father, Terah, and entering the land of Canaan at age 75 (Gen. 12:4) 2,083 years after the Creation (AM 2083 – see Chart 1, patriarchal genealogies of Genesis 5 and 11) and terminates at the Exodus. As will presently be proven beyond all doubt, the Scriptures describe this epoch to be of 430 years' duration. Just previously it has been

shown that Joseph died in 1635 BC which converts to AM 2369 (4004 − 1635 = AM 2369). Thus Abraham's entry unto the death of Joseph is an interlude of 286 years.

$$2083 - 2369 = 286 \text{ years}$$

It is also known that from the birth of Moses to the Exodus was a period of 80 years (Exo. 7:7; Act. 7:23–30). If we add these numbers (286 + 80 = 366) and subtract their sum from the number of years across the entire period (430 − 366 = 64), the 64 remaining will be the exact number of years between the death of Joseph and the birth of Moses (the whole being equal to the sum of its parts) − the number of years between the close of the Book of Genesis and the beginning of the Book of Exodus.

Observe that there has been neither an appeal to extra-biblical aids, consulting of Josephus nor the making of speculative hypothesis, assumption or conjecture. The answer has been calculated by means of an historical induction taken from the facts and figures given in the Text itself and is mathematically exact.

Many similar chasms are encountered in the detailed events found in the text of Scripture but, as in the foregoing example, they may always be resolved by the use of statements giving numerical data of a longer period which thus bridges the gulf and establishes a new fixed date. Beginning at that established new date, one may work backward, closing the gap toward his original point of departure from whence he had leapt.

Thus whether it be with the simple "chasm" type problem such as the age of Noah at the birth of Shem (see Chart 6, left side), the age of Terah at the birth of Abraham (Charts 1 and 6) or the more complex ones that lie ahead such as the chasms relative to Joshua-Judges or Artaxerxes-Christ, the solution is always given within Scripture with such precision that the chronology may be ascertained with as great a degree of certainty as the chronology of any period in ancient secular history.

Coming back from the preceding digression, it is noted that by working backward and forward from the Exodus, the life span of Moses can be depicted and the historical events associated with his life dated. This we shall continue to do, but by our simpler technique.

Now Genesis 50 and Exodus 1 make very clear that as long as Joseph lived, he and his family were well treated; thus the maximum period of hard bondage was 144 years[1] (Joseph's death year minus the year of the Exodus, 1635 − 1491 = 144). Obviously, the minimum length of the affliction was 80 years, the span from the birth of Moses unto the Exodus at which time he was that age (Exo. 2:1–12; cp. 7:7). This enables us to set the year of Moses' birth as 1571 BC, the date of the Exodus having already been established as 1491 BC.

$$1491 + 80 = 1571 \text{ BC (Moses' birth)}$$

D. HARMONIZING AND RESOLVING EXODUS 12:40

Having determined that the children of Israel abode in Egypt but 215 years by direct dead reckoning calculation, one final point needs to be addressed in order to leave the issue as forever set right. This is necessary due to the fact that many may still somehow be convinced that Exodus 12:40 demands a 430-year stay. Of course such a view sets one Scripture at variance with another; yet God has promised to preserve His Word such that neither jot nor tittle be altered.

Nevertheless, wanting to clarify beyond reasonable doubt the problem at hand and realizing that confusion may still persist over the "400-year" statement in Genesis 15:13 and Acts 7:6, the following explanation is offered. The passages in question read:

> Now the sojourning of the children of Israel, who dwelt in Egypt, was four hundred and thirty years (Exo. 12:40).

> And he said unto Abram, Know of a surety that thy seed shall be a stranger in a land that is not theirs, and shall serve them; and they shall afflict them 400 years; (Gen. 15:13).

By comparing Genesis 12:4, Exodus 12:40 and Galatians 3:17 the much debated 430-year epoch can be properly understood. Never is it said in these Scripture references that the Jews *dwelt* in or were *slaves* in Egypt for 430 years. Rather, they teach that the duration of their

---

[1] Exodus 1:6-8 imply the hard bondage did not begin until after all the brothers etc. died. Levi, the only brother of Joseph whose life-span is recorded, died 16 years after Joseph (in 1619 BC, see Chart 3a). Thus, the actual duration was less than 128 years (1619 − 1491 = 128).

sojourn from the time Abraham (Abram) entered the Promised Land (Gen. 12:1) until the giving of the Law three months after the Exodus was that of 430 years. The *sojourning* commenced at Genesis 12:1 and is quite a different subject from the *dwelling* in Egypt. The Scripture does not say the "sojourning" of the children of Israel in Egypt, but rather who "dwelt" in Egypt. As we have seen, the *dwelling* in Egypt was only 215 years. The dwelling is to be distinguished from the broader "sojourning," which was over another 215 years. Galatians 3:17 makes all this both clear and certain:

> And this I say, that the covenant, that was confirmed before of God in Christ, the law, which was four hundred and thirty years after, cannot disannul, that it should make the promise of none effect.

The Galatian text unequivocally declares that the interval from the Covenant with Abraham (context, cp. Gal.3:16) to the giving of the Law at Sinai (on the Day of Pentecost 53 days after Passover, see page 56, fn. 2) was 430 years.

That is, Exodus 12:40 does not say that the children of Israel sojourned (or dwelt) 430 years *in* Egypt. It does say that the sojourn of that particular branch of Abraham's lineage as traced through Isaac and Jacob, with which we are specifically concerned, was the group which eventually went down to Egypt. In other words, it is a statement defining and identifying with which of Abraham's lineages the narrative is dealing as Abraham had numerous other lineages. It is through Isaac and Jacob and not by way of Ishmael, Esau or Abraham's many offspring by Keturah whom he wed after Sarah died (Genesis 25).

The verse is telling us *which* children of Abraham are being focused upon, not how long they were in Egypt. That the lineage of Isaac was the branch selected by God is indisputable for "in Isaac shall thy seed be called" (Genesis 21:12c, cp. 17:19, 21 and Hebrews 11:17–18; all Moslem claims for Ishmael notwithstanding).

And yet there is more Scripture that supports and demands the "short sojourn." Judah's genealogy confirms and verifies that it was 430 years from the covenant with Abraham unto the receiving of the Law as his offspring made their way to obtain the land God promised in Genesis 12:7, not 430 years from Jacob and his family's

coming to Egypt unto the Law (see Chart 3b and Gal 3:17).

Four generations of Judah's family came down to join Joseph in Egypt during the year 1706 BC. These were Jacob, Judah, Perez (or Pharez and his twin Zerah), and Hezron (and his brother Hamul, see Gen. 46:8,12). Hezron fathered Caleb who begat Hur (1 Chronicles 2:1–5,18–20).

This is that Hur[1] who, with Aaron's help, supported the arms of Moses when the Amalekites attacked the tired and weary stragglers at the rear of the column of the exiting Israelites less than 50 days after the Exodus (Exo. 17:10–12; 19:1–2; Deut. 25:17–19).[2] Hur was the grandfather of Bezaleel (Exodus 31:1–11; 1 Chron. 2:20). Bezaleel was a most skillful craftsman whom God filled with His Spirit and granted special wisdom, understanding and knowledge to empower him as the chief designer and builder of the tabernacle.

Bezaleel worked in carving the wood, working the gold, silver and brass used in making the furniture as well as the other furnishings while at the same time overseeing the construction of the tabernacle. As the tabernacle was completed almost one year after the Exodus (Exo. 12:2, 6; 13:4, cp. 40:17 and Num. 1:1), Hur is an old man at this time for his grandson, Bezaleel, is fully mature (1 Chron. 2:20; Exo. 31:1–11; 35:30–35).

---

[1] Flavius Josephus, *Josephus Complete Works,* trans. by William Whiston, (Grand Rapids, MI: Kregel Publications, 1960), *Antiquities of the Jews,* III, 2, 4. Hur is called the husband of Miriam (Greek = Mary), the sister of Moses and Aaron.

[2] The oral giving of the Law was on the 7th day of the 3rd month (Sivan), 1491 BC. Moses and the children of Israel came to Sinai in the 3rd month, "the same day" (Exo. 19:1) which means the 3rd day of the 3rd month. Moses "went up unto God" on Mt. Sinai the following day which was the 4th of Sivan (Exo. 19:3). The people were to come back to the Mount 3 days after this (Exo. 19:9–19 where verse 10 speaks of the 5th day of the 3rd month, i.e. *today* and the 6th day, i.e. *tomorrow* – see chart, p. 276).

Thus they came back on the 7th day of the 3rd month which is permanently fixed as a Sunday by Lev. 23:4–22 as being the "Feasts of Weeks" (Pentecost). Therefore the Law was first given on what later came to be observed as the Day of Pentecost once the Jews entered the Land of Promise (Abib 10, 1451 BC, cp. Joshua 4:19). As the Amalekite attack was prior to this, Moses was 80 and Aaron 83 years old at the time (Exo. 7:7).

The point is that the entire interlude from the arrival of Judah with the rest of his kindred in Goshen to the Exodus must be spanned by only three lives, Hezron, Caleb and Hur. If, as has been shown, this intervening period is 215 years it would require a scenario whereby beginning with Hezron as an infant (a fact, see Chart 3f) each would be required to *father* around age 65 at a time when men's life spans had been foreshortened to almost that of the present day.

However, if the duration of the dwelling in Egypt had been 430 years instead of the correct 215, a scenario would be required whereby Hezron would have fathered Caleb about age 145, Caleb fathered Hur about 145 and Hur would have been around 140 at the Exodus. Any such scenario is inconsistent with Bible data and thus highly unlikely as during this period other men's life spans were not compatible with such a great age for the begetting of sons. For example, Jacob died at 147, Joseph 110, Moses 120, Aaron 123, and Levi as well as his son and grandson died between the ages of 133–137 (Exo. 6:16–20, cp. Gen. 47:28; 50:26; Num. 33:39; Deut. 31:2). Thus Judah's genealogy is seen to support the 215-year sojourn, but it militates against its being 430 years as is often wrongly supposed.

In addition, the genealogy of Moses is inconsistent with so long an interval as 430 years between Jacob's 130th year and the 80th year of Moses. Genesis 15:14–16 states:

> And also that nation, whom they shall serve, will I judge: and afterward shall they come out with great substance. And thou shalt go to thy fathers in peace; thou shalt be buried in a good old age. But in the fourth generation they shall come hither again: ...

A possible yet well mathematically controlled scenario depicting the "four generations" of the 16th verse has been constructed (Chart 3a). The problem is that the entire period under analysis must be spanned by only four generations yet Chart 3a reveals that it is impossible for a 430-year sojourn in Egypt to be spanned by these four lives. For example, the chart enables us to see that if Levi had come to Goshen at age 50 with his son Kohath as a newborn (Gen. 46:11), even had Kohath fathered Amram at age 133, the year of his death, Amram's age of 137 still would fail to fill the gap over to the birth of his

son Moses by 80 years! Thus even if Levi were much, much younger, there would still not be enough years to fill the void. Biblically, the matter is not merely settled; it is engraved in stone.

E. 430 OR 400 YEARS OF AFFLICTION?

The final piece of the puzzle deals with the "400-year prophecy" found in Genesis 15:13 (cp. Acts 7:6):

> And he said unto Abram, Know of a surety that thy seed shall be a stranger in a land that is not theirs, and shall serve them; and they shall afflict them four hundred years;

Several avenues must be explored in the resolving of this bothersome enigma.

First, beginning at Genesis 12 and reading through Exodus 15, the Scriptures disclose that the Jews were afflicted in some measure not only during the bondage while in Egypt, but the entire time they lived in Canaan and even during previous short periods of residence in Egypt. For example, being afflicted by a famine, Abraham departed almost immediately after arriving in the land of Canaan and went down into Egypt seeking relief (Gen. 12:4–10).

In Egypt, he was afflicted by the fear that Pharaoh would slay him in order to obtain for himself the beautiful Sarah (Sarai), Abraham's half sister whom he had taken to wife (Gen. 11:29; cp. Gen. 20:12). Other afflictions were the battle of the four kings against five resulting in Abraham's having to rescue his nephew Lot (Genesis 14) and the incidents concerning the wells of Abraham and Isaac being violently taken away and/or plugged (Gen. 21:25; 26:12–33).

The word "affliction" simply means "trouble" and Abraham and his descendants had trouble off and on the entire time from leaving Haran unto the Exodus. Therefore, the 430-year period could apparently be understood as one of *affliction* and not just bondage.

Indeed, as Abraham almost immediately went down into Egypt, there is a sense in which it could be said to have taken 430 years to finally totally depart from there, namely at the Exodus. Although this may appear reasonable to some, this facile solution is not satisfactory.

┌─────────────────────────────┐
│ Isaac's age at his weaning │
└─────────────────────────────┘

1921 BC = 2083 AM + 430 yrs	Abraham – age 75 – leaves Haran and enters the Land and begins the 430-year sojourn (Exo. 12:40–42, Gal.3:17)
1491 BC = 2513 AM – 400 yrs	Year of the Exodus. Number of years back to the promised seed (Gen. 15:3)
1891 BC = 2113 AM	Isaac *established* as the seed lineage.
1896 BC = 2108 AM	Year Isaac is born (Gen. 21:5, see Chart 3)
= 5 yrs	Isaac's age when he became *established* as the seed lineage and *heir* at the *weaning*. Ishmael who is 14 years older than Isaac is now 19. He mocked and persecuted Isaac and is cast out (Gen. 21:8–10; Gal.4:29; Gen. 17:24–25; 21:5).

In the first place the prophecy does not merely say "affliction," it also says "and they shall serve them" (Gen. 15:13). Besides this, the time mentioned is that of 400 years, not 430. Hence two different subjects are before us.

Coming to the 400 years of "affliction," some have offered that it began with Abraham's half-Egyptian son Ishmael's mocking Isaac at the feast celebrating his weaning (Gen. 21:8–9). Ishmael was Abraham's son through his Egyptian concubine Hagar (see Chart 3b). A tabular presentation summing all of these points is given above for clarity.[1]

As Anstey said, the fixing of the date of Isaac's weaning is both logical and mathematically exact. The testimony of the Hebrew Text is that the "seed" of Abraham would be strangers and sojourners for a period of 400 years. That period clearly ended with the AM 2513 Exodus; therefore it began AM 2113 (2513 – 400 = 2113). Since Isaac was born 1896 BC (Chart 2), or AM 2108 (4004 – 1896 = 2108), he was 5 years old at the beginning of the 400-year epoch (2113 – 2108 = 5) as demonstrated on the above outline.

It is at the weaning that Isaac became the sole *heir* with which the term "seed" may be connected. On that day Abraham made him a great feast to celebrate the event. Ishmael was Abraham's heir no longer; he had been officially replaced by little Isaac.

Weaning in the Middle East takes place much later than here in the western world. There it normally transpires between one and three years of age.[2] Weaning refers to more than just withdrawal from breast-feeding in the Bible. It marks the end of infancy and the onset of childhood (compare 1 Sam. 1:22–2:11; Isa. 28:9; Heb. 5:11–14; I Pet. 2:1–3).

Having waited 25 years for the son of God's promise, and thus very old when Isaac was born, Abraham and Sarah apparently indulged the boy and postponed the weaning. Ishmael's mocking of Isaac may now be comprehended more clearly.

Children do not accept withdrawal from being suckled without much protest. Truly, apart from one's considering the miraculous birth as well as the supernatural rejuvenation of the physical body enabling the 95-year-old Sarah to nurse, the scene must have appeared ludicrous.

As stated heretofore, Ishmael is 14 years older and thus is about 19 when 5-year-old Isaac is weaned. He mocks his young half brother's plight, but Isaac now outranks him. Isaac has been named as the "seed," the heir of Abraham who is a mighty prince of Canaan (Gen. 23:6).

---

[1] Anstey, *The Romance of Bible Chronology, op. cit.*, pp. 113–114. See also Ussher, *Annals, op. cit.*, pp. 26-27 (1658 ed., p. 6).

[2] II Maccabees 7:27; also 2 Chron. 31:16: "From 3 years old and upward" – apparently the age the priests began receiving public support from the offerings; those younger were probably not yet considered weaned.

Also see Lev. 27:5–6 where five years of age may be conjectured as pertaining to weaning.

Ishmael mocked his young master, therefore he was cast out.[1]

In support of this concept, it is worthy to note that before the weaning, Ishmael is called Abraham's son (Gen. 17:25), but afterwards he is called the son of "the Egyptian," son of "this bondwoman" (Gen. 21:9–10), and "lad." Moreover, as a child's attitude usually reflects that of its parents (i.e., Hagar), Abraham must "cast out this bondwoman and her son."

So for some, here in small measure began the 400 years of affliction by Egypt (Gen. 15:13). Yet although much of what has been said concerning the significance of the weaning, the public placing of Isaac as "seed" and heir, the meaning of the feast, etc. is legitimate and instructive, the explanation is not sufficient for most in that it does not satisfactorily fulfill the Egyptian "affliction" prophecy. Further, it again does not deal with the "servitude" portion of Genesis 15:13 for Isaac did not thereafter serve either the Egyptian bondwoman, her son or any other Egyptian.

This author considers the best solution to be that found in the *Companion Bible*[2] which is to give attention to and recognize the significance of the structure of Genesis 15:13 (cp. Acts 7:6). The text is known as an *introversion* as shown:

(A) Thy seed shall be a stranger in a land that is not theirs
   (B) and they shall serve them
   (B) and they shall afflict them
(A) four hundred years.

A and A correspond to the same event and to each other. They define the whole period of the seed (through Isaac when weaned) sojourning in Canaan and dwelling in Egypt without permanent land holdings in either as being 400 years.

B and B likewise correspond to each other but relate to a different event from that of which A and A speak. B and B are parenthetic and only relate to the dwelling, servitude, and affliction in Egypt. As has been demonstrated, that was of 215 years' duration. Further details concerning the servitude in Egypt referred to in clauses B and B in Egypt are given in Genesis 15:14-16.

> And also that nation, whom they shall serve, will I judge: and afterward shall they come out with great substance. And thou (Abraham) shalt go to thy fathers in peace; thou shalt be buried in a good old age. But in the fourth generation they shall come hither again: for the iniquity of the Amorites is not yet full.

All which has been under investigation relating to the 430, 400, and 215-year difficulties is succinctly summarized on the small chart located in upper right corner of Chart 3b. This has been lifted almost verbatim from Anstey[3] because it so simply and clearly portrays in an uncomplicated visual form the entire matter which has required pages of detailed explanation and because this author could find no significant way to improve the graphic display.

---

[1] Again the LXX is found wanting, for Gen. 21:14 reads that here Abraham put Ishmael on Hagar's shoulder, yet he was 19!

[2] E.W. Bullinger, *The Companion Bible*, (Grand Rapids, MI: Kregel Publications, 1990), Genesis 15:13 note, p. 22. This is not to be taken as a general endorsement of the notes in the *Companion Bible*. For this writer, Bullinger, like Dake and many others who have produced reference Bibles, is "feast or famine". When he is on the mark he can be very perceptive, but the pendulum often swings to the extreme; for example, his totally biblically erroneous conclusion that Adam died lost in his sin (see Appendix 50, note on Gen. 6:3, p. 45). Here he is not only wrong, he displays a lack of basic understanding regarding Adam's accepting the animal skin covering from God (Gen. 3:21) which finds full explanation in the Gospel of Matthew Chapter 22:1–14; i.e., no one will be admitted to the marriage feast for the King's Son without first accepting a free gift, the covering furnished by the King Himself.

In accepting this garment the recipient so does with full knowledge that the purpose for his entrance to the feast is that the Son is to be therein honored and that he is to wholeheartedly participate in the praise and homage to this Son. To refuse the glorious free and gracious gift from the King is to dishonor both the Father and the Son. Moreover, refusal declares the intention of entering on one's own terms rather than those imposed by the King, a condition which is altogether intolerable. Ruth 3:9, II Chronicles 6:41, Isaiah 61:10, Ezekiel 16:8–14 and Revelation 19:7–8 to but name a few all enlarge upon this

theme. Indeed, only the burnt offering was skinned, and that sacrifice was done voluntarily to symbolize total consecration (Lev.1:3–9 & 7:8). Esther 6:7–9 enlarges on all this by teaching that the greatest honor one can receive is to be clothed in the king's garments, and in the NT Adam is called a son of God (Luk.3:38).

Further, after the Fall we find Eve gratefully praising and giving thanksgiving to Jehovah upon the birth of Cain (Gen. 4:1) as well as Abel (Gen. 4:25), and Adam obviously taught these two sons God's blood atonement requirement for sin (Gen. 4:2–7). More could be said but, having given the gist, we forbear while at the same time proclaiming that our first parents are with the LORD.

[3] Anstey, *The Romance of Bible Chronology, op. cit.*, p. 130.

A thoughtful perusal of this graph will prove most instructive and beneficial. On it we see that the key to the entire problem rests in perceiving that the Genesis 15:13 text distinctly states that the 400-year sojourn related only to *Abraham's seed*; hence it does not include the 30 additional years of Abraham's own sojourning.

Indeed, the 430 years of Exodus 12:40 is 30 years longer than the 400 years of Genesis 15:13 because it includes the sojourning of Abraham himself as well as that of his Seed. The term "children of Israel" (Exo. 12:40) would include Abraham. A short definitive note to the left of Chart 3 summarizes the result of our research which has firmly led us to the "short sojourn" conclusion.

In closing this section the reader is reminded that the interpretation which this work has placed upon the Hebrew Text of Exodus 12:40 is undeniably correct as it is the one the Apostle Paul, himself a Pharisee and a Hebrew of the Hebrews (Phil. 3:4–6), placed on it under the inspiration of the Holy Spirit. To this we add that in view of that which we have just disclosed, the meaning of the Hebrew is completely clear when the Text is properly understood. The chronology of the Old Testament is exact, accurate in every detail and will stand forward and answer any scientific test to which it is subjected.

F. THE PHARAOH(S) OF THE BOOK OF EXODUS

An Egyptian chronology (there are many from which to choose) has been superposed at the lower right of the chart for general reference in identifying the pharaohs that ruled during the various segments of the life of Moses.[1] In so doing, it should not be understood that this writer considers these Egyptian identifications or dates as fixed. The accuracy with regard to the years the pharaohs actually reigned is, by the admission of the writers themselves, somewhat subjective. The author merely sees

them as being substantially correct and reasonably suitable from a time perspective.

To the extent that they are correct, Amosis then would be the Pharaoh that initiated the oppression after the passing of Joseph and his brothers and Thutmose III would be the Pharaoh of the Exodus. Although as of this research, Egyptian writings and monuments give no clear mention of Moses, the plagues, the death of the firstborn, or his having led the children of Israel out of Egypt with the subsequent parting of the Red Sea and the drowning of the Egyptian charioteers, a study of the man Thutmose III[2] makes such a condition readily understandable.

Thutmose III's aunt (or mother-in-law, or wife) Hatshepsut reigned as a prominent queen with many notable accomplishments. She dominated young Thutmose for a period while they co-reigned, causing him to increasingly come to hate her. Upon her death, Thutmose wreaked his revenge by having her name obliterated from the monuments, the annals and all official documents. Our only extant information concerning this powerful queen is that which has been recovered by the archaeologists from the records of the neighboring nations with whom Egypt had contact during her reign.

Indeed, Thutmose III had a reputation of destroying from the archives every mention of those whom he held in disfavor. This also quite naturally would have been applicable to Moses and would account for the absence of his name. In fact, the same petulance and vengeful attitude toward their enemies could well be said of most of the other kings of Egypt. Moreover, the Egyptians, as well as the other nations of antiquity, were disinclined to chronicle their misfortunes, disasters or defeats. Only their good fortune and triumphs are left preserved for posterity.

If the period of the Hyksos Dynasties (XV and XVI), referred to in the literature as the foreign "shepherd kings" who controlled Egypt for

---

[1] Walton, *Chronology and Background Charts of the Old Testament, op. cit.,* p. 31. Sir J. Gardiner Wilkinson's classic study yields the same Pharaoh's as Walton for each of the major events in the life of Moses, but his dates are a few years earlier [*Manners and Customs of the Ancient Egyptians,* vol. I, (London: 1837), pp. 34–39].

[2] Carlton J.H. Hayes and James H. Hanscom, *Ancient Civilizations,* (New York: The Macmillan Co., 1968), pp. 83, 121–124. Many sources may be consulted to ascertain a more detailed account concerning Thutmose III as well as Hatshepsut. The cited reference was selected due to its clear, concise yet careful treatment.

about 150 years, is superimposed on this chart it would seem that they are the rulers of Egypt with whom Joseph and his family found favor. The Hyksos were also Semites, hence related to the Hebrews, reigning over the entire western portion of the fertile crescent from about 1730 to 1580 BC.

The older Bible expositors insisted this was the correct identification and history, but most of the more recent scholars have gone amiss by moving the dates of all the Bible people and events forward. In so doing, they "create" history but it is erroneous for it violates the most accurate continuous historical record extant of ancient man. Again, part of the goal of this inquiry is to expose, explain, and correct such anachronisms.

G. CHART 3A

This chart is largely self-explanatory and has already been referenced earlier. Its primary purpose is to assist in substantiating and resolving the length of time the Hebrews dwelt in Egypt by graphically depicting the lives of Moses' forefathers over a four generation span back to Levi. From Chart 2, the year Joseph's family came down to Egypt (1706 BC) is selected in order to obtain an approximate age for Levi, Jacob's third born son (see Chart 3a, upper left):

1759 BC 77-year-old Jacob fled to Laban (Chart 2)
 – 3 yrs Levi was the 3rd son born to Leah (Gen. 29:32–34)

1756 BC Approximate birth year of Levi
–1706 BC Jacob's family went to Egypt (Gen. 47:9, Chart 2)

50 yrs Levi's approx. age upon coming to Egypt (Gen.46)

Taking Levi's age to be about 50 at the time of their arrival in Egypt, a possible scenario has been constructed based on the ages of Kohath and Amram (Levi's son and grandson respectively) as given in Exodus 6:16–20 unto the birth of his great-grandson Moses. Being unable to scripturally determine the precise dates of the births of Kohath and Amram or when they bore children, the 145 years from 1706 BC (when Levi went to Egypt) and 1571 BC (when Moses was born, see Chart 3) were divided between their life spans. From Chart 3 it was determined that as Moses was 80 years old at the 1491 BC Exodus (Exo. 7:7), his birth year was 1571 BC.

1491 + 80 = 1571 BC (Moses' birth year)

Again, Genesis 15:14–16 states:

> And also that nation, whom they shall serve, will I judge: and afterward shall they come out with great substance. And thou shalt go to thy fathers in peace; thou shalt be buried in a good old age. But in the fourth generation they shall come hither again: ...

As discussed previously, the plausible mathematically controlled scenario depicting the "four generations" of the 16th verse reveals that the sojourn in Egypt can readily be bridged by these men's lives if the period is but 215 years as demanded by Galatians 3:17. However, Chart 3a discloses that it is impossible for a 430-year sojourn in Egypt to be spanned by only these four lives (see note at lower left of chart and page 57).

Although the "four generations" could be comprised of Jacob, Levi, Jochebed (Levi's daughter, wife of Amram and mother of Moses, Exo. 6:20) and Moses, it is felt that the selected lineage is better if it passes through the male descendants as is the biblical norm. Whereas some have complained that "names or generations" could be missing in the Levi, Kohath, Amram to Moses descent, the data contained in Exodus 6:20 is pertinent as it demands four generations.

H. CHART 3B

For the most part, the material found on this chart has been previously utilized in Section C (see page 53) in order to substantiate the "short sojourn" as the correct duration of Israels having dwelt in Egypt. As far as could be ascertained, this chart employs biblical data not used by any other study; consequently it not only authenticates our "short sojourn" determination, the uniqueness of its testimony powerfully undermines and refutes the "long sojourn" position (see note, lower center and lower right).

The importance of Chart 3b lies not only in this or its confirmation of Chart 3, but in that it both illustrates the Bible's built-in internal safeguard system as well as the necessity of checking for other evidence relative to given areas of chronological inquiry. Fully explored on page 57 ff. is the explanation on the left side of 3b offering two credible biblical interpretations of the 400-year prophecy found in Genesis 15:13–16.

I. CHARTS 3C AND 3D

These two charts are largely self-explanatory. Not only are they of great instructional value but are foundational in the drawing and solving of other chronological problems in the Book of Genesis.

Graph 3c is a stick diagram of Jacob's life prepared from material obtained from Chart 2 and 3. Charts 3d, 3e, and 3f were constructed by lifting well-defined segments from Jacob's life displayed on this seemingly inconsequential diagram. These sections then become the start and end points for a more detailed examination of that phase of Jacob's activities.

Here is a simple form of the chasm or gulf predicament encountered and discussed earlier in the chapter. The problem is to ascertain the time Jacob and his family lived in Canaan after he returned from the stay with Laban before they went down to Egypt during the great famine. From Chart 2 it was established that Jacob was 97 years old at his departure from Padan-aram. There it was also seen that he was 130 at the coming to Egypt (Gen. 47:9), thus bridging the chasm and fixing the stay in Canaan at 33 years.

130 − 97 = 33 years (Jacob's 2nd Canaan stay)

The most immediate and meaningful discovery obtained from perusing this chart is the realization that all of the events recorded from Genesis 38 to 46:12 transpired during these 33 years.

This is most significant for it allows a study to be constructed focusing on the life of Jacob's fourth born son, Judah. Being the recipient of the blessing in Reuben's stead (Gen. 49:8–12, cp. Psa. 78:67–68), Judah began to take his place alongside Joseph as a principal person through whom God chose to fulfill His will, purpose, and plan.

While the biblical account discloses Judah's enormous character flaws and general unworthiness, under the molding and shaping by the Lord's hands over the years, he becomes a true man of God. All the kings of Judah from David onward as well as Messiah Jesus (insofar as the flesh is concerned, Rom.1:3–4) are of Judah's direct lineage. The chronology of these episodes becomes the next focus of this study, but the solving of other related previous events must receive priority.

The 20-year span Jacob spent with Uncle Laban (see Gen. 31:38, 41) has been lifted out and enlarged, forming the basis for Chart 3d. The time required for Jacob to father his twelve sons and daughter Dinah, as well as affixing their ages in context for the remaining Genesis narrative, bears heavily on ascertaining the correct chronology over the second sojourn in Canaan.

J. CHARTS 3E AND 3F

The 33-year interim during which Jacob's family dwelt in Canaan is lifted from Chart 3c, enlarged and embellished forming Chart 3f. The data accompanying Chart 3e, as well as the chart itself, substantiates and demonstrates the correctness and plausibility of the decisions attendant to the preparation of 3f.

The issue now becomes whether Jacob obtained his wives before or after his first seven-year dowry period. Fortunately, the Word of the Living God has not been left to the *subjective* whims and interpretations of mere men. The matter may be known with *objective* certainty for it is the will of God that His Spirit guide us into all truth (John 16:13). The Scriptures contain within themselves all the data necessary to ascertain the truth of any specific issue. First, we "study to show ourselves approved." Then we wait for the Spirit's revelation for He rewards those who diligently seek Him (Heb.11:6).

Although not common knowledge, the mathematics imposed upon the chronology by Scripture context demand that Jacob took his wives, Leah and Rachel, almost immediately upon coming to his Uncle Laban's in Haran of Padan-aram (northern Syria). Otherwise, Judah would have been born too late for all the details of his life given in Genesis 38 to have occurred. As has just been established, there are but 33 years for Judah to return with his father to Canaan, marry a Canaanite girl, beget Er, Onan, and Shelah, commit adultery with his daughter-in-law Tamar who subsequently bore him twin sons Perez (Pharez) and Zerah, and Perez's having begotten two sons by the time Jacob's family went down to Egypt.

A perusal of the lower portion of Chart 3f as compared to the upper section illustrates some of the great difficulties that would arise were Judah's age shortened by seven years, which would have been the case if Jacob had to wait seven years before he married Leah and Rachel. Beginning with Judah's marriage, all the incidents recorded in Genesis 38 would have to be postponed until he came of age, thereby effectively reducing the already incident-laden period of available time for the events to have occurred. As we shall see, such a happenstance would result in Dinah's being about 13 at the time of her rape (Gen. 34), and Judah's sons, Er and Onan, not only marrying and supposedly capable of fathering around the ages of 12 and 11 respectively (or even 9 and 8 as some reckon!) but the Lord's judging them as wicked and slaying them for this at such young ages.

Obviously the context of these stories does not fit into such a scenario. In fact, this is what brought Dr. Kennicott and his Mr. Skinner, with Adam Clarke's blessing,[1] to the conclusion that something was wrong; and there was. As mentioned previously in the discussion of Chart 2, their solution was that Jacob left home and went to Haran at age 57 rather than 77.

This contrivance enables Jacob to begin generating his offspring when he is much younger resulting in Dinah's being about 16 at the time of her defilement and Er around 19 (Onan *circa* 18) when God slew them. Their scheme has Jacob remaining with Laban for 40 rather than 20 years, thus this compensating error correctly places that patriarch at 97 when he departed Haran and returned to Canaan. The problem is that in order to so do they transgress two Scriptures, giving us their own private interpretation in order to justify their solution. The violated passages are:

> This twenty years have I been with thee; thy ewes and thy she goats have not cast their young, and the rams of thy flock have I not eaten (Gen. 31:38).

> Thus have I been twenty years in thy house; I served thee fourteen years for thy two daughters, and six years for thy cattle: and thou hast changed my wages ten times (Gen. 31:41).

---

[1] Clarke, *Clarke's Commentary, op. cit.*, vol. I, pp. 176, 196–199.

Their recommended alteration in verse 38 is from "This twenty years have I been with thee" to "During the *one* twenty years I was with thee." In verse 41 they alter "Thus have I been twenty years in thy house; I served ..." to read "During the *other* twenty years for myself, in thy house, I served ... ."

Such is not the way of the biblicist. Anyone can "solve" a difficult chronological problem if he is free to resort to altering Scripture or declaring the problem passage as being corrupt as the need arises. Indeed, most of the many works examined during this study are guilty of such unworthy practice, but it is neither necessary to address the perceived uncertainties nor allowable as God has promised to preserve His Word.

Kennicott, Skinner, and Clarke wrongly discern the matter, not realizing that here Bishop Lloyd (by altering Ussher) has failed us and in so doing, created an anachronism which gives the appearance of a problem or even an error in the text. Assuming the "Ussher" date (though it is actually Lloyd's) to be correct, they reject the Text and proceed to "correct" the Holy Writ rather than to stand on it as the continuing infallible deposit from God to man. Without ever considering alteration of the Text as an option, it became necessary to reexamine the problem in order to discover where the usually reliable Ussher had missed the mark and after correcting the matter, continue.

Whereas Ussher had placed Jacob's arrival at Haran in 1759 BC and his marriage to Leah and espousal to Rachel during that same year[2] (he is seldom wrong in the Book of Genesis), Bishop Lloyd altered Jacob's wedding date, having him wait seven years before marrying Leah (1753 BC). This mistake necessitated the ages of Dinah and Judah to be lessened.[3] Accordingly, Dinah's birth is forced closer to the

---

[2] Ussher, *Annals of the World, op. cit.*, p. 29 (1658 ed., page. 8–9).

[3] Clarke, *Clarke's Commentary, op. cit.*, vol. I, page 199. In this commentary, Adam Clarke references Kennicott and Skinner as correctly crediting Ussher with asserting that Jacob married almost as soon as he arrived at Haran, ascribing sons to him very soon after his coming to Laban (Clarke agreeing by inference). This was, in fact, the actual case and is the correct solution to the dilemma; however most are unaware that such was Ussher's position as Bishop Lloyd altered his dates allowing a seven-year delay from the arrival unto the weddings.

1739 BC return to Canaan making her about 13, far younger than implied by the context of the story (Gen. 34). Likewise, Judah's birth year approaches the year of the return so that he is only about 9 that year. As alluded to heretofore, the years from 9 to his marriage to the daughter of Shuah the Canaanite must be subtracted from the 33-year total time spent in Canaan (prior to the move to Egypt) resulting in the ages of Er and Onan being only 12 and 11 in the lower scenario of Chart 3f (or about 9 and 8 as Kennicott, Skinner, and Clarke reckon to Lloyd: Clarke, pages 197–198, see fn 3, p. 63), much too young to either marry, procreate, or be slain for having been judged as wicked.

Again, the context tells us that something is amiss, but the rectification hardly requires Kennicott's or Skinner's radical recommendation of mutilating the Sacred Text. All that is required to untangle this is to acknowledge that it could not have been after waiting for seven years that the marriage contract was fulfilled; Ussher had been right all along. The force of the sum of the following five recapitulating proofs is irresistible.

1. Jacob did not say "Give me my wife, for my *years* are fulfilled." He said "for my *days* are fulfilled" (Gen. 29:21). This implies a certain number of days from the time the contract was made until he could actually take Rachel to wife. The number itself was always left to the determination of the contracting parties. The seven years (vs.18) of service were the total dowry and *not* the customary waiting period. The "few days" of Gen. 29:20 could have been the month of verse 14, and the contract could have been made at the beginning of these 30 days. Verse 15 implies that Jacob had already been working or "serving" Laban in order to earn his keep.

2. Jacob actually received both wives within a week of each other (vv.27–30). He was told that if he would "fulfill her (Leah's) week" (vs.27) Rachel would then be given to him. Verse 28 declares: "And Jacob did so, and fulfilled her week: and he gave him Rachel his daughter to wife *also*." As it may be proved that Leah became his wife at the beginning of the total 14-year dowry period (see reasons #3 and #4), then Rachel had to have *also* become his wife at that time.

3. It is not feasible that Jacob obtained Leah (and Rachel a week later) at the *end* of the first seven-year period because that would not allow enough time for all the children to be born. Birthed at the end of the 14-year dowry period, Joseph was the last of Jacob's sons born before the return to Canaan. After his delivery and having fully paid for Rachel (Gen. 30:24–26), Jacob desired to return to Canaan, but Laban persuaded him to remain 6 more years (for the cattle, Gen. 30:24–28; 31:41). Thus all the other children, except Benjamin,[1] had to be born in either a 7 or a 14-year span.

Now Leah had six sons and a daughter *before* Joseph was born (30:20–24). Furthermore, there was a period when she "left (off) bearing" after having birthed four sons (29:35; 30:9). During this interval of barrenness, she gave her handmaid Zilpah to Jacob that she might have more children through her. As Zilpah bore two sons *before* Leah herself began to bear again, the childless interval had to have been close to a minimum of two years. Thus, it is not possible that Leah could have had seven single births and an approximately two-year unfruitful interval in only seven years. Moreover suckling tends to delay ovulation, making this even less conceivable. Therefore Jacob received his wives at the *beginning* of the entire 14-year dowry period.

4. As alluded to earlier, Judah could not have been born in the second seven-year period because the events relating to his life recorded in Genesis 38 require more time than that would allow. This episode occurs before Judah's family went down to Egypt. Jacob departed from Laban in Haran when he was 97 years old (see Chart 3c), and he was 130 when he and his family entered Egypt (Gen. 47:9). Thus the family only dwelt in Canaan 33 years (130 − 97 = 33, see Chart 3c) during which time Judah married a Canaanitess, the daughter of Shuah of Adullam. They begat a son named Er who married Tamar. The LORD slew Er, and his younger brother Onan wed Tamar.

---

[1] Benjamin was "begotten" or conceived in Padan-aram (Gen. 35:26 where ילד is translated "born"; this Hebrew word is also often rendered as "begotten," "beget," or "begat" meaning "to impart life"), but he was born of Rachel near Bethlehem on the 1739 BC return to Canaan just before coming to Isaac at Hebron (Gen. 35:16–20, 27; cp. Gen. 48:7).

After God also slew Onan for his wickedness, Judah refused to let his youngest son, Shelah, marry Tamar. Later, after Judah's wife had died, Tamar disguised herself as a harlot and seduced her father-in-law Judah that she might give birth to a son in order to "raise up seed" to Er (Gen. 38:8; cp. Deut. 5:5–10). She gave birth to twins, and when Jacob and his clan came to Joseph in Egypt, they were of sufficient age that one of them, Perez (Pharez), was married and had two sons (Gen. 46:12).

Judah was Jacob and Leah's fourth son (Gen. 29:31–35). Chart 3d depicts the 20 years that Jacob spent with Laban in which he worked 14 years for his two wives and 6 years for his cattle (Gen. 31:41). It exhibits two possible scenarios for the birth year of Judah. Chart 3f portrays both for comparison.

The upper scenario reflects the difficulty of compressing the account of Judah's family given in Genesis 38 into the biblically required 33-year span, even when the maximum conditions that make use of Judah's being born in the first 7-year period are considered. This scenario assumes that Jacob took his wives at the beginning of the first 7 years of his 20-year sojourn in Haran and allows that Judah was born after 4 years.

Even this requires four generations (Judah, Er, Perez and his two sons) be born in only 49 years, i.e., Judah's birth in 1755 BC (Chart 3d) minus 1706, the year the family entered Egypt (Chart 2 and 3c). This could permit Judah to be about 16 when his father took him to Canaan whereupon he soon wed, fathered by age 17 so that Er, Onan and Perez (Pharez) could have been around 14 to 15 years old when they married.

However, if we attempt to place the time of Judah's birth in the second 7-year period, we lose 7 years, forcing all these births and marriages into only a 42-year term (1748 – 1707 = 42) as displayed in the lower scenario of Chart 3f. Here the marriage ages become so small such that the setting does not ring true. Furthermore, the ages of Er and Onan become generally too young (c. 11 or 12) to procreate or to incur the judgment that fell upon them. Moreover, it is difficult to imagine God as describing boys of 12 and 11 years as "wicked."

Therefore, in view of the above four considerations one must conclude that Jacob took his wives at the beginning of the entire 14-year dowry period, working for Laban to pay off the dowry while living with both Leah and Rachel. How else could it be said of a love-smitten suitor that the time "seemed unto him (Jacob) but a few days" (Gen. 29:20)? Yet there is still more confirming evidence.

5. Dinah's age is a restricting factor with regard to when Jacob obtained his wives (see Chart 3f and diagram on page 66). Upon his return, Jacob built a home as well as shelters for his cattle at Succoth. At this time, his sons were referred to as "tender children" (Gen. 33:2–13). Later, Jacob sojourned at Shalem, a city of Shechem, where he purchased "a parcel of a field" (Genesis 33:18–19). There, Dinah (Jacob's daughter by Leah) "went out to see the daughters of the land" (Gen. 34) at which time Shechem, the Hivite prince, raped her. At the time of Dinah's defilement, Jacob's sons were then called "men" (Gen. 34:7,21,22,25). Thus, Jacob lived a considerable time at Succoth.

Jacob had gone to Laban in 1759 BC. Joseph was born in 1745 at the end of the 14-year dowry period which he served to pay for his two wives (Gen. 30:24–26; cp. 29:18–28), and Dinah was born before Joseph (Gen. 30:19–26). Later while living in Hebron with Isaac, Joseph's brothers sold the 17-year-old into slavery in 1728 BC (Gen. 37:2,28,36; cp. 35:27). This and Joseph's birth date place restrictions on Dinah's age at the time of her defiling.

As she was Leah's youngest child and since the rape took place before Joseph's 17th year, Jacob could not have waited 7 years until 1752 BC (1759 − 7 = 1752) before he received his wives for Dinah could not feasibly be born during the first 7-year span as demonstrated in reason #3. Even in the extreme unlikelihood of this having happened, at best, her birth would have had to have been in the same year as that of Joseph (1745 BC). Such a scenario would place her age around 13, too young to fit the context of the incident; so young a maiden would hardly go unescorted among the ungodly in that day. The additional seven years brings her age much more in line with the story.

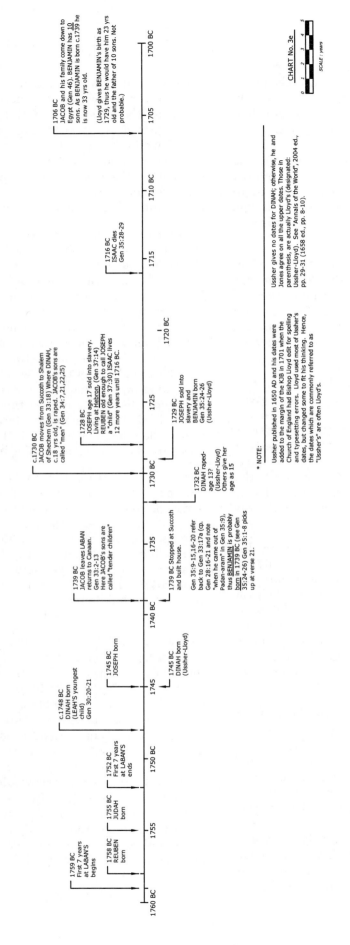

1706 BC
JACOB and his family come down to Egypt (Gen 46). BENJAMIN has 10 sons. As BENJAMIN is born c.1739 he is now 33 yrs old.

(Lloyd gives BENJAMIN's birth as 1729, thus he would have him 23 yrs old and the father of 10 sons. Not probable.)

1716 BC
ISAAC dies
Gen 35:28-29

c.1730 BC
JACOB moves from Succoth to Shalem of Shechem (Gen 33:18) Where DINAH, c.18 yrs old, is raped. JACOB's sons are called "men" (Gen 34:7,21,22,25)

1728 BC
JOSEPH age 17 sold into slavery. Living at Hebron (Gen 37:14) REUBEN old enough to call JOSEPH a "child" (Gen 37:30) ISAAC lives 12 more years until 1716 BC.

1729 BC
JOSEPH sold into slavery and BENJAMIN born Gen 35:24-26 (Ussher-Lloyd)

1732 BC
DINAH raped-age 13? (Ussher-Lloyd) Others give her age as 15

1739 BC
JACOB leaves LABAN returns to Canaan. Gen 33:2-13

Here JACOB's sons are called "tender children"

1739 BC Stopped at Succoth and built house.

Gen 35:9-15,16-20 refer back to Gen 33:17a (cp. Gen 28:16-21 and note "when he came out of Padan-aram" in Gen 35:9), thus BENJAMIN is probably born in 1739 BC (see Gen 35:24-26) Gen 35:1-8 picks up at verse 21.

c.1748 BC
DINAH born (LEAH'S youngest child) Gen 30:20-21

1745 BC
JOSEPH born

1745 BC
DINAH born (Ussher-Lloyd)

1759 BC
First 7 years at LABAN'S begins

1758 BC
REUBEN born

1755 BC
JUDAH born

1752 BC
First 7 years at LABAN'S ends

1760 BC   1755   1750 BC   1745   1740 BC   1735   1730 BC   1725   1720 BC   1715   1710 BC   1705   1700 BC

* NOTE:

Ussher published in 1650 AD and his dates were added to the margin of the KJB in 1701 when the Church of England had Bishop Lloyd edit for spelling and typesetting errors. Lloyd used most of Ussher's dates, but changed some to fit his thinking. Hence, the dates which are commonly referred to as "Ussher's" are often Lloyd's.

Ussher gives no dates for DINAH; otherwise, he and Jones agree on all the upper dates. Those in parenthesis, are actually Lloyd's (designated: Ussher-Lloyd). See "Annals of the World", 2004 ed., pp. 29-31 (1658 ed., pp. 8-10).

CHART No. 3e

SCALE : years
0   1   2   3   4   5

66

This concludes our thesis concerning the chronology of Jacob's life, especially with reference to his marriages. Significantly, in nearly a century, not one other chronologist has corroborated Skinner's thesis, Kennicott's and Clarke's verbal approval notwithstanding. No such contriving is necessary; all his perceived paradoxes have been satisfactorily resolved by the present research on the accompanying charts that sustain Chart 3 (3c–3f). The five-point exegesis is absolutely decisive. With the foregoing as a guide, the story can be read and understood without violence to the Text.

K. JACOB'S "KINDRED"

A final point pertaining to this time frame concerns a perceived problem with respect to the register of the children of Israel who came down to Joseph in Egypt (1706 BC). A comparison of Genesis 46:5–27 with Acts 7:14 reveals three different statements as to the number of family members in that southward moving caravan: 66, 70, and 75.

As a result, when interpreting the Acts 7:14 passage nearly all modern scholars inform us that the Septuagint (LXX) *conforms* in reading "75" in Genesis 46:26–27 (and at Exo. 1:5) whereas the Hebrew text supposedly errs and contradicts Acts in recording "70" in the Genesis passage. Although the highly spurious nature of the Septuagint was covered in our first chapter, Section H, this specific problem dealing with Jacob's joining Joseph in Goshen was judged to be better addressed at this point due to its relevant context.

The scholars continue by adding that the five missing names in the Hebrew text are preserved in the LXX at Genesis 46:20 where Machir, the son of Manasseh, and Machir's son Galaad (Hebrew = Gilead) are recorded along with Ephraim's two son's Taam (Hebrew = Tahan) and Sutalaam (Hebrew = Shuthelah) and his son Edom (Hebrew = Eran). We are further informed that as the Hebrew text contradicts the Acts account regarding the number of Jacob's family that traveled down to Egypt during the severe famine, the Hebrew text is corrupt here (and at Deut. 10:22 as well as Exo. 1:5 as they also record "70") and must be corrected by the LXX to bring the count into agreement.

Here is a straightforward example of scholars placing the Septuagint on a level equal to, yes — at times even above — the Hebrew text. But such recourse is totally unwarranted. All that is required is to begin with faith in God's many promises that He would preserve His Word — forever! Then careful prudent examination will expose that there is no real contradiction at all.

However, even a casual reflection on the ramifications involved in accepting the reading of the LXX in the Acts 7 and Genesis 46 passages under discussion will disclose the fallacious nature of so doing. Is it really reasonable or likely that Stephen (having been dragged in before the Sanhedrin by a mob and now in the middle of a Spirit-filled address before the very men who had caused the death of his Lord – while speaking as a Hebrew to the Hebrews) would have quoted from a GREEK Old Testament manuscript of Genesis in which five names had been added in violation of the Hebrew laws governing Scripture transmission? We trow not! Deuteronomy 4:2, 12:32; Psalm 12:6–7 and Proverbs 30:6 all declare to neither add nor subtract from God's Word.

Are we to suppose that Stephen is going to convert the Sanhedrin who have already crucified Christ and/or possibly save his own life by quoting to them from a verse that added five names to the Scriptures which they used in the synagogue every Sabbath? No small wonder they killed him! They would have looked upon him as a perverter of Scripture. Such an act is not that which is recorded in the account.

They slew Stephen for confronting them with the person of the Lord Jesus – that He was Christ indeed and, rather than receive Him as such, they had murdered Him as their fathers had done to His predecessors, the prophets (Acts 7:51–53)! They were further enraged by Stephen's call to repentance and his accusation that they had broken the Law. *Never* is there any suggestion that their rage resulted from consternation over Stephen's having perverted the Scriptures.

Acts 7:14 and Genesis 46:27 are not referring to the same entity. Stephen is speaking of something else – a different entity, a different total. Again, three totals (66, 70, and 75) are given in the Scriptures under investigation.

Genesis 46:26–27 (cp. Exo. 1:5 and Deut. 10:22) records two, 66 and 70.

First, Genesis 46:26 states that 66 souls came "*with*" Jacob to Egypt.

Jacob's 11 sons and 1 daughter	12	Genesis 5:22
Reuben's sons	4	Genesis 46:9
Simeon's sons	6	Genesis 46:10
Levi's sons	3	Genesis 46:11
Judah's 3 sons and 2 grandsons	5	Genesis 46:12
Issachar's sons	4	Genesis 46:13
Zebulun's sons	3	Genesis 46:14
Gad's sons	7	Genesis 46:16
Asher's 4 sons, 1 daughter & 2 grandsons	7	Genesis 46:17
Dan's son	1	Genesis 46:23
Naphtali's sons	4	Genesis 46:24
Benjamin's sons	10	Genesis 46:21
total	66	Genesis 46:26

All the souls that came with Jacob into Egypt, which came out of his loins, besides Jacob's sons' wives, all the souls were threescore and six;

Furthermore, these 66 are said to have come "out of his loins." Beginning at Genesis 46:9 and going through verse 25, we find 66 males listed of which two (Er and Onan, vs. 12) have already died leaving a total of 64 males.

If we now add the two girls from verses 15 (Dinah, a daughter) and 17 (Serah, a grand-daughter), we account for the 66 souls "from Jacob's loins" who came *with* him to Egypt (Gen. 46:26). These facts are reflected in the preceding chart. Thus, the first of the three numbers has been verified.

The solution to the 66 and 70 predicament is quite unambiguous. Genesis 46:27 says:

And the sons of Joseph, which were born him in Egypt, were two souls: all the souls of the house of Jacob, which came into Egypt, were threescore and ten.

Here, Genesis 46:27 adds Joseph and his 2 sons (Manasseh and Ephraim, vs. 20), all 3 of whom were already down in Egypt. This brings our running total to 66 + 3 = 69. As the "66" are said to have been those who came *with* Jacob, he has not yet been included. Now we so do and obtain the 70 souls included in the term, "the house of Jacob" (vs. 27). Indeed, the biblical definition for "the house of Jacob" is clearly stated as being Jacob and "all his seed" which would include Joseph and his two sons (vs. 27, cp. vs. 6). This total may also be obtained by

merely adding the 33[1] of verse 15, the 16 (vs. 18), the 14 (vs. 22), and the 7 (vs. 25). That is: 33 + 16 + 14 + 7 = 70. The second of the three seemingly contradictory numbers has thus been established.

The problem now reaches a crescendo for Acts 7:14 declares:

Then sent Joseph, and called his father Jacob to him, and all his kindred, threescore and fifteen souls.

Here a genuine contradiction is perceived by many; were there 70 or 75? Stephen is neither mistaken nor is he citing from the LXX[2] when he gives the number as 75. He is speaking of a different entity which he calls Jacob's "*kindred*." The terms "house of Jacob" and "kindred," though similar, are not synonymous. As we have shown, the "house of Jacob" numbered 70, and it consisted of only Jacob as well as "his seed" – those who were said to have "come out of his loins."

---

[1] This "33" actually includes Jacob himself. Beginning at vs. 8, Reuben and his sons number 5, Simeon and his sons = 7, Levi and sons = 4, Judah and his "sons" total 8, Issachar and sons = 5, and Zebulun and his sons number 4. These sum to 33 (5 + 7 + 4 + 8 + 5 + 4 = 33), but as Er and Onan (two of Judah's sons, vs. 12) died in Canaan, they must be subtracted. This leaves 31. We now add Jacob's daughter, Dinah, bringing the total to 32. We have already established above that Jacob must be included in order to obtain the 70 of verse 27; hence, we go back to verse 8 and now include him and establish the 33 of vs. 15. Keil and Delitzsch concur: *Commentary on the Old Testament in Ten Volumes, op. cit.*, vol. I, p. 370.

It should be noted that as Gen. 46:15 reads "daughters" (plural) the temptation is to conclude that the 33rd person must surely refer to an unnamed 2nd daughter rather than Jacob. But the temptation must be resisted as this reasonable solution immediately fails upon further analysis. As already stated in the text of the main body, Genesis 46:9 through verse 25 lists a total of 66 males, and when we subtract Er and Onan (vs. 12) we arrive at 64. Dinah (vs. 15) and Serah (vs. 17) bring the total back to the 66 souls "from Jacob's loins" who came *with* him to Egypt (Gen. 46:26; see preceding chart).

Obviously, then, adding another daughter at vs. 15 would yield 67 and exceed our stated limit; thus it must be incorrect (it would also bring the final total to 71 rather than 70). Accordingly, vs. 15 is seen as a cumulative running statement, i.e., total sons = 31, total daughters = one, and therefore we must now include Jacob to obtain 33.

[2] Many commentaries imprudently reason that as Stephen was a Hellenistic Jew, he would naturally use the Septuagint.

However Jacob's "kindred" that Joseph "sent" for to come "to him" (Acts 7:14) are the 66[1] already cited plus *the wives*[2] of his sons that came down to Egypt with their father. Moreover, it is back in Genesis 46:26 where we are given the clue that these wives are the key to differentiating between the "70" and the "75." There we read that 66 souls came with Jacob down to Egypt: "besides Jacob's sons' wives." These daughters-in-law were not included as having to do with the "house of Jacob" (Gen. 46:26) which numbered only those "who came out of his loins," but they are part of Jacob's "kindred"[3] that Joseph sent for.

Now Jacob had 12 sons (Gen. 35:22). To determine how many of their wives went down to Egypt, we simply take the 75 "kindred," subtract the 66 who came from Jacob's loins (as they are included in the "kindred") and obtain only 9 rather than 12. That is, 9 of the 75 "kindred" that came to Egypt *with* Jacob did not come from his loins, and Gen. 46:26 has alerted us to the fact that they are the sons' wives. Therefore, 3 of the 12 son's wives (12 − 9 = 3) were not numbered in the "kindred."

Of course, we must immediately exclude Joseph's wife for she was already in Egypt and thus was not "sent" for (Acts 7:14). This accounts for one of the three. A second is found earlier at Genesis 38:12 where we learn that Judah's wife had died previously.[4] Thus, one of the other sons must also have become a widower. We may deduce that it was almost certainly Simeon as special attention is called to the fact that Shaul, his youngest son, was by a Canaanitess (Gen. 46:10). The three differing totals — 66, 70, and 75 — have now all been established and explained. Yet more to the point, the real issue is still the "five missing names" which are "preserved" in the LXX. What of these five names? They are man's forgery, not the words of God!

The proof is straightforward and undeniable. Joseph wed at age 30 (Gen. 41:45–46). His father Jacob and kindred joined him in Egypt nine years later (Gen. 41:53; cp. 45:6; after the seven years of plenty and near the end of the second year of the famine that followed). Manasseh and Ephraim were born to Joseph *during* the seven years of plenty (41:50–53). Further, the context of Acts 7:14 is unmistakable — it refers to Joseph's family that joined him in Egypt at the end of these nine years. Manasseh, the elder son, could therefore be no more than eight years of age at that time!

Manifestly, the LXX that is today extant has been proven spurious, for Manasseh and Ephraim are far too young to be fathers when Joseph's "kindred" went down to him in Egypt — much less grandfathers![5] The reading in the LXX is grossly untenable.

Thus, the "five missing names" in the Hebrew text at Genesis 46:20 (Machir, the son of Manasseh, Machir's son Gilead, Ephraim's two sons, Tahan and Shuthelah, along with his son Eran) are seen to have been interpolated by conjecture from Genesis 50:23 and Numbers 26:29, 35–36 (vv. 33, 39 and 40 in the LXX). The author of the LXX has tried to force Gen. 46:20 to conform to Acts 7:14. This shows that the LXX in use today was *not* written BC, and its editor had a NT before him as he wrote.

The painfully obvious conclusion before us is that — by not grasping the true explanation of the 66, 70, and 75 — the translator of the Septuagint tried to "correct" what he perceived as a "scribal error" in the Hebrew text. In so doing, he *created* one.

---

[1] Obviously, neither Joseph and his sons (Gen. 46:27) nor Jacob are included in Acts 7:14 (note: "to him").

[2] Scripture records Jacob as having only one biological daughter (Dinah, Gen. 46:15; 30:21); thus, Genesis 46:7 which mentions his "daughters" (plural) must refer to Jacob's daughters-in-law (cp.46:5 and 26).

[3] This author is not the first to recognize this distinction. It has recently come to my attention that Dr. William Hales also realized this as far back as 1809: *A New Analysis of Chronology*, 2nd ed., vol. 2 of 4, (London: 1830, first ed. 1809), p. 159. See my p. 93, footnote 1.

[4] As a passing interest, Jacob's wives (Rachel, Gen. 36:19 and Leah 49:31 with context, etc.) are also dead.

---

[5] Having uncritically accepted the Septuagint's reading of Genesis 46:20 where Machir the son of Manasseh, Machir's son Gilead, Ephraim's two son's Tahan and Shuthelah as well as his son Eran have been added, Dr. Hales (fn. 3) failed to detect this fatal flaw in his beloved LXX. The reader will note from this brief paragraph that the most modest investigation would have exposed the error of recording these five names here. Indeed, all commentaries, Bible encyclopedias, biblical footnotes, seminarians, pastors, scholars, etc., that likewise promote this flaw stand equally guilty of failing to trust God's infallible preserved Word as found in the Hebrew Masoretic Text and are to be further blamed for not having done their basic homework. Shame!

THE 10 PLAGUES ON EGYPT

DAY	EXODUS							
1	7:11–13	Aaron's rod turns to a serpent – Egypt's Magicians defeated – Pharaoh's heart hardens, hence …						
	CYCLE 1		"IN THE MORNING" (1st, 7:15)					
2	7:14–25	**[1] Water** **to blood**	Goshen spared of all plagues	Moses **Warns** 7:16–18	Used Aaron's staff (7:19)	Fish die (7:21)	Pharaoh's heart hardens	
3								
4								
5								
6								
7								
8								
9	7:25	7 days were fulfilled *after* the waters of Egypt had been turned into blood						
10	8:1–7	**[2] Frogs**		Moses **Warns** 8:2	Used Aaron's staff	Magicians duplicate		
11	8:8–11		Pharaoh sends for Moses			Frogs to be removed		*"tomorrow"*
12	8:12–15		Frogs die, piled into heaps			Pharaoh says they can go	but hardens, hence —	
13	8:16–19	**[3] Lice**		**No Warning** (1st)	Used Aaron's staff	Magicians can't duplicate	Pharaoh's heart hardens	
	CYCLE 2		"EARLY IN THE MORNING" (2nd, 8:20)					
14	8:20–23			Moses **Warns** 8:21		Flies		*"tomorrow"*
15	8:24–29	**[4] Flies**	Goshen spared		No staff used	to be removed		*"tomorrow"*
16	8:30–32		Flies removed			Pharaoh says they can go	but hardens, hence —	
17	9:1–5			Moses **Warns**		Plague on cattle "in the field"		*"tomorrow"*
18	9:6	**[5] Murrain** (plague)	No animals die in Goshen		No staff used	all animals in the field died		
19	9:7					No Israelite cattle killed	Pharaoh's heart hardens	
20	9:8–12	**[6] Boils**	Magicians have boils	**No Warning** (2nd)	No staff used	Magicians again defeated	Pharaoh's heart hardens	
	CYCLE 3		"EARLY IN THE MORNING" (3rd, 9:13)					
21	9:13–21			Moses **Warns**		Hail to fall on all in the field		*"tomorrow"* at this time
22	9:22–26	**[7] Hail and Fire**	Early Abib		Used Moses' staff	Barley & flax smitten, v.31		
23	9:27–35		Moses sent for		Hands to God	Hail stops		*"that day"*
			Wheat and rye not yet up			Pharaoh says they can go	then hardens heart, hence –	
24	10:1–13a			Moses **Warns**		Locust plague		*"tomorrow"*
25	10:13b–15	**[8] Locust**	Brought in by the east wind		Used Moses' staff			*in the morning*
26	10:16–20		Strong west wind			Locust cast in the Red Sea	Pharaoh's heart hardens	
27	10:21–23	**[9] Darkness** **for 3 days**	Goshen had light	**No Warning** (3rd)	Used Moses' hand			
28								
29								
30	10:24–29	Moses sent for – Pharaoh declares he will slay Moses if he sees him again. ……………					heart hardened	
	11:1–10	Moses **Warns** – death to firstborn, leaves in anger – tells Israelites to ask goods of Egyptians						
31	12:1–20	God **instructs Moses** regarding the beginning of months and **Passover**: time of the death of the firstborn foretold (11:4–5, cp. 12:6, 12, 22–23)					→ *night of 15*	
32	12:21–28	Moses instructs the elders regarding Passover:						
33		the elders then instructed *all* the people						
34		(time was required to assemble *all* the people, instruct them, and return)						
35	12:3, 28	10th of Abib (Nisan) — Passover lamb **selected** — examined until the 14th — no spot or blemish.						
36		11th of Abib						
37		12th of Abib						
38		13th of Abib						
39	12:28	14th of Abib Passover lamb killed at evening — blood **applied** to door as instructed in 12:22						
40	12:29–36	**[10] Death of the firstborn** – at midnight, 15th of Abib (Nisan) 1491 BC, ate lamb after sundown – the Exodus begin						

CHART FOUR

A. BIBLICAL JUDGES DESCRIBED AND DEFINED

This chart covers the period of the judges through the first three kings. Many have been caused great consternation over the Book of Judges; thus, although the broad overview is mathematically simple, there are several critical problems which have to be faced. Even among the most outstanding scholars, seminary professors, and pastors, much misunderstanding exists as to the nature and duties of biblical judges.

Hence at the onset a definition based solely upon the internal content and context of Scripture must be formed, not only for the sake of accuracy and clarity but in order that such a statement, if correct, may keep us from falling into the old mistakes of past chronologers and from creating new ones as well. As will be seen, the Scriptures do not portray these individuals in the same light as the judges with whom twentieth century man is familiar.

The judges were raised up by the Lord, especially during the times of spiritual decline or backsliding of Israel. During these periods, God would bind Israel over to an enemy for the purpose of bringing her to her senses, causing the nation to acknowledge her sin in forsaking the Lord which invariably involved the worship of other gods, and to again rely upon Him. A rather general definition as to the essence of biblical judgeship is:

> Nevertheless the LORD raised up judges, which delivered them out of the hand of those that spoiled them. And when the LORD raised them up judges, then the LORD was with the judge, and delivered them out of the hand of their enemies all the days of the judge; ... (Judg. 2:16 and 18a).

The scriptural qualifications for the judgeship were that they be Hebrew men who reverenced Jehovah, were able, had wisdom and understanding in the ways of the Lord, were truthful, hating covetousness, and well known throughout the Twelve Tribes for those attributes (Exo. 18:21–22; Deut. 1:13–17).

Although the nature of the function discharged by the judges is not distinctly defined by the above, a more thorough description is readily ascertainable from within the course of the narrative. For example, even though some fathers did appoint their sons as co-judges and successors, the "office" of judge was not hereditary as was the priesthood. It was conferred successively upon each individual who sustained it by the immediate appointment of God himself.

At the time of his call from God, the judge's primary function was to bring the people to judgment. This was done by the judge and/or a prophet (or prophetess) first confronting the people so as to bring them to judge their sins with God's viewpoint. This having been done, the people were called upon to repent and return wholeheartedly to following the living and true God with singleness of purpose.

Once the judge had succeeded in bringing the people to judge their sin (cp. 1 Cor. 11:31–32), the Lord would then use that judge as His instrument of deliverance. The judge then became their savior-deliverer, leading the people to victory over their sin and then over their oppressors. In so doing, they served as types of Jesus the Christ, the Savior-Deliverer over sin, Satan, and his hordes.

This pattern may be noted throughout the book (Judg. 3:7–10; cp. Neh. 9:26–28). This definition is further substantiated in the Book of 1 Samuel which discloses that Samuel was not referred to as anything other than a prophet until chapter 7 whereupon, acting as outlined above, he became a judge (1 Sam. 7:6: Samuel *judged* Israel at Mizpeh, after calling on the people to repent, vs. 3 ff.).

Therefore, it was not in the civil sense of the word that these people were referred to as judges during the first phase of their service. It was not like Moses and others that "sat on the bench" (Exo. 18:13–27; Deut. 1:15–18) that this term is to be understood. Thus, two different shades of meaning are seen to apply to the word "judge" at this period of Israel's history.

Of course, after having restored the people to the Lord and delivered them from their oppressors, he would thereby be established as the spiritual Shepherd, overseeing the children

of Israel. Quite naturally, during the remainder of his lifetime the judge would be that individual to whom the people would resort for direction, leadership, and counsel. Thus, he served in different capacities, initially as a preacher, then a warrior and finally as an administrator of civil and ceremonial justice by the application and enforcement of the Mosaic law until the time of his death (1 Sam. 7, especially vv. 15–17). Considerable reflection upon the biblical narratives with respect to the individual judges should substantiate the correctness of the above definition and reveal that it is neither an artificial contrivance nor a private interpretation.

Moreover, the Scriptures state that Moses was a judge and the incidents recorded therein clearly depict that he and Joshua functioned as previously described. Hence, both are to be included as part of the period of the judges and not merely those men whose exploits are given in the actual Book of Judges, beginning with Othniel (Judg. 3:8–11).

Moses performed according to the above biblical definition in bringing the children of Israel out of Egypt and also during the 40-year trek in the wilderness as did Joshua throughout the time of the conquest of Canaan and the subsequent division of the land among the Twelve Tribes. Indeed then, Moses functioned in two distinct and diverse roles, yet both bore the single title judge.

Accordingly, the period of the judges is seen to begin at the 1491 BC Exodus and end with the death of Samuel about 1060 BC (431+ years, cp. Acts 13:20: "about" 450 years). As Samuel's life span overlaps and intertwines with those of Saul, the first king, and David, their reigns and Solomon's are depicted on Chart 4 so that the period of the divided monarchy may be treated as a single and separate unit.

1. THE SPAN OF THE JUDGES – 480 OR 450 YEARS?

The first major chronological problem in the period of the judges, therefore is that of its duration. As alluded to in the discussion of Chart 3, a paradox is perceived to occur between 1 Kings 6:1, (stating that from Solomon's fourth year to the Exodus was 480 years) and Acts 13:17–21 (apparently giving about 450 years for only the judges). With regard to this apparent discrepancy, Scaliger long ago termed Acts

13:20 as the "Crux Chronologorum."[1] One of the two must somehow be selected as "correct" and the other understood in its context – but which, and how can one be certain?[2] The 480 years is the correct number of consecutive linear years; therefore, the verse to be used as the standard for the following reasons.

(1) Beginning with the weakest, it is offered that the Acts 13 passage is from the New Testament; hence, if its 450 years were the standard to which the 480 must somehow be reconciled, no Old Testament man of God could have solved the paradox. He would, in fact, have been led into error as he would only have had access to the 1 Kings 6:1 passage. This author is of the conviction that the Old Testament saints could calculate their own history and chronology in order that they could know the "time of their visitation" by Messiah.

---

[1] Joseph Scaliger, *De Emendatione Temporum* (1596). A Frenchman (1540–1609) of exceptional genius and consummate scholarship who is everywhere accepted as the forefather of the science of modern chronology.

[2] Seemingly endless schemes have been put forth over the years to solve this anomaly. One of the more original attempts was offered by the world-renown self-educated Scottish minister John Brown of Haddington (1722–1787) in the footnotes at the end of the Book of Judges in his AD 1778 reference Bible (*Self-Interpreting Bible*, p. 295). Brown actually attempts to reconcile by harmonizing the two verses in question by way of a unique speculation. He says: "Supposing the time 'when the children of Israel were come out of the land of Egypt,' to be the period when their escape out of the house of bondage was consummated by their *entrance* into the land of Canaan; and supposing that the apostle's reckoning of the 450 years begins at the same point, (which the context naturally leads us to conclude,) and closes with the death of Samuel the prophet — two years before the fall of Saul — we may combine the two calculations thus:

434 Period of the judges, from the entrance into Canaan to the death of Samuel, about 450 years.
+ 2 From the death of Samuel to the death of Saul
+ 40 David's reign
+ 4 Solomon's reign before the erection of the Temple
480 Period from entrance into Canaan to the building of the Temple (1 Kings 6:1)."

Hence, by redefining the meaning of "when the children of Israel were come out of the land of Egypt," to be the entrance into the land of Canaan rather than the Exodus, Brown feels that he has put the problem to rest. To this author's knowledge, few if any have accepted this supposition (present writer included); however it has been placed herein for its illustrative merit and historic interest.

(2) The patent fact gleaned from reading the narratives concerning the various judges is that the stories, men, and periods mentioned in Acts 13 overlap one another. Failure to see this leads one, as do many, to take the Acts 13:17–21 data, i.e., the 40 years in the wilderness, the "about" 450 years for judges and 40 years for Saul's reign obtaining a subtotal of 530 years.

They then add 40 years for David's reign and 3⁺ (or 4⁻) years for the beginning of Solomon's reign to the building of the Temple and obtain 573 (or some similar number by the same reasoning) as the total years (*Anno Mundi*) for the period described in 1 Kings 6:1 as being only 480 years.

Next they sum all the years of servitude as punishment for idolatry, etc., thus 8 + 18 + 20 + 7 + 40 are 93 years.[1] This 93 is then subtracted from the 573 *Anno Mundi* years yielding 480 which are designated as "*Anno Dei*" years (or some similar method).[2]

The advocates of the "450" position feel this solves the problem by stating that God did not "count" (?) the years of punishment in 1 Kings 6:1; He only "counted" the 480, hence the designation *Anno Dei*. Others insist that more overlaps are also possible; hence, to them the paradox is insolvable.

True, the possibility exists of the individual judges overlapping rather than following one another in succession. However, it is believed that God's main purpose in giving the time periods of rule and authority as well as the ages of the begetting of sons, etc., was to make possible the ascertaining of the chronology and dates within the Holy Writ. Therefore, as the Scriptures list the judges successively, Chart 4 does likewise.

However, rather than adding 40 + 450 + 40 = 530 years, the 40's were found to overlap the period of 450 and thus should be subtracted from the total. That is, in the Book of First Samuel, Samuel's life as a judge overlaps Saul's reign until almost its end. Comparing 1 Sam. 25:1 with 1 Sam. 27:7 reveals that Samuel died at least one year and four months before Saul was slain on Mount Gilboa. Consequently Saul's 40 years should not be added as though they consecutively followed those of Samuel's judgeship.

As Samuel is the last judge, most of Saul's years must be taken from the 450-year total. Further, as Moses is one of the judges, his last 40 years are included in the "about 450 years" of Acts 13:20 as are the years of Joshua's judgeship. When this is understood and drawn, the 480 years of 1 Kings 6:1 are verified, becoming a major chronological key.

Furthermore, an overlap exists in the stories in Judges where the period of servitude is given along with the time of rest for the land in order to complete the 480-year scenario as heretofore justified. For example, the verses relating to judge Ehud are interpreted as meaning that due to disobedience and sin, Israel served Eglon the king of Moab 18 years. God raised up Ehud as His instrument to judge and deliver her, and then the land had rest. A break or pause in thought is construed as following after the word "rest" (vs.30) so that the next two words are taken as a recapitulation whereby the total time elapsed for the whole story (Judg. 3:12–30) was fourscore or 80 years.

To elaborate, the defenders of the 450-year position are forced by that number to interpret the Eglon episode as meaning that the whole period comprised the 18 years of servitude plus 80 years of peaceful living under Ehud, totaling 98 years (Judg. 3:14, 3:30). To the contrary however, of those 80, the first 18 were under Eglon's control. Hence rather than 98 years, the interval is actually only 80 during which 80 – 18 or 62 years of peace follow Ehud's slaying of Eglon and his subsequent deliverance from Moab's overlordship.

The 480 years of 1 Kings 6:1 demand this manner of interpretation of the narrative, not only for Ehud-Eglon but for the other judges as well. The problem is that English punctuation

---

[1] *The Companion Bible*, Study Notes by E. W. Bullinger, *op. cit.* Appendix 50, p. 55. This method places the 18 years of being "vexed and oppressed" by the Philistines and Ammonites within Jair's judgeship. There are almost as many solutions offered for this as the number of researchers who have investigated the paradox. For example, another similar approach sums 8 + 18 + 20 + 7 + 18 + 20 (40–20) where they include Samson's 20 in the Philistines' 40 obtaining a total of 91 years. This 91 is then subtracted from 573 yielding 482 or "nearly" 480.

[2] Anstey, *The Romance of Bible Chronology, op. cit.*, pp. 157–158. Anstey arrives at 480, but he obtains 594 rather than 573 and 114 instead of 93.

and syntax suggest that the land had rest for a period of 80 years after Moab's defeat; however Hebrew contains no punctuation.

Thus Judges 3:30 should be understood as saying "and the land had rest" followed by a pause in thought whereby the following "80 years" is a summary statement referring to the entire period of time covered by the story. Accordingly, each biblical episode records the period of time from one period of rest to the following period of rest, and included within this span is the time of oppression.[1]

The story of Samson, recorded in Judges 13–16 is offered as further scriptural precedence and justification for this conclusion. Samson's 20-year period of judgeship was within the 40 years during which the Philistines held dominion over Israel, thus his 20 and their 40 are not to be summed. The obvious undeniable overlap of the 40 years of Philistine domination (Judg. 13:1; 14:4; 15:11, 20) and Samson's 20-year judgeship (Judg. 13–16) are seen as a precedent in illustrating that which is true concerning the relationship of the other servitudes and their accompanying judgeships.

(3) The aforementioned conclusions in the above numbers (1) and (2) are confirmed and sustained by Judges 11:26. This reveals that from the conquest of Heshbon during the year before the entry until Jephthah was 300 years. Though most critics ignore or ridicule this number, the 300-year statement and the 480-year declaration of 1 Kings 6:1 beautifully sustain one another.

Moreover when believed and taken literally, the 300-year pronouncement is the chronological key to Judges. This value for the time period in question militates against adding the other values to the 450 years of Acts 13:20. Further, it enables one to solve the "Judges-Joshua chasm" between the division of the land under Joshua to the beginning of the oppression by Cushan-rishathaim. It also confirms as well as demands the overlap interpretation of Eglon's account given in (2) above and strengthens the Samson-Philistine overlap observation at the end of that section as 8 + 18 + 20 + 7 sum to a value greater than the possible maximum gap between the division of the land to the oppression by Cushan.

---

[1] This is how the Jews reckon, *Seder Olam* (2005) p. 121 ff.

(4) Lastly, Judah's lineage yields data that confirms and supports the 480 years of 1 Kings 6:1 and Jephthah's 300 years, but militates against the aforementioned consecutive adding technique as being applicable to Acts 13. That is, Judah's offspring Amminadab had a son named Nahshon as well as a daughter named Elisheba who married Aaron (Exodus 6:23). Nahshon was a contemporary of Moses and was the leader (Prince) of the tribe of Judah during the Exodus and wilderness wanderings (Num. 1:7; 2:3; 7:12; 10:14). His son, Salmon, entered the land with Joshua and married Rahab, the converted prostitute, who had hidden the spies (Josh. 2, cp. Mat. 1:5).

As the generation of Joshua and Caleb and those older perished during the 40-year wilderness wanderings, Salmon is of the next generation (Joshua lived 110 years, Judg. 2:8). Salmon begat Boaz who begat Obed who begat Jesse, the father of David. Now, Jesse was alive with Samuel and Saul (1 Sam. 16:1–5). This means that from the entry into Canaan to the last judge and the first king covers the life spans of only four men, i.e., Salmon, Boaz, Obed, and Jesse (Chart 4a).

A possible scenario of just these four generations, based on using the 480 years of 1 Kings 6:1 and the 300 of Judges 11:26, over the time frame for only the magistrates covered in the Book of Judges yields a time span of:

299 yrs: Othniel (1400 BC) to Samson (1101 BC) or
305 yrs: Othniel (1400 BC) to Saul (1095 BC)

With only four life spans to fill this time gap and taking Salmon's age to be about 20 at the entry would require Salmon to have fathered Boaz around 100 years of age. Boaz would also have had to father Obed at nearly 100 who, in turn, would have had to begat Jesse around age 100. Jesse would then had to have begotten David about age 86 and been about 100 when David (c. 15 years old) was anointed by Samuel. Comparative ages of the oldest biblical contemporaries over this interval are: Moses 120, Aaron 123, Ehud c. 110, Eli 98 and David, "old" at age 70 (Chart 4a).

As these decreasing ages depict, during this era life spans continued to shorten after the time of the global Deluge and finally reached modern life expectancies. Thus even this scenario requires a series of miracle births whereby men

begot sons at nearly 100 across a span of time when most men were scarcely living that long.

A scenario that would include the 450 years as though they were consecutive linear years for the span describing the eight-year servitude to Cushan (Judg. 3:8) as its beginning and Saul's year of enthronement as its end (rather than the 305 years as shown above) would require adding to the life spans and increasing the ages of Salmon, Boaz, Obed, and Jesse as to when they fathered one another over and above the years as depicted on Chart 4a. This strongly argues against the span's being 450 years.

Indeed, Moses' ancestry through his second son, Eliezer, yields similar results and thus confirms the information concerning Judah. The lineage continues from Eliezer down to Rehabiah, Jeshaiah, Joram, Zichri, and Shelomoth. This Shelomoth was an overseer of the treasury during the reign of King David (1 Chron. 26:24–28). A possible scenario of this data indicates that each of the above descendants of Moses would have to have begotten a son when they were around 80 years of age (see Chart 4b).

If Acts 13 were forced to mean that the period from Israel's servitude for Cushan-rishathaim (Judg. 3:8) to Saul's enthronement is 450 years, the span over which these offspring lived and gave birth would have to be expanded by 150 years. This would necessitate increasing the ages in which Moses' lineage fathered to c. 110 in this instance and to 130 for Judah's lineage.

Again, these are not reasonable values for the begetting of sons when compared to biblical life spans for that period. Increasing the length by nearly 150 years would therefore have the highly improbable effect of two distinct lineages begetting sons at an age equal to – and beyond – that which men were living!

Hence, the 40 years, etc., referred to in Acts 13:17–22 must overlap the "about" 450 years and be subtracted from it, not summed. This Gordian knot is cut by simply seeing that the "about 450" is not referring to the length of the period of the judges at all in Acts 13:17–22! Instead, it is either:

(a) A parenthetic remark concerning the span of time of this whole thought from the Exodus in 1491 BC until 1048 BC when David became king of all 12 tribes (i.e., c. 443 years).

(b) The 400 years of affliction (vs.17 cp. Gen. 15:13) by Egypt plus the 40 years in the wilderness (vs.18) and the 7 years of war until the actual distribution of the land (vs.19) totaling 447 years.

(c) A parenthetic remark beginning when the covenant ritual with Abraham (initiated in Genesis 15; cp. "chose our fathers," Acts 13:17) was consummated in his 99th year (born 1996 BC – 99 = 1897 BC) in Genesis 17 by the changing of his name from Abram and the seal of circumcision. The period ended in 1444 BC when the land was divided among the last 7 tribes (1897 – 1444 = 453 years).

(c) is self explanatory and well may be the actual solution. (a) and (b) are markedly different in content. (b) is actually saying the 450 years all transpired prior to the events recorded in the Book of Judges. Here, it is a parenthetic remark summing the years from verse 17 up to the time of the division of the land after the defeat of the seven nations that dwelt in Canaan.

This means that the 20th verse is not telling us the duration of the period in which God gave Israel judges, rather it is telling us *when* they were given. Thus the first part of this verse is referring back to the first part of the 17th to the time when "the God of this people of Israel chose our fathers."

This "choosing" has been established in the discussion of Chart 3 regarding God's selection of Isaac out of the children of Abraham as the lineage through whom the covenant was to be established: "for in Isaac shall thy seed be called" (Gen. 21:12c, cp. 17:19 and 21). The 20th verse of Acts 13 now informs us that God chose Isaac about 450 years before the division of the land (vs. 19). Remember, the words "unto them" and "for" are in italics and thus are not in the Greek New Testament Text. They are interpretative and have been added by the King James translators for clarity and smoothness. This latter interpretation is well-substantiated by the literal reading in the Greek of verses 19 and 20 (cp. Acts 7:6):

> And having destroyed nations seven in [the] land of Canaan, he gave by lot to them their land. And after these things about years four hundred and fifty he gave judges until Samuel the prophet. (*Textus Receptus*; the critical text reads similarly.)

Portraying the calculation of this thought should clarify that which is being said. From the birth of Isaac to the birth of Jacob are 60 years (Gen. 25:20, cp. vs. 26; Chart 3, upper left); from there to Jacob's going to Egypt, 130 (Gen. 47:8–9); from there to the Exodus, 215 (Chart 3); from thence to the entrance into Canaan, 40 (Acts 13:18, etc.); from that to the division of the land among the last seven tribes,[1] 7 years (Chart 4); which totals 452:

$$60 + 130 + 215 + 40 + 7 = 452 \text{ years}$$
("about" 450; 1896 BC – 1444 = 452).

Of course it could be argued that instead of commencing at the birth of Isaac the initiation point should be that of the feast of his weaning at which time he is placed as the heir and seed lineage, Ishmael being set aside and sent away. The above would then be adjusted to:

$$55 + 130 + 215 + 40 + 7 = 447 \text{ years}$$
("about" 450; 1891 BC – 1444 = 447)

and should this be numbered inclusively, one more year could be obtained bringing the sum to 448. Obviously 453, 452, 447 or 448 are all more than sufficient to satisfy any reasonable person with reference to the Apostle Paul's "about" 450 years. Neither should the reader have undue concern over this forthright solution as though it were merely the desperate resolution of a single individual.

Over a decade after making this determination, the author learned that in his annotations upon difficult texts, Sir Norton Knatchbull had reached similar conclusions as had Calmet and others.[2] Indeed, even more recently the following quote from Ussher, written prior to AD 1658, was located which succinctly embodies that which is stated in (b) as well as all that preceded it:[3]

---

[1] After seven years of war, Joshua began dividing the land west of the Jordan River near the end of 1445 BC, but he did not finish distributing it among the last seven tribes until after the tabernacle was moved to Shiloh early in 1444 (see page 289).

[2] Clarke, *Clarke's Commentary*, op. cit. vol. V, pp. 784–785. An excellent summary of Calmet's and Knatchbull's findings may be found in Clarke's work. *Liberty Bible Commentary*, among others, also has captured and embraced the general thrust of that which has been set forth herein (p. 2163).

[3] Ussher, *Annals*, op. cit., "The Epistle to the Reader" p. 8 and p. 26 (1658 ed., p. iii and p. 28).

In the year after the Elections of the Fathers, much about 450 [Acts 13:17, 19–20] for from the birth of the promised seed Isaac, to this time [i.e.: the division of the land in 1444 BC – as seen from his preceding paragraph. He gives 1896 as the birth year for Isaac on page 26 (1658 ed., p. 6)], are reckoned 452 years: and from the rejection of Ishmael, 447 but between both, we may count, 450 years (author's brackets).

Thus all the principal difficulties long associated with this troublesome verse have been removed so that it may be seen to perfectly harmonize with the 480 years of 1 Kings 6:1 and, as shall be established presently herein, with Jephthah's 300-year declaration in Judges 11:26. This brings all the key passages long believed either to be in error or at variance with one another into concord resulting in a flowing concert of melodious mutual confirmation.

Again, we see that God did not leave the matter to the mere subjective whims of man. The context of the stories contained within the Book of Judges along with the testimony of 1 Kings 6:1 make clear that overlaps as described heretofore exist and therefore years must be subtracted, not added. The basic rule of interpretation that takes precedence with regard to this entire section is that an "iffy" Scripture (one whose context is at all ambiguous or difficult) must never be used to override the testimony of a crystal clear verse which can only have one meaning such as 1 Kings 6:1.

2. THE SKELETAL OUTLINE

Having established the validity and reliability of the 480-year span from the Exodus to the commencement of the building of the Temple, a skeletal outline may be constructed for the sake of clarity. The general stick diagram for this period may quickly be displayed by extracting the established biblical anchor points 1491 and 975 BC from within the rectangles on Chart 1 (see page 77).

Thus, this graph will exhibit the period of the judges, beginning with Moses at the time of the Exodus, and extending through the first three kings of the united monarchy unto Solomon's demise and the ensuing disruption of the kingdom into two factions.

Diagram 1

The
Exodus
1491

Death of
Solomon
975

It should be seen that Chart 4 is essentially a visual display of the aforementioned 480-year interval from the Exodus to the beginning of Solomon's fourth year when he began to build the Temple. However it extends 36 years and about 11 months longer to include all of Solomon's reign and not merely his first 3 years 1 month and 2nd day (same as 4th year, 2nd month, 2nd day; 2 Chron. 3:1–2). The interval between these two fixed points must now be filled in with the pertinent data extracted from the biblical record, especially that contained within the Book of Judges.

Beginning on the left side at the 1491 BC Exodus, 40 years is scaled off for the wilderness wandering under Moses' judgeship. Another gulf known as the Joshua-Judges chasm is encountered at this point as the Scriptures do not contain data which directly mathematically connect Joshua's life to the oppression by Cushan-rishathaim and Israel's subsequent deliverance under Othniel (Judg. 3:8–11) so that the chronology may be continued.

As shall be demonstrated, the duration of the wars with the various Canaanite kings from the entry to the division of the land among the Twelve Tribes of Israel was seven years. Although this information closes the gulf somewhat, it is not of sufficient extent to bring the chronology forward to Cushan. The solving of this problem will be enlarged upon presently

at which time there will be an accounting for these seven years. However for the purpose of describing the outline, it is sufficient for the time being to demonstrate the ease with which the gap may readily be bridged.

Although Sihon, King of the Amorites, and his capital city, Heshbon, were captured only months before the entry under Joshua (see Chart 4, lower right), its fall took place during the prior year (1452 BC). Judges 11:26 relates that from this triumph to the incident which led to the commencement of Jephthah's judgeship, a span of 300 years ensued. This brings us to the year 1152 BC and establishes this as an intermediate fixed point within the interval under investigation from which one may work backward or forward in time (Diagram 2).

Closing the void back toward the time of Joshua from this date is accomplished by beginning at the tenth chapter of Judges and incorporating the historical information contained unto the third chapter where the story of Cushan and Othniel is recorded. This will fix the date of Cushan's dominion over Israel. The remaining gap must then be the time allotted for the remainder of Joshua's life after the division of the land unto his death at age 110, the rule of the elders that outlived him, and the subsequent forsaking of the Lord by the generation that followed them.

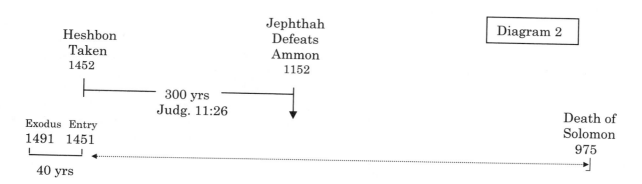

Diagram 2

Heshbon
Taken
1452

Jephthah
Defeats
Ammon
1152

300 yrs
Judg. 11:26

Exodus Entry
1491   1451

40 yrs

Death of
Solomon
975

Moving to fill in the gap toward Solomon's death, Jephthah's six-year judgeship is first measured off bringing the mark to 1146 BC (1152 – 6 = 1146). At this juncture, the correct path becomes uncertain, hence a leap is made to the right side of the outline to 975 BC (the whole is equal to the sum of its parts). Working from the opposite direction, the gap between 975 and 1146 BC is closed by scaling off the 40 years of the dominion of Solomon bringing us to 1015 BC (1 Kings 11:42). David's 40-year reign (2 Sam. 5:3–5) takes us back to the 1055 BC termination of the 40-year rule of Saul (Acts 13:21), which thus began in 1095 (Chart 4 and Diagram 3 on the following page).

The numerous problems normally associated with this section have now been mathematically reduced to a very small period. All that is remaining to close this portion of the stick diagram is the 51 years from the end of Jephthah's judgeship to the inception of the monarchy under Saul (1146 – 1095 = 51 years) with the men whose judgeships followed Jephthah.

However, here another great "Gordian knot" is encountered. All the obtainable former studies also floundered at this crossroad, each producing a unique solution. In fact, one of the authors actually left a huge breach in his work for the period of the judges, bemoaning that due to "overlapping" there was "no method to date these periods of judges at the present time."[1]

Nevertheless, the skeletal outline is well in place and all that remains is to add meat to the bones. Thus it cannot be overemphasized that even should one or more of the decisions relevant to any of the individual judges later be proven incorrect, the fabric of the overall chronology will not be marred for the skeleton is firm and sound. Again, the nature of the sections or blocks of data with which we are dealing is such that any error in judgment is not cumulative for an indefinite duration as the next fixed point serves as a buttress of correction. The solution to this part of the puzzle awaits our attention.

---

[1] Walter R. Dolen, *The Chronology Papers,* (San Jose, CA: The Becoming-One Church Pub., 1977), p. 11. Although Dolen feels that a workable solution to the chronology of the Book of Judges is unobtainable, his abbreviated study has much to recommend it.

3. THE FORTY-YEAR PHILISTINE DOMINION

It is the conviction of this author that the key to the Jephthah-Saul gap resides in a 40-year span occurring within this 51-year interval during which the Philistines had dominion over the children of Israel (Judg. 13:1; 14:4; 15:11, 20). If only an anchor point could be located with certainty somewhere within the 51-year period to attach one end of the "days of the Philistines" (Judg. 15:20), this troublesome zone could be resolved.

The uniqueness of the word "dominion" is seen as "the sword of the Lord" with which to sever this Gordian knot. One may have only partial control over a person or nation, but the peculiar meaning of "dominion" will not allow such a condition. There is no such thing as partial dominion. One either has dominion or he does not. If it is partial, it is not "dominion." The realization of this gives one something tangible for which to search. Could the point be determined when either the dominion began or when it terminated?

First, Samson's 20-year judgeship transpired somewhere within the 40-year Philistine dominion (Judg. 15:20). Second, the Scriptures clearly declare that Samson "began" to break that dominion (Judg. 13:5). Again, due to the singular meaning of the word "dominion," it logically follows that if Samson's act of pulling down the temple of Dagon in which the governmental, military and religious leadership of Philistia were decimated almost to the point of extinction "began" the liberation from that oppressive dominion, then the culmination of the deliverance must follow very close at hand.

The occasion of that overthrow is unmistakable. At Mizpeh, the Lord used Samuel to complete the toppling of the Philistine dominion of Israel (1 Sam. 7:13).

Moreover, the story of Israel's 40-year Philistine domination had been left hanging in suspense back in Judges 16 with Samson's defeat and humiliation of the Philistine god Dagon when he destroyed that pagan deity's temple and by that same act slew more than 3,000 of their foremost military and civil leaders. The Philistines, who had absolute lordship over Israel, would have been furious!

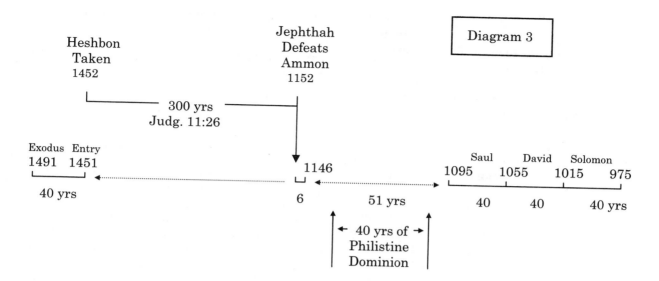

Diagram 3

Thus should arise the questions: "And then what happened? What did the Philistines do to the despised Jews in retaliation?" God answers this, but before revealing the conclusion of the story, He interjects two bloody and dreadful incidents.

a. Micah's "Priest" and the Tribe of Dan

The first is the story of the young Levite of Bethlehem-judah named Jonathan whom a certain unscrupulous "Micah of Mount Ephraim" unlawfully ordained and hired as his personal priest. A portion of the tribe of Dan left its original inheritance which Joshua had apportioned to them because their allotment was small, and they had been unable to dispossess the tall Amorites (Amos 2:9, cp. Num. 13:32–33). The Amorites had forced the Danites to dwell on the mountain, not allowing them to come down into the valley (Joshua 19:47–48; Judg. 1:34; cp. Judg. 18).

After sending out five spies to discover a favorable location, 600 warriors and their families eventually migrated about 110 miles northward to the city of Laish and its environs. While passing Mount Ephraim they stopped, hired Jonathan away from Micah and continued their journey. Arriving at Laish, the 600 slew all its inhabitants, burned the city, rebuilt it in the secluded valley, and renamed it "Dan" after their progenitor, Dan the son of Jacob. They then established Jonathan and his male descendants, who were not of the lineage of Aaron, as their idolatrous priesthood until the

year Tiglath-pileser, the great Assyrian monarch, carried the inhabitants of this northern settlement into captivity (c. 740 BC, Judg. 18:30, cp. 2 Kings 15:29).[1]

Many of these Danites were originally from Zorah, thus not only were they of the same tribe – they were of the same town from whence came Samson (Judg. 18:2,11, cp. 13:2,25). God's purpose in placing this account immediately following the story of Samson rather than in its chronological position was to reveal and underscore that it was not only Samson whose morals were of a low and degenerate nature, but nearly everyone from his hometown had for a long time been hardened and wicked against the ways of the Lord. This emphasized the righteousness of the Lord in allowing the long term vexation and dominion of that tribe in particular, especially by the hands of the Philistines whose northern border was contiguous to that of the tribe of Dan.

Although the biblical narrative does not include data which would enable one to establish the precise chronology, there are indications which allow an approximation of the time frame to be

---

[1] Nearly all modern scholars date this event along with the fall of Damascus as having transpired in the year 732 BC, but this date is based upon the Assyrian Eponym List rather than on the Hebrew history as recorded in the Old Testament. The flawed logic involved in imposing the fragmented Assyrian data on and over the continuous, unbroken testimony of Scripture as well as the problems associated with the Assyrian records will be examined at length under that subject in the discussion of Chart 5.

firmly set. First, the story occurred before the time of Samson, hence before Judges chapters 13–16. This may be seen in that it was at the time of the migration of the 600 families of Dan that the township of Kiriath-jearim became known among the Danites as Mahaneh-dan (i.e., "the camp of Dan") because of their encampment there just prior to their enticing Jonathan, the hireling "priest," away from Micah (Judg. 18:12–13); yet Samson is said to have frequented the "camp of Dan" (Judg. 13:25).

Another evidence, one which places the events under discussion very close to the customary beginning of the time of the judges, is the well-known apparent reference to Moses (Judg. 18:30) where Jonathan is said to be the son of Gershom, the son of Manasseh (Moses).[1] It is generally believed by modern scholarship, and perhaps correctly so, that as Jonathan had dishonored his distinguished descent from Moses, the scribes inserted the letter "nun" (נ) in the Hebrew word for Moses in this passage thereby changing it to Manasseh.

Actually, the "nun" is neither inserted nor incorporated into the Hebrew Text; it is suspended and squeezed in above the line. It is for this last reason that the present author gives some credence to the connection to the name of Moses. Supposedly this was done in order to spare the name and reputation of the great lawgiver from having an idolater and, as he was not a male progeny of Aaron, an unqualified self-styled priest among his immediate descendants. If Jonathan is the grandson of Moses, and this admittedly seems likely, it places the story after the death of Joshua, and near the time of Cushan.

As appealing as the above may be, it is still somewhat enshrouded in speculation. Of course, the raised "nun" in the Hebrew Masoretic Text must somehow be explained; accordingly, the given anecdote is a most plausible resolution. In any case, there exists other evidence as to the season of these

happenings which does agree with the time setting as already determined.

The irrefutable chronological key is to be found in the 1st verse of the 18th chapter:

In those days there was no king in Israel: and in those days the tribe of the Danites sought them an inheritance to dwell in; for unto that day all their inheritance had not fallen unto them among the tribes of Israel (Judg. 18:1).

When this verse is compared to Josh. 19:47–48 and Judges 1:34, the fact that the Danites had not yet obtained the mastery over the Amorites betrays the fact that only a relatively short span of years had transpired from the 1444 BC final distribution of the land until this occasion, certainly not a century or so as many would have it. Yet there is one more factor to be considered.

The ensuing historical account recorded in Judges 19–21 contains unmistakable documentation which allows the chronologer to considerably narrow the time frame for the story. As will be shown, it places the near annihilation of the tribe of Benjamin incident after Joshua's death, before the rise of Cushan, hence very near the time of the demise of the elders who outlived Joshua. As the story of Micah, Jonathan, and the Danites precedes this, it may be somewhat safely inferred that it also antedates it.

It is held by this writer that although no single portion of evidence offered relevant to the time frame under investigation is in and of itself conclusive, the sum of the whole body of that which has been presented is exceedingly formidable. Its attestation is considered sufficient to the extent that a point of certainty has been established.

b. The Levite's Concubine – Benjamin Decimated

The Danite episode is followed by the sordid story of the Levite and his concubine which resulted in the near annihilation of the tribe of Benjamin (Judg.19–21). Phinehas, the grandson of Aaron, had become the high priest upon the death of Eleazar, a contemporary of Joshua who seems to have died soon after the passing of that renowned conqueror (Josh. 24:29–33).

Phinehas had been a young warrior priest around the time of the conquest of Sihon, king of Heshbon (1452 BC). He proved himself

---

[1] See "Jonathan" or "Manasseh" in almost any Bible dictionary such as Merrill F. Unger, *Unger's Bible Dictionary,* (Chicago, IL: Moody Press, 1966), pp. 602–603 or Henry S. Gehman, (ed.), *The New Westminster Dictionary of the Bible,* (Phil., PA: The Westminster Press, 1970), p. 510.

zealous for the Lord during the encounter with the hireling prophet Balaam and the king (and women) of Moab which followed immediately thereafter (Num. 25:1–13), as well as the punitive expedition against the Midianites in which Balaam was slain (Num. 31:6–8). Nevertheless he was of sufficient age so that directly after the 1444 BC division of the land, it was his leadership under whom Joshua placed the army in the matter of "Ed," the altar which the tribes of Reuben, Gad, and the half tribe of Manasseh had erected at the Jordan River (Josh. 22, esp. vs.13).

This places Phinehas' priesthood as beginning during the rule of the elders who outlived Joshua and extending reasonably close to the Cushan-Othniel period, thus dating the debased story of a Levitical priest who not only had a concubine but permitted her to be repeatedly raped all night resulting in her death in order to save himself from the bisexual perverts in Gibeah of Benjamin. Her "husband" chopped her body into 12 pieces, sending one to each of the tribes and demanded retribution against the perpetrators. When the tribe of Benjamin refused to surrender the guilty over for punishment, a civil war ensued, and except for 600 men, the entire tribe of Benjamin was exterminated.

The whole sorry affair ends with an account in chapter 21 which reveals debauchery, mockery, and apostasy in Israel's worship and in her dealings with the Lord in general. Not only had the three annual feasts called for by the Law been reduced to but one, the manner in which the feast was kept by the dancing of the virgins was likewise unscriptural (Although only the men were commanded to attend the three feasts [Exo. 23:14–17, 34:22–23; Deut. 16:16–17; cp. Judg. 21:19], the ideal was for all the family members — as well as the servants, Levites, foreigners, widows, and orphans — to join in the celebration [Deut. 16:11, 14]).

Indeed, Leviticus 5:4–6 gave clear instructions for the proper handling of a foolish vow before the Lord and the proper sacrifices attendant thereunto, rendering unnecessary all of their machinations in circumventing their pledge not to give any of their daughters to Benjamin in marriage. The explanation for such degeneracy, sham, and false worship is recorded in the final verse; there was no God-established human authority to whom the people had to give account (Judg. 21:25).

God's purpose in further interposing between the account of Samson's act against the Philistines at the temple of Dagon and Samuel's deliverance at Mizpeh was to clearly depict that it was not just Samson and the men of his own city or even merely those of his tribe who were wicked and thus deserving judgment. These five chapters show explicitly the full depths of moral declension of the nation as a whole at the inception of the period. Only the strong leadership of Moses, Joshua, and the elders had been able to hold the people's allegiance to the Lord, and even then it was often only partial and sporadic.

With the death of these committed men of God, the faithfulness and moral fabric of the people waned such that the nation of Israel stood guilty before the Lord at one time or another over the entire period of the judges. Wherefore God's delivering her over to her enemies was both justifiable and righteous; thus His deliverances sprang forth from His compassion and grace. God's intent in allowing Israel's enemies to vex and oppress her was to bring the people under enough pressure that they would repent and thereafter God could restore blessings unto them. More importantly, He wanted them to see the need for a leader far greater than Moses, Joshua, or the elders so that they would call upon Him to send to them the promised Messiah. Even so, return quickly Lord Jesus.

c. Eli and His "Judgeship"

Nevertheless, the question remains, with their leadership slain by the champion of the despised Jews, in what manner and when did the Philistines wreak vengeance? Again, God leaves the reader in suspense at the end of the story of Samson. He interjects the episode of Jonathan and the 600 of the tribe of Dan (Judges 17–18) followed by that of the Levite and the decimation of the tribe of Benjamin (Judges 19–21) for the reasons given previously.

Then, coming to the Book of Samuel, He introduces Eli for the purpose of letting the reader know something about the judge who immediately followed Samson as well as the new hero who completed the task of breaking the 40-year Philistine dominion over Israel which the now

dead blinded warrior had initiated. To accomplish this, the biblical narrative digresses far back before the time of Samson in order to lay the groundwork as to who he was and from whence he came. Hence, one of the main purposes of the story of Eli was to introduce the last judge, Samuel.

The necessity of the digression at the point of Samson's mighty delivering act has been made apparent. Now when the enraged Philistines seek vengeance on Israel for Samson's deed, the student will know from whence came this new champion. Consequently, the story from Judges 16 then continues chronologically at 1 Sam. 7 with the Philistine's avenging attack at Mizpeh. As God's prophet, Samuel had already "judged" the people and led them to repentance. God then delivered Israel with a mighty rout of the Philistines so that within a few days after the death of Samson, Samuel had been established as the new judge succeeding Samson – not Eli as most suppose.

Scripture records that Eli lived 98 years (1 Sam. 5:15–18). He would have become fully established as a priest at age 30 after serving a five-year apprenticeship (Num. 4:1–3, 22–23, 29–30, 46–47 cp. 8:24–26). After serving about 28 years in that capacity, Eli would have eventually succeeded his father as the high priest for the remainder of his life. This tenure almost certainly covered his last 40 years (see Eli's life-line display, Chart 4).

Eli's judgeship of 40 years would then best be understood as that of his role as high priest. To serve as a judge was included in the duties of the high priest (Num. 5:11–31; Deut. 17:9; 19:17–19; and 2 Chron. 19:5). As high priest, Eli would assist the judges in accord with their duties described at the beginning of this chapter much as Eleazar assisted Joshua (Num. 27:18–23) and Jeshua assisted Zerubbabel (Hag. 1:1; Zech. 3:1–5; Ezra 3:2; and Neh. 12:1).

So Eli, as an associate, would assist the various judges in accordance with their duties, helping them bring the people to repentance, etc., thereby functioning as a savior and deliverer. This is the correct biblical understanding, and actual meaning of his judgeship (cp. 1 Sam. 14:3 where Eli is called "the Lord's priest," not His "judge").

Hence, his 40-year judgeship is not to be added consecutively to the spans of the judges. He was a high priest whose job description caused him to function with and as a judge. Consequently, his judgeship is to be understood as overlapping and be included within the time frames of several judges whose official terms of service he outlived. Note that there is not one instance in which Eli functioned in the sense of a judge as outlined in the biblical definition as formerly set forth on page 71.

d. Contrasting Samson and Samuel

Thus the lives of Samson, Samuel and Eli overlapped one another in part. The 40-year Philistine dominion of which the Scripture speaks covers the 20 years of Samson's judgeship, a large portion of the story of Eli and his "judgeship," and part of the story of Samuel.

Although the lives of Samson and Samuel were in tremendous contrast, they had several notable particulars in common. Both were supernaturally conceived, selected before birth as God's deliverers over the Philistines, and were types of Christ. For example, as the Lord Jesus, Samson did all of his great feats apart from any outside human assistance. Of course, the reason was different. Samson did not attract followers because he was a hypocrite; his life and morals did not equal his message.

Although God raised up Samson as a deliverer of Israel, He foreknew the people would not follow him, thus Samuel was already there as an established prophet waiting in the wings to succeed him. The people did follow Samuel because of the faithfulness and sincerity of his commitment to the Lord and because of his shepherd's heart toward them. Even though the two were probably born about the same time, the Lord granted Samuel to live almost twice as long as Samson.

Samuel did not receive the gift of great physical strength which God imparted to Samson when the Holy Spirit came upon him. Nevertheless, God's power was mightily evidenced in Samuel's life through answers to his prayers.

e. Establishing Samson's Judgeship

With this understanding and returning to Jephthah's 1152 BC defeat of the forces of Ammon, his six-year "governing" filled in the gap toward the 1095 BC commencement of the

reign of Saul unto the year 1146. This left only the 51 years mentioned at the onset of this topic to be filled in order to complete this segment (Diagram 3, page 79 and Chart 4):

$$1146 - 1095 = 51\text{-year gap}$$

Several approaches were examined and considered in working out the last 51 years. From the reading of Judges 12, the simplest most direct method was to begin listing the successive judgeships of Ibzan (7 years), Elon (10 years), and Abdon (8 years). This secured the final year of Abdon at 1121 BC and closed the gap to but 26 years:

$$1146 - 7 - 10 - 8 = 1121 \text{ BC and}$$
$$1121 - 1095 = 26\text{-year gap remaining}$$

Obviously the 40-year Philistine overlordship of Israel could not begin at 1121 BC as the remaining span was 14 years too short ($40 - 26 = 14$). To so do would carry beyond the onset of the reign of Saul, yet Samuel's deliverance had occurred several years prior to that event.

At that point the decision had to be made whether to have Samson follow Abdon or to back up so that his judgeship would begin during the first part of the Philistine domination. At the same time, great care had to be exercised in order not to fall into subjectivity and mere conjecture.

With regard to the latter possibility, logic demanded that Samson could not be said to have begun breaking the dominion if his judgeship began at its onset. This is evident for then his 20 years would end upon his death at the mid-point of the "days of the Philistines" in which case the Philistines would still have had dominion for 20 more years.

In addition, if Samson's judgeship were placed such that his 20 years were at the beginning of the 40-year dominion, this would position his birth before the 18 years of oppression and vexation by the Philistines and Ammonites described in the tenth chapter of Judges. The significance of this can hardly be overstated for unless Israel were already under Philistine bondage when the angel told his parents that Samson would begin to deliver his people, such a promise would have had little meaning for them.

Moreover, if it is supposed that he was at least 30 years of age when he began to judge, which is a biblically reasonable assumption, such would have been precisely the case had Samson immediately succeeded Abdon in 1121 BC and terminated 20 years later at the end of the 40-year dominion as shown on Chart 4.

$$1121 \text{ BC} - 20 = 1101 \text{ BC}$$
(the year Samson died and Samuel succeeded him)

That would result in his conception and birth as having probably occurred near the end of the 18-year Philistine and Ammonite oppression; hence the Angel of the Lord's promise would have been extremely meaningful to Samson's mother and father, Manoah.

As the context of the story so reads and in view of all that has been stated, the given solution must be seen as both reasonable and logically correct (it would be almost as logical for Samson to have been born in 1140, one year after the "40-year dominion" began, and die at 39 in 1101 BC; hence, 1140 is a viable alternative).

Thus by continuing from Jephthah to Ibzan, Elon, Abdon and placing Samson's 20 years immediately following, as the natural flow of Scripture also implies, 1101 BC is established as shown above as the year of Samson's death and Samuel's signal victory over the Philistines (Judg. 12:8–15; 15:20; 16:31). Immediately afterward Samuel succeeded to the judgeship, having served theretofore as prophet (1 Sam. 3:20, cp. 7:2–6).

After breaking the Philistine dominion in the seventh chapter of 1 Samuel, the remaining accounts through the anointing and confirmation of Saul as king in chapters 10 and 11 all take place during the six-year gap from 1101 to 1095. These years to the 1095 BC commencement of the reign of Saul describe the first six years of Samuel's judgeship, closing the "51-year gap." Remember, Samuel was not referred to as anything other than a prophet until the defeat of the Philistines at Mizpeh. Furthermore, he is said to have continued judging Israel all the days of his life, thus most of his time spent so functioning overlapped Saul's kinghip (1 Sam. 7:15).

The current interpretation sets Samuel's age around twelve and Eli's at 80 when the Lord revealed himself to the still-growing "child"

(1 Sam. 3:1, 8, 19; cp. 2:22 where Eli is said to be "very old"). Several such generalized age related statements relevant to Samuel are given and serve as guides to assist in properly delineating this difficult 51-year span (e.g., 1 Sam. 8:1, 5).

f. Establishing Eli's Death Year

Having established 1101 BC as the year in which Samuel completed the breaking of the Philistine hold over Israel, the year of the capture of the ark of the covenant by that arch enemy may now be ascertained. As 98-year-old Eli's death was caused by his learning of the ark's having been taken, the securing of this date enables us to graph his life (1 Sam. 4).

The ark of the Lord remained in the country of the Philistines for seven months (1 Sam. 6:1). However, when the leaders of Philistia saw that the hand of Jehovah was hard upon their god, Dagon, as well as all the inhabitants of each of the cities in which the ark was placed, they became desperate. The plague of "emerods" in the people's private parts led the lords of Philistia to seek the counsel of the priests and diviners for a solution. This resulted in their sending the ark back on a cart drawn by two milk cows whereupon it went first to the Levitical city of Beth-shemesh (1 Sam. 5–6).

Upon learning of its return, the ark became something of a sightseeing attraction, for apparently Israelites from all the neighboring villages and cities gathered unto it. At that time 50,070 men were slain by the Lord for their having looked into the ark. This presumptuous act broke His clear instructions as to the proper handling of that consecrated object, thereby ignoring God's warning that such violation would result in death (1 Sam. 6:19, cp. Num. 4:15–16).

After this, the ark was brought into the house of Abinadab of Kiriath-jearim (1 Sam. 7). There it remained for 20 years until the day Samuel summoned all Israel to Mizpeh where he rendered judgment and, calling upon Jehovah, saved them from the Philistines who were still enraged over Samson's having just pushed down the temple of Dagon. This is the unmistakable context of 1 Sam. 7:2–3.

By calculating back 20 years from this event, the return of the ark can be dated:[1]

1101 + 20 = 1121 BC (year ark returned)

That the Lord withdrew the plague from the Philistines immediately upon the return of the ark is not stated. Regardless, God's hand was still heavy upon them for it was during the same year of this incident that He began to use Samson as His scourge against them "in the camp of Dan between Zorah and Eshtaol" (Judg. 13:25).

As the ark's return occurred at the time of the reaping of the wheat harvest (1 Sam. 6:13), the year of the capture of the ark and the death of Eli may quickly be fixed. In Israel, wheat harvest takes place during the months of May/June.[2] Since the ark abode in Philistia seven months, the death of Eli upon hearing the dreadful news of its capture, not to mention the slaying of his two wicked sons, must have taken place around November or December of the previous year (1122 BC).

---

[1] Frank R. Klassen, *The Chronology of the Bible*, (Nashville, TN: Regal Pub., 1975), p. 33. At this point, Klassen took the 20-year period of 1 Sam.7:2 out of its immediate context and made it refer to the interval of time from when the ark was sent to the house of Abinadab until David sent for it after becoming king (2 Sam.6; 1 Chron. 13; 15:12–15). However, the reading of the chapter reveals that the context is speaking of the period of time from when the ark went to Abinadab's house until Samuel brought the people to judgment and repentance, delivering them out of the hands of the Philistines at Mizpeh. During that period, Samuel was functioning as a prophet and not as a judge.

This error in judgment significantly flaws his undertaking over this interval. One clear example may be seen on his sketch depicting Samuel's life on page 33. Due to the above mentioned error, Klassen is forced to show him to be approximately 38 years of age (1103 – 1065 BC = 38) around the year that 1 Sam.8:1 describes Samuel as being "old" and having two grown sons who were serving as judges; thus both in all likelihood were at least 30 years old. To describe a man of 38 as "old" is obviously inappropriate, and for such a man to have grown sons of 30 years of age is likewise incongruous as it is most doubtful that the people of Israel would have accepted 20-year-olds as judges. Our study portrays Samuel as being a minimum of nearly 58 (1152 BC – 1095 = 57, or 58 by inclusive numbering), which is much more appropriate and believable. Whatever his age at the time the people demanded a king unto the anointing of Saul, Samuel lived about thirty-five years past that event (1 Sam.25:1, cp. 27:7; continued p. 104).

[2] Walton, *Chronological And Background Charts of The Old Testament, op. cit.*, p. 17.

g. Philistine Dominion Thesis Confirmation

During the above portion of inquiry, the posted dates in the margin of the Authorized Version had not been consulted for a considerable time. Whereas the differences between the two investigations had been reasonably minimal in going from the entry to the time of Ehud's deliverance, its dates suddenly markedly diverged from those of the present study. After completing the 51-year gap portion as described, these dates were again examined. Surprisingly, although the results differed as to the death of Samson and Samuel's ensuing breaking of the Philistine dominion by 19 years, Bishop Lloyd (KJB margin) also had dated the two events as having occurred in the selfsame year.

Faulstich concurs; thus other notable workers have also concluded that Samuel's judgeship immediately followed that of Samson.[1] This strongly infers that they drew the same conclusion from the data as did the current author with regard to the aforementioned "dominion" thesis, yet to our knowledge this concept has not been verbalized heretofore in writing. This "happening" is considered as most significant with regard to the validity of the dominion deduction as set forth in this discourse.

B. JEPHTHAH'S 300-YEAR DECLARATION

Amplification of the 300-year span associated with Jephthah is deemed necessary as it has been the object of considerable skepticism over the years. Over and over, critics complain that the number cannot be taken literally as no commander in the heat of the eve of battle would possibly be able to recall so precise a fact. However, such is not at all the case.

Indeed, the Scriptures are very meticulous concerning such matters. When a number is approximate, the Word of God so records by using the word "about" to delineate that fact.

One example is found in Acts 19:7 where we learn that the number of disciples to whom Paul ministered at Ephesus included "about" 12 men.

Other examples are that there were "about" 3,000 souls saved shortly after the resurrection of the Lord Jesus on the day of Pentecost, and that "about" 5,000 more believed the gospel as a result of the healing of the lame man at the gate of the Temple called "Beautiful" and Peter's declaration concerning Christ Jesus which followed (Acts 2:41 and 4:4 respectively). Clearly "about" is a word with which God is more than familiar, and He uses it when apropos.

The Ammonites had oppressed and vexed Israel for 18 years (Judg. 10:6–9). As the land of Ammon juxtaposed Gilead, the Hebrews in that region had especially suffered at the hands of their oppressors. This duress brought the children of Israel to call again upon the Lord to deliver them. After their turning from following Baal and other heathen gods in true contrition, the Lord raised up Jephthah as their champion.

The Ammonites were poised to launch another attack against Gilead prompting the elders to send for Jephthah in the land of Tob where a band of malcontents had gathered themselves under his leadership (Judg. 11). Accepting the elders' offer as commander-in-chief of the army, Jephthah dispatched messengers to the Ammonite king inquiring as to why he had come to invade Israel. The Ammonite king responded that it was because Israel had taken his land between the Arnon and Jabbok Rivers and unto the Jordan when they came up out of Egypt.

To this charge Jephthah replied that Israel, under Joshua's command, had taken the land in dispute from Sihon, king of Heshbon, who was an Amorite, not an Ammonite, and that Sihon previously had conquered the land from the Moabites, not the Ammonites.[2] Thus Jephthah contended that the king of Ammon had no claim or quarrel with Israel as she had not wronged

---

[1] See back left side of Faulstich's Chart X, 1237–927 BC. Keil and Delitzsch also came to this determination (at least for all practical purposes) as they show a slight two-year overlapping of their judgeships in their *Commentary on the Old Testament in Ten Volumes*, reprint, (Grand Rapids, MI: Eerdmans Pub. Co., 1986), vol. II, p. 289.

[2] As shown on the chart under the "Chronology for the Conquering of Heshbon," Heshbon was conquered between the sixth and eleventh month of the Jewish year previous to the crossing.

Ammon. Moreover, if a legitimate complaint between the two nations existed, why had not Ammon pressed the matter long before as 300 years had passed since the conquest of Sihon and his kingdom (Judg. 11:26)?

Thus, a reading of the account reveals that Jephthah, in the safety of his homeland and camp, calmly dictated the bygone facts relevant to the inception of the current dispute between Ammon and Israel. Moreover, he gives a precise, abbreviated yet detailed historical account relating to the facts involving the final months of the 40-year wilderness wanderings just prior to the crossing of the Jordan. This demonstrates beyond question that his knowledge concerning the history of his roots was both well known by him and at his fingertips (Judg. 11:15–26).

Indeed, he was surrounded by many officers and elders, one of whom would surely have known the correct span. Jephthah had ample time and opportunity to recall or otherwise obtain the exact number of years that had transpired with respect to the disputed land over which the king of Ammon contended.

Furthermore, other Scripture demonstrates that the Jews in general well knew their own history (as do many even today). For instance, Joab lucidly recounted an event to David that had taken place about 160 years earlier while he was engaged in besieging the city of Rabbath-Ammon (2 Sam. 11:21).

The account recorded in Judges 11 recounts that as a Jew, Jephthah knew the history of his nation which, at that time, was extremely young. As Jephthah was growing up, he would have known exactly the number of years involved. Doubtless, the older men and women kept up with the history of their deliverance and often rehearsed it to the children as God had often commanded them to so do – much as we study American history today.

More to the point, it was not merely up to Jephthah's intellect or ability to remember these details that are involved in this matter. The substantial amount of biblical data of a precise chronological nature bears indisputable testimony that the Holy Spirit guided the writing of the Scripture with the intent that the chronology could be known. Seeing this truth

logically leads one to understand that the same Spirit oversaw the statement as to the number of years involved, its faithful recording into Scripture,[1] and its preservation down to the present so that the chronology of the Book of Judges could be ascertained.

Remember, Heshbon had been conquered merely months before Israel crossed the Jordan at flood stage, the waters miraculously parting as the feet of the ark-bearing priests entered the water (Josh. 3:13). This supernatural event occurred on the tenth day of Nisan (Abib, Josh. 4:19) only four days before Passover (Josh. 4:10). Besides, it was only seven days from the 40th-year anniversary after the miraculous parting of the Red Sea; all the Jews would have kept up with that momentous event. Consequently, the individual Hebrew would know and venerate that date much more readily than Americans would 1492, July 4, 1776, or the 7th of December, 1941 – yet nearly all U.S. citizens are aware of the significance of those dates.

We therefore aver and asseverate that Jephthah knew the exact span and further declare that the 300 is a decisive component which has largely been dismissed by most chronologists, thereby compromising (to a great extent) the accuracy of their endeavors. By their rejection of Jephthah's statement as anything other than a general approximation, they fail to see that the time periods in the Book of Judges can no longer be accurately calculated. Not only this, but in so failing to fix a firm date within the large time segment under investigation, they also lose the ability to greatly limit the size of any error that they may interject.

Remember, the main reason this number has not been accepted is because if the chronological calculations are based on the 300 years of Judges 11:26, it will absolutely militate against the summation technique which is invariably applied when Acts 13:20 is taken as meaning the span from Cushan to Saul's enthronement. However, as previously stated, rather than summing the numbers associated with Acts

---

[1] The Book of Judges was probably written, as Jewish tradition relates, by Samuel. It was definitely written before David's conquest of Jerusalem (Judg.1:21), apparently during Saul's reign.

13:20, some must be subtracted because they overlap, as a reading of the narratives denotes; hence, Jephthah's 300 confirms the subtracting technique. It also confirms absolutely 1 Kings 6:1 which unmistakably states it was 480 years from Solomon's fourth year when he began to build the Temple back to the Exodus.

In other words, this 480-year Scripture confirms that the 300 years verse is authentic as well as precise, and vice versa. The 300 and 480 also militate against summing the years of oppression with the time given during which the land is said to be at rest in the Book of Judges (such as Othniel's 8 and 40 or Ehud's 18 and 80 in Judges 3). To insist, as do most scholars, that Jephthah neither did nor could have known the explicit time span from his own day to the conquest of Heshbon is clearly not tenable with regard to the facts of Scripture; it is a poor subjective surmising, nothing more.

C. THE JOSHUA-JUDGES CHASM

Having solved, at least for the most part, the chronology from the time of Jephthah (1152–1146 BC) unto the 975 BC death of Solomon, attention must now turn toward an enlargement upon the filling in of the gap back to Joshua as promised. Beginning at the 1491 BC Exodus, the 40 years during which Moses functioned as a judge must be subtracted bringing us to 1451, the year that Joshua entered the land. Again, Heshbon was conquered only a few months earlier, but during the previous year of 1452:

$$1491 - 40 = 1451 \text{ BC} + 1 = 1452 \text{ BC}$$
(Heshbon conquered)

Again, if one attempts to continue from 1451, the year Moses died and Joshua brought the children of Israel across the Jordan during the spring floods on the tenth day of the month Abib (Josh. 4:19), an impenetrable wall is soon met.

Beginning at 1451, the duration of the wars with the Canaanite kings from this entry to the division of the land among the Twelve Tribes of Israel may be readily obtained (Chart 4, upper middle). At the occasion wherewith Joshua gathered all the tribes to Shiloh for the distributing of the land, Caleb relates that he was 40 years old when Moses sent him and the

other 11 from Kadesh-barnea to spy out the land of Canaan (Josh. 14:7). The time of wandering from leaving Kadesh-barnea unto the crossing of Brook Zered (southern boundary of Moab) just prior to their conquest of Sihon, king of Heshbon, and Og, king of Bashan was 38 years (Deut. 2:14).

The overthrow of these two Amorite kingdoms (Deut. 3:8) occurred only a few months before Israel crossed the Jordan (see "Chronology for the Conquering of Heshbon," Chart 4, lower right). Thus the spies were sent from Kadesh in the second year after the Exodus, Caleb's being 38 (40 – 2 = 38) at the 1491 BC (2513 AM) departure from Egypt.

Caleb continues, declaring that he was 85 years old at the time the division of the land of Canaan began west of the Jordan among the tribes of Judah and Joseph (Josh. 14:10), hence he was:

40   at Kadesh, in second year after the Exodus.
+38   years of wandering left before crossing Zered.
78   Caleb's age at the crossing of Brook Zered.

As Caleb was 85 when the land had rest from the wars for its dividing (Josh. 11:23; 14:10) and was about 78 when Israel crossed the Jordan, the wars with the various Canaanite nations must have lasted seven years (85 – 78 = 7, cp. Josh. 11:18). Since the crossing of Jordan took place in 1451 BC (AM 2553), the land was therefore divided among the last seven tribes in 1444 BC (1451 – 7 = 1444).

Although this closes the gulf somewhat, it is not of sufficient extent to bring the chronology forward to Cushan. As previously stated, the problem is that Judges 2:8 records that Joshua died at age 110 but Scripture gives neither the year of his birth, his age at the Exodus, nor his age at the time of any of the other events during his life. Thus the Scriptures do not allow one to directly mathematically connect Joshua's life to Israel's oppression under Cushan-rishathaim and her deliverance by Othniel (Judg. 3:8–11) so that the chronology may be continued.

The 300-year bridge from the 1452 conquering of Heshbon to the 1152 deliverance over Ammon by Jephthah has already been authenticated and upheld.

$$1452 - 300 = 1152 \text{ BC}$$

As stated earlier, closing the void back toward the time of Joshua from this date is accomplished by beginning at the tenth chapter of Judges and incorporating the historical information from Jair to Tola, Abimelech, Gideon, Deborah, Barak, and Ehud unto the third chapter where the story of Cushan and Othniel is recorded. This will "fix" the date of Cushan's dominion over Israel at 1400 BC (Chart 4). Since the whole is equal to the sum of its parts, subtracting the 1400 from 1444, the year of the division of the land among the last seven tribes, resolves the Joshua-Judges chasm as being a span of 44 years.

1444 – 1400 = 44 (the Joshua-Judges chasm)

This remaining 44-year gap must then be the time allotted for the remainder of Joshua's life after the division of the land in 1444 BC unto his death at age 110, the rule of the elders that outlived him, and the subsequent forsaking of the Lord by the generation that followed them.

As noted earlier, adding the years of servitude is not workable as from Cushan-rishathaim to Jephthah yields 319 years, yet there remains seven years of war, the remainder of Joshua's life, the rule of the elders, etc. Plainly this would more than close up the Joshua-Judges chasm and extend back into the period of the wilderness journey. Thus the 300 years is proven to be the critical factor in solving the Joshua-Judges gap as its application reveals the fact that the periods of servitude must not be added to the time in which the land is said to enjoy rest. Rather, they must be subtracted from it.

At this point another great weakness in using the 450 years of Acts 13:20 as the standard is accentuated and underlined. As with this author, its proponents cannot hurdle the void from Moses' death and the entry under Joshua unto Cushan (moving from left to right on the chart) so they also have to begin with the division of the kingdom and work back from the right side. Eventually they still end up with a time gap and no mathematical or chronological data with which to appeal and are forced into speculation and conjecture.

An example would be from the time Saul was anointed king back to when Samuel delivered the people at Mizpeh. Having ignored the 300-year declaration of Judges 11:26 which is the

chronological key to that entire book, they have no anchor point of reference and must now resort to guess work producing as many different solutions as the number of researchers looking into the matter. They are equally at a loss to solve the Joshua-Judges chasm.

This, in addition to the general failure among those who (like the present author) have used the 480 and 300-year Scriptures in their chronologies but failed to recognize the significance of the Samson-Samuel "deliverance" from the Philistine connection, has resulted in a total lack of consensus with regard to the length of the gap. This along with the fact that such failure leaves the solution open to subjective hypothesis and speculation may be readily noted in the wide range of variation seen by sampling the chronologers, ancient and modern, as the following list discloses:

The Joshua-Judges Chasm
From the Division of the Land to the Oppression by Cushan

Keil-Delitzsch	10 years
Beecher, Willis J.	11 years
Anstey, M.	13 years
Petavius, D.	18 years
Clinton, H.	20 years
Clement of Alexandria	20 years
Hales, Dr. W.	29 years
Ussher	32 years
Faulstich, E.	36 years
Strong-McClintock	37 years
Josephus	38 years
AV margin, Bp. Lloyd	42 years
Klassen, F.	43 years
Jones, Dr. F.N.	44 years
Africanus, J.	48 years
Pezron	61 years
Serrarius	71 years

D. JOSHUA'S AGE

Another often overlooked factor necessary for determining and assessing the Joshua-Judges connection has to do with the pertinent facts associated with Joshua's life. When viewed logically and prudently, certain events in the life of Joshua place very restrictive limits on chronological conclusions with respect to this particular time frame and may thus be used not only to guide one's judgment with regard to his own work but also in appraising the validity of the inquiries of others. Yet it is precisely here

that care must also be exercised in discerning between that which is known and that which is surmised, between Scripture and tradition.

Although the Sacred Writ records that Joshua lived 110 years (Josh. 24:29; Judg. 2:8), it does not give any other precise data from which to reckon. Again, neither the year of his birth nor death is absolutely ascertainable nor can any episode in his life be dated with relation to his age. Nevertheless, several particulars are given which bear significantly upon the chronology.

First, we note that very shortly after the 1491 BC Exodus (before the third month third day, Exo. 19:3) the Amalekites attacked the weary stragglers at the rearward of the column of Israel near Rephidim (Exodus 17:8–16; Deut. 25:17–19). Moses installed Joshua as commander of the army, a position which he held at least to the time of the division of the land 47 years later, and sent him against the forces of Amalek. Before that year ended, Scripture calls Joshua a "young man" (Exo. 33:11, cp. 40:17). The question becomes "How young was he?"

As formerly stated, we are not told, however we are certain that he was at least 20 for that was the minimum age given by the Lord for military service (Num. 1:1–3). Further, it may be inferred that he was over 30 at the time. Scripture did not consider a man mature and thereby qualified to function in any capacity as a leader or eligible to fully serve as a priest until he had attained at least the age of 30. Hence, it is very unlikely the army would have followed a man under that age.

From the biblical narrative, Joshua seems generally to be of the same age and generation as Caleb. Again, Caleb was 40 years old when Moses sent him, Joshua and the other ten spies, all "young" rulers from their respective tribes,[1] from Kadesh-barnea to reconnoiter the land of Canaan (Josh. 14:7). As the spies were sent in the second year after the Exodus, Caleb would have been thirty-eight (40 – 2 = 38) at the 1491 BC (2513 AM) departure from Egypt. Thus from these scriptural facts, it would appear that

Joshua was "near" the age of 38 at the time of the battle with the Amalekites.

Secondly, Caleb was 85 years old in 1445 BC at the time Joshua began dividing the land among the Twelve Tribes at the end of the seven-year war with the various Canaanite nations (Josh. 14:10–11, cp. Joshua. 11:18 and 23). Caleb testified that God had maintained his health such that he was as strong a warrior at 85 as he had been at 40, yet at the same time Joshua was said to be "old and stricken in years."

Thus a chronology that solves the Joshua-Judges chasm must take into account both that at the 1491 BC Exodus Joshua is said to be a "young" man whereas at the 1445 BC division of the land to the tribes of Judah and Joseph, an interval of 46 years (1491 – 1445 = 46), he is said to be old and stricken in years. Such is not as simple a matter as one might imagine.

If, for example, Joshua's age is taken as being about that of Caleb's as mentioned above, an explanation must be given for the vast discrepancy between their physical condition at the time of the division of the land. Of course, this can be explained in that there is clear indication from Scripture that Caleb's vigor was abnormal, a special blessing from the Lord much as had been done for Moses before him (Deut. 34:7). Indeed, the tenth verse of the 90th Psalm, penned by the hand of Moses himself, validates beyond question this very point:

> The days of our years are threescore years and ten; and if by reason of strength they be fourscore years, yet is their strength labour and sorrow; for it is soon cut off, and we fly away (Psa. 90:10).

Such a scenario would maintain that Joshua's condition was the result of a more normal aging process compounded with the added strain and stress of decision making associated with leadership and command over the entire nation, and not merely over that of a single tribe. Of course, he still would not die for quite a few years for he lived 110 years.

On the other hand, if one takes Joshua as being significantly older than Caleb in order to account for the physical disparity at the end of the seven-year war, he causes Joshua to be correspondingly that same number of years

---

[1] Nahshon was the actual leader over the tribe of Judah at the time Caleb was selected and said to be a "ruler" of Judah whereas Elishama was the head of the tribe of Ephraim when Joshua was selected and said to be a "ruler" of that tribe, Num. 1:4–7, 10, 16; cp. 13:1–8, 16.

older than Caleb at the Exodus when Caleb is 38. Taking Joshua's age as 15 years above Caleb's will illustrate the dilemma. He would thus be 100 when he was said to be stricken with age and live only 10 more years — so far so good — but wait. That would place his age at 53 when he is said to be "young."

Now the oldest person referred to as "young" in Scripture was Rehoboam when he was 41 (by implicit inference, see 1 Kings 14:21, cp. 12:8). For most, 53 would not so qualify. Yet it could be contended, with some merit, that Moses was eighty during the year of the Exodus at which time Joshua was said to be a young man; hence, perhaps the term "young" is to be understood in a relative sense.

Thus a certain tension is seen to exist relevant to Joshua's age and the Joshua-Judges chasm. The various scholars have approached the matter quite differently. A significant number seem to be completely unaware of the ramifications involved with where they place the death of Joshua. Others undoubtedly feel that one of the two options given above adequately addresses the difficulty. Most turn to Josephus for the solution.[1]

Josephus relates that during the fifth year after the entry, Joshua divided the land among the tribes.[2] He goes on to say that Joshua died 20 years later at the age of 110, having led the people 25 years after the death of Moses.[3]

This brings us to a major point of clarification. The author has no objection in appealing to a secular source, but such is allowable in the mind of a true biblicist as long as (1) by so doing, neither the letter nor the Spirit of Scripture is in any way compromised, and (2) it is understood that the validity and the authority of the incorporated profane data is not equal to that of Scripture. Thus, although it is deemed essentially legitimate and accurate as it does not offend in the first canon, it may still be faulty whether one is able to so demonstrate or not. The prudent researcher

must never allow himself to accept such testimony without being constantly aware of this limitation, hence recognize it as a constant potential source of error in his findings.

Of course, appeal to Josephus has the merit of utilizing the facts, conjectures, and considerations of a somewhat ancient authority. However, it is well known that his work has been edited and revised over the years;[4] consequently "Josephus" often contradicts himself. Whether these are actual errors made by Josephus or merely perceived contradictions and are in fact statements not properly understood, or those caused by a redactor may not always be known.

Therefore proceeding with caution, it is noted that Josephus is wrong as to his statement that Joshua divided the land among the tribes during the fifth year after the entry. It has already been scripturally documented that this occurred after seven years of war, not five. Here he is wrong, yet he is not unreasonably inaccurate.

Moreover, the fact that this assertion has been proven flawed does not preclude the possibility that his second statement is accurate. Accordingly, as there is nothing better apart from a purely subjective estimate, this work accepts his testimony that Joshua died 20 years after the 1444 BC final division of the land at the end of the seven years of war with the Canaanites:

1444 − 20 = c. 1424 BC (year Joshua died)

As Joshua was 110 when he died (Josh. 24:29; Judg. 2:8), his birth year may now be calculated:

1424 + 110 = c. 1534 BC (year Joshua born)

[1] For example, Bishop Lloyd in the margin of the *King James Authorized Version* and Faulstich (see back left side of his Chart IX, 1547–1237 BC).

[2] Josephus, *Antiquities, op. cit.*, V, 1, 19 and 23.

[3] *Ibid.*, V, 1, 28–29.

[4] McClintock and Strong, *Cyclopedia of Biblical Theological and Ecclesiastical Literature, op. cit.*, vol. II, p. 299. That Josephus has been edited and revised by redactors is so widely admitted that the matter is not at all controversial.

Strong and McClintock have summed the situation as well as any: "The text of Josephus is too corrupt in its numbers to be at all relied upon, as may be seen from the slightest comparison of the sums in the title of the chapters with the detailed contents, having doubtless been tampered with by readers who used only the Sept.[uagint] or Vulg.[ate] versions."

The assumption and admission of this declaration relevant to the death of Joshua by Josephus is deemed acceptable only because, as shall be shown, in so doing the sum and substance of Scripture is at all points maintained. That is, there were eight generations in the lineage between Joseph's son Ephraim and Joshua (Num. 13:8, and 16, cp. 1 Chronicles 7:22–27), and Ephraim was born during the seven years of plenty prior to the seven years of famine (Gen. 41:50–53, Chart 3).

Accordingly when Jacob and the rest of the family came down to Egypt after two years of famine, Ephraim would have been about 7 years old (Gen. 45:1–6). As this gives an interval of nearly 180 years from the birth of Ephraim (c. 1713 BC, Chart 3) to the birth of Joshua (c. 1534 BC), his tenth descendant, an average of about 20 years per generation would result, depicting that Joshua would have to have been at least 40 at the Exode.[1]

The reader will observe that the result of this inclusion from Joseph's lineage brings Joshua's age at the Exodus as being 43:

1534 − 1491 = 43 (Joshua's age at Exode)

This places him but 5 years older than Caleb, relatively young yet mature enough to be commander-in-chief of the army at the Exodus and 90 at the time of the final tribal allotments when he is "old and stricken in years."

1534 − 1444 = 90 (Joshua's age at the conclusion of the land apportionments)

This scenario provides a span of 24 years for the godly rule of the elders who outlived Joshua until they and all their generation died out (Josh. 24:31; Judg. 2:7, 10), the story of Micah with his appointed priest (Judg. 17–18), the depraved story of the Levite and his concubine which resulted in the near annihilation of the tribe of Benjamin (Judg. 19–21), and the eventual bondage to Cushan-rishathaim:

1424 − 1400 = 24 (number of years from Joshua's death to Cushan-rishathaim).

Of course, it rightly could be argued that as there is no definitive biblical data other than

his life span from which to reckon, a chronology may be calculated and/or drawn which simply omits dating key events such as the year of Joshua's demise altogether. This is true; however in so doing one is merely ignoring the issue. A time span of sufficient duration must still be allowed for the remainder of Joshua's life after the division of the land unto his death at age 110, the rule of the elders who outlived him, the story of Micah's priest and the tribe of Dan (Jdg. 17–18), the story of the Levite and his doomed concubine (Jdg. 19–21), the subsequent forsaking of the Lord by the generation that followed the elders, and the bondage to Cushan.

The primary point of that which has been said concerning the events relevant to Joshua is that most chronologists do include a death date for Joshua in their works. That date must be seen as the true test of that individual's comprehension and overall grasp of the entire matter concerning the period of the judges; hence it will reflect the general reliability and trustworthiness of his labor over this segment.

Failure to properly perceive and prudently deal with this problem is commonplace. For example, Keil and Delitzsch, whose ten volume commentary on the Old Testament is widely considered a standard and is usually scholarly and generally reliable, places Joshua's death date such that his age would be 61 at the Exodus.[2] Willis J. Beecher falls into the same pit as his dates place Joshua at 62.[3]

---

[1] Clinton, *Fasti Hellenici, op. cit.*, vol. I, p. 294. This was first demonstrated by Henry Fynes Clinton who rightly concluded "Joshua was born at least 40 years before the Exode."

[2] C.F. Keil and F. Delitzsch, *Commentary on the Old Testament in Ten Volumes*, Reprint, (Grand Rapids, MI: Eerdmans Pub. Co., 1986), vol. II, p. 289.

[3] Willis J. Beecher, *The Dated Events of the Old Testament*, (Phil., PA: The Sunday School Times Co., 1907), pp. 32, 75. Dr. Beecher was professor of Hebrew language and literature at Auburn Theological Seminary in Auburn, New York. On the whole, there are but few authorities on biblical chronology that equal or surpass him. His dates differ little from Ussher, usually only between 4 and 11 years.

This author regards Beecher's greatest error on the subject as that of his view relating to the chronology of the pre-Abrahamic patriarchs. He stated "There is no biblical chronology for the times before Abraham. ... The pre-Abrahamic tables of numbers (Gen. 5 and 11:10–25) are ethnical ... and we have no key to the duration of time intended in them." This position has already been logically and mathematically refuted under the Chart 1 discussion in the section dealing with the second Cainan. Professor Beecher tentatively places Joshua's death year as 1450 BC, hence Joshua would, by that scheme, have

Sixty-one or 62 hardly qualifies as being the age of a "young" man nor does that age really fit the general context. Caleb was selected as one of the spies not only because he was one of the princes of the tribe of Judah but, at 38, he was young and strong enough for undertaking the extremely dangerous journey of nearly 600 miles over very rugged terrain in only 40 days (Numbers 13:21–25), and at the same time, supposedly mature enough to accurately interpret that which he saw and encountered.

The same requirements would naturally apply to the other 11 spies as well. Thus, although Keil and Delitzsch do indicate that Joshua's death year is approximate, this strongly argues against the validity of their interpretation of the judges. This period is further weakened by several unwarranted subjective decisions reflected on their tabular presentation (p. 289). Attention is not being called to this defect to unduly criticize; rather this work has been singled out because of its deserved reputation for excellence.

The subtleties and difficulties associated with the period of the judges is greatly underscored and accentuated when men of their metal fall into one of the ever present vortices. The *Companion Bible* would have Joshua "young" at 53[1] whereas Lloyd better places him as 45 at the Exodus.[2] Many others could be cited but, as the point has been made, their addition would be superfluous.

Now, at long last, enough has been placed before the reader so that the real application of the entire matter related to Joshua's age, etc. may be addressed and understood. It has been vigorously emphasized that the entire crux of the chronology of the judges resides in the proper solution of the 480 (1 Kings 6:1) and the 450 (Act.13:20) year conflict. This author has

sharply contended that the selection of the 450 as one's standard for the span from Cushan to Saul's coronation is erroneous and that 1 Kings 6:1 is correct when it states that the interval from the Exodus to the inception of Solomon's fourth year at which time he began the building of the Temple is 480 years (completing it in the year 3,000 after the Creation).

Further, it has been demonstrated that Jephthah's 300 years from the defeat of Sihon at Jahaz unto the year in which he was installed as judge upon his defeat of the Ammonite oppressors (Judg. 11:26) confirmed and substantiated the 480 years of 1 Kings 6:1. Now we shall see that Joshua's age also supports these two Scriptures, but protests against there being 450 years from Cushan's oppression of Israel to Saul. If this be demonstrable, it should add convincing credibility to the interpretation given to Acts 13:20 in this study. Let us therefore put this thesis to the test.

For our test, the 1913 work of Martin Anstey is selected. Anstey's work is singled out for several pertinent reasons. First, he believed the Scriptures, had read a wide range of classic works (ancient and modern), was a careful student producing an excellent and useful treatise, and defended the 450-year position as ably and vigorously as any this writer has encountered.

Unfortunately, his erroneous final conclusion that the Canon of Ptolemy grossly blundered with respect to the duration of the Persian Empire such that the BC dates from there back are wrong by 82 years greatly damaged his reputation and credibility to the extent that his work has largely been ignored. This writer is aware of instances in which his work has been used by others without their having given Anstey proper credit for fear that the reference might in some way be taken to align them with his *outré* deduction. Unlike Jackson,[3] who

---

been born in 1560 BC (1450 + 110 = 1560). As he dates the Exodus as 1498, 1560 – 1498 would give Joshua an age of 62 at that event.

[1] Bullinger, *The Companion Bible, op. cit.*, p. 53. Bullinger does not actually give Joshua's age at the Exodus. It must be calculated from the fact that he gives 1434 BC as the year of Joshua's death at age 110 and 1491 BC as the date of the Exodus.

[2] *The Authorized Version* margin (Lloyd) places the Exodus at 1491 BC and the death of Joshua in the year c. 1426 BC; see Judg.2:8.

[3] John Jackson, *Chronological Antiquities*, (London: 1752), volume I, page 163–164. Jackson was the first English chronologer of the "modern" school to break away from the true foundation of the Hebrew Text, which had been previously adhered to by Scaliger, Petavius, and Ussher. He adopted the longer chronology of the Greek LXX, hence all his brilliance and ingenuity were for naught. His work is rife with unconventional changes, ingenious criticisms, and conjectural emendations of the received systems.

rejects the value as spurious or the LXX which alters it to 440, Anstey does not reject the 480.

Despite the fact that many other distinguished chronologers before his time such as Hales[1] and Clinton[2] also dismissed the 480, Anstey accepted the value but, like many others, he took it to apply only to the years in which Israel enjoyed peace and prosperity while following God under the various judges. It did not include the years of servitude under the several oppressors mentioned in the Book of Judges.

Again, for Anstey and those of this persuasion, the actual number of years from Cushan to Saul is around 594 years (others give varying amounts down to 573).[3] The years of servitude (114 in Anstey's case, which they maintain God didn't count?) are subtracted from the 594 in order to obtain 480 (or thereabout) and thus "defend" the 1 Kings 6:1 passage.

Another major error was his introduction of a span of 130 years for the Second Cainan between Arphaxad and Salah which he based solely upon the LXX at Genesis 11:13. His errors were further compounded by his conclusion that Terah was 70 years old at the birth of Abraham when Ussher had already proven that he was 130. Jackson's best effort is his critical determination of his fundamental date for the destruction of the Temple as being 586 BC.

[1] Dr. William Hales, *A New Analysis of Chronology*, 2nd ed., (London: 1830), vol. I, p. 17; vol. II, p. 87. This technical comprehensive work at once commends Hales' abilities as a thinker, however he followed Jackson by adopting the LXX's longer chronology and lowered the "superstitious veneration of the Hebrew Verity or supposed immaculate purity of the Masoretic editions of the Hebrew Text to the proper level of rational respect." He professed that his chronology was based upon the LXX, rectified by the aid of Josephus. His three-volume 1809–12 first edition was extended to four and largely confirmed many of the conclusions of Jackson. Dr. Hales set the Creation at 5411 BC and concluded that "the period of 480 years is a forgery, foisted into the text."

[2] Clinton, *Fasti Hellenici, op. cit.*, vol. I, p. 313. A most complete and detailed work, replete with references and footnotes. Although he makes many positive statements with regard to the Hebrew Scriptures, he is to be faulted for his assertion that the numbers recorded in the Books of Kings and Chronicles are sometimes "corrupt" and thus to be rejected. Thus he sometimes follows the Hebrew while at others, the Samaritan (p. 289) and corrected Greek copies supported by Josephus. He obtained 4138 BC as the year of the Creation.

[3] Anstey, *The Romance of Bible Chronology, op. cit.*, pp. 157–158.

Although Anstey does not actually give a death year for Joshua, he discusses the problem during his treatment of the Joshua-Judges connection.[4] In the 16th chapter, Anstey determines the Joshua-Judges chasm to be from AM (or AH) 2560 to 2573, a 13-year interval (the correct discovery of this interval he credits to the *Companion Bible*, p. 137, also see pp. 139, 145–149).

However, it is at this very point that the fallacy of the entire 450-based scheme becomes manifest. Indeed, this is Anstey's Achilles' heel for not only must Joshua die within these scant 13 years, time must be allowed for:

(1) the remainder of Joshua's life after the division of the land unto his death;

(2) the rule of the elders who outlived him unto their ends;

(3) the subsequent forsaking of the Lord by the generation that followed the elders; as well as

(4) include time for the story of Micah's priest and his involvement with the tribe of Dan (Judg. 17–18); followed by

(5) the story of the Levite and his concubine which results in the near extinction of the tribe of Benjamin (Judg. 19–21), all before the period ends with Cushan subjugating Israel.

A feasible scenario could take Joshua's demise to come after six of the 13, leaving but seven years for the elders, etc. and bringing the arrangement to:

2560 AM + 6 = 2566 AM (Joshua died)

consequently the year of Joshua's birth would have been:

2566 AM − 110 = 2456 AM (Joshua born)

When this birth year is subtracted from AM 2513, the year of the Exodus, Joshua's age at that historic event is:

2513 AM − 2456 = 57 (age at the Exodus)

Hence in this scenario, Joshua would be 57 at which time he is said to be "young." No

[4] *Ibid.*, pp. 137–149.

adjusting of the parameters with regard to the 13 years, Joshua's death date, and the elders' rule unto Cushan actually does any better. As Joshua's data is altered to make him somewhat younger, the time for the deaths of the elders and the remainder of their generation, etc. must be correspondingly shortened such that a point of no credibility is quickly reached.

Thus, Anstey's solution — indeed his whole premise based upon interpreting the 450 years of Acts 13:20 as being the interval from Cushan-rishathaim to Saul (which admittedly seems a feasible explanation and exegesis until other Scripture is brought to bear on the matter) – is finally fully exposed as insufficient. Further, it must be seen and admitted that the Scriptures incorporating the 480-year and 300-year proclamations not only support and confirm one another, their validity is substantiated to an even greater extent by the biblical data relevant to the life of Joshua; and as Solomon has rightly observed: "a threefold cord is not quickly broken" (Eccles. 4:12).

E. DAVID'S AGE AT HIS SLAYING OF GOLIATH

The establishing of David's age when he slew Goliath, the Philistine giant of Gath, in single combat is an important reference from which the dating of many other biblical events depends. Although the Scriptures do not furnish the data required for an exact derivation of his age at that singular episode, they do provide enough information to enable the chronologer to determine within very narrow limits an accurate approximation.

It is offered that David was about 18 years of age at the time of his conquest of Goliath. The logic behind this determination begins with the genealogy of the eight sons of Jesse, David's father (see visual aid below).

A comparison of the account of David's anointing by Samuel (1 Sam. 16:5–13) with that of the battle scene prior to David's encounter with the giant of Gath reveals that Eliab was the eldest of the eight, followed by Abinadab and Shammah (1 Sam. 17:12–14), David being the youngest. This is confirmed by Jesse's lineage as registered in Chronicles which gives the order shown below with the exception that the Chronicler only lists seven sons (1 Chronicles 2:13–15).

It is widely accepted that such an occurrence is probably the result of one son having died young and leaving no issue. The Book of Chronicles was written around 500 years after that of Samuel; hence such a son would have been of no genealogical importance, especially after so long an interval.

1. DAVID'S MINIMAL AGE

Beginning on the low side of David's possible age at the time of the encounter with the Philistine, David related to Saul that while tending his father's sheep he had, in single combat on separate occasions, slain a lion and a bear that had taken a lamb out of the flock (1 Sam. 17:32–37).

Jesse was a long-time, experienced shepherd who well knew the dangers and the various wild beasts that frequented the hills around Bethlehem. A good father, which the Scripture indicates to be the case concerning Jesse, would never send a small, physically undeveloped boy (say 10–14 years old) to guard livestock all alone under such circumstances.

In the account, David relates "I went out after him," not "we" went, emphasizing that he was unaccompanied at the time.

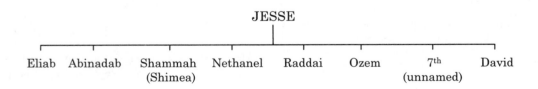

JESSE

| Eliab | Abinadab | Shammah (Shimea) | Nethanel | Raddai | Ozem | 7th (unnamed) | David |

Even if such a glaring mistake in judgment had somehow transpired in the first instance, all precautions would have been taken to insure its not having reoccurred. Rest assured, had Jesse himself been so calloused as to not being more prudent concerning the safety of such a young lad, Mrs. Jesse would have more than attended to the matter. There is a vast difference between the meaning of the word "youth" used to describe David's age at this time as opposed to "boy" which nearly all artists' conceptions of the episode portray him as being.

In fact it was upon his awareness of these incredible deeds that one of Saul's servants recommended David to his king as both an accomplished musician as well as a mighty and valiant man of war (1 Sam. 16:18). Soon after coming to minister before Saul, David became his armor-bearer in training (1 Sam. 16:21). The verse is taken to mean "in training" because as Saul's armor-bearer proper, David's place would have been with him as such in the following chapter when Israel was engaged in confrontation with the Philistines.

This also strongly implies that David was of sufficient age to be of full stature at the time. Yet there is much more evidence to be gleaned from Scripture to substantiate our assertion.

Moreover, David was of sufficient physical size that Saul, who was a whole head taller than any other Israelite at the time of his coronation (1 Sam. 9:2; 10:23), did not consider it incredulous to have David gird himself in the king's armor and helmet in preparation for the combat (1 Sam. 17:38–39). As God's selection as king of His people, Saul was hardly intellectually dull, nor was David.

Indeed, David did not protest that as Saul was so large and he but a small boy, such would be obviously ridiculous; hence there was no need to try on the weaponry. To the contrary, David declined after putting the armor on because he was unaccustomed to wearing such cumbersome gear; he had not proved or tested them to the point that he felt unconstrained and comfortable for combat.

If reservations still persist, it is to be remembered that after he had slain the giant, crown prince Jonathan entered into covenant with the victor, giving David his weaponry, as well as his robe and other garments (1 Sam. 18:3).[1] As shall be demonstrated, Jonathan was not only a grown man at the time (and probably tall via Saul), he was far older than David. Again this shows David to be a youth who had developed to full size.

Lastly, it is to be remembered that the context concerning Saul's offering a daughter in marriage to the man who successfully engaged the giant and the actual time of the wedding were not separated by an interval of significant duration. Therefore David was not a mere boy of 10 to 14 years, but was a fully developed youth. It only remains to ascertain the upward limit of his years.

2. DAVID'S MAXIMUM AGE

Further logic and deductive reasoning based solely upon Scripture will now be brought to bear to demonstrate conclusively that David, though physically mature, could not yet have attained 20 years. Referring back to the illustration depicting Jesse's eight sons in the order of their births, a tension will be seen to exist tempting the chronologer to push David's age younger than has already been validated. Therefore it must first be demonstrated that David is undeniably under 20 years of age.

This may be seen in that the biblical norm called for all males from twenty unto some undisclosed advanced age to serve in the army (Num. 1:3). As the narrative clearly relates that at this time David returned from his duties as musician and armor-bearer in training to tend his father's sheep in Bethlehem rather than accompany the army to the battle, he must be under 20 (1 Sam. 17:14–15). *Vis-à-vis* this understanding, some have supposed that although David was of military age he was on special leave to aid his aging father (17:12).

The obvious flaw in this may be immediately seen in the angry remark of Eliab, Jesse's firstborn, given at the occasion when under Jesse's bidding David visited the battle scene: "Why camest thou down here?" Were David 20 or above, this question would not have been asked; it would have been out of place for his presence would then not have seemed irregular. This clue is greatly accentuated by Eliab's

---

[1] The Hebrew word for covenant is "berith" meaning "to cut," i.e., to cut covenant by the shedding of blood.

further remark: ."... thou art come down that thou mightest see the battle."

Indeed, David has obviously not come with the intent of "rejoining" his fellow soldiers and taking part in the fray. This is evidenced by the fact that he came to the battle scene totally lacking any normal weapons for such a conflict. David had no armor, spear, sword, helmet, etc.; he had only his shepherd's sling, rod and staff ("staves," vs. 43). He was sent by his father merely to bring supplies to his brothers, learn of their welfare and then return with news of them to Jesse (1 Sam. 17:17–18, note 18c "and take their pledge").

Moreover, were he 20 or more he should have been with the army as Jesse had at least three sons, all older than David yet for some reason were not engaged in the battle (as will be enlarged upon), who could have helped the aged patriarch. Had David been 20-plus, he should and would have been with the army.

The problem is that of Jesse's eight sons only Eliab, Abinadab, and Shammah are said to be under Saul's command against the Philistines. As David was the youngest, this could be taken to imply that his four older brothers who were not engaged in the military action with Philistia were less than 20 thus pushing David's age to a minimum of 15 and very likely even lower. How then can this be reconciled with all that Scripture has demanded concerning his minimum age as formerly set forth?

Again, Scripture does not answer this question directly, nonetheless it supplies us with much information that allows the construction of biblically valid explanations and scenarios. Many possible answers could be developed; however the few offered should suffice to demonstrate the principles involved.

For example, as one son had probably died young and without children, Scripture nevertheless demands that he was alive at the anointing of David (1 Samuel 16:10–11; 17:12). Therefore conceivably he died after the anointing, but before David slew Goliath. This likely happenstance would account for one and leave but three other older brothers to consider. As twins had long run in this family (Esau and Jacob, Pharez and Zerah, etc.), perhaps Raddai and Ozem were 19-year-old twins. Nethanel

could have been around 22, but was sick and at home. Possibly the three were triplets, all being 19 or maybe all three were ill (with the sickness that took their unnamed brother?). Perchance one or more had married within the year of the battle, they would have been exempt from military service for the entire year (Deut. 24:5). Moreover, the God-given laws of warfare decreed that if any man had built a new home and not yet dedicated it, planted a new vineyard and not yet eaten of it, become betrothed and not yet taken the girl to wife, or was fearful and fainthearted concerning the impending military action such would be excused from taking part in that war (Deut. 20:1–9).

Obviously many varied combinations of these could be made. Thus it should be most apparent that, as stated earlier, there exists more than enough plausible as well as reasonable biblical solutions to allow for intellectual reconciliation with all that Scripture demands concerning David's minimum age. In summary, at this time David was:

1. said to be "but a youth" (1 Sam. 17:33), yet adult to the point of trying on Saul's armor (17:38) and Jonathan's clothing (18:3);

2. disdained by Goliath who regarded him as "a youth ... of fair countenance" yet he was able to wield that giant's sword (18:51);

3. referred to by Saul as a "youth" and "stripling" yet he was of sufficient age as to be in training as Saul's armor bearer (1 Sam. 16:21; 17:55–56);

4. old enough, prior to 1–3 above where he was described as a "youth," that his father allowed him to tend sheep alone in a region where bears and lions were known to roam;

5. old enough for Saul to address him as "young man (17:58);

6. of ample age, maturity, and wisdom such that shortly after slaying the giant, Saul could set him over many seasoned warriors who accepted and wholeheartedly followed him (1 Sam. 18:5, 13–16);

7. old enough to marry Saul's daughter shortly after slaying Goliath, yet not of sufficient age to go to war (Num. 1:3).

Accordingly, it may be concluded that David's age has been logically and biblically established as being about 18 when he faced Goliath of Gath.

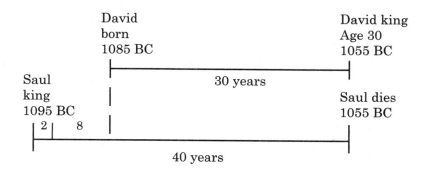

F. JONATHAN'S AND DAVID'S AGE DISPARITY

An interesting and somewhat surprising consequence of this study was to learn of the wide difference between the ages of David and his covenant brother and friend, Jonathan son of Saul. Although the disparity between the two friends' ages has been clearly established long ago by chronologers, their story is almost always taught presenting them as youths of about the same age, being either in their late teens or early 20's.

The simple stick diagram above illustrates that this is far from the actual case and serves to underline and accentuate the importance of and need for the study of Bible chronology (also see Chart 4).

As Saul occupied the throne 40 years (Acts 13:21),[1] it should be readily apparent that the dates assigned to the beginning and termination of his reign will not alter the legitimacy of the following proposition. Jonathan is said to have led a thousand men in an assault against the Philistine garrison at Geba after Saul had reigned two years over Israel (1 Sam. 13:1–3).[2] Thus at that time Jonathan is at least 20 years old (Num. 1:3).

Upon the death of Saul (1 Sam. 31), 30-year-old David became king over Judah and ruled from the capital at Hebron for seven years and six months (2 Sam. 2:1–11; 5:3–5). This allows us to fix the year of David's birth as being ten years into Saul's reign and about eight years after Jonathan's sortie against the Philistines.

Therefore Jonathan's age must exceed that of David's by no less than 28 years.[3] Whereas the scriptural data permits neither a precise calculation of Saul's birth year nor his age, judging from Jonathan's age it may be reckoned that he was approximately 40 years or more older than David.

How different, more beautiful and moving the story becomes in the proper chronological setting. Jonathan, heir to his father's throne

---

[1] The giving of Ish-bosheth's (Esh-baal) age as being 40 (2 Sam. 2:10) when his father died is a major chronological key. Since he is not listed as one of Saul's sons when Saul began to reign (1 Sam.14:49) but is included in the much later written complete listing (1 Chron. 8:33; 9:39), he must be the youngest and been born after Saul became king, thereby indicating at least a 40-year reign for Saul. Thus, Acts 13:21 should be seen as confirmatory (and vice versa! See fn. 1, page xiii).

Again, from this we learn that the Hebrews had access to all the information necessary for them to trace their own history from only the Old Testament, and thus no New Testament information was or is necessary whatsoever to construct the chronology from Creation to the time of Christ. The OT is a complete self-contained revelation in all chronological matters.

Furthermore, this is why the 480 years from the Exodus to the start of the Temple in the fourth year of Solomon's sole reign must be taken as the factual chronological key for that period and the Acts 13:17–22 passage understood and interpreted accordingly – and not the reverse as so

many would have it. We again assert that the 300-year statement of Judges 11:26 absolutely confirms 1 Kings 6:1 and its 480-year declaration.

[2] Saul reigned unchallenged for one year; opposition arose after his second, and he raised an army. This interpretation is attested to by the AD 1560 Geneva Bible.

[3] As David was 30 and Ish-bosheth (Esh-baal) 40 when Saul was slain (2 Sam. 2:10), Ish-bosheth was 10 years older than David. The original heir to Saul's throne (1 Sam.20:30–31), Jonathan was clearly eldest of the four brothers and thus at least 3 years older than Ish-bosheth — thereby proving Jonathan's age to exceed David's by a minimum of 13 years.

(1 Samuel 20:30–31), forsakes the crown submitting himself to the will of God (1 Sam. 23:16–17) and to the much younger David. This man who has long awaited his day to rule gives up a kingdom for the love of a youthful friend and duty to God.

Contrariwise, how much darker Saul's demon oppressed hounding of David must be viewed. As a mere youth, his life was sought by the aging yet most powerful male authority figure on earth – the king.

Having validated logically as well as biblically David's age as being about 18 and Jonathan's as approximately 46 (28 + 18 = 46) at the slaying of Goliath, the following chronology containing most of the major events in David's life is offered. This corrects those dated events in the older editions of the Authorized King James margin, many being Bishop Lloyd's, which were based on David's being about 22 at the time of this conflict.

G. DAVID'S CHRONOLOGY

BC Yr Ussher	BC Yr FNJ	EVENT	{ Jonathan is c. 28 yrs older than { David; Saul is c. 40 to 44 yrs older
1085	1085	**Birth** of David.	
1063	c. 1070	**Anointed by Samuel** to succeed Saul (1 Sam. 16).	
1063*	c. 1067	David plays harp at palace and becomes member of royal court	
1063*	c. 1067	Slays **Goliath**	
1063*	c. 1066	Marries Michal (1 Sam. 18:17–30)	
1062*	c. 1065	**Flees from Saul to Samuel** at Ramah (1 Sam. 19:18)	
1062*	1065	Hides near Gibeah of Saul – Jonathan warns him to flee (1 Sam. 20:1–23)	
1062*	1065	Flees to Nob (1 Sam. 21) – David c. 20 years old	
1062*	1065	Flees to King Achish of Gath (1st time) – feigns madness (1 Sam. 21:10)	
1062*	1065	Cave Adullam – joined by family and **400** men (1 Sam. 22:1)	
1062*	1065	Takes father (Jesse) and mother to Mizpah of Moab and leaves them with the king (1 Sam. 22:3–4)	
1062*	1064	In the stronghold (Masada? – not in Judah, 1 Sam. 22:4–5)	
1062*	1064	God instructs David thru Gad to go to Forest of Hareth (1 Sam. 22:5)	
1062*	1064	Doeg (Edomite) slays Ahimelech, 85 priests, and all alive in Nob – **Abiathar** flees to David (1 Sam. 22:6–23)	
1062*	1064	David delivers Keilah from Philistines (1 Sam. 23:1–13)	
1061*	1064	Abiathar joins David at Keilah (1 Sam. 23:6) and inquires of God via the Ephod. David's warriors now number **600** men	
1061*	1064	Wilderness strongholds of Ziph – **Jonathan** visits David (1 Sam. 23:16)	
1061*	1063	Ziphites betray David (1st time) – Saul pursues David (1 Sam. 23:19–24a)	
1061*	1063	Flees to wilderness of Maon – Saul breaks off manhunt to fight off Philistine invasion (1 Sam. 23:24b–28)	
1061*	1063	Flees to Engedi (1 Sam. 23:29)	
1061*	1062	David cuts off Saul's robe in cave of Engedi – **Saul spared** (1st time) – Saul and 3000 soldiers depart (1 Sam. 24:1–21)	
1061*	1062	Flees back to the stronghold (Masada? — 1 Sam. 24:22)	
1060*	c. 1060	**Samuel dies** (1 Sam. 25:1) – David c. 25 years old	
1060*	1060	Wilderness of Paran – near Maon and Carmel – Nabal and **Abigail** (1 Sam. 25:2)	
1060*	c. 1059	Ziphites again betray David who hides in hill in Hachilah wilderness of Ziph; Saul and 3000; David steals spear and water, Abner blamed; **spares Saul** (2nd time) 26:1–25	
1058*	c. 1058	Flees to Achish of Gath (2nd time)	
1057*	c. 1058	Achish gives David and the **600** Ziklag (1 Sam. 27:1–7) (1 year 4 mos.; cp. <u>29:3</u>)	
1055	1055	Saul and **Witch of Endor** – Saul and Jonathan slain on Mt. Gilboa – David's 600 dismissed by Philistine Lords; Ziklag razed by Amalekites (1 Sam. 28–2 Sam. 1)	
1055	1055	David is anointed **king over Judah** at **Hebron – age 30** – Abner brings 40-year-old Ish-bosheth eastward over the Jordan, establishes Mahanaim as the capital and makes him king over Gilead (2 Sam. 2:1–11). During the next two years, Abner completes the liberation of the western portion of the Northern Kingdom from the Philistines and Ish-bosheth (Esh-baal) is then established as king over "all" Israel (2 Sam. 2:9–10)	

BC Yr Ussher	BC Yr FNJ	EVENT
1053	1053	After 2 years without conflict with David (2 Sam. 2:9–10; cp. 1 Sam. 13:1), Ish-bosheth has been secured as king over "all" Israel. Abner then slays **Asahel** and initiates the "long war" (2 Sam. 3:1, c. 5 ½ years duration) between Israel and Judah (2 Sam. 2:18–32)
1048	1048	David gets wife (Michal) back – Joab murders Abner. Ish-bosheth is assassinated at age 47. David becomes **king over all 12 tribes** – age 37 – (2 Sam. 3–5:5)
1044	1047	David desires to build Temple – Davidic Covenant (2 Sam. 7)
1044–34	1047–40	David defeats his enemies – expands the kingdom (2 Sam. 8)
1040*	c. 1040	Mephibosheth (Jonathan's son) found and raised to the king's table (2 Sam. 9)
1038	1038	Young new king of Ammon humiliates David's Ambassadors – Joab and Abishai defeat Ammon and Syria (2 Sam. 10)
1035	1037	David comits adultery with **Bathsheba** – Uriah slain (April) (2 Sam. 11)
1034	1037	Nathan brings David to repentance (2 Sam. 12) – but his child dies c. December
1034	1036	Solomon born (See 1 Chron. 3:5 – Bathsheba – if Solomon were her 4th born son then this would be 3+ yrs after the child dies) (2 Sam. 12:24)
1033*	1036	Joab and David take Rabbah (Rabbath-ammon) (2 Sam. 12:26–31; 1 Chr.20:1–3)
1032	c. 1035	**Amnon rapes Tamar** (2 Sam. 13:1–22)
1030	1033	Absalom murders Amnon 2 yrs after his raping of Tamar (2 Sam. 13:23–38)
1027	1030	Joab and woman of Tekoa (2 Sam. 14; 13:38), Absalom comes home after 3 yrs
1024	1028	Absalom at the gate 2 yrs after his return (cp. 2 Sam. 14:28; 15:1–6) c. 25 yrs. old
1023	1027	Absalom's revolt – slain – stole men of Israel's hearts from David **40 yrs**. after David had won them by slaying Goliath (2 Sam. 15:7) – David is 58 yrs old (2 Sam. 15–19)
1023	1025	Sheba's revolt suppressed – Joab murders Amasa (2 Sam. 20)
1021	1024	3 year Famine – due to Saul slaying Gibeonites (2 Sam. 21:1)
1018	1022	7 of Saul's sons hung by Gibeonites – Rizpah's 6 month vigil (2 Sam. 21:2–14)
1018	1021	Philistine wars – **Abishai saves David from a Giant** – David told he can no longer go to war – age 64 – (2 Sam. 21:15–22)
1017	1020	Numbered the people – threshing floor of **Ornan** the Jebusite (2 Sam. 24 and 1 Chr.21:1–17) (9 months 20 days; vs.8)
1017	c. 1018	David begins preparation for building **Temple** (1 Chr.22:2–5)
1017	1017	After *abundant* preparation, David charges Solomon and the Princes (1 Chr.22:6–19)
1015	c. 1016	David old and stricken in health – Abishag the Shunammite (1 Kings 1:1–4)
1015	1015	Adonijah, Joab, and Abiathar revolt – Nathan, Bathsheba, Zadok, and Benaiah are loyal and plan to preserve the kingdom for Solomon (1 Kings 1:5–37)
1015	1015	David proclaims Solomon king [**pro-rex**] during the last year of his life (1 Chr.23:1; cp. 1 Chr.26:31; 1 Kings 1:38–53)
1015	1015	David addresses a great convocation, gives Solomon the "**Pattern**" for the **Temple** (1 Chr.28), and exhorts the people to give willingly – joyful worship. Solomon anointed **2nd time** (publicly) as **co-rex** (1 Chr.29:1–25). He became sole rex when David died.
1015	1015	David's last charge to Solomon – in private – walk with God and deal with Joab and Shimei (1 Kings 2:1–9)
1015	1015	David dies–age **70** (2 Sam. 5:4–5; 1 Kings 2:10–11; 1 Chr.29:26–30; cp. 1 Kings 2:12)

*Places where Bishop Lloyd added his own dates or slightly altered Ussher's in the KJB margin.

H. "FORTY YEARS" AFTER WHAT?

Having presented the tabular outline of David's chronology, a persisting problem with regard to his time frame may now be addressed. The anomaly is found in 2 Sam. 15:6–7:

> And on this manner did Absalom to all Israel that came to the king for judgment: so Absalom stole the hearts of the men of Israel (the context). And it came to pass after forty years, that Absalom said unto the king, I pray thee, let me go and pay my vow, which I have vowed unto the LORD, in Hebron.

Many of the modern translations have followed the Syriac version and read "after four days" even though every extant Hebrew manuscript reads "forty." Admittedly, two of the Hebrew manuscripts have the novel, yet obviously erroneous, rendering "forty days" rather than "forty years." However, as it is impossible that Absalom could have won the hearts of all Israel in so short a time, all scholarship has conceded that this is a corrupted reading of the text.

Nearly all commentaries conclude that the "forty" is also corrupt, but they discount that God has promised many times to preserve His Word. Accordingly, we shall exercise faith in those promises and proclaim with absolute calm assurance that "forty" is the correct reading.

Moreover, a so-called "scribal" error is not an acceptable solution as the Hebrew word for "four" (aleph-beth-resh-ain = אברע) is significantly different from the Hebrew "forty" (aleph-resh-beth-ain-jod-mem = ארבעים).

QUESTION: Since 40 is the correct number, to what does it refer?

CONSIDERATIONS:

1. The 40th year of David's reign?
2. Absalom's age?
3. David's age?
4. The years Absalom politicked at the gate?
5. Other?

PERTINENT FACTS:

a. David reigned 40 years (2 Sam. 5:4–5)

b. David began to reign over Judah at age 30 (2 Sam. 5:4)

c. David reigned 40 years, whereupon he died at age 70 (30 + 40; 2 Sam. 5:4)

d. Absalom was the third son born to David at Hebron during the first 7½ years of his rule (2 Sam. 3:3; cp. 1 Chron. 3:1–4; David was about 33 years old at the time)

e. Thus, Absalom's "potential" age at David's death would be 70 – 33 = about 37 years (maximum age would be 70 – 31 = 39 if David's oldest three sons were all born during the first year at Hebron).

POSSIBLE SOLUTIONS:

The 40 years are:

1. Not 40 years into David's reign for this incident did not occur at the end of David's life. 2 Sam. 21:1 makes clear that a minimum of 4 years remained unto David for the famine and the census, not to mention the Temple preparations (cp. vv.9-10 and 24:8).

2. Not Absalom's age. We have already shown that Absalom's "potential" age at David's death would have been 70 – 33 = 37 years old (or 39 max.). As we have also shown that the rebellion and death of Absalom took place at least 4 years prior to David's decease, Absalom's life span cannot exceed 37 – 4 = 33 years (or 39 – 4 = 35).

3. Not David's age. Were David 40, Absalom would be only about 7 years old – hardly the age of a murderer and leader of a rebellion.

4. Not the number of years Absalom was at the gate winning the hearts of Israel for he did not live that long (see #2 above).

SOLUTION: The answer is number five under "Considerations" – other! The explanation is ascertained by deriving the context which is given in the sixth verse: "so Absalom stole the hearts of the men of Israel." Note, the verse does not say Absalom "won" their hearts; it says he "stole" them. Therefore, we must ask the question: from whom did Absalom steal these hearts? Absalom stole the hearts of the men of Israel *from* David and joined them to himself.

When had David won over and bonded unto himself the hearts of the men of Israel? Forty years earlier when he slew the Philistine giant, Goliath, followed quickly by a succession of victories in the months that ensued (1 Sam. 18:5, 16, 30). The 2 Samuel 15:6-7 passage thereby allows us to place David's age as c.58 at the time of Absalom's rebellion (chart p. 102).

101

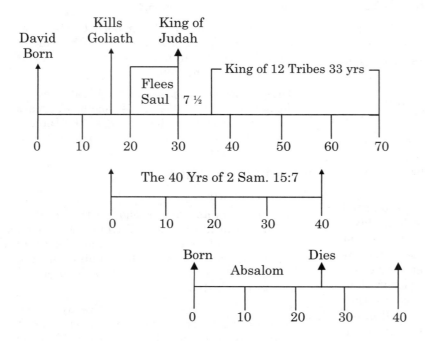

Thus the "forty" years is not an error, it is a major key in the chronology of David's life (tabular display, page 99 ff.). The biblicist must exercise faith rather than doubt when he doesn't understand.

I. FINAL CONSIDERATIONS

Special attention is called to the derivation and scriptural verification of the 40-year wilderness journey at the top of Chart 4 just under the year "1500 BC" as well as the two computations which derive the length of time from the entry under Joshua to the dividing of the land among the Twelve Tribes. They are worthy of perusal and reflection.

Again, Chart 4a and 4b confirm the "short sojourn" contention by applying Scriptures that deal with the lineages of Judah and Moses to the controversy. Here it may once more be seen that the God-breathed but oft ignored genealogies, apparently unused by most investigators, contain significant corroborating information which is capable of keeping the chronologist from going astray.

Despite all that has been presented and laboriously documented, most scholars have considered the era of the judges as being the least precise of the chronological sections into which the Scriptures are usually divided, especially with regard to the explicit detailed dates for the individual events recorded. Doubtless, many will continue to so believe; however it is felt that the foregoing has scripturally met and logically answered the vast majority of the principal points of historical contention and confusion. Yet it is not meant to be inferred that the author is convinced that some refinements will not be forthcoming as study and time continue.

Indeed, after all that has been said and done, this researcher considers the single area of least certainty and potential weakness that of the positioning of the 18-year segment of vexation and oppression of Israel at the hands of the Philistines and the children of Ammon (Judg. 10:7). The reason for this relative ambiguity and hesitancy is largely due to a general lack of definitive scriptural evidence upon which to base a firm decision.

As Anstey pointed out in 1913, Judges 10:8 is a most difficult verse to exegete.[1] Thus, it is at

---

[1] Anstey, *The Romance of Bible Chronology, op. cit.*, pp. 144–145.

this juncture that our undertaking has of necessity departed from the point of maximum certainty and is left teetering between two uncertain alternatives.

The present interpretation has this 18-year period concomitant with the judgeship of Jair. Many past chronologers have reached the same determination. This treatment has in its favor that it is consistent with the known case involving Samson's judgeship with relation to the 40-year Philistine dominion as well as that involving those judges prior to the interval in question.

The only real problem entailed with this resolution is that the natural progression in reading Judges 10 is that the servitude seems to follow the abbreviated story of Jair. Of course, this happens often both in Scripture and in everyday life as one cannot narrate two happenings at the same time. However in this instance Jair is from Gilead (10:3), the very province mentioned as particularly being under Ammonite oppression (10:8, 17-18).

If these 18 years should immediately follow Jair's 22 rather than overlap them so as to be inserted between Jephthah's fixed 1152 BC date and Jair, the net result would be that all the judgeships prior to Jair would slide to the left toward the secured 1444 BC date at which the land was divided among the last seven tribes. That is, each judge would be pushed 18 years farther back in time resulting in Cushan-rishathaim's initial oppression date becoming 1418 BC rather than 1400. Thus the Judges-Joshua chasm would be reduced by that same amount so that instead of its being a 44-year gap as diagrammed, it would become only 26 years:

1444 − 1418 = 26 yrs. (Judges-Joshua chasm)

Insofar as the heretofore discussed problems related to allowing for a time span of sufficient duration for the remainder of Joshua's life after the division of the land unto his death, the rule of the elders who outlived him, the story of Micah's priest and the tribe of Dan (Judges 17-18), the story of the Levite and his concubine (Judg. 19–21), the subsequent forsaking of the Lord by the generation that followed the elders, and the bondage to Cushan – a feasible solution could be managed. For example, if Joshua died around 1430 BC, he would have been 49 at the Exodus (young) and 96 at the division of the land (old and stricken). This would leave at least 12 years for the elders, etc. (1430 − 1418 = 12).

The main objection to this is that selecting 1430 BC is mere conjecture, an accommodation and nothing more. It may be correct, or at least nearly so, but for now it lacks any known method for confirmation.

Moreover, appeal to Josephus is no longer practicable as his 20-year statement from the final division of the land (1444) to Joshua's decease (1444 − 20 = 1424 BC) would leave but 6 years for the elders and all that follows (1424 − 1418 = 6). This stretches credulity beyond that which this author can bear.

Thus, in the final analysis the present interpretation of the 18-year period of oppression as concomitant with the judgeship of Jair has only in its favor that it is consistent with the known situation whereby Samson's 20-year judgeship transpired during the 40-year Philistine dominion as well as the similar overlap condition found existing in those judgeships which occurred prior to Jair and the 20-year statement of Josephus. True, this latter is an ancient historic link but a most tenuous one upon which to cling as resorting to Josephus is hardly "thus saith the Lord."

It has been stated that there is a lack of definitive scriptural evidence upon which to make a firm decision with respect to this matter. It is not intended that this be taken as a final assessment. This author is convinced that there exists such a clue within the bounds of the Holy Writ that will militate against one of these two solutions in favor of the other. He confesses that neither his arduous searching nor the Lord has as yet revealed that fact to him as of this writing; thus the investigation continues.

Finally, it should be noted that the beginning and ending of the period of the judges is marked by the judgeships of the two greatest such men, Moses and Samuel (Jer. 15:1, cp. Psa. 99:6). Nevertheless, this form of government which persisted about 300 years failed to keep the people as a whole in the ways of God. The heart of the majority was not after His paths.

Among the system's main shortcomings was that it lacked the ability to bring about sufficient personal accountability. Among the lessons learned is that, even with such outstanding men of God at the helm, man simply cannot govern man under a form of government where the leader lacks absolute authority. The final result of such an administration will always end in failure for it cannot bring the hearts of the people into submission to either the leader or to the God who appointed him. The inevitable result will always be that every man will do that which seems right in his own eyes (Judg. 17:6; 21:25).

Thus this 300-year trial, like the patriarchal period before it, terminated having demonstrated conclusively the need for more authority to be invested in the uppermost representative's position. Yet even with that, the question still remains – can any form of human government really achieve such lofty goals as bringing mankind to love and obey his human regnant and God – to change his allegiance from self to God?

The period ends with the elders of Israel coming to Samuel and, being dissatisfied with the judgeship structure as a whole, demanding that he appoint a king to rule over them as was the manner of all the other nations about them (1 Sam. 8:4-5,19-20). Until this, God had been their unseen King, but they were breaking His covenant, rejecting His laws and leadership, as well as that of His human representatives. To these sins, they now add the demand of a mere human to replace Him as King. Thus the next grim lesson begins.

Other than that already cited, the major shortcomings are that the work is small, cramped, and cluttered - a great shame for these discourage examination and use. That notwithstanding, besides its many thoughtful insights, its great appeal lies in its simple pictorial presentation making Bible chronology appealing to the man on the street.

Despite its many strong points, it unfortunately contains a fatal flaw with respect to the period of the disruption of the monarchy. This defect which relates to King Hoshea is to be found on the 41st page of his book. The problem is that 2 Kings 17:1 states: "In the twelfth year of Ahaz king of Judah began Hoshea the son of Elah to reign in Samaria over Israel nine years." Unfortunately, Klassen has made it 12 years to the end of Hoshea's reign rather than to the beginning as the Scripture indicates. The result is that he has the reign of Ahaz beginning in 732 BC and Hoshea's commencing in 729, a difference of only three years. This oversight on his part not only mars the biblical relationship of the reign of King Ahaz of Judah to that of Hoshea of Israel, it has led to other problems in this time zone as well.

The only other questionable decision in this period worthy of comment is on page 40. There, without biblical direction, he used the date of Uzziah's birth from which to fix the regnal dates of other sovereigns whereas in all other cases he measured from the beginning of the various kings reigns. However this latter is a judgment problem while the 2 Kings 17:1-4 case is an actual Scripture violation.

The net result of these two instances is that the date for the death of Solomon and the ensuing schism of the kingdom is 29 years too recent as well as all the dates of the events anterior to that happening.

(Klassen continued from footnote 1, page 84)
Nevertheless, that which we have said must not be taken as an undue criticism of either Klassen as a man or his overall effort. Frank Klassen is a dedicated and committed Christian who has produced a fine work. This author has benefited much in his study of it and did, in fact, enlarge and draft the judges and kings of the divided monarchy portions for personal contemplation and reference.

Indeed, the popular *Reese Chronological Bible* (Minn. MN: Bethany Fellowship, Inc., 1980) has admittedly heavily leaned upon Klassen as the major source for its dates (See unnumbered pages at the front under the headings "Some of the Unique Features of This Bible, #5" and "A Final Word About the Dating").

CHART FIVE

A. BRIEF CHART FAMILIARIZATION

At the onset, the reader is reminded that the major part of this dissertation is to be found on the charts themselves. In a very real sense, they are the treatise. Therefore attention is directed to the pertinent information concerning the period of the kings of the divided monarchy (the "disruption" or "schism") found in the guidelines on the left side, in the seven columns at the lower right, including other vital data dispersed randomly throughout the body of the entire chart.

The purpose of this chart's arrangement is so that the user may learn exactly how each decision was made and be able to check the result for himself. The two columns on the left side, elaborated upon in this written discourse, have been condensed and so placed that one may grasp the basic chronological fundamentals and techniques entailed in the construction of such an outline.

Due to its overall size and complexity, a brief survey and review of some of the basic fundamentals is deemed necessary. With reference to the chart, observe that a timeline consisting of BC and AM values is located across the top. As the Creation has been calculated on the first chart as being 4004 BC, any BC number added to its corresponding AM counterpart will always yield the value 4004. For example, on the left end of the chart this topmost line begins with 975 BC and 3029 AM (years from Creation). These sum to 4004. Conversely, if we have either a BC or an AM value, subtracting it from 4004 will always obtain the other. Thus in the example just given, the year 4004 − 975 BC = 3029 AM

On the left side, we also find a long extended rectangle entitled "The Kingdom of Israel". Beneath it is another such rectangle designated "The Kingdom of Judah". Special attention is called to the arrow and text box immediately below the Kingdom of Judah. This alerts the reader that the regnal dates on the chart are *not* portrayed against a January-to-January BC year backdrop as was the case on the copies of this chart made before the year 2003.

The updated work now displays the BC years along the top and bottom hatchered lines, but as the biblical Hebrews were actually using Nisan-to-Nisan years (about 1 April to 1 April), the data concerning the various kings have been shifted to the right three months so as to place their reigns at their true chronological positions (again, see the arrow). To illustrate, Rehoboam's first official year of reign was from Nisan (c.April) 975 BC to Nisan (c.April) 974.

The advantage of reconstructing the chart to a Nisan-to-Nisan year presentation is best appreciated when positioning the death of King Josiah (just before 1 Nisan 609 BC, see Chart 5 and 5c, as well as page 188) and the short three-month and ten-day reign of Jeconiah (also known as Coniah or Jehoiachin), both of Judah. The correct placement of Jeconiah's brief rule is absolutely necessary or else the relationship of his rule to that of Jehoiakim, Zedekiah, and the years 598-597 will be distorted. As Ezekiel received his vision of the Millennial Temple on 10 Nisan (Ezek. 40:1) and since he declared this date was, to the very day, the 25th anniversary of Jeconiah's deportation (referred in Scripture as the "captivity", cp. Ezke. 33:21; 2 Chr. 36:10), Jeconiah's reign is precisely fixed.

As his reign terminated only ten days after the Jewish new years day, the very exact detailed nature of the chronological data concerning Jeconiah allows us to properly display his short rule. As it ended 10 Nisan in 597 (16 April, Gregorian), we merely go back 3 months and 10 days which places the beginning of his reign at 1 Tebeth (11 December) 598 BC. Thus, Chart 5 and 5c now place the reigns of the kings of Israel and Judah at their true positions in time.

A major feature of Chart 5 and 5c is that they depict the "triangulation" technique, discovered and developed as a result of this research, which synchronizes absolutely the data of the Northern to the Southern Kingdom (see page 135 ff.). Chart 5c, a less cluttered version of Chart 5, better displays the Hebrew Nisan-to-Nisan years in their proper BC settings. It was released in 2003 (see back of this book).

About an inch and a half *above* the Kingdom of Israel rectangle and the same distance *below* the rectangle containing the data for the Kingdom of Judah are two lines bearing supplemental support data for the respective

kingdom in its proximity. That is, the upper line supports the Kingdom of Israel and the lower the Kingdom of Judah. This was done to "unclutter" the rectangles. Other elongate rectangles delineate several other kingdoms mentioned in Scripture such as Assyria, Neo-Babylonia, Persia, and Greece that played a significant role in the history from the division of the kingdom to the time of Alexander.

B. THE BIBLICAL-HEBREW YEAR

Several pertinent matters must be addressed before continuing with the discussion of the fifth chart because much has been written in the literature of a contradictory nature which has resulted in general confusion regarding the Hebrew year. The first concerns the method in which the Scriptures portray the reckoning of time by Israel.

The biblical year is the luni-solar year. It is designated "luni-solar" because this calendar uses the lunar (moon) cycles to determine months and solar (sun) cycles to govern the year. This was the method used by most of the ancient world. The solar year averages 365.24219879 days or 365 days, 5 hours, 48 minutes, 45.975 seconds.[1]

The revolution of the moon or the completion of a lunar cycle such as the new or full moon varies slightly in length, but averages 29.530587 days. Thus 12 lunar cycles take only about 354 days (354.367056), approximately 11¼ days less than the length of the solar year. This difference is referred to as the "epact." These facts, of course, are well known and may be checked in any standard reference.

With regard to the biblical Hebrew calendar, Sir Isaac Newton penned:[2]

> All nations, before the just length of the solar year was known, reckoned months by the course of the moon; and years by the returns of winter and summer, spring and autumn: (Gen. 1:14, 8:22; Censorinus c. 19 and 20; Cicero in Verrem. Geminus c. 6.) and in making calendars for their festivals, they

reckoned thirty days to a Lunar month, and twelve Lunar months to a year; taking the nearest round numbers: whence came the division of the ecliptic into 360 degrees. So in the time of Noah's flood, when the Moon could not be seen, Noah reckoned thirty days to a month: but if the Moon appeared a day or two before the end of the month, they began the next month with the first day of her appearing: ...

Newton, the greatest scientist and mathematician the world has yet known, continued:[3]

> That the Israelites used the Luni-solar year is beyond question. Their months began with their new Moons. Their first month was called Abib, from the earing of Corn in that month. Their Passover was kept upon the fourteenth day of the first month, the Moon being then in the full: and if the Corn was not then ripe enough for offering the first Fruits, the Festival was put off, by adding an intercalary month to the end of the year; and the harvest was got in before the Pentecost, and the other Fruits gathered before the Feast of the seventh month.

This venerable chronologer has, for the most part, correctly and concisely stated the case. However, elaboration on several salient points relevant to Newton's observations still require our attention.

God does declare that one of His main intended purposes for the creation of the sun and moon was so that man could use them for the measuring of time. The sun allowed the setting of days and years; the moon was given to set the feasts or festivals and the months began at each new moon (Gen. 1:14-16; Psa. 104:19; etc.). Indeed, the Hebrew word "month" is derived from the word "moon."

Having noted that the lunar year consists of but about 354 days or approximately 11¼ days less than the length of the solar year, the difficulty with merely using a lunar calendar becomes readily apparent. Being shorter than the solar year, the seasons would occur at earlier and earlier dates through the years.

As the Jewish feasts unto the Lord were to be regulated according to the harvest of the various crops (Exo. 34:22, etc.), such a departure from the actual season would be totally

[1] Jack Finegan, *Handbook of Biblical Chronology,* (Princeton, NJ: Princeton University Press, 1964), p. 19. These values may be consulted in any standard Encyclopedia.

[2] Sir Isaac Newton, *The Chronology of Ancient Kingdoms Amended,* (London: 1728), p. 71.

[3] *Ibid.*, p. 77.

impracticable as the feast days would move "backward" each year by nearly 11 days in relation to the solar seasons. If this had been allowed, the commemoration of the Exodus from Egyptian bondage would have "wandered" throughout the four seasons and its agricultural significance would have diminished. However, a specific biblical commandment prevented this:

Thou shalt keep the feast of unleavened bread: (thou shalt eat unleavened bread seven days, as I commanded thee, *in the time appointed of the month Abib*; for in it thou camest out from Egypt (Exo. 23:15, author's italics).

Observe the month of Abib, and keep the passover unto the LORD thy God: for in the month of Abib the LORD thy God brought thee forth out of Egypt by night (Deut. 16:1).

To offset this effect, the lunar calendar is "solarized" among today's Jews by intercalating (inserting or adding) a month. Having been initiated by Hillel II in the fourth century AD, their present day calendar is no longer an *observed* calendar. In order to keep the seasons from drifting from their normal solar positions, an extra month of 29 days (known as either Veadar or Adar II) is added every 3rd, 6th, 8th, 11th, 14th, 17th, and 19th year of a 19-year cycle just before the month of Nisan (Abib).

The modern Hebrew colloquially refers to the 13-month-year as a "pregnant year" and is the Jewish variant of the Gregorian leap year. By the periodic addition of this 13th or leap month 7 times in a 19-year cycle, the correlation of the lunar month with the solar year is assured.

Formerly, a most clever system was adopted. After being exposed to the Babylonians and their astrology and astronomical calculations during the captivity, the following simple expedient whereby an intercalary or 13th month (Veadar) was inserted in the 3rd, 6th, and 8th years of each 8-year cycle in order to keep the seasons from drifting as mentioned above.[1]

After 3 years of drifting by 11¼ days per year, a 30-day-month was inserted bringing the drift back from 33¾ (3 x 11¼ = 33¾) to only 3¾ days (33¾ − 30 = 3¾). To this three and three-quarter-day carryover was added the next cumulative 33¾-day drift over years 4, 5, and 6 so that at the end of year six the calendar had moved against the natural season by 37½ days necessitating a second 30-day intercalation.

This resulted in a 7½-day carryover (37½ − 30 = 7½) to which was added the drift for years seven and eight or 22½ days for a total of precisely 30 days (2 x 11¼ = 22½ + 7½ = 30). Thus after the third intercalation of a 30-day-month, the days of drift were for all practical purposes reduced to zero.

Of course, as noted earlier, the actual lunar-solar discrepancy is not exactly one-fourth day, hence further adjustments would eventually be needed. Still this adroit yet unadorned solution nearly perfectly accommodated the difficulty after every eight-year cycle. As the maximum drift was but 37½ days, the season would not have been unduly affected. Its use seems to have terminated at some unknown date after Julius Africanus (c. AD 200–245) yet prior to Hillel II (c. AD 350).

Year

1	11¼	days drift of lunar year from the solar year
2	11¼	
3	11¼	
	33¾	total days drift after three years
	− 30	insert first leap month (Veadar or Adar II)
	3¾	days of drift remaining
4	11¼	
5	11¼	
6	11¼	
	37½	total days drift after six years
	− 30	insert second leap month (Veadar or Adar II)
	7½	days of drift remaining
7	11¼	
8	11¼	
	30	total days drift after eight years
	− 30	insert third leap month (Veadar or Adar II)
	0	with no drift (epact) remaining.

[1] Anderson, *The Coming Prince, op. cit.,* pp. 103–104. Sir Robert Anderson both quotes and enlarges somewhat on Henry Browne from his *Ordo Saeclorum,* "Chronology of the Holy Scriptures," (London: 1844), p. 473. However the first mention of this approach found by my study was: Julius Africanus, *Anti-Nicene Fathers,* vol. VI, Roberts and Donaldson, eds., (Grand Rapids, MI: Eerdmans, 1885), "Pentabiblos" (Five Books of Chronology) or *Chronographies,* ch. xvi., para. 3, p. 135.

All of this notwithstanding, the luni-solar biblical year in which the feasts and months were regulated by the revolutions of the moon was adjusted to the solar year, not by astronomical or mathematical calculation, but by direct observation of the state of the crops and the physical appearance of the moon. Thus the months, beginning at the new moon, were lunar but the year, which controlled the condition of the crops, was solar. It was this latter feature that kept the calendar from drifting. As we shall see, the resulting system was complete, faultless, and self-adjusting. It required neither periodic correction nor inter-calation.

The Israelites would know when each new moon would appear; for experience would have taught man from the earliest days that it would occur the second or third day after they observed the old or "dark" moon. Biblical proof of this assertion may be seen in that David and Jonathan *knew* that the following day would be a new moon (1 Sam. 20:5,18). Experience would also teach them that the new moon could only be seen at sunset, near the sun as it travels toward the north.[1]

Obviously, weather conditions would be a constant threat to a calendar based upon observation and could complicate its precision. The advantage of using lunar months is that the phases of the moon remain precisely fixed, and the observed calendar is self-correcting. As indicated by the account of the Deluge (Gen. 7:11,24; 8:3-4), some method was available by which Noah could still mark the months. Of course, this recorded data may have been given by revelation to Moses as he wrote of the account over eight centuries after the actual time of the Flood. However, as can be seen in the first quote from Newton (p. 106, and also according to Talmudic tradition) should fog, clouds or a prolonged period of overcast prevent the moon from being seen, the 30th day after the previous new moon was reckoned and the new month began on the morrow.

This may be the case, but such is not certain or necessary. The correction could inherently be made as soon as visibility returned for whether one can actually see the moon on a given day or

night does not alter its precise period of revolution. These revolutions remain constant over time and thus allow a precision that is unattainable in a calendar which is calculation dependent.

As stated heretofore, at the Exodus when God had the Jews change the beginning of their year from Tishri (Autumn, September-October) to Abib (Spring, March-April; Exo. 12:2; 13:4; cp. 9:31 and 23:15) the resulting Hebrew new year began when the crops reached a certain degree of maturity in the spring. Again, their first month was called "Abib" meaning "first ear of ripe grain" or "green ears." Abib was the time marked by the stage of growth of the grain at the beginning of its ripening process after the stalks had hardened.[2] The first new moon after the full ripe ear would begin the next year. Fourteen days later they killed the Passover lamb, and shortly thereafter began the harvest.

A little-known yet equally significant factor assisting the Jews in regulating their calendar was that of the presence of the almond tree which was indigenous to the land of Israel. The Hebrew word for almond is "shaked" (שקד) which means the "watcher," "awakener," "alerter" or "to watch." The tree was so named because it is the first to awaken from the dormant sleep or "death" of winter,[3] putting forth its conspicuous white (or possibly roseate) blossoms in profusion around February.[4]

The appearance of these early bright blooms, viewed in stark contrast to the landscape still shrouded by the drab shadow of winter, was the annual clarion announcing the impending arrival of spring. From their first sighting, the Jews would be alerted to observe closely the status of the "corn" (barley, not Indian corn) in the field with relation to the following new moons. Again, as both these occurrences were dependent upon the sun's light and warmth as related to the tilt of the plane of the ecliptic, the

[1] Faulstich, *History, Harmony, And The Hebrew Kings, op. cit.*, p. 42.

[2] Nogah Hareuveni, *Nature in Our Biblical Heritage,* (Israel:Neot Kedumim Ltd., 1980), p. 49.

[3] Henry S. Gehman, (ed.), *The New Westminster Dictionary of the Bible,* (Phil., PA: The Westminster Press, 1970), page 29.

[4] Walton, *Chronological And Background Charts of The Old Testament, op. cit.*, p. 17.

year could not drift. Since plant growth and development are controlled by the sun, the biblical month "Abib" occurs at the same solar season each year.

Accordingly, it should be seen that all the other months are lunar being determined by the first appearing of the new moon, but Abib is solar as its beginning is first determined and governed by the sun. The continual connection of the historical event of the Exodus with the agrarian month Abib by means of the luni-solar year is the Lord's way of reminding Israel that the success of the crops is dependent on the same God who brought them out of the land of Egypt.

Moreover, although in more recent years the Jews have referred to the intercalary 13th month as Veadar, there is no such designation or even the hint of such a concept in Scripture. It is almost certain that the early Hebrews never employed such a concept in their calendar. For example, David's assignment of the monthly captains "who came in and went out month by month throughout all the months of the year" were but 12 (1 Chron. 27:1-15). This is confirmed by Solomon's 12 monthly officers who looked over the king's food supplies "each man his month in a year" (1 Kings 4:7).

Indeed, such was totally unnecessary under the conditions as described in the preceding. After seeing the almonds blossom and waiting for the first new moon after this event in which the barley was also fully ripened, the new year would begin automatically. If by the middle or end of Adar the barley was not at the "Abib" stage of maturity (and thus ripe enough for offering the firstfruits, second quote, p. 106), the following new moon would not be declared. Thus the 12th month, called Adar (Esther 3:7, 9:1), would simply become an extended long month rather than adding a 13th.

The almond tree brought forth its fruit in late February or early March[1] before the time of the Passover on the 14th of Abib (Nisan) and the Feast of Firstfruits which took place on the following Sunday (the 17th, Lev. 23:9-14, cp. 1 Cor. 15:20,23). Thus, the almond blossoms and fruit became natural representations or symbols of spring's resurrection victory of life over the cold bleak death of winter.

In keeping with this symbolism, God instructed that the almond tree's nut, bud, and flower be placed on the central shaft and six branches of the golden lampstand (menorah, Exo. 25:31-40, 37:17-24) as prophetic tokens of Messiah's resurrection. As in the instance of Aaron's dead staff (or rod) which brought forth buds, blossoms, and yielded almonds, God demonstrated that authority is based on resurrection power and as it was a resurrection which proved that Aaron was the chosen of the Lord even so the Lord Jesus was authenticated as Messiah by the resurrection (Greek = Christ; Num. 17, cp. Rom.1:3-4).

C. THE PROBLEM STATED

The great problem in working out the chronology for the period following Solomon's death (c. 975) whereupon the kingdom divided into the Kingdoms of Israel and Judah until the destruction of the Temple, Jerusalem and the carrying away of Judah to Babylon (c. 586 BC) is well known to all Bible chronologists. It faces each squarely, like an implacable stone wall.

This problem is made readily apparent when we sum the length of the reigns of the kings of Israel beginning at the reign of Jeroboam (the son of Nebat), through its collapse in the ninth year of Hoshea, viz.,

1.	Jeroboam I	22 yrs.
2.	Nadab	2 yrs.
3.	Baasha	24 yrs.
4.	Elah	2 yrs.
5.	Zimri	(7 days only)
6.	Omri	12 yrs.
7.	Ahab	22 yrs.
8.	Ahaziah	2 yrs.
9.	Joram	12 yrs.
10.	Jehu	28 yrs.
11.	Jehoahaz	17 yrs
12.	Jehoash	16 yrs.
13.	Jeroboam II	41 yrs.
14.	Zachariah	6 mos. (or 12 yrs.?)
15.	Shallum	1 mo.
16.	Menahem	10 yrs.
17.	Pekahiah	2 yrs.
18.	Pekah	20 yrs.
19.	Hoshea	9 yrs.

---

[1] McClintock and Strong, *Cyclopedia of Biblical Theological and Ecclesiastical Literature*, *op. cit.*, vol. 1, p. 170.

These reigns total 241 years, 7 months and 7 days.

If we then total the length of the reigns of the kings of Judah for the same period of reign, that is from Solomon's son Rehoboam through the sixth year of Hezekiah (which was the ninth year of Hoshea, 2 Kings 18:10), we obtain 261 years as the length of the span – a difference of nearly 20 years.

1.	Rehoboam	17 yrs.
2.	Abijah	3 yrs.
3.	Asa	41 yrs.
4.	Jehoshaphat	25 yrs.
5.	Jehoram	8 yrs.
6.	Ahaziah	1 yr.
7.	Athaliah	7 yrs.
8.	Joash	40 yrs.
9.	Amaziah	29 yrs.
10.	Uzziah	52 yrs.
11.	Jotham	16 yrs.
12.	Ahaz	16 yrs.
13.	Hezekiah	6 yrs. of his 29 total

Thus, a built-in dilemma confronts the student from the onset.

From the earliest works, there have been offered two, and only two, possible solutions to the paradox. Either:

1. The chronologist accepts Israel's 241-plus years as the correct length of the period and adjusts off the nearly 20 years of Judah by *assuming periods of co-regencies,* whether the Scriptures actually say this to be the case or not. This *effectively subtracts* these 20 years as the lengths of the various kings reigns are made to *overlap* one another rather than to run in a linear, consecutive manner.

However, as shall be seen, the *only scriptural co-regency* is that of Jehoshaphat and his son, Jehoram (2 Kings 8:16).

2. Or the chronologist accepts the 261 years as the length of this span of time by using Judah as the standard. He then "hangs" Israel from this standard, the 241 years being "stretched" by the insertion or addition of a period of years for one or more interregna. An *interregnum* is a period of time in which there is no king occupying the throne. Whereas the concept of a co-regency is familiar to most, the concept of an interregnum is probably a new one to the typical reader although such has occurred fairly often throughout history. Scripturally, an example of having

no reigning king is clearly stated in 1 Kings 22:47 with regard to the Kingdom of Edom.

Babylonian history records an interregnum of two years which has been dated as 703–704 BC by secular historians, and another of eight years duration from 688–681 BC. A more recent and familiar instance is that period in England's past from AD 1653–1658 when Oliver Cromwell governed as "protectorate" bringing the monarchy to a temporary halt. This circumstance was an interregnum.

As is true in the instances concerning the six to eight co-regencies proposed by various proponents who have accepted Israel as the criterion from which to work, no actual mention of the term "interregnum" appears in the Holy Writ.

Thus from the onset, every worker has faced this paradox. The majority have selected Israel's 241-plus span as being the correct length based upon the purely *subjective* reason that the concept of the existence of co-regencies was more palatable to their taste than that of the existence of interregna. Those who selected Judah with its 261-year time span did so for the most part because:

(1) Judah was the more faithful kingdom – Israel having produced 19 kings from 9 different dynasties, all of whom were rebellious against Jehovah – whereas during its existence, Judah's 19 kings, some good and some evil, were all from one dynasty – namely, that of David's. And

(2) Judah was the chosen kingdom "The scepter shall not depart from Judah ... until Shiloh come" (Gen. 49:10), and its kings are the direct lineage to the Messiah – King Jesus.

To the true Bible believer, these last two reasons are compelling; but do they actually lead us to the correct chronological picture? Is there a way to know – to be sure? The result of the latter decision was that as the data was plotted using Judah as the hallmark, one or more interregna had to have occurred in order to honor the Scriptures. If, on the other hand, Israel were selected, co-regencies of various numbers and durations had to be included in order to accommodate the data.

But, which was actually correct? Would the God of Creation, the God of Order actually leave the solution in the form of a *subjective* decision

such that man would be left with the choice as to whether he had a propensity toward co-regencies over interregna or not?

Heretofore, all the workers to our knowledge (with the possible exception of Ussher) tried to solve the problem by *beginning* at the death of Solomon (c. 975 BC) and working from that point in time *toward* the subsequent collapse of the northern Kingdom of Israel via Assyrian capture and dispersion. This approach *always* forced the worker to choose at the onset which kingdom he would select to "hang" the other's data from, and placed him on the horns of uncertainty.

1. THE SOLUTION

The Gordian knot is cut by simply approaching the problem from the *opposite* end. That is, we leap to the data *beginning* at *the fall of the Kingdom of Judah* (c. 586 BC) and *work backward* to the sixth year of Hezekiah (Hoshea's ninth), which is the year of *the fall of the Kingdom of Israel*.[1] Now the problem becomes clear and direct as there is only one kingdom and the data relevant to that kingdom to consider. First, we sum the years of reign of these final kings of the Judaic monarchy.

1.	Zedekiah	11 yrs.
2.	Jehoiachin (Jeconiah)	3 mos. 10 days
3.	Jehoiakim	11 yrs.
4.	Jehoahaz	3 mos.
5.	Josiah	31 yrs.
6.	Amon	2 yrs.
7.	Manasseh	55 yrs.
8.	Hezekiah	24 yrs. (29 – 6 = 24 yrs. *inclusive* of his 6th year)

The total of 134 years, 6 months and 10 days, carries us *into* the 135th year of that time frame.

Thus, all the uncertainty has been reduced to one simple yet vital question. If we mark off

135 squares, one for each of these 135 years, can we take the biblical data as to the length of the reigns of the kings of Judah and exactly fill in and account for the 135 years? The problem should be straightforward as there is no other kingdom's data to consider for this span. If this proves out, then Judah will be seen to furnish its own exact regnal data necessary to enable us to chronologically order its monarchs.

If this is successful, why – when we pick up Israel's data in the sixth year of Hezekiah – would we ever even consider leaving Judah as our foundation? We would have proven that Judah was trustworthy and that the data pertaining to its kings was complete, self-contained and *independent* for solving the remainder of the puzzle.

Conversely, would it be logical or reasonable to then suddenly change our standard by *subjectively* going to Israel as our standard when we would have already established *objective* reasons for remaining with a proven entity – namely, the data concerning the kings and Kingdom of Judah. Would this not clearly establish Judah as the true criterion for the entire period of the divided monarchy?[2] Even a superficial check will prove and document the above thesis.

2. THE ASSYRIAN SNARE

One more grave related problem must be noted before proceeding to test our thesis. The above discussed dilemma has led many to resort to reliance upon the data gleaned from archaeological studies of the nearby nations that came into intercourse with Judah and Israel. This especially is true with regard to the Assyrian Eponym Lists as well as Babylonian and to a lesser measure, Egyptian data.

The Assyrian Eponym List, which will be dealt with in much more detail later in this chapter, is a compilation of kings and important generals, officials and nobles after whom the years were named. Each year was named in honor of one such man, and that man became the designated "eponym."

---

[1] Faulstich, *History, Harmony and the Hebrew Kings, op. cit.*, pp. 43,78. Faulstich affirms that Hebrew chronology is so written from the division of the kingdom to the fall of Jerusalem as to be "ill-suited" to the point of "an impossibility" for one to work backward through it. He declares that one may only work forward. This may well be true if one uses Israel as the standard from which to "hang" Judah's data, but it is certainly not correct if Judah is chosen as the standard.

[2] Again: "The sceptre shall not depart from Judah, nor a lawgiver from between his feet, until Shiloh come; and unto him shall the gathering of the people be" (Genesis 49:10, note: Shiloh is a "him") confirms our selection.

Eleven or so such lists are extant, though only four are usually referred to in the literature. None is complete, each is broken in places, and all but one of the four is very short. From these fragments a composite has been constructed.

During the year when a certain Bur-Sagale was eponym, the record states that "In the month of Simanu an eclipse of the sun took place." Astronomical computations have supposedly "fixed" this date as June 15, 763 (Julian calendar, Gregorian = June 7, 763 BC). Thus, with the epony of Bur-Sagale established, the year of every other name on the list has also presumably been "fixed" as "absolutely reliable" by merely numbering consecutively in both directions from that anchor point. Nearly all scholars consider the matter to be closed and settled beyond doubt or discussion.

This would be true *if* somehow we *knew* that the Assyrian lists were *complete* and *without error*. To the contrary, at least two clear contradictions are known to exist. These are (1) the addition on one of the main four lists (designated as Ca3) of the name "Balatu" at the year 787 BC and (2) another name (Nabu-shar-usur) which is out of sequence when compared to the other three lists. Other eponym difficulties will be disclosed in a subsequent section within this chapter. All these problems are merely ignored or glossed over in almost all of the pertinent literature.

Furthermore, every competent historian, archaeologist, Egyptologist, Assyriologist, etc., knows that inscriptions and other ancient records are not always reliable in all details. The account given in one place may vary considerably from that found in another. An achievement of one king may be claimed by the king who succeeds him. Sometimes both opposing kings claim a victory for the battle. Specific details of a victory may grow in splendor and magnitude in the reports of succeeding years.

In point of fact, it is extremely rare that the loss of a battle or war is admitted by these nations. This stands out in bold contrast to the Hebrew record contained in the Holy Scriptures. Even the names of kings and other important personages who later came into disfavor may be completely obliterated from that nation's historical records, only to show up in the

preserved records of contiguous, contemporary kingdoms. A well-known example of the latter is that of Thutmose III (c. 1504–1450 BC) who had all mention of his aunt's name (Hatshepsut, 1504–1482 BC) obliterated from the Egyptian annals. He had come to the throne as a child. She arrogated a co-regency with him at that time and dominated him for years.

Examples of this in our lifetime are the removal of Joseph Stalin from the annals of Russian history and the name of Mao-Tse-Tung from China's ("the People's Republic of China") records. Both, of course, are preserved in the histories of other nations.

Thus, the strong possibility that such has happened to the Assyrian records exists, though modern scholars are loathe to admit this. This is especially evident where the Assyrian and biblical records of the Hebrew kings are not apparently in harmony (although there are places where clear agreement exists).

The problem is then, that at such places of apparent disagreement the trend in modern scholarship for the past 150 years has been to accept these secular materials, especially the Assyrian Eponym List, as correct. This data is then imposed upon the biblical record and where there are discrepancies, the biblical record is overruled and forced to fit the secular outline by the arbitrary invention of many non-biblical co-regencies. That is, they assign the label of infallibility to the Assyrian, and to a lesser degree the Babylonian and Egyptian historical records (such as they are) where they relate to the biblical time frame while they admit that errors exist elsewhere.

All this is done as though the Hebrew record, which is by far the most complete and uninterrupted, is of no consequence as to its veracity. Even if one were to disregard the supernatural nature of the Scriptures, he would expect these men to accept the Hebrew record as valid an historical witness as the records of any other kingdom. Such treatment is, to say the very least, inconsistent with the usually accepted practice in history and archaeology.

The net result of all this is that some have reduced the actual length of the Kingdom of Judah's existence by 30 years, and as much as 44 (E.R. Thiele) and even as much as 53 years

(William F. Albright). These men, including Christian scholars, feel completely justified in this wicked practice because of the aforementioned eclipse calculation concerning the eponym of Bur-Sagale as being 763 BC. The author is not altogether unfamiliar with such calculations having been formally introduced to the same while engaging in the discipline of astronomy in his university days.

As to eclipse calculations, we mention that though eclipses occur at very precise, predictable intervals – the famous eclipse of Thales recorded by Herodotus has been awarded *five different dates* ranging from 607 to 585 BC by different astronomers. The reader should be thereby warned of the danger and mistake of regarding a single astronomically determined date with the infallibility of a mathematical calculation.

These differences may be due to errors of observation by the historian, calculation error by the astronomer, and errors of identification on the part of the chronologist who may wrongly conclude that the dated eclipse calculated by the astronomer is the same one described by the historian. For example, it could have been cloudy, etc., so that the phenomenon which was calculated to be seen, was not seen.

Such calculations are often given as final authority, but this mistake is basic. It assumes that the strength of a chain is the strongest link rather than its weakest link. In his addressing of this problem, Beecher rightly observed:[1]

> Modern Egyptologists make much of astronomical data. Each advocate of a scheme regards his scheme as having the certainty of a mathematical calculation. But there are many schemes and they disagree by centuries. Each chain has links of the solid steel of astronomical computation, but they are tied together in places with rotten twine of conjecture.

Although most of today's schemes are no longer discrepant by spans as large as centuries, to a disturbingly large extent Beecher's complaint and comment holds as true as when he penned it in 1907, and the overall tenor is true of the

[1] Willis J. Beecher, *The Dated Events of the Old Testament, op. cit.*, p. 19.

chronologies of other ancient nations besides that of Egypt. Of course, such weaknesses as these would not hold true for a group of eclipses that occurred over a relatively short span.

3. THE CORRECT AND ONLY TRUE SOURCE

As stated at the onset, the author is persuaded that the Word of God is *its own commentary* and that it contains within itself all data necessary for its complete chronology. The secular-profane data may be examined along with the Scriptures, but it must not and will not be taken as judge. It is merely a witness. The Holy Scriptures – in context – are the only and final authority on the matter. Thus, where the secular fits, its witness has spoken the truth, where there is disparity – the witness has been misunderstood or has lied.

This is the very opposite mind-set which we see in vogue before us today. Such imprudent men dare to place their intellects above the Word of the Living God and impiously sit in judgment over the biblical account. This mind-set says in effect, "If I cannot understand or ferret out the meaning of this verse or that statement from the Holy Writ, then the Scripture must be wrong." Far better and wiser would such be to humble one's intellect and education before Him "with whom we have to do" and admit to ignorance and the need for revelation from the Spirit of that same LORD. Prudence demands this since it is these very words that will judge the souls and deeds of all when we stand before the Lord Jesus on that day.

Truly, the Hebrew record of the kings of the disruption is a cohesive unified entity. It forms a single orchestrated unit based on an unbroken chain of intertwined events between the kings of Judah and Israel beginning at the accessions of Rehoboam and Jeroboam in 975 BC and extending to 721, the ninth and final year of Hoshea, last monarch of the Northern Kingdom.

To the contrary, all too often the secular material has been found to be a staff of a bruised reed which we have leaned upon. It has broken and pierced us through (2 Kings 18:21; Isa. 36:6).

The serious, prudent student – the true biblicist – must then retrace the steps of the church and find where we ventured off the right path.

After the following explanation which will acquaint the reader with some basic principles of chronology, the above thesis will be proved.

4. EDWIN R. THIELE

It is obligatory at this juncture to discharge an unpleasant duty and address the claims of Edwin R. Thiele (1895–1986). He has professed to have resolved the issues concerning the chronology of the period of the kings of the divided monarchy of the Hebrews. For nearly half a century his dates, and to a far lesser degree those of Professor William F. Albright, have dominated this segment of Bible chronology to the extent that nearly all Bible commentaries, dictionaries, encyclopedias, etc. in the marketplace reflect his views. Thiele's dates are used and sanctioned by nearly every Bible college and seminary, conservative or liberal, on the globe today. As the general views of Thiele and Albright differ little with regard to the unfailing trustworthiness of the Assyrian documents, they obtained somewhat similar results.[1]

It is incontrovertible that with respect to the chronology of the period of the Hebrew kings, Professor Edwin R. Thiele has, by the near unanimous consensus of academia, attained the undisputed first chair; William F. Albright is a far distant second. Thiele's own assessment of his chronology is given in the 1983 revised edition:[2]

> In the pages of this volume are found the links of a chain of chronological evidence ... This chain we believe to be complete, sound, and capable of withstanding any challenge that historical evidence may bring to it.

It may truly be said that his results have completely replaced those of Ussher and Lloyd, long held in veneration by nearly all. Throughout his various works, Dr. Thiele professes to champion the Hebrew Scriptures.[3]

Over and over he claims that his solutions are superior to those of the past as he has not only brought the archaeological findings, especially those of the Assyrian Empire, to bear on the problem involved in Israel's monarchical period but that he has at all points honored the lengths of reign as recorded in the Hebrew Text.

The frustration for this author is that having so said, Thiele did not do that which he stated. He did not honor the Hebrew Scriptures.[4] He did not even come close. Careful study reveals that his faith and loyalty were totally to the Assyrian Eponym List (to be addressed presently). When the Hebrew Text did not directly fit into the Assyrian chronological scheme, it was contorted and disfigured until it apparently conformed. The following reveals his true world view with regard to Scripture:[5]

> The only basis for a sound chronology of the period to be discussed is a completely unbiased use of biblical statements in the light of ... the history and chronology of the ancient Near East. ... If biblical chronology seems to be at variance with Assyrian chronology, it may be because of errors in the Hebrew records, ...

Moreover, Thiele developed a "dual dating" technique which supposedly is responsible for his success in solving the "mysterious numbers" of the Hebrew kings. He maintains that "more than anything else" it is the failure of perceiving this technique heretofore that has been responsible for the "confusion and bewilderment that has arisen concerning the data in kings."[6] Thiele has also stated:[7]

> Whether or not the dates here provided are actually final and absolute will be determined by the test of time ... It is only proper that the dates herein set forth for the kings of Judah and Israel should be subjected to every possible test.

Thus at his bidding we shall in the proceeding pages be constrained to subject Thiele's methods and dates to "every possible test." That Thiele placed the Assyrian data as his

[1] *Oxford Bible Atlas,* H.G. May, ed., (New York: 1970), pp. 16–17. This may be verified by a direct comparison as found in this atlas. Thiele feels that his system has solved and corrected Albright's errors of judgment (E.R. Thiele, *The Mysterious Numbers of the Hebrew Kings, op. cit.,* pp. 84–85, 114).

[2] Thiele, *The Mysterious Numbers of the Hebrew Kings, op. cit.,* p. 211.

[3] *Ibid.,* pp. 208–211. See for an example.

[4] *Ibid.,* p. 199.

[5] *Ibid.,* preface, pp. 16 and 34.

[6] *Ibid.,* p. 55.

[7] Edwin R. Thiele, *A Chronology of the Hebrew Kings,* (Grand Rapids, MI: Zondervan, 1977), pp. 71–72.

infallible guide over the Scriptures is his own choosing and although his right to so do is freely acknowledged, it is a decision for which he and all others who follow his example must give an account, though certainly not to this writer. Although this deed is disturbing, that which most distresses is that nearly all conservative, evangelical scholars and schools alike have endorsed Thiele's dates even though they do constant violence to the written Word of God.

Thus it must be seen that the challenges which follow are never intended to reflect disdain for Professor Thiele as a man or to impugn his monumental efforts, historical research or scholarship. In these he has earned much personal respect; hence any remark, no matter how strongly against his findings it may be, should in no way be interpreted as an *ad hominem* toward Professor Thiele.

The real discomfiture that may be sensed in the remainder of this chapter is toward the many conservatives who did not question Thiele's work but merely accepted his results; or if examined, such men are even more guilty for then they, for their own reasons, did not speak out to protect the flock of God which He purchased with His own blood (Acts 20:28).

Indeed, the present writer has learned much from and is greatly indebted to Dr. Thiele for his extensive toils. This is most especially true of his second chapter in *A Chronology of the Hebrew Kings* in which he explains basic chronological procedures.[1] Although issue will be taken with several of his proposals contained within this pericope, here Thiele exhibits a rare gift for compiling the most pertinent findings over the centuries, adding his own touch while refining and distilling them in the clearest, most concise, and informative manner.

This may be seen in the following section by comparing Beecher's four rules, published in AD 1880, with Thiele's aforementioned second chapter. Much of Beecher's thought is there, but it is better and more simply stated. The present author has attempted to achieve the

same clarity and conciseness for his reader. In so endeavoring, some of the fundamental principles explained in that which ensues is admittedly directly attributed to that which was gleaned from Dr. Thiele's labors. However, due to our different frames of reference, major dissimilarities will be seen in applying them to the Scriptures.

D. BASIC CANONS OF HEBREW CHRONOLOGY

As stated earlier, this segment is considered the great unsolvable Gordian knot of biblical chronology. Over the centuries, rudimentary concepts and principles have been noted, developed and utilized as aids in understanding and unraveling the study of synchronous kingdoms. These principles, when properly understood and applied, unravel seemingly irresolvable difficulties and ambiguities such that even apparent contradictions become intelligible.

Over a century ago, Willis J. Beecher published the following four "rules" as keys to unlock nearly all the principal difficulties encountered in attempting the synchronization of the Kingdoms of Israel and Judah.[2] Beecher wrote:

> In recording dates these narratives follow a simple and consistent system. The following rules are obeyed with entire uniformity in all the dates of the period under consideration:

1. All the years mentioned are current years of a consecutive system. The first year of a king is not a year's time beginning with the month and day of his accession, but a year's time beginning (1) the preceding, or (2) the following New Year's Day – the New Moon before the Passover, Nisan 1st.

2. When a reign closes and another begins during a year, that year is counted to the previous reign (Judaite mode).

3. Regularly in the case of the earlier kings of Israel, and occasionally in other cases, the broken year is counted to the following reign as well as to the previous reign (Israelite mode).

4. When we use the ordinal numbers (1st, 2nd, 3rd, etc.) which date the beginning or the end of a reign to check the cardinal numbers (1, 2, 3,

---

[1] Thiele, *A Chronology of the Hebrew Kings, op. cit.*, pp. 14–22. A more detailed explanation may be found in the second chapter of another of Thiele's Books, *The Mysterious Numbers of the Hebrew Kings, op. cit.*, pages. 43–60.

[2] These four rules were initially published in *American Presbyterian Review*, "The Kings of Israel and Judah," April, 1880.

etc.), which denote its duration, we must count both sets as designating complete calendar years. That is, we must count the date given in the ordinal as being either the opening or the close of the year designated by the ordinal. Otherwise the units represented by the two sets of numbers are of different sorts, and cannot be numerically compared.

At this point, it must be reiterated that the authentic Hebrew Text for this period is continuous, uninterrupted, and self-contained. The Text itself embodies all the data needed to resolve *any* difficulty that may be encountered. There is no need to resort to Josephus, the LXX, or even "emendations," "restorations" or any "corrections" of the Text by modern critics. Even "Sothic Cycles," eclipse calculations or other astronomical techniques and expedients are inadmissible for setting biblical dates if such entails the violation – either by the letter or spirit – of the Sacred Writ.

All of these are open to errors of observation on the part of the original eyewitness and to calculation errors as well as to proper identification of the observed and recorded eclipse with that which has been determined by astronomical computation. If they agree with the fabric of Scripture, the work has been properly done and thus can be used in support but if not, they are ignored. Such may or may not be correct, but either way it must not be taken as a standard to which the data in the Hebrew Text must be forced to conform.

These have become the favorite tools of the modern scholar which he employs to establish dates in support of his presuppositions, assumptions, and conjectures in amending and overturning the testimony of Scripture. Of course, it is the duty of each investigator to make certain that he has understood the Scripture properly before declaring the testimony of these lesser witnesses as invalid.

Unfortunately, all too often well-meaning biblicists have done this very thing. Having missed the import of the Scriptures on a given matter, they then continue to weave a doctrine or chronology around their private interpretations, all the while proclaiming to have defended the integrity of the Sacred Writ. In so doing, they blindly harm the reliability of that which they have set out to establish.

1. THE REGNAL YEAR

The first problem in understanding basic chronology in the Books of Kings and Chronicles is determining from Scripture the month used by a king and/or nation in beginning the regnal year. Most ancient nations used either spring or fall months (i.e., around April first or October first) as beginning the new year.

The majority began their new year at a new moon near the spring or vernal equinox although some adhered to one close to the fall or autumnal equinox.[1] From the diagram on page 117 it can be seen that if king "A" used a fall date for the official beginning of his reign and king "B" used a spring date, apparent contradictions could arise.

For instance, both kings could have ascended to the throne on the same day yet one could reference a certain event as having occurred during the first year of King "A" whereas another could ascribe that same incident as having taken place in the second year of the reign of King "B." Both reports would be historically correct for no discrepancy actually exists. This is due to the fact that these calendar schemes offset one another by six months.

As indicated previously, the beginning of the new year by the various nations may have been determined by astronomical computation, observing the stage of development of the crops, noting the point in time when the days and nights were of equal length, etc. The point is that the new year was regulated by some type of natural phenomena, and not by merely numbering the months and days.

Most are aware that the modern Jews have two calendars, a secular and a sacred (religious) year. The secular year begins in the fall on the first day of the Hebrew month called Tishri whereas the sacred begins six months later in the spring on the first of Abib or Nisan.

---

[1] Still, much variation existed. For example, the ancient Greek new year began at different points in different city states. It began c.July 1 in Athens and Delphi hence some uncertainty is encountered when dating with the Greek Olympiads (Finegan, *Handbook of Biblical Chronology, op. cit.*, pp. 57–59, 108–117).

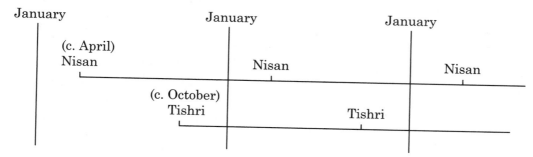

Although this may seem strange at first, other modern nations have similar dual calendars. For example, the United States not only observes its normal new year on the first day of January near the winter solstice, it also recognizes a fiscal year which both ends and the new one begins on July 1. At its end, all books are closed and the financial standing of business and government are determined.

From the days of Josephus, Old Testament chronology has been greatly impeded by a vocal minority who have wrongly assumed that secular events such as the coronations of the kings of either or both the Kingdoms of Judah or Israel were dated from autumnal years much as the above Hebrew custom could lead one to conclude. It is at this point that a collision with Thiele occurs.

Most biblical chronologers such as Sir Isaac Newton,[1] Sir Robert Anderson,[2] Willis Judson Beecher,[3] K.F. Keil,[4] E.W. Faulstich,[5] and the Jewish *Mishna*,[6] etc., have followed a Nisan-to-Nisan year in their dealings with the Hebrew kings. Thiele acknowledged this, but credited the practice as largely being the result of the

tendency of most chronologers to follow the *Mishnah's* testimony.[7]

Thiele correctly concluded that the apparent discrepancies in the synchronisms between the two Hebrew kingdoms could not be reconciled until this issue be determined with certainty. Attempting to resolve the matter, he reasoned that the biblical data concerning the building of the Temple indicated that Solomon had used a Tishri-to-Tishri year:[8]

> Work on the Temple was begun in the second month of the fourth year of Solomon (1 Kings 6:1, 37), and it was completed in the eighth month of Solomon's eleventh year, having been seven years in building (1 Kings 6:38). *In the Hebrew Scriptures the months are numbered from Nisan, regardless of whether the reckoning of the year was from the spring or fall.* And reckoning was according to the *inclusive* system, whereby the first and last units or fractions of units of a group were included as full units in the total of the group.

> If Solomon's regnal year began in Nisan, then according to the above method of counting, the construction of the Temple would have occupied eight years instead of seven [i.e., seven years and six months were required in the building which is "in the 8th year" if one numbers inclusively, F.N.J.] ... the figure of seven years for the building of the Temple can be secured only when regnal years are computed from Tishri-to-Tishri but with a Nisan-to-Nisan year used for the reckoning of ordinary events and the ecclesiastical year (author's italics).

[1] Newton, *The Chronology of Ancient Kingdoms Amended, op. cit.,* p. 296.

[2] Anderson, *The Coming Prince, op. cit.,* pp. 237–240.

[3] Beecher, *The Dated Events of the Old Testament, op. cit.,* pp. 11–14.

[4] Keil and Delitzsch, *Commentary on the Old Testament, op. cit.,* vol. III, p. 187.

[5] Faulstich, *History, Harmony and the Hebrew Kings, op. cit.,* pp. 16–18.

[6] *Babylonian Talmud,* Tract Rosh Hashana ("New Year"), 1.1.

[7] Thiele, *The Mysterious Numbers of the Hebrew Kings, op. cit.,* pp. 51–52.

[8] *Ibid.*

From this reasoning, Dr. Thiele continues and draws the further conclusions:[1]

> If the regnal years of Solomon were figured from Tishri-to-Tishri, this would almost certainly be the method used by the successors of Solomon in the Southern Kingdom. That Judah almost at the close of its history was still counting its regnal years from Tishri-to-Tishri is indicated by 2 Kings 22:3 and 23:23, for it was in the eighteenth year of Josiah that the work of repair was begun on the Temple; and it was still in the same eighteenth year, after 1 Nisan had passed, that the Passover was celebrated on 14 Nisan. The proof turns on the fact that there are too many events to be performed in a short two-week period narrated between 2 Kings 22:3 and 23:23.

Thiele follows this by listing the events recorded in Scripture which he deems to be in excess of that which could reasonably have been accomplished in so short a duration; then he adds the candid admission:[2]

> If all this could have been performed in the short period of two weeks between 1 and 14 Nisan, then there would be no evidence here for beginning the regnal year with 1 Tishri.

The quotes have been extensive in order to fairly place Professor Thiele's position before the reader and to escape the potential criticism that the excerpts had been too brief and the present author had taken them out of context. Now a point by point assessment of Dr. Thiele's statements as compared to Scripture is in order. The significance of that which follows can hardly be overstated; for if he is wrong here as he sets forth his "Fundamental Principles of Hebrew Chronology," that which follows from an erroneous foundation will, as we shall see, surely become even more corrupt.

To begin with, Dr. Thiele is correct in the initial italicized portion in the first citation in stating that the Scriptures number the months from Nisan. Moreover, he gives a footnote at the end of his sentence giving many biblical examples documenting this critical admission.[3]

The testimony from these verses alone should have alerted him to the true situation and that his thesis was tenuous at best. However, he omits several others which unmistakably establish that Judah's kings reckoned their reigns from a Nisan-to-Nisan year.

a. Nisan or Tishri Regnal Years for Judah

Scripture clearly portrays the undeniable fact that the Judaic monarchy used the Nisan-to-Nisan year for dating the reigns of their kings. For example, the Book of Jeremiah records:

> Now the king sat in the winterhouse in the ninth month: and there was a fire on the hearth burning before him (Jer. 36:22).

The king referred to in the citation above is wicked Jehoiakim, son of Josiah — the very Josiah in question (Jer. 36:1, 9). From the verse, the ninth month ("Chisleu," Zech. 7:1) is obviously a winter month and the ninth month of Jehoiakim's fifth year (36:9) can only fall in the winter season if the year begins on 1 Nisan, not 1 Tishri in which case the ninth month would fall around May.

A second example is also found in Jeremiah:

> And in the eleventh year of Zedekiah, in the fourth month, the ninth day of the month, the city was broken up (Jer. 39:2).

A comparison of the data found in chapter 52 dates the 8th through the 14th verses of chapter 39 as having taken place in the 5th month of the 11th year of the reign of Zedekiah, the ruling monarch of the Kingdom of Judah:

> So the city was besieged unto the eleventh year of king Zedekiah. And in the fourth month, in the ninth day of the month, the famine was sore in the city, so that there was no bread for the people of the land. Then the city was broken up, and all the men of war fled, and went forth out of the city by night by the way of the gate between the two walls, which was by the king's garden; (now the Chaldeans were by the city round about:) and they went by the way of the plain (Jer. 52:5-7).

> Now in the fifth month, in the tenth day of the month, which was the nineteenth year of Nebuchadrezzar king of Babylon, came Nebuzaradan, captain of the guard, which served the king of Babylon, into Jerusalem,

[1] Thiele, *The Mysterious Numbers of the Hebrew Kings,* op. cit., pp. 52–53.

[2] *Ibid.*, p. 53.

[3] Beecher, *The Dated Events of the Old Testament,* op. cit., pp. 11–14. A concise yet excellent exposition documenting that Nisan-to-Nisan was the Old Testament year and the method used in counting the regnal years of the kings.

And burned the house of the LORD, and the king's house; and all the houses of Jerusalem, and all the houses of the great men, burned he with fire: And all the army of the Chaldeans, that were with the captain of the guard, brake down all the walls of Jerusalem round about. Then Nebuzaradan the captain of the guard carried away captive certain of the poor of the people, and the residue of the people that remained in the city, and those that fell away, that fell to the king of Babylon, and the rest of the multitude (Jer. 52:12–15, compare 2 Kings 25:8).

The Jeremiah 39:2 narrative continues without a significant time interruption into chapter 40 for when we come to the forty-first chapter it is but the seventh month (Jer. 41:1). Verses 10 and 12 of chapter 40 reveal that it was the time of gathering the wine and summer fruits. This unmistakably fixes the time of year in question for this ingathering occurs during the Hebrew fifth or sixth month[1] (our August or September) and perfectly fits the context, being confirmed by the time of the burning of the Temple and Nebuzaradan's releasing Jeremiah and giving him food and money (40:5c). For the fifth or sixth month of Zedekiah's reign to fall around the vintage and gathering of summer fruits demands that his years of rule be reckoned from 1 Nisan, not 1 Tishri.

A third example is to be found nearly a century earlier at the time of Hezekiah. The first month of the first year of Hezekiah's rule over the Kingdom of Judah was also the Passover month (2 Chron. 29:3,17; 30:1–5,13,15); thus he was using the Nisan method of reckoning, not the Tishri. Indeed, 2 Sam. 11:1–2 demands that the Nisan year was being used in David's day.

The biblical principle that by the mouth of two or more witnesses "shall the matter be established" has been met (Deut. 17:6a; 19:15; Mat. 18:16; John 8:17). The cited scriptural examples are conclusively against Dr. Thiele's assertion. It has been established on the authority of the Holy Scriptures that the Judaic kingdom observed the Nisan-to-Nisan regnal system. Having validated this, Professor Thiele's other major propositions can now be analyzed.

b. The Inclusive Reckoning Question

Dr. Thiele's next mistake is to be found in his reasoning regarding the Temple data. He correctly saw that the Temple was seven years and six months in its building. However he then inflexibly insisted that the Scriptures demand inclusive reckoning, footnoting several proofs from the biblical text, and stated that according to the inclusive method of counting, the construction of the Temple would have occupied eight years instead of seven had the regnal year of Solomon begun in Nisan.

For Thiele, and those who have followed in his footsteps, this conclusively proved "the regnal years of Solomon were figured from Tishri-to-Tishri" and his entire system was based upon this as an established fact. Yet all of this was founded upon a commonly encountered error, the unwarranted assertion that from the internal evidence of Scripture the Hebrews always numbered inclusively. At the onset the reader may be assured that Scripture does often so enumerate and that many more examples than those cited by Dr. Thiele could be given in evidence. The problem is that in his presentation, Dr. Thiele does not inform his reader of the undeniable fact that Scripture does not always number inclusively as the following examples depict.

1. The text of the Bible states that David reigned seven and one half years in Hebron and thirty-three years in Jerusalem, yet it gives the total length as being forty years, not forty-one as would be true if one were numbering inclusively (2 Sam. 5:4–5, cp. 1 Kings 2:10). As shall be explained in that which follows, this actually shows that David was using the accession method of reckoning regnal years. And this is why the kings of the southern monarchy normally followed that system;

2. The drought which produced a great famine in the days of Elijah was said to have lasted three years and six months, but the same period is also referred to as having been three years, not four as would be demanded by inclusive reckoning (1 Kings 17:1; 18:1, cp. Luke 4:25; Jam. 5:17);

3. Jehoiachin (Jeconiah), king of Judah, is declared to have ruled three months and ten days, a period which is also referred to as being that of but three months, not four as required by inclusive enumeration (2 Kings 24:8; 2 Chron. 36:9–10, cp. Ezek. 40:1); and

---

[1] Walton, *Chronological And Background Charts of The Old Testament, op. cit.,* p. 17.

4. Another example is found in the Book of Nehemiah: "Moreover from the time that I was appointed to be their governor in the land of Judah, from the twentieth year even unto the two and thirtieth year of Artaxerxes the king, that is, twelve years, I and my brethren have not eaten the bread of the governor" (Neh. 5:14). The duration of Nehemiah's governorship is said to be 12 years, but from the 20th to the 32nd year of his administration would be 13 if computed inclusively.

More examples could be cited but by now surely the point has clearly been established by the testimony of the above Scriptures that Dr. Thiele has badly overstated his position. Naturally it would be a most convenient and happy circumstance for today's scholar if the Hebrews had always reckoned by the inclusive method but, as has been shown, they did not consistently so do. Yet Thiele has based his entire approach on the supposition that they did and erected his system on that conjecture.

Dr. Thiele has been shown to have failed to establish his point for if it cannot be proven that inclusive numbering must be applied to the Temple construction, there is no irrefutable proof that Solomon used the Tishri procedure. Moreover, the mathematics simply do not demand a Tishri-to-Tishri calendar for the ascendancy of Solomon to the throne.

Surely by now the truth must be evident to all alike, for if the 2nd month of the 4th year of Solomon's reign was "Zif" (called "Iyyar" since the captivity) and the 8th month of his 11th year was "Bul" (called "Marchesvan" since the captivity), the writer of Kings was reckoning from Nisan – not from Tishri (1 Ki. 6:1, 37–38, cp. 2 Chron. 3:1–2) as Thiele has claimed. Thus the internal biblical data has been shown to reveal that the Hebrew kings were using the Nisan-to-Nisan regnal year near the inception of the monarchy (David and Solomon), near the middle of the monarchy (Hezekiah), and very near its termination (Josiah, Jehoiakim and Zedekiah).

Thiele's attempt to circumvent this obvious fact by stating: "In the Hebrew Scriptures the months are numbered from Nisan, regardless of whether the reckoning of the year was from the spring or fall" seems at best a *non sequitur*. Behind this innocuous quote hides volumes of error and ignored scriptural testimony.

Moreover, the 1 Kings 6 example wrongly used by Dr. Thiele in attempting to make his point should be seen for that which it actually is — another example where the Hebrew Text does not always number inclusively. Thiele's Diagram 5 on page 52 and his conclusions taken from it would be correct if, and only if, the Scriptures concerning the Temple in 1 Kings 6 were to be taken inclusively, but this cannot be the case if Solomon were using Nisan years. As it has been shown that Solomon was reckoning by the Nisan method, Diagram 5 is rendered nonfunctional. Thus almost inexplicably Thiele has not arrived at the true state of the matter but at its antithesis on both counts.

c. The Excessive Events of Josiah Question

The reader is enjoined to recall that Thiele's second proffered scriptural proof of his Tishri-to-Tishri thesis for the Judaic kingdom hinged on his conviction that the events recorded in 2 Kings between 22:3 and 23:23 were in excess of that which could reasonably have been accomplished in only 14 days' duration. Over the years, this "intellectual problem" has been addressed by many who, like Thiele, feel that this is a decisive indicator; however the argument is completely without force.

First, it should be remembered that Josiah was king. In point of fact, he was king over a small nation yet, judging by other Scriptures which enumerate the strength of the Judaic military as being several hundred thousand strong, had an army of significant numbers at his beckoning. Indeed, he would have had at least 24,000 soldiers stationed in Jerusalem month by month at his immediate disposal (1 Chron. 27:1–15), not to mention the various courses of Levites which would have included armed temple guards, e.g., "porters" or "keepers of the door" and guardians of the treasury (2 Kings 23:4; 1 Chron. 9:17–27; 26:1–28).

With such resources at his disposal and maximizing his authority as king, Josiah would have readily been able to accomplish the numerous projects listed. Truly, the narrative implies that all the men of the kingdom took at least some part in the proceedings (2 Kings 23:1–3; 2 Chron. 34:29–32).

More to the point, it cannot be overemphasized that a careful reading of the narrative under analysis in either the Books of Kings or

Chronicles does not in any way demand or even suggest that the Temple renovation had to be or had been completed by the time of the Passover on 14 Nisan. The work may have been accomplished by then, but the project merely had to have been initiated in order to satisfy the data in the biblical account.

There is no scriptural reason why it could not have been finished after the Passover and the Feast of Unleavened Bread which would have immediately followed. When this is seen, the major intellectual stumbling block for Dr. Thiele and those who have likewise so viewed the problem simply vanishes for all of the other recorded events could have easily been performed in a two week period. Furthermore, the internal evidence of the Hebrew Text will not permit one to impose a Tishri-to-Tishri system upon the Josiah episode under inquiry.

The undertaking of the repair and renovation on the Temple would, under all normal circumstances, have been a springtime project. Certainly it would not usually have begun during the time of the cool fall rains. Besides, such an undertaking could have run into difficulties which would thus have continued into the cold of winter, the time of the heaviest rainfall in the land of Palestine. A prudent planner would have allowed for such a possibility and scheduled so as to avoid such a possibility. Moreover, in a very real sense, Josiah had gone to war against idolatry and immorality throughout the land, and most students are aware that the time for such actions as found both in the secular history of the neighboring kingdoms as well as the testimony of Scripture is that of springtime (compare 2 Sam. 11:1; 1 Kings 20:21–26).

Thus the Scriptures distinctly imply that Josiah's initiation of the Temple refurbishment in 2 Kings 22:3 transpired in the springtime, around 1 Nisan. Further, its initiation was in the 18th year of Josiah's reign, not the 18th year since his birth (2 Kings 22:3, cp. 2 Chron. 34:8). As the great Passover celebration also took place in the 18th year of the reign of Josiah on the 14th day of Nisan (2 Chron. 35:1, 19), the two events had to have transpired during the same year and not in successive years as Thiele would have it.

Further, it is demanded from the biblical narrative that the cleansing or purifying project in which Josiah ordered the vessels that were made for Baal, etc. to be taken from the Temple and burned had to have begun concomitant with the undertaking of the renovation on the Temple. Josiah certainly would not have repaired the House of God and left those pagan idols and relics within it for a year (or even six months according to anyone's mode of reckoning). This work was said to have been carried out by the priests of the *second order* (2 Kings 23:4).

This is a reference to David's having divided the priests into 24 courses for their carrying out the various duties at the Temple (1 Chron. 24:1–19). Now the Scriptures reveal, and Josephus concurs,[1] that the courses of priests and Levites would rotate throughout the year, each term at the Temple lasting one week from Sabbath to Sabbath (1 Chron. 9:23–25; 2 Chron. 23:4, 8). This scheme would have satisfied the needs and requirements for the sacrificial system, temple upkeep, etc. for 48 of the 52 weeks in the year allowing the priests to spend most of the year at home with their families in one of their 13 appointed cities (Josh. 21:10–19).

The other weeks were those of the three great yearly festivals (Feasts of Unleavened Bread, Pentecost, and Tabernacles) during which all the males of Israel had to come to the Temple (Exo. 23:14–17; 34:22–24; Deut. 16:16–17). Due to the vast number atttending these feasts, all the courses would have to be on duty.

Depending upon whether a Nisan or Tishri year was being implemented, the second course would thus officiate its first term either the second week of Nisan or Tishri. Whichever system was being invoked, the second term would take place nearly six months later in either Tishri or Nisan. However, in the case in question there can be no doubt as to which system was in force, for it is impossible to have begun the project in the spring of the 18th year of Josiah's reign in a Tishri-to-Tishri year and have a second Nisan in which the great Passover was kept also occur in that same 18th year. Besides, it has already been documented beyond any reasonable doubt that the kings of

---

[1] Josephus, *Antiquities, op. cit.*, VII, 14, 7.

Judah made use of the Nisan reckoning for dating the regnal years.

Therefore the sequence of events continued whereby 2 Kings 23:4 was almost certainly the first day of the second week of Nisan, about a week after 2 Kings 22:3, at the time the second course of priests reported for their first ministration of the year. Accordingly, all the recorded acts between 2 Kings 22:4–20 were carried out by various members of the aforementioned enormous manpower pool at Josiah's disposal during the second week of Nisan, yet prior to Passover on the 14th. Indeed, it may fairly be noted that the entire narrative does flow in accordance with the chronological presentation given in the above exegesis.

In view of the foregoing, it should be remembered that Professor Thiele admitted:[1]

> If all this could have been performed in the short period of two weeks between 1 and 14 Nisan, then there would be no evidence here for beginning the regnal year with 1 Tishri.

This author agrees with the doctor, hence there is no evidence in this instance for the Judaic regnal year as beginning 1 Tishri. Having therefore answered Dr. Thiele with the internal evidence as found within the Hebrew Text, his final comment on the matter:[2]

> Perhaps the strongest argument for the use of a Tishri-to-Tishri regnal year in Judah is that this method works, giving us a harmonious pattern of the regnal years and synchronisms, while with a Nisan-to-Nisan regnal year the old discrepancies remain.

must be taken as a gross misstatement and tragically incorrect insofar as the Hebrew Text is concerned.

d. Hebrew Method of Reckoning Foreign Regnal Years as Revealed in Judah's Closing Period

A continuing problem for biblical chronologers lies in the particular that most scholars attribute Nisan-to-Nisan years to the Assyrian, Babylonian, and Persian monarchs. Although it is generally acknowledged that such custom was not always adhered to, most also conclude

that the Assyrians, Babylonians, and Persians usually called the year in which a king first came to the throne his "accession" year rather than his first official year of dominion. They would begin dating events from his own first year on the first day of the first month of the following new year.[3]

When these conclusions are employed in an attempt to synchronize various dated historic events of these kingdoms with the biblical framework, they are sometimes found to mismatch on the order of about six months which usually places these kingdoms' dates in a different year from that of the Hebrew. The normal result is frustration and doubt in the veracity of the Hebrew Text.[4]

The Babylonian records refer to the accession year of Nebuchadnezzar and give a sequence of events dated by month and year closely following so that one may determine with certainty that the Babylonian sovereign did indeed use the accession method as well as Nisan-to-Nisan reckoning.[5]

---

[1] Thiele, *The Mysterious Numbers of the Hebrew Kings*, op. cit., p. 53.

[2] *Ibid.*, p. 53.

[3] *Ibid.*, p. 43.

[4] *Ibid.*, p. 180. This is an example of the complete confusion that one habitually encounters.

[5] A.K. Grayson, *Assyrian and Babylonian Chronicles*, [hereafter designated *ABC*] Texts From Cuneiform Sources, A. Leo Oppenheim et al., ed., (Locust Valley, New York: J.J. Augustin, 1975), Chronicles 5, p. 100; D.J. Wiseman, *Chronicles of Chaldaean Kings (626–556 B.C.) in the British Museum*, (London: 1956), BM 21946 (Obverse), p. 69.

It is at this very juncture that Dr. Thiele deemed it necessary to force the Tishri-to-Tishri reckoning on Judah. Having already committed to the commonly accepted methods given above for Assyria, Babylon, and Persia and having encountered the usual frustrations in his attempt to synchronize these kingdoms' data with that of the Hebrews, he concluded that the problem could be resolved if differing regnal systems were involved between the other nations and Judah. This tension between the evidence is what pushed Dr. Thiele to override the obvious meaning of the many scriptural examples already addressed, and it accounts for how he was driven to force the Hebrew witness to say "Tishri" when it loudly and continually proclaims "Nisan." However, this fallacy would not have arisen and been perpetuated had Thiele trusted the Holy Scriptures or even considered that these Gentile records may have been misunderstood.

After nearly a decade of re-examining the data, the present author has come to arrive at different conclusions regarding what the biblical Text was revealing on this

Surprisingly, there are no Persian sources to invoke in order to learn first hand which procedures they used. The Persians were so hated by the Greeks and later by the Moslems that these two conquerors destroyed nearly all of the Persian records. However, the Hebrew Text is most clear in this matter. Nehemiah's speaks of his being at the Persian palace at Shushan (Susa) in the month of Chisleu (Kislev = the Hebrew 9th month, November/December) in the 20th year of Artaxerxes.

He goes on to record that the month of Nisan (spring) that followed was still in the same 20th year of that selfsame Persian monarch. Therefore, he is referencing by Tishri reckoning because the month of Nisan following the Chisleu of the 20th year would have to have been in the 21st year if Nisan-to-Nisan counting had been invoked (Neh. 1:1, cp. 2:1).

This is confirmed by double-dated papyri written by the Jews of Elephantine during the same century as Nehemiah.[1] On the papyri the reigns of the Persian kings were dated by the Tishri-to-Tishri method. The importance of this cannot be overstressed, as many scholars tend to deride the testimony of "mere" Scripture. This piece of hard external evidence makes it much more difficult for men of such disposition

to lightly sweep aside that which is recorded in the Sacred Writ.[2]

As formerly set forth, the year of Nebuchadnezzar's accession to the throne of Babylon is that point of contact between secular kingdoms and the Hebrew which enables the chronologer to assign dates in terms of the years of the Christian or BC era. Nebuchadnezzar's accession year is fixed by a lunar eclipse which was recorded by Ptolemy as having taken place on 22 April, −620 (Julian Period, all astronomers uniformly use JP dates [see page 287], the historical Gregorian date is April 15, 621 BC) during the fifth year of Nabopolassar, king of Babylon.[3]

---

[2] Thiele, *The Mysterious Numbers of the Hebrew Kings, op. cit.*, p. 180. Thiele acknowledged the witness of this biblical example as well as the significance of the Elephantine papyri. He also concluded that Daniel, writing from outside the Promised Land, used Tishri years when referencing Hebrew kings. This last assertion could be true, but it should be acknowledged that it is only necessarily so from a mathematical-chronological standpoint if the year of the destruction of Jerusalem is indeed 586 BC. Were 587 the correct year for this calamity, such would be needless.

[3] Claudius Ptolemy, "The Almagest," *Great Books of The Western World*, (Chicago, IL: William Benton Pub., 1952), Book 5, p. 172. "For in the year 5 of Nabopolassar (which is the year 127 of Nabonassar, Egyptianwise Athyr 27–28 at the end of the eleventh hour) the moon began to be eclipsed in Babylon; ..." Yet it is exactly at this point that the impossibly of arguing for an absolute chronology is most clearly seen. Ptolemy places the eclipse in the fifth year of Nabopolassar because he has assigned 13 years to Assaradinus (Esarhaddon) in the Canon; however in three different places the Babylonian Chronicles records his reign as but twelve years. Which then is the correct number? Of course, both positions have able defenders. Recently, this has led Eugene Faulstich to date this eclipse as April 15, 621, but in Nabopolassar's sixth year rather than his fifth. From that determination he computed 588 BC as the year of Nebuchadnezzar's destruction of the Temple which Solomon built (Faulstich, *History, Harmony and the Hebrew Kings, op. cit.*, pp. 218–219). Thus, the project of establishing biblical chronology, though well determined and contained within very certain narrow bounds, must be seen as an ongoing project whereby some small refinements remain possible.

For this date, cp. Ussher, *Annals, op. cit.*, p. 93 (1658 ed., p. 80) and Christian Ludwig Idler, *Abhdll. der Berliner Academie de Wissensch. fur histor.*, (Klasse, 1814), pp. 202, 224. Originally entitled *Mathematike Syntaxis* meaning Mathematical System, Ptolemy's book came to be known by many titles in different languages including *Megiste Syntaxis* (Greek for "Great System") and *The Almagest* (Arabian for "The Great Work").

---

matter. Many chronologists imagine, as did this author in the past, that the Jews had their own system for referencing foreign regnal dates which did not take into account the regulations used by that foreign government for setting their regnal years. Moreover, that the encountered seeming inconsistencies in the Hebrew Text followed a clear pattern whereby the biblical authors who were writing from *outside* the land of Israel (Nehemiah Ezra, and possibly Daniel) referenced the regal years as Tishri-to-Tishri whereas the books of Jeremiah, Haggai, Zechariah, Kings, and Chronicles (having been composed from *within* the land of Israel during the same time period) all used Nisan years for regal dating Hebrew monarchs as well as the kings of Babylon. Therefore, a king's first regnal year using one method could be his second year by the other method. However, no error or contradiction would actually exist.

It is not now being proposed that all these views are indefensible or wholly without merit, but rather that a simpler, less complex solution has been found and is deemed to more probably reflect the actual history.

[1] S.H. Horn and L.H. Wood, "The Fifth-Century Jewish Calendar at Elephantine," *Journal of Near Eastern Studies*, 13 (Jan., 1954), pp. 4 and 20. Elephantine is an island at the first cataract of the Nile opposite Aswan.

The Canon of Ptolemy and the Babylonian Chronicles tell us that Nabopolassar, the father and immediate predecessor of Nebuchadnezzar, reigned 21 years;[1] hence, the year of his death and the accession of his son are set as 605 BC. Again, Jeremiah 25:1 states that Nebuchadnezzar's 1st year was the 4th year of the reign of Jehoiakim thus establishing a BC date for that Judaic sovereign. Jeremiah goes on to record that the Temple was burned in the 19th year of Nebuchadnezzar (Jer. 52: 12–14, also 2 Kings 25:8).

As determined by the vast majority of chronologists, Dr. Thiele and the present author included, the date of that conflagration has been set at 586 BC (see page 309). In attempting to synchronize this data, Thiele supposed such could only be accomplished using the above dates if differing regnal systems were involved between Babylon and Judah.[2]

---

[1] Grayson, *ABC, op. cit.*, p. 99.

[2] The present author also originally thought the chronology could not be resolved unless Babylon and Judah were employing different regnal systems. All my editions prior to AD 2000 reflect this view. Although not true, Thiele was seemingly correct in this assessment, as all who so attempt will soon discover. As has been demonstrated, in desperation he saw a mirage of hope at 1 Kings 6:1 and necessity led him to violate the clear message of the Hebrew Text, forcing the Tishri-to-Tishri system on the Kingdom of Judah.

Still, even this would not be enough to place that Babylonian monarch on the throne in 605 BC. For if the Tishri scheme is forced on Judah and if one uses 586 for the nineteenth year of Nebuchadnezzar in which Jerusalem was burned and its walls cast down, one must also suppose that the Hebrews reckoned the regnal years of foreign kings by their own unique method. Specifically, that the Jews uniformly considered the year in which the outsider ascended to the throne as his first official year, never his year of accession.

By taking into account these two factors, Dr. Thiele seemed to have resolved all the difficulties attendant to this troublesome yet most critical segment of Bible chronology. Moreover, accounting for these two components is also the reason his charts are so complex across this time frame (*A Chronology of the Hebrew Kings, op. cit.*, pp. 179–184; e.g., see Charts 28–31). As the current author also used 586 BC as the year of the destruction of the Temple, he encountered the same two considerations. Yet whereas it does *appear* that this data will not yield itself to synchronization apart from using differing regnal systems between Babylon and Judah (but as we shall soon see, such is not true), it is at this seeming *cul-de-sac* that the contrast between the two world views as discussed in the initial portion of this research becomes most conspicuous.

The table at the top of the next page portrays how these data would synchronize with the Babylonian kings in the middle column using Tishri years and those of Judah on the bottom using Nisan years (cp. my Chart 5's dated before the year 2000).

Let us now examine the pertinent data and see whether different regnal systems must be used.

The Babylonian Chronicles (5:10–13, Obverse side) indicates that Nebuchadnezzar began his reign as sole rex over the Babylonian Empire on the first day of Elul.

Dr. Thiele's frame of reference with regard to the infallible nature of Scripture *vis-à-vis* the absolute certainty with which he viewed the Assyrian/Babylonian records brought him to conclude that somehow the Hebrew Text had to be forced to conform to the secular. He could do no other.

This author's frame of reference led him to the opposite conclusion. As the Hebrew Text does demand Nisan-to-Nisan reckoning, if the two kingdoms in question could not be synchronized apart from their using different methods for setting regnal dates, it should be the Babylonian data that must yield. The solution would become the antithesis of that which Thiele introduced.

Remember he proposed that the ancient Kingdom of Judah used two calendars, one religious and the other civil, and that the regnal dates for Judah had been set from a civil Tishri-to-Tishri calendar. Having already shown this to be erroneous, it stands thoroughly refuted. Furthermore, my study acknowledges that the Babylonian Chronicles do contain data conclusively depicting that Nebuchadnezzar's deeds were recorded reflecting the Nisan-to-Nisan mode.

If no other avenue of reconciliation existed, this author would be forced to urge in the strongest of terms that this would bear evidence that it was the Babylonians, not the ancient Hebrews of the Old Testament, who had engaged in a two calendar system. Moreover, it would be proposed that the Babylonian Chronicles and other records were engraved by scribes who were Chaldean priests and that, although they did not write the text in religious form, they dated the deeds of the kings of Babylon by their religious calendar's Nisan reckoning whereas the actual functions of their government and business were set to the Tishri calendar.

This proposition reflects all of Dr. Thiele's reasoning except, as the old chess expression goes, with "colors reversed." Judah is fixed as using Nisan-to-Nisan reckoning and Babylonia is set at Tishri.

Finally, it should be noted that either 587 BC or 588 can be reasonably defended as the year of the destruction of Jerusalem and its Temple. However, the selection of either will also encounter difficulties, none of which is insurmountable but which nevertheless strains the assurance with which the chosen year can be held. Again, the problem is that of obtaining an "absolute" chronology when areas of uncertainty persist.

606	605	604	603	602	601	600	599	598	597	596	595	594	593	592	591	590	589	588	587	586
20	AC 21	1	2	3	4	5	6	7	8	9	10	11	12	13	14	15	16	17	18	19
3	4	5	6	7	8	9	10	11	AC	1	2	3	4	5	6	7	8	9	10	11

Jehoiakim   Jeconiah   Zedekiah

This computes to August 30, 605 BC (See 2 Kings 24:1, 7; Jer. 46:2). Grayson translates Chronicles 5:10–13 as follows:[1]

10 On the eighth day of the month Ab, he [Nabopolassar] died. In the month Elul Nebuchadnezzar (II) returned to Babylon and
11 on the first day of the month Elul he ascended the royal throne in Babylon.
12 In (his) accession year Nebuchadnezzar (II) returned to Hattu. Until the month Shebat
13 he marched about victoriously
12 in Hattu.

As commander of the army and crown prince of the Babylonian Empire, Nebuchadnezzar had just weeks previously engaged Pharaoh Neco in battle at Carchemish. Returning soon thereafter, he subjugated Judah in the fourth year of King Jehoiakim (Jer. 46:2, 605 BC) whereupon Jehoiakim, who had been paying annual tribute to Neco, became Nebuchadnezzar's vassal for three years. Thereafter, in his eighth year, Jehoiakim rebelled against that mighty Babylonian monarch (2 Kings 24:1, cp. Jer. 25:1).

As manifested in the foregoing excerpt from Chronicle 5, the Babylonians used the accession method of reckoning. Hence they counted Nebuchadnezzar's reign from his coronation on the first of Elul (Aug. 30, Gregorian); thereby his first official year did not commence until the first of Nisan the following year. Now if we allow both Judah and Babylon to employ the accession method for regnal years as well as Nisan-to-Nisan years as their respective historical data records, the chronology in the table on the next page emerges.[2] The only

change is the Babylonian data shifts six-months to the right.

The 8th year of Nebuchadnezzar synchronizes with Jeconiah's captivity as required by 2 Kings 24:8, and the 11th year of Zedekiah is seen to synchronize with the 19th of Nebuchadnezzar as required by 2 Kings 25:2, 8 and Jer. 52:5, 12. However, three particulars still require clarification.

First, it will be observed that the fourth year of Jehoiakim is placed in the year of the Battle of Carchemish (605 BC) in agreement with Jer. 46:2. However, Jer. 25:1 also speaks of the fourth year of Jehoiakim saying: "that was the first year of Nebuchadrezzar king of Babylon" (see diagram on page 126). How may this apparent discrepancy be reconciled?

The Hebrew words for "first year" in Jer. 25:1 are השׁנה הראשׁנית (hashshanah haroshniyth). Not being found elsewhere in Scripture, the phrase is unique and the feminine singular form of the adjective modifying the word "year" can mean either "first or beginning."[3] Thus the phrase in Jer. 25:1 is seen as not referring to Nebuchadnezzar's *official* first year but to his initial year on the throne, the year of his accession.[4]

Taking this as the intended correct meaning, the synchronism in Jer. 25:1 will agree with Jer. 46:2. The fourth year of Jehoiakim, the accession of Nebuchadnezzar to the throne, and the Battle of Carchemish all transpired in the same year, 605 BC (see table on the following page).

---

[1] Grayson, *ABC, op. cit.*, pp. 99–100. D.J. Wiseman, *Chronicles of Chaldaean Kings (626–556 B.C.) in the British Museum*, (London: 1956), BM 21946 (Obverse), p. 69.

[2] Significantly, Josephus utilizes his own unique system. Displaying a thorough understanding of the Hebrew manner of reckoning, he references the reigns of the Hebrew kings by the Hebrew system, but foreign kings such as Nebuchadnezzar are reckoned in accordance with their own method. The present author so does in the new chart on page 126.

[3] Finegan, *Handbook of Biblical Chronology, op. cit.*, p. 202.

[4] Hayim Tadmor, "Chronology of the Last Kings of Judah," *Journal of Near Eastern Studies,* 15 (1956), p. 227. Finegan concurs (*Handbook of Biblical Chronology, op. cit.*, p. 202); cp. Albright [Journal of Biblical Literature 51 (1932), p. 102.

Professor Tadmor was an Assyriologist at Hebrew University of Jerusalem.

606	605	604	603	602	601	600	599	598	597	596	595	594	593	592	591	590	589	588	587	586
20	AC 21	1	2	3	4	5	6	7	8	9	10	11	12	13	14	15	16	17	18	19
3	4	5	6	7	8	9	10	11	AC	1	2	3	4	5	6	7	8	9	10	11

Jehoiakim   Jeconiah   Zedekiah

Second, the Babylonian Chronicles date the siege and, apparently, the deportation of King Jehoiachin (Jeconiah) of Judah from the seventh year of Nebuchadnezzar.[1]

> 11 The seventh year: In the month of Kislev the king of Akkad mustered his army and marched to Hattu.
> 12 He encamped against the city of Judah and on the second day of the month Adar he captured the city (and) seized (its) king.
> 13 A king of his own choice he appointed in the city (and) taking the vast tribute he brought it into Babylon.

However, the Hebrew account seems to conflict with the Babylonian record. It declares that the second deportation which brought Jehoiachin to Babylon, whereupon Zedekiah was placed on the throne in Jerusalem, occurred in the 8th year of Nebuchadnezzar.

> At that time the servants of Nebuchadnezzar king of Babylon came up against Jerusalem, and the city was besieged ... And Jehoiachin the king of Judah went out to the king of Babylon, he, and his mother, and his servants, and his princes, and his officers: and the king of Babylon took him in the eighth year of his reign (2 Kings 24:10–12).

The "discrepancy" resolves itself when it is seen that the Babylonian account has Jerusalem falling into their hands on 2 Adar.[2] Now Adar is the 12th and final month of the 7th year. It naturally follows that selecting a vassal, establishing a new government, cutting in pieces the gold vessels in the Temple (2 Kings 24:13) and preparing the vast booty for transport before returning to Babylon requires time. Moreover,

2 Kings 24:14–16 tells us that the populace was divided and all the leaders, the most affluent, the surviving warriors of valor, masons, smiths, and carpenters – at least 10,000 of the cream of Judah's citizenry – were separated from the poorest of the common people and then carried away to the Chaldean homeland. Such an undertaking would also have required time.

Indeed, the Hebrew Text reveals the precise length of that interval! In 2 Chron. 36:9–10 we learn that, after a reign of three months and ten days, "when the year was expired" Jeconiah (Jehoiachin) was brought to Babylon. Hence, this very brief but undefined time after 1 Nisan of the next year would fall in the eighth year of Nebuchadnezzar.

Ezekiel, who was carried away with Jeconiah, enlarges on this by writing that this "deportation" began 10 Nisan ("in the beginning of the year"). In fact, he says that his vision of the Millennial Temple was given on the 25th anniversary to the very day of this "captivity" (Ezek. 40:1, cp. 2 Chron. 36:10; Ezek. 33:21). From the 2nd day of the 12th month to the 10th day of the first month of the following year is a 38-day span (inclusive). Further, backing up 3 months and 10 days places us at 1 Tebeth (December 11, 598 BC), the date Jeconiah began his brief reign after the death of Jehoiakim.

Thus, there is no contradiction. Nebuchadnezzar entered Jerusalem in the final month of the 7th year of his official reign and set up Zedekiah as king of the new vassal government. Then the king of Babylon deported Jeconiah, along with 10,000 captives, to Chaldea the following month on 10 Nisan 597 BC (16 April, Gregorian) which was the 8th year of that Babylonian king's official reign (see the above table).

The third particular is the apparent conflict over the date of the fall of Jerusalem. It is given as having occurred in the 19th year of Nebuchadnezzar and the 11th of Zedekiah in the following accounts.

---

[1] Grayson, *ABC, op. cit.*, Chronicles 5:11–13, Reverse side, p. 102.

[2] Of course, the "discrepancy" could also be resolved by accepting that the Babylonian government was actually using Tishri-to-Tishri years and that the Hebrews counted the accession year of foreign monarchs as their first year of reigning. Then Nebuchadnezzar's 7th year by Babylonian dating would have been his 8th year by Jewish reckoning.

And in the fifth month, on the seventh day of the month, which is the nineteenth year of king Nebuchadnezzar king of Babylon, came Nebuzaradan, captain of the guard, ... And he burnt the house of the LORD, and the king's house, and all the houses of Jerusalem, and every great man's house burnt he with fire. And all the army of the Chaldees, that were with the captain of the guard, brake down the walls of Jerusalem round about (2 Ki. 25:8–10).

Now in the fifth month, in the tenth day of the month, which was the nineteenth year of Nebuchadnezzar king of Babylon, came Nebuzaradan, captain of the guard, ... And burned the house of the LORD, and the king's house; and all the houses of Jerusalem, and all the houses of the great men, burned he with fire: And all the army of the Chaldeans ... brake down all the walls of Jerusalem round about" (Jer. 52:12–14).

These passages agree with Jer. 32:1 where the 18th of Nebuchadnezzar is said to coincide with the 10th year of Zedekiah. Yet, inconceivably, the later portion of Jeremiah 52 records the fall and burning of Jerusalem as having taken place in the 18th year of Nebuchadnezzar.[1]

This is the people whom Nebuchadnezzar carried away captive: in the seventh year three thousand Jews and three and twenty: In the eighteenth year of Nebuchadnezzar he carried away captive from Jerusalem eight hundred thirty and two persons: In the three and twentieth year of Nebuchadrezzar Nebuzaradan the captain of the guard carried away captive of the Jews seven hundred forty and five persons: all the persons were four thousand and six hundred (Jer. 52:28–30).

To begin with, these verses are not recorded in 2 Kings 25. Jeremiah 52:28–34 seems to be an addendum – possibly written by Ezra in Babylon after Jeremiah's death (It is noteworthy that it is *not* part of the text of the LXX.).

Being so small a number, most suppose verses 28–30 are referring to only the adult males of importance. Yet, how can we conclude that only 4,600 Jews were carried away in all of Nebuchadnezzar's expeditions when we know at least 10,000 of prominence were carried away at

one time with Jeconiah in 597 BC (2 Kings 24:12–16)?

Indeed, the very fact that 2 Kings 24:12–16 records the removal of these 10,000 in the eighth year of Nebuchadnezzar demands that Jer. 52:28 where 3,023 were said to have been carried away in that monarch's seventh year is referring to a completely separate event. The differing numbers should alert us that it is not merely a matter of attempting to reconcile Nebuchadnezzar's seventh with his eighth year by "Hebrew reckoning" or "Babylonian reckoning" that is in view here. Two different happenings are before us.

It follows that if these are not equivalent, and thus should not be associated, then the same is true for trying to force the "18th year" of Jer. 52:29 to match the "19th year" of Jer. 52:12 and 2 Kings 25:8. Hence, it seems most reasonable to conclude with Ussher that there were three significant deportations – in 606 BC when Nebuchadnezzar was a crown prince (Dan.1:1), his 8th, and 19th year — which are to be distinguished from the minor ones Jer. 52:28–30 lists in his 7th, 18th, and 23rd years.[2] These latter, then, were likely added after the fact to complete the historical record.

If so, the first minor deportation, reported by Jeremiah to have transpired in Nebuchadnezzar's 7th year, would have been those seized by the bands of Chaldeans, Syrians, etc. whom the king of Babylon sent against Judah prior to his coming (2 Kings 24:2). That in the 18th year would correspond to when the Chaldeans broke off the siege of Jerusalem to meet Pharaoh's approaching army. Afterward, it may have been deemed prudent to march the swelling number of Egyptian and Jewish prisoners in the camp off to Babylon.

The 23rd year would have been when Nebuzaradan (vs. 30) was sent against the Moabites, etc. during the siege of Tyre (Jos., *Antiq, op. cit.*, X, 9, 7), at which time the remaining 745 Jews were gleaned from the land and carried away. Thus, the third enigma vanishes.

---

[1] Obviously, the fire was started on the 7th day of the 5th month, and it continued burning until the 10th of the same month.

[2] James Ussher, *Chronologia Sacra*, (1660) and reported in *Clarke's Commentary, op. cit.*, vol. IV, p. 395; see Ussher, *Annals*, p. 98, year 600 BC (1658 ed., p. 85).

e. Ezekiel's Regnal Dates

Like Josephus (see fn. 2, p. 125), Ezekiel also has a singular method of dating which, at first glance, seems enigmatical and contradictory to other Scripture; however it also is uncomplicated, clear and consistent once the confusion is resolved. All of Ezekiel's dates are referenced to the 597 BC deportation of Jehoiachin (the first occurring in 606 when Daniel was carried away, Dan. 1:1–6) which is designated scripturally as the "captivity" (Ezek. 1:2; cp. 33:21).

That is, Ezekiel's dates are all referenced from the year of the "captivity" (Zedekiah's accession year), not from Zedekiah's official regnal years (cp. Ezek. 1:1–2, 40:1 and 33:21 with 32:1 and note the "12th" year which cannot be Zedekiah's as, according to 2 Kings 24:18, he reigned only 11 years). The year labeled the "captivity" is the year preceding Zedekiah's regnal years. Thus, all Ezekiel's dates are one year prior to that which we would normally anticipate.

For example, chapter 8 begins with a reference to a "sixth" year. This is not to be counted from Zedekiah's first official year of reigning (596 BC) in which case one would erroneously fix the "glory" as departing from the Temple in the year 591 (inclusive numbering). Instead, Ezekiel intends us to begin one year prior at the 597 BC "captivity," and number to 592 BC (inclusively), the correct year for the departing of the "glory."

This manifests that in God's view, Jehoiachin (Jeconiah) is still the anointed king of Judah[1] even though exiled and captive in a Babylonian dungeon.[2] This is the reason Ezekiel dates in terms of the years of Jehoiachin's deportation rather that from those of Zedekiah, his successor (2 Kings 25:27; Jer. 52:31). This is why Zedekiah, Jehoiachin's uncle, is occasionally referred to as merely the "prince" of Judah rather than its "king" by the prophet Ezekiel (Ezek. 12:10,12; 21:25).

Moreover, in the first year of his reign, Evil Merodach (Amel-Marduk), Nebuchadnezzar's son and successor, liberated Jehoiachin from prison and raised him to a position of honor at the palace (562 BC, the 18th Jubilee — Jer. 52:31–34). Evil Merodach's kind, respectful treatment of Jehoiachin after 37 years' imprisonment further substantiates the correctness of the above assertions.

Additionally, Ezekiel uses King Jehoiachin's deportation as his point of reference because he himself was also carried away to Babylon with the monarch at that time (Ezek. 40:1) as was Mordecai of the Book of Esther (Esther 2:6, cp. 2 Kings 24:6).

f. The Regnal Year Query Concluded

As for the northern kingdom of Israel, Thiele writes:[3]

> For Israel there seems to be no direct scriptural evidence as to the time of the beginning of the regnal year. However, when a Nisan-to-Nisan regnal year is used for Israel together with a Tishri-to-Tishri year for Judah, the perplexing discrepancies disappear and a harmonious chronological pattern results.

With regard to the regnal question, nearly every possible solution has been championed. Kleber argued for a Nisan-to-Nisan year for Judah but a Tishri-to-Tishri year for Israel, the very antithesis of Thiele's position.[4] Mowinckel concluded that both kingdoms followed a Tishri-to-Tishri policy[5] whereas still others have held that a shift was made from Tishri-to-Tishri reckoning in the initial period to a Nisan-to-Nisan year in the later years for both kingdoms.

More recently Faulstich judged that no data existed within or without the Hebrew Text that demands the regnal reckoning of the kings of

---

[1] The Babylonians also so viewed; the Jehoiachin Tablets, found in the ruins of a vaulted building near the Ishtar Gate of Babylon (dated 595–570 BC), provide evidence that even after he was replaced by Zedekiah the Babylonians continued to regard Jehoiachin as the legitimate King of Judah (Pritchard, *ANET, op. cit.*, p. 308.).

[2] Further, it sustains the logical deduction that Josiah must have anointed Jehoiachin, his grandson, to succeed him just prior to his encounter with Pharaoh Neco. This conclusion will be fully biblically substantiated later in this chapter.

[3] Thiele, *The Mysterious Numbers of the Hebrew Kings, op. cit.*, p. 53.

[4] Albert M. Kleber, "The Chronology of 3 and 4 Kings and 2 Paralipomenon," *Biblica* 2 (1921), pp. 3–29, 170–205.

[5] Sigmund Mowinckel, "Die Chronologie der israelitischen und judischen Konige," *Acta Orientalia*, 10 (1932), pp. 161–277.

Judah or Israel from any date other than the first of Nisan.[1] In so concluding, Faulstich agreed with Thiele's findings given in the last quote concerning the Northern Kingdom, but not with his Tishri-to-Tishri position for Judah.

The findings of this research agree with Faulstich's evaluation[2] with the exception of the final monarch of the Kingdom of Israel, Hoshea. In harmonizing all of the data concerning his reign, the best synchronization with Judah favors Hoshea's having used the Tishri system. This he may have done either due to Assyrian influence or the desperate circumstances overhanging his kingdom as a result of the precarious Assyrian presence in the area, much of the Northern Kingdom having already been subjugated into captivity during Pekah's reign by Tiglath-pileser III (2 Kings 15:29; 1 Chron. 5:26; Isaiah 9:1). Of course insofar as the Kingdom of Israel was concerned, as King Hoshea could choose any method he desired.

Yet the question of why Dr. Thiele reached the opposite result from the undeniable witness of Scripture with regard to the data concerning the Temple construction and Solomon's regnal year, as well as his poor handling of the facts relevant to Josiah's 18th year, remains unanswered. The undeniable reason for these distortions is the world view and frame of reference which he brought to the task. Professor Thiele betrays a "hidden" agenda in his previously quoted statement (page 122) where he says:[3]

> Perhaps the strongest argument for the use of a Tishri-to-Tishri regnal year in Judah is that this method works, giving us a harmonious pattern of the regnal years and synchronisms, while with a Nisan-to-Nisan regnal year the old discrepancies remain.

He thereby admits that although the biblical data clearly called for Nisan regnal years, it could not be made to synchronize exactly with the Assyrian and Babylonian materials – thus "the old discrepancies remain." Since for him

---

[1] E.W. Faulstich, *History, Harmony and the Hebrew Kings,* op. cit., p. 18.

[2] For example, see 1 Kings 20:22 and 26 as well as 2 Sam. 11:1–2.

[3] Thiele, *The Mysterious Numbers of the Hebrew Kings,* op. cit., p. 53.

the Assyrian and Babylonian records, often fragmented, discontinuous, and self-contradictory, are the standard to which all other historic data must be brought in line, Professor Thiele came to an impasse with the Hebrew regnal system as it would not directly fit into his preconceived commitment.

Because of this frame of reference, he could not conceive that the problem could have lain with the determination he and others had reached from the Assyrian and/or Babylonian records. This forced him to conclude that the problem lay within the Hebrew Text and, in desperation to achieve his goal, he became so enmeshed in attempting to resolve the enigma that he made "black" read "white."

Thiele's own admission alluded to above that: "In the Hebrew Scriptures the months are numbered from Nisan" reveals that he could discern their message yet he did not heed them. Rather, he invented a contrivance to circumvent the testimony of Scripture which the world of scholarship has followed.

Yet this was unnecessary. As shall be seen, all that was needed was to recognize that either the Assyrian/Babylonian records had been misunderstood or, even more to the case in point, the Hebrew Text simply did not reckon the regnal years for foreign monarchs according to the regulations used by that foreign government.

If this were the only place Dr. Thiele applied such a stratagem, one could justly wonder if such an appraisal as that just given were justly warranted and accurate, yet assuredly he has done far worse and much more blatant violation to the text of the Holy Scriptures. This shall be demonstrated and enlarged upon in the sections dealing with the Assyrian eponyms and the northern kings, Pekahiah and Pekah.

The real question here, however, is why have nearly all the fundamental and conservative scholars followed Dr. Thiele's results for the past half-century as though the Scriptures had been honored, recommending them to the church as well as to interested secular inquirers and thereby giving their "approval" to his findings? As this has already been addressed in the first chapter of this dissertation, we forbear.

JUDAH	OFFICIAL YRS.	ISRAEL	OFFICIAL YRS.	ACTUAL YRS.
Rehoboam	17	Jeroboam	22	21
Abijah	3	Nadab	2	1
Asa	41	Baasha	24	23
Jehoshaphat	18	Elah	2	1
		Omri	12	11
		Ahab	22	21
		Ahaziah	2	1
Total	79		86	79

2. ACCESSION OR NON-ACCESSION DATING

In addition to the regnal year, the second major basic principle of Hebrew chronology is that of the *method* used in reckoning regal years. If a king reckoned his reign beginning with New Year's Day *after* his accession as the first official year of reign, he called that part of the year in which he came to the throne his "accession" year. Thus this method is called "accession year dating" or "postdating." But if he called the year in which he ascended to the throne his first official year, regardless of the number of months in which he actually reigned during that year, he was using the "non-accession year" method (also called "pre" or "antedating").[1] The following depicts the salient differences between the two methods.

Accession Year Dating:
    (Accession year) (1st year) (2nd year)

Non-accession Year Dating:
        (1st year)   (2nd year)   (3rd year)

As king, each sovereign could choose which method he desired. Observe that in non-accession year dating, the *last* year of one king was the *first* official year of his successor even if he reigned but one day in that year. In this method, that year was counted *twice*; consequently, reigns so reckoned give one year more than the actual elapsed time. Hence with both sovereigns claiming the same year, it becomes necessary to subtract one year when computing the actual number of elapsed years. Conversely, accession reckoning gives official years equal to actual years.

Customarily, the kings of Judah used accession dating while those of Israel most often chose the non-accession method. Judah adopted the non-accession method when Jehoshaphat's son, Jehoram, married Athaliah, whose parents were Ahab, the wicked king of Israel, and Jezebel, the depraved Sidonian princess. When Athaliah's influence was broken, the Kingdom of Judah returned to the accession method.

When the month used by a king (or nation) to begin his (its) regnal year is determined and the actual method of reckoning regnal dates is understood, the apparent chronological discrepancies between the Kingdoms of Israel and Judah disappear. To illustrate, in the example above the accessions of Rehoboam in Judah and Jeroboam in Israel transpired in the same year.

Furthermore, the Scriptures declare that the 18th year of King Jehoshaphat of Judah was the year when Ahaziah of Israel died and Joram (NK) took his place, therefore near identical periods for the two nations are represented (2 Kings 3:1). Accordingly, their regnal data should total to the same value; however, as shown above, the official years of reign between the two kingdoms seem to reflect a seven-year discrepancy (86 − 79 = 7).

Nevertheless, as the chart depicts, recognizing accession year reckoning for Judah and non-accession year for Israel shows the data to harmonize. By merely subtracting one year from each of the reigns of the kings of Israel (due to the overlapping feature of the non-accession method), the paradox is resolved. How one determines which method a given king or kingdom employed will be explained in the subsequent description of the "triangulation" technique.

---

[1] Finegan, *Handbook of Biblical Chronology, op. cit.,* pages 85–92.

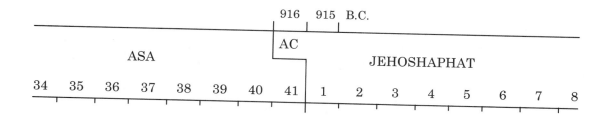

The above is a typical example as to how the *accession* year method works and appears on the chart.

The offset indicates that Asa died during the 41st year of his reign. In that year (916 BC) Jehoshaphat ascended to the throne but called it his "accession year" giving full credit for that year to his father, Asa. He began his 1st official year (915 BC) after the first of the year (1 Nisan). Again, note that the official years and the actual linear years are the same in this method.

At the bottom of the page is an example of the *non-accession* year method. Here, the offset indicates that Omri died in 919 BC during the 12th year of his reign. Within that year, Ahab ascended to the throne and also claimed the year as his first rather than as his accession year. It will be observed that the official years would now exceed the actual linear years by one year as both men claimed the year 919 BC.

3. THE BASIC PRINCIPLES SUMMARIZED

It should be recalled that with regard to the problems inherent with the chronological computations of this period, chronologists have from the onset sought to reconcile the apparent discrepancies by assuming co-regencies (overlapping reigns), interregna, or inaccuracies in the biblical account. For the biblicist, the latter is not an acceptable alternative. As for the first two, synchronization between the northern and southern Hebrew kingdoms will be found impossible without them, yet their application to the distinct problems encountered is not dependent upon mere caprice. The harmonization of their data must be such that co-regencies and interregna be implemented only where there are clear indications in the text.

The apparent discordances can be reconciled by the careful application of the two basic principles described heretofore along with the Talmud's assertion that even a single day before or after 1 Nisan is reckoned as one year. This latter statement becomes most important in fixing regnal years. If these three be prudently heeded, it will be found that there was not a single interregnum during the entire span of the Kingdom of Judah's existence, only one co-regency — that being Jehoram with his father Jehoshaphat as the Text clearly relates (2 Kings 8:16) — and three short pro-rex periods (Jehoram before becoming co-rex, Ahaziah, and Jotham).

This is most important for, as previously stated, Judah is the standard from which Israel's data is to be measured [Jewish chronology concurs, *Seder Olam Rabbah*, (2005), pp. 154, 192] and if the guiding foundation is straightforward, that which is fitted alongside it should be equally trustworthy. Indeed, the arrangement of the chronological data of the biblical text upon these principles produces a result that has the added assurance of its correctness by the fact that it intermeshes and synchronizes with the established chronological data of the universal history of the ancient world as demonstrated by Ussher, Clinton, and astronomically established events recorded by Ptolemy.

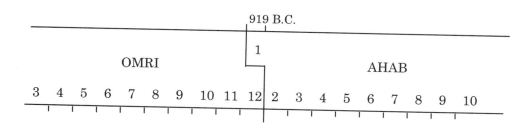

E. THE 390 YEARS OF THE KINGDOM OF JUDAH

Perhaps the most decisive factor in determining the chronology of the period of the "disruption" of the monarchy is that of establishing with certainty its *terminus a quo* and *terminus ad quem*, hence its duration; for without absolute boundaries, the door is left wide open for unbounded flights of imagination and conjecture on the part of the individual. Of course, the span to be determined is the length of time from Solomon's death, with the subsequent division of the kingdom, to the termination of the Kingdom of Judah at the hand of King Nebuchadnezzar of Babylonia in 586 BC.

The interval was found to be 390 years. It has already been stated as being a key biblical anchor point in the second chapter dealing with Chart 1 and also may be found as such on the first chart itself.

As indicated earlier, this length was determined by first adding the years of the reigns of the kings of Judah from the fall of Babylon to the sixth year of Hezekiah, when Israel was carried away to Assyria. This span is 134 years, 6 months and 10 days or "in the 135th year" (Chart 5). Again, the regnal data of the kings of Judah fits this time span perfectly without reference to any other kingdom, thus demonstrating that it would be illogical to suddenly resort to using Israel as the chronological guide at the point where they begin to coexist.

Next, the reigns of Judah's monarchs from the *terminus a quo* to the *terminus ad quem* was summed yielding 394 years, 6 months and 10 days. To this, we must add the year designated in Scripture as "the captivity" (see chart 5 at 597 BC with its accompanying note designated * * and p. 128, "Ezekiel's Regnal Dates"). Thus, the total becomes 395 years, 6 months and 10 days.

Again, the *only* scriptural co-regency between these kings is that of Jehoshaphat and his son Jehoram:

> And in the fifth year of Joram the son of Ahab king of Israel, Jehoshaphat being <u>then</u> king of Judah, Jehoram the son of Jehoshaphat king of Judah began to reign. (2 Kings 8:16)

This verse requires that Jehoram was placed upon the throne while his father was still alive and reigning. From 2 Kings 3:1; 8:16; 8:25; and 9:29, the length of this overlapping co-regency was unequivocally determined to be four years (Chart 5 and Chart 5c). Subtracting the 4-year overlap from the total, leaves 391 years, 6 months and 10 days:

$$395 \text{ yrs. } 6 \text{ mos. } 10 \text{ days } - 4 \text{ yrs.}$$
$$= 391 \text{ yrs. } 6 \text{ mos. } 10 \text{ days.}$$

As formerly mentioned, Athaliah seems to have been the source who influenced her and Jehoram's son, Ahaziah, to resort to the non-accession method which was then operative in her father's northern dynasty. Athaliah usurped the crown, temporarily breaking the Davidic line, for six years (2 Kings 11:1–3). She was slain shortly thereafter thus reigning part of a seventh year (2 Kings 11:4, 21; 2 Chron. 22:12, 23:1). Of course the true monarch, little Joash of the lineage of David, was being hidden inside the Temple.

When Jehoram died, Ahaziah claimed his father's last year as his first official year. Then upon Ahaziah's being slain that same year, his mother Athaliah seized the throne and also made that her first official year. Consequently, Jehoram, Athaliah, and their son Ahaziah all three occupied the throne in 886 BC, and all laid claim to that year (see Charts 5 and Chart 5c).

As a result, the official years become two years more than the actual years. Therefore, these extraneous years must be subtracted from the 391 years, 6 months and 10 days in order to obtain the true interval of the period of the "disruption":

$$391 \text{ yrs. } 6 \text{ mos. } 10 \text{ days } - 2 \text{ yrs.}$$
$$= 389 \text{ yrs. } 6 \text{ mos. } 10 \text{ days.}$$

Now 389 years, 6 months and 10 days places one "in the 390th year." Furthermore, this 390-year time span is confirmed by Ezekiel 4:4–8. There God instructed the prophet to lie on his left side each day for 390 days in solemn protestation against the "iniquity" of Israel as a sign unto the people that they would know that the fall of Jerusalem was the LORD'S work. Moreover, each day was said to represent one of the years during which the house of Israel had lived in open sin against its God until which

time He was to bring judgment.[1] The biblical data reveals that this prophecy was given before, yet very near, 586 BC, the time of God's recompense against the nation through His vessel, Nebuchadnezzar (Ezek. 1:1–2, cp. 8:1; see Chart 5, 5c, and Appendix N, page 309).

Moreover, Ezekiel 35:5 (cp. Psa. 137:7) undeniably marks the "end" of Israel's "iniquity" (cp. Ezek. 4:4–6) as being the time of her "calamity" (cp. Obadiah 10–13; especially note the play on the word "calamity" in vs. 13). The context[2] of these verses demonstrates beyond any reasonable doubt the correctness of our interpretation regarding the 390 years of Ezekiel 4:4–6. Therefore, the fulfillment and *terminus ad quem* of the prophecy was at the 586 BC "calamity" when Jerusalem was carried away captive, thus ending Israel's "iniquity."

With the *terminus ad quem* thus firmly established, we need only number back 390 years inclusively to establish the prophecy's *terminus a quo*. This places us precisely at the event which marked both the issue of the controversy that Jehovah had with Israel and the occasion when it originated. The iniquity for which Israel was being called into account was that of idolatry and the specific case in point began when the Kingdom of Israel was founded under Jeroboam I, the son of Nebat, at

which time he set up the golden calves at Dan and Bethel (1 Kings 12:26–33; 13:33–34).

At that time he also consecrated priests who were not of the tribe of Levi and instituted a counterfeit Feast of Tabernacles in the eighth month rather than in the seventh as God had ordained. There can be no doubt that this is the prophecy's *terminus a quo* as over and over Scripture records the oft repeated refrain that Jeroboam "caused Israel to sin" (1 Kings 14:16; 15:26, 30; 16:2, 19, 26; 22:52, etc.).

It must be noted that even though the Kingdom of Israel had been terminated and all but the poorest of its people carried away from the land and resettled in the farthest regions of the Assyrian Empire back in 721 BC (2 Kings 17; 18:9–12), Judah had long before become a truly "representative" kingdom. On several occasions, mass emigrations of people from all the tribes left the Northern Kingdom and went down to live in the Southern Kingdom (2 Chron. 11:1, 13–17; 12:1,6; 15:8–9; 35:17–19). In this manner, the Kingdom of Judah became not only heavily populated, but around a century after the fall of Samaria, capital of the northern realm, members of all the tribes of Israel were still said to be living there (2 Chron. 35:17–19).

Thus, the Ezekiel 4:4–8 passages are completely apropos in assigning the 390-year prophecy to "Israel" over a century and a quarter after that kingdom had ceased to exist as an entity. Hence, in time the realm of Judah came to consist of all "Israel" (thus there are no "ten missing tribes") and the sin of idolatry begun by Jeroboam I continued to be a snare to "Israel" and the Southern Kingdom in the days of Ezekiel (4:13; 5:4; 6:2,4–5,11; 8:4,10–11, etc.).

Thus it has been shown that the context of Ezekiel 4:4–8 and 35:5 with regard to the 390-year segment of the history of the Hebrew people confirms the exact interval derived by summing the regnal years of all the kings of Judah and removing the two small overlapping periods mentioned at the onset of this subject thereby fixing precisely the duration of the period of the divided monarchy (Chart 1). Having independently discovered these facts, this author was most gratified years later to learn that other workers had come to the same conclusions (or very nearly so), especially with

---

[1] Another judgment of 40 years against Judah is also mentioned. The author's interpretation of this may be found on Chart 5 between the years 627 and 588 BC where the interval is shown as being that of Jeremiah's prophecies from their commencement in the 13th year of Josiah to the 9th year of Zedekiah in which the final siege of Jerusalem began (numbered inclusively). Although idolatry was also among Judah's sins, others were specified by the Lord, especially through the prophet Jeremiah, which brought about this additional judgment. Sir Robert Anderson (*The Coming Prince, op. cit.,* p. 26) and Anstey (*The Romance of Bible Chronology, op. cit.,* p. 225) are among those who reckoned similarly.

In addition, the 40 years of Judah's iniquity and its association to a siege of Jerusalem in Ezekiel 4:4–7 is taken to be a double reference prophecy with its second fulfillment being the 40 years from the Crucifixion of our Lord to the destruction of the city and Temple by Titus in AD 70 (see page 238 for an amplification on this).

[2] The immediate context of Ezek. 4:4–8 was that after Nebuchadnezzar routed the Egyptian army which had come to aid Zedekiah, he would return and re-initiate the siege of Jerusalem 390 days before the city fell (= mid 3rd month of Zedekiah's 10th).

regard to the significance of the 390 years of Ezekiel. Clinton concurred with my results.[1]

Several others of notable eminence and ability considered the 390 years to be taken from the ninth year of Zedekiah when Nebuchadnezzar began the final siege of Jerusalem (about 18 months before the final fall, cp. Jer. 39:1; 52:4,12; 2 Kings 25:1–4, 8). Accordingly, Sir Isaac Newton determined that, rather than the 390-year span defining the duration of the Judaic kingdom, it marked the interval from the death of Solomon with the ensuing emergence of the divided kingdoms to the year Nebuchadnezzar initiated the siege.[2]

Sir Robert Anderson also understood the 390 to be taken from the commencement of the final siege, but he judged that those years encompassed the period from that date to the year the prophet Ahijah promised Jeroboam (I) that he would receive the ten tribes (1 Ki. 11:29–39).[3] Browne also took the 390 as beginning with Ahijah's promise to Jeroboam, but he ended the span at the fall of Jerusalem.[4] Ussher began on the 15th day of the eighth month of Jeroboam's first year at his counterfeit Feast of Tabernacles and ended in Nebuchadnezzar's 23rd year when the final 745 Jews were carried to Babylon (1 Kings 12:32–33; Jer. 52:30).[5] Beecher[6] and Anstey[7] both understood the period to encompass the year Ezekiel began to prophesy (30 years after Josiah's second reform and great Passover in the 18th year of his dominion, Ezek. 1:1–2) unto the "disruption."

It is most important to consider the gravity of this last particular. First, like the author, all these scholars took the Hebrew Text literally and attempted to allow it to speak for itself. This world view led them all to conclude that the 390-year Ezekiel prophecy was of major

significance in correctly deriving the chronology of the period. Once the scholar establishes the date of the 19th year of Nebuchadnezzar as best as the data and conscience allows (be it 588, 587, or 586), he may readily use that mainstay to firmly fix another major biblical anchor point by the simple addition of this large time interval. Thus in this chronology:

586 BC + 390 years = 975 BC
(year of the schism, inclusively numbered).

The fact that its application from a contextual standpoint was not understood as defining exactly the same boundaries by all of these dedicated biblically conservative men serves to underscore that which has been formerly mentioned, namely, the limitations involved in such an undertaking as computing a chronology of the Old Testament. This further helps explain why this author has stated his doubts that, apart from divine revelation, an "absolute" chronology, though a goal to which one should aspire, is almost certainly unattainable. This 390-year element should help all to see that the preparation of a "standard" chronology, which may from time to time undergo modifications as new insights and even perhaps new data arises, is a more realistic attainment. Each should be true to oneself.

Yet at the same time the 390-year prophecy serves to accentuate something even more meaningful. Even though the interval was somewhat variously perceived, the literal acceptance and utilization of the number resulted in narrowing the deviation between the work of the individuals involved to that of a maximum of eight years for the date of the disruption – less than a decade. Of course, differences of this magnitude are not desirable, but the biblical events are kept well within chronological bounds so that the narratives do not completely lose their historical perspective.

Such cannot be said for Thiele's work or the school of thought and philosophy he represents. Like the present author, Dr. Thiele placed the date of the destruction of Jerusalem at 586 BC, but he held to the Assyrian data as his certain guide rather than the Scriptures (though all the while professing to honor them) and, as so many others, ignored the context of the Ezekiel passage. In so doing, he and nearly all modern scholars have set themselves to the problem

[1] Clinton, *Fasti Hellenici, op. cit.*, vol. I, pp. 314, 328.

[2] Newton, *The Chronology of Ancient Kingdoms Amended op. cit.*, p. 298; also see Newton's pp. 20, 39, 52, and 126.

[3] Anderson, *The Coming Prince, op. cit.*, footnote pp. 26–27.

[4] Browne, *Ordo Saeclorum, op. cit.*, p. 230.

[5] Ussher, *Annals, op. cit.*, pp. 68, 108 (1658 ed., pp. 41, 93).

[6] Beecher, *The Dated Events of the Old Testament, op. cit.*, pp. 156–157. See his p. 123 and compare dates to determine how he understood the 390-year span.

[7] Anstey, *The Romance of Bible Chronology, op. cit.*, p. 225.

lacking the proper tool which would place stringent limitations and firm boundaries on the matter.

Tragically, the result is that Thiele has placed the date of the disruption at 931/930 BC, only 345 years from the date of Jerusalem's fall – an error of 45 years (390 − 345 = 45)! This 931/930 date (either or both) serves to "tag" Thiele's material thus allowing its immediate recognition regardless of the source being referenced.

Although Thiele believed he had correctly synchronized the Hebrew record by bringing it in line with the Assyrian annals, he actually placed the biblical events completely out of their historic settings. Albright's dates, identifiable at once by his 922 BC year for the schism, are even farther out of their true positions.

The 390-year declaration, taken in context, is most significant for it takes the date of the schism (or there about by anyone's consideration) out of the hands of men and places it on a firm foundation. This passage serves to inhibit and constrict the fanciful imagination and conjecture of scholars from all the various disciplines (be they chronologers, archaeologists, theologians, etc.) and sets a fixed mathematical value of 390 years on the period.

Moreover, this span has been shown to be absolutely confirmed by the lengths of the reigns of the kings of Judah. It is the mathematical key to correctly founding the chronology of the kings of Judah and Israel. By this, the chronological configuration of Dr. Edwin R. Thiele must be seen as refuted. Not only should fundamental conservatives so concede, but all fair thinking people as well, for such should be willing to, at the very least, give the Hebrew Text its day on the witness stand.

Before closing this section, it must be acknowledged that some would also claim a co-regency (hence an overlap) for Uzziah and his son Jotham (2 Chron. 26:21). However, a most careful examination of the wording in these Scriptures discloses otherwise, i.e., Jotham *"Began to reign"* versus *"was over the king's house, governing the people."* The marked contrast between the two statements reveals that Jotham held only a pro-rex post at this time as 2 Chron. 26:23 confirms:

So Uzziah slept with his fathers, and they buried him with his fathers in the field of the burial which belonged to the kings; for they said, He is a leper: and Jotham his son reigned in his stead.

This verse unmistakably states that Jotham did not begin to "reign" until his father died, hence he did not bear the title of king when Uzziah became a leper.

F. THE TRIANGULATION FORMULA

Now to the dynamics of the scheme itself. For the most part, Chart 5 has been constructed by using a series of "scriptural triangles." The discovery and development of this triangulation formula over the period whereby the kingdoms of Israel and Judah existed simultaneously is solely that of the author of this dissertation. It is offered as a new and decisive tool in the outworking, systematizing, and synchronization of this segment of the disruption.[1]

To illustrate the technique, let us begin with Asa of the Kingdom of Judah (see the following page, Charts 5 and 5c). Beginning at Asa's first official regnal year, the 41 years of his reign are numbered along a horizontal line (1 Kings 15:10). This will be the base of the triangle under construction.

The lower line extending diagonally upward from his year of accession (956 BC) has the message "38th year 1 Kings 16:29" inserted along its length, hence 38 years of Asa's dominion must be counted off along the length of the triangle's base. The long slanted line above this base becomes an upper "arm" of the triangle which is in the process of being formed, and it connects the Kingdom of Judah's data with that of the Kingdom of Israel. This line or "arm" terminates at the year 918 BC, the 12th year of Omri (1 Kings 16:23b) and/or the first year of Ahab.

---

[1] This triangulation formula may be imagined as being akin to or even the same technique as that used by Frank R. Klassen, but the affinity is totally superficial; any resemblance is purely that of optics, not of substance. Whereas it is acknowledged that the intricacies of the formula came to this author during the time while Klassen's work was under close analysis, even a most casual examination of his work will readily document that Klassen himself neither utilized nor embraced the triangulation scheme herein presented. Moreover, at no place does he so claim in his somewhat diminutive but accomplished text (See Frank R. Klassen, *The Chronology of the Bible, op. cit.*, pp. 38–41.).

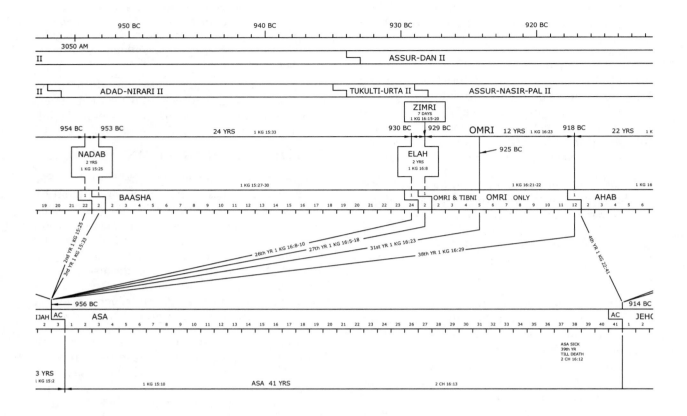

At this point a major subtlety is introduced. One of the most difficult tasks was to devise a visual display that would clearly and simply depict this subtlety. A comparison of 1 Kings 16:29 and 16:23b reveals that the 38th year of the reign of Asa must coincide with both the beginning of Ahab's dominion and the termination or 12th year of Omri (non-accession). Hence beginning at Asa's first official regnal year, we again locate the position of Asa's 38th year along the base of the triangle which we are in the process of forming. Then, looking directly above to the Kingdom of Israel's data, one may observe that Ahab is properly located. Two sides, the base and the arm above, of the first triangle have now been formed.

Next, beginning at Ahab, we note another angular directive reading "4th year 1 Kings 22:41" bounded by a line drawn from the first year of that monarch down to the end of Asa's and the commencement of Jehoshaphat's reign. This means First Kings 22:41 relates that Jehoshaphat began his rule in the 4th year of Ahab. Therefore, if we ascribe four years to Ahab and drop straight down to the rectangle

containing Judah's data, our plat should show Asa's son, Jehoshaphat succeeding him – and it does. The third side has now been formed, closing the triangle.

The reader has already been familiarized with the concept of "accession" and "non-accession" dating. Before now, one could fairly levy the complaint that although these two concepts are both interesting and historically applicable where other kingdoms are concerned, neither is to be found mentioned in the pages of the Holy Writ. Whereas it is true that the Scriptures do not actually use these terms, they do utilize both concepts without so verbalizing. The casual reader would never notice this for it is only by extremely careful observation (or revelation) that it can be ascertained. Indeed, few would so notice apart from making a drawing.

What is being said is that the Hebrew Scriptures are so written that inexorably embedded within the text concerning the regnal information is recorded precise mathematical data which, if heeded, demands the chro-

nologers' choosing the correct method of reckoning over the period wherein the two kingdoms coexist. The proof and explanation of this phenomenon may be seen in that which follows.

Below Asa's numbered extended rectangle is Judah's "supplemental data" line as previously described. On it are inscribed two Scriptures, 1 Kings 15:10 and 2 Chron. 16:13 and the words "ASA 41 YRS" in larger print. This means these two verses record the number of years Asa governed as being 41. However, now something seems amiss with our triangulation technique. The first arm (long side above the base) containing 1 Kings 16:29 tells us that Ahab began to reign in Asa's 38th year; the third arm (short arm) bearing 1 Kings 22:41 indicates that Asa's reign ended in Ahab's 4th – yet 38 and 4 are 42, not 41!

This kind of anomaly runs throughout the entire fabric of the Books of Kings and Chronicles often causing chronologists to lose their way, if not their faith in the reliability of the Sacred Writ. In fact, it is at this very point that many scholars so do. The truth is there is no error at all. Most are simply not familiar enough with the intricate subtleties of accession and non-accession reckoning, and hence do not recognize that which bewilders them as being such.

Yet, the solution and understanding of the same is very simple and forthright. Observe that the year "one" of Ahab's reign is above the 12th year of Omri. How is one to know to put it there? Why not in the year to the right side of the 12? If one mentally visualizes placing it beside the 12, it will be evident that now Ahab's 4th year is one year to the *right* and *beyond* the 41 years that the two heretofore mentioned verses demand for Asa. Thus, these two "witnesses" force the chronologist to place Ahab's first official year of rule above and in the same year as Omri's 12th. Accordingly, the reconciliation of all the God-given data teaches and demands that Ahab was employing the non-accession method of reckoning.

Consequently as each triangle is forged, the internal facts embedded within Scripture will compel the student to see which method is being used by that particular monarch. Indeed, now that the system has been demonstrated, a shortcut becomes apparent. Specifically, the moment it was seen that 38 and 4 summed to a value greater than the stated length of Asa's reign, the chronologist should be alerted to the fact that a non-accession relationship must exist with regard to the other part of the triangle.

Again, the Bible does not contain the words "accession" or "non-accession" yet it teaches and applies the principles of each. As one continues building the graph, he merely adds one triangle after another, connecting the two kingdoms *synchronously* as he goes. The advantage of this system is that if a mistake or oversight is made with one triangle, the arms of the following triangle will not meet; hence the error is quickly noted and may be corrected. Thus, plotting the Scriptures will reveal whether accession or non-accession reckoning was the method of choice of a given king.

Even though several judicious conservative chronologers such as Ussher and Clinton were able to very nearly achieve the same results as produced by this analysis by simply being careful to honor the scriptural data without being aware of "triangulation," this system now elevates the study of the Hebrew kings to an unprecedented height. It places the study on objective scientific grounds, reducing subjectivity and speculation to near non-existent levels.

Doubtless, critics and skeptics will always be with us, but their standard objections and past challenge that a given Bible honoring solution by some biblicist is merely his "opinion" has been forever removed. Those who have considered the Holy Scriptures as the mere works of men now have something tangible, systematic, and scientific with which to cope.

Verily, does not this rigid mathematically embedded triangulation formula loudly speak and bear undeniable testimony, not only to encourage the Christian but the honest seeker of truth and skeptic as well, that a mighty and personal God – one of great purpose, providence and intelligence – exists to have produced, interwoven, and preserved so intricate a design within the Sacred Hebrew history? Does the history or chronology of any other kingdom boast a design so simple yet so grand? Does not this render the Holy Bible of the Reformation (Masoretic and *Textus Receptus*) as totally unlike all others, a text *sui generis*?

G. USING CHART OPTICS AS A PROBLEM SOLVING AID

Because it is so difficult to mentally visualize the apparent scriptural contradictions which exist across the interval of the disruption, the inquirer is often left in doubt or even reduced to unbelief in the veracity of the biblical text. Of course, the preparation of diagrams takes time and so often this time is deemed as too great a sacrifice for such little benefit, but this point of view is the enemy of obtaining and verifying the truth with regard to the matter at hand.

However, when these "problem" passages are graphed, they immediately become clarified and their meaning and context become manifest thereby removing at once both the paradox and doubt. If the entire matter is not totally resolved, it is reduced to the point of mere fine tuning, but the stumbling block is at once removed.

All of this is never more apparent than in the positive advantages derived from a visual exhibit of the Hebrew chronological data covering the period of the schism as readily displayed on Chart 5. More than on any of the preceding charts, this chart brings the trouble areas into focus and aids in resolving the un-resolvable. Beginning on the left side near the time of the division of the monarchy, several of these problems will be addressed briefly thus demonstrating the above proposition as we move along the chart to the right.

Before we so embark, it is important to bear in mind that nearly all of the solutions which will be set forth have been given long ago and by many different biblical scholars. The problem has not been that the paradoxes have not been resolved; it is that, due to their world view, the majority of twentieth century academia have not accepted the answers.

It is the sincere hope of this chronologist that the visual enhancement before the reader will assist him in breaking through any honest mental reservations he may have and enable him to, perhaps for the first time, perceive and "see" that the Scriptures are in fact perfectly reliable and self-correcting through their own internal system of mathematical "checks and balances" which serves to maintain absolute accuracy.

1. BAASHA'S 36TH YEAR

The problem encountered here is how Baasha can be said to come up against Asa in the 36th year of that Judaic king's reign (2 Chron. 16:1) when other Scripture declares that Baasha died in the 26th year of Asa's regime (1 Kings 16:6,8, cp. verse 23). Is not this a clear contradiction between "infallible" passages?

As will be seen, the individual's reaction upon his being made aware of such a circumstance as this depends solely upon his world view and the accompanying frames of reference which it brings to bear upon not only the example before us, but all that follows. It does not depend upon the scriptural statements themselves. The humanistic man-centered world view will lead one to the immediate conclusion that an un-deniable error exists between the accounts. Unfortunately, as has often been stated throughout this paper, many conservative fundamental, evangelical Christians concur. The true biblicist, due to his world view, merely exercises faith in God's many promises to forever preserve His Word, knowing that somehow both statements must be accurate as well as trustworthy – and so they are.

From viewing the chart, it becomes apparent that the chronicler is referencing the 36 years from the division of the monarchy at which time the Judaic dynasty, of which Asa belongs, began under Rehoboam. Hence, the Hebrew phrase which includes the "reign" of Asa in 2 Chron. 16:1 references the kingdom over which Asa had dominion and is to be understood in the sense of "the kingdom of Asa" (Judah) as distinguished from the Northern Kingdom, *not* the number of years he had occupied the throne in actual reign.[1]

Gleason Archer correctly points out that the Hebrew *"malkuwth"* is used elsewhere in Scripture to denote "realm," "dynasty," or "kingdom," rather than "reign" (2 Chron. 1:1; 11:17; 20:30; Neh. 9:35; Esther 1:14, etc.).[2] Thus it is 36 years from the schism (1 Kings 12, 13) to Baasha's attack on Asa in the 16th year since the latter was enthroned. In addressing Asa's 35th year, the 15th chapter of 2 Chronicles uses the same differentiation.

---

[1] Jewish reckoning agrees; *Seder Olam* (2005) pp. 150-151.

[2] Gleason L. Archer Jr., *Encyclopedia of Bible Difficulties,* (Grand Rapids, MI: Zondervan, 1982), p. 225.

The proof that this interpretation is undeniably correct lies in the fact that it actually resolves two significant chronological problems. First, it completely eliminates the anomalous circumstance in which Baasha otherwise apparently waited 21 entire years before blocking the exodus of his citizens to Judah (2 Chron. 14:1; 15:10,19; and 16:1).

An aftermath of Asa's startling victory over the enormous host of Zerah the Ethiopian was that many of the people of Israel deserted that kingdom for Asa and Judah: "for they fell to him [Asa] out of Israel in abundance, when they saw that the LORD his God was with him" (2 Chron. 15:9). Baasha would certainly have lost little time before taking appropriate measures to insure his borders, thereby halting the southern flow out of Israel.

Zerah's invasion took place in the 15th year of Asa (2 Chron. 15:10, cp. 14:9) or the 35th year of the Kingdom of Judah. Consequently, in the year following the crushing defeat of Zerah (36 years after the kingdom of Judah was born and in the 16th year in which Asa sat upon the throne) Baasha fortified Ramah in order to stop the departure of his citizens. Although all of this is conceded by Thiele,[1] it must be acknowledged that Ussher reached the same conclusion before AD 1650.[2]

Of course the second problem is that the above interpretation removes the absurdity of Baasha's having invaded Judah ten years after his death (cp. 1 Kings 15:33). Not only has all of the Baasha difficulty been resolved, it should be noted as to how much easier the explanation is to follow when one makes use of the visual aid.

2. AHAZIAH'S AGE UPON HIS ACCESSION

The age in which Jehoshaphat's grandson Ahaziah took the throne is another apparent error in Scripture:

> Two and twenty years old *was* Ahaziah when he began to reign; and he reigned one year in Jerusalem. And his mother's name *was* Athaliah, the daughter of Omri king of Israel (2 Kings 8:26).

> Forty and two years old *was* Ahaziah when he began to reign, and he reigned one year in

Jerusalem. His mother's name also *was* Athaliah the daughter of Omri (2 Chron. 22:2).

Ahaziah was 22, not 42 when he became sovereign of Judah. That this is the undeniable case may be seen in the simple fact that Jehoram, Ahaziah's father and predecessor, was 40 years old at the time of his death. This may be seen in that Jehoram was 32 when he ascended to the crown as co-regent with Jehoshaphat and ruled 8 years (32 + 8 = 40; 2 Kings 8:16–17). Obviously a son cannot be 42 when his father is 40 (unless adopted? 2 Chron. 22:9, but we think not), thus 22 is the correct age for Ahaziah; but what of the number 42 as given in 2 Chron. 22:2?

For the non biblicist, the solution is quite simple. The 42 is merely another scribal error where 42 was mistakenly written for 22. Whereby it might seem reasonable that a four could have inadvertently been written for the two, such is simply not the case.

A crucial problem with this rationale is that the Hebrew Text does not give numbers. Instead, the words "forty and two years" and "twenty and two years" are written out and the words for 20 and 40 are considerably different. In Hebrew, 20 is spelled "ain-sin-resh-jod-mem" 40 is written "aleph-resh-beth-ain-jod-mem," a significant difference requiring far more than a mere slip of the pen or blink of the eye on the part of a scribe.

In the first place, the believing biblicist would never have accepted such a solution as his frame of reference begins with a position of faith. Thus he reasons: "As both statements have been faithfully preserved by God to the 'jot and tittle', how can both be true – for they must so be."

The solution for this problem has been given by so many conservative scholars over the years that an attempt at referencing becomes unending. A careful comparison of the two passages reveals that the word "was" is in italics in the Authorized Version (King James) meaning that it is not actually present in the Hebrew Text. The words in italics have been added by the translators in an attempt to make the rendering smoother and clearer. They have so designated to distinguish God's words from man's.

Thus the literal Hebrew idiom reads "a son of 42 years" (very similar to 1 Sam. 13:1 where that "problem" passage translates "a son of one

---

[1] Thiele, *The Mysterious Numbers of the Hebrew Kings, op. cit.,* p. 84.

[2] Ussher, *Annals, op. cit.,* p. 69, 951 BC (1658 ed., p. 43).

year in his reigning") and in so doing, 2 Chron. 22:2 does not demand that Ahaziah be 42 years old upon his ascension. The idiom can only be properly understood in its context. That is, the same expression may be understood differently if the context is not the same.

The solution becomes forthright as a precedence has already been established. Observe that the "problem passage" is in the Book of Chronicles. As stated heretofore, Chronicles was written around five centuries after Kings. Furthermore, as we have seen in the case concerning Baasha, Chronicles recorded an incident and referenced it to the beginning of Asa's dynasty rather than to his actual years of reign. Ahaziah's mother is Athaliah, daughter of Ahab and granddaughter to Omri; hence he is in the direct lineage of both the dynasties of Israel and Judah and moreover is said to be of "the house of Ahab" (2 Chron. 22:3–4).

Now the benefit of a visual display in aiding the seeker to solve the puzzle may be truly appreciated. As one refers to Chart 5 in an attempt to discover the intended context of the Chronicler and remembering that he has used regnal statements with reference to the beginning of Asa's dynasty just prior to this thus establishing a nearby precedent, the solution immediately stands forth. Note that the verse in question calls attention to Omri and it may readily be seen that it is exactly the 42nd year (Judaic reckoning) of the dynasty in Israel which he founded in 929 BC when he slew Zimri.

Thus the sense of Ahaziah's being "a son of 42 years" in his reigning is seen to refer to his being a son of the dynasty of Omri which was in its 42nd year. Putting the two Scriptures together reveals that Ahaziah was 22 years old when he began to reign during the *42nd year of the dynasty of Omri*, of which he is also an integral part.

The point that is being stressed by the Holy Spirit who inspired the Chronicler to so write is that Ahaziah is as much the "son of Omri" as he is "the son of David." Since the Messiah was foretold as being "the son of David" (Mat. 22:42), and not the "son of Omri," Ahaziah's name is deliberately omitted in the official genealogy of Christ Jesus in Mat. 1:8. That is, Ahaziah, his son Joash, and Joash's son Amaziah have been judicially removed by the

Holy Spirit in Matthew due to their relationship to Ahab and Jezebel's wicked daughter, Athaliah.

Her idolatrous influence infected, as it were, the Judaic lineage and these three kings of Judah were all charged with idolatry:

1) Ahaziah, 2 Chron. 22:3–4, the "ways of the house of Ahab";

2) Joash, 2 Chron. 24:17–18;

3) Amaziah, 2 Chronicles 25:14–15, "gods of Edom."

As the sins of the parents are visited to the third and fourth generations (Exo. 20:5, cp. Psa. 109:13–14), three generations are passed over in the register in "cleansing" the Messianic lineage so that Messiah may be said to be the "son of David" and none other. Thus it may be seen that these two Scriptures (2 Chron. 22:2; Mat. 1:8), both long held to be erroneous, actually sustain and explain one another.

If it be doubted that the Holy Spirit's omission of these three names in Matthew 1:8 is deliberate, let the skeptic note that the names of three high priests, (Amariah [Jehoshaphat's], Jehoiada [Athaliah's, etc.], and Zechariah [Joash's]) all of whom officiated during this time frame, are also not found in the official register. Moreover Jehoiada was one of the finest priests since Samuel (2 Chron. 24:16) and yet his name is omitted from the genealogical roll (1 Chron. 6:1–15, cp. Ezra 7:1–5; also see 2 Kings 11:4–19; 12:2; 2 Chron. 22–24).

Jehoiada lived 130 years (2 Chron. 24:15) so he was alive in the days of Rehoboam, perhaps even back to the time of Solomon. He would have reached the age of assuming the full priesthood during the middle of the reign of Asa and was the high priest at the time of Athaliah's overthrow and the installment of little Joash to his rightful throne (2 Chron. 23:8c, 18–20; 24:6).

Why are their names missing? Although a conclusive answer for all three is not known, perhaps it was due in part to their association with several of the monarchs. That notwithstanding, sufficient reasons are to be found related to Jehoiada's having been excluded.

First, it was he who made the plural marriages for young Joash, undoubtedly in an attempt to insure a male heir to David's throne. Such marriages were not only wrong in God's eyes, but by so doing Jehoiada displayed a lack of faith that God himself would perform the promise to David that he would not lack a son who could occupy the throne (2 Sam. 7; Psa. 89:19–37).

In addition, Jehoiada, for unexplained cause, was not diligent in obeying the king's orders to raise funds and repair the Temple which had suffered damage at the hands of the sons of Athaliah and Jehoram (2 Chron. 24:7), a deed for which they lost their lives (2 Chronicles 21:16–17). Especially in his position as high priest, Jehoiada's delay was an affront both to Joash and the Lord. After being reproved by Joash, Jehoiada did repent and actively pursued the king's wishes (2 Kings 12:4–16; 2 Chron. 24:4–14).

Lastly, it is also possible that, in deference to Jehoshaphat, Jehoiada may have performed the marriage of Jehoram to Athaliah – if indeed such ceremonies were required to be discharged by the Hebrew priests at that period. Though Jehoram can in no way be conceived as having been a man of God, this marriage between the Baal worshiping family of Ahab to the dynasty supposedly committed to Jehovah was opposed, at least in principle, to the many scriptural instances which teach against such an unequal yoke. Through this union Jehoshaphat apparently hoped to secure the peace and eventually reunite the divided kingdom, but this attempt in the wisdom of the flesh proved disastrous for his realm.

In any event, by his omission, the Lord showed that He was no respecter of the person of men and that even the names of godly high priests would be removed in order to underscore God's displeasure with some of their deeds. The fact that three high priests' names are found to be omitted over the same general time frame as that of the three missing monarchs in Matthew 1:8 must be viewed by all honest students of Scripture as more than mere coincidence. Such must be seen as confirming the affirmed deliberate nature of the happenstance found in Matthew.

Finally, to any who may still harbor doubt over this matter, the converse is there, still

confronting him and requiring a responsible explanation. That is, whereas he may continue discounting the validity of the 2 Chron. 22:2 passage, the undeniable awkward fact glares back at him from the chart – it just happens to be precisely 42 years from Ahaziah's enthronement back to the commencement of his maternal great grandfather's dynasty. Is not this more than an unhappy circumstance to be brushed aside as meaningless, and does it not enjoin the deepest reflection by all lettered men of integrity?

3. THE JEHOAHAZ-JEHOASH CONNECTION

A difficulty is often perceived in relation to Jehoahaz, king of Israel, and his son Jehoash. The problem arises because Jehoahaz is said to (1) succeed his father Jehu on the throne in the 23rd year of Joash, king of Judah (2 Kings 13:1), and (2) reign 17 years; yet Jehoash is said to have begun reigning in the 37th year of King Joash of Judah, and continued for 16 years (2 Kings 13:10). The enigma is compounded by the fact that Joash is said to have ruled over the Southern Kingdom 40 years, being followed by his son Amaziah in the 2nd year of Jehoash of Israel (2 Kings 12:1, cp. 2 Kings 14:1; Chart 5).

However contradictory all of this appears, when the triangulation formula is applied and the data diagrammed, the problem is quickly resolved. A small three-year gap appears between the long side opposite the base and the short third side of the triangle indicating that Jehoahaz installed Jehoash as his pro-rex during the 37th year of Joash. After a term of nearly three years of so functioning, Jehoahaz died leaving the throne to Jehoash who continued 16 years as sole rex.

The distinction between the positions of pro-rex and co-rex is significant in that a pro-rex does not possess the broader authority and powers of a co-regent. A further distinction which naturally follows is that years served in the capacity as co-regent are included along with the years served in the capacity of sole rex in reckoning the total term of reign whereas the years passed as merely a pro-rex are not.

An example of the former is that of Jehoshaphat's son Jehoram who is credited with an eight-year tenure even though about half of it was served as a co-regent with his

father and only about four years as sole rex (2 Kings 8:16–17).

The latter (pro-rex) may be seen in regard to this same Jehoram as he is also said to have been placed in some royal capacity during the 17th year of Jehoshaphat; yet this undisclosed term is not added to his total (2 Kings 1:17, cp. 1 Kings 22:51). This action was necessitated due to Syrian incursions originating from the strategically located fortress city of Ramoth-gilead on the eastern border of the Northern Kingdom which had been taken some three years earlier and/or due to Jehoshaphat's preoccupation with his shipbuilding venture at Ezion-geber at the north end of the eastern arm of the Red Sea (modern Gulf of Aqaba near Elath) with Ahaziah of Israel who was serving as co-regent with his father Ahab that year.

The following year, Jehoshaphat agreed to join Ahab in retaking Ramoth-gilead from Ben-hadad (II), the king of Syria. The battle itself took place in Jehoshaphat's 18th regnal year at which time Ahab was slain by a Syrian arrow (1 Kings 22:1–40).

Jehoram's son, Ahaziah of Judah, provides us with a clear uncluttered example of this principle. Two verses associate Ahaziah with the throne, one in the 11th year of Joram, the crowned head of Israel (2 Kings 9:29), whereas the other does so in Joram's 12th year (2 Kings 8:25, Chart 5); yet Ahaziah is said to have only reigned one official year (2 Kings 8:26). Thiele interprets this anomaly as follows:[1]

> The introduction of nonacccession-year reck-oning into Judah at this time explains the seemingly contradictory synchronisms for the accession of Ahaziah in Judah: ... The first synchronism [the 11th year of Joram] is in accord with the former accession-year system, while the second [Joram's 12th year] is in accord with the newly adopted nonaccession-year method (author's brackets).

However this hardly seems the correct explanation, for Joram's 11th year is concurrent with the 7th of Judah's Jehoram; it is difficult to envision reckoning that year as having been designated Ahaziah's accession year when his father was still alive and did not expire until the succeeding year. As earlier described, the

accession year is the last year of the deceased former monarch during which a new sovereign mounts the throne but attributes that entire year to his predecessor's regime.

Therefore the proper answer is that in his 7th year (the 11th year of Joram the son of Ahab) Jehoram, being grievously ill with an incurable disease in his bowels with which God had stricken him during the last two years of his life (2 Chron. 21:15, 18–19), made Ahaziah his pro-rex, not his co-regent. The proof of this lies in the fact that had Ahaziah been named co-regent, this year would have been credited to him along with Jehoram's 8th, and he would thus have been said to have worn the crown two years instead of only one.

In 886 BC, the second year of his sickness which was also the eighth year of his reign, wicked Jehoram died and Ahaziah became king. Invoking his kingly prerogative, Ahaziah chose to reckon his regnal years by the non-accession method and thus claimed the year in which his father died as his own first (and last) official year. Jotham of Judah and now also Jehoash of Israel are seen as further examples of a period of pro-regency in which the years so served are not added to the years of sole reign. Since the years as pro-rex are not counted, the official years of reign and the term of sole reign are one and the same.

4. THE JEROBOAM (II) DILEMMA

Another commonly reported contradiction in the biblical text is that concerning the synchroniza-tion involving the reigns of Amaziah and Uzziah (Azariah) of Judah as compared to that of Jeroboam (II) of Israel. This perception arises as a result of Amaziah's being credited with a 29-year rule (2 Kings 14:1–2) followed by the statement that Jeroboam (II) began his 41-year reign in Amaziah's 15th (2 Kings 14:23). So far so good, for this precisely fits with the 16th and final year of Jehoash, Jeroboam's father and immediate predecessor.

The triangle closes with the testimony that Amaziah of Judah lived 15 years after the death of Jehoash, son of Jehoahaz of Israel (2 Kings 14:17). As the base is that of 29 years and the two arms of 15 each totals 30, these seemingly antagonistic results simply reveal that a non-accession relationship existed between the

---

[1] Thiele, *The Mysterious Numbers of the Hebrew Kings*, op. cit., p. 38.

regimes of Jehoash and his son Jeroboam (II) (Chart 5).

Were that all the data to consider the problem would thus have been resolved; however such is not the case for the scriptural record goes on to add that Uzziah (Azariah) began to reign over the Southern Kingdom at age 16 in the 27th year of Jeroboam (II) and continued in his post for 52 years (2 Kings 15:1–2). Unhappily, from the previous scriptural determination which fixed the first year of Jeroboam at 825 BC, the 27th year of Jeroboam's dominion falls not on Uzziah's first official year but at his *12th*. This disturbing result causes nearly all modern scholars to hurl anathemas against the 2 Kings 15:1–2 passage as 2 Kings 14:17 which assigned 15 years to Amaziah after the death of his antagonist, King Jehoash of Israel, is confirmed by the Chronicler (2 Chron. 25:25).

Once again, the biblicist merely stands firm knowing that both Scriptures are true, and a reasonable way to reconcile them must exist. To reject this position denies and demeans God's promises to preserve His Word. Once this is done, it leaves open to the subjective whim of man the depraved notion that he has the right to select which Scripture should be accepted and which rejected. Such is an open-ended argument and, being the wrong path to follow, neither will ever be acknowledged as fully resolved by either side nor even a consensus reached within the respective camps.

Whereas the author does not pretend to *know* the true historic details with regard to the question, several viable answers are available which do not violate any of the known facts and at the same time allow one to honor the testimony of all of the Scriptures involved. Three solutions are offered and displayed on the chart.

It is most significant to note that whichever of the three is correct, or accepted as so, the relative chronological positions and dates of all the kings involved do not change. As resolving the problem does not rely upon any of the admittedly somewhat subjective judgments, the chronology is independent of the solution and stands correct.

The first and very probably correct answer is that which has been offered many times in the past, yet without just cause steadfastly rejected by liberal and secular scholarship alike. Namely, that upon Jehoash's going to face the Syrians in a war in which he overthrew Ben-hadad (III) in three pitched battles and recovered out of his hands the cities which his father (Jehoahaz) had lost to Hazael (Ben-hadad's father), he placed Jeroboam (II) as pro-rex over the government.[1]

A second explanation is that when young Uzziah ascended the throne, he inherited a kingdom in dire circumstances from his father, Amaziah, who had not only been soundly defeated by Jehoash of Israel in open battle, but had been captured and brought back in shame to Jerusalem by that northern monarch (2 Kings 14:8–14; 2 Chron. 25:17–24). Jehoash added to this humiliation by making an approximately 200-yard breach in the wall of Jerusalem, plundering all the treasure in the Temple and Amaziah's house, and returned to Samaria with hostages thereby reducing Judah to vassalage, or at least nearly so, under the Kingdom of Israel.

Thus the 2 Kings 15:1 passage could be understood to mean that in Jeroboam's 27th year an older maturing Uzziah finally succeeded in strengthening himself and his kingdom to the point in which he was able to break out from under the heavy hand of the Northern Kingdom (cp. 2 Chron. 26:15b) and from thence govern as indisputable sovereign.

A third possible solution is that 2 Kings 15:1–2, which mentions Uzziah's age as being 16 years upon his enthronement, is also giving forth Jeroboam's age at that occasion so that the year of his birth may likewise be ascertained. Other possibilities may also be uncovered, but for now these three must be seen as not only feasible but far superior to the capricious casting aside of any verse containing data causing difficulty.

It is simply unworthy of chronologists and scholars to resolve chronological problems by such a practice. This is even more especially true when the anomaly has practicable conceivable solutions as demonstrated in this instance.

[1] This solution goes back at least as far as AD 1650 when Ussher first published his chronology in Latin under the title *Annales Veteris et Novi Testamenti*, see: Ussher, *Annals, op. cit.*, p. 73, 836 BC (1658 ed., p. 52).

5. THE ZACHARIAH QUANDARY

Still another issue is that associated with the reign of Zachariah, son and successor of King Jeroboam (II) of Israel. Uzziah had come to the throne of Judah following 29 years under the government of Amaziah, his father, in the 15th year of Jeroboam (II) (2 Kings 14:1–2; cp. 14:23 and 14:17, also Chart 5). Jeroboam (II) brought the Northern Kingdom to its zenith, holding governmental authority 41 years which would have ended in the 26th year of Uzziah (2 Kings 14:23–29).

The problem arises when the Scriptures continue by saying that Zachariah reigned 6 months over Israel and was assassinated during the 38th year of Uzziah. This seems to require an interregnum of about 11 and a half years. Such could have been due to an anarchy resulting from a power struggle upon the death of Jeroboam (II), especially if he had failed to name his successor. Of course, as formerly noted, the term "interregnum" is not actually mentioned here by the Scripture although the data seems to require one.

Again, though known to have occurred from time to time throughout the history of various empires, interregna are not generally palatable to the scholar's taste. This is all the more true here since the word does not appear within the account; hence most moderns are certain that an error of some kind must surely be present with regard to the data germane to Zachariah.

For the biblicist no real problem is seen, for throughout history, multiple assassinations of top leaders and interregna have often been signs that a regime was in its death throes. As Israel is undeniably at that threshold, resolving the issue by placing an interregnum between Jeroboam (II) and Zachariah is not only an acceptable resolution – it may well be the historical fact. However, it is not the only biblical possibility. Although this author is not certain whether or not the answer originated with Dolen, that analyst has offered the following interesting and attractive solution:[1]

> Zachariah reigned 6 months and then was killed ... in the last 6 months of Azariah's [Uzziah] 38th year ... This 6 months was the first 6 months of his would be 12th year [of reign]. ... Note: the total years of Zachariah's

reign is not mentioned in the Bible (author's brackets).

Upon reading this concise unsupported declaration, the present author was thunderstruck by its possibilities and immediately began to investigate to see whether scriptural verification was possible. Significantly, an imperceptible clue was uncovered which gives credibility to Dolen's assertion that Zachariah actually ascended the throne of Israel immediately following Jeroboam's death and maintained that position for 12 years unto the 38th year of Uzziah (Azariah), king of Judah.

The clue is that the verses describing the time of enthronement of all of the kings mentioned in the proximity of Zachariah's brief account include the single word "began" as in "began to reign" *but* not so with Zachariah (2 Kings 12:1; 2 Kings 13:1, and vs. 10; 2 Kings 14:1, cp. 2 Chronicles 25:1; 2 Kings 14:23; 2 Kings 15:1; 2 Kings 15:7, compare verse 32; 2 Kings 15:13, 17, 23, 27; 2 Kings 16:1; 2 Kings 17:1; 2 Kings 18:1, etc.)!

> And Jeroboam slept with his fathers, even with the kings of Israel; and Zachariah his son reigned in his stead (2 Kings 14:29).

> In the thirty and eighth year of Azariah king of Judah did Zachariah the son of Jeroboam reign over Israel in Samaria six months (2 Kings 15:8).

As can be seen, in stark contrast to all of the other monarchs listed in the above cited Scriptures there is no "began" associated with any of the verses concerning Zachariah's reign. Thus the justified conclusion may be reached that 2 Kings 15:8 is not speaking of the total length of his regime but rather is merely giving the data for establishing the *termination* of both his personal reign and that of the Jehuic dynasty (see 2 Kings 10:30), which had its prophetic duration fulfilled in Zachariah (2 Kings 15:12). If this be the actual case, his ascension would have been assumed by the Author of the Holy Writ to be understood as having directly followed his father to the throne after his death during his 41st year. This find should be regarded worthy of due consideration as the likely answer to this heretofore unsettled question by all interested parties regardless of world view. We await the reaction of academia with hopeful anticipation of a favorable reception.

---

[1] Dolen, *The Chronology Papers, op. cit.*, p. 13.

H. THE ASSYRIAN EPONYM LIST

One of the great problems in biblical chronology is that of converting Bible dates (i.e.: *Anno Mundi* = year of the world) to years BC. This is accomplished by establishing with certainty a point (or points) of contact between the history of the Hebrews and that of some other nation whose chronology is known to the extent that it will render an absolute date at the contact(s). The record of Scripture contains such points of definite contact with the Assyrian and the Neo-Babylonian empires during the period of the divided Hebrew monarchies.

Most scholars believe that the chronologies for these two nations are firmly determined, at least for this span. Other nations such as Egypt also came in touch with the kingdoms of Judah and Israel during this time frame, but the chronologies of these are not yet fully established.

Today, the Assyrian chronology for this span is especially accepted as being absolute. The reason for this is due to the practice utilized by the Assyrians in recording their years.[1] Each year was individually named to honor a significant person within the government. The person is the *eponym* (or limmu) holding the office for a given year and historical events or documents in Assyria were usually dated in terms of these men's names. Normally, the king would be honored as *limmu* during the first full year of his reign. He would usually be succeeded by a high official in the court; first the Tartan or commander-in-chief of the army (2 Kings 18:17; Isa. 20:1), who would be followed in succession by the grand vizier (Rab-shakeh, Isa. 36:2, 4, 11–13, etc.), chief musician, chief eunuch, and then the governor of a city or province.

Between the years 859 to 703 BC, an outstanding event or activity occurring during that particular eponymous year would follow in the second column after the man's name for whom the year was assigned. Thus, if we have a complete list of eponyms, we have a list of successive years in Assyrian history.

In AD 1846, Sir Henry Rawlinson, the famous British Assyriologist, discovered among the inscribed cuneiform terra cotta tablets four copies of the Assyrian Eponym Canon (list) which had been recovered by Austen Layard at Nineveh. He designated the four as Canons I, II, III and IV. Covering the period from 911 BC according to Assyrian reckoning (actual date = 956 BC) to 659 BC, Canon I is the foremost and standard copy. Canon II extended from 893 (Assyrian, actual = 938 BC) to 692, III from 792 BC (Assyrian, actual = 837 BC) to 649, and IV from 753 BC (Assyrian, actual = 798 BC) to 701. None of these lists is perfect for the entire period, each being broken in places.

Since then, other fragments of Canon I have been found as well as many additional fragmentary copies. Some contain but a few names; others catalogue several hundred. Often where one tablet may be broken, the missing name or names may be supplied from the other lists such that a single composite[2] of the annual eponyms has been constructed for the period from 1030 BC (Assyrian, actual = c. 1075 BC) to 648 BC (see Appendix G, page 281 ff.).

The composite list is then synchronized with the King List found in the 1932/33 excavations at Khorsabad,[3] the ancient capital of Sargon II, and the SDAS King List. These two registers are practically identical, except that the SDAS ends with the names of Tiglath-pileser (III) (18 years, 745–727 BC) and Shalmaneser IV (V) (5 years, 727–722 BC). The Khorsabad List bears an inscription which states that it was copied from a king list in the city of Ashur in the eighth year of Tiglath-pileser (III) (738 BC) during the second eponymy of Adad-bel-ukin.

As the King List very closely approximates the number of names between the kings listed among the eponyms, a fairly close synchronization between most of the data is achieved which leads the majority of scholars to conclude that the problems are minor and almost inconsequential. However, as we shall presently see, such is an illusion and a deception.

---

[1] George S. Goodspeed, *A History of the Babylonians and Assyrians*, (Cambridge, MA: University Press, 1902), pp. 40–42.

---

[2] Daniel David Luckenbill, *Ancient Records of Assyria and Babylonia* [hereafter designated *ARAB*], (New York: Greenwood Press, 1968), vol. II, sec. 1197–1198, pages 430–438.

[3] Pritchard, *ANET*, op. cit., pp. 564–566.

It will be noted in the preceding paragraph that two Roman numeral designations have been assigned to some of the Assyrian monarchs. This is because a conflict exists among the works of various Assyriologists as to the number of Assyrian monarchs bearing the same name. In general, the older works give the numerical value outside the parentheses.

Thus, when consulting the older studies the reader will find "Shalmaneser II", but the works after AD 1912[1] designate him as "Shalmaneser III". To circumvent the confusion, he is herein designated "Shalmaneser II (III)". However, even this attempt to allay the confusion by always placing the modern Assyrian school's assignments in parentheses falls short of its intended goal as all scholars do not uniformly follow the above conventions.

1. THE ECLIPSE OF BUR-SAGALE

There now arises the problem of assigning precise dates to each of the eponyms. The prevailing position is that this has been solved by the footnote accompanying the eponym of Bur-Sagale which states that an eclipse of the sun took place in the month of June. Astronomical computations yielding a Julian calendar date of 15 June, 763 have become widely accepted for this event (Gregorian = 7 June 763 BC). Hence, with the year of the eponymy of Bur-Sagale "established," one merely assigns BC dates in both directions from that foundation. Based upon these Assyrian lists, nearly all Assyriologists consider the matter firmly settled from 1030–648 BC.

2. THE CANON OF PTOLEMY

The Canon of Claudius Ptolemy (AD 70–161) is utilized to check the accuracy of the eponyms from 747–648 BC. Over 80 solar, lunar and planetary positions are recorded and dated by this astronomer in his *Almagest*. Thus, Ptolemy's Canon gives much precise data beginning at 747 BC and as the Assyrian Eponym Canon goes down to 648 BC, an overlap of a century exists between the two.

[1] The year C.H.W. Johns published his book *Ancient Assyria,* in which he made known new findings regarding earlier kings bearing the same names as those already known. The Assyrian king dates given on the charts and in the text of this dissertation are those adopted by E.A. Wallis Budge in his *Annals of the Kings of Assyria,* (London: BM, 1902).

This overlapping allows the two works to serve as a check one upon the other.

Hence, for most investigators the entire matter is settled. For them, the Assyrian records are absolute and all other national chronologies for the period in question must be made to conform to whatever mold is imposed upon them by the Assyrian data. Although it seems so facile and tidy, is it an accurate portrayal of the actual history and is such unqualified trust warranted?

3. ASSYRIAN INCONSISTENCIES

With regard to these eponyms, a truly strange phenomena is encountered. When one gleans the reference material readily available to the typical reader, the glaring overstatements relative to their reliability as though no significant problems or uncertainties exist become a matter of major concern for such is not an accurate presentation of the facts.

For example, the Assyrian Eponym Canon has 33 eponyms assigned to Tiglath-pileser (II) but the Assyrian King List ascribes to him only 32 years. By the number of eponyms between King Tukulti-urta (II) and King Ashur-nasir-apli, the eponym lists assign Tukulti-urta a six-year reign, yet the Assyrian King List gives him a seven-year reign. This suggests that a name has been *removed* from the eponym register.

Moreover, on one eponym list an extra eponym — Balatu — is supplied as compared to three other lists that cover the period. Either the first list is correct and the others have omitted Balatu or the three are correct necessitating a clarification as to why the name has been inserted on the first. The first list reads:

788 Sil-Ishtar	785 Marduk-shar-usur
787 Balatu	784 Nabu-shar-usur
786 Adad-uballit	783 Ninurta-nasir

The other three lists contain the following sequence:

787 Sil-Ishtar	784 Marduk-shar-usur
786 Nabu-shar-usur	783 Ninurta-nasir
785 Adad-uballit	

It should be noted that the first list not only contains the additional name, Balatu, but the name Nabu-shar-usur is discordant. It appears

in a different sequence than on the other registers.

There is a discrepancy involving an incursion into "Hatte" which is associated with the eponym Daian-assur (Assyrian dating = 853 BC). The Assyrian Eponym List places this event in the sixth year of the reign of Shalmaneser II (III) whereas the Black Obelisk Inscription places the eponymy of Daian-assur in the fourth year of Shalmaneser.[1] Further, the eponym of Naidi-ili is listed twice in the annals of Tukulti-urta II[2] but is not found on the Assyrian Eponym Canon. The Assyrian King List gives Adad-nirari (III) a reign of 28 years, yet the Eponym Canon records 29 names. Also, there are several gaps in which a number of names have been lost.

Moreover, the June 15, 763 BC date for the eclipse of Bur-Sagale has been challenged several times in the past. Some have fixed this solar phenomena as that of June 24, 791; others identified it with the eclipse of June 13, 809.[3]

It is neither the purpose of this endeavor to attempt identifying the eclipse nor undertaking the solving of any aforementioned problems with regard to the Assyrian Eponym registers. We merely note them and are amazed at how lightly they are passed over by most modern Assyriologist as well as other scholars. For the most part, they contemplate these problems as amounting to no more than that of whether the so-called "long chronology" or the "short chronology" is the correct solution – a difference of but one year in the entire Assyrian scheme. Moreover, after assuring us that no evidence exists of any type break in the Eponym Canon, particularly during the eighth century BC,[4] Edwin R. Thiele goes on to state:[5]

It will be noted that this accord between the chronological evidence provided by the lengths of reign of the Assyrian kings for this period and of the names on the limmu lists makes utterly untenable the postulation of a gap in the eponym canon, for it is in this period that the existence of such a gap has been proposed.

We take great issue with Thiele's comment that there is no evidence indicating a break in the Assyrian Eponym List. Thiele's chronology tortures and contorts the Hebrew record in order to make it fit the Assyrian framework. In so doing, many clear forthright Scriptures suffer violence.

Apparently, for Thiele, the Scriptures fall into the category of being "no evidence" for they do much protest against the current Assyrian interpretations. It is obvious from the cited quote Thiele never considered that an official decree issued by a new monarch (perhaps as the founder of a new dynasty) wishing to obliterate a predecessor(s) would necessitate not only removing the name of that king from all chronicles, inscriptions, etc. but the names of the limmu within his reign as well.

Indeed, such limmu represents the names of men associated with the hated predecessor, hence loyal and usually supportive of his views and goals. Both the newly copied resulting king list and Eponym Canon would contain an absolutely indistinguishable gap, almost incapable of detection. Only by some reference among the records of neighboring countries might the deleted monarch escape historical obliteration.

Nor is it an altogether unfamiliar circumstance to find the removal of all reference to past rulers from the history of a nation. Such events are well documented in antiquity. For example as mentioned previously, Thutmose III had the name of his co-regent aunt, Queen Hatshepsut, obliterated from all the Egyptians records. We know of her only through the annals of other kingdoms which came into contact with Egypt during that period.

Such confidence and faith in the Assyrian data is all the more puzzling when one considers that the single addition of "Cainan" to the genealogical list recorded in Luke 3:36 causes liberals and even staunch conservatives to call into

[1] Luckenbill, *ARAB, op. cit.,* vol. I, sec. 610, pp. 222–223; see also sec. 561, p. 202.

[2] A.K. Pritchard, *Assyrian Royal Inscriptions* [Hereafter denoted *ARI*], (Wiesbaden, Germany: Otto Harrassowitz, 1972), vol. II, sec. 469, p. 101; sec. 483, p. 105.

[3] Thiele, *The Mysterious Numbers of the Hebrew Kings, op. cit.,* footnote 3, p. 69 and George Smith, *Assyrian Eponym Canon,* (London: Oxford UP, 1875), p. 4ff.

[4] Thiele, *The Mysterious Numbers of the Hebrew Kings, op. cit.,* footnote p. 75.

[5] *Ibid.*

question the validity of the strict chronology interpretation of the 11th chapter of Genesis.

The Assyrian data has been noted as having the aforementioned uncertainties, yet it is viewed by most modern scholars as not being capable of a disparity of more than a single year over the entire 382-year span from 1030 to 648 BC. The Bible, on the other hand, has but one departure between the registers in Luke chapter 3 and the 11th chapter of Genesis and yet it is seen as a totally disqualifying consequence. Does not this strike our reader as being that of a double standard to say the very least?

4. THE FACTS EXPOSED

As hundreds of these ancient chronicles in their actual unedited form came under the focus of this analysis, this writer was shocked, not only by the overall marred condition of the vast majority of the relevant data but by the extensive amount of unsubstantiated filling in of words, names, phrases, clauses, etc. that had been added by the various translators. Some seemed justifiable but others, flights of a most fertile imagination. Yet when published, quotes and even extended quotes taken from these records are usually presented without any qualifying parenthesis, brackets or the like and thus the reader is not made aware of the often loose and expanded liberties made during translation.

Much of the supposed "translation" consists of an interpretation laced with conjecture, creative imagination, paraphrase and that often based upon preconceived ideas of the editor. This is especially true with regard to nearly all materials written for laymen, secular or Christian, and even pastors. Indeed, for the most part, only a relatively small esoteric group of scholars are cognizant of such information, thus becoming the "trade secret" of the elite. Several examples will be given presently so that the reader may judge for himself.

The undeniable reality is that the history of Assyria and Babylonia, although sometimes giving detailed dates, exists only in a mutilated condition with no continuous chronology. This fact cannot be overstated. This is especially true with regard to the time traverse in question.

Even the "history" of Assyria is highly interpretive, subjective and contradictory. This fact is not readily apparent when one peruses standard reference materials which usually describe a rather straightforward flowing albeit abbreviated account over the span from c. 900 to c. 605 BC. However, careful scrutiny reveals much conjecture and many gross discrepancies between the various accounts. For example, one reference source[1] relates that near the end of Shalmaneser's II (III) reign, his eldest son revolted against him. The revolt is said to have been put down by his second son, Shamshi-Adad (V), who succeeded his father on the throne.

Continuing, we read that Shamshi-Adad died young and his widow, Sammuramat (Semiramis), assumed control until their son, Adad-nirari (III) came of age.[2] The encyclopedia continues stating that "Assyria made little real advance" under Adad-nirari's rule. It concludes in stating that he died young without issue thus creating a problem over his successor. Other sources mention the revolt but make no mention of Sammuramat or Adad-nirari's being so young upon his accession.

Yet another general source[3] has nothing to say of the revolt but states that under the leadership of three great warrior-kings the Assyrians again secured their northern and eastern frontiers, reached the Mediterranean Sea on the west and penetrated Babylonia. The three great warrior-kings are listed as having been Ashur-nasir-pal (II), Shalmaneser II (III) and *Adad-nirari* (III)! Some of these statements will seem all the more ambiguous before this pericope is concluded. Numerous other examples could be cited but as the point has been made, we refrain.

No history of any ancient peoples is even minutely comparable to the detailed and flowing continuous record of the Hebrew

---

[1] *The Zondervan Pictorial Encyclopedia of the Bible,* Merrill C. Tenney General Editor, (Grand Rapid, MI: Zondervan, 1978), vol. I, p. 376.

[2] J. Oppert, *Chronologie des Assyriens et des Babyloniens,* (1857). According to Dr. Oppert, she controlled the Empire alone for 17 years.

[3] *Collier's Encyclopaedia,* (New York: Macmillan Pub. Co., 1981), vol. III, p. 428.

witness nor is there any nation of antiquity other than that of the Hebrews whose annals record their military defeats. The force of these facts cannot be overly emphasized. They transcend all miraculous and religious overtones which some could otherwise perceive as adequate reason for disqualifying or lessening their testimony, explicitly attesting to the preeminent integrity of the Bible.

It becomes painfully apparent that were it not for the religious and spiritual overtones of that witness, no clear thinking unbiased scholar would ever set aside its testimony in favor of the extant, yet fragmented and disfigured, data of the various countries contiguous to the Hebrew nation. Indeed, few seem aware of these circumstances.

Moreover, it seems to be a requirement for acceptance as a peer among those involved in such investigations that they play down the accuracy of the Hebrew testimony while extolling that of not only the Assyrian, but any other record than that of the people of the Word. The desire to obtain such recognition is a most powerful, intimidating and driving force. This pressure, acting in concert with the aforementioned presuppositions, must be seen as that pall which overshadows not only the area under discussion but all other related fields as well. Christian and secular inquirers alike seem unable to stand free of this ever compelling vortex.

Here then is unmistakable proof of the lack of an objective dispassionate approach to biblical related research. We find not the slightest evidence of any "neutral" approach. Of a truth, the unprejudiced mind would without controversy never overthrow the lucid historical data embedded in the pages of Scripture for the other stale fragmented crumbs as is the vogue in today's so-called "scholarly" cliques. This is not to say this data is valueless and devoid of merit. Its testimony deserves a hearing but is not worthy of its current place on the bench.

5. MORE EPONYMOUS INCONSISTENCIES

Nor is our list of aforementioned problems concerning the composite Assyrian Eponym List exhaustive. There are other particulars, regardless of whether due to tampering or simple error, which cast doubt and uncertainty with respect to their being unconditionally unblemished. To mention but a few, we note the following:

857	Shulman-asharid	king of Ashur (Shalmaneser)
856	Ashur-bel-ukin	field marshal
855	Ashur-bunaia-usur	chief cupbearer

as compared to:

827	Shulman-asharidu	king of Ashur (Shalmaneser)
826	Daian-Assur	field marshal
825	Ashur-bunaia-usur	chief cupbearer

There is a most conspicuous similarity between the two triads yet they are presumably separated by thirty years. First, each trio begins with the same king's name save the additional "u" at the end of the latter. We note that the titles are in the same usual descending order: king, field marshal and chief cupbearer.

Although the second names are not identical (not uncommon with regard to Assyrian personal names relating to the same individual) "Ashur" is part of both names. In and of itself, this would seem inconsequential were it not for the fact that both the third name and title are identical. Hence, we find an "Ashur" twice sandwiched between two men bearing the same name and titles – the titles of both triumvirates being in the same descending progression.

This highly suspicious condition bristles with most disturbing possibilities for the promoters of an invincible, certain Assyrian chronology. Are these really different kings, we wonder? Could not these be the same king and an abbreviated repetition with names missing from the earlier part of the Canon?

We also observe that the name "Nabu-shar-usur," which appeared in our first listing on page 146, is found not only at the year 786, but also 104 years earlier at 682 BC. Of course they could be different men who merely happen to have precisely the same name, but we wonder. This is especially true since we also note other such cases as a "Tab-bel" at both 859 BC and 762 and an "Urta-ilia" at 863, 837, 801, 736 and 722.

Obviously, these cannot all be one and the same person but as it is rare for men to have the exact same names, we ponder whether these represent in some cases different men or flaws – and precisely how one is to be certain in each instance? Indeed, is it not curious or at least

noteworthy that after Sennacherib's reign, neither Esarhaddon nor Ashur-banipal, the succeeding monarchs, are found among the eponyms.

Thus, it has been demonstrated that the Assyrian Eponym Canon is fraught with uncertainties and is not the solid unquestioned foundation upon which to base all other chronologies as is published and proclaimed by today's scholars in nearly all quarters.

6. TAMPERING COMMONPLACE

Inexplicably, the defenders of the Assyrian evidence often lament its inconsistencies and the fact that there exists obvious indication of its having been altered. Faulstich cites many such corruptions. For example, he concludes that the reason for the discrepancy between the activity during the Daian-assur eponym, listed as occurring in Shalmaneser's fourth year on the Black Obelisk Inscription but said to have transpired in his sixth on the Monolith Inscription, is because Shalmaneser "stole" the Monolith Inscription from his father, Ashur-nasir-pal (II).[1] That is, Faulstich accuses Shalmaneser II (III) of removing his father's name along with the eponym years coinciding with his father's reign from the Monolith Inscription, placing his own name in its stead along with eponymous persons into the text to parallel his first six years.

Whereas most of the information contained on the Black Obelisk is apparently correctly attributable to Shalmaneser II (III), there also are appalling indications of forgery. For example, an inscription over a relief catalogs animals received as tribute from Africa[2] yet there is no evidence documenting that he extended his sphere of influence that far south. Moreover, a near identical inventory has been found on the "Broken Obelisk" in which the animals were presented to King Ashur-bel-kala, c. 150 (Assyrian = 200) years previously, hence Shalmaneser has apparently claimed for himself tribute belonging to a former monarch.[3]

It is well known and accepted by most Assyriologists that a significant number of the

inscriptions claimed by Tiglath-pileser (III) deal with events that precede his reign. A mutilated brick inscription states that he is the son of Adad-nirari (III), however, the Assyrian King List makes Tiglath-pileser (III) the son of Ashur-nirari (V), son of Adad-nirari (III).[4] This is quite a discrepancy for the King List places Adad-nirari III four monarchs before Tiglath-pileser's reign and depicts Ashur-nirari (V) as both his father and immediate predecessor upon the throne. The List goes on to relate that Shalmaneser III (IV), and Ashur-dan III (III) were brothers, being the sons of Adad-nirari (III). Ashur-nirari (V) is also said to be a son of Adad-nirari (III), implying brotherhood with Shalmaneser III (IV), and Ashur-dan III (III).

The Assyrian records contain very little information concerning Adad-nirari (III) and nothing about Shalmaneser III (IV) or Ashur-dan III (III). Significantly, an alabaster stele was discovered in 1894 at Tell Abta displaying the name Tiglath-pileser imprinted over that of Shalmaneser (IV), a successor of Adad-nirari (III) and the third sovereign prior to Tiglath-pileser (III).[5] This find coupled with the aforementioned absence of information relative to Shalmaneser III (IV) and Ashur-dan III (III) strongly implies that Tiglath-pileser was a usurper to the throne and that he destroyed the records of his three immediate predecessors — Ashur-nirari (V), Shalmaneser III (IV), and Ashur-dan III (III).

No less Assyrian authority than Daniel David Luckenbill, commenting on the brick inscription, was led to pen .".. whether we err in ascribing these texts to Tiglath-pileser III is still to be determined."[6] Again we note that the Assyrian evidence is lacking the towering degree of reliability generally ascribed to it. We do not mean to suggest that all such records should be counted as unworthy of merit, but intend to underscore with what great prudence and skepticism their testimony should be regarded when unsupported by other certified

---

[1] Faulstich, *History, Harmony and the Hebrew Kings, op. cit.*, pp. 153–154.

[2] Luckenbill, *ARAB, op. cit.*, vol. 1, sec. 591, p. 211.

[3] Grayson, *ARI, op. cit.*, sec. 248, p. 55.

[4] Pritchard, *ANET, op. cit.*, p. 566)

[5] *Ibid.*, vol. 1 sec. 824, p. 295.

[6] Luckenbill, *ARAB, op. cit.*, vol. 1 sec. 822, pp. 294–295.

historical data. Pertaining to this subject, Dr. Thiele candidly admits:[1]

> Every Assyriologist knows that Assyrian inscriptions are not always reliable in all details. The account given in one place may vary from that found in another place. An achievement of one king may be claimed by his successor. The specific details of a victory reported in one year may grow in magnitude and splendor in the reports of succeeding years. The fact that Sargon claimed to have captured Samaria does not prove that he did so.

Is it not most incongruous that in light of so explicit an admission, the eminent Doctor along with nearly all modern scholars not only follows the Assyrian data to the near exclusion of all others, but wholeheartedly endorses its chronological implications allowing possible no more error than that of a single year? Does not this contradict all logic and common sense? All fair minded men, secular or Christian, should wonder with great amazement how it is that such well educated, informed intellectuals can so continue. Were it not so obvious, we would answer herewith. Presently we shall as we may forbear only so long.

We have not exhausted the matter as though these were the only imaginable faults to which the data regarding these two monarchs may be called into question for other Assyrian sovereigns are likewise guilty of such unseemly behavior against the records of their predecessors. So widespread were these alterations that some, hoping to discourage any from changing the records by which they hoped their fame might continue throughout time, had curses inscribed against anyone so brash and profane. The following specimen is from a stele of Ashurnasir-pal (II), father of Shalmaneser II (III), who plainly feared that his name would otherwise be removed from the archives and his achievements claimed by some future prince of Assyria.

> As for the one who removes my name: May Ashur and the god Ninurta glare at him angrily, overthrow his sovereignty, take away from him his throne, make him sit in bondage before his enemies, (and) destroy his name with mine (and) his seed from the land.[2]

> ... O later prince among the kings my sons whom Ashur will name for the shepherdship of Assyria: [restore] the weakened (portions) of that temple; [write] your name with mine (and) return (my inscription) to their places so that Ashur the great lord (and) the goddess Ishtar, mistress of battle and conflict, [in wars] with kings on the battlefield will cause him to achieve success.[3]

> ... As for the one who sees my stele, reads (it), anoints (it) with oil, makes sacrifices, (and) returns (it) to its place, Ashur, the great lord, will listen to his prayers (and) in wars with kings on the battlefield will cause him to achieve success.[4]

> ... O later prince, do not erase my inscribed name! (Then) Ashur, the great lord, will listen to your prayers.[5]

7. TRUTH REVERSED

As previously stated, it is affirmed by most modern scholars that as the Assyrian Eponym List confirms the Assyrian part of the Canon of Ptolemy, the validity of the rest of the Canon should be accepted with complete confidence and trust. This may be true, but as Beecher[6] and Anstey[7] pointed out as far back as AD 1907 and 1913 respectively, wherever the Assyrian list of eponyms confirms the Assyrian part of the Canon of Ptolemy, it confirms also the biblical record!

Strangely, the world of scholarship seems unable to perceive this fact. Since the Canon of Ptolemy agrees with the Assyrian Eponym List in those places where the biblical record also agrees with it, why is this not seen by the scholars as confirming proof of the authenticity of the record of the Scriptures instead of assessing the situation as being that of having authenticated the Canon of Ptolemy?

---

[1] Thiele, *The Mysterious Numbers of the Hebrew Kings, op. cit.*, p. 137.

[2] Grayson, *ARI, op. cit.*, vol. 2, sec. 660, p. 168.

[3] *Ibid.*, sec. 666, p. 170.

[4] *Ibid.*, sec. 697, p. 180.

[5] *Ibid.*, sec. 771, p. 195.

[6] Beecher, *The Dated Events of the Old Testament, op. cit.*, p. 18.

[7] Anstey, *The Romance of Bible Chronology, op. cit.*, pages 39–40.

Let it be said, the Canon of Ptolemy's agreement with the Eponym List at the occasion where the Assyrian data is contiguous to the biblical record serves as positive external attestation to that account as being a verifiable and actual historical chronicle of the Hebrew people. Therefore, all religious and supernatural overtones aside, due to its uninterrupted, continuous record as compared to the mutilated records of all their neighbors, the Hebrew record deserves at least equal, if not preferred, esteem in establishing the chronology of the ancient world.

Then why, we ask, do we find the opposite to be true? Why instead do today's scholars proceed to "correct" the biblical record with the Canon of Ptolemy from 648 BC to the time of Christ during which there is no Assyrian record and by the Assyrian Eponym List prior to 747 BC where there is no record in the Canon of Ptolemy? The biblical chronology is clear, uninterrupted, unambiguous, and precise. In light of the facts, to displace it in favor of the Assyrian data demonstrates one's lacking not only scientific bearing with respect to approach and concept, but logic as well. Is not our earlier thesis thus documented?

It must be seen that most have allowed their world view, their bias and presuppositions against the Hebrew record and against all the Holy Writ to blind them leaving them unable to do objective scientific investigations. Yet these very scholars boldly assert that their methods and arguments represent the truly scientific approach void of "biblical" prejudices. Conversely, they contend that those with a biblicist bent are guilty of creating "some system of Assyrian chronology that will be more in keeping with certain preconceived ideas of 'biblical' chronology" and that all such work should be "disdained by the careful historian."[1]

The author freely admits that he has encountered some shoddy work by would-be defenders of Scripture founded upon preconceived views causing the workers to disregard all facts contrary to their theses. Yet for the most part the non-biblicists, be they Christian or not, have been found more guilty of the very faults which they so piously charge their

antagonists. And to worsen an already lamentable condition while wishing to appear scientific, progressive, and intellectually acceptable by the hierarchy of academia, many Christian quasi scholars add their voice to that bandwagon being unwilling to stand in faith against the tide that would sweep away the infallible witness of Scripture.

If agreement with the Assyrian Records authenticates Ptolemy's Canon, it must of necessity authenticate the biblical record as well. Furthermore, it should be noted that wherever these three witnesses meet, they are in accord. The real problem between the Assyrian and biblical records is at but one point and, as we shall see, that point of contact may not even exist!

8. INSCRIPTIONS OF SHALMANESER II (III)

Simply stated, the problem begins with the fact that the "Monolith Inscription" documents that in the sixth year of his reign, Shalmaneser II (III), son of Ashur-nasir-pal (II), fought against a 12-king alliance at the battle of Qarqar (Karkar) during the eponymous year of Daian-Assur. The inscription states that one of the kings against whom King Shalmaneser II (III) engaged was a certain "A-ha-ab-bu Sir-i-la-a-a."

Most Assyriologist understand this to be Ahab, the Israelite. This may be true, but there are problems associated with this identification. First, the identification may be incorrect.[2]

"A-ha-ab-bu Sir-i-la-a-a" may be some other historically obscure ruler, perhaps of something no more than a city-state anywhere along the nearly 300-mile seacoast area of the Fertile Crescent. Some researchers go so far as to accuse Shalmaneser II (III) of taking credit for

---

1 Thiele, *The Mysterious Numbers of the Hebrew Kings, op. cit.*, footnote 3, p. 69.

2 Ahab is supposed to have furnished 2,000 chariots at Qarqar [and 10,000 infantry, *New Westminster Dictionary of the Bible, op. cit.*, p. 21 (Ahab)], yet at the height of his power, Solomon had but 1,400 (1 Kings 10:26). Only five biblical citations record Israel as having them in large quantity. Indeed, a 3½-year drought/famine had earlier destroyed most of Israel's livestock. When Ben-hadad II invaded Israel five years afterward, Ahab could only assemble 7,232 *footmen* to oppose the Syrians (1 Kings 18:1–5, 20:1–21). While it is possible that Ahab took chariots and horses from among these and the following year's spoils, such is not recorded and it seems improbable that only two years later he could have placed so vast an armada in the field at Qarqar.

this and other events which actually belonged to his father, Ashur-nasir-pal (II). Among them, Faulstich addresses several perceived inconsistencies and/or contradictions regarding military expeditions and warns:[1]

> Some of the claims of Shalmaneser are preposterous, and it would be ill-advised to reconstruct the Hebrew chronology to satisfy his inaccurate boasting.

After advancing examples, he concludes:[2]

> ... that the inconsistencies in Shalmaneser's annals would make it impossible to accurately date the battle of Qarqar.

Whereas we do not concur with or endorse all of Faulstich's determinations, we cite him to expose the uncertain nature of much of the oft cited Assyrian assertions. Nor is Faulstich alone. Daniel David Luckenbill cautions in his comments prior to Shalmaneser's royal annals that: "It is possible that the first of these, which contained a full account of the events of the year of accession, belongs to a much earlier period."[3]

A fragment of an annalistic text from Shalmaneser's 18th year declares that upon an incursion against Damascus (Di-mas-qi), the Assyrian ruler received tribute from "Ia-u-a mar Hu-um-ri-i."[4] Also the Assyrian Black Obelisk,[5] which has 20 small reliefs engraved on its four sides, depicts a ruler with a short trimmed beard bowing down to the ground in submission before Shalmaneser.

The inscription reads: "Tribute from 'Ia-u-a mar Hu-um-ri-i'." The majority of Assyrian scholars conjecture this to translate "Jehu, son of Omri." Thus, it is insisted that the reign of Jehu,

monarch of the northern kingdom of Israel, must overlap that of Shalmaneser II (III). The Black Obelisk does not give the year of Jehu's (?) tribute; the year is ascertained by comparing it to the aforementioned fragment from Shalmaneser's annals.

However, we hasten to caution that the identification by way of the translation is not certain[6] nor is the incident mentioned in the Bible. Though not to be taken as conclusive by itself, we observe that the Jews were forbidden by Jehovah to trim or round off the corners of their beards.[7] Of course, Jehu may have ignored this injunction as he certainly did others, due mainly to his syncretistic religious practices in simultaneously serving both Jehovah and the golden calves. That notwithstanding, we note that he did acknowledge Jehovah had placed him upon the throne.

Further, Jehu was neither Omri's son, his kin, nor even of his dynasty. Moreover, it was Jehu who personally slew Omri's grandson, King Joram of Israel, thus bringing that dynasty to an end (2 Kings 9:26). At the same time, Jehu had put to death Omri's great grandson, King Ahaziah of Judah (2 Kings 9:27–28). He rapidly followed these deeds by coercing the elders and rulers of Samaria to behead Ahab's other 70 sons leaving none remaining of the house of Ahab (2 Kings 10:1–11). He even had 42 of Ahaziah's kinsman executed, extirpating the last of Omri's lineage.

Finally, we add that prior to his enthronement, Jehu is portrayed in Scripture as having been a mighty warrior. He had become a general in the army of Israel and held in such repute and esteem among his fellow commanders that upon their learning of his having been anointed king at Ramoth-gilead by the young prophet whom Elisha had appointed to the task, to the man they immediately submitted to his authority placing their garments beneath his feet and hailing him king (2 Kings 9:1–13).

[1] Faulstich, *History, Harmony and the Hebrew Kings, op. cit.*, p. 144. See pp. 143–157 where he details his thesis.

[2] *Ibid.*, p. 157.

[3] Luckenbill, *ARAB, op. cit.*, vol. 1, sec. 626, p. 232.

[4] Pritchard, *ANET, op. cit.*, p. 191.

[5] Oliver R. Blosser, "The Synchronization of Jehu with Shalmaneser III," *It's About Time*, (Spencer, IA: Chronology-History Research Institute, March, 1986), p. 4. During excavations at Calah (Nimrud) in 1846, Austen H. Layard discovered this six and one-half foot high four-sided black limestone pillar with five rows of bas reliefs extending around the pillar. Between and below the reliefs, cuneiform inscriptions (wedge-shaped writing) explain each of the twenty small reliefs.

[6] "There is no evidence, however, that the obelisk was actually depicting the Israelite monarch Jehu." "Shalmaneser, Black Obelisk of," *New International Dictionary of Biblical Archaeology*, (Grand Rapids, MI: Zondervan Pub. House, 1983), p. 409.

[7] *Holy Bible* (Authorized), Lev. 19:27.

As a charioteer, Jehu's skill and style acquired legendary proportions. It made him a byword in all Israel (2 Kings 9:20). His personal presence, adroitness, and valor as a warrior commanded instantaneous allegiance. It invoked immense fear in those who might oppose his will (2 Kings 9:24,25, 31–34; 10:4, 16–28). Yet most Assyriologists, chronologists, and other scholars would have us believe that the man seen fawning obsequiously before Shalmaneser is this same Jehu. We think not.

Such sycophantic behavior scarcely seems befitting so valiant a soldier. Such men die first. But in view of their presuppositions, we wonder if such considerations have even been taken into account by these accomplished intellectuals as they proceed with their etymological endeavors and identifications. The overwhelming biblical evidence throws serious doubt upon this identification.

The situation before us is this. If neither of the cited references from Shalmaneser's records is actually referring to Ahab or Jehu, there exists no conflict between the Assyrian and biblical accounts. Thus there would be no point of synchronization between the two nations extant during this period, and as such, the Assyrian and Hebrew dates would stand independent of one another, without cross-verification or conflict. No less authority than the late George Smith championed this very assessment.[1]

We do not "know" or assert that such is the status; indeed, allowance for the accurateness of both identifications has been given on Chart 5. The point being made is that the manner in which these considerations is usually reported does not reflect the amount of conjecture, speculation and uncertainty that is involved in these and many other determinations. Regardless of anyone's personal convictions, it must be acknowledged that neither of the two postulated identifications may reflect the actual historical situation.

If, however, either or both of the cited references from Shalmaneser's time refers to Ahab or Jehu, then obviously a synchronistic

relationship must be taken into account. It is at this possible happenstance that the entire issue between the two schools with regard to the period of the divided monarchy of the Hebrew kings focuses and the battle lines are sharply drawn. Each school has its own approach based upon its presuppositions.

a. Assyrian Academy's Solution to the Shalmaneser Problem

Adherents of the Assyrian School, presupposing that the Eponym List is precise, will "fix" Shalmaneser II's (III) accession to the throne at the "Assyrian" date 859 BC (or 858). Then, having accepted "A-ha-ab-bu Sir-i-la-a-a" as being Ahab of Israel, they deduce that these two sovereigns engaged one another at the Battle of Qarqar 853 BC (or 852) in Shalmaneser's sixth year. Thus, for this school, the term of Ahab's reign is forced to correspond to that year, even though the Hebrew record clearly places him about 45 years back in time.

"Ia-u-a mar Hu-um-ri-i" is also embraced as "Jehu, son of Omri"; hence they compel Jehu to be on the throne in the 18th year of the reign of Shalmaneser, about 841 (Assyrian date). But again, this does violence to the Hebrew account which would place Jehu 45 years earlier.

How then does the Assyrian Academy contend with and remove this 45-year excess? They reduce the span by contriving and interjecting a series of unsubstantiated co-regencies upon the lengths of reign of the Jewish monarchs. By overlapping the biblically stated regnal years of these kings, the epoch is shortened, bringing the Hebrew to conform to the Assyrian outline which has been superimposed upon it. Each Assyriologist and chronologist of that school has his own peculiar solutions, but the results are basically the same. Dr. Thiele, for example, proposes nine such overlapping co-regencies.[2] However, of the nine, five are neither mentioned nor demonstrable in the Holy Text.

Thiele's first co-regency, that of Tibni and Omri of the Kingdom of Israel, and his seventh, between Jehoram and his father Jehoshaphat

[1] George Smith, *The Assyrian Eponym Canon*, (London: Oxford UP, 1875), pp. 154, 185. This famous English Assyriologist and cuneiform expert was affiliated with the British Museum.

[2] Thiele, *The Mysterious Numbers of the Hebrew Kings, op. cit.*, pp. 61–65; *Chronology of the Hebrew Kings, op. cit.*, pp. 23–28.

in Judah's realm, are demanded by the biblical text. His fifth, involving Jotham and his father Uzziah (Azariah), and his eighth, that of Jehoshaphat with his father Asa, do superficially appear possible from the biblical perspective but upon more thorough analysis, the context becomes more certain and the support vanishes. Again, Thiele completely ignored the Hebrew Masoretic Text, choosing instead to follow the witness of the thoroughly corrupt LXX manuscript, *Vaticanus* B, which credits Asa with but 39 years rather than 41.[1] Thus Thiele's frame of reference with regard to the Scriptures and the Assyrian archives has betrayed him into fabricating and imposing these five contrivances.

Inconceivably, Thiele's slavish allegiance to his presuppositions drove him to ignore the biblical witness to the extent that he actually concocted from a single abused Scripture (Hosea 5:5) an unprecedented third Hebrew kingdom, the nation of Ephraim. As a consequence, he was forced to violate the testimony of at least six other clear Scriptures in order to maintain his third kingdom. This fanciful invention will be dealt with presently.

For now, it should be manifestly clear that the chronology of the Hebrew dynasties becomes no more than historical nonsense when adjusted to conform to such corruptions and/or forgeries as we have thus far enumerated. Other faulty insights coupled with numerous misapplications and misrepresentations of the Assyrian materials which follow will only widen the already strained credibility gap.

b. Biblicists' Solution to the Shalmaneser Problem

Adherents of the "biblicist" school, placing their faith and trust in the far more complete self-consistent biblical account and presupposing that the Creator has both given His Word as an infallible deposit to man and kept His many promises to preserve that Text, are not hostile to the Assyrian data in and of itself. It is the relative value placed upon it; hence it is the manner in which its witness to history is "honored" that is contrary to the Assyrian School's beliefs. Our frame of reference with its accompanying presuppositions forces us to observe its testimony as secondary; thus if

usable at all, a way must be found to blend it into the outline that the Scriptures demand – a position which is the antithesis of that of the Assyrian School.

(1) No Point of Contact

The posture of the biblicists is divided with some holding that neither of the cited references from Shalmaneser's records is actually referring to Ahab nor Jehu. For them, no conflict exists over this period between the Assyrian and biblical accounts as there is no point of synchronization between the two kingdoms. The Assyrian and Hebrew dates are viewed as independent of one another here and are without cross verification or conflict. Again, we acknowledge the possibility of this resolution. Of course, the disciples of the modern Assyrian Academy do not concur.

(2) Contact Exists

The other solution is based upon the biblicists' accepting as correct both or either of the aforementioned postulated interpretations. Namely, that "A-ha-ab-bu Sir-i-la-a-a" is Ahab of Israel and/or "Ia-u-a mar Hu-um-ri-i" is Jehu.[2] However, as the biblical record unmistakably places the reigns of these two Israeli sovereigns farther back in time, a gap must exist in the Assyrian data. That is, the testimony of that data is flawed and this flaw must be taken into account to accurately reconstruct the history in question.

If indeed Ahab and Shalmaneser II (III) made contact with one another, Shalmaneser's accession year becomes 903 BC, not 859, and the Battle of Qarqar in Shalmaneser's 6th year becomes 898 rather than 853. In this scenario, Jehu has contact with the Assyrian monarch's 18th year about 886 instead of 841 by Assyrian

---

[1] Thiele, *The Mysterious Numbers of the Hebrew Kings, op. cit.*, footnote, p. 97.

[2] Other Assyrian data, if it is correctly understood, does seem to link Shalmaneser (III) to this general time frame. Shalmaneser apparently refers to the "Hazael" King of Syria mentioned in 2 Kings 8:15; 10:32; 12:17; 13:7, 32; 2 Chron. 22:5–7, etc. who ruled during the reigns of Joram, Jehu, and Jehoahaz of Israel and Ahaziah, Athaliah, and Joash of Judah. David Daniel Luckenbill translates that Shalmaneser (III) called Hazael "the son of a nobody," strongly implying that Hazael did not come from royal stock. This agrees with the biblical account where "Hazael" was but a courtier to Ben-hadad II who usurped the throne of Syria after murdering his lord (Grayson, *ARI, op. cit.*, vol. I, p. 246).

reckoning. It must be borne in mind that only one of these two identifications may be correct.

If both are, the gap must be at least 45 years in length. However, if but one is the actual circumstance, the gap could be smaller. That is, if the Shalmaneser/Jehu contact is the only state of affairs, an exact year for Shalmaneser's eighteenth could not be determined and it could be accommodated to match Jehu anywhere along a 29-year span (Jehu's 28 plus his year of accession). Thus the gap could be foreshortened by 29 years to but 16 (45 − 29 = 16).

The point is that the Assyrian information is being forced to fit the "known" biblical data and regardless of which biblicist's chronological arrangement one prefers, a gap in the Assyrian annals is necessary to align the sovereigns under discussion. The size of the gap will depend upon the commitment of the individual to the doctrine of inerrancy of Scripture, his discernment, insight, prudence and especially the revelation given to him as he examines and weighs the various Scriptures germane to the problem. If, for instance, his commitment to inerrancy is not firmly established or if it only extends to the "originals," he will be tempted and almost invariably eventually succumb to relegating difficulties to the category of so-called "scribal errors" in the text in order to ameliorate the problem.

It must not be supposed that the postulation of the existence of a gap in the Assyrian evidence at this period is novel. One school of past Assyriologists stood similarly convinced that a whole block of consecutive names had somehow been removed.[1] Again, this view of the Canon is the one that agrees with the chronological data as found in the Sacred Writ if, indeed, a point of contact between Shalmaneser II (III) and either or both Ahab and Jehu did historically occur.

If such a connecting synchronization did transpire, is there an explanation for the discrepancy between the Assyrian and biblical accounts? This longer chronology as derived from the biblical evidence is supported by:

(1) the long numbers given in Josephus;

(2) the synchronism of the Egyptian date of the invasion of Shishak, during Rehoboam's reign (2 Chron. 12:2–9) as the biblical date, 971 BC, harmonizes well with the Egyptian data but the Assyrian date, c. 926 BC, can be made to do so only by injustice to the evidence;[2] and

(3) the ancient work of Georgius Syncellus (c. AD 800). Syncellus writes: "... Nabonassar, after compiling the acts of his royal predecessors, did away with these records so that the numbering of the Chaldean kings commences from himself."

As Nabonassar began to reign over Babylon in 747 BC, his tampering with the earlier records is the reason why Ptolemy took his Canon back no farther than that year.[3]

Anstey voices his support and enlarges upon Beecher's proposal that the Assyrians were overtaken by some national disaster resulting in a large block of eponymous names (c. 51) being lost either by accident or destroyed by design.[4] He concludes, with some justification, that this unknown calamity probably occurred shortly after the reign of the powerful Assyrian sovereign Ramman-nirari (III) [Adad-nirari (III)] stating:[5]

> For in his time we find the Assyrians taking tribute from the whole region of the Mediterranean, Judah alone excepted, whilst at the end of the blank period, in the reign of Asshur-daan III, we find that their power over this region had been lost, and that they were now engaged in a desperate struggle to regain it.

However, if the synchronization under inquiry did transpire, the real reason for the disparity

---

[1] Anstey, *The Romance of Bible Chronology, op. cit.*, p. 220.

[2] Beecher, *The Dated Events of the Old Testament, op. cit.*, pp. 21–23. Although Beecher gives the biblical date as 978 BC and the Assyrian date as 927 rather than 971 and 926, his reasoning is incisive, thoughtful, and compelling. He well demonstrates the error in appealing to the Assyrian data to correct not only the Hebrew, but the Egyptian chronology over this period as is the current fashion. This custom should be seen as all the more dangerous when, as in this case, the two are supportive against the standard Assyrian interpretation.

[3] Georgius Syncellus, *Historia Chronographia*, (Paris, France: c. AD 800), pp. 244–245.

[4] Anstey, *Romance of Bible Chronology, op. cit.*, p. 40. Beecher, *Dated Events, op. cit.*, pp. 18–19, 30, 138.

[5] *Ibid.*

between the two records and the missing block of names is implied within Scripture. To begin with, 2 Kings 14:23–27 records that the prophet Jonah ministered to Israel during the reign of Jeroboam II. The Book of Jonah (3:7–10) relates that the king of Assyria ("Nineveh" being the capital) and all his nobles repented, turning in faith to the true God. That this was a true act of contrition is verified by the Lord, Christ Jesus, in Luke 11:32.

Now this unnamed monarch and his nobles are the very men for whom the years would have been named – they would be the limmu in the Assyrian scheme. With the passing of time and the subsequent enthronement of different kings, eventually one would come to power who reverenced the ancestral gods of Assyria. The general spiritual condition of the people, as has befallen all nations throughout recorded history, would tend to diminish and gravitate back to the old paths as well.

Regardless of the number of kings who had reigned remaining loyal to Jehovah, how would this new ruler behold his immediate predecessors? Would he not consider and mark them as sacrilegious apostates, blasphemers all? And from the testimony of history, what might we expect as to this recent king's reaction? The answer is manifestly obvious. The natural response would be to obliterate every mention of such "wicked" men from all the archives in order to "purify" the land, creating as they did holes or gaps in their records.

Whereas we freely admit that such a scenario is neither directly so stated nor capable of certification, it should be taken as more than a passing "coincidence" that the potential for so lucid and rational a resolution is found embedded within the Sacred Text at the very time span in dispute. The fact that the Assyrian archives catalogue Tiglath-pileser (III), Ashur-nirari (V), Shalmaneser III (IV), and Ashur-dan III (III) as all being sons of Adad-nirari (III) may well be the signal indicating an effort by each of them to distance himself from the apostate king or kings who repented under Jonah's message, embracing Jehovah.

Yet despite all the uncertainty and lack of consensus, particularly among past Assyriologists, involved in both of these identifications, inexplicably nearly all modern scholars hold to

them even though it causes much abuse and contortion to the plain reading of the Hebrew Text. It would seem that were there not an obvious bias against the Hebrew authority, it would be utilized by these scholars as the deciding factor in "clarifying" the uncertainties regarding the persons in question. Instead, one incessantly finds the Shalmaneser/Ahab/Jehu connection referred to as "having provided tremendous help" in dating the regnal years of the Hebrew kings of both kingdoms as they are "cross-referenced in the Bible" but, to the contrary, when Scriptures are forced to so fit the Assyrian scheme an anachronism is created.

To our knowledge, the foregoing solution has never appeared in print and may well represent a novel explanation with reference to the issue. The question has been biblically answered.

9. TWO FRAMES OF REFERENCE CONTRASTED

This, then, is the method utilized by the Assyrian Academy. Despite the many deficiencies and uncertainties alluded to previously, the disciples of this school still have great "faith" in their conclusions. After applying these multiplied assumptions, conjectures and, at times, fanciful flights of the imagination, we are told and assured by these intellectuals that the Assyrian records have "thrown much light on the Hebrew." Yet assuredly, any true enlightenment received from these and other records apart from the Hebrew only "add" and illuminate when the biblical account has first been taken as true and authentic. If the reverse practice is accepted confusion, haze, and even darkness will follow. Hence, let us return to the basics.

This author's practice, the biblicist's frame of reference, is that whenever possible, without violating the scriptural data in its proper context, the integrity of the Assyrian, etc. records has been maintained. When there is an irreconcilable conflict, the integrity of the Holy Writ is placed above, not only the Assyrian, but all other documents. In such instances, it is presumed that the documents are either in error, suffer scribal emendation or their testimony has simply been misunderstood or misinterpreted by the archaeologist, Assyriologist, etc. Thus it is the Assyrian et al. documents which require confirmation.

The actual situation is that the Scriptures are needed to "throw light" upon the other nations' chronologies, not the reverse as is the current vogue. The fact is that if truth is reversed 180 degrees, the reverser will always be deemed profound, even a visionary.

10. THE CURRENT SORRY STATE OF AFFAIRS

We find it most disconcerting that these devotees, without the slightest reservations, now pretend they have taken a purely dispassionate scientific position and approach free of presuppositions, all the while decrying that the methodology of their biblical opponents is founded on no more solid a foundation than "religious blind faith," holding back progress and the cause of science and history. Again, both sides are saturated with presuppositions and are exercising great faith in their extant documents and techniques.

One side admits to this, the other more or less blindly denies it. The multitudes sit on the sidelines mesmerized and intimidated. Not wishing to be deemed unprogressive, uninformed, and unaware of the true state of the matter, they invariably buckle and gravitate toward the views of the Assyrian School.

Unfortunately, all the great champions of the past are dead and too few have dared to seize the fallen torch and stand in the gap to protect the faithful from the critical attacks on the validity and veracity of the Word of God. Not willing to spend the enormous time and intellectual energy necessary to become adequately informed so that their own faith will be rooted and grounded, few have been able to answer the call. As a result, most are not "ready always to give an answer to every man that asketh ... a reason of the hope that is in you"[1] and thus be able to "convince the gainsayers."[2] Truly, these are evil days. Christian, gird up the loins of your mind.

It is not that the biblicist is blindly opposed to the "hard facts" of archaeology. The Assyrian data is of considerable value, but its limitations must be taken into account. It must be seen that it is not the "facts" that are at issue. The real difficulty lies in the presuppositions, goals and hidden agendas brought to the problem. The data is the same for both camps. The crux of the matter is in the relative value each researcher places upon the various inscriptions and writings of antiquity.

All too often the modern Christian who has far better data from which to forge his judgments but being desirous of acceptance by those at the higher echelons of academia, has shamefully compromised in order to achieve that end. In this rarefied domain of Olympus, an academic fraternity dwells and the desire for acceptance by those who have already scaled the pinnacle often overcomes any loyalty to "earnestly contend for the faith which was once delivered unto the saints."[3] After all, to be labeled a biblicist by those who have so scaled is to be deemed uninformed and unworthy; such is appraised as worthy of non-admission or expulsion.

Nor may the works of these Olympians be denigrated if one is to remain in the graces of these esoteric fraternities. They must ever be treated with courtesy, even praised and any aberrations criticized with extreme caution. Nor should this be interpreted or confused as an expression of "being Christian" toward the opposing view.

It is a self-serving, fawning attempt to raise one's status, gain the esteem and respect of those on the "upper tier" by means of a mutual admiration pact in order to promote oneself among the fraternities of academia. Shame! Faith should be founded on better than this.

The facts and implications elucidated in this section should not only be illuminating to the biblicist, but be of equal concern to the liberal theologian and secular inquirer as well. Irrespective of world views and presuppositions, honest inquirers deserve the right to be privy to all data, suppositions, and opinions that they may form logical intelligent decisions. As our adversary's position is everywhere publicized and generally accepted, we are grateful for having had this opportunity to present the contrary view as a service to all fair-minded men.

---

[1] *Holy Bible* (Authorized), 1 Pet. 3:15.

[2] *Ibid.*, Titus 1:9.

[3] *Ibid.*, Jude 3.

11. THE PREVAILING STATUS EXPLAINED

How did the evangelical conservative wing of the Church allow itself to descend into such a sorry state of affairs? Its scholars and leadership began to compromise their long standing commitment and views on inerrancy, altering them into a new doctrine. Namely, that inerrancy only held true with regard to the "original" manuscripts. As the autographs of the prophets and apostles are no longer extant and with the discovery of the existence of variant readings with regard to a minor portion of the text, the faith of these defenders slowly succumbed over the years. The result on American conservatism was that lower criticism came to be viewed as "safe."

The traditional fundamental belief in "preservation" of Scripture was soon replaced by the doctrine of "restoration." That is, the bizarre notion that over the years some of the true text had become corrupted resulting in the loss of a small yet significant portion of the original readings. The opinion among scholars of the upper echelon was that they could take the numerous extant manuscripts and ancient versions and, by applying the supposed "scientific" techniques and methods of "lower" or textual criticism, restore to the Church and the world at large the original wording.

But God had often promised to preserve His Word. It was never implicit in these many promises that He would miraculously preserve the original stones, scrolls, or manuscripts upon which the prophets and apostles wrote. All that was necessary was that the text itself be preserved. This, we aver and asseverate, He has done — not by a continuing miracle but as the late conservative text critic Edward F. Hills correctly advocated, by providentially preserving it over the centuries, thus fulfilling the aforementioned promises.[1]

In short, most evangelicals have not realized that what they correctly recognize as "that dangerous higher criticism" is inexorably interwoven with and subtly tied to the "safe" discipline of lower criticism. Many, intending to defend "verbal inspiration" from German higher

criticism attacks but naively thinking that lower criticism, dealing as it does with the "concrete facts," was immune to the "speculations" of the higher critics, have in fact betrayed both the truth and the cause of Christ Jesus. Truly, one of the greatest deceptions Satan has foisted upon the Church in the past century is the lie that text criticism does not affect doctrine. With it, he has subverted almost the entire Christian Church.

Once the conservative leadership accepted the so-called "fact" of the presence of emendations, embellishments, and scribal errors within the text of the Sacred Writ, faith in its integrity and authority waned. The result has been that appeal to final authority among Protestants shifted from being that of the Word of the Living God to the varied opinions of incalculable numbers of mere men. It is an incontestable natural consequence that whenever and wherever the authority of Scripture is diminished in the minds of a people, the power of a priesthood of men is proportionally increased.

The Roman Catholic structure has long played down the accuracy and faithfulness of God's Word and will continue to do so in order to maintain its dominion over the laity through its pope and priesthood. This ungodly dominion has been historically facilitated in great measure by the practice of using a language no longer familiar to the people in which to conduct the service.

Tragically, the Protestant churchmen are rapidly, and often unknowingly, succumbing to the same snare, enmeshing their flocks and going about establishing their own personal control over the faith of the people by a constant overemphasis of Hebrew and/or Greek. Again, that which is being said is that the laity, not knowing the language of the pastor/scholar and having no reliable written witness as his guide, simply cannot correctly understand or approach the Deity for himself and must depend upon some other man or religious organization to do this for him. Did the reformers suffer and perish in vain?

Consequently, as the Scriptures which the Deity gave as a deposit to man came to be looked upon in its current form as error-pocked and no longer esteemed inerrant by the fundamental conservatives, churchmen — often

---

[1] Edward F. Hills, *The King James Version Defended*, (Des Moines, IO: The Christian Research Press, 1988), pp. 106–107.

with no more than a mere two-year introduction to the Hebrew or Greek languages — began to unceasingly "correct" the text for the "benefit" of the flock. Having themselves lost confidence in God to honor His oft given assurances that He would oversee and safeguard its text, these men began to look to other fields and other sources for more reliable data upon which they could place their trust.

Many of them felt that this was justifiable as modern science had supposedly "proven" by various radiometric dating techniques that the earth and the universe were far, far older than indicated by the ancient yet "outmoded" Scriptures. Besides, had not geology and pale-ontology demonstrated that man himself was but an animal having arisen from a primeval "soup" and subsequently from lower animals in an ongoing unending struggle where only the fit survive?

Supposedly, those individuals possessing slight advantages for survival in the environment which the organism finds itself are "naturally selected" by nature to survive in the struggle. The successful individuals are said to then pass on via reproduction to their offspring the favorable traits which had given them their edge in this great conflict. Over many generations, the presumed cumulative effect of these slight advantages eventually are postulated to give rise to new species and, in time, new genera, orders and even phyla. Indeed, has not science proven that all forms of life evolved from the primeval ocean through the strictly mechanistic, naturalistic process of evolution to the extent that all informed thinking persons have accepted it as an incontestable fact?

The answer is a resounding "no," they have not so proved. It is merely their belief.

I. DATING THE FOURTEENTH YEAR OF HEZEKIAH

Since the days of Thiele's influence, the establishment of the date of Hezekiah's 14th year has become a major point of contention in Bible chronology. The Assyrian records indicate that in the 3rd year of his reign, Sennacherib directed a military campaign against Hezekiah of Judah. The biblical text records an incursion

by this same Sennacherib in the 14th year of Hezekiah. Thiele has insisted that the two military operations are identical, hence the date of Hezekiah's 14th must be the same as Sennacherib's third year – a date which has been firmly fixed by dead reckoning from the aforementioned June 15, 763 BC eclipse during the eponymous year of Bur-Sagale (Gregorian = June 7, 763 BC).

On the basis of this supposition, Thiele has taken the liberty to adjust the Hebrew chronology to fit the Assyrian scheme. He has dated the 3rd year of Sennacherib at 701 BC and declared that as the 14th year of Hezekiah.[1]

> The date of 701 for the attack of Sennacherib in the fourteenth year of Hezekiah is a key point in my chronological pattern for the Hebrew rulers. This is a precise date from which we may go forward or backward on the basis of the regnal data to all other dates in our pattern. Full confidence can be placed in 701 as the fourteenth year of Hezekiah, and complete confidence can be placed in any other dates for either Israel or Judah reckoned from that date in accord with the requirements of the numbers in Kings.

Thiele further stated:[2]

> A solid synchronism between Judah and Assyria at which our pattern of Hebrew dates could begin is 701 BC. That is a definitely fixed date in Assyrian history and is the year in which Sennacherib in his third campaign 'went against the Hittite-land' (Aram) and shut up 'Hezekiah the Jew ... like a caged bird in Jerusalem, his royal city.' That took place in the fourteenth year of Hezekiah (2 Kings 18:13), that is, in the year 701.

The result of this erroneous assumption is the production of a regnal chronology for the Hebrew monarchs which neither harmonizes with the biblical record nor secular history. As shall be demonstrated, by so doing Thiele has created problems with the integrity of the Hebrew Text. Actually even Thiele's Assyrian date is not precise as the Assyrian records indicate that 705 BC is Sennacherib's accession year; thus his third year is 702, but that is not the real issue here.

---

[1] Thiele, *The Mysterious Numbers of the Hebrew Kings*, op. cit., p. 175.

[2] *Ibid.*, p. 78.

The real problem is that the Scriptures have recorded the accounts of two Assyrian invasions; one being briefly described in 2 Kings 18:13–16 and the other from 18:17 to 19:37 (also in 2 Chron. 32:1–23; Isa. 36:2–37:38), but Thiele has combined them into a single event and then forced the Assyrian account and its date upon this composite. Yet the two are not equivalent events; they are different encounters altogether (but see fn. 2, page 164).

This problem is compounded in that most scholars have followed Thiele in noting the similarities between the Assyrian account and the Hebrew Text but have somehow been blind to the striking *differences*. These loudly proclaim that two separate accounts regarding two distinct invasions by Sennacherib are being presented. Indeed, this fact is so incontestable that it should no longer be a matter worthy of serious academic consideration.

To begin with, the Hebrew Scriptures declare that Samaria, capital and last stronghold of the Kingdom of Israel, fell after a three-year siege begun during the reign of the Assyrian monarch, Shalmaneser IV (V). They further record that this took place in the sixth year of Hezekiah:

> And it came to pass in the fourth year of king Hezekiah, which was the seventh year of Hoshea son of Elah king of Israel, that Shalmaneser king of Assyria came up against Samaria, and besieged it. And at the end of three years they took it: even in the sixth year of Hezekiah, that is in the ninth year of Hoshea king of Israel, Samaria was taken (2 Kings 18:9–10).

The ensuing assault against Judah was conducted by Sennacherib during the 14th year of Hezekiah:

> Now in the fourteenth year of king Hezekiah did Sennacherib king of Assyria come up against all the fenced cities of Judah, and took them. And Hezekiah king of Judah sent to the king of Assyria to Lachish, saying, I have offended; return from me: that which thou puttest on me will I bear. And the king of Assyria appointed unto Hezekiah king of Judah three hundred talents of silver and thirty talents of gold. And Hezekiah gave him all the silver that was found in the house of the LORD, and in the treasures of the king's house. At that time did Hezekiah cut off the gold from the doors of the Temple of the LORD, and from the pillars which Hezekiah

king of Judah had overlaid, and gave it to the king of Assyria (2 Ki:18:13–16).

Again, Thiele advanced 701 BC as the 14th year of Hezekiah. He also fixed the fall of Samaria as 723 BC,[1] a date which places these two events 22 years apart (723 BC – 701 = 22). However, as Faulstich pointed out in 1987,[2] 2 Kings 18:9–10 state that Samaria fell in the sixth year of Hezekiah and that in his 14th Sennacherib invaded his domain, thereby defining the two episodes as being separated by only 8 years (14 – 6 = 8). Thus by wrongly determining the two different accounts to be the one and the same and then forcing the 701 (702) Assyrian date to be the 14th of Hezekiah, Thiele has created an anachronism.

Furthermore, in order to maintain this error he has employed his "dual dating" technique to develop a chronological scheme which denies the testimony of 2 Kings 18:9–10 that synchronizes the sixth year of Hezekiah with the ninth year of Hoshea, king of Israel. Indeed, Thiele's pattern places both the fall of Samaria and the *end* of Hoshea's reign as occurring *before* the year Hezekiah began to reign despite the clear wording of the biblical text which states that the two transpired in the sixth year of that Judaic monarch's rule.[3]

This not only disregards 2 Kings 18:9–10, it also violates 2 Kings 17:1, 6, and 18:1 (cp. diagram, page 174). Yet this is not all for, as shall be seen in the next major section of this paper, in establishing 701 BC as the 14th of Hezekiah, Thiele then used that dated occurrence as one of his major anchor points from which to chronologically "fix" and date many other biblical events. In so doing, he engaged in further compromises through which he overthrew other Scriptures thus creating more distortions in Hebrew history.

---

[1] Thiele, *The Mysterious Numbers of the Hebrew Kings, op. cit.,* pp. 163–166.

[2] Faulstich, *It's About Time, op. cit.,* Jan. 1987, p. 14 and *History, Harmony and the Hebrew Kings, op. cit.,* pages 99–118. Although the present author does not concur with all his conclusions, the latter work is very incisive and represents Faulstich at his best.

[3] Thiele, *The Mysterious Numbers of the Hebrew Kings, op. cit.,* p. 121.

Moving from the 701 anchor point toward younger dates, Thiele is forced to fabricate an 11-year co-regency between Hezekiah and Manasseh in order to compensate for his error. This is immediately compounded for he associated Manasseh on the throne during Hezekiah's final 11 years while stating that he had been so elevated at the age of 12.[1] Yet the context of 2 Kings 20:1–11 and 21:1 is that Manasseh was only 12 when his father died.

This is the clear explanation for Hezekiah's weeping and his petition before God; he did not yet have a male heir to succeed him and thus fulfill the Lord's promise to David that he would not lack a son who could occupy his throne. This is the reason for the 15-year extension of Hezekiah's life, and it rules out Thiele's conclusion. Traveling the other direction toward older dates, he even invented an unprecedented third Jewish kingdom which completely misplaces a Hebrew king in time in order to maintain this 701 judgment!

Due to his world view, Thiele felt free to pick and choose which portions of Scripture to honor and which to reject; yet all the while he claimed to be defending the Hebrew Text. Cast aside as flawed and meaningless, these ignored portions of Scripture were actually the guideposts intended to point him to the fact that the invasion recorded as having taken place in the third year of Sennacherib was not the same as that of the sixth year of Hezekiah. Had these Scriptures been observed, they would have kept Thiele from the manipulation of data to which he resorted but having removed "the ancient landmark" (Prov. 22:28), he found it obligatory to adopt conjecture upon conjecture.

Although it may be fairly said that the academic world as a whole follows Thiele in this identification, it is important to note that not all scholars have embraced the view that Hezekiah's 14th year is identical with Sennacherib's 3rd. Faulstich mentions that, in addition to himself, W.F. Albright, Jack Finegan, John Bright, et al. recognized the discrepancies between the biblical and Assyrian accounts of Sennacherib's besiegement of

Jerualem and concluded that two different events were being described.[2]

Although for the biblicist the evidence already cited would be enough for him to disregard Thiele's 701 anchor date for the 14th of Hezekiah, the fair question could be asked: "Other than the attestation of 2 Kings 18:9–10, is there any additional evidence upon which these men and the present author have founded their position? The answer is a resounding "yes" and several of the more incontestable proofs are given in that which follows.

1. THE PASSOVER IN HEZEKIAH'S FIRST YEAR

It is evident that if 701 BC were the 14th year of Hezekiah, his 1st year would have been 714 and his 6th 709. By Thiele's reckoning, Samaria fell 14 years prior to 709 BC. Hence Hezekiah would have to have begun his reign 9 years *after* the collapse of the Northern Kingdom rather than 6 years *before* as required by the biblical text formerly presented. And yet the Scriptures give further proof that Hezekiah began his reign *prior* to the fall of Samaria:

> Now it came to pass in the third year of Hoshea son of Elah king of Israel, that Hezekiah the son of Ahaz king of Judah began to reign. ... And the LORD was with him; and he prospered whithersoever he went forth: and he rebelled against the king of Assyria, and served him not (2 Kings 18:1,7).

This portion of text describes Hezekiah's revolt against the king of Assyria. Hezekiah's wicked father, Ahaz, had appealed to Tiglath-pileser III to aid him against Rezin, king of Syria, and Pekah, king of Israel (rather than repenting and calling upon Jehovah), who were oppressing his kingdom. The Assyrian monarch came at Ahaz' request, taking Damascus and slaying Rezin as well as causing the Northern Kingdom to break off her military engagement. However this help came at a far greater price than Ahaz had realized for Tiglath-pileser III placed him under tribute at that time (2 Kings 16:5–9; 2 Chron. 28:16–21).

In the first year of his reign, Hezekiah rebelled against the Assyrian yoke. As the Temple had

---

[1] Thiele, *The Mysterious Numbers of the Hebrew Kings, op. cit.*, p. 177.

[2] John Bright, *A History of Israel*, (Philadelphia, Pa: The Westminster Press, 1959), pages. 282–287; Faulstich, *History, Harmony and the Hebrew Kings, op. cit.*, p. 113.

fallen into disarray during the rule of Ahaz, Hezekiah immediately instituted a repair project to bring Judah back to the Lord (2 Chron. 29:3–36, cp. 28:24). Hezekiah then called for a Passover celebration during which he also invited the Northern Kingdom to participate, and a great spiritual revival took place:

> And Hezekiah sent to all Israel and Judah, and wrote letters also to Ephraim and Manasseh, that they should come to the house of the LORD at Jerusalem, to keep the passover unto the LORD God of Israel. For the king had taken counsel, and his princes, and all the congregation in Jerusalem, to keep the passover in the second month. For they could not keep it at that time, because the priests had not sanctified themselves sufficiently, neither had the people gathered themselves together to Jerusalem. And the thing pleased the king and all the congregation. So they established a decree to make proclamation throughout all Israel, from Beersheba even to Dan, that they should come to keep the passover unto the LORD God of Israel at Jerusalem: for they had not done it of a long time in such sort as it was written (2°Chron. 30:1–5).

These passages do not describe the circumstances one would expect from Thiele's findings. They clearly portray a condition in which the kingdom of Israel is still in existence in the first year(s) of Hezekiah, not one that has been ravaged by Shalmaneser IV (V), deported to the far reaches of the Assyrian Empire by Sargon II and the land repopulated by non-Israelis. In attempting to maintain Thiele's theory, some have taken the clause "he will return to the remnant of you, that are escaped out of the hand of the kings of Assyria" in the following passage

> So the posts went with the letters from the king and his princes throughout all Israel and Judah, and according to the commandment of the king, saying, Ye children of Israel, turn again unto the LORD God of Abraham, Isaac, and Israel, and he will return to the remnant of you, that are escaped out of the hand of the kings of Assyria. And be not ye like your fathers, and like your brethren, which trespassed against the LORD God of their fathers, who therefore gave them up to desolation, as ye see. Now be ye not stiffnecked, as your fathers were, but yield yourselves unto the LORD, and enter into his

sanctuary, which he hath sanctified for ever: and serve the LORD your God, that the fierceness of his wrath may turn away from you. For if ye turn again unto the LORD, your brethren and your children shall find compassion before them that lead them captive, so that they shall come again into this land: for the LORD your God is gracious and merciful, and will not turn away his face from you, if ye return unto him (2 Chron. 30:6–9).

to refer to a remnant of Hebrews remaining in the land of Israel after the devastation of Samaria by Shalmaneser IV (V). However, this clause refers to earlier deportations of only the trans-Jordan and northern tribes of the Israelite kingdom at the hands of two of the Assyrian kings, Pul and Tiglath-pileser III and not to those related to the time of the final fall at the hands of Shalmaneser IV (V), i.e.,

> And they [the northern tribes] transgressed against the God of their fathers, and went a whoring after the gods of the people of the land, whom God destroyed before them. And the God of Israel stirred up the spirit of Pul king of Assyria, and the spirit of Tilgathpilneser king of Assyria, and he [Jehovah] carried them away, even the Reubenites, and the Gadites, and the half tribe of Manasseh, and brought them unto Halah, and Habor, and Hara, and to the river Gozan, unto this day (1 Chronicles 5:25–26, author's brackets).

> In the days of Pekah king of Israel came Tiglathpileser king of Assyria, and took Ijon, and Abelbethmaachah, and Janoah, and Kedesh, and Hazor, and Gilead, and Galilee, all the land of Naphtali, and carried them captive to Assyria (2 Kings 15:29).

The Scriptures reveal that though many from Ephraim, and Manasseh unto Zebulun laughed to scorn and mocked the messengers bearing Hezekiah's invitation to attend the Passover at Jerusalem, significant numbers from Asher, Manasseh, Ephraim, Issachar, and Zebulun did come and participate in the great feast (2 Chron. 30:10–11, 18; 31:1, 6). Thus it is evident that the 726 BC Passover during the first year of Hezekiah took place *before* the fall of Samaria and *not afterward* as Thiele would have it.

Here it is important to note that the problem does not lie with the Assyrian data *per se*, but merely with Thiele's interpretation of it in relation to the biblical record. As shall be shown, the solution neither necessitates altering the

Hebrew Text as Thiele chose to do, nor altering the chronology of the Assyrian kings. All that is required is to recognize that the biblical account of Sennacherib's attack against Judah in the 14th year of Hezekiah and the incursion by that same Assyrian monarch in his third year as described by the Assyrian chronicles are not one and the same historical events, but rather two disconnected happenings.

2. 701 (702) BC – THE THIRD YEAR OF SENNACHERIB

The Assyrian account describes Hezekiah as being shut up in Jerusalem "like a caged bird." Let us now examine the entire narrative.[1]

> As for Hezekiah, the Jew, who did not submit to my yoke, 46 of his strong, walled cities, as well as the small cities in their neighborhood, which were without number – by escalade [by causing them to tread the ramp or incline] and by bringing up siege engines(?), by attacking and storming on foot, by mines, tunnels, and breaches(?), I besieged and took (those cities) 200,150 people, great and small, male and female, horses, mules, asses, camels, cattle and sheep, without number, I brought away from them and counted as spoil. Himself, like a caged bird, I shut up in Jerusalem, his royal city. Earthworks I threw up against him, – the one coming out of his city gate I turned back to his misery. The cities of his, which I had despoiled, I cut off from his land and to Mitini, king of Ashdod, Padi, king of Ekron, and Silli-bel, king of Gaza, I gave them. And (thus) I diminished his land. I added to the former tribute, and laid upon him (var., them) as their yearly payment a tax (in the form of) gifts for my majesty. As for Hezekiah, the terrifying splendor of my majesty overcame him, and the Irbi (Arabs) and his mercenary (? lit., choice or picked) troops which he had brought in to strengthen Jerusalem, his royal city, deserted him (lit., took leave). In addition to 30 talents of gold and 800 talents of silver, (there were) gems, antimony, jewels(?), large sandu-stones, couches of ivory, house chairs of ivory, elephant's hide, ivory (lit., elephant's "teeth"), maple (?), boxwood, all kinds of valuable (heavy) treasures, as well as his daughters, his harem, his male and female musicians, (which) he had (them) bring after me to Nineveh, my royal city. To pay tribute and to accept (lit., do) servitude he dispatched his messengers (author's bracket).

The similarities between the biblical and Assyrian versions are that the same two kings are involved, the city of besiegement is Jerusalem, many of the northern cities of Judah were taken before the siege of Jerusalem began, and the number of talents of gold exchanging hands in both records was 30. However, even these are not as persuasive and forceful as might be taken at first glance for the first three would be an expected natural result of nearly any invasion from the Assyrians; the northern cities, walled and otherwise, would be the first to fall. But now let us consider a few of the more important variants.

a. The Earthen Siege Mounds

The Assyrian description mentions earthworks thrown up against the city wall of Jerusalem, but the biblical account distinctly says this did not occur during the Sennacherib encounter:

> Therefore thus saith the LORD concerning the king of Assyria, He shall not come into this city, nor shoot an arrow there, nor come before it with shield, *nor cast a bank against it.* By the way that he came, by the same shall he return, and shall not come into this city, saith the LORD. For I will defend this city, to save it, for mine own sake, and for my servant David's sake (Two Kings 19:32–34, author's italics).

This does not at all fit the Assyrian description of the encounter between the two nations in the third year of Sennacherib. One notable discrepancy is that of the siege banks. In fact, at no point does the Hebrew Text mention earthen siege mounds in relation to any of Sennacherib's activities regarding Jerusalem.[2]

b. Tribute Disparities

The account from Sennacherib's third year includes 800 talents of silver in addition to

---

[1] Luckenbill, *ARAB, op. cit.,* vol. II, sec. 240, pp. 120–121.

[2] Still, the Assyrian account could be reconciled with the biblical if Sennacherib's 3rd campaign is not referring to the 3rd year of his sole reign (701 BC) but rather the 3rd of his co-rule with Sargon. Then the Assyrian account is that of the 713 BC first invasion in Hezekiah's 14th year (see "c." on following page). Shutting Hezekiah up in Jerusalem "like a caged bird" would not then refer to a direct besiegement against the capital but be seen in the context that, as the surrounding cities had already fallen or were under siege, Jerusalem was left isolated. The siege mound statement would thereby refer to those other besieged cities, not to Jerusalem; and the 300–800 talents of silver discrepancy taken as an error in the Assyrian record (both do give 30 talents of gold). Although this resolution may appeal to a biblicist, the Assyrian Academy would never so concede.

several other forms of spoil whereas the Hebrew record states that the Assyrian monarch imposed but 300 talents of silver upon Hezekiah in his 14th year. Again, it is not being said that the Assyrian is necessarily erroneous in any of the particulars. What is being said is that the various discrepancies are indicative that two different military engagements are before us.

c. No Siege in Hezekiah's Fourteenth Year

As shall be explained and proven presently, no besiegement took place during Sennacherib's first incursion into Judah. The encounter which transpired in the 14th year of Hezekiah's reign is described in 2 Kings 18:13–16. The biblical evidence is unmistakable that the seventeenth verse of 2 Kings 18 through 2 Kings 19:37 is speaking of a later "second" invasion.

The first penetration was the Assyrian's punitive action for Hezekiah's earlier revolt. After Sennacherib had left Jerusalem exposed by first taking all the outlying fortified cities of Judah, Hezekiah capitulated while the Assyrian forces were at Lachish (2 Kings 18:14, see fn. 2, page 164). At that time the Assyrian monarch imposed a tribute of 300 talents of silver and 30 talents of gold which Judah paid (2 Kings 18:14–16). Having met the Assyrian demands, the matter was concluded until four years later when Hezekiah, counting upon help from Egypt, again revolted against the Assyrian yoke and the Assyrians quickly returned (2 Kings 18:20–21; Isa. 36:6).

d. Events Relevant to Merodach-Baladan

Sennacherib records that at the beginning of his reign when he first took his place on the throne (i.e., his first year), King Merodach-baladan of Babylonia revolted from under his authority. The Assyrian account goes on to say that during the ensuing battle, Merodach-baladan fled into a swamp alone and that after five days the search for him was abandoned. He apparently was never heard from again.[1]

Yet 2 Kings 20:12 has that Babylonian monarch sending an embassy with letters and a present to Hezekiah during (or just after) his 14th year (and supposedly Sennacherib's 3rd) following Hezekiah's recovery from an infection which nearly brought about his death (2 Kings 20:12;

Isaiah 39:1, cp. 2 Kings 20:1, 6). This Scripture demands that the 14th year of Hezekiah preceded Sennacherib's 3rd (if his 3rd is taken as that of his sole reign in 701; again, see fn. 2, page 164).

e. Tirhakah, King of Ethiopia

Finally, were the 3rd year of Sennacherib and the 14th of Hezekiah concurrent, the Assyrian records are found lacking as they say nothing of a major encounter with an Ethiopian (Egyptian)[2] army under King Tirhakah at that time (see 2 Kings 19:8–9). A scenario in which Sennacherib:

(1) departed from Libnah to meet the relief column under Tirhakah (or at least made plans to so do),

(2) awoke to find his army decimated by the loss of 185,000 men in a single night at the hands of an angel from Jehovah,

(3) departed from Judah and returned to his own land "with shame of face" (2 Chron. 32:21)

is in no way descriptive of the Assyrian account of his third year in which he is portrayed as returning in triumph with the spoils of war. Clearly, these accounts are not parallel.

3. JUBILEE – THE CHRONOLOGICAL KEY

Since the discovery of the Assyrian documents, it has been postulated, especially by conservative scholars, that there are two distinct invasions in view within the biblical record. Such is the case, but neither has anything to do with the third year of Sennacherib. The data establishing that fact and which allows the setting of the date for the second Assyrian movement into Judah is found in 2 Kings 19:29 and Isaiah 37:30.

After prophesying against Sennacherib because of his letter of reproach, Isaiah gives a sign to Israel that God will defend her against the invaders from the north:

> And this shall be a sign unto thee, Ye shall eat this year [a 49th Sabbatic year] such things as grow of themselves, and in the second year

---

[1] Luckenbill, *ARAB, op. cit.,* vol. II, sec. 255–267, pages 128–133.

[2] The kings of the Twenty-fifth Dynasty of Egypt were of the Ethiopian dynasty, hence Tirhakah is also referred to as the Pharaoh of Egypt in the text (2 Kings 18:21; Isa. 36:6). See James H. Breasted, *Ancient Records of Egypt,* (New York: Russell & Russell, 1962), vol. 4, pp. 451–455.

[*Jubilee*] that which springeth of the same; and in the third year sow ye [*the year following Jubilee*], and reap, and plant vineyards, and eat the fruits thereof (Isa. 37:30 author's brackets).

This prophetic promise clearly describes a Jubilee condition.[1] Thus the "this year" must refer to the year of Sennacherib's invasion in which his Rab-shakeh sent the threatening letter to Hezekiah after learning of the approaching Egyptian legions under Tirhakah (2 Kings 19:8–14).[2] The date of the second year,

---

7th

[1] Speak unto the children of Israel, and say unto them, When ye come into the land which I give you, then shall the land keep a sabbath unto the LORD. Six years thou shalt sow thy field, and six years thou shalt prune thy vineyard, and gather in the fruit thereof; But in the seventh year shall be a sabbath of rest unto the land, a sabbath for the LORD: thou shalt neither sow thy field, nor prune thy vineyard. That which groweth of its own accord of thy harvest thou shalt not reap, neither gather the grapes of thy vine undressed: for it is a year of rest unto the land. And the sabbath of the land shall be meat for you; for thee, and for thy servant, and for thy maid, and for thy hired servant, and for thy stranger that sojourneth with thee. And for thy cattle, and for the beast that are in thy land, shall all the increase thereof be meat. And thou shalt number seven sabbaths of years unto thee, seven times seven years; and the space of the seven sabbaths of years shall be unto thee forty and nine years. Then shalt thou cause the trumpet of the jubile to sound on the tenth day of the seventh month, in the day of atonement shall ye make the trumpet sound throughout all your land. And ye shall hallow the fiftieth year, and proclaim liberty throughout all the land unto all the inhabitants thereof: it shall be a jubile unto you; and ye shall return every man unto his possession, and ye shall return every man unto his family. A jubile shall that fiftieth year be unto you: ye shall not sow, neither reap that which groweth of itself in it, nor gather the grapes in it of thy vine undressed. For it is the jubile; it shall be holy unto you: ye shall eat the increase thereof out of the field (Lev. 25:2–12).

JUBILE 49

[2] Attempts to date this invasion by the reference to Tirhakah (Taharqa or Tirhaqa) are without force. In the first place, there is insufficient evidence to support the contention by some scholars that this engagement must have taken place around 686 BC on the grounds that Tirhakah was merely a boy at this time and thus incapable of commanding the army. (See *The Bible Knowledge Commentary*, J. Walvoord and R. Zuck, eds., (Wheaton, IL: Victor Books, 1985) p. 576.

Gleason Archer Jr. informs us that this conjecture was based on an interpretation of the Egyptian *Kawa Stela IV* by M.F.L. Macadam. However, a later edition of Kawa Stela IV by Leclant and Yoyette in 1952 revealed that Macadam had misinterpreted the data. They determined it was actually Tirhakah's father, Piankhy, who died in 713 (or more likely in 717 or 716), hence Tirhakah would have been much older than nine in 701 (Archer, *A Survey of Old Testament Introduction*, op. cit., p. 294).

descriptive of a Jubilee, may be determined by the chronology of previously established events thereby fixing the year of this assault.

The year Moses died and Joshua entered the land was long ago determined by Ussher, Bishop Lloyd, Nicholas Toinard, William Whiston and now independently confirmed by this author as 1451 BC. However, the year of Jubilee did not have to do with merely being in the land but with its actual possession and cultivation (Lev. 25).

After seven years of conflict with the Canaanites, the wars ended at the close of 1445 BC (c. April 1451 to 1445 = 7 years, inclusive). From the base camp at Gilgal, Joshua then gave the tribes of Judah and Joseph their portions. Early in 1444, the tabernacle was moved to Shiloh. The rest of the land west of the Jordan was then divided among the remaining seven tribes, and the men from the 2½ tribes east of the Jordan returned home.

Until this, Israel had lived off the crops of the Canaanites, volunteer crops and supplies from the eastern 2½ tribes (Josh. 24:13). Israel's tillage thus began in 1444.

Archer goes on to report that the 1952 edition showed that Macadam had mistakenly assumed a co-regency of six years between Tirhakah and his older brother, Shebitku. Moreover, that he had also been wrong in placing Tirhakah's age as twenty (Kawa Stela V:17) in 690/689 BC for it actually was pointing to a time immediately after Shebitku's accession in 702. Thus the Leclant-Yoyette edition concluded that Tirhakah was twenty years old in 701 when his brother summoned him to take charge of the campaign into Judah. Although it is most probable that Tirhakah was not yet king at this time, Scripture is merely referring to him as such in that the biblical scribes are not writing prophetically concerning this episode. They are writing after the event before us took place, perhaps even during Tirhakah's actual reign.

The same is done today. If one were introducing Ronald Reagan, he would not present him as Ronald Reagan the movie actor or the ex-governor of California, but as former President Reagan. Accordingly, though Tirhakah is probably only the commander-in-chief of the armies at this time, in retrospect he is referred to as "King." Indeed, the later edition interprets Kawa Stela IV:7–8 as referring to Tirhakah by the title of "His Majesty," i.e., "His Majesty was in Nubia, a goodly youth ... amidst the goodly youths whom His Majesty King Shebitku had summoned from Nubia."

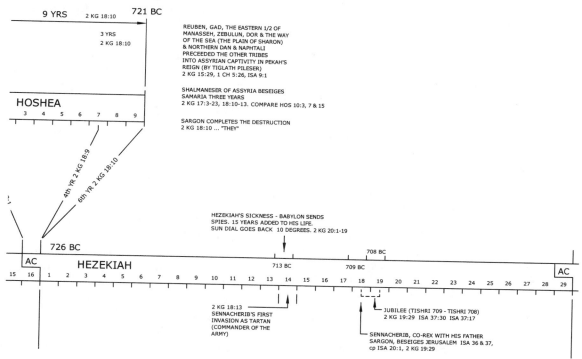

Hence, from this year are reckoned Sabbatic and Jubilee years (1444 − 49 = 1395 BC, the first Jubilee; see page 289 ff.). Thus, the 15th Jubilee commenced in the autumn of 709 BC and ended in the autumn of 708 (2 Kings 19:29; Isa. 37:30, cp. 2 Kings 18:32 and Isa. 37:17).[1]

The significance of the Lord's answer to Hezekiah's prayer may be seen when compared to the Assyrian Rab-shakeh's declaration that he intended to soon come and take the warriors of Judah who were defending the wall of Jerusalem away to a foreign land (2 Ki. 18:32). God's reply was that not only would they not be carried away that year, but He would bless them with bumper volunteer crops and a Jubilee in their own land the following year to the extent that the surplus would last until the crops came up in the year after Jubilee at which time they would still be in their homeland.

This incursion by Sennacherib must have taken place earlier in 709, during the preceding Hebrew year (Hezekiah's 18th, hart 5, 5c, and above). As the date of the 14th year of Hezekiah has been derived by the triangulation method as 713 BC and confirmed by adding the 134 years 6 months and 10 days remaining to the Judaic monarchs from the fall of Samaria in

Hezekiah's sixth to 586 BC (the year of the fall of Jerusalem to Nebuchadnezzar), two separate invasions by Sennacherib are proved to be recorded in the biblical account.

Thus the Assyrian account, if it is in fact true, is a third and later encounter. Further, this 709/708 Jubilee documents that a significant error exists in Thiele's and the Assyrian Academy's scheme.

4. THE CORRECT CHRONOLOGICAL SEQUENCE OF EVENTS

From all that has been examined, the following chronology may be set forth:

726 B.C.   The reform and great Passover in the first year of Hezekiah in which he invited Israel to participate (2 Chron. 30:1–31:1; note the time element in 2 Chron. 29:3–17; 30:2, 13 and 15): As Israel was still a kingdom at that time, the first year of Hezekiah occurred before the 721 BC fall of Samaria. It is therefore impossible to date his fourteenth in 701 (702) for that would place his first year as 714 BC, at least seven years too late for the many individuals from the nation of Israel to take part in that Passover. Hezekiah rebelled against Assyria (2 Kings 18:7).

723 B.C.   Shalmaneser's initiation of the siege of Samaria was in the fourth year of King Hezekiah of Judah (2 Kings 18:9).

---

[1] See Appendix I, pages 288–292.

721 B.C.   Fall of Samaria in the sixth year of Hezekiah: Shalmaneser died during the siege. Sargon, his Tartan and successor, took the city carrying away Israel unto Assyria ("they," 2 Kings 18:10–11).

713 B.C.   The 14th year of Hezekiah and ninth of Sargon: Sennacherib, Tartan and co-regent (or viceroy), went to punish Hezekiah for his earlier revolt. After the fortified cities of Judah fell, Hezekiah submitted to the Assyrian yoke and paid a large tribute before Jerusalem was endangered (2 Kings 18:13–16). As Hezekiah reigned 29 years (2 Kings 18:2), his sickness and that which followed had to have transpired in that same year for it is said that he was given 15 more years at that time (14 + 15 = 29, 2 Kings 20:1, 6).

711 B.C.   City of Ashdod taken (Isa. 20:1, cp. *ARAB*, Vol. II, sec. 30, p. 13): Upon learning that the king of Ashdod plotted to withhold his tribute, in his eleventh year Sargon sent his Tartan (almost certainly Sennacherib) and conquered the city.

709 B.C.   Hezekiah's second rebellion against the Assyrian yoke (2 Kings 18:20–24): This was either as a result of hearing of Egypt's (Ethiopia) stand against Assyria or due to a treaty with the southern Pharaoh. This time the Assyrian's reacted quickly. The ensuing invasion, ending in the slaying of 185,000 of Sennacherib's troops in one night, is that with which the majority of Scripture deals.

A brief chronological overview of Hezekiah's reign is that upon ascending the throne at age 25 (2 Kings 18:1–3), he opened the doors of the Temple which his wicked father Ahaz had closed, initiated repairs and a spiritual revival. This included inviting the people of the Northern Kingdom to come to Jerusalem and take part in the great Passover (2 Chronicles 29:3–30:27). Other religious reforms soon followed (2 Chron. 31:1–21). He rebelled against Assyria and defeated the Philistines (2 Kings 18:7–8). After a three-year siege beginning in Hezekiah's fourth year and ending in his sixth, the fortress city of Samaria fell to the Assyrians. The people were carried away to Assyria, and the Northern Kingdom ceased to exist (2 Kings 18:9–12).

In the 14th year of King Hezekiah's reign Sennacherib, co-regent (or viceroy) with his father Sargon, came at last to punish Hezekiah for his earlier revolt. After the fortified cities of Judah fell, Hezekiah submitted to the Assyrian yoke and paid a large tribute before Jerusalem was attacked and the Assyrians withdrew (2 Kings 18:13–16). As Hezekiah reigned 29 years (2 Kings 18:2), his sickness, recovery and the visit of the embassy from Babylonia had to have also transpired during his 14th year for he was given 15 more years to live at that time (14 + 15 = 29, 2 Kings 20:1, 6).

Four years later, due to Egyptian military influence in the area, Hezekiah seized the opportunity to once more rebel against the Assyrians (2 Kings 18:20–24). This time Sargon responded quickly by again sending his son and co-regent, Sennacherib, at the head of his army (2 Chron. 32:1). Hezekiah reacted by stopping up all the water supplies outside Jerusalem, repairing the city wall and taking other defensive precautions (2 Chron. 32:2–8). While Sennacherib was besieging Lachish, a fortress city about 28 miles southwest of Jerusalem, with his main force, he dispatched his Tartan (commander-in-chief), Rabsaris and Rab-shakeh (two high ranking officials) along with a great host of warriors to Jerusalem to sue for its unconditional surrender (2 Kings 18:17–36, cp. 2 Chron. 32:9).

Eliakim and the other two Hebrew officials brought Sennacherib's blasphemous words as delivered by the Rab-shakeh to Hezekiah who went into the house of the Lord while dispatching an embassy to seek out Isaiah, the prophet, for a word from Jehovah (2 Kings 18:37–19:5). Speaking through Isaiah, the Lord promised to send a "blast" upon the Assyrian monarch, that he would "hear a rumor" and return to his own land where he would be slain by the sword (2 Kings 19:5–7).

Meanwhile the Rab-shakeh returned to Sennacherib who had left Lachish and was attacking Libnah, a city 10 miles north of Lachish and 25 miles west/southwest of Jerusalem (2 Kings 19:8). Upon hearing that Tirhakah, king of Ethiopia, was coming to engage him in battle (fulfilling the prophecy that the Assyrian king would "hear a rumor," 2 Kings 19:7), Sennacherib again sent messengers bearing a God-defying letter to Hezekiah. Attempting to frighten Hezekiah into immediate surrender and thus gain Jerusalem without a prolonged battle, the railing letter said in effect that neither Tirhakah nor Jehovah could

save Jerusalem for he would return after defeating the Egyptian army and take it (2 Kings 19:7–13). Hezekiah retired with the letter to the Temple, spread it out before the Lord and prayed for deliverance (2 Kings 19:14–19).

God's second answer through Isaiah included the aforementioned promise that Judah would celebrate Jubilee the following year in her own land. The Lord added that the king of Assyria would not enter Jerusalem, shoot a single arrow against it or cast a siege mound against the city for Jehovah himself would defend it (2 Kings 19:20–34, esp. vv.29 and 32).

That very night the angel of Jehovah slew 185,000 Assyrian soldiers (the "blast"), and Sennacherib returned "with shame of face" to Nineveh where he was later assassinated by two of his sons while worshiping in the temple of his god (2 Kings 19:35–37, cp. 2 Chron. 32:21). An ironic ending as Hezekiah's God had defended him, but Sennacherib's was unable to deliver him even in its temple.

5. CONCLUDING REMARKS

The Assyrian records are silent relevant to the invasion of Judah and Sennacherib's humiliating departure during the 18th year of Hezekiah as well as any conflict with Tirhakah. This should not be seen to militate against the biblical account for, as formerly mentioned, none of the nations in the ancient near-east other than the Hebrews recorded their inglorious defeats in battle.

As to why Scripture is silent concerning the assault against Judah in the third year of Sennacherib, one can but speculate. Perhaps this incident was recorded in the unpreserved non-canonical "Book of the Kings of Judah" (2 Chron. 32:32). Yet one can but wonder if the account is nothing more than a greatly exaggerated fabrication by Sennacherib in an attempt to cover and eradicate his humiliating reversal at the hands of the Living God.

The mind set of that time would clearly lead Sennacherib to view the slaying of 185,000 of his troops as an act and victory of Jehovah over his god, Nisroch (2 Kings 19:37). It is difficult to imagine a superstitious pagan king returning to take reprisals against another king whose God so decimated his army in only one night. Nevertheless, this is not to be taken as a complete rejection of the account, and the interpretation given herein has allowed for its possibly being an historic happening (see fn. 2, page 164).

Before closing this section, the author is compelled to again note that once the conservative scholar takes the bait by accepting the Assyrian Academy's final conclusions (Thiele being their chief spokesman in the area of the chronology of the kings of the schism), he invariably is seduced into further compromises with Scripture. For example, with regard to the 14th year of Hezekiah and Sennacherib's 701 BC invasion, Gleason Archer Jr. carefully chooses his wording in order to support Thiele as best he can although he admits that Hezekiah's "Great Passover" did not take place after the fall of Samaria but rather early in that king of Judah's reign.[1] Reluctantly, Archer admitted that Thiele's solution had caused a "clear discrepancy between 2 Kings 18:13 and all the other passages" related to the problem. Yet his frame of reference, especially with regard to textual criticism, caused him to entirely miss the moment.

Rather than realizing that this "clear discrepancy" was the signal that something was very wrong with Thiele's line of logic therefore calling for a complete reexamination of the whole matter as presented herein, Archer instead sided with E.J. Young offering as a solution that "fourteenth" was a scribal error and therefore should be amended to "twenty-fourth" year. This would result in 725 BC as being the commencement year of Hezekiah's sole reign and apparently resolve the issue.

The Hebrew language presents "fourteen" as "four (and) ten" (aleph-resh-beth-ayin and ayin-siyn-resh), which transliterates as "arba eser." The Hebrew for "twenty-four" is "four (and) twenty (aleph-resh-beth-ayin and ayin-siyn-resh-yod-mem). This transliterates into "arba esrim."

Archer is inaccurate when he understates that which would have been necessary to bring

---

[1] Archer, *A Survey of Old Testament Introduction, op. cit.*, pp. 291–292.

about the proposed scribal error. He basically said that all that would have been required was the "misreading of one letter," the miscopying of the "mem." However, as can be seen from the above, it would have required the copyist to have dropped out two letters – the "yod" and the "mem."

Regardless, such is hardly in keeping with the testimony of Christ Jesus who positively declared that neither jot nor tittle had been altered in the Hebrew Text during the nearly 1,500 years from Moses to His day (Mat. 5:18). Archer's proposed solution is certainly a far cry from this avowal of Christ's, yet it serves to demonstrate the attitude and place to which most modern conservatism has plummeted. Simply stated, that posture has the mind set that when a problem is encountered which the intellect cannot readily solve, merely alter or reject the Scriptures.

Finally, a Jubilee did occur beginning in the autumn of 709 BC[1] and if Sennacherib's account actually transpired during the 3rd year of his sole reign (and not the 3rd of his co-reign, fn. 2, page 164), then there were three encounters between the two monarchs.[2] Regardless, as Thiele and the Assyrian Academy remove at

least 45 years from the period of the Hebrew kings and date Hezekiah's 14th year as 701 BC, they fail to honor this biblical Jubilee. Hence, this Jubilee completely exposes their historical reconstruction as flawed and invalid. Taken with all the preceding, Thiele stands refuted in the matter of Hezekiah's 14th year, one of his major anchor points.

J. THE IDENTITY OF "PUL"

Most modern scholars insist that the Assyrian annals record Tiglath-pileser (III) as claiming to have received tribute from Menahem, king of Israel. This has led nearly all scholars to identify the biblical "Pul" as being Tiglath-pileser (III) rather than his immediate predecessor as stated in the Authorized Bible:

> And the God of Israel stirred up the spirit of Pul king of Assyria, **and** the spirit of Tilgathpilneser king of Assyria, and **he** [Tiglath-pileser, cp. 2 Kings 15:29] carried them away, even the Reubenites, and the Gadites, and the half tribe of Manasseh, and brought them unto Halah, and Habor, and Hara, and to the river Gozan, unto this day (1 Chron. 5:26, author's emphasis & brackets).

In order to "honor" the Assyrian data, the New King James translation alters this Scripture to read, "So the God of Israel stirred up the spirit of Pul king of Assyria, *that is*, Tiglath-pileser king of Assyria. ..." rather than the more correct word "*and*" as the King James Bible faithfully records.[3] Thus two problems arise. Do the Assyrian records say that Menahem paid tribute to Tiglath-pileser and were Pul and Tiglath-pileser one and the same Assyrian sovereign?

1. MENAHEM AND THE ASSYRIAN ANNALS

There are only two extant Assyrian texts that mention Menahem. The following Assyrian quote is an undated fragmentary annalistic text ascribed to Tiglath-pileser (III) and is the one to which appeal is invariably made regarding this matter. This identification may be seen as correct as it apparently references both Pekah

---

[1] Editions prior to the 15th and Chart 5's dated before the year 2003 erroneously reported 588 as a Sabbatical year. Many take the freeing of the Hebrew servants in Jer. 34 as a Sabbatical year. As Nebuchadnezzar initiated the siege of Jerusalem in Zedekiah 9th year, they make a Sabbatic calculation, obtain 590 BC, and take it as Zedekiah's 9th as well as the year of Jer. 34. With Zedekiah's 9th year fixed as 590 and as the city fell in his 11th, they conclude the fall was 588 BC.

But it is a mistake to suppose that the manumission of the Hebrew slaves took place in a Sabbatic year. Leviticus 25:1–7 speaks only of rest for the land. There is no mention of the release of slaves. Only the suspension of debts was added later (Deu.15:1–11). The freeing of Hebrew slaves had to do with the 7th year from the time of their purchase — the 7th year of their servitude (Exo.21:2; Deut.15:12–15). This is that which Jer. 34 has to do and not with a Sabbatical year. Thus, Jer. 34 does not have to be synchronized with the Sabbatical year 590 BC and that Sabbatical year does not have to correspond with the 9th year of Zedekiah (see pp. 291–292; Browne, *Ordo Saeclorum, op. cit.*, p. 293; McClintock & Strong, *Cyclopedia, op. cit.*, vol. IX, pp. 200–201).

[2] Were 2 Kings 19:29 (also Isa. 37:30) not what it clearly is, namely a Jubilee, then the biblical account would contain only one Assyrian invasion – that of the 14th year of Hezekiah in 713 BC – and the Assyrian account would then have to be rejected as spurious. The Assyrian Academy uniformly ignores the Jubilee issue.

[3] The NIV is similar; the NAS, etc. renders "even." These renderings are possible, but usually the grammar would call for "and." Most noteworthy is the fact that, to our knowledge, none of the numerous older versions in any language ever translated the Hebrew other than "and."

and Hoshea of Israel, a synchronism which the biblical text confirms:[1]

> ... the town Hatarikka as far as the mountain Saua, [...the towns:] Byb[los],...Simirra, Arqa, Zimarra, ... Uzno, [Siannu], Ri'-raba, Ri'-sisu, ... the towns ... of the Upper Sea, I brought under my rule. Six officers of mine I installed as governors over them. [...the town R]ashpuna which is (situated) at the coast of the Upper Sea, [the towns...]nite, Gal'za, Abilakka which are adjacent to Israel (Bit Hu-um-ri-a) [and the] wide (land of) [...]li, in its entire extent, I united with Assyria. Officers of mine I installed as governors upon them. As to Hanno of Gaza (Ha-a-nu-u-nu al Ha-az-za-at-a-a) who had fled before my army and run away to Egypt, [I conquered] the town of Gaza, ... his personal property, his images ... [and I placed (?)] (the images of) my [...gods] and my royal image in his own palace...and declared (them) to be (thenceforward) the gods of their country. I imposed upon th[em tribute]. [As for Menahem I ov]erwhelmed him [like a snowstorm] and he ... fled like a bird, alone, [and bowed to my feet(?)]. I returned him to his place [and imposed tribute upon him to wit:] gold, silver, linen garments with multicolored trimmings, ... great ... [I re]ceived from him. Israel (lit.: "Omri-Land" bit Humria) ... all its inhabitants (and) their possessions I led to Assyria. They overthrew their king Pekah (Pa-qa-ha) and I placed Hoshea (A-u-si-') as king over them. I received from them 10 talents of gold, 1,000(?) talents of silver as their [tri]bute and brought them to Assyria.

The continual assertion that the Annals of the Kings of Assyria record Tiglath-pileser (III) as claiming to have received tribute from Menahem is seen as false as the name "Menahem" appears in *brackets* meaning that the annals is unreadable and the word has been supplied by the translator.[2] Thus, this identification rests solely upon conjecture.

The rationale behind this supposition is to be found in the second Assyrian annals text which refers to the tribute of a "Menihimmu of Samerina" (Menahem of Samaria?).[3] This fragmentary text has been assigned to Tiglath-pileser (III). Based on this data, the name "Menahem" was added and inserted in the bracket in the preceding text.

However Tiglath-pileser's annals were engraved upon the slabs of the rebuilt central palace at Calah (Nimrud) and were later removed by Esarhaddon to be used in his southwest palace of the same city. Removal and trimming of the stone have resulted in reducing the annals to a fragmentary state, and thus it is possible that these texts are actually those of a previous monarch(s). With regard to this and the uncertainty surrounding the reliability of these particular fragments, Daniel David Luckenbill has written:[4]

> Without the aid of the Eponym List with Notes it would have been impossible to arrange the fragments in their chronological order, and, even so, future discoveries are likely to show that the arrangement now generally accepted is wrong.

Thus it is seen that there is no compelling Assyrian data demanding the placing of the reigns of Menahem and Tiglath-pileser (III) as parallel. On the authority of the Hebrew Text, this author positively asserts that the second "slab" inscription has been wrongly assigned to Tiglath-pileser (III) whereas in truth it should be credited to an earlier Assyrian monarch whom the biblical text calls "Pul" (Ashur-dan III). The testimony of the Hebrew Text unmistakably places Pul in the days of Menahem's reign (772–761 BC) and states that he extracted tribute from that king of Israel:

> And Pul the king of Assyria came against the land: and Menahem gave Pul a thousand talents of silver, that his hand might be with him to confirm the kingdom in his hand. And Menahem exacted the money of Israel, even of all the mighty men of wealth, of each man fifty shekels of silver, to give to the king of Assyria. So the king of Assyria turned back, and stayed not there in the land (2 Kings 15:19–20).

---

[1] Pritchard, *ANET, op. cit.,* pp. 283–284, 2 Kings 15:29–30.

[2] Italic designates a doubtful translation of a known text or for transliterations. Square brackets indicate restorations in the text due to damage and unreadability; parentheses are placed around interpolations made for better understanding of the translation, that is the words so enclosed are not part of the original text; obvious scribal omissions are placed between triangular brackets. A lacuna (a blank space or missing part, i.e., a gap) is indicated by three dots, four if the lacuna comes before a final sentence dot (period). Pritchard, *ANET, op. cit.,* Intro. p. xxii.

[3] Luckenbill, *ARAB, op. cit.,* vol. 1, sec. 761–772, pages 269–276.

[4] *Ibid.,* vol. 1, sec. 761, p. 269.

Hence the situation is that one Assyrian text has the name "Menahem" placed in brackets by conjecture based solely upon another fragmented text which reliable external evidence shows to have been mistakenly assigned to Tiglath-pileser (III). Yet it is this identification that has been used by the Assyrian Academy to overrule the Hebrew chronology, cause anachronisms, and in so doing violate and cast biblical passages aside as erroneous. As shall be shown, Pul and Tiglath-pileser (III) are *not* one and the same.

Moreover, only a few lines down in this same fragmentary annals appears the name "Pa-qa-ha" (Pekah, see quotation on page 171), the king of Israel who began his reign only two years after Menahem's death. The context indicates – the biblical chronology demands – that the missing name in the first mentioned damaged Assyrian annalistic text should be Pekah, not Menahem. Thus, there is no Assyrian historical text which says or even infers that Tiglath-pileser collected tribute from Menahem of Israel, although almost all scholarly sources proclaim that he so did.[1]

2. TIGLATH-PILESER (III) IS NOT "PUL"

Doctor Thiele has compared two Babylonian documents, King List A and the Babylonian Chronicle.[2] The first document mentions that a "Pulu" (or Porus in Ptolemy's Canon) reigned two years in Babylon following a three-year reign by Ukin-zer. The second states that Tiglath-pileser took the throne of Babylon after Ukin-zer had reigned three years and died the following year.[3] The comparison brought him to the conclusion that "Pulu" (or "Porus") was Tiglath-pileser (III), and in this determination he apparently is correct. Thiele then assumes that the similarity of these names to the "Pul" in the Hebrew Text must insure that they are one and the same individual.

The academic world has accepted this assumption, especially in light of the general absence of the name "Pul" in the existing Assyrian data. Yet this absence cannot be taken as final. For example, at one time the name "Sargon" was not accepted as genuine by secular scholars until Paul E. Botta's 1843 discovery of that now celebrated Assyrian monarch's palace at Khorsabad. Prior to this archaeological find, the only mention of him was by the prophet Isaiah (Isa. 20:1), which of course was not considered conclusive by academia.

Anyone can see the obvious similarity between the words "Pul", "Pulu" and even somewhat to "Porus", and "Pileser". However, as Faulstich has well pointed out, this does not prove that Tiglath-pileser is the biblical "Pul" any more than the form of "Pul" in the name of Ashur-nasir-pal, another Assyrian ruler, makes him to be the "Pul" of Scripture.[4] Indeed, the word "Pul" is a title, not a proper or forename. It means "Lord" and could therefore refer to *any* Assyrian ruler.

Actually, the name of the principal Assyrian god from their older works is "Val" (or Vul in its Hebrew form). The letter "V" is identical to the letter "P" in their language such that Pul is also the name of their god. He is identical to the Canaanite god, Baal, as our letters "v" and "b" are the same letter in Semitic languages.[5] Hence, here an Assyrian monarch took the name or title of his god unto himself or his position.

Moreover, even a casual glance at 1 Chron. 5:26 reveals the obvious truth that Pul and Tiglath-pileser (III) are not the same man but two different Assyrian monarchs; and with this Josephus completely concurs.[6] If they were one and the same ruler, why does the title "king of Assyria" follow after both: "And the God of Israel stirred up the spirit of Pul king of Assyria, and[7] the spirit of Tiglath-pileser king of Assyria"…? Were they the same man, the verse would only have the title "king of Assyria" *once*, reading "And the God of Israel stirred up

---

[1] Citing, as they do, David Daniel Luckenbill, *ARAB, op. cit.*, vol. I, sec. 772, p. 276.

[2] Pritchard, *ANET, op. cit.*, p. 272, and Grayson, *ABC, op. cit.*, Chronicle 1. i. 17–26, pp. 72–73.

[3] Thiele, *The Mysterious Numbers of the Hebrew Kings, op. cit.*, pp. 125, 139–141.

[4] Faulstich, *History, Harmony and the Hebrew Kings, op. cit.*, pages 119–142. Faulstich has done an excellent analysis on this entire matter.

[5] *Ibid.*, pp. 130–134.

[6] Josephus, *Antiquities, op. cit.*, IX, 11, 1. All older English Bibles (Geneva, etc.) read as the KJB.

[7] Editions before the 16th were supposed to show the KJB wording here, but the NIV was mistakenly given instead.

the spirit of Pul, that is, Tiglath-pileser king of Assyria." The redundancy, although not mentioned heretofore in the literature to our knowledge, is an unmistakable indication that we are dealing with two distinct monarchs – not one. As to "and he carried them away" that follows after "...Tiglath-pileser king of Assyria" in I Chronicles 5:26, the "he" contextually refers to Tiglath-pileser there and also back to verse six! (note: Reubenites in vv. 6 & 26, Gad vv. 11, & 26, & half tribe of Manasseh vv. 18 & 26)

Furthermore, Eugene Faulstich asserts that the Hebrew language will not permit the association of Pul with Tiglath-pileser (III). He states that the phrases "the spirit of Pul" and "the spirit of Tiglath-pileser" in the text are followed by the Hebrew symbol for the direct object indicating "definiteness" and that the double use of that symbol demonstrates two definite spirits of two different kings.[1] Indeed, the context of this passage requires that the biblical "Pul," though not mentioned in any extant Assyrian document by that appellation, is a king prior to Tiglath-pileser (III).

If the Assyrian records are accurate in this time period, Pul is Ashur-dan III. As Assyrian names usually consisted of compounds of two, three or more elements, his complete name may well have originally been Ashur-danin-pal. Pul is the Hebrew form of the Akkadian name "Pal." It is known that this name was given to the eldest son of Shalmaneser II (III).[2]

Shalmaneser II's (III) son, Shamasi-adad V, was also known as Shamas-Pul (Vul = Pul as "V" and "P" are interchangeable). Moreover, Shamas-Pul was Ashur-dan III's "grandfather" and Ashur-dan III's "father," Adad-nirari III, was known as "Pullush." Thus the word "Pul" is firmly attached to his immediate lineage and fits the biblical narrative.

Therefore, when the New King James Version and nearly all others make Pul and Tiglath-pileser III one and the same person, such is *not* a translation, rather it is an *interpretation* based on a faulty archaeological judgment. This misidentification is directly opposed to the actual translation and is absolutely shown to be

false by the biblical chronology of the Hebrew kings. The erroneous identification of Pul to be the same Assyrian ruler as Tiglath-pileser III creates grave chronological problems with the Hebrew Text. It renders biblical chronology impossible unless, as the following section will reveal, one ignores many other Scriptures in order to compensate as Thiele has done.

K. THE MENAHEM-PEKAHIAH-PEKAH CONNECTION

Allusion has already been made to the fact that by wrongly assigning the third year of Sennacherib as the 14th of Hezekiah, Thiele was forced to erect compensating anachronisms. When the formerly mentioned mishandled fragmentary text involving the incorrect insertion of "Menahem" in brackets is combined with the "fourteenth year of Hezekiah" error, the resulting "chronology" violates the Hebrew Text with rampant disregard. The diagram on page 174 has been constructed after Thiele's interpretation so that the former statement may be judged as to its validity and allow the reader to see the lengths Thiele went, as well as all who have walked in his footsteps, in unashamedly perverting Scripture.[3]

Remember, this is not a matter of rejecting the actual testimony of the Assyrian data in favor of the biblical. Both cases have been shown to be examples of wrong handling of the Assyrian records in places where the data was fragmented, missing and thus restored by conjecture, etc. Thus, untrustworthy Assyrian information has consistently been given precedence over the unmistakably clear Hebrew historical account.

1. THIELE'S "KINGDOM OF EPHRAIM"

As one peruses Thiele's rationale where he forces the biblical text to conform with conjectured and abused secular history, the first shock is that of his totally unwarranted creation of a *third* Hebrew kingdom which he entitled "Ephraim" (see diagram on next page and compare to Charts 5 and 5c).[4]

---

[1] Faulstich, *History, Harmony and the Hebrew Kings, op. cit.*, footnote 4, p. 139.

[2] *Ibid.*, p. 133.

[3] Thiele, *The Mysterious Numbers of the Hebrew Kings, op. cit.*, diagram 17, p. 121, and *A Chronology of the Hebrew Kings, op. cit.*, p. 47.

[4] *Ibid.*, pp. 124–135. *Ibid.*, pp. 24–25, 46–47.

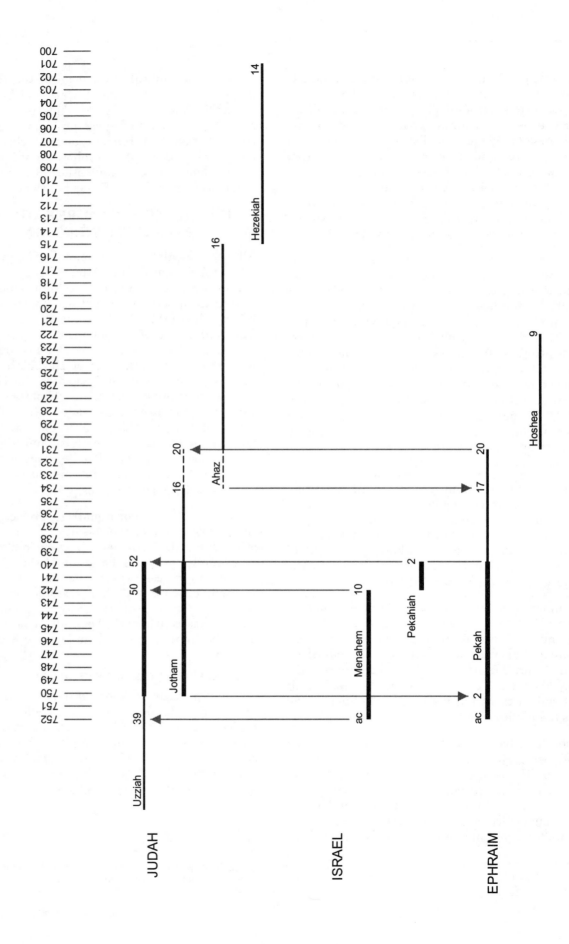

After Thiele

JUDAH

ISRAEL

EPHRAIM

Thiele, *The Mysterious Numbers of the Hebrew Kings*, p. 121

174

Thiele's entire justification and "proof" for this new kingdom, aside from the fact that the aforementioned errors of judgment in dealing with the fragmented Assyrian data have caught up with him and now force him to admit to their wrongness or to resort to inventing history, rests solely upon several verses from the Book of Hosea:

> And the pride of Israel doth testify to his face: therefore shall Israel and Ephraim fall in their iniquity: Judah also shall fall with them (Hos.5:5; also 7:1 and 11:12).

Desperate to now somehow produce a chronology, Thiele grasps on the inclusion of the name "Ephraim" in the Hosea passages along with the names of the Kingdoms of Israel and Judah. He then promotes "Ephraim" to kingdom status in order for him to subtract years from the Hebrew data by promoting Pekah to king of this fictitious realm. Thiele continues by placing Pekah as contemporaneous first with Menahem and then Pekahiah, rather than as the king of Israel who succeeded the latter. The result is that, according to Thiele, there then existed concomitantly two Northern Kingdoms – Israel and Ephraim – as well as the Kingdom of Judah in the south.

Thiele continues by taking the phrase "Shallum son of Jabesh" in 2 Kings 15:13–14 and surmises that "Jabesh" might be the town in Gilead named Jabesh rather than a personal name. As Menahem had seized the throne by assassinating Shallum, Thiele further reasoned that the citizenry of Gilead would have given Pekah strong support and thus been part of the so-called "kingdom of Ephraim."

As his proof, he cites the fact that "fifty men of Gilead" aided him in his *coup d'etat* over Pekahiah and the taking of the throne in Samaria (2 Kings 15:25).[1] However plausible all of this may seem to some, it is superficial speculation and has nothing whatever to do with actual history.

2. THE "KINGDOM OF EPHRAIM" REFUTED

In the first place, as Faulstich has well pointed out, Hosea 5 and almost all of the remainder of that book was written in poetic form. Throughout the text, Israel and Ephraim are used as synonyms. Moreover, Hosea parallels the words "Israel," "Ephraim," and "Samaria" in saying:

> When I would have healed Israel, then the iniquity of Ephraim was discovered, and the wickedness of Samaria: for they commit falsehood; ... (Hosea 7:1)

This is the very same manner in which Hosea 5:5 uses "Israel" and "Ephraim"; yet neither Thiele nor anyone else has been so ridiculous as to interpret this as positive evidence for the existence of *three* concurrent kingdoms in the North. Indeed, Hosea 12:2 refers to the Southern Kingdom by way of parallelism as "Judah" and "Jacob"; yet none has suggested this as proof of two distinctly different kingdoms coexisting in the South.[2]

That the Holy Writ would use "Ephraim" in parallel or as a synonym for "Israel" throughout much of Scripture is natural and easily understandable. In the first place, of the ten tribes comprising the Northern Kingdom it was Joseph who received the birthright (i.e., the double portion albeit the blessing went to Judah, Genesis 49:8–12, 22–26, cp. 48:1–22; 1 Chron. 5:1–2; Psa. 78:67–68, etc.) and of his sons, it was Ephraim for whom the tribe was named who received the blessing from Jacob.

Thus Ephraim became the preeminent tribe among Israel and as such, that name became a common byword or synonym for that kingdom. Still another most significant reason for this phenomenon may be seen in the fact that the founder of the Kingdom of Israel, Jeroboam (I) the son of Nebat, was himself from the tribe of Ephraim (1 Kings 11:26).

Yet the most telling reason that the Book of Hosea uses the word "Ephraim" so often in parallel with Israel is because of the fact that the town of Bethel, lying within its southernmost border, became the prominent idolatrous religious center of the Northern Kingdom. The golden calf worship, instituted by Jeroboam and set up at Bethel of Ephraim and in Dan to the north, flourished mainly in the southern city as opposed to Dan partly due to its geographic location and nearness to Samaria and Jerusalem. Undoubtedly, the main reason was

---

[1] Thiele, *The Mysterious Numbers of the Hebrew Kings*, op. cit., p. 129.

[2] Faulstich, *History, Harmony and the Hebrew Kings*, op. cit., footnote 24, p. 141.

because it was at that site that the kingdom's founder ordained a yearly feast of idolatry on the 15th day of the 8th month to compete with the Feast of Tabernacles. This Jeroboam (I) did hoping to secure the hearts of the people to himself lest they return to Rehoboam, Solomon's son and king of Judah, and slay him in so doing (1 Kings 12:26–33). Once established, the tradition would naturally continue.

That this is the actual fact of the matter and not that of a third kingdom as Thiele has conjectured may be seen by observing the *context* of the Hosea 5:5 passage. This may first be seen in two verses that immediately precede Thiele's "proof text," viz.,

> Ephraim is joined to idols: let him alone (Hos.4:17).

This is telling, but the next is even more so for it is only two verses prior to Hosea 5:5:

> I know Ephraim, and Israel is not hid from me: for now, O Ephraim, thou committest whoredom, and Israel is defiled (Hos.5:3).

The context is unmistakable. The idolatry involved in the golden calf worship in Ephraim had polluted all Israel. Ephraim was singled out above and yet representatively of all the ten tribes because it was the focal point of the sinful practice. The ninth verse makes undeniably plain this entire argument:

> Ephraim shall be desolate in the day of rebuke: among the tribes of Israel have I made known that which shall surely be (Hos.5:9).

Here in the very immediate proximity where Thiele has taken for his proof of a third kingdom named "Ephraim," the text refers to it as no more than one of the tribes of Israel.

By now the matter should be finally settled, yet another proof shall be given from which Thiele's hypothesis cannot possibly survive:

> And it came to pass in the days of Ahaz the son of Jotham, the son of Uzziah, king of Judah, that Rezin the king of Syria, and Pekah the son of Remaliah, king of Israel, went up toward Jerusalem to war against it, but could not prevail against it. And it was told the house of David, saying, Syria is confederate with Ephraim. And his heart was moved, and the heart of his people, as the trees of the wood are moved with the wind. Then said the LORD unto Isaiah, Go forth now to meet Ahaz, thou, and Shearjashub thy son, at the end of the conduit of the upper pool in the highway of the fuller's field; And say unto him, Take heed, and be quiet; fear not, neither be fainthearted for the two tails of these smoking firebrands, for the fierce anger of Rezin with Syria, and of the son of Remaliah. Because Syria, Ephraim, and the son of Remaliah, have taken evil counsel against thee, saying, Let us go up against Judah, and vex it, and let us make a breach therein for us, and set a king in the midst of it, even the son of Tabeal: Thus saith the Lord GOD, It shall not stand, neither shall it come to pass. For the head of Syria is Damascus, and the head of Damascus is Rezin; and within threescore and five years shall Ephraim be broken, that it be not a people. And the head of Ephraim is Samaria, and the head of Samaria is Remaliah's son. If ye will not believe, surely ye shall not be established (Isa. 7:1–9).

Who can honestly read these verses and not see that Israel and Ephraim are being used interchangeably and synonymously? Pekah is said to be the king of Israel and united with Syria yet in the following sentence Syria's confederate is identified as Ephraim. The eighth verse is conclusive for it states that within 65 years Ephraim would be broken and no longer be a people. Was not this the fate of Israel?

If they were two different kingdoms, where is Israel's judgment declared? After all, the passage began by making mention of her. The ninth verse forever seals the argument for it declares that the head (capital or seat of government) of Ephraim is Samaria – and Samaria *was* the capital of the northern kingdom of Israel from the days of Omri (1 Kings 16:23–24, cp. vs.29, etc.).

The 17th verse, though not given above, adds a crushing encore for it refers to "the day that Ephraim departed from Judah." Not even Thiele had Ephraim departing from "Judah"! He had her split off from *Israel*. The *only* departing from Judah was that of the Kingdom of Israel in the days of Jeroboam (I) and thus verse 17, speaking of the same time frame as Hosea, demands that Ephraim is but another name by which the Northern Kingdom was known (2 Chron. 25:7 unmistakably so states this fact).

Finally, Thiele's position is totally untenable for 2 Kings 15:25, a verse to which he often alludes, distinctly states that Pekah was merely "a captain" of Pekahiah's, not even "the" captain (i.e., the commander-in-chief) of his army — much less the king of a concurrent rival kingdom in the north! Yet Thiele would have us believe that while king of the "Kingdom of Ephraim," Pekah concurrently accepted such a position in the legions of Pekahiah.[1] How can such a declaration be either offered or taken as serious?

As "king," Pekah would never have accepted so lowly an offer. Indeed, Pekahiah could hardly have been expected to have even made it in the first place for, according to Thiele's conjecture, Pekah rebelled against Pekahiah's father, Menahem, and in so doing divided the Northern Kingdom. No! It was only upon his assassination of Pekahiah that Pekah assumed the title of "king" and at that time he was said to be king of Israel (2 Kings 15:27). Thus Thiele's hypothesis is shown as thoroughly destitute and devoid of merit.

3. THIELE'S HOSHEA-HEZEKIAH ANACHRONISM

As formerly reported, Thiele employed his "dual dating" technique to develop a chronological scheme that denies the testimony of 2 Kings 18:9–10 which synchronizes the fourth and sixth years of Hezekiah with the seventh and ninth of Hoshea respectively. (Again, see Thiele's exposition on page 174 of this dissertation; cp. Charts 5, 5c and see page 167.) Thiele is also seen to violate 2 Kings 18:1 which synchronizes the beginning of Hezekiah's reign with the third year of Hoshea, king of Israel. Note that Thiele's pattern places both the fall of Samaria and the *end* of Hoshea's reign as occurring about *seven years before* Hezekiah began to reign despite the clear wording of the biblical text which states unequivocally that the two events transpired in the sixth year of that Judaic monarch's rule.

He also violates 2 Kings 17:1 and 17:6. Thus, Thiele's anti-biblical scheme has been shown to violate the plain teachings of 2 Kings 17:1, 17:6, as well as 18:1, 9–10 which place Hoshea and Hezekiah as having overlapping reigns, a fact which Thiele himself acknowledges having done.[2]

4. MENAHEM-PEKAHIAH-PEKAH-HEZEKIAH SUMMARY

It has been demonstrated that because of Thiele's

1. uncritical acceptance of the Assyrian documents at face value (although as shown, due to their fragmented condition much of a conjectural nature has been added by the translators);

2. erroneous identification of Pul with Tiglath-pileser; and

3. incorrect handling of the 14th year of Hezekiah with reference to the 3rd year of Sennacherib,

he has violated much Scripture while at the same time he has claimed to defend its authority. Yet instead, he has forced the biblical text to conform to a tainted secular history. The extant Assyrian data itself is not so much at fault; rather, the major cause of the problem is the often highly speculative emendations and interpretations given to the damaged areas which are then taken as historical fact. It was this, in part, that caused Thiele to erect a biblically unsupported second Hebrew kingdom in the north in direct violation against much Sacred Scripture.

Yet it must be seen that even more at the heart of the problem as to how Thiele and the vast majority of academia who followed him were so easily lead astray in all this was due to their world view and frame of reference regarding textual criticism. Once he and they had accepted as "fact" that the biblical text was not preserved as God had promised, but contained many scribal errors, emendations, omissions, additions, etc. they felt no compunction in altering or setting aside the testimony of that record in favor of the data of other nations.

Yet, as has been demonstrated again and again in this work, it is the continuous uninterrupted flowing Hebrew history that should be utilized in amending and interpreting the often fragmented discontinuous records of the kingdoms contiguous to those people – not the reverse, as is the custom in this day. Truly, the prongs of

---

[1] Thiele, *The Mysterious Numbers of the Hebrew Kings, op. cit.,* p. 129.

[2] Thiele, *The Mysterious Numbers of the Hebrew Kings, op. cit.,* p. 130.

the "Trident" blind all alike, Christian or non-Christian, regardless of brilliance, dedication, and scholarship.

Although he may be referred to on occasion, the thrust of this work will now remove Dr. Thiele out from under the spotlight. The field of education has been properly served by that which has already been said. Although other salient points could well be addressed, it should be remembered that this research was never intended as a point-by-point refutation of Thiele's chronology of the kings of the divided monarchy. Nevertheless, due to the vaunted position to which he has been placed, the foregoing detailed analysis of many of his major points has been deemed necessary in order to allow the reader to bring clearly into focus the matter at hand.

It is most important that the secular as well as the Christian reader bear in mind that the actual issues covered on this subject have had nothing whatever to do with "religion." The real issue has been to lay before the world of academia and the general public the true nature of the condition and handling of the ancient records of the neighboring kingdoms of the Hebrew people, especially those of the Assyrians, to the intent that all may see the unfair practices, extravagant claims, and brain-washing which has for years gone on in the name of scholarship and education.

Again, such dishonest and unscientific practices against the records of any people other than the Hebrews is totally without precedent. This bears testimony to our previous charge that an undercurrent of absolute prejudice exists in the realm of academia with regard to the Jewish people of the Bible, their ancient records, and the God of Abraham, Isaac, and Jacob.

L. OTHER MISCELLANEOUS PROBLEMS RESOLVED

In this section, an assortment of varied problems will be addressed. With regard to chronological importance, its significance is not always of equal standing with some issues dealt with earlier. Moreover, it is beyond the scope of the present treatise to attempt at this writing to meet every pertinent question or problem; although to some degree each has been

confronted by the various charts presented herein.

1. THE PEKAH-HOSHEA CONNECTION

In comparing and/or triangulating the Scriptures relating to the reigns of Pekah and Hoshea of Israel with those of Ahaz and Hezekiah of the Kingdom of Judah, an interregnum or period of time in which no king occupied the throne of Israel for a space of about nine years is demanded by the data (2 Kings 15:30; 16:2; 17:1–4; 18:1–2, 9–10; see Chart 5). This problem is well known and, as the Scriptures do not specifically use the term "interregnum" to identify this phenomenon, it has become a stumbling block for many. Yet an understanding of the problem is actually very straightforward.

Ahaz had called Tiglath-pileser (III) to come to his aid against Rezin, King of Syria, and Pekah of Israel. The Assyrian monarch came at Ahaz's request. He took Damascus and slew Rezin. Tiglath also caused the Northern Kingdom to break off her attack at which time he placed Ahaz under tribute (2 Kings 16:5-9; 2 Chron. 28:16-21). With Pekah still enthroned, at this time Tiglath carried the tribes of Reuben, Gad, the eastern half of Manasseh, Zebulun, the area around Dor and the plain of Sharon ("the way of the sea") into captivity. These thereby preceded the other tribes who were not removed to Assyria until Hoshea's ninth year (2 Ki. 15:29; 1 Chron. 5:26; Isa. 9:1).

About that time and during the "twentieth year of Jotham, the son of Uzziah" (740 BC),[1] Hoshea led a conspiracy against Pekah, slew him and took the reigns of the government – although not as king at the time (2 Kings 15:30, cp. 17:1 and 15:30; 16:2; 17:1–4; 18:1–2, 9–10; again, see Chart 5).

---

[1] Although Jotham reigned only 16 years and not 20, the date is probably reckoned from the beginning of his rule to underscore the Lord's displeasure against wicked Ahaz for: (1) calling upon Tiglath-pileser for help instead of the Living God, (2) having Urijah, the high priest, build an altar like that at Damascus at which he might inquire, (3) cutting off the borders of the bases, removing the laver from off them, and taking down the laver from off the brasen oxen that were under it, (4) sacrificing unto the gods of Damascus, (5) shutting up the doors of the Temple in Jerusalem, (6) making altars and placing them at every corner of Jerusalem, and (7) making high places to burn incense unto other gods in every city of Judah, etc. (2 Kings 16:7–18; 2 Chron. 28:19–25).

Undoubtedly, the reason for this short suspension of the monarchy, during which some sort of an uneasy and confused anarchy must have prevailed, was the impending danger presented by the immediate presence of the Assyrians. The full impact of this threat can only be appreciated if one marks off the tribes, cities, and land areas mentioned as having fallen to Tiglath-pileser near the end of Pekah's reign (2 Kings 15:29; 1 Chron. 5:26; Isa. 9:1).

The result will show that the areal extent of the Northern Kingdom was reduced by nearly 75 percent. The remaining quarter, about 35 miles wide by 45 long, was enclosed on three sides by Assyrian occupation. The enemy controlled a 10 to 15 mile wide strip on the west side along the Plain of Sharon ("the way of the sea," Isa. 9:1) to just south of the town of Aphek, all of the upper portion of Israel from the town of Megiddo northward, and a nearly 30-mile-wide band along the entire eastern side of the Jordan down to the Arnon River.

Thus, enveloped by a people well known for their barbaric actions, especially toward opposing monarchs (e.g., 2 Kings 16:9, Assyrian records being replete with boasts concerning such deeds by her various kings), is it any wonder that no one could be found possessing the ability to unite the differing factions under his leadership? Indeed, under such tenuous and precarious conditions could any be found who would take the reins of the kingdom? Consequently, there exists a clear forthright reason for the interregnum and yet, in a very real sense, there was none! The Scriptures proclaim that Israel had a "king" during this period, at least in God's sight, and he was not Hoshea!

Scripture refers to Ahaz not only as the king of Judah, but also as bearing the title "King of Israel" (2 Chron. 28:19, cp. vv. 26–27). Hence it would appear that upon the death of Pekah, the Assyrian vassal Ahaz, having the heart and religious demeanor of the kings of Israel (2 Kings 16:1–4 and 9–18), was viewed as then being "king" of Israel as well. After all, most of the Northern Kingdom was then under the heel of the Assyrian boot. Perhaps Tiglath-pileser placed his vassal in authority over the conquered NK and bestowed the title "King of Israel" upon Ahaz, though he remained in

Jerusalem and Hoshea functioned as the "on site" overseer in Samaria. In any case, that Ahaz bore that appellation is confirmed by a comparison of the following Scriptures:

> Now the rest of the acts of Ahaz which he did, are they not written in the book of the chronicles of the *kings of Judah*? And Ahaz slept with his fathers, and *was buried with his fathers* in the city of David: and Hezekiah his son reigned in his stead (2 Kings 16:19–20).

> Now the rest of his acts and of all his ways, first and last, behold, they are written in the book of the kings of Judah *and Israel*. And Ahaz slept with his fathers, and they buried him in the city, even in Jerusalem: but *they brought him not into the sepulchres of the kings of Israel*: and Hezekiah his son reigned in his stead (2 Chronicles 28:26–27, author's italics).

The italicized words in the above passages give bold contrast to each other for 2 Kings 16 proclaims that Ahaz's deeds were recorded with the other kings of Judah and that he was buried with its former kings in the city of David; whereas 2 Chron. 28 adds that his deeds were also recorded in the annals of Israel as well as Judah and accentuates the fact that he was not buried with the other kings of Israel. How could the situation have been more clearly stated?

Then, apparently after about nine years in which he maintained some lesser position at the head of the tiny nation, Hoshea ascended the throne in the 12th year of Ahaz (c. 731 BC, 2 Kings 17:1–4), probably as an Assyrian vassal. Tiglath-pileser claims to have so placed him:[1]

> The land of Bit-Humria ... all of its people, together with their goods I carried off to Assyria. Pakaha, their king they deposed and I placed Ausi' (Hoshea) over them as king. 10 talents of gold, x talents of silver, as their tribute I received from them and to Assyria I carried them.

It is admitted by all Assyriologists that her monarchs often overstated the facts. As the Hebrew Text does not confirm the above claim, it is viewed by this author with considerable caution. Thus, whereas Tiglath-pileser may or may not actually have placed Hoshea upon the throne, the Assyrian and biblical accounts

---

[1] Luckenbill, *ARAB, op. cit.*, vol. I, sec. 816, p. 293.

indicate that his enthronement had Assyrian approval.

Hoshea seized upon the death of that Assyrian sovereign to rebel and was again subjugated, this time by King Shalmaneser IV (V) (see 2 Kings 17:3). After about three years, Shalmaneser learned of a conspiracy whereby Hoshea had sent messengers to So, king of Egypt, for help and sent no tribute to the Assyrian king as he had done year-by-year. Shalmaneser responded by taking Hoshea, casting him in prison, and besieging Samaria three years. In the ninth year of Hoshea, the king of Assyria took Samaria and carried Israel away into Assyria (2 Kings 17:4–6).

2. DATING THE FALL OF PEKAH, REZIN, AND DAMASCUS

The conflict between the confederacy of Pekah of Israel and Rezin of Syria against Ahaz is recorded in 2 Kings 16:5–9,18; 2 Chronicles 28:5–25; and chapters 7–10 of Isaiah. The Assyrian School assigns 732 BC as the year in which these three events transpired; however as can be seen on Chart 5, this study places it in the year 740. The question naturally arises as to how Thiele and others have arrived at 732 and whether my study has ignored *bona fide* historical data and thus contains an error?

The Assyrian date is based upon the information contained in the third column of the eponymous years assigned 733 BC and 732, both of which read "against the land of Damascus",[1] and this is thereby deduced as referencing the same encounter as that of the biblical account. This is the sum of the Assyrian data with reference to these incidents. However, this may merely refer to a later conflict with resurgent Syrian forces. After all, it is certain that the Syrian army was not totally obliterated or ceased to function as a military force for the eponym designated 727 BC gives the fact that they again fought "against Damascus."[2]

The point to keep in mind is that this author knows of no Assyrian document discovered as of this writing which actually bears decisive

information as to the death of Rezin and/or the fall of Damascus. It is a curious circumstance indeed that this date has been so firmly "fixed" and so widely accepted throughout academic circles on such scant and flimsy evidence.

Conversely, as stated in the previous problem (the Pekah-Hoshea connection), the Hebrew historical record as preserved in the Scriptures contains data that unmistakably places these events some nineteen years prior to the fall of Samaria in Hezekiah's sixth year. Therefore, the positioning of these events in the year 740 BC does not violate any firm historic data which states the contrary. Further, it honors that which is far and away the most reliable chronological record available.

To the charge that "the Assyrian Eponym List says nothing of an incursion against Damascus in the year 740 BC" which might be laid against this, the reader should be aware that of the 157 limmu that have a third column only 12 contain an extra entry concerning a second subject. Further, beginning in the eponym of Tukulti-apal-esharra (Tiglath-pileser III) which is set as 743 BC, one finds the major event of the year recorded as being a conflict with the city of "Arpadda."[3] Reading down the list, the following year states "against Arpadda" and the year designated 741 BC reads "against Arpadda. After three years it was conquered." The next eponym, Nabu-etirani, which Assyriologists assign the year 740 BC again says "against Arpadda."

Now since the Eponym List almost exclusively names but one event per limmu (the most outstanding of that year) and the ongoing struggle with Arpadda had been the paramount focus of the Assyrian military thrust for the three preceding years, if Tiglath-pileser opened up action on a second front in the general vicinity of the first and in so doing Damascus fell in the succeeding year, is it any wonder this event would be seen as secondary when compared to the status of the persistent defenders of the city of Arpadda? Therefore, one should not be surprised that the 740 BC fall of Damascus was not selected as the foremost event of that year. In comparison, the Syrian capital

---

[1] Thiele, *The Mysterious Numbers of the Hebrew Kings, op. cit.,* p. 224.

[2] *Ibid.*

[3] *Ibid.*

gave far less resistance and thus its taking would not have been deemed as glorious an act.

Moreover, this writer would not at all be surprised to learn that subsequent archaeological discoveries uncover just such a finding. Yet it must be added that even in the eventuality such would be found at some future date, it would not "throw more light" upon Scripture. Its testimony is already true and secure. What is needful is for all to see and acknowledge that it is Scripture which should be consulted to "throw more light" on the secular dates for this period. For now, there is no explicit decisive Assyrian data that militates against the 740 BC date as set forth by this research for the death year of Pekah, Rezin, and the fall of Damascus.

3. DATING THE FALL OF SAMARIA

The Assyrian Academy follows Thiele in assigning 723 BC as the year of the fall of Samaria, however the data contained in the Hebrew Text more readily lends itself to the placing of this event in the year 721 BC. Most of the past chronologists concluded the latter. This is not to say that the biblical data "demands" the year 721, but it is the most natural resolution. This is especially true if one places the fall of Jerusalem at 586 BC. It is not being said that Scripture will support no other date but rather that this author could not stretch it to support 723 unless he moved the date for Jerusalem's razing to at least 587 BC.

Attention is not being called to this matter merely over this two-year discrepancy between the Assyrian School's result and this work. As stated at the onset, the goal of this study was to erect a "standard" Hebrew chronology, not a so-called "absolute" one. Therefore, in that spirit Thiele's 723 date in and of itself is neither being challenged nor is an issue being made over this small two-year disparity.

That which is being called into question is the technique, method, and general handling (or mishandling) of the Assyrian documents by the Assyrian Academy. Again the question must be answered: "How did Thiele, etc. arrive at 723 BC for the fall of Samaria and is the research herein disregarding genuine historic data and thus contains an error?"

With regard to this date, a problem exists among Assyriologists due to the fact that

Sargon II seems to claim he was responsible for the capture of Samaria. Luckenbill has supplied the restoration: "[At the beginning of my rule, in my first year of reign]" to Sargon's annals.[1] According to the Assyrian dating, Sargon ascended the throne 12 Tebeth (December, 20th 722 BC), and his first year began in 721.[2]

As has been formerly demonstrated, Thiele's mishandling of the Hoshea/Hezekiah connection led him to set Hoshea's ninth year during which Samaria fell to the Assyrians as 723 BC. Thus, Luckenbill's restoration which places Sargon as taking Samaria in 721 creates a great difficulty for Thiele and those who follow his chronology. At this point Thiele appealed to Olmstead's earlier work which concluded that the fall of Samaria occurred in 723 and that Sargon's claim was not true,[3] thereby erecting a division of opinion among Assyriologists.

Olmstead correctly pointed out that the biblical account of Samaria's fall made no mention of Sargon, and that Shalmaneser was twice mentioned as the Assyrian king who initiated the military action against Hoshea's rebellion which ended after a three-year siege (2 Kings 17:3–7; 2 Kings 18:9–11).[4] Of course, one cannot help but find it amusing that now at last the Hebrew record is resorted to as a final "court of appeal" when so many other times its testimony has been so flagrantly set aside by the pundits of this school.

Olmstead further noted that the Babylonian Chronicle gave only one citation concerning the reign of Shalmaneser, and that was his destruction of the city of "Sa-ma/ba-ra-'-in"

---

[1] Luckenbill, *ARAB*, op. cit., vol. II, sec. 4, p. 2.

[2] Professor Jack Finegan's recent edition is the source for the 12 Tebeth = 20 December computation: *Handbook of Biblical Chronology*, Revised Edition (Peabody, MA: Hendrickson Pub., 1998) p. 250. Also see: Grayson, *ABC*, op. cit., Chronicle 1:31, p. 73; cp. Thiele, *The Mysterious Numbers of the Hebrew Kings*, op. cit., pp. 163–164. Finegan's 1964 publication, as well as Thiele, simply stated that Sargon's enthronement of 12 Tebeth was "late in December of 722 BC."

[3] Thiele, *The Mysterious Numbers of the Hebrew Kings*, op. cit., p. 164.

[4] A.T. Olmstead, "Fall of Samaria," *American Journal of Semitic Languages and Literatures* 21 (1904–05): pages 179–182.

which Tadmor concluded was Samaria.[1] However, this identification has long been the subject of debate with only Olmstead, Delitzsch, Haupt, and Boree concurring (as of AD 1982) leaving the deciding factor as the witness of the Eponym Chronicle.[2] Unfortunately the register is badly mutilated for the years 725–720, nonetheless Luckenbill has restored them to read:[3]

726 Marduk-bel-usur	(governor) of Amedi	in the land
725 Mahde	(governor) of Nineveh	against [Samaria]
724 Ashur-ishmeani	(governor) of [Kakzi]	against [Samaria]
723 Shalmaneser	king of Assyria	against [Samaria]
722 Urta-ilia	[field marshal]	[The foundation of the temple of Nabu was torn up (for repairs)]
721 Nabutaris	[high chamberlain]	[Nabu entered the new temple]

However the fact is the eye/mind cannot properly appreciate the full significance of the fragmented nature of the above even with the brackets and parenthesis present.

The true extent of the mutilation can be seen below. Bear in mind that this is how the register actually appears, only without the years being listed.

726 Marduk-bel-usur	of Amedi	in the land
725 Mahde	of Nineveh	against
724 Ashur-ishmeani	of	against
723 Shalmaneser	king of Assyria	against
722 Urta-ilia		
721 Nabutaris		

This then is the *only* Assyrian evidence which is uncontested. The rationale for using it to establish the date for the fall of Samaria is:

1. the biblical account states that the siege of Samaria lasted *three* years,

2. the Eponym List has the word "against" *three* years in succession (725–723) with the name of the enemy location completely missing, and

3. the coincidence of the "three's" in 1 and 2 above was deemed by Luckenbill (Olmstead also) as sufficient cause for the "restoration" as shown in the first listing and the subsequent "fixing" of the date of the fall of Samaria as being 723 BC.

1 Grayson, *ABC, op. cit.,* Chronicle 1:28, p. 73.

2 Thiele, *The Mysterious Numbers of the Hebrew Kings, op. cit.,* footnote 4, p. 165.

3 Luckenbill, *ARAB, op. cit.,* vol. II, p. 437.

There we have it! Although Thiele offers in evidence several other far weaker supportive arguments on pages 166–167, each based upon still more speculation, this is the real thrust of the Assyrian Academy's thesis. These are its strong points.

The third particular may have a ring of being reasonable or logical, but it certainly cannot be construed as a settled historic fact although it has been so made at the expense of Hebrew history. Whatever else may be said with regard to this matter, the fact is that the scholars of the Assyrian School must be seen as guilty of having reached their final conclusion as to the 723 BC date for the fall of Samaria based upon the *absence* of data!

To say the least, this seems an embarrassing circumstance upon which to lay a foundation. As to the 721 date used by this research, it should be noted that again this violates no real substantiated Assyrian data for the information in the third column of the Eponym List is in brackets for both 722 and 721; thus the outstanding event for the year rests upon nothing more than Luckenbill's speculation.

Insofar as the complaint that the Hebrew record does not mention Sargon by name with regard to the besiegement and fall of Samaria, the following verses are again appealed to for consideration:

> And it came to pass in the fourth year of king Hezekiah, which was the seventh year of Hoshea son of Elah king of Israel, that Shalmaneser king of Assyria came up against Samaria, and besieged it. And at the end of three years **they** took it: even in the sixth year of Hezekiah, that is in the ninth year of Hoshea king of Israel, Samaria was taken (2 Kings 18:9–10, author's boldface font).

This author finds no real fault in the long-standing argument that Shalmaneser began the siege in 723 BC with Sargon probably his tartan. Toward the end of 722 BC, with the siege still in full effect, Shalmaneser died and Sargon ascended the throne exactly as the Assyrian annals seem to indicate. Thus, Sargon was the Assyrian monarch who actually carried the Northern Kingdom away upon Samaria's collapse the following year.

The biblical evidence for this admittedly is quite modest; however the above text may be alluding to this very scenario by the boldfaced "they" in

the phrase "they took it" (Samaria) in the tenth verse. Is it not possible, even plausible, that this is a veiled reference to the fact that two Assyrian monarchs were involved in the final days of Samaria, namely Shalmaneser and his successor Sargon?

Still, the real issue which must not be lost here is that of the degree of confidence which abounds throughout the literature as to the certainty of the termination date of the Kingdom of Israel based upon the Assyrian records in light of the reality of the situation as presented herein. As in this case and others already discussed, time and time again excessive extravagant conclusions and judgments are made based on the most flimsy evidence and/or a misunderstanding of that which is before the interpreter.

This may be due to the damaged condition of the data, preconceived ideas based upon his frame of reference or, as in the example under discussion, much has been made from nothing; yet its reliability is amazingly still placed above that of the biblical testimony. The scriptural witness, although often spoken of as if it were held in some esteem, is actually hardly referenced except where there is nothing else or when it can be used to support hypotheses which are too weak to stand alone on the fragmented meager evidence upon which they were erected.

Considering all that has been said from the section on the Assyrian Eponyms to this point, it should be readily apparent how reasonably conservative scholars have been deceived into believing and/or writing much that is half-truth. Gleason Archer Jr. is typical of the problem when he wrote:[1]

> In the earlier days of Old Testament scholarship, considerable difficulty was encountered in harmonizing the numbers given in the Books of Kings for the reigns of the various rulers of the Northern and Southern Kingdoms ... when all the regnal years were added, they came to a total considerably greater than that which could have elapsed between the death of Solomon and the fall of Jerusalem. Later research, however, demonstrated the fact that in many instances the crown prince or immediate

successor to the throne was formally crowned and his reign officially begun even in the lifetime of his father. ... between 743 and 739 Judah was ruled over by no less than three kings at once: Uzziah, Jotham, and Ahaz.

Where did Archer get the erroneous idea that the regnal years of Judah summed to a value far greater than the time span from the death of Solomon to the fall of Jerusalem? The answer reveals the real problem confronting Christian (and secular) scholarship today.

Like so many others, Archer began by accepting Thiele's final results as his starting point thereby moving from one error to another although at the same time offering much intermingled insight. Archer uncritically accepted as established fact the entire Eponym Canon with its dates and that Ahab and Jehu were positively synchronized with the realm of Shalmaneser II (III). Not trusting in the faithfulness of the Hebrew Text and faced with the dilemma of about 45 years having been removed from the biblical chronological records by that determination, Archer could come to no other conclusion.

Yet it has been shown that he and all others who so do are grasping at a mirage, an evanescent cloud which vanishes upon thorough analysis. Later it will be shown that this same error has also led many to place Shalmaneser I (II) as a contemporary adversary of David by more mishandling of the historical data.

Having fallen into the first pit, Archer quickly fell into the next snare by declaring the contrived biblical co-regencies by Thiele, etc. as "demonstrated" fact. This led him to the thoroughly non-scriptural determination that Uzziah, Jotham, and Ahaz all reigned over Judah between the years 743 to 739 (Charts 5 and 5c for biblical portrayal).

Nor should this be taken as conjecture on the part of this author, for on the following page Archer refers to several Assyrian monuments stating: "From such data as these it has been established that there were numerous co-regencies in both Judah and Israel, and that the years of the co-regency were reckoned in the total figure for the reign of each king involved." It is truly an amazing phenomenon with what inconsequential data chronologists will assign co-regencies to the Hebrew kings in order to

---

[1] Archer, *A Survey of Old Testament Introduction, op. cit.,* p. 291.

make matters "work out," yet reject so doing with regard to their neighboring nations even when the records present justification.

4. JOSIAH, NECO, AND THE KING OF ASSYRIA

Another problem somewhat different from those dealt with previously in that it does not directly deal with the constructing of a chronology yet still related to such studies, is that found concerning Josiah, the last godly king of the kingdom of Judah. In the strictest sense, the problem is one of apologetics, the branch of theology concerned with the defense or proof of the Christian faith and Scripture. Nevertheless, as one may readily comprehend from all that has gone before in this treatise, there is an obvious close relationship of biblical chronology to such a defense or proof and hence, it is appropriate to address the issue herein.

a. "Against" or "To the Aid Of"

The controversy revolves about the following passage:

> In his days Pharaohnechoh king of Egypt went up against the king of Assyria to the river Euphrates: and king Josiah went *against* him; and he slew him at Megiddo, when he had seen him (2 Kings 23:29, author's italics).

The problem arises over the italicized word "against" as rendered by the King James translators. The New King James Version gives the verse as:

> In his days Pharaoh Necho king of Egypt *went to the aid of* the king of Assyria, to the River Euphrates; and King Josiah went against him. And Pharaoh Necho killed him at Megiddo when he confronted him (2 Kings 23:29, NKJV, author's italics).

The phrase "went to the aid of" the king of Assyria as found in the NKJV is certainly not the same as "against" the king of Assyria in the KJB. The New International Version, Revised Standard Version, New English Version – indeed the majority of the modern translations – read similar to the New King James Version which strangely relegates to a footnote the alternative "or to attack."

However, the old AD 1560 Geneva Bible along with all the old English translations prior to AD 1611 such as Wycliffe's, Coverdale's, Matthew's, The Great Bible, The Bishop's Bible, etc., as well as the American Standard, and Amplified are among those whose reading is "against" in agreement with the Authorized King James Bible. The highly touted New American Standard compromises stating simply "Pharaoh Neco king of Egypt went up *to* the king of Assyria to the river Euphrates" and thus one way or the other perverts the Scripture.

What then is at the heart of this discrepancy? Did Pharaoh Neco go to help or fight against the king of Assyria, and why cannot the various translators make up their minds? The forthcoming analysis reveals the tragic current state of affairs with regard to textual criticism and translation prevailing in today's academia.

First, the Hebrew word in question here is transliterated "al" (Hebrew = ayin-lamedh = על, Strong's Concordance number 5921). It is a preposition which occurs 1896 times in Scripture and has a wide variety of meanings depending upon syntax and context. According to computer analysis, the 47 King James translators rendered "al" as "against" 542 times, "over" 409, "on" 292, "at" 83, "concerning" 78, and "above" 68 times.

Further, in descending order of usage it was translated as "off," "into," "thereon," "because," "according," "after," "toward," "beside," "about," "before," "therein," "under," "thereto," "within," "among," "than," "through," and the word "forward" bringing the study down to being so referenced but 3 times with quite a few other less frequent meanings having been recovered as well. However, *not one time* was it rendered "to the aid of" or even "together with" as the NKJV margin suggests (and never as "to" as in the NAS version).

In fact, not once was a word found which bore any resemblance whatsoever to that meaning and neither Strong, Gesenius, nor Jay P. Green offers any support to such a translation. Keil and Delitzsch accepted unreservedly that the "against" rendering was correct.[1] So again the question must be asked: "Why this discrepancy between the various translations?"

This alteration in wording is not at all the result of a different translation of the Hebrew word "al" (על). Actually the Hebrew Text has been *rejected* by most scholars as corrupt. The

---

[1] Keil and Delitzsch, *op. cit.*, vol. 3, pp. 492–493.

change which states that rather than opposing the king of Assyria, Pharaoh Neco (Necho) went to *join* the king of Assyria is based totally upon a conjectured restoration of a portion of the historical records of Babylon. Hence an alteration has been made in the biblical text based upon the assumption that some *other* nation's historical writings are correct, true and have no "scribal blunders" or misstated facts rather than the God-inspired Hebrew Scriptures.

b. Egypt Allied with Assyria

As a matter of fact, the archaeological records upon which the reading in the NKJV (and many others) are based *do not even say* that the king of Egypt joined with the king of Assyria. With reference to the years of Nabopolassar's reign and recalling that the Babylonian records habitually refer to their various monarchs as "the king of Akkad," what they actually say is:

58   The sixteenth year: In the month Iyyar the king of Akkad mustered his army and marched to Assyria. From [the month ...] until the month Marchesvan

59   he marched about victoriously in Assyria. In the month Marchesvan the Umman-manda, [who] had come [hel]p the king of Akkad,

60   put their armies together and

61   marched

60   to Harran [against Ashur-uball]it (II) who had ascended the throne in Assyria.

61f. Fear of the enemy overcame Ashur-uballit (II) and the army of Eg[...] had come [...] and they aban[...] the city [...] they crossed.

62

63   The king of Akkad reached Harran and [...] he captured the city.

64   He carried off the vast booty of the city and the temple. In the month Adar the kings of Akkad left their [...]

65   He went home. The Umman-manda, who had come to help the king of Akkad, withdrew.

66   <The seventeenth year>: In the month Tammuz Ashur-uballit (II), king of Assyria, the large army of Egypt [...]

67   crossed the river (Euphrates) and marched against Harran to conquer (it) [...] they [capture]d (it).

68   They defeated the garrison which the king of Akkad had stationed inside. When they had defeated (it) they encamped against Harran.

Babylonian Chronicle 3:58–68 has been interpreted by Albert Kirk Grayson such that 61f. reads:

61f. Fear of the enemy overcame Ashur-uballit (II) and the army of Eg[ypt which] had come [to help him] and they aban[doned] the city [...] they crossed.

However possible this rendering may be, it represents conjecture on the part of the translator. The words contained in brackets and parentheses are not found in this Assyrian document.[1] The reader can also see for himself that the numbers have been arranged *out of order* to facilitate the translation as given. It is further most instructive to note that, as this author has often asserted, the Babylonian records are not nearly as complete or flowing as the Hebrew Old Testament record.

We hasten to add that the letters which precede each of the brackets (i.e., in 61f., "Eg[...]" and "abon[...]") may also be viewed as being of an extremely doubtful nature as letters from one language do not readily lend themselves to be translated unless one has the whole word before him. In many languages, the endings of many words make a great difference as to the correct meaning. Nearly always in such circumstances, all that can be done is to merely transliterate the letters into the other alphabet, the result of which is usually nonsensical. Such seldom results in the forming of a word or even part of a recognizable word in the other language.

Thus the questions may be fairly asked, does Chronicle 3:61f. actually testify to and prove that the word "Egypt" is present in the text and/or to the fact that whatever army it may be, they have come to "help" the Assyrian king, Ashur-uballit (II)? Indeed, does 3:66–67 really state that the Egyptian army united with Ashur-uballit's Assyrian forces against the Babylonian army? When taken alone, the truthful reply must be declared as "no, they do not so state." Wiseman underscores this fact in his work by adding a question mark within the bracket, viz. "Eg[ypt(?)]."[2]

As a result of the above stated weaknesses and overstatements concerning the Babylonian records and, in the hope that the matter may be put to rest for all interested parties on both

---

[1] Grayson, *ABC, op. cit.*, pp. 95–96.

[2] D.J. Wiseman, *Chronicles of Chaldaean Kings (626–556 B.C.) in the British Museum*, (London: 1956) BM 21901, Reverse side, p. 63.

sides of the question, a thorough examination seems in order before concluding with a solution to this issue. In order to realize this intended goal, further weaknesses must first be raised that nothing be left undisclosed now only to be brought up at some later occasion and thus undo that which has been accomplished. These will be followed by factual rejoinders which heretofore have been generally lacking in the literature thereby possibly leaving much in doubt and unsettled in the minds of many.

First, the Assyrian word for Egypt transliterates "mi-sir." It occurs frequently throughout the Babylonian records. Only the "mi" portion is legible in 61f., however as the context relates to an army, "mi" must be a portion of the word for some nation. Chronicle 3:66, referring to the following year (substantiated by the months mentioned from 58–69) contains the word "mi-sir" in clear un-mutilated condition[1] and as this study has found no other nation designated in the Chronicles as beginning with "mi" the matter would appear to be resolved. Therefore the restoration "Eg[ypt]" by Grayson seems justified, yet Wiseman's question mark within the brackets still enjoins caution.

The second part of the problem as to whether the Egyptian army came to "assist" the Assyrian forces against the Babylonian's is not so straightforward. First, Chronicle 3:66–68 has been said to substantiate the interpretation rendered to 61f.; however this testimony alone would not be truly sufficient for, due to its fragmented condition, the same data could have just as easily been rendered:

61f. Fear of the enemy overcame Ashur-uballit (II) and the army of Eg[ypt stood firm which] had come [to assist the king of Akkad (ie: from the south)] and they aban[doned] the city [...] they crossed.

66 <The seventeenth year>: In the month Tammuz Ashur-uballit (II), king of Assyria, the large army of Egypt [having withdrawn,]

67 crossed the river (Euphrates) and marched against Harran to conquer (it) [...] they [...]d (it).

68 They defeated the garrison which the king of Akkad had stationed inside. When they had defeated (it) they encamped against Harran.

or some similar reading (e.g., 61f. ... and the army of Eg[ypt arrived which] had come [to

---

[1] Wiseman, *Chronicles of Chaldaean Kings, op. cit.*, pages 62–63. Cp. plates III and XI.

resist him] and they aban[doned] the city ..., etc.). Obviously, this approach has the advantage in that appeal for such a "speculative" interpretation could be made to the Hebrew Text for substantiation.

Indeed, the overall historical setting would certainly seem against Egypt's coming to assist the Assyrian forces, and this fact has been appealed to over the years by more than a few. The Assyrian Empire had long held prominence in the area. Josiah died about the year 609 BC. As recently as 671, Esarhaddon, the Assyrian monarch, had conquered Egypt. Ashur-banipal, his son and successor, made a new conquest (667 or 666), advancing as far as Thebes. In his second campaign, Ashur-banipal took and sacked Thebes (the biblical city "No"), the great capital of Upper Egypt (663).

The Assyrians were infamous for their great cruelty as noted in profane history as well as the biblical narrative (for example, Nahum, especially chapter 3). It seems almost inconceivable that only 54 years later and after the ensuing years of enduring these ruthless brutalities, suddenly these same beleaguered Egyptians would travel nearly 500 miles over rugged terrain in an attempt to rescue the barbarous and hated Assyrians from the upstart Babylonians.

The Babylonians had successfully revolted from under the Assyrian yoke in 625 BC under the leadership of King Nabopolassar, founder of the Neo-Babylonian Empire. His son and commander of the army, crown prince Nebuchadnezzar, was to become king of Babylonia shortly after the Josiah confrontation with Neco. It had been hundreds of years since the Babylonians had been an empire of distinction and might. Over these many years, the Babylonians had been no threat to Egypt, having several times become vassals to Assyria as far back as around 824 BC.

In view of all of this historical background between these two empires one is certainly justified to doubt, asking why the Egyptians would have feared or hated the Babylonians enough to put aside their recent viciously cruel persecutions at the hand of the Assyrians. Nevertheless, the Babylonian records declare

that they so did. Chronicle 3:1 identifies itself as being the account of the tenth year of Nabopolassar and states:[1]

10   In the month of Tisri the Egyptian army and the Assyrian army marched after the king of Akkad as far as the town of Qablinu but
11   did not overtake the king of Akkad and then went back. ...

Therefore we have an un-mutilated portion of Babylonian history linking the Egyptian and Assyrian armies as allies against the king of Akkad (Babylonia) only six years prior to the event in question.

c. Resolving the Josiah-Neco-Assyrian Question

As has been documented, the context and frequency analysis presented on page 184 justifies the King James rendering of the Hebrew word "al" (על) in 2 Kings 23:29 as saying that Pharaoh Neco went up to the River Euphrates "*against* the king of Assyria." Yet at the same time it has been shown that one seems warranted in concluding that the Babylonian Chronicles possibly do testify that Neco joined with the Assyrian forces against Babylonia in the Euphrates area during both the 16th and 17th years of Nabopolassar.

However, on the basis of the Hebrew Text (viz. 2 Kings 23:29; 2 Chron. 35:21–25), it must be conceded that at some point during the six years (from Nabopolassar's 10th to his 16th) the Egyptians could have found cause to change allegiances. Then, in this scenario, after the Assyrian Empire's total collapse the Egyptian rulers, unable to maintain a peace with the Neo-Babylonian monarchy, eventually engaged them in battle at Carchemish during Nabopolassar's 20th and 21st years (Chronicle 4:16–28; 5:1–11). At present, this author knows of no data which would refute such a contention and has no objection to it as a viable solution to the problem.

Notwithstanding, perhaps the best resolution is that given well over three hundred years ago by Ussher.[2] First, bear in mind Josephus' statement with regard to this incident. He says that the occasion in which Neco slew Josiah was the result of the Egyptian army's passing through Judah on its way to the River Euphrates to engage the *Medes and Babylonians* who had just overthrown the Assyrian Empire.[3] With Nineveh's fall to the allied forces in 612 BC, followed by that of the city of Haran 610 BC, the Assyrian Empire collapsed, forever ceasing to exist. As the leader of the allied forces, Nabopolassar, king of Babylonia, now engaged in the well known and commonplace ancient custom of taking unto himself the title of any and all kings whom they conquered.

Thus with its land nearly totally occupied by the allied forces, in 609 BC the kingdom of Assyria was no longer an entity. Its remaining army was in hiding and regrouping near the Euphrates for its doomed counterattack and siege which attempted to retake Haran in 609, the 17th year of Nabopolassar.[4] The land had now become mainly the property of the king of Babylonia who therefore also captured for himself the appellation, "King of Assyria."

A scriptural example of this practice may be seen in Ezra 6:22 where Darius (I, Hystaspis) the king of Persia, having overcome Babylonia and Assyria, also bore the title "King of Assyria" (Compare with vs. 15 and consider that, as Ussher states, heathen authors relate how Babylon was formerly part of Assyria. Scripture also mentions that the kingdom of Chaldea was founded by the king of Assyria, Isa. 23:13.).

Thus, taking into account Josephus' statement along with the aforementioned Babylonian Chronicle record, the 2 Kings 23:29 passage is seen to refer to Neco's going up to join the beleaguered remnant of the Assyrian army which had been driven out to only a small corner of the kingdom and thereby engage Nabopolassar, the new possessor of the title "King of Assyria," and his allies near Carchemish on the Euphrates and Haran. Keil and Delitzsch acknowledge this as a viable solution[5] as well as that of the first offered possibility given above.

[1] Wiseman, *Chronicles of Chaldaean Kings, op. cit.,* BM 21901, Obverse side, p. 55.

[2] Ussher, *Annals, op. cit.,* p. 94 (1658 ed., p. 81).

[3] Josephus, *Antiquities, op. cit.,* X, 5, 1.

[4] Grayson, *ABC, op. cit.,* Chronicle 3, p. 96.

[5] Keil and Delitzsch, *op. cit.,* vol. III, p. 493.

d. Remaining Limitations

Most sources place Neco's slaying of Josiah in the 17th year of Nabopolassar; however upon referring back to Chronicle 3:58–70 and comparing this to the relevant Scriptures, it will be seen that the death of Josiah cannot be readily fixed with certainty and thus could have taken place in either the 16th or 17th year of Nabopolassar. Being fixed by the heretofore mentioned 22 April, – 620 (Julian Period, Gregorian = 15 April, 621 BC, page 123) lunar eclipse recorded by Ptolemy which took place during the 5th year of Nabopolassar, the year for this and other various Babylonian dates are usually given as unquestionably certain. However, things are not so simple or positive.

For example, Faulstich has recently challenged this assignment. Ptolemy placed the eclipse in the fifth year of Nabopolassar because he assigned 13 years to Assaradinus (Esarhaddon) in the Canon; however, in three different places the Babylonian Chronicles records his reign as but 12 years. Which then is the correct number? This has led Eugene Faulstich to date this eclipse as 15 April 621, but in Nabopolassar's sixth year rather than his fifth.[1] Thus, biblical chronology, though well determined and contained within very certain narrow bounds, must be seen as an ongoing project whereby some small disagreements, uncertainties, and refinements remain.

Thiele has placed the Josiah-Neco confrontation in the 17th year of Nabopolassar. He adds that Josiah perished in the month of Tammuz (June–July) of 609 BC as Chronicles 3:66–67 gives that month as the beginning of the Assyrian and Egyptian counterattack against Haran.[2] This decision resulted in his placing the three-month reign of Jehoahaz from Tammuz (June–July) to sometime in September or October,[3] but this cannot be as accurate as Thiele would have us believe.

It could have taken as much as several months for Neco to regroup and rest his troops after the Battle of Megiddo, march his massive army nearly 425 miles over often rugged to mountainous terrain, join with the Assyrian's under Ashur-uballit, lay out battle plans, and finally launch the attack. Thus, Josiah could hardly have been killed in the month Tammuz. Accordingly, he was slain months earlier.

Moreover, charting the data quickly clarifies the matter (see next page and Chart 5c). From this, it will be seen that Josiah died near the very end of Nabopolassar's 16th year (609 BC), shortly *before* 1 Nisan (the beginning of Nabopolassar's 17th). Otherwise, he would have received credit for a reign of 32 years instead of 31. Of course, this would also mark the inception of Jehoahaz's three-month reign.

e. Concluding Remarks

Finally, it has been shown that there is no legitimate reason to reject either the Hebrew or the Babylonian accounts of this incident. The alteration of the Hebrew Text from "against" to "to the aid of" the king of Assyria by the NKJV, NIV, RSV, NEB, etc. is totally unwarranted and unnecessary.

The Hebrew record must not be altered; and even more especially, it must not be so capriciously changed over the latest often mutilated or misunderstood archaeological discoveries. As the divine historical Hebrew Text relates, Neco "went up *against* the king of Assyria to the river Euphrates."

The reader can now judge for himself and see that the Babylonian account does not actually contradict the King James Bible which is a faithful rendering of the Hebrew Text. Part of the problem is due to the fragmented nature of the Chronicle, leaving much to the imagination and subjective will of the translator.

Has it not been appalling to see to what lengths critics and translators will go in their exaggerated and, at times, dishonest reporting of facts as well as in their interpretations and translating where the Holy Writ is concerned? Yet such is the pit into which modern scholarship in general has plummeted.

---

[1] Faulstich, *History, Harmony and the Hebrew Kings, op. cit.*, pp. 218–219 (referred to earlier in footnote 3, p. 123).

[2] Thiele, *The Mysterious Numbers of the Hebrew Kings, op. cit.*, p. 181.

[3] *Ibid.*, p. 182.

623	622	621	620	619	618	617	616	615	614	613	612	611	610	609	608	607	606	605	604	603
3	4	5	6	7	8	9	10	11	12	13	14	15	16	17	18	19	20	AC 21	1	2
18	19	20	21	22	23	24	25	26	27	28	29	30	31	AC	1	2	3	4	5	6

Josiah   Jehoahaz   Jehoiakim

5. DANIEL 1:1 AND CARCHEMISH

The following chart is constructed from the data contained in the first and second chapters of the Book of Daniel. Beginning in the third year of the reign of Jehoiachin (Dan. 1:1), the first chapter is said to span a three-year period (vv. 4, 5, 18). Since the events recorded in chapter 2 transpired in the second year of Nebuchadnezzar's reign, the question arises – does the story contained in chapter 2 occur *within* the three-year span of chapter 1 or does it take place *afterward*? In other words, does chapter 2 follow chapter 1 chronologically or not? Moreover, what is the relationship of the years of King Jehoiachin of Judah's reign to those of Nebuchadnezzar's?

The first step in resolving this issue revolves around the fact that it simply would not be possible that Daniel and his three friends could be so highly elevated in the affairs of the government of Babylonia in chapter 2 (Dan. 2:48, 49) and afterward still have to appear before King Nebuchadnezzar to obtain his approval by proving their abilities "to stand in the king's palace" (Dan. 1:4, 18–20) as though they were yet mere students. But such would be the case were the happenings of chapter 2 imbedded somewhere within the three-year time frame of chapter 1. Accordingly, the context of chapter 2 clearly follows *after* chapter 1 chronologically.

Since chapter 1 encompasses most of a three-year span (cp. vv. 4, 5, 18), then the events in chapter 2 must have occurred after Daniel's schooling. Thus, the second year of Nebuchadnezzar's reign must take place after Daniel's and the other princes of Judah's "graduation."

Furthermore, Jeremiah 25:1 reveals that Nebuchadnezzar's first regnal year was Jehoiakim's fourth regnal year. Consequently, Nebuchadnezzar's second year of reign (Dan. 2:1) was during Daniel's third year in the school of the Chaldeans. Further, the events of chapter 2

must occur *during* that year (604 BC) but *after* Daniel's face-to-face "final exam" (Dan. 1:18–20) with Nebuchadnezzar.

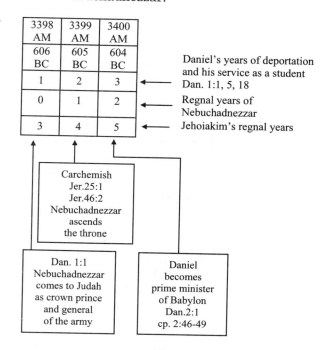

3398 AM	3399 AM	3400 AM	
606 BC	605 BC	604 BC	
1	2	3	← Daniel's years of deportation and his service as a student Dan. 1:1, 5, 18
0	1	2	← Regnal years of Nebuchadnezzar
3	4	5	← Jehoiakim's regnal years

Carchemish
Jer.25:1
Jer.46:2
Nebuchadnezzar
ascends
the throne

Dan. 1:1
Nebuchadnezzar
comes to Judah
as crown prince
and general
of the army

Daniel
becomes
prime minister
of Babylon
Dan.2:1
cp. 2:46-49

By numbering backward from that point, it will be seen that Daniel's first year of deportation and schooling must have occurred one year prior to Nebuchadnezzar's actual accession to the throne (see above chart where year 1 for Daniel is thereby compelled to equal year 0 for Nebuchadnezzar).

Jeremiah 46:2 states that Jehoiakim's fourth year was the year in which Pharaoh Neco was defeated by Nebuchadnezzar at the battle of Carchemish on the Euphrates River. The date of this battle has been established as firmly as possible by secular scholars and astronomers, assigning it the year 605 BC. If this date is correct, it in turn serves as one of the two great connecting links between Bible chronology and secular dating (the other being the 15th year of Tiberius Caesar in which Christ Jesus was "about 30 years of age," cp. Luke 3:1, 23). Therefore, the "first" year of Nebuchadnezzar

(which is the 21st and last year of his father, Nabopolassar; see page 125 ff. where "first" equals the accession year) is the 4th year of Jehoiakim, 605 BC, the same year in which the Battle of Carchemish was fought.

Considering the chart and comparing these last facts to the first paragraphs in which chapters 1 and 2 of Daniel were examined, it is concluded that this data demands both an invasion and a deportation by Nebuchadnezzar in the year *before* that king began to reign, that is, the year prior to Carchemish. The fact is that Daniel chapter 2 is contextually after the final testing of Daniel, and chapter 1 states the examination took place during the third year of Daniel's deportation (Dan. 1:5, 18). Furthermore, when this is compared to Jeremiah 25:1, which states that Nebuchadnezzar's first year of reign was Jehoiakim's 4th, it demands the conclusion that the 3rd year of Daniel's deportation was the 2nd year of Nebuchadnezzar's reign (plat, p. 189).

It follows then that Daniel 1:1 does not conflict with Jeremiah 25:1 as is often claimed. Observe that Daniel 1:1 does not say that the third year of the reign of Jehoiakim is the first year of Nebuchadnezzar's *reign*. As illustrated, such would be impossible from the data in chapter 1 when compared to 2:1 which is said to occur in Nebuchadnezzar's second year of dominion. Moreover, Daniel 1:1 is merely a statement of *identification*, i.e., the Nebuchadnezzar who came and besieged Jerusalem in Jehoiakim's third year is the same man who ascended to the throne and became sole rex the following year (Jer. 25:1). The apparent contradiction has been resolved by simply allowing the Scriptures to speak for themselves, apart from profane materials.

This simple chart also corrects the current vogue of making Daniel's deportation occur in the year of the Battle of Carchemish. Those who so insist consider the opening verse of Daniel as being a blunder for it states that Nebuchadnezzar besieged Jerusalem "in the third year of Jehoiakim." To prove their point they invariably invoke a quote from Berosus, the Babylonian priest and historian.

Berosus was a Chaldean priest of Belus residing at Babylon who lived at the time of Alexander the Great (356–323 BC). About 268 BC, he wrote a history of Babylonia in Greek, beginning from the Creation unto his own time.

Preserved in quotes within the works of Apollodorus (144 BC), Polyhistor (88 BC), Abydenus (60 BC), Josephus (AD 37–103), and Eusebius (AD 265–340), only fragments of this work remain. Berosus says he obtained the materials for his history from the archives of the temple of Belus.

According to the Babylonian Chronicles, almost every year during the period from 609–598 BC, a Babylonian army under the command of Nabopolassar or his son Nebuchadnezzar entered the area along the Mediterranean coast toward Judah to oppose Egyptian domination of that part of the Fertile Crescent. The Battle of Carchemish, and consequently Jehoiakim's fourth year, has been dated by Babylonian evidence as having taken place the 21st and last year of King Nabopolassar.[1] The Babylonian Chronicles go on to say that Nabopolassar died on the 8th of Ab (8 August) 605 BC, and that Crown Prince Nebuchadnezzar returned to Babylon from the fighting near Hamath and took the throne on 1 Elul (30 August).

The critics pretend that this account of the 605 Carchemish expedition extended into Judah, and that this is when Daniel, etc., were carried back to Babylon in Jehoiakim's fourth year in order to make it "fit" Jeremiah 25:1 and 46:2. The former cited account of the battle in the Babylonian Chronicles states that the Egyptians fled from Carchemish to Hamath where they were overtaken and slain to the last man. Combining portions of Berosus' account with that of the Chronicles, scholars commonly report that after the Carchemish victory, Nebuchadnezzar hastened back to Babylon "over the desert" to secure the throne. The particular quote from Berosus relating to one of these incursions is preserved by Josephus:[2]

When his father Nabopolassar heard that the governor whom he had set over Egypt, and the places about Celesyria and Phoenicia, had revolted from him, while he was not himself able any longer to undergo the hardships (of war), he committed to his son Nebuchadnezzar, who was still but a youth, some parts of his army, and sent them against him. So when Nebuchadnezzar had given battle, and fought with the rebel, he beat him and

---

[1] Wiseman, *Chronicles of Chaldaean Kings, op. cit.*, pages 67–69.

[2] Josephus, *Antiquities, op. cit.*, X, 11, 1.

reduced the country from under his subjection and made it a branch of his own kingdom; but about that time it happened that his father Nabopolassar fell ill, and ended his life in the city of Babylon, when he had reigned twenty-one years; and when he was made sensible, as he was in a little time, that his father Nabopolassar was dead, and having settled the affairs of Egypt, and the other countries, as also those that concerned the captive Jews, and Phoenicians, and Syrians, and those of the Egyptian nations, and having committed the conveyance of them to Babylon to certain of his friends, together with the gross of his army, ... he went himself hastily, accompanied with a few others, *over the desert*, and came to Babylon. (author's italics)

So he took upon him the management of public affairs and of the kingdom which had been kept for him by one that was the principal of the Chaldeans, and he received the entire dominions of his father and appointed, that when the captives came, they should be placed as colonies, in the most proper places of Babylonia; but then he adorned the temple of Belus, and the rest of the temples, in a magnificent manner, with the spoils he had taken in the war.

It should be pointed out that the account as recorded by Berosus differs from the Chronicles' account in that Berosus says that the governor whom Nabopolassar had set over Egypt rebelled and that this is he with whom Nebuchadnezzar did battle and subdued. In contrast, the Battle of Carchemish was fought against Pharaoh Neco. Neco was a king, not a governor. Neither was he appointed by Nabopolassar. He inherited the throne from his father, Psammetik.

Another question arises concerning these accounts; how could Nebuchadnezzar return to Babylon "over the desert" from Carchemish on the Euphrates? Not even from Hamath would he have crossed the desert. Of course the supposed answer is that he was far to the south having just raided Syria, Phoenicia, Egypt, and Judah as Berosus states, but the Chronicles merely say that "at that time Nebuchadnezzar conquered the whole area of the Hatti-country." Wiseman asserts that the geographical term "Hatti" included "*at this period*" all of Syria and Palestine;[1] however this is not as certain as he indicates (author's italics).

The key italicized words from the quote underscore the fact that conjecture is involved in this identification. Only several hundred years previous, the region known as "Hattina" (Hatti) was far to the north in the Hamath-Orontes River-Aleppo area, starting about 50 miles southwest of Carchemish and more than 150 miles north of the Sea of Galilee.[2]

In any event, the Babylonian Chronicles and the account by Berosus exhibit a number of other significant discrepancies between them justifying one to doubt and wonder if the Berosus narrative is little more than his confused compilation of several different incursions. As it stands, the modern practice of combining these two accounts into one whereby after the 605 BC Carchemish victory Nebuchadnezzar, after already having subjugated Judah such that Daniel was carried back to Babylon in Jehoiakim's fourth year, hastened back to Babylon "over the desert" to secure the throne does not actually "fit" Jeremiah 25:1 and 46:2. Instead, the contrivance invents a direct contradiction with the faithful testimony of Daniel 1:1. The Scriptures clearly declare that Nebuchadnezzar came against Jerusalem in Jehoiakim's third year, the year before Carchemish (Dan. 1:1, cp. Jer. 25:1; 46:2), and the Lord Jesus endorsed these Scriptures.

The construction of an elementary chart depicting the data in Daniel chapters 1 and 2 enables us to clearly identify the third year of Daniel's deportation as the 2nd year in which Nebuchadnezzar reigned as sole rex (see plat, page 189). This in turn leads one to the inescapable determination that Nebuchadnezzar could not be reigning as sole king when he carried Daniel away to Babylon (the Babylonian records state he was merely the crown prince at the time, see page 310). The removal of Daniel, the other "princes" of Judah, and part of the vessels of the House of God had to have occurred in 606 BC, the year prior to Carchemish.

This finding harmonizes the paradox between Daniel 1:1 and Jeremiah 25:1, leaving us to see that no contradiction exists between these two passages as is often reported. Indeed, the cited Babylonian record indicates their army was

---

[1] Wiseman, *Chronicles of Chaldaean Kings, op. cit.*, pages 67–69.

[2] Yohanan Aharoni and Michael Avi-Yonah, *The Macmillan Bible Atlas*, (New York: The Macmillan Co., 1968), p. 88.

south of the Euphrates in Nabopolassar's 20th year (606 BC) for perhaps as much as four months[1] — which was time enough for an incursion against Jerusalem.

To try to force the Babylonian account of the Battle of Carchemish from either Berosus or the Babylonian Chronicles to be the year in which Daniel is deported is unwarranted. This is all the more so since these accounts have been shown to contradict one another with respect to important particulars. As the Chronicles have been found reliable many times over, Berosus' description must come into question.

Furthermore, were Daniel 1:1 in error as compared to Jer. 25:1 and 46:2, his contemporaries would not have regarded him as a true prophet, but Ezekiel so did (Ezek. 14:14,20; 28:3) as did the Lord Jesus about 600 years afterward (Mat. 24:15). Thus, not only should the matter be settled in the mind of the interested secular inquirer, for the biblicist it should be without the slightest doubt or hesitancy.

6. JEHOIACHIN (JECONIAH) — 8 OR 18?

Another well-known problem whose solution is facilitated by use of the visual benefits derived from Charts 5 and 5c is that which results from comparing the following.

> Jehoiachin was eighteen years old when he began to reign, and he reigned in Jerusalem three months. And his mother's name was Nehushta, the daughter of Elnathan of Jerusalem (2 Kings 24:8).

> Jehoiachin was eight years old when he began to reign, and he reigned three months and ten days in Jerusalem: and he did that which was evil in the sight of the LORD (2 Chron. 36:9).

The problem is that the first verse relates that Jehoiachin was 18 years old when he began to reign yet the second states that he was only 8. As the two verses appear to contradict one another, this is commonly touted as a scribal error in the Hebrew Text. Surely in view of all the foregoing proofs and solutions which consistently have borne out the faithfulness and accuracy of the Holy Scriptures as well as the testimony of the manner in which we have seen the many mathematical chronological statements contained within that same Book perfectly fit together time and time again; by

now, we "know" there is a Bible-honoring solution. In fact, three feasible as well as possible answers are offered, none of which violates either the context or veracity of Scripture.

As may be viewed on Charts 5 and 5c, the first is that Jehoiachin was actually 18 years old upon his ascension (see 2 Kings 24:8) whereas the 2 Chronicles 36:9 passage, which literally translates that he was "a son of eight years," is referencing the fact that his dynasty or kingdom had been under Nebuchadnezzar as its suzerain since the fourth year of his father, Jehoiakim (605 BC, Jer. 25:1, cp. 2 Kings 24:1). From that year until Jehoiachin succeeded his father on the throne, an eight-year span had elapsed during which he was a vassal crown prince. Thus, upon his accession, the beginning of his reign could be rightly referenced to the time in which Nebuchadnezzar placed the Babylonian yoke upon him and his kingdom; thereby, he was "a son of eight years" under Nebuchadnezzar's dominion.

Moreover, the Chronicles passage is looking back nearly 500 years after the fact. It is so relating to emphasize the fact that upon Jehoiachin's coming to the throne, Nebuchadnezzar was already conducting a siege against Jerusalem (in punishment for Jehoiakim's rebellion) which, along with the new king, had already been under Babylonian authority for the past eight years.

A second alternative explanation for the confusion is that, taking both statements as being factual, Jehoiakim named or anointed his son to succeed him at an early age (Judaic reckoning) in an attempt to secure the throne through his lineage by way of Jehoiachin (Jeconiah). This would have been done in order to deny the throne to his weak and ineffective younger brother, Zedekiah.

The third solution offered, and that preferred by this author in light of that which follows, is that Josiah must have anointed Jehoiachin, his grandson, to succeed him just prior to his encounter with Pharaoh Neco. This answer, along with the two previous, has been proffered many times in the past. However this study has developed and refined this third resolution with additional internal biblical evidence to a far higher degree of certitude and believability than that given in the past.

---

[1] Wiseman, *Chronicles of Chaldaean Kings, op. cit.*, p. 67.

Realizing that his sons were wicked, godly Josiah must have hoped that his grandson Jehoiachin (Jeconiah), though only eight years old at the time, would turn out better. As Josiah himself was but eight when he began to reign, he would have few qualms in placing so young a child upon the throne of Judah. Josiah fully realized that he might not return from this conflict with the Egyptians.

In the first place, he was going up against a much larger contingency. Secondly, it had been prophesied that he would die young and also prior to the judgment that God would send upon the Kingdom of Judah (2 Kings 22, 2 Chron. 34). Having already reigned 31 years, Josiah was now about 39 years of age. Thus he knew that his time was very possibly at hand.

The only biblical and legal way that a grandson, etc., could be made to inherit the throne while his father and uncles were still alive was that of *adoption* to the status of a full son. (See Genesus 48 where Joseph's sons, Ephraim and Manasseh, are placed as sons, adopted by Jacob [verse 5, cp. vv. 12 and 16 for the ritual] so that they could become equal heirs with his other sons.) It is the contention of this writer that Josiah did adopt and name as his successor young Jehoiachin (Jeconiah) just prior to departing for his fatal encounter with Neco at Megiddo. Moreover, this scenario enjoys scriptural corroboration:

> And Josiah *begat Jeconiah* **and** *his brethern*, about the time they were carried away to Babylon (Mat. 1:11, author's emphasis).

This Scripture occurs in Matthew's roll of Christ Jesus' ancestors. Beginning with David and Solomon at the 6th verse, it continues through the 11th listing the kings of Judah in His lineage. Verse 11 asserts that Josiah *begat* Jeconiah (Jehoiachin being his "throne" name) though he was not his son. Although in a larger biblical sense, it is permissible to speak of "begetting" descendants beyond the generation of one's own offspring, the context of this "begetting" would have occurred at the time of the adoption. The truth of this is clearly seen in that which follows: "and his brothers."

Now this is indeed very strange, for the allusion is clearly to Josiah's sons and as such, are Jehoiachin's uncles and father — unless — unless he had been adopted. Then and only

then could it be said that Josiah's sons are Jehoiachin's brothers! Lest there remain any reservations, consider:

> And when the year was expired, king Nebuchadnezzar sent, and brought him (Jehoiachin, see vs.9) to Babylon, with the goodly vessels of the house of the LORD, and made *Zedekiah his brother* king over Judah and Jerusalem (2 Chronicles 36:10, author's italics).

Again, how can Zedekiah be Jehoiachin's brother? Only by his being adopted to full sonship. However the people of the land did not abide by Josiah's decision, placing instead Josiah's 23-year-old son Jehoahaz (not his eldest, 2 Kings 23:36) on the throne (2 Kings 23:8). After reigning but three months, Jehoahaz was removed by Pharaoh Neco and carried prisoner to Egypt where he died. Placing the land under tribute, Neco installed Jehoahaz's older brother Jehoiakim (father of Jehoiachin) as his vassal on the throne of Judah (2 Kings 23:33–37) where he reigned 11 years.

Of course, this does not demand that he reigned 11 years to the very day. For example, if he reigned 10 years and 3 months, that would qualify as being "in his eleventh year." Thus, whereby Jehoiachin (Jeconiah) was *anointed* to *be* king when but a child (2 Chron. 36:9), he did not actually occupy the throne until he was 18 years of age (2 Kings 24:8–12) — a span of 11 years when numbered inclusively. Moreover, Chronicles is stating the situation as viewed from the priest's, the Temple's, and God's perspective whereas the Book of Kings is presenting it from the historical political/throne view.

The "discrepancy" or "scribal error" between 2 Kings 24:8 and 2 Chronicles 36:9 is thus resolved. The verses are seen to signify that Jehoiachin's first year upon the throne would have been his "year of accession"; hence he would have been eight during his first official year of reign (Judaic method of reckoning). Thus 2 Kings 24:8, 2 Chron. 36:9, and Matthew 1:11 — Scriptures long held by liberals, agnostics, infidels, and most scholars to be in error — when placed together, actually explain, confirm and sustain one another.

Yet once again Archer misses the mark, considering this as another scribal mistake.

Tragically failing to grasp the import of the mischief against the Word of God which the Assyrian Academy has brought about with its various mishandling of the ancient records, he naively states that "even Thiele" readily acknowledges 2 Chron. 36:9 as an error.[1]

Further, we know that Jehoiachin (Jeconiah) was actually 18[2] and not 8 when installed to reign as we are informed by the writer of Kings that after reigning only 3 months and 10 days, he and *his wives* were carried away to Babylon (2 Kings 24:15). An 8-year-old would hardly be married, much less have multiple wives. Neither is it tenable that God would brand an 8-year-old as "evil" (2 Chron. 36:9).

Thus, like his "father" David, Jehoiachin was anointed to reign, but many years passed before he actually ascended to the head of the monarchy. The first time "he came unto his own" and presented himself as their anointed king, "his own received him not" (John 1:11) saying "we will not have this man to reign over us" (Luke 19:14). The second time, he was welcomed as king, for no one is said to have installed him.

Both thereby become types of another and far greater in this same dynasty, even the Lord Jesus, the Christ. Jesus was anointed to rule by the last of the Old Testament prophets, John the Baptist. The Father confirmed the same at that occasion by audibly speaking from heaven (Mat. 3:13–17; 11:7–15); yet the Lord Jesus has not yet occupied "the throne of His father, David" (Luke 1:31–32). "Oh, that thou wouldest rend the heavens, that thou wouldest come down ..." (Isaiah 64:1a).

7. THE ADAD-GUPPI STELAE

Of special interest is the document recorded on two stelae found in Haran which is the tomb inscription of Adad-guppi, mother of Nabonidus — the last king of Babylon. One stele was found in AD 1906 and the other in 1956. On these two stones, Adad-guppi relates that she was born in the 20th year of the reign of Ashurbanipal, king of Assyria (650 BC) and that from her birth into the 4th year of Neriglissar, the Babylonian monarch, was a span of 95 years. She also relates that the city of Haran fell in the 16th year of Nabopolassar. A postscript adds that she died a natural death in the 9th year of her son, Nabonidus (at age 104).

This valuable information, taken from James B. Pritchard's classic anthology of the ancient near East,[3] was discovered by the author long after the completion of Chart 5 and thus served as a most stringent test on the work. This find is of immense value in bridging the complex and often puzzling section from Josiah across the life span of Nebuchadnezzar. Charts 5 and 5c honor this data by placing the 4th year of Neriglissar as 556 BC, 95 years after Ashurbanipal's 20th (650 BC − 556 = 95 years, inclusive numbering).

The significance of this can hardly be overstated for it allows one to close with certainty the span around 560 BC where the Hebrew record is suddenly becoming almost devoid of data, and brings the chronology into very close proximity to the lunar eclipses of 523, 502 and 491 BC[4] (Gregorian) thereby establishing the bridge. The Adad-guppi stelae also confirm the accuracy of the 621 BC lunar eclipse in the fifth year of Nabopolassar with regard to this later trio of eclipses, as well as authenticate the synchronization of the Assyrian monarchs with the Babylonian and hence with the kings of Judah over this time period.

All of this valid profane data places exceedingly rigorous mathematical restraints and demands upon the analysis depicted on the fifth chart. Thus, the complex area around the time of Nebuchadnezzar and the fall of Jerusalem is not only "date attested" by the many Scriptures referred to on the chart (none of which has been violated), much secular data of a precise nature has been interwoven into the warp and woof of the fabric. Recalling that two of the three "Bible to secular" bridges are located along this sector, such interlocking becomes significantly meaningful and final.

---

[1] Archer, *A Survey of Old Testament Introduction, op. cit.,* p. 292.

[2] A youth of 18, Jeconiah could not have a son capable of reigning. As his nearest kin, Zedekiah was first in line to rule.

[3] Pritchard, *ANET, op. cit.,* pp. 560–562.

[4] Ptolemy, "The Almagest," *Great Books of The Western World, op. cit.,* Bk. 4, pp. 136–137; Bk. 5, p. 172.

8. DAVID AND SHALMANESER I (II)

Chronologically, this problem belongs to a much later period. However, its discussion has been postponed until after the former examples which showed the mishandling or misreporting of the Assyrian data so that it may better be appreciated. The problem here is that many of the Assyrian Academy scholars attempt to force a synchronization between Shalmaneser I (II) and David. As a result, many conservatives, intimidated by Academy publications, follow them in this determination. Recently, Eugene W. Faulstich has fallen into this classification.

Relying solely on Scripture, this study (also Ussher, Clinton, Anderson, etc.) places the reign of David around 1055 to 1015 BC. Faulstich dates David as reigning between 1026 to 985 BC, and he has set 1018 BC as the year in which David and Shalmaneser I (II) engaged in battle. The year 1018 therefore becomes a principal anchor date in his chronology.

Faulstich's deductions are typical of those who make this determination; hence his work is cited. He contends that 2 Kings 10 in the Septuagint (our 2 Samuel 10) and Josephus (*Antiquities*, VII, 6, 3) indicate that King David fought the Assyrian monarch Shalmaneser I (II) the year David took Jerusalem.[1]

Faulstich continues by insisting that "Chalamak" in the LXX and "Chalaman" in Josephus are Greek variations of the same name and that they refer to Shalmaneser I (II). He further states that 1 Chron. 19:16 refers to this same Shalmaneser, "the king of Assyria beyond the river" (i.e., the Euphrates). These are the central proofs in his argument.

First, it should be noted that this crucial anchor date is actually based solely upon extra-biblical data plus, as we shall see, much erroneous surmising. Next, the LXX neither supports Faulstich's claim that "Chalamak" is the

"Chalaman" of Josephus nor that they both are referring to Shalmaneser I (II); it unmistakably calls "Chalamak" a river!

> And the Syrians saw that they were worsted before Israel and they gathered themselves together. And Adraazar [the biblical king of Syria, Hadarezer] sent and gathered the Syrians from the other side of *the river Chalamak*, and they came to Aelam; and Sobac [the biblical captain of the Syrian forces, Shopach] the captain of the host of Adraazar was at their head. (2 Kings 10:15, LXX; 2 Sam. 10:15 in the King James Bible, author's brackets and italics)

Moreover, the word "Chalamak" is not even to be found in the Hebrew Text with reference to this military engagement.

It should also be noted that the Hebrew Text, as well as the LXX and Josephus, states that this battle was fought between David and the Syrian's, not the Assyrians as Faulstich and many others maintain. Faulstich's rationale for this is that the name "'Syria' is a Greek term which is derived from Assyrios, 'Assyria(n)'." To this it must be replied that the Hebrew Text is careful to always clearly distinguish between the two different nations, Syria is always unmistakably spelled Syria when those people are in view and Assyria is always so denoted when that empire is the subject.

It is true that the king of the Syrians is called "Chalaman" in the Josephus account; however this has nothing whatever to do with the Septuagint's identification as Faulstich relates. The fact that Josephus calls him "the Syrian king of Mesopotamia" (*Antiquities*, VII, 6, 1) is self-explanatory; he is a Syrian king who has added Mesopotamia to his realm. Indeed, whether the name "Chalamak" referred to a man or a river would still miss the point and must be seen as even more ludicrous for the king of Syria is "Adraazar" (Bible = Hadarezer) in the LXX passage before us, not "Chalamak." "Chalaman" is either an error by Josephus or it is another designation for Hadarezer.

In summation, David fought the Syrians, not the Assyrians and Hadarezer was their king – not "Chalamak." Furthermore, "Chalamak" is the name of a river, not that of a king of Syria.

---

[1] Faulstich, *History, Harmony & the Hebrew Kings, op. cit.*, pages 84–86, 201. More than any other decision, it is this one that causes Faulstich to violate the testimony of Scripture in his chronology of the divided monarchy. He has been found to transgress the witness of 1 Kings 22:51; 2 Kings 3:1; 2 Kings 13:1; 2 Kings 15:8–18; 2 Kings 15:30; 2 Kings 15:32; and 2 Kings 16:1 as well as Acts 13:10 which assigns 40 years to the reign of Saul, yet Faulstich allows him but 11 years on the throne (1031–1020 BC).

Faulstich's identification and date must therefore be rejected.

9. THE MOABITE STONE

This inscription was discovered intact in 1868, and it was later deciphered by the Arabs. It was placed in the Louvre museum in Paris, France in 1873 where it currently resides. The translation of the stele seems to indicate that it is a victory monument carved and raised by Mesha, king of Moab. The date of the stone is approximated by the biblical reference to Mesha in 2 Kings 3:4–5:

> And Mesha king of Moab was a sheepmaster, and rendered unto the king of Israel an hundred thousand lambs, and an hundred thousand rams, with the wool. But it came to pass, when Ahab was dead, that the king of Moab rebelled against the king of Israel.

The first verse of 2 Kings 3 relates that Joram came to the throne of Israel upon the death of his father Ahab in the 18th year of Jehoshaphat, king of Judah. As this was about the year 897 BC (Charts 5 and 5c), the time of Mesha's rebellion against Joram in the above citation is set as being very close to that date. This, along with the translation of Elijah, places the ensuing defeat of Mesha by the alliance of Israel, Judah, and Edom as probably occurring early during 896 BC (2 Kings 3:6–27).

The stone inscription claims that Mesha conquered most of the territory beyond the Jordan River belonging to the tribe of Reuben including the cities of Dibon, Nebo, and even drove the king of Israel out that had built Jahaz and attached the city to the district of Dibon. Mesha also states that, located within Reuben's territorial boundary, he took the Gadite city of Ataroth and ruled over a hundred towns which he had annexed to his land. Mesha claims to have built several cities including Baal-meon, Aroer and a highway in the Arnon (valley).

Comparing these statements to 2 Kings 3, it would seem that the two are not differing versions of the same story; thus it appears that Mesha must have rebelled twice against Israel. The Scriptures say nothing of these Moabite victories; however both 2 Kings 3:4–5 and the Moabite Stone begin by stating that King Mesha had been a vassal to the king of Israel and had rebelled in the days of Omri's (grand) son. Omri had founded a new dynasty in the Northern Kingdom which endured over the span of only four monarchs. This dynasty was founded by Omri who was succeeded by his son, Ahab, and his two grandsons, Ahaziah and Joram (Jehoram).

From a chronological standpoint, the most important data on the stone is that Moab had been under subjection to Israel for 40 years:[1]

> I (am) Mesha, son of Chemosh-[...], king of Moab, the Dibonite – my father (had) reigned over Moab thirty years, and I reigned after my father ... As for Omri, king of Israel, he humbled Moab many years (lit., days), for Chemosh was angry at his land. And his son followed him and he also said, "I will humble Moab." In my time he spoke (thus), but I have triumphed over him and over his house, while Israel hath perished for ever! (Now) Omri had occupied the land of Medeba, and (Israel) had dwelt there in his time and half the time of his son (Ahab), forty years; but Chemosh dwelt there in my time.

Thus, the Mesha Stele declares that Moab's vassalage began during the reign of Omri and ended 40 years later after "half the time of his *son*." Once again it is to be noted that the word "Ahab" is in parenthesis and is not in the original text. Several possibilities are open concerning the data on the Moabite Stone.

First, if it is to be understood that the stele means that Omri himself was responsible for the vassalage of Moab and that he was king when this event took place, then the 40-year period would have as its maximum beginning 929 BC (see page 140 and Chart 5). The "son" would not then be Ahab, but Omri's grandson, Joram, whose reign covered the years 897–886 BC. It is well known that such extended usage of the middle eastern words for "son" is commonplace and that often only the context will enable one to know if a son, grandson, great grandson, etc. is intended.

The mid-point or half of this would bring the date down to 891 (maximum) and thus a span of 38 (929 − 891 = 38) or 39 years (inclusive) is obtained (the same as Thiele). In this scenario, the "forty" years would be seen as a rounded

---

[1] Pritchard, *ANET, op. cit.*, pp. 320–321.

figure, not having been intended as a precise number. This position is certainly tenable, especially in view of the fact that Mesha clearly is given to exaggeration when he says "Israel has perished for ever!"

However, the more probable and better answer is that "half the time of his 'son'" is intended as a rounded off or approximate statement and nothing more. After all whether he meant them to be taken as such or not, Mesha has given precise numbers for the length of his father's reign (30 years) and Moab's vassalage to Israel (40 years). From this it would seem both reasonable and logical to conclude that if he had known the exact duration of Joram's reign, he would have stated it with a explicit numerical value as he had done in the other two instances. Actually, the very nature of his wording: "half the time of his 'son'" (like similar expressions "middle, at the beginning, or at the end" of his reign) is one that is normally understood as being an approximation.

The possibility of a small latitude to either side of the exact middle is implied although unspoken. Therefore the expression should be seen in this context thereby allowing it to include another year or so into Joram's reign and thus arrive at the exact 40-year terminus. To interpret the phrase as having been intended as anything more than a general approximation seems in itself an act of pressing the data beyond that which the overall setting demands.

Still another, and perhaps the correct solution, is that the subjugation of Moab began prior to Omri's enthronement – at the time when he was the "captain of the host" (2 Kings 16:16) under either King Elah or King Baasha. This would allow for a precise 40-year span to the middle of Joram's reign, thereby completely honoring the stele's testimony. In any case, the Moabite Stone data does not justify one in taking a dogmatic stand as to its actual chronological resolution; hence, the fifth chart cannot rightly be said to have not harmonized this secular witness with the biblical history.

10. THE KINGS OF SYRIA

It will surprise most to learn that in the biblical narrative, the role of the kings of Syria over the time frame in which the kingdoms of Israel and Judah coexisted was far greater than that of

any of the Assyrian or Babylonian monarchs. The problem is, there are no extant Syrian records of that period; hence we have no king list bearing names, lengths of reign, or other synchronous data to assist in a biblical chronological study. Actually the reverse is the case, the biblical record is that source used to reconstruct this period of Syrian chronology. However, as has been explained and demonstrated, the true biblical record has been placed in subjugation to the Assyrian documents, usually wrongfully, and thus the resulting contorted Hebrew chronology is that which is used to construct and fix the Syrian dates. The previously cited work of John Walton is a typical example of this practice.

Walton's charts contain much fine material presented in an easy-to-follow format but, as may be seen from his dates, he uses Thiele's chronology for the period of the disruption.[1] As Walton's resulting regnal years reflect the general consensus of modern scholarship, the following king list and regnal dates reflecting the results of a prolonged and detailed study into the matter are offered as a brief summation of that effort. A more delineated account would go beyond the present scope of this dissertation. Although many of the dates on the ensuing diagram are not necessarily precise and could be inexact by several years, they enjoy the benefit of generally matching the recorded Hebrew history and thus synchronize well with that record.

SYRIAN KINGS	DATES	SCRIPTURE
Rezon	c. 980-970	1 Ki.11:23-25 (father = Eliada)
Hezion*	c. 970-960?	1 Ki.15:18
Tabrimmon	c. 960-945	1 Ki.15:18
Ben-hadad I	c. 945-905	1 Ki.15:18, 20
Ben-hadad II	c. 905-886	1 Ki. 20; 2 Ki. 6:8, 24; 8:7–15
Hazael	c. 886-840	1 Ki.19:17; 2 Ki. 8:15; 10:32; 12:17; 13:7, 13:22; Jer. 49:27; Amos 1:2–5
Ben-hadad III	c. 840-804?	2 Kings 13:3, 22-25; Jer. 49:27; Amos 1:2–5
Rezin	c. 757-740	2 Kings 15:37; 16:5–9; Isa. 7:1–17

* May be the same as Rezon.

As demonstrated, Dr. Thiele's many forced synchronisms produced anachronisms in the

---

[1] Walton, *Chronological And Background Charts of The Old Testament, op. cit.,* pp. 56–59.

Hebrew records even though many of the Assyrian king dates, at least from about 609 to 783 BC, seem basically correct when compared to the biblical chronology. Thus by using Thiele as his guide, Walton has dated the Syrian kings mentioned in Scripture in that distorted scheme, thereby imposing those erroneous dates on the Syrian dynasties and reigns.[1]

11. HIGH PRIESTS — DARIUS THE PERSIAN

The Scriptures tell us that Seraiah, Ezra's father (Ezra 7:1) was the high priest in 586 BC when Nebuchadnezzar's army captured Jerusalem and burned the Temple (2 Kings 25:18–21, cp. 1 Chron. 6:14). Seraiah was then taken to Nebuchadnezzar in Riblah of the land of Hamath and slain. At that time, Jehozadak succeeded his father, Seraiah, as high priest and was carried away with Judah and all Jerusalem to Babylon. He apparently died there as his son Jeshua (Joshua) was high priest at the time of the return (1 Chron. 6:15, cp. Ezra 2:2; 3:2).

The Book of Nehemiah (12:10–11) lists the six high priests who followed Jehozadak as being:

1. Jeshua (Joshua, returned from captivity with Zerubbabel, held office from at least 536 BC to c. 519 – the 2nd year of Darius I, Ezra 2:2, 3:2; Neh. 12:10; Hag. 1:1; Zech. 1:7; 3:1; 6:11.),

2. Joiakim (contemporary with Nehemiah, Ezra, and Xerxes I; Nehemiah 12:10,12,36; Josephus, *Antiq.* XI, 5, 1),

3. Eliashib (allied to Tobiah – a younger contemporary of Nehemiah in the 20th year of Artaxerxes; Neh. 3:1, 20, 21; 6:18; 12:10; 13:4–7),

4. Joiada,

5. Jonathan (Johanan, Grk. = John; 2 Maccabees 1:23 speaks of him as contemporary with Nehemiah; the Elephantine papyri possibly places him [Yedoniah?, texts 30 and 31, Cowley edition] in the 14th and 17th years of Darius II Nothus [c. 410–407 BC]; Jos. *Antiq.* XI, 7, 1), and

6. Jaddua (Neh. 12:1–11, 22, cp. Ezra 3:2).

Nehemiah goes on to say that the names of the heads of the Levitical houses and the chief priests were recorded down to Jaddua's administration which extended to the reign of "Darius the Persian" (Neh. 12:22). The phrase "until the days of Johanan, the son of Eliashib" (Neh. 12:23) indicates that Johanan also officeated during part of this Persian king's reign.

Josephus identified this Darius the Persian as Darius III (Codomannus), the ruler whose empire fell to Alexander the Great in 331 BC. Thus, beginning at Eliashib, Josephus lists the same high priests as Neh. 12:10–11 (albeit with spelling differences) and relates in great detail that Jaddua was serving as high priest when Alexander came to Jerusalem shortly after decisively defeating Darius III.[2]

However, as Sir Isaac Newton pointed out over 250 years ago, this creates a difficulty for it leaves only seven high priests to serve from 586 to 331, a span of 255 years. Thus, the average term of service for each would be a little more than 36 years. As one had to be at least 30 years old before he could serve as high priest (Num. 4:3), and since the tenure ended only at death, an age question arises.

Further, over the 390-year period from the beginning of the schism until Nebuchadnezzar destroyed Jerusalem in 586, 17 high priests served yielding an average term of only about 23 years. This problem has caused some scholars to wrongly conclude that Nehemiah's roster was merely an appendix, even though the line of succession was basically confirmed by Josephus.

Contrary to Josephus, the Talmud states that the high priest who came out to meet Alexander when he marched on Jerusalem in 331 BC was Simon, son of Onias, not Jaddua.[3] Hence Jaddua did not live to the end of the Persian Empire as Josephus stated. Thus, taking 23 years for an average as derived above and applying it from both Jehozadak in 586 and Jeshua in 540 to Jaddua, averaging the two results (425 [7 x 23] + 402 [6 x 23] ÷ 2 = 414), then searching for a Persian monarch called

---

[1] Walton, *Chronological And Background Charts of The Old Testament, op. cit.,* p. 65.

[2] Josephus, *Antiquities, op. cit.,* XI, 7 and 8. Josephus also says Jaddua and Alexander died about the same time; *Antiq.* XI, 8, 7. Josephus adds that Jaddua's son, Onias, succeeded him as high priest (*Antiq.* XI, 8, 7) and that Eleazar, Onias' son who was also called "Simon the Just," replaced his father (*Antiq.* XII, 2, 5).

[3] Beecher, *The Dated Events of the Old Testament, op. cit.,* page 172; *Talmud,* Soma fol. 69, I. The *Encyclopedia Judaica* sides with the Talmud against Josephus, vol. 9, p. 1246.

"Darius" near 414 BC, one would conclude that "Darius the Persian" was likely Darius II Nothus.

The Talmud relates that Simon had been preceded by Onias who is said to have served 19 years, Onias by Jaddua for 20 years and Jaddua by Johanan for 32. If these numbers are correct, they may be summed and added to 331 BC, obtaining the year 402 which represents the latest possible date for the accession of Johanan to the high priesthood. Adding to 402 the number of years Simon had held that post prior to Alexander's arrival will push that date farther back in time and again place Jaddua as well as Johanan near Darius II Nothus.

This conclusion was also made by Archbishop Ussher[1] and set forth with great logic and care long ago by Sir Isaac Newton.[2] Although Beecher did not reach the identical conclusion, his excellent detailed study produced similar deductions.[3] Note that the average lengths of officiating for Onias, Jaddua, and Johanan also comes to nearly 23 (19 + 20 + 32 = 71 and 71 ÷ 3 = 23.67).[4]

Although it is concluded that Darius II Nothus is "Darius the Persian," as long as Eliashib is seen as a younger contemporary of Nehemiah in the 20th year of Artaxerxes the biblical chronology will not fall or rise on this assessment. Whether one places his confidence in Josephus or the Talmud is not the real issue for the chronology may be determined without taking into account the conflicting information contained in these non-biblical sources.

M. THE IDENTITY OF AHASUERUS IN THE BOOK OF ESTHER

The identification of the Persian Monarch portrayed in the Book of Esther under the title "Ahasuerus" has caused much debate over the

centuries. The Book of Esther begins with a great feast "in the 3rd year of the reign of Ahasuerus" (Esther 1:3). Although at one time or another nearly every monarch from Cyaxares (624–586 BC) to Artaxerxes III Ochus (358–338 BC) has been declared as the Medo-Persian ruler in question, in nearly all theological circles today it is conceded almost beyond question that the man is Xerxes I of Thermopylae (486-465 BC).

This identification was initially offered by Scaliger, the first modern chronologer. The proofs offered are: (1) a supposed congruity of the character of Ahasuerus with that of Xerxes as portrayed by Herodotus and other classic writers and (2) a philological conjecture.

These will be examined in that which follows, comparing secular data with Scripture. The secular will not be taken as judge but merely as a witness. Where the secular fits – if it does – it will be incorporated, but the framework will be based upon the Scriptures which, in context, are the only and final authority on the matter, not the reverse.

Before proceeding, it should be noted that although the duration of the Persian empire is probably accurately established, it is not based upon eye witness accounts. Secondly, the exact listing of kings and the lengths of their reigns are not verifiable with absolute certainty and thirdly, the same Persian monarch may have possessed two or more different titles or "throne" names.

Profane literature will now speak and testify as to the identity of this Ahasuerus. It shall be shown that this material declares him to be Darius Hystaspis (of Marathon, the Great or Darius I), and not Xerxes, as is commonly believed. Darius I, a kinsman of Cyrus II (The Great, the Cyrus of Scripture), recorded: "Eight of my family have been kings before me. I am the ninth. In two branches have we been kings."[5]

---

[1] Ussher, *Annals, op. cit.,* p. 160 (1658 ed., p. 146).

[2] Newton, *The Chronology of Ancient Kingdoms Amended, op. cit.,* pp. 363–373.

[3] Beecher, *The Dated Events of the Old Testament, op. cit.,* pp. 164–165, 170–175.

[4] A workable scenario that also honors Scripture is: Jehozadak 586–c.540 BC, Jeshua 540–c.500, Joiakim 500–c.468, Eliashib 468–c.442, Joiada 442–c.438, Jonathan 438–c.406, Jaddua 406–c.386, Onias 386–c.367, and Simon the Just 367–c.327.

[5] *Sculptures and Inscriptions of Darius the Great on the Rock of Behistun, in Persia,* (London: British Museum, 1907). This quote, taken with the Cylinder Inscription of Cyrus (*ANET, op. cit.,* p. 316), yields the genealogy of Darius as given on page 200. See Anstey, *The Romance of Bible Chronology, op. cit.,* p. 260.

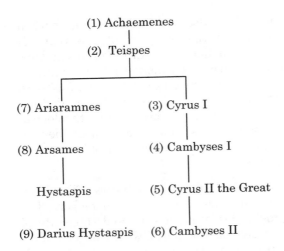

(1) Achaemenes

(2) Teispes

(7) Ariaramnes   (3) Cyrus I

(8) Arsames   (4) Cambyses I

Hystaspis   (5) Cyrus II the Great

(9) Darius Hystaspis   (6) Cambyses II

1. BRIEF HISTORIC BACKGROUND

As one can see, both are related to Teispes (Kishpish). Darius was an officer in the famous "Ten Thousand Immortals," the special elite portion of the Persian army under Cyrus' son, Cambyses II. Cambyses had contracted the murder of his brother, Smerdis, to secure the throne. Leaving Patizithes in control of the government, Cambyses embarked on a campaign into Egypt and succeeded in conquering that empire in the fifth year of his reign (525 BC). He then invaded Ethiopia, but the swamps, deserts, etc. frustrated his attempts for its complete annexation.

During this later engagement, Patizithes usurped total control placing his brother Gomates on the throne in the year 522 BC.[1] These brothers were Magians, a priestly cultic caste similar to the Druids and often referred to as the *"magi."* It was proclaimed to the populace that Gomates (identified by the Behistun Inscription and Ctesias) was actually Smerdis (Xenopion); hence his name commonly appears in the literature as "Pseudo-Smerdis."[2] These *magi* ruled seven months.

When Cambyses learned of this betrayal, he intended to return and retake his throne. History here gives differing accounts.[3] Some authorities say he was murdered on the way back to Babylon; others that he died of an infected wound en route. Still others insist that he committed suicide, fearing either the assassin had not carried out the deed or that Smerdis had somehow come back to life.

Regardless, as Cambyses had no son, Darius, his 28-year-old[4] captain and distant relative, moved to claim the kingship. This seizure was greatly facilitated by the fact that Darius was related to Cyrus. He took charge of the whole army and marched toward Babylon. Upon nearing the seditious city, six young Persians from noble families having learned of his arrival met Darius and pledged their support, forming a seven family pact.

Darius entered Babylon and slew the brothers. These six Persian families, linked to each other by intermarriages, became established as counselors to the king with special privileges. They even bore the right to rule their estates as semi-independent princes for the duration of the Persian empire.

2. SECULAR DATA IDENTIFYING AHASUERUS

Firstly, Esther 1:14 refers to "The seven princes of Persia and Media." As the Book of Esther mentions Persia *before* Media (1:3,18,19), this Ahasuerus *cannot precede* Cyrus' first year as sole king over the expanded empire (536 BC) for during Darius the Mede's short reign[5] (539–537

---

[1] Herodotus, *The Histories*, 4 Vols., Loeb Classical Library, III, 65.

[2] Pseudo-Smerdis is in all likelihood the Artaxerxes of Ezra 4:7–23 as the implication of the word "kings" in Ezra 4:13,22 implies a plural reign.

[3] Hayes and Hanscom, *Ancient Civilizations, op. cit.*, page 175.

[4] *Collier's Encyclopedia, op. cit.*, vol. VII, page 718, referencing Ctesias. Ctesias of Cnidus (flourished 401–384 BC) was a Greek physician to Artaxerxes Mnemon, residing at court for 17 years in Susa. Based upon the Persian Royal Archives, he wrote *Persica*, a history of Assyria and Persia in 23 books. Like most ancient authorities, Ctesias often exaggerates and is not always reliable. He gives Darius' life span as 73 years. This would give him 44 years (73 − 28) of sole reign. See *The New Westminster Dictionary of the Bible, op. cit.*, p. 210 under "Darius" #2.

[5] Darius the Mede, son of Ahasuerus, was the uncle of Cyrus (II) the Great (Xenophon, *Cyropaedia*, I, ii, 1 [or Grandfather? Herodotus, *op. cit.*, I, 107–108]). He was Cyaxares II, son of Astyages (Jos., *Antiq.* x. 11. 4 = the Ahasuerus of Dan.9:1). Belshazzar, son and pro-rex of Nabonidus, king of the Babylonian empire, was on the throne in the capitol city, Babylon, during the prolonged absence of his father. A great pagan feast was being held in the besieged city celebrating the impregnability of its famed walls. As the prophet Daniel predicted when he interpreted the cryptic message scrolled miraculously upon the wall by a bodiless hand, the confederate armies under the Median and Persian leadership of Cyrus entered Babylon that selfsame night, 16 Tishri, 539 BC

BC) the Medes were named *before* the Persians (Dan. 6:8, 12, 15). During Cyrus' "first year,"[1] the Persians gained political ascendancy over the Median constituency and were thereafter consistently mentioned *ahead* of the Medes.

Secondly, King Darius the Mede had set 120 princes over the kingdom (Dan. 6:1). At the time of Esther, King Ahasuerus' Medo-Persian Empire, extending from India to Ethiopia, had increased into 127 provinces or "satrapies" (Esther 1:1). These satrapies constitute a major key as to the correct identity of Esther's "Ahasuerus."

Although today's standard chronologies would have Esther the wife of Xerxes (485–464 BC), by the *beginning* of his reign the Persian empire had begun to *lose* satrapies.[2] Therefore, the name "Ahasuerus" must refer to a monarch *after* Darius the Mede, but *before* the reign of Xerxes (refer to the following diagram). Conventional chronological schemes have completely ignored this problem choosing instead to give preference to and place reliance upon a tenuous etymological identification, the merit of which will be presently examined.

THE PERSIAN KING LIST FOR THE
PERIOD UNDER DISCUSSION

2 yrs	9 yrs	8 yrs	36 yrs	21 yrs	41 yrs
Darius the Mede	Cyrus the Great	Cambyses II	Darius I Hystaspis	Xerxes I	Artaxerxes Longimanus

Furthermore, Esther 1:1 declares: "This is (that) Ahasuerus which reigned from India even unto Ethiopia over 127 provinces."[3] During the fifth year of his reign, all Egypt had submitted to Cambyses (525 BC) and he also subdued the Ethiopians, at least in part.[4] Having already inherited Cambyses' conquests in Egypt and Ethiopia, Darius I Hystaspis invaded and conquered India (506 BC).[5] Therefore, the Ahasuerus of Esther cannot be a Persian *before* Darius Hystaspis (Darius of Marathon) because it was not until Darius that the Empire extended from "India unto Ethiopia." These hard facts are decisive, yet there is more:

> And King Ahasuerus laid a *tribute* upon the land and upon the Isles of the Sea (Est. 10:1).

During 496 BC, the fleet of Darius conquered Samos, Chios, Lesbos and the rest of the islands of the Aegean Sea.[6] Herodotus says that Egypt, India, the Island of Cyprus and the Islands of the Erythraean Sea paid tribute to this Darius Hystaspis.[7] He also says that "The Ethiopians bordering upon Egypt, who were reduced by

---

(6 October, 539, Gregorian). Belshazzar was slain and Cyrus placed his 62-year-old relative, Darius the Mede, on the throne to rule over Babylon while he personally continued his military conquest at the head of his armies, annexing the remainder of the empire (Dan.5:30–31; note: Darius was "made" king, Dan.9:1).

[1] Henry Browne, *Ordo Saeclorum, op. cit.*, p. 173. That is, the first year of his sole reign over his newly enlarged empire (536 BC), not the first year in which Cyrus became a sovereign. When Cambyses I died in 559, Cyrus inherited the throne of Anshan, a Persian kingdom but vassal of the Medes. Cyrus became king over all of Medeo-Persia in 550. Scripture makes no reference to these earlier accounts as they had no bearing upon Israel. He conquered Babylon in 539, placed his uncle on the throne while he continued at the head of the army, annexing territory. In 536, Cyrus returned to resume control of the government. Thus 536 is his "first year" in the connotation that: (a) Cyrus' kingdom more than doubled in extent, his power and prestige soared proportionately, and (b) it was Cyrus' first year as suzerain over the Jews. Xenophon indicates this reign over Babylon was 7 years by recording that Cyrus went from Babylon to Susa every Spring and that he made this trip 7 times (*Cyropaedia, op. cit.*, VIII, vi, 22 and VIII, vii, 1).

[2] Herodotus, *The Histories, op. cit.*, VII, 4. After the Persian defeat by the Greeks at Marathon, not only were the Ionian states in revolt, Egypt also revolted. When Xerxes ascended the throne, the empire was beginning to crumble; the number of provinces began to diminish.

[3] This statement proves that Ahasuerus was a throne name and that more than one Persian monarch bore that title. At this point it must be acknowledged that although this author had already discovered and put in writing much of that which follows in identifying Ahasuerus, upon finding Anstey's excellent summation in which he had uncovered and organized even more references than had previously been found, his discoveries were checked and added to my original research. Therefore, much of the credit for this disclosure rightly belongs to that indefatigable scholar as well as to Ussher whom I later discovered to be Anstey's source for the data in paragraph 3 on my p. 202. Whereas Anstey's association of Darius I Hystaspis as being the Artaxerxes of Ezra 7:1–21 and Neh.2:1, 5:14, 13:6 (with which Faulstich agrees) is deemed by this study to be totally faulty, his carefully documented research with regard to the Artaxerxes in Esther is that of a chronologer par excellence. See: Anstey, *The Romance of Bible Chronology, op. cit.*, pp. 240–243 and Ussher, *Annals, op. cit.*, page 134 (1658 = p. 119).

[4] Herodotus, *The Histories, op. cit.*, III.

[5] *Ibid.*, III and IV.

[6] *Ibid.*, VI.

[7] *Ibid.*, III, 89–97.

Cambyses" paid no fixed tribute but like others, brought gifts regularly to Darius Hystaspis:[1]

> The Ethiopians paid no settled tribute, but brought gifts to the King. Every 3rd year the inhabitants of Egypt and Nubia brought 2 quarts of virgin gold; 200 logs of ebony, 5 Ethiopian boys and 20 elephant tusks.

When compared to the previously cited Esther 10:1 passage, this secular data testifies and declares that Ahasuerus is Darius Hystaspis. Moreover, upon being chosen as his royal residence, Susa (or Shushan) was embellished and extended by Darius Hystaspis (521 BC).[2] There he built his palace and kept all his treasures within.[3] These data militate against Cambyses, or anyone before him, as being the Ahasuerus of the Book of Esther for the palace therein *was* at Shushan (Esther 1:2).

This excluding determination is especially legitimate when coupled with Esther 1:14 concerning the "seven princes of Persia." It was Darius I who established the Persian tradition of having a council of seven wise and powerful men at court to serve and assist the king. This custom was a continuation of the policy resulting from the Persian noblemen's aiding Darius in procuring the throne from the Magians. Obviously then, no monarch prior to Darius Hystaspis could be the "Ahasuerus" in question.

Moreover, Thucydides (571–396 BC) tells us that Darius Hystaspis used his Phoenician fleet to subdue all the islands in the Aegean Sea,[4] and Diodorus Siculus relates that they were all lost again by his son Xerxes immediately after his 479 BC defeat to the Greeks – *before* the 12th year of his reign.[5] Yet it was *after* the 12th year of the reign of Ahasuerus of Esther that he imposed a tribute upon the Isles (Esther 3:7,12,13; 9:1,21; 10:1) or at least during the very last days of that 12th year. Further, as Ussher pointed out, the terms of the 387 BC

"Peace of Antalcidas" recorded by Xenophon shows that, except for Clazomene and Cyprus, Xerxes' successors held none of these islands.[6]

All of this external secular data tells us that the Ahasuerus of Esther is *not* Xerxes, and it harmonizes with the internal evidence contained in Scripture. Cyrus and Cambyses never imposed tribute, although they did receive presents. Polyaenus writes that Darius was the first of the Persians to impose a tribute on the people.[7] This act led Herodotus to pen that the Persians called Cyrus a father, Cambyses a master, but Darius a huckster, "for Darius looked to make a gain in everything."[8]

This description of Darius is consistent with Haman's behavior in the account. Being aware of this aspect of his king's character and in order to secure approval to massacre all the Jews within the empire, Haman offered to pay the monarch 10,000 talents of silver to offset the expenses that would be incurred in his proposed plan (Esther 3:9). Esther also seems aware of this trait as she mentions in her petition that the king would lose revenue if the exterminations were carried out (Esther 7:4).

Although the Old Testament Apocrypha is not the inspired Word of God, hence is neither authoritative nor trustworthy, it does reveal how the writers of that time interpreted the story of Ezra. The first Book of Esdras (c. 140 BC) recites verbatim Esther 1:1–3, the only change being that of replacing the name "Ahasuerus" with "Darius" (1 Esdras 3:1–2). This Darius is later firmly identified as Darius Hystaspis by relating that it was in the sixth year of this king's reign that the Temple was completed (1 Esdras 6:5, cp. Ezra 6:15).

In the Apocrypha account of "The Rest of Esther" as well as in the LXX, Ahasuerus is everywhere called "Artaxerxes"; however these are not necessarily attempts to identify him as the Persian king of Ezra chapter 7 and/or the Book of Nehemiah. Though there have been able, conservative Christian chronologers who have made this connection, two things must be

1 Herodotus, *The Histories, op. cit.*, III, 97.

2 Pliny, *Natural History*, vol. XX, Loeb Classical Library, VI, p. 27.

3 Herodotus, *The Histories, op. cit.*, V, 49.

4 Thucydides, *History of Peloponnesian War*, vol. I, Loeb Classical Library, (Cambridge, MA: Harvard UP, 1980), Bk. I, Ch. 16.

5 Diodorus Siculus, *The Library of History*, Book XI, 36–37 and Bk. XII (Loeb, vol. IV, 1968, pp. 221, 223, 375).

6 Ussher, *Annals, op. cit.*, p. 134 (1658 = 119). Xenophon, *Hellenica*, Book V. i. 31–36 (Loeb, vol. II, pp. 21–25).

7 Polyaenus, *Stratagematum*, (Chicago, IL: Ares Pub., 1974), Book 7, 11.

8 Herodotus, *The Histories, op. cit.*, III, 89.

remembered. First, "Artaxerxes" may here only be intended as an appellation meaning "king" (as "pharaoh" or "caesar").

Secondly, none of these books is inspired. They do not contain God-breathed words, thus they are not authoritative and are only useful as incidental witnesses. Nevertheless, Sir Isaac Newton took the Book of Esdras to be the "best interpreter of the Book of Ezra" and thus, although he never refers to the Book of Esther anywhere in his discussion of the Persians, his chronology accepted Esdras to be correct in identifying the Ahasuerus of Esther as Darius Hystaspis.[1] Ussher and Bishop Lloyd made the same identification.[2]

3. THE TESTIMONY OF MORDECAI'S AGE

The last and most pertinent data necessary in correctly identifying Ahasuerus is the direct *internal evidence* within the biblical story itself concerning the age of Mordecai. The erroneous identification of Ahasuerus with Xerxes, compounded by other poor judgments, has caused most modern scholars to reject that Mordecai was taken away from Jerusalem with Jeconiah in "the captivity" of 597 BC despite the clear declaration of Esther 2:5–6 which so proclaims.

This biblical assertion is rejected because, having already erroneously presumed that Ahasuerus is Xerxes, the acceptance of the verse as it stands would force Mordecai to be at least 113 years old (597 – 484 BC [the 3rd year of Xerxes; Esther 1:1–3]) at the beginning of the story (if he were a newborn when carried away). Moreover, Mordecai would have been a minimum of 125 at the close of the book when

he became "prime minister" in the king's 12th year (Esther 10:3, cp. 3:7). Though this would be possible, it is somewhat unlikely as only one man's age has been reported in Scripture as being that great since the days of "the judges" (over 700 years!). Besides, as Esther is Mordecai's first cousin (Esther 2:7), she would tend to be too old to fit the context of the story.

The solution to the dilemma, accepted by nearly all, has been to impose an unnatural rendering of the Esther 2:5–6 passage compelling the verse to read as though it were Kish, Mordecai's great-grandfather, who was carried away in 597 BC with Jeconiah rather than Mordecai himself. Notwithstanding, this interpretation is neither true nor an accurate rendering of the Hebrew construction which affirms that it *was* Mordecai who was carried away with Jeconiah. Only by a tortured, forced grammatical construction could this sentence ever be applied to his great-grandfather Kish.

The entire matter is resolved by simply letting the Bible speak for itself. This excessive age problem is simply due to a failure to accept the obvious which is that the Ahasuerus of Esther is actually Darius Hystaspis and not Xerxes. When this is seen, the age of Mordecai will be significantly reduced to a more reasonable and believable value (as will Ezra's and Nehemiah's, see fn. 1, p. 204). Moreover, it is the persistent insistence by most modern scholars that "Ahasuerus" is Xerxes that has caused the problem.[3]

With the Ahasuerus of Esther as Darius I Hystaspis (of Marathon, the Great), his third year would fall in 519 BC. Thus, Mordecai could have been as young as 78 in the first chapter of Esther and ten years older (88) rather than 125 years old when promoted to prime minister during the 12th year (509 BC) of that Persian monarch (597 BC – 519 = 78 years;

---

[1] Newton, *The Chronology of Ancient Kingdoms Amended*, *op. cit.*, pp. 368–370. When Newton calls Ahasuerus "Xerxes," he means the Ahasuerus in Ezra 4:6 and not the Ahasuerus of Esther. Newton so did because Xerxes succeeded Darius on the throne and the Ahasuerus in Ezra 4:6 follows Darius in Ezra 4:5. By the same reasoning, he identifies the "Artaxerxes" that followed in Ezra 4:7–23 as being Artaxerxes Longimanus.

[2] Ussher, *Annals*, *op. cit.*, pp. 127–129 (1658 edition, pages 112–114). Josephus also calls the Ahasuerus of the Book of Esther "Artaxerxes," but he does not mean the Artaxerxes of Ezra 7 and Nehemiah. Josephus identified him as "Cyrus the son of Xerxes whom the Greeks called 'Artaxerxes'." In other words, Josephus makes Ahasuerus to be Artaxerxes I Longimanus. The point is, he does not corroborate the testimonies of "The Rest of Esther" and the LXX even though he refers to Ahasuerus as "Artaxerxes" because he does not intend the same "Artaxerxes" that they propose. Josephus, *Antiquities, op. cit.*, II, 6, 1.

[3] The Book of Esther says nothing about Xerxes' attempt to avenge his father's humiliating 490 BC trouncing by the Greeks at Marathon. After his defeat at Salamis (end of September) in 480 (his 6th year), Xerxes fled 400 miles in 45 days to the Hellespont (mid-November) – still 1,300 miles from Shushan. Now Esther was brought into the house of the women in the 6th year of Ahasuerus and into the king's house in his 7th (Est.2:16; cp. vv. 8 & 12). Were Ahasuerus Xerxes, the search for the "fair young virgins" would have begun in 480 (his 6th year, see Chart 5c) or 481 – the very years Xerxes was at war in Greece – yet Ahasuerus was at the palace in Shushan at the beginning of the search (Est.2:4-5)! Thus the events in Esther do not fit well with the historical facts regarding Xerxes.

Esther 1:3, cp. 2:5–7, 3:7, hence 12 − 3 = 10 years inclusive). Indeed, the Mordecai of Ezra 2:2 and Nehemiah 7:7 should, in all likelihood, be identified as the Mordecai of the Book of Esther such that we have only one Mordecai, not two as is being taught today.[1] This is much more in line with other Bible ages for this period and unifies the Books of Ezra, Nehemiah, and Esther into one continuous story with only one principal person named Mordecai (and as we shall soon see, probably only one Nehemiah and one Ezra, not two).

The sum of all the foregoing particulars is conclusive evidence offered both for the proper identification of the Ahasuerus of Esther as Darius Hystaspis and against his being Xerxes I or any Persian ruler after Xerxes I. Evidence has also been presented as to why Ahasuerus cannot be an occupant of the throne preceding Darius I Hystaspis of Marathon.

4. AMBIGUOUS CONTRARY EVIDENCE

What then is the overwhelming evidence to the contrary upon which all modern scholarship has succumbed? As mentioned in the second paragraph at the onset of this subject, the first consideration is that of the descriptions passed

---

[1] A check of almost any recent Bible dictionary will identify the Ezra of Neh.12:1,7 as a chief priest and leader who returned with Zerubbabel in the first year of Cyrus as different from the one in the Book of Ezra who is also a priest (Ezra 7:1–12) and leader. Yet "both" men are clearly alive during the reign of the same Persian monarch, Artaxerxes (cp. Ezra 7:1,12,21 with Neh.2:1; 5:14; 8:1–4,9; 12:1). "Both" are contemporaries of Zerubbabel and associated with a Nehemiah who is a leader (Neh.8:1–4,9) and a Nehemiah who is associated with Zerubbabel (Neh.7:7). It is equally dismaying to "learn" that the Nehemiah who returned from Babylon as a leader with Zerubbabel (Ezra 2:2; Neh.7:7) is not supposed to be the same Nehemiah of the Book of Nehemiah who succeeded Zerubbabel as governor under Artaxerxes. A further check will almost certainly "uncover" that the Mordecai of the Book of Esther will not be seen as the leader who returned with Zerubbabel (Ezra 2.2; Neh.7:7).

Apparently Nehemiah, Mordecai and possibly Ezra, as key Jewish leaders, were recalled to serve various Persian kings who followed Cyrus. The biblical narrative reveals the circumstances as to what became of them, how Nehemiah and Ezra, undoubtedly young among the leaders in the days of Cyrus and Zerubbabel, were subsequently allowed to return in the wisdom of their gray heads and be used by the LORD in Jerusalem while God's purpose for Mordecai was for the good of His people back in Persia who had chosen not to return from the captivity.

down to our day by Herodotus (484–425 BC). Although Herodotus is reasonably authoritative for the period of the great Persian War with Greece (490–485 BC), his accounts of older periods are not always reliable. Vivid pictures are given in his writings concerning the first four Persian kings, i.e.,[2]

1. Cyrus, the simple hardy, vigorous mountain chief, endowed with vast ambition, and with great military genius, changing as his Empire changed, into the kind and friendly paternal monarch, clement, witty, polite familiar with his people;

2. Cambyses, the first form of the Eastern tyrant, inheriting his father's vigour and much of his talent, but violent, rash, headstrong, incapable of self-restraint, furious at opposition, not only cruel, but brutal;

3. Darius Hystaspis, the model Oriental prince, brave, sagacious, astute, great in the arts of both war and peace, the organizer and consolidator as well as the extender of the Empire; and

4. Xerxes, the second and inferior form of tyrant, weak and puerile as well as cruel and selfish, fickle, timid, licentious and luxurious.

The first argument put forth by those who favor Xerxes as the Ahasuerus of Esther is that the character of Ahasuerus fits that of Xerxes as given by Herodotus and other classic writers. But this is highly subjective and hardly tenable or admissible in light of all that we have offered to the contrary. Indeed, were we to ask twenty or so historians, news commentators, etc. to describe the character of a certain world leader, what would we actually hear in reply? Widely varied opinions would issue forth. Much would depend upon the writer's ethical views, political affiliations, prejudices, etc.

When human beings judge others, there is no such thing as being purely objective. Moreover, Herodotus' descriptions are neither first nor secondhand information. They are hearsay portrayals gleaned from various sources over the course of his many travels.

Besides, from our knowledge of the classic literature there is nothing in the character of Ahasuerus which could not equally apply as well to Darius I Hystaspis. In fact, the money

---

[2] George Rawlinson (ed.), *History of Herodotus*, 4 vols., (London: n.p., 1858), Introduction.

matters mentioned as well as his friendly attitude toward the Hebrews agree exactly with what one would expect from Darius the "huckster," the money-maker and organizer of the empire.

The second and supposedly conclusive argument that Ahasuerus is Xerxes is derived from the similarity between a name found on an inscription in a ruin with the name "Xerxes." A young student at the University of Gottingen, Georg Friedrich Grotefend, deciphered the inscriptions of Persian characters found among the ruins of the ancient Persian city, Persepolis. The name of the son of Darius Hystaspis was deciphered as "KHSHAYARSHA" which is the "old" Persian. Grotefend translated this into Greek as "Xerxes." When "KHSHAYARSHA" is transposed into Hebrew, it becomes almost letter for letter "AKHASHVEROSH," which is rendered "Ahasuerus" in English. Thus the "Ahasuerus" of the Book of Esther was established to be Xerxes.

At first glance this seems decisive. However, this is actually of no force when we recall that the word "Xerxes" in any form, regardless of spelling, simply means "SHAH" (king) and as such could be applied to *anyone* sitting upon the throne of Persia. Moreover, sound exegesis dictates that no etymology may ever take precedence over a clear context.

The opposite is quite popular today among both those who overemphasize lexical word studies and Greek dilettantes; however, it is the path to error. Etymology may *confirm* a context or even assist in clarification, but it is not an exact science and thus should be used as sole judge with extreme caution – and then only when there is nothing else available to consult. It must *never* be used to overturn clear context!

Finally, there is something amiss with the above etymological reasoning inasmuch as "Ahasuerus" means "the mighty" (Aha) and "king" (Suerus). How then in translating does this suddenly reduce to "Xerxes" which means only "shah" or "king"? Actually it would seem that "Artaxerxes" would have been a more faithful rendering. The translators of the Septuagint certainly so concurred (Esther 1:1, etc., LXX). What, we ask, happened to "The Mighty" portion during the translation? Selah.

N. DANIEL'S 483 (490) YEAR PROPHECY

The ninth chapter of the Book of Daniel contains the well known "seventy weeks" prophecy which has become the subject of many varied interpretations and disagreements without end. The setting for the prophecy is that of the period of the servitude of Israel to Babylonia (606–536 BC). Specifically, it was the year the Medes and Persians had conquered the Neo-Babylonian Empire, the first year of the reign of Darius the Mede, son of Ahasuerus (c. 539 BC, Dan. 5:25–31; 9:1; cp. 2 Chronicles 36:21–23; Ezra 1; 6:3–5).

Daniel was studying the writings of Jeremiah, his contemporary, and was given to realize that along with the fall of Babylon and the empire, the seventy-year servitude and especially the seventy-year span of the desolations of the city of Jerusalem and its temple were all soon to end (Daniel 9:2, 16–19; see various seventy-year prophecies depicted on Charts 5 and 5c). While Daniel was praying and confessing his sins and those of his people at the time of the evening sacrifice (about mid-afternoon or c. 3:00 P.M., Dan. 9:21), the angel Gabriel came to him.

Gabriel had appeared to Daniel nearly 13 years earlier to explain a former vision concerning the future conquest of the Median-Persian Empire (the ram with two uneven horns) by Alexander the Great (the he-goat with one large horn, Dan. 8), etc. The purpose of this second visitation was to explain a new vision to the prophet. The prophecy, given to Daniel and interpreted for him by the angel Gabriel, was:

> Seventy weeks are determined upon thy people and upon thy holy city, to finish the transgression, and to make an end of sins, and to make reconciliation for iniquity, and to bring in everlasting righteousness, and to seal up the vision and prophecy, and to anoint the most Holy. Know therefore and understand, that from the going forth of the commandment to restore and to build Jerusalem unto the Messiah the Prince shall be seven weeks, and threescore and two weeks: the street shall be built again, and the wall, even in troublous times. And after threescore and two weeks shall Messiah be cut off, but not for himself: and the people of the prince that shall come shall destroy the city and the sanctuary; and the end thereof shall be with a flood, and unto the end of the war desolations are determined.

And he shall confirm the covenant with many for one week: and in the midst of the week he shall cause the sacrifice and the oblation to cease, and for the overspreading of abominations he shall make it desolate, even until the consummation, and that determined shall be poured upon the desolate (Daniel 9:24–27).

It is not the purpose of this undertaking to examine the eschatological aspects of this prophecy, but those which are of a chronological nature. In so doing, it will be assumed that the reader has a background in the study of the prophecy.[1]

Accordingly, that which is before the reader will begin with the acceptance of the position that the terminology of the "seventy weeks" or, more properly in the Hebrew, the "seventy sevens" prophecy is speaking of "seventy sevens" of *years* or a total span of 490 years (70 x 7 = 490). Further, that there is a natural break in the prophecy (actually several breaks exist) after the completion of "sixty-nine sevens" or at the end of a 483-year period (69 x 7 = 483) which relates to the First Advent of the Messiah, Jesus the Christ.

As a definitive *terminus a quo* is given with reference to a specific decree locatable within the Holy Writ and since its *terminus ad quem* is in the time of Christ Jesus, this prediction becomes a most invaluable chronological tool in spanning from the period of the Persian rule over the Hebrew people to the era of New Testament times.

1. WHICH DECREE?

Four decrees regarding the restoration of the Jews from the Babylonian captivity are mentioned in the Books of Ezra and Nehemiah. Each has been offered by able advocates as being the *terminus a quo* for the Daniel 9:25 prophecy. They are:

1. The decree issued to rebuild the Temple in the first year of Cyrus, 536 BC (2 Chron. 36:22–23; Ezra 1:1–6; Ezra 5:13–17);

2. The decree issued to complete the Temple in the second year of Darius (I) Hystaspis, 519 BC (Ezra 4:24; 6:1–12);

3. The decree issued to beautify the Temple in the seventh year of Artaxerxes (Ezra 7:7–28); and

4. The decree issued to build the city of Jerusalem and its wall in the twentieth year of Artaxerxes (Neh. 2:1–8,13,17).

One of these must be identified as being the specific decree which included "the commandment to restore and to build Jerusalem ... the street shall be built again, and the wall, even in troublous times." As may be seen and verified, the first three have only to do with the Temple proper; nothing was said concerning the rebuilding of the city, the street in the plaza area and its walls. Indeed, the reconstruction of the Temple was stopped because the Jews were rebuilding the city without authorization (Ezra 4:1–4). Thus, the conditions of Daniel 9:25 were not met in any of the first three decrees.

Despite the fact that the first three decrees do not fit the conditions of the Daniel prophecy, several of them have had strong proponents over the years. Anstey and others have strongly advocated the decree of Cyrus on the grounds that other Scripture in Isaiah demands it was under this Persian monarch that the city would be built.[2]

The notes in Doctor C.I. Scofield's Study Bible originally favored the decree in the 20th year of Artaxerxes I as being that 20th fulfilled the Daniel 9:25 prophecy. However, after reading Anstey's book, Scofield became convinced, concluding that it was the decree of Cyrus which was the proper starting point for the "seventy weeks." In AD 1918, he published a book in which he stated this decision and added: "whatever confusion has existed at this point has been due to following the Ptolemaic instead of the biblical chronology, as Martin Anstey in his 'Romance of Bible Chronology.'"[3]

---

[1] For those lacking such a background, the marketplace is rife with works which address the "seventy weeks" of Daniel. The classic composition cited by all who have investigated the matter during the past century is *The Coming Prince* by Sir Robert Anderson, *op. cit.* Many other books from various Dallas Theological Seminary graduates such as Walvoord, D. Pentecost, Lindsey and Hoehner as well as the Scofield notes, McClain, Willmington and Jeffrey, to name but a few, may be readily found for consultation. However, as shall be shown, this subject was thoroughly addressed much earlier by Sir Isaac Newton, Ussher, many of the Reformers, and Julius Africanus in the 2nd century AD.

[2] Anstey, *The Romance of Bible Chronology, op. cit.*, pp. 277–293.

[3] C.I. Scofield, *What Do the Prophets Say?*, (Phil., PA: The Sunday School Times Co., 1918), p. 142.

Interestingly, those dates have never been changed in any of the Scofield Bible notes.

The decree issued in the seventh year of Artaxerxes (Ezra 7:7–28) has also had a strong following, not because it matched the conditions of the Daniel 9:25 prophecy but more by virtue of the fact that of all the four possibilities it seemed to best "fit" the prescribed time frame. The seventh year of Artaxerxes I Longimanus fell about 458 BC (or 457) and 483 years (or as some reckon, 483 + 3½, etc. = c. 487) after that date would fall around AD 24–28.

This brings the chronology to about the 15th year of the reign of Tiberius Caesar (AD 26–28 at which time Christ Jesus, being about 30 years of age, was baptized by John, Luke 3:1–3, 21–23). Among those championing this position was the redoubtable Sir Isaac Newton.[1] He was later followed by Dr. Humphrey Prideaux[2] and, more recently, by Frank Klassen.[3]

2. DANIEL FULFILLED – ARTAXERXES' DECREE

However at least as far back as the days of Julius Africanus (c. AD 200–245), it has been widely accepted by historians, chronologers and biblical commentators (i.e., Africanus, Petavius, Ussher, Lloyd, Marshall, Anderson, McClain, Walvoord, D. Pentecost, Hoehner, Unger, and most present day students of Daniel's prophecy) that only the decree issued in the 20th year of Artaxerxes I granted permission for the rebuilding of the city of Jerusalem, along with its plaza street and walls, and thus fulfilled the conditions of the prophecy. With regard to this, Africanus wrote:[4]

> And the beginning of the numbers, that is, of the seventy weeks which make 490 years, the angel instructs us to take from the going forth of the commandment to answer and to build Jerusalem. And this happened in the 20th year of the reign of Artaxerxes king of Persia.

The present author's study has led him to the same conclusion (see Appendix M, page 300 ff.), thus establishing the date of the 20th year of Artaxerxes becomes paramount.

O. THE TIME OF THE SAVIOR'S BIRTH, MINISTRY, & CRUCIFIXION

Over the years Cyrus the Great, Darius I Hystaspis, Artaxerxes I Longimanus, and Artaxerxes II Mnemon have been offered as being the Artaxerxes of Ezra 6:14, Ezra 7, and the Book of Nehemiah. Nevertheless, at least three clear guiding parameters do exist to assist the historian or chronologist in making the correct association.

Taking the Scriptures at face value, one looks for the first "Artaxerxes" who reigned *after* Darius Hystaspis (Ezra 6:14) whose dominion extended for at least 32 years (Neh. 5:14) and whose accession to the throne was at least 483 years from the time of Christ Jesus' first advent (Dan. 9:24–27). Accordingly, Longimanus (465–424 BC) has been generally acknowledged for many years as the correct choice and that his 20th year would fall c. 445 BC (though some argue for 446 or 444).

However, it is at this very point that a long debated problem arises. The Christian Era began with the birth of Christ Jesus; however, the exact date of this event has given rise to much controversy. It is true that 483 years (or 483 + 3½ years or 483 + 7 as some insist) from 445 BC does take one to AD 39 or around the lifetime of Christ Jesus. Nevertheless, when compared to other biblical data which places the Lord as "about thirty years of age" (Luke 3:23) in the "fifteenth year of Tiberius Caesar" (Luke 3:1, AD 26–28 depending upon whether one begins when Tiberius was made co-rex with Augustus or when he became sole rex), it would seem that His crucifixion and resurrection could not have extended far past AD 33.

The fact that the Gospel of John mentions only four Passovers (at most) during Christ's earthly ministry tends to confirm this conclusion. Many arrangements have been made in the past attempting to reconcile all the facts attendant to the birth and crucifixion of Christ, and some have indeed set AD 39 (or AD 38 if

[1] Newton, *Observations Upon the Prophecies of Daniel, op. cit.*, pp. 130–143.

[2] Humphrey Prideaux, *The Old and New Testament Connected in the History of the Jews*, 25th ed., 2 Vols., (London: 1858; orig. pub. 1718). See Anstey, *The Romance of Bible Chronology, op. cit.*, pp. 279–280.

[3] Klassen, *The Chronology of the Bible, op. cit.*, pp. 46–54.

[4] Julius Africanus, *Chronographies, Anti-Nicene Fathers*, vol. VI, Roberts and Donaldson, eds., (Grand Rapids, MI: Eerdmans, 1885), chapter xvi., para. 3.

446 BC is taken as Artaxerxes' 20th year) as the death and resurrection year of the Lord Jesus.

The Holy Scriptures do not record information that will allow us to calculate the precise day of this singular event. As the early Christian church did not celebrate our Lord's birth, the exact date has not been preserved in its festivals. Although this study will show that biblical data does exist that will allow us to narrow His birth day down to two closely approximated "seasons" which are six months apart, it should be obvious that had God wanted the date known and/or celebrated He would have recorded it plainly in Scripture much as He did the precise months and days of the "Feasts of the Lord" as recorded in Leviticus 23.

Of course, as there is also no biblical injunction against setting aside a day to observe the divine birth it would seem we are free to so do at any date we might choose. That which follows are the biblical facts as best as this author can determine.

1. THE YEAR OF THE SAVIOR'S BIRTH

The Nativity year in use today was established in AD 525 by Pope John I who commissioned Dionysius Exiguus the Little, a Roman abbot, to prepare a standard calendar for the Western Church.[1] Not wanting the years of history to be reckoned from the life of a persecutor of the church, Dionysus modified the Alexandrian system of dating which used as its foundation the reign of Diocletian, the Roman Emperor. He calculated the commencement of the Christian Era as being on January 1, 754 A.U.C. (anno urbis conditae = from the foundation of the city of Rome) and Christ's birth was thought to have been the preceding December 25th.

Thus 754 A.U.C. (also called YOR = years of Rome) became AD 1 on Dionysius' calendar. Unfortunately his date, which has secured wide adoption in Christian countries, apparently errs

in placing the birth of Christ about four years after the fact (i.e., too late).

The Scriptures reveal that Jesus' birth occurred very shortly before the death of King Herod the Great (Matthew 2, compare Luke 2:21–39). Consequently, Herod's death has been universally relied upon as the most significant and reliable data upon which to fix the year of Christ Jesus' birth. Josephus mentions an eclipse of the moon which occurred shortly before Herod died.[2] This eclipse is the only one alluded to by Josephus and, as the Lord Jesus was born while Herod was still living (Matthew 2:1–6), it thus serves to fix with "absolute" certainty the time after which the birth of Jesus could not have taken place.[3] Astronomical calculations locate a partial eclipse of the moon March 12/13 in the year of Rome 750; no eclipse occurred the following year that was visible in Palestine.

Josephus also says that Herod died 37 years after he was declared king by the Romans.[4] According to Jewish reckoning, Herod was proclaimed king in 714 bringing his death (at the age of 70)[5] to the year from 1 Nisan 750 to 1 Nisan 751 (Josephus normally counts from Nisan to Nisan). Josephus further states that Herod died just before a Passover.[6]

As there was no eclipse in 751,[7] Herod's death is firmly placed shortly before the Passover in the 750th year (April 7) from the foundation of Rome. Accordingly, the death of Herod must have taken place between 12 March and 7 April in the year 4 BC. This is four years before the

---

[1] Harold W. Hoehner, *Chronological Aspects of the Life of Christ*, (Grand Rapids, MI: Zondervan, 1977), p. 11. Although Dr. Hoehner is the actual reference used, this information may be found in nearly any encyclopedia under the topic of "calendar" as well as in many other standard references. Whereas this author does not agree with some of Hoehner's conclusions, the work is highly recommended. It is lucid, well-researched, factual, and God-honoring.

[2] Josephus, *Antiquities, op. cit.,* XVII, 6, 4.

[3] A.T. Robertson, *A Harmony of the Gospels for Students of the Life of Christ*, (New York: Harper & Row, 1922), p. 262. Whereas the material in this study was originally researched from Dr. Robertson years ago, many other publications have since been considered in checking and verifying his findings. This section of his "Notes on Special Points" (pp. 262–267) is deemed by this author to be among his finest and most incisive. Nevertheless, it is not intended that his statements should be taken as final. As noted in footnote 1, page 209, a very strong case can be made for 1 or 2 BC as the birth year of our Lord.

[4] Josephus, *Antiquities, op. cit.,* XVII, 8, 1.

[5] Samuel J. Andrews, *The Life of Our Lord upon the Earth*, 4th ed., (New York: Charles Scribner & Co., 1867), p. 1.

[6] Josephus, *Antiquities, op. cit.,* XVII, 8, 1, cp. 9, 3.

[7] Robertson, *A Harmony of the Gospels, op. cit.,* p. 262.

usual period fixed as the beginning of Christian chronology according to the eclipse and the length of his reign[1] Thus it would seem that four years must be counted between the first year of the Christian Era (754) and the birth of Christ; that is, He was born about 750 A.U.C. or 4 BC (see table, page 255). Some make this difference as much as five or six years.

Other ancient authorities also testify to a 4 BC birth year (or at least to its near proximity). Around AD 180, Irenaeus penned: "Our Lord was born about the 41st year of the reign of Augustus."[2] Tertullian, another early church father, writing about AD 198 stated that Augustus began to reign 41 years before the birth of Christ[3]. This also converts to a 4 BC date (see table, page 256, Augustus = Octavian began to reign March 15, 44 BC).

About AD 194 Clement of Alexandria wrote that Jesus was born in the 28th year of the reign of Augustus.[4] Finegan correctly understands Clement as not meaning 28 years from 44 BC when Augustus succeeded Julius Caesar which would place our Lord's birth in 17 BC but rather 28 years from when Augustus began to reign over Egypt following the death of Anthony and Cleopatra.[5] The 28th year of the Egyptian reign of Augustus is 3 BC.[6]

Julius Africanus (AD c. 160–c. 240) also dated the birth of Christ. His dating method converts to Olympiad 194, year 2 which is 3 BC.[7] Africanus' contemporary, Hippolytus of Rome (AD circa 170–236), indicates the same date in his *Chronicle*.[8] In a Greek fragment of the *Homilies*, Origen (c. AD 185–c. 254) says that Christ Jesus was born in the 41st year of Caesar Augustus (4 BC).[9] Eusebius of Caesarea (c. AD 325) places the Savior's birth in the 42nd year of the reign of Augustus and/or 28 years "after the submission of Egypt and the death of Anthony and Cleopatra" (= 3 BC).[10]

In addition to these, Epiphanius (about AD 315–403, born in Palestine, became bishop of Salamis on the island of Cyprus in AD 357) wrote that Jesus was born in the 42nd year of Augustus.[11] Writing in his *Panarion* or "medicine chest" for the healing of all heresies, Epiphanius mentions a group which he designates as the Alogi (so named Αλογοι because they did not receive the Logos proclaimed by John and rejected the books John wrote) and says that they placed Christ's birth in the 40th year of Augustus.[12] Finally, we mention Cassiodorus Senator (AD c. 490–585), a Roman monk and historian who in his

---

[1] However there was a total lunar eclipse visible at Jerusalem on 9 January, 1 BC which may well have been the one referred to by Josephus [Sir Robert Anderson, *The Coming Prince*, (Grand Rapids, MI: Kregel Pub., 1882), p. 262]. Although 4 BC currently receives the majority support among conservatives, the 1 BC date also has had staunch supporters in the past and presently is making somewhat of a comeback. The result has been in placing the Nativity at 1 or 2 BC (continued p. 250).

[2] Irenaeus, *Against Heresies, Anti-Nicene Fathers*, vol. I, Roberts and Donaldson, eds., (Grand Rapids, MI: Eerdmans, 1885), Bk. III, xxi, 3.

[3] Tertullian, *An Answer to the Jews, Ante-Nicene Fathers*, vol. III, Roberts and Donaldson, eds., (Grand Rapids, MI: Eerdmans, 1885), Part I, vii, 8. However, he also gives the Lord's birth as being 28 years "after the death of Cleopatra."

[4] Clement of Alexandria, *Stromata, Anti-Nicene Fathers*, vol. II, Roberts and Donaldson, eds., (Grand Rapids, MI: Eerdmans, 1885), Bk. I, xxi, 145.

[5] Finegan, *Handbook of Biblical Chronology, op. cit.*, p. 223 (see footnote 3 above, "Tertullian"). The actual year depends upon whether accession or nonaccession year systems were being used as well as to which nation's calendar the various ancient writers were referring.

Often, the answers to these questions are not obtainable with certainty.

[6] *Ibid.*

[7] Africanus, *Chronographies, op. cit.*, I; Finegan, *Handbook of Biblical Chronology, op. cit.*, p. 225; also see pages 143–144.

[8] Finegan, *Handbook of Biblical Chronology, op. cit.*, pp. 225, 228–229 and also 145–147.

[9] Cited by Finegan, *Handbook of Biblical Chronology, op. cit.*, p. 226.

[10] Eusebius, *Ecclesiastical History*, 2 Volumes, The Loeb Classical Library, trans. by Kirsopp Lake, (Cambridge, MA: Harvard UP, 1980), vol. 1, v, 2.

[11] Epiphanius, *Panarion haereses*, 20, 2; and cited by Finegan, *Handbook of Biblical Chronology, op. cit.*, pp. 227–228. Epiphanius compiled this work in which he described and attempted to refute no less than 80 heresies, 20 of which were extant before the time of Christ [Elgin S. Moyer, *Who Was Who in Church History*, (Chicago: Moody Press, 1962), p. 134].

[12] Epiphanius, *Panarion haereses*, 51, 3, 2; and cited by Finegan, *Handbook of Biblical Chronology, op. cit.*, p. 228.

Chronica placed the Savior's birth as occurring in the 41st year of the reign of Augustus.[1]

Despite the slight variations found in the preceding sources, they support the aforementioned scriptural requirement that our Lord's birth must be placed within the reign of Herod. Their overall testimony confirms our conclusion that the best date to satisfy both Scripture and the data found in Josephus concerning Herod is 4 BC.

2. THE DAY OF OUR LORD'S BIRTH

That which remains then is to attempt to ascertain as best as possible the actual day upon which Messiah was born or failing at so precise a date as that, to establish the time or season of the year during which the event took place. Moreover, it has long been acknowledged by the most learned students that the day of our Lord's birth cannot be determined and that within the Christian Church the festival of Christmas was completely unheard of until the 3rd century AD. Indeed, it was not until well into the 4th century that the celebration became widely observed.[2]

When Constantine issued forth his decree of religious tolerance known as the Edict of Milan (AD 313), it suddenly became fashionable to profess Christianity. Overwhelmed by thousands upon thousands of new but unregenerate members, the "Church" soon became the State Church of the Roman Empire. Bringing their traditions and religious holy days with them, these pagans gradually subverted the Church and eventually installed the 25 December birthday of the Egyptian god Horus (Osiris) as being that of our Lord.[3]

The earliest allusion to December 25 (modern reckoning) as the date of the Nativity is by Clement of Alexandria (c. AD 155–220), around the beginning of the third century.[4] However, Clement is somewhat vague and merely mentions several dates which others have given as the birth day of the Lord. He does not actually give us his view. Further ancient evidence offering December 25th as the Savior's birthday is from as early as Hippolytus[5] and the Calendar of Furius Dionysius Filocalus (or Philocalus, AD 354) which placed Jesus' birth as Friday, December 25,[6] AD 1. This day was officially accepted by the church fathers in AD 440. The date was selected to coincide with the Roman heathen festival of Saturnalia which was held annually in honor the birth of the son

---

[4] Clement, *Stromata*, op. cit., Bk. I, xxi.

[5] Hoehner, *Chronological Aspects of the Life of Christ*, op. cit., p. 25. Hoehner also accepts a near 25 December birth, p. 27.

[6] The main arguments against December 25 as being the Nativity date are: (1) That Mary, being in her 9th month and "great with child" (Luke 3:5), could hardly have undertaken a journey of about 70 miles (as the crow flies) through a rugged hill region which averages about 3,000 feet above sea-level in the depth of winter. Moreover, Mary's sacrifice at the Temple on the 40th day after the birth is unmistakable evidence that she and Joseph were poor (Luke 2:21–24, cp. Lev. 12:8) and therefore probably did not own a donkey for her to ride upon for the journey to Bethlehem [however the gold from the Wise Men would have made such a purchase possible for the trip to Egypt]; (2) Shepherds would not normally be "abiding" with their flocks in the open fields at night in December (Tebeth), not only due to the cold but primarily because of the lack of pasturage at that season. It was the custom then as now to bring the flocks out of the field in the month Bul (Oct.–Nov.) and house them for the winter (still, see page 210, fn. 3); (3) The Roman authorities would hardly impose the census for the purpose of the hated and unpopular "foreign" taxation (Luke 2:1) at the most inconvenient, inclement season of the year.

To force the subjugated populace to enroll at their respective cities in December would cause great inconvenience and interfere with the habits and pursuits of the Jewish people. A competent Roman administrator would tend to take advantage of the annual agricultural festivals such as Unleavened Bread (which marked the beginning of the barley or grain harvest) or the Feast of Tabernacles (which was the celebration of the end or completion of the final ingathering of the years harvest) when all the males were commanded by God to go up to Jerusalem and thus already be engaged in travel. To enforce the edict of registration for the purpose of imperial taxation in the depth of winter when traveling for such a purpose would have been all the more resented and could even have led to open revolt would hardly have been attempted by such an astute ruler as Augustus [see Bullinger, *The Companion Bible*, op. cit., Appendix 179, pp. 199–200.].

---

[1] Finegan, *Handbook of Biblical Chronology*, op. cit., pp. 229 and 95.

[2] Alexander Hislop, *The Two Babylons*, (Neptune, NJ: Loizeaux Bros., 1916), p. 93; Andrews, *Life of our Lord*, op. cit., p. 19.

[3] Andrews, *Life of our Lord*, op. cit., p. 15. Although it is widely accepted by nearly all recent scholars that Christ's birth could not possibly have been on 25 December, such a conclusion has not been without defenders in the not too distant past. Andrews, for example, sets forth a strong argument in its favor (continued p. 250).

of Semiramis, the Babylonian "queen of heaven" (cp. Jer. 7:18, 44:15–30).[1]

Known as Isis in Egypt, this "Queen's" son was said to have been born "about the time of the winter solstice."[2]   Observed near the winter solstice, it was among the many pagan traditions the compromising organized Church absorbed from the ancient Babylonian priesthood.

3. THE COURSE OF ABIJAH (ABIA) – LUKE 1:5

It is the intent of this author to examine the matter before us by depending as nearly as possible solely upon the testimony of Scripture as well as regarding the correct context of those selfsame passages. In so endeavoring, it is first noted that many workers in the past have given much weight to the Luke 2:8 passage and concluded the impossibility (or at least the high improbability) of the shepherds around Bethlehem being in the field "keeping watch over their flocks by night" as far into the winter as the end of December, and thus they have ruled out Christmas day as having been a possible birthday for our Lord.

Whereas the result of this study concurs that 25 December is neither the date nor season of His birth, Luke 2:8 is viewed as having little or no force in determining the matter one way or the other. Indeed, many strong arguments have been presented in the past which reflect the possibility of shepherds pasturing their animals near Bethlehem even at so late a date (see page 210, fn. 3 and page 210 fn. 6).

The real reason that the Nativity did not transpire on the 25th of December has to do with the circumstances centered around a statement found in Luke 1:5. Here we read that John the

Baptist's father, Zacharias, was a priest of the course of Abia (Greek, Hebrew = Abijah). Abijah was a descendant of Aaron. By the time of David, Abijah's family had grown and risen to prominence as a "father's house" among the priests. It became the eighth of the 24 divisions (called a course) into which David separated the Aaronic priesthood just prior to his death when he organized the kingdom for his son, Solomon (1 Chron. 24:1, 6, 10).

Each course ministered in its turn at the Temple for a week from Sabbath to Sabbath biannually or twice during the year.[3] The first course fell by lot to Jehoiarib, the eighth to Abijah, and so on. As all the males of Israel were commanded by the Lord to come to Jerusalem at the time of the three great feasts (Unleavened Bread, Pentecost, and Tabernacles, Deut. 16:16), all 24 courses would be required to serve during those days in order to minister to so great a multitude. Thus these great feasts must be taken into account when arranging the various times of administration for the 24 courses. Unfortunately, this last fact has been overlooked by many in the past.

Obviously then, if we knew when the reckoning commenced we could determine the dates of the first and second administrations of the 8th course of Abijah for any given year. Although the Scriptures do not state with absolute certainty when the reckoning began, we conclude that it began on the first Sabbath of the first month of each year. This deduction is based upon the fact that when David organized the kingdom for the youthful Solomon (1 Chron. 23–27), he established a military sentinel to guard the capital city of Jerusalem.

This consisted of 12 changes of the guard (each of which contained 24,000 warriors), one for each month throughout the year beginning at the first month (1 Chron. 27:1, 2 and 15). As there is no other Scripture nor any reliable profane data relating to the question,[4] it seems

---

[1] Hislop, *The Two Babylons*, op. cit., pp. 91–103, esp. p. 93. The origin of this may be traced back to Babylon at the time of the Tower of Babel. The Tower was built under the direction of the founder of the world's first kingdom, Nimrod-bar-Cush, the son of Cush ("the black one") and grandson of Ham ("the dark or the sunburned one"). Secular records state that Nimrod (Orion, or Kronos [a corona or crown] "the horned one") married the infamous Semiramis I. She is reputed to have been the foundress of the Babylonian "Mysteries" and the first high priestess of idolatry. Tradition also ascribes the invention of the use of the cross as an instrument of death to this same woman (continued p. 250).

[2] Sir J. Gardiner Wilkinson, *Manners and Customs of the Ancient Egyptians*, vol. IV, (London: 1841), p. 405.

[3] 2 Chron. 23:4 and 8; also see Josephus, *Antiquities, op. cit.*, VII, 14, 7.

[4] Bullinger, *The Companion Bible, op. cit.*, Appendix 179, p. 200. Bullinger states that the reckoning commenced on "the 22nd day of Tisri or Ethanim" which was the 8th and last day of the Feast of Tabernacles = the "Great Day of the Feast" (John 7:37); however, he gives no source.

Moreover, after carefully studying and charting his work, it would seem that Bullinger began with a preconceived

logical that the reckoning of the priesthood would begin at the same time.

The only remaining question withholding us from calculating the approximate time of the Savior's birth is the kind of year that was being used – was it Tishri-to-Tishri or Nisan-to-Nisan? As it has already been categorically demonstrated that the Scriptures uniformly depict the Hebrews as using a Nisan-to-Nisan year,[1] we therefore conclude that the reckoning commenced in the spring on the first Sabbath after the first day of Nisan (Abib) on the Jewish calendar. Then after all 24 courses had served (taking one half year) the first course would again minister for a week beginning in the autumn.

4. THE COURSE OF ABIJAH AND NISAN YEARS

As scriptural as all has been so far, the resolving of the problem still is limited in that we have no sure way of determining whether Zacharias was ministering at the Temple during the first or second yearly administration of the course of Abijah. We shall therefore give both solutions and examine them as best we can.

a. The Course of Abijah – First Administration

According to my ephemeris-generating calendar conversion new moon program developed by the Harvard Center for Astrophysics,[2] 1 Nisan of 5 BC was a Sabbath.[3] As all the priests would be serving the third week during the Feast of Unleavened Bread, the third course would not begin until the following Sabbath (Nisan 22). Thus the first administration of the 8th course whereby Jesus would be born in the year 4 BC would fall between Zif 27–Sivan 4 which is June 1–7 (Gregorian calendar) in the year 5 BC.

Were this the course during which the angel Gabriel announced the conception of John the Baptist (Luke 1:11–15), Zacharias would have departed to his own home which was in the hill country of Judah (Luke 1:23) on the 7th of Sivan (Luke 1:39).[4] Consulting Joshua 21, we learn that of the 48 cities assigned to the Levites 13 were set aside for the priests (21:4, 10–19). Of these, three were located in the Judean hills. They were Hebron, Juttah, and Eshtemoa (see a Bible-land map).

As Scripture does not designate and since it is located between Hebron and Eshtemoa, we will take Juttah as the home of Zacharias. Bearing in mind he was old (Luke 1:7), possibly traveling on foot and that the Judean hill country is very rugged terrain, we estimate the time for Zacharias to travel the 25 or so miles – perhaps rest a bit – unto the conception of John to have been about three to four days. This brings us to around Sivan 10.

Luke records the begetting of our Lord as six months after the conception of John the Baptist (vv. 1:26, 36). Now the average gestation period for humans is about 270–290 days. If we take 280 as the mean, we may solve the simple ratio: if 280 days are 9 months, how many days are in 6 months = 186+.[5] Thus, we count 186 days from Sivan 10 and approximate the conception

---

idea and actually worked backwards from 25 December (which he maintains is the day Mary miraculously *conceived* Christ, the day on which Jesus was "begotten of the Holy Spirit" and "the Word became flesh") in order to obtain the 22 Tishri date. Not only does Bullinger's scheme feature these "special" days, he has Christ's birth falling on Tishri 15, AD 4 (the first day of the Feast of Tabernacles) thus making his design quite theologically aesthetic. The current author (FNJ) has no theological objection to 25 December as being the day in which Christ Jesus was "begotten," but for this to be an ascertainable fact, authentication by a reliable near contemporaneous source is deemed necessary.

Also see page 250 where Andrews cited the Talmud as saying that at the destruction of the Temple by Titus on the 4th August, 823 (AUC or YOR, i.e., AD 70 on the 10th day of Ab, FNJ), the first class of the priesthood had just entered on its course. Again, when one checks the calendar, it does not seem feasible that the first course could have had either of its administrations begin 10 Ab (the 5th Jewish month); thus for me Andrews' calculations and conclusion cannot be accepted.

[1] See "B. The Biblical Hebrew Year," page 106 ff. as well as "1. The Regnal Year," page 116 ff.

[2] The benefit of such a program can hardly be overstated. Remember biblical months were regulated by the new moon.

[3] The calendar on pages 222–223 will assist the reader in following the reckoning of the days (both Hebrew and Gentile) concerning the Lord's birth.

[4] Zacharias would not have departed Jerusalem on Sivan 4 at the end of his administration as Sivan 7 was the day of Pentecost.

[5] If we simply count ahead 6 Hebrew months (which well may be that intended by Scripture), Chisleu 10 becomes the day of Christ's conception.

day of Christ Jesus as Chisleu 19.[1] Numbering forward another 270–290-day swath from Chisleu 19 brings us to the time of the Savior's birth: Elul 23–Tishri 14 (see calendar on page 222 ff.) – in the fall around the time of the Feast of Trumpets and the Day of Atonement.[2]

b. The Course of Abijah – Second Administration

Beginning again at 1 Nisan of 5 BC (April 6 and 7), which was when the first course began its ministration, we number backwards so that Veadar 23–Nisan 1 would have been the 24th course and establish the second administration of the 8th course whereby Jesus could be born in the year 4 BC. The 8th course would have fallen between Chisleu (modern = Kislev) 30 and Tebeth 7 which is December 9–16 (Gregorian calendar) in the year 6 BC. If this were the course during which the angel Gabriel announced the conception of John the Baptist (Luke 1:11–15), Zacharias would have departed to his own home (Luke 1:23) about Tebeth 8, and John would have been conceived around Tebeth 11.

Counting off 186 days (6 months) from there, we approximate the conception day of Christ Jesus as being around Sivan 20. Numbering forward another 270–290-day swath from Sivan 20 brings us to the time of the Savior's birth – Adar 23 to Nisan 14 (again, see calendar on pages 222–223). As Nisan 14 is Passover day, we see that in this scenario it becomes possible that our Lord could have been born on Passover and, if so, would have been crucified on His birthday. Regardless, the general time for the Nativity is springtime in this outline – not summer or the dead of winter.

c. The Course of Abijah — Conclusion

But which of the two scenarios is correct? Though admittedly a weak argument, we mention that springtime is the lambing season and as the "Lamb of God, which taketh away

the sin of the world" (John 1:29) it would seem fitting if the Savior were born at this time. More significantly, the second administration of Abijah commends itself to us in that it results in Mary's conception of Jesus occurring around Sivan 20 (June 23).

Remembering that at this time Elizabeth (John the Baptist's mother) was six months along in her pregnancy and that Mary traveled from Nazareth to Juttah (?) – a distance of about 100 miles – to visit cousin Elizabeth (Luke 1:36 and 39–40), it is noted that the trip would have taken place in the summer. However, if we consider the timing for the first course of Abijah, this hundred-mile journey would have taken place near mid-December.

Winter travel in Israel is arduous, but it is far from impossible.[3] Indeed, recall that our Lord was crucified on the 14th of Nisan (springtime) and that His ministration spanned 3½ years (see page 220). If we go back these 3½ to the beginning of the ministry – when He was 30 years old – we come to the fall of the year. Simple and engaging as it is, this argument is obviously not absolutely conclusive. Thus we still cannot differentiate with certainty between the two scenarios as to the season of the Birth.

We add that a December 25th Nativity not only would place Mary as undertaking a most difficult journey of at least 70 miles over rugged hill country in her ninth month in the depth of winter, she and Joseph would then also have made the 120 to 200-mile trip from Bethlehem to Egypt with the newborn king almost immediately after having given birth. They would then have to return all the way to Nazareth during that same bitter cold season (see the chronology, page 215 ff.).

Not only is this most unlikely, the witness of Chrysostom writing in Antioch c. AD 380 seems to add the death knell to December 25. He

---

[1] Note, John the Baptist is said to have been born three months later, Luke 1:56, 57. Also note that 19 Chisleu is only c.8 days before December 25; hence, in this scenario it is possible that Christ could have been conceived on Christmas day.

[2] Had Hebrew months been used (see page 212, fn. 5), the birth swath would have been 9 days earlier, i.e., Elul 14 to Tishri 5, near the Feast of Trumpets which is always 1 Tishri (Lev. 23:24).

[3] Many years of eschatological study has convinced this author that as the Lord fulfilled the first group of feasts given in Leviticus 23 (Passover, First-fruits, Unleavened Bread, and Pentecost) at the first advent, He will fulfill the second group (i.e., Trumpets, Tabernacles along with its accompanying 8th day, and the Day of Atonement with its affliction of soul and mourning) at the second coming when Israel fulfills Atonement Day by looking upon "me whom they have pierced" and *mourn* (Zech. 12:10 and Mat. 24:30). This is another reason to favor a springtime birth over a fall "Tabernacles" date.

complained that it had not yet been ten years since that date had been made known as the birthday of the Lord to the Church of Antioch which lay on the very border of the Holy Land. Yet, incredulously, it had been well known as such from "ancient and primitive times" in all the European region of the west from Thrace to Spain![1]

Before closing this section, the reader is reminded to consider the many limiting uncertainties involved in that which has been presented. For example, the number of days after the ending of the eighth course that John was conceived, exactly how many days to allow for the six months of Elizabeth's pregnancy and thereby for the conception day of Christ Jesus, the actual gestation span for Christ, from which administration of the course of Abijah to calculate, etc.

Furthermore, it cannot be overstated that time in Scripture is always based on *observed* time (moon, going down and rising of the sun, crop maturation, etc.) whereas "Gentile" time is the result of calculation (this is why we must rely on aids such as clocks and calendars) Therefore, it must be understood that any astronomical calculation, no matter how carefully it may be obtained and scientific it may seem, may not yield – indeed, probably will not yield – the actual Hebrew day one is trying to establish in the biblical past. All of our computers calculate using Veadars to keep the calendar from drifting but, as we have already explained, the ancient Jews used no such expediency.

Thus, without a reliable near contemporaneous written witness (which remains undiscovered as of this writing), the actual day of our Lord's birth cannot be determined. The various unknowns place it beyond the scope of calculation.

5. EVENTS ACCOMPANYING JESUS' BIRTH

Many have attempted to demonstrate from Matthew 2:16 that the visit of the Wise Men (*Magi* = Latin from Greek *Magoi*, plural of *Magos*) and Herod's subsequent slaughter of the infants in Bethlehem occurred when Christ was about two years old.

Then Herod, when he saw that he was mocked of the wise men, was exceeding wroth, and sent forth, and slew all the children that were in Bethlehem, and in all the coasts thereof, from two years old and under, according to the time which he had diligently enquired of the wise men.

To strengthen their thesis, they note that the Lukan account uses the Greek term *"brephos"* (βρεφος, 2:12) which they say is used to pertain to an unborn, newborn, or an infant whereas Matthew uses the words *"paidion"* (παδιον, 2:8, 9, 11, 13, 14, 20, and 21) and *"pais"* (παις, 2:16) which supposedly designates a child of at least one year of age rather than an infant.[2] They add that the Wise Men came to the house in Matthew's account (2:11) rather than a manger as Luke records (2:16), indicating that a different time frame is involved in the two narratives. Thus, they insist, Luke is speaking of the time of Christ's birth whereas Matthew is referring to events about two years after His birth.

However, the distinction is neither that precise in the Greek nor in the Scriptures.[3] The word *"Paidion"* **is** used of infants. John the Baptist is said to be a *"paidion"* when he is but 8 days old (Luke 1:59, 66, 76), as is Christ Jesus at the time of His birth (Luke 2:17) and when He was 40 days old (Luke 2:27; also see John 16:21; Heb.11:23). Indeed, *"brephos"* **is** used of a young child (2 Tim. 3:15; Luke 18:15–17). Furthermore, *"pais"* would fall into the same age group as *"paidion"* in Mat. 2:16 since the latter term is used nine times in the same context in that chapter.

To insist that Jesus was no longer an infant because the *Magi* visited Him in a house rather than a stable is imprudent. His parents would have moved into a house as soon as possible. After all, Bethlehem was the city of Joseph's birth (Luke 2:2–3), and he would be known there. Further, the whole tone of Matthew 2:1 ff. is that the *Magi* visited the Christ child soon after His birth. This is seen by their question: "Where is he that *is* born King of the Jews?"

---

[1] Hislop, *The Two Babylons, op. cit.,* fn., pp. 92–93; citing Chrysostom, *Monitum in Hom. de Natal. Christi,* vol. ii, p. 352.

[2] Leslie P. Madison, "Problems of Chronology in the Life of Christ," (unpublished Th.D. dissertation, Dallas Theological Seminary, 1963), pp. 25–27.

[3] Hoehner, *Chronological Aspects of the Life of Christ, op. cit.,* p. 24.

They did not say "was" born (past tense) which would have been proper had two years elapsed.

The timing in the Authorized Version is clear that "When[1] Jesus was born in Bethlehem ... there came wise men from the east to Jerusalem." As far back as c. AD 135, Justin Martyr wrote in support of this thesis saying, "the Magi from Arabia, who as soon as the Child was born came to worship Him" as did Tertullian (c. AD 200).[2]

Indeed, they were directed to go to Bethlehem as it was the foretold place of the child's birth. Were Jesus two years old when the Wise Men came, they should then have been led to Nazareth not Bethlehem, for that is where he was living at that time (Mat. 2:23; Luke 2:39–40). Yet no mention whatsoever is made of Nazareth in the verses that follow until after the return from Egypt.

Moreover, the "two years" of Matthew does not demand that Jesus be of that age. Herod's slaughter of children up to two years of age was only to make certain that his infant rival did not escape. This is in keeping with his documented wicked and ruthless character. He already had 3 of his own sons murdered, 45 members of a rival faction slain, his wife's 17-year-old brother drowned in a bath, her 80-year-old grandfather put to death, and even had her falsely accused and executed — all in order to secure the throne for himself.[3]

So desperate a man would neither take chances nor have any compunction for slaying additional innocent children to maintain that security. Herod's natural propensity for over-kill, inherent in his makeup, is unmistakably demonstrated by the salient fact that his edict did not merely call for the destruction of the male children in Bethlehem. He extended the blood bath as far as Ramah, a village in the tribal allotment of Benjamin some ten miles north of the City of David (Mat. 2:16–18).[4]

Finally, if Matthew is telling us of a time when Jesus is two years old and living in Nazareth (Matthew 2:23; Luke 2:39), why should God instruct Joseph to flee to Egypt in order to escape Herod? The children were only being slain in the area around Bethlehem. This would hardly seem prudent as in order to reach Egypt from Nazareth they would have to pass through or in close proximity to Herod's domain of Judea.

They would be manifestly safe where they already were, being about 70 miles north of the slaughter. Indeed, the same reasoning applies to the fact that the Wise Men returned to their own country "another way" (Mat. 2:12).

Were they in Nazareth such action would have been unnecessary for they would have been well out of harms way by simply returning back up the "Fertile Crescent" to the "east" as King Herod was in Jerusalem (Mat. 2:3). However, such evasive steps would have been judicious had they have been south of Jerusalem in Bethlehem.

> Now **when** Jesus was born in Bethlehem of Judaea in the days of Herod the king, behold, there came wise men from the east to Jerusalem, (Mat. 2:1)

Thus, the correct order of events concerning the birth of Christ Jesus is:

1. He was born in Bethlehem – five miles south of Jerusalem (Mat. 2:1). The shepherds came that night (Luke 2:11–16).

2. **When** He was born in Bethlehem, the *Magi* (or Wise Men) came (Mat. 2:1, KJB; compare "having been" or "after" in other versions).

   Thus the *Magi* came before Herod's presence the following morning or afternoon and, being warned of God in a dream that night, departed to their own country (singular! thus they are all from the same country, not 3 different ones as tradition relates) from Bethlehem by a route that would by-pass Jerusalem and Herod (Luke 2:12).

---

[1] William Tyndale's 1534 New Testament, the 1557 Geneva Bible, the 1380 Wycliffe, the 1539 Great Bible (Cranmer's), as well as other pre-King James English versions also read "When" here at Matthew 2:1.

[2] Justin Martyr, *Dialogue with Trypho, Ante-Nicene Fathers*, vol. I, Alexander Roberts and James Donaldson, eds., (Grand Rapids, MI: Eerdmans Pub. Co., 1885), 88; Tertullian, *On Idolatry, Ante-Nicene Fathers*, vol. III, ch. ix, p. 65. Jack Finegan reached the same conclusion: *Handbook of Biblical Chronology, op. cit.*, p. 248.

[3] Gehman, (ed.), *The New Westminster Dictionary of the Bible, op. cit.*, pp. 379–382 (Herod).

[4] Flavius Josephus, *Josephus Complete Works*, trans. by William Whiston, (Grand Rapids, MI: Kregel Publications, 1960), *Wars of the Jews*, I, 29, 2; *Antiquities, op. cit.*, XVI 11, 7; XVII 3, 2, etc.

He was born in a manger because there was no room for them in the inn (Luke 2:7) and was moved into a house almost certainly on the following day (Mat. 2:7) as word of the birth had not yet reached Jerusalem (a point which will be explained subsequently).

Note: There is no mention of a cave or is the number of the *Magi* given as 3; their names are not given or their races. The number 3 was selected because three gifts were brought (Mat. 2:11), but such reasoning is pure conjecture and constitutes adding to Scripture. This is all based on Roman Catholic tradition and is unsupported by Scripture.

3. They fled to Egypt before news of His birth could reach Jerusalem, Jesus being only a day or so old.

4. He was circumcised on the 8th day (Luke 2:21), almost certainly while en route to Egypt – as was done to Moses' "firstborn" son, Gershom, on the way down to Egypt (Exo. 4:21–25, 2:22, cp. 18:4).

5. Herod dies within 40 days of his edict to slaughter the male children (like Pharaoh's attempt to kill the male babies – again similar to Moses) so that Joseph and Mary returned from Egypt to Jerusalem by the 40th day after Jesus' birth in order to dedicate Jesus at the Temple (Luke 2:22; Lev. 12:26; see Mat. 2:22, and note: "notwithstanding," KJB).

6. Immediately afterward, they left to return to Nazareth (Luke 2:39, cp. 2:4 and Mat. 2:19–23), being warned of God in a dream and not wanting to tarry there for fear of Herod's son, Archelaus.

So Joseph and Mary fled to Egypt very soon after Jesus' birth. Herod died within a few days so that they can return back to Jerusalem by the 40th day after the birth for the Temple dedication.

Luke 2:11, 17–18 teach us that the shepherds gave testimony as to the message which the angels had given unto them:

For unto you is born this day in the city of David a Saviour, which is Christ the Lord (Luke 2:11).

These verses tell us that this event was made known throughout all the region. Bethlehem is only about five miles south of Jerusalem. It is inconceivable that two years could have elapsed and such a momentous story had not yet reached Herod or the priests in Jerusalem.

The entire religion of Judaism is founded upon the coming of a Messiah. The whole expectancy of that religious order was looking forward to His appearance. Yet when Herod inquired of all the chief priests and scribes as to where the Messiah should be born, not one of them made mention of the testimony of the shepherds. Rather, they quoted from Micah 5:2:

But thou, Bethlehem Ephratah, though thou be little among the thousands of Judah, yet out of thee shall he come forth unto me that is to be ruler in Israel; whose goings forth have been from of old, from everlasting (Mic. 5:2).

Are we to believe that the rabbi from the synagogue in Bethlehem did not report this message to his superiors in Jerusalem? Are we actually expected to think that in two years no layman had carried this story to the Temple and that so ruthless a despot as Herod had no "ears" to hear of his rival's birth – that he knows nothing of an event which is being told openly and that has occurred under his very nose? The answer is obvious.

This constitutes irrefutable proof that the Wise Men came at Jesus' birth for if *two* years had elapsed, Herod would surely have already heard of the birth. The priest and scribes did not mention the testimony of the shepherds when Herod inquired of them (Mat. 2:1, 4) because the story had not yet had time to travel the five miles to Jerusalem.

This point is greatly strengthened when Luke 1:57–66 and 76 are considered. A similar series of events had occurred only six months earlier at the birth of John the Baptist; namely, a supernatural birth (Luke 1:7, 18), an angel's presence, and the whole matter being published throughout all the hill country of Judea (Luke 1:65–66). Furthermore, this wonder child was to be the forerunner of the Messiah (Luke 1:76, cp. Mal. 3:1, 6). Moreover, not only was no effort made to keep these happenings "under wrap," they were openly proclaimed abroad.

Lastly, the account of Mary's purification at the Temple in Jerusalem on the 40th day after the birth of Jesus (Luke 2:22–39, cp. Lev. 12:2–6) relates that two credible witnesses, Simeon and Anna, gave public testimony as to Jesus' personage. Again, this was all done openly at the Temple.

Could two years have passed and *none* of these events come to the attention of Herod, much less to that of the priests and scribes who ministered at the Temple daily? Do not these simple considerations from the Holy Writ instruct all would-be scholars and laity alike as to the actual circumstances attendant to the birth of our Lord?

Indeed, the prophecies foretold Messiah's birth – the birth of the God-King, of Immanuel – that God would become flesh. Thus, the *birth* was the momentous event. There is neither mention nor allusion to His second year anywhere in the Old Testament; hence, no significance whatever can rightly be attached to it.

Moreover, the reason the Lukan account of the Birth and that in Matthew are so dissimilar is that they are from two different perspectives. The Holy Spirit directed Matthew to record the events attendant to the birth of Christ Jesus from the husband's point of view. This is obvious for in it we find Joseph featured as the main personage (second only to Christ).

Matthew depicts:

(1) Joseph's struggle with Mary's "premature" pregnancy;

(2) the angel's appearance giving him encouragement and instructions as to the baby's name (Mat. 1:18–25);

(3) the dream wherein the angel tells him (not Mary) to flee to Egypt (2:13);

(4) instructions to him by the angel to return from Egypt (2:19–21); and

(5) his bringing his family to dwell in Nazareth (2:23).

Clearly, Joseph is prominent in this account revealing that Matthew is recording the "father's" viewpoint of the Birth. Thus the genealogy in Matthew 1:1–17 is that of Joseph. It depicts him as a direct descendant of King David through whom Messiah Jesus (as Joseph's adopted son) obtained the **royal right** to David's throne as prophesied in many Scriptures (2 Sam. 7:4–29; Psa. 89:3–4, 19–37; Luke 1:30–33).

Conversely, Luke records the events relevant to the Birth from the mother's perspective featuring Mary as the central character. In Luke we find:

(1) the angel Gabriel appearing to Mary to explain the impending supernatural conception (Luke 1:26–38);

(2) her reception and commendation from her cousin Elisabeth (who had been carrying John the Baptist in her womb six months, Luke 1:31–45);

(3) Mary's "magnificat" (Luke 1:46–56);

(4) her purification and sin offering 40 days after Jesus' birth during His dedication at the Temple; and

(5) Mary "kept" all the happenings surrounding these days and "pondered" them in "her heart" as is twice recorded in the second chapter (Luke 2:19, 51).

Even at the Passover episode at the Temple in Jesus' 12th year, it was Mary's words that were recorded – not Joseph's (Luke 2:48). Therefore it must be seen that the genealogy preserved in the third chapter of Luke is that of Mary's.

This genealogy shows that although she was maternally of the tribe of Levi (Luke 1:5, cp. vs. 36), she was also of the family of David and thus of the Tribe of Judah but through a different non-kingly lineage than Joseph (cp. Rom.1:3; Heb.7:14; Rev.22:16). Therefore, it is through Mary's egg that Jesus obtained the **legal right** to David's throne, fulfilling many OT Scriptures that Messiah would be a *physical* descendant of that son of Jesse (several Scriptures demand this in stating that there was a genuine "conception," e.g., Gen. 3:15; Isa. 7:14; Mat. 1:21; Luke 1:31, cp. vs. 36).

Hence, the Matthew and Lukan genealogies are identical in the generations from Abraham to David, but Matthew traces our Lord's ancestry from the royal line through David's son Solomon. However Luke follows the lineage through another of David's sons, Nathan – who did not inherit the throne. Thus the differences between the two Gospel accounts may be appreciated and understood.

The Wise Men (Jews whose ancestors had remained in Persia after the Babylonian exile and had not returned under Zerubbabel) were *not* astronomers or astrologers as is often surmised, but were Jewish rabbis or priests who were looking for the promised "Star out of Jacob" (Num. 24:17–19; Esther 1:13).

Furthermore, the star was neither the result of a conjunction of the planets nor was it a comet. It was a miraculous supernatural occurrence as the Scriptures demand; it moved, disappeared, reappeared and *stood still* over the place where Jesus lay. These then are the scriptural facts attendant to the birth of Jesus the Christ, the Son of the Living God.

6. TIBERIUS' 15TH – PREPARATION YEAR FOR PUBLIC MINISTRY

Fortunately, there is far less uncertainty about the starting point of Christ's ministry, since it is set forth very clearly in Luke (3:1–3, 21–23) as beginning in the 15th year of the reign of Tiberius Caesar. Tiberius reigned jointly as co-regent with Caesar Augustus from AD 12–14, when the latter died. Velleius Paterculus (c. 19 BC–AD 30+), a friend of Tiberius,[1] relates in his history that at the request of Augustus, Tiberius was invested with equal authority in all the provinces.[2] Tacitus (*circa* AD 55–120) confirms this in stating that Tiberius was adopted by Augustus as his son and was named colleague in the empire.[3]

Thus in AD 12, Tiberius' power was already equal to that of Augustus in the provinces. As he had become the practical ruler in the provinces, many would well argue that it would be natural for Luke to use the provincial point of view.[4] Adding 15 years to the first year of Tiberius' reign would bring us to AD 26 (numbering inclusively), when Pilate was procurator of Judea, Herod Antipas tetrarch of Galilee, with Annas (probably the president of the Sanhedrin) and Caiaphas being the high priests – as Luke relates. Taken together, these historic facts would lead us to determine and

establish that John the Baptist began his ministry AD 26. This also sets the year of the baptism of the Lord Jesus Christ (Luke 1:35–36; cp. 3:23).

Note that this date establishes a more direct and absolute method of determining the birth year of Christ. Now beginning at AD 26 and working backward, the year of the birth of the Lord Jesus may be established. Luke 3:23 records that Jesus was baptized by John the Baptist in His 30th year which places the Nativity at 4 BC. In determining the length of time covered, one year must be deducted from the total when moving from BC to AD as there is no year zero. However the span remains 30 years as the Jews, although not without exception, commonly numbered inclusively.[5]

This date is also somewhat confirmed by the statement of the Jews (John 2:20), made soon after Jesus' baptism: "Forty and six years was this temple in building." The rebuilding of the Temple by Herod was begun in the 18th year of his reign which is c. 20 BC.[6] Although Josephus possibly contradicts himself elsewhere (not uncommon) by mentioning work that was done on the Temple in Herod's 15th year,[7] he says that the Temple was begun the year that the Emperor came to Syria. Dio Cassius places this visit in 20 BC.[8] If we presume that the 46 years had elapsed when the remark in John was given, we come again to AD 26.

Again, Matthew 2:1 states that Jesus was born "in the days of Herod the king"; and Luke 1:5 likewise fixes the annunciations to Zacharias and Mary as being "in the days of Herod, king of Judea." Now Josephus states that Herod received the kingship from Antony and Augustus (Octavian) "in the hundred and eighty-fourth Olympiad" when Calvinus was

1 Sir William M. Ramsay, *Was Christ Born at Bethlehem?*, 2nd ed., (London: Hodder and Stoughton Pub., 1898), p. 200.

2 Velleius Paterculus, *Roman Histories,* The Loeb Classical Library, trans. by F.W. Shipley, (Cambridge, MA: Harvard UP, 1924), Book II, 121, 1.

3 Cornelius Tacitus, *Annals,* The Loeb Classical Library, (Cambridge, MA: Harvard UP, 1931), Book 1, 3.

4 Charles Merivale, *History of the Romans under the Empire*, 7 Vols., (New York: D. Appleman & Co., 1896), vol. 4, p. 367; Robertson, *A Harmony of the Gospels, op. cit.*, p. 264. Ussher, Bengel, Jarvis, and Greswell (to name but a few) favor the computation from the colleagueship.

5 See "inclusive reckoning" p. 119 ff.

6 Josephus, *Antiquities, op. cit.*, XV, 11, 1.

7 Josephus, *Wars of the Jews, op. cit.*, I, 21, 1. Many apparent discrepancies in Josephus can be resolved by consulting the table on the following page which depicts Herod's regnal years.

8 Dio Cassius, *Roman History*, vol. VI, The Loeb Classical Library, trans. by Earnest Cary, (Cambridge, MA: Harvard UP, 2000), Book LIV, p. 299.

consul for the second time.[1] The consular date of Calvinus corresponds with the year 40 BC.[2] Josephus further indicates that Herod did not actually go from Egypt to Rome until winter,[3] thus the date Herod was named king was late in 40 BC (Oly. 185, 1, the year 40 began Oly. 184, 4 but as Greek years began c. July 1 winter would fall during the following Greek year as indicated).[4]

Josephus also records that Herod actually began his reign upon his taking of the city of Jerusalem by force "during the consulship at Rome of Marcus Agrippa and Caninius Gallus, in the hundred and eighty-fifth Olympiad" at which time his rival Antigonus was slain.[5] The consular date for Agrippa et Gallo is 37 BC (Oly. 185, 4 — extending from c. July 1, 37 to June 30, 36 BC) which is the year Herod became king in fact by actual residence in Jerusalem.[6]

Josephus further relates that Herod died "having reigned thirty-four years, since he had caused Antigonus to be slain, and obtained his kingdom; but thirty-seven years since he had been made king by the Romans."[7] From these two starting points Herod's years of reign may be depicted as given in the following table.

7. THE BEGINNING YEAR OF OUR LORD'S PUBLIC MINISTRY

Further, biblical chronological studies with regard to the years of Jubilee (especially note Isa. 37:30) yield the result that AD 27 was a Jubilee year (Whiston in Josephus concurs, see

Appendix I, page 289).[8] This is manifestly confirmed by Jesus' message at the synagogue at Nazareth near the onset of His ministry when He read from Isaiah 61:1–2a. This portion of Scripture is an undeniable offer of Jubilee (i.e., the kingdom; "to set at liberty them that are bruised, To preach the acceptable year of the Lord," Luke 4:18–19).

HEROD THE GREAT'S REGNAL YEAR[9]

BC	Years since being named king at Rome	Years since becoming king in fact by taking Jerusalem	Olympiad
40	1		185, 1
39	2		2
38	3		3
37	4	1	4
36	5	2	186, 1
35	6	3	2
34	7	4	3
33	8	5	4
32	9	6	187, 1
31	10	7	2
30	11	8	3
29	12	9	4
28	13	10	188, 1
27	14	11	2
26	15	12	3
25	16	13	4
24	17	14	189, 1
23	18	15	2
22	19	16	3
21	20	17	4
20	21	18	190, 1
19	22	19	2
18	23	20	3
17	24	21	4
16	25	22	191, 1
15	26	23	2
14	27	24	3
13	28	25	4
12	29	26	192, 1
11	30	27	2
10	31	28	3
9	32	29	4
8	33	30	193, 1
7	34	31	2
6	35	32	3
5	36	33	4
4	37	34	194, 1

Jubilee begins on the 10th day of the Jewish 7th month (Lev. 25:8–12). This computes to the Gregorian date of Tuesday, September 28, AD 27 according to astronomical computer calculation, six months after the first Passover of our Lord's earthly ministry (John 2:13). The

---

1 Josephus, *Antiquities, op. cit.,* XIV, 14, 5.

2 Finegan, *Handbook of Biblical Chronology, op. cit.,* p. 230, cp. Finegan's table 38, p. 96.

3 Josephus, *Antiquities, op. cit.,* XIV, 14, 2.

4 Finegan, *Handbook of Biblical Chronology, op. cit.,* p. 230.

5 Josephus, *Antiquities, op. cit.,* XIV, 16, 4.

6 Finegan, *Handbook of Biblical Chronology, op. cit.,* pp. 230–231, again cp. Finegan's table 38, p. 96. Dio Cassius (AD c.155–c.235) gives as the consuls for this event Claudius and Norbanus who precede Agrippa and Gallus on his list, hence that Herod took the city in 38 BC *Roman History,* XLIX, 22–23). However, writing nearly a century afterward, he is probably less accurate in this than Josephus.

7 Josephus, *Wars, op. cit.,* I, 38, 8; *Antiquities, op. cit.,* XVII, 8, 1.

8 Flavius Josephus, *Josephus Complete Works,* trans. by William Whiston, (Grand Rapids, MI: Kregel Publications, 1960), appendix, Dissertation V., 55, 56.

9 Adapted after Finegan, *Handbook of Biblical Chronology, op. cit.,* p. 232.

beginning of the ministry of Jesus the Christ seems to be firmly fixed by this data.

8. THE YEAR OF THE CRUCIFIXION

These facts also help establish the date of His crucifixion and resurrection as the spring of AD 30. Several diverse interpretations have been placed on the identification of the feast in John 5:1 largely because it reads "feast" without any qualifying words (i.e., of Passover, Pentecost, etc.), especially since the definite article "the" is absent. Notwithstanding, this author is confident that it was with reference to Jesus' second Passover, bringing the total of Passovers recorded by John to four (2:13; 5:1; 6:4; 13:1).

The issue over the proper identity of this feast bears significantly on the length of Christ's ministry and thereby on establishing the year of His crucifixion. Briefly, it is offered that the word "feast" without the article occurs with specific reference to the Passover in Matthew 27:15, Mark 15:6, and Luke 23:17[1] (cp. John 18:39) thus diminishing the force of that objection.

As this feast brought Christ from Galilee up to Jerusalem (cp. John 4:46, 54 and 5:1), John 5 is most probably one of the three annual feasts held at that ancient capital city (Deut. 16:16). Further, as John 4:35 places us around the first of December, John 5 is seen as a feast held *after* December and, as the general setting of the story best fits a time when the weather is warm, before the cooler fall Feast of Tabernacles. Whereas a Pentecost is possible, taking this occurrence as chronologically following John 4:35 whereupon it would be the first of the three great feasts after December, Passover appears to be the simplest and best solution.

Purim, observed the 14th and 15th of Adar (c. March 1), may be eliminated from consideration even though it is only one month before Passover as the Jews did not go up to Jerusalem to celebrate that festival. The worldwide observance of Purim consisted solely of reading the Book of Esther in the synagogues on those days and making them "days of feasting and joy and of sending portions [food] one to another and gifts to the poor."[2] Indeed, as Edward Robinson noted, "the multitude" of John 5:13

would seem to contextually require that one of the three great feasts is intended.[3]

Lastly, the controversy between the Pharisees and Jesus' disciples over their plucking ears of grain as they walked through the fields on the Sabbath recorded in Matthew 12:1–8, Mark 2:23–28 and Luke 6:1–5 is seen by nearly all to chronologically follow John 5. In these passages, Jesus and the disciples are probably on the way back to Galilee from Jerusalem having left for the reason given at John 5:16 and 18 (Mark 3:7 recording that they then withdrew to the Sea of Galilee). The point is that the plucking of the ears of grain indicates a time shortly after the Passover yet before Pentecost. This exactly ties in with the visit of the Lord to Jerusalem and verifies our identification.

Since the first chapter of John's gospel records that Christ Jesus was baptized a few months before the first of the four Passovers in that same gospel (2:13) and as it seems best to conclude that His ministry ended at the 4th, the duration of our Lord's ministry must have been about three and a half years in length. Therefore He was crucified and died near 3:00 P.M. Thursday the 14th of Nisan (Heb. = Abib = an ear of ripe grain) – Passover day – in the year AD 30 by Jewish reckoning (April 4th Gregorian). Further reasons for accepting this date will soon be forthcoming.

Christ Jesus was triumphantly resurrected from the grave three days and three nights later[4] (Mat. 12:40) near, but before, sunrise (Mat. 28:1–4, cp. John 20:1) Sunday the 17th of Nisan (Jewish reckoning = April 7th Gregorian).

9. THE CRUCIFIXION YEAR AND DANIEL'S 483-YEAR PROPHECY

These conclusions have important bearing on the matter of biblical chronology. We have seen that Jesus must be "about 30 years of age" in the 15th year of Tiberius Caesar (Luke 3:1, 23). Secular history has been examined and it declares this to have been about AD 26. Profane material has established the death of Herod as being in the spring of 4 BC (some give

---

1 Robertson, *A Harmony of the Gospels, op. cit.*, p. 269.

2 Esther 9:22; Josephus, *Antiquities op. cit.*, XI, 6, 13.

3 Edward Robinson, *Harmony of the Gospels in English*, (Boston: Crocker & Brewster, 1846), p. 177.

4 Compare Jonah 1:17; Gen. 7:12; 1 Sam. 30:12. In Esther 3:12, 4:16, & 5:1 the 3 nights & 3 days are 3 full nights, 2 full days, & part of the 3rd day – not 72 hours. Thus, biblically the term includes all or at least part of each of the 3 days as well as all or part of each of the 3 nights.

3 BC). Obviously if Jesus were two years old when the *Magi* came, then He would have been born in 6 BC and would be *above* 30 years of age in the 15th year of Tiberius. Jesus' birth, therefore, occurred *circa* 4 BC.

These conclusions also well fit the prophecy given in Daniel 9:25–26, which foretold that the Messiah would come 483 years after the decree was given allowing the Jews, having returned from their deportation, to rebuild the city of Jerusalem and its *wall* "in troublous times."

The return and rebuilding of the Temple began in 536 BC, the first year in which Cyrus, king of Persia, became *sole* ruler over the people of Israel (Cyrus having placed his uncle, Darius the Mede, on the throne to run the affairs of government from Babylon, 539 BC, while he continued at the head of his army conquering and adding to his kingdom until 536 BC). The story of this decree of Cyrus is recorded in the Book of Ezra.

However, the decree concerning the rebuilding of the city of Jerusalem (Although some homes had been rebuilt at the 536 BC return under the leadership of Zerubbabel — cp. Isa. 44:28, 45:13 and Neh. 7:4, Appendix M, p. 308) and its walls was issued after Cyrus' decree in the 20th year of the reign of Artaxerxes Longimanus, king of Persia (Nehemiah 2:1,9 — c. 454 BC, not c. 445 as most suppose; the proof is given in next sections and Charts 5 and 5c). This rebuilding undertaking is recorded in the Book of Nehemiah.

As the correct determination of Artaxerxes' 20th year allows an independent method for the verification of the crucifixion year of the Lord Jesus, its importance with regard to Bible chronology can hardly be overstated. This derivation will be given beginning at the following new heading. For now, it will suffice to merely give our conclusion which is that in the year 473 BC, Xerxes installed Artaxerxes I Longimanus as his co-regent.

As that would have been the first year the Jews began to have dealings with him as their sovereign, they would quite naturally begin to reference the dates associated with him from that year. Starting at that date would place his 20th year over the Jews as 454 BC (or AM 3550 inclusive) and the 483 years of the Daniel 9:25 prophecy would bring us to AD 30 for its

fulfillment[1] at the time of our Lord's crucifixion (454 BC + AD 30 = 484 less 1 for going from BC to AD = 483).

As will be shown in that which follows, Jesus the Christ, Immanuel – GOD from everlasting (Mic. 5:2), was born in Bethlehem of Judea of the lineage of David. He was crucified and resurrected from the dead precisely 483 years after the decree of Artaxerxes and thereby fulfilled the Scriptures. "Let God be true, but every man a liar" (Rom.3:4).

---

[1] Eusebius and Ussher (*Annals, op. cit.*, p. 822 (1658 ed., p. 847) arrived at AD 33 largely due to Phlegon of Tralles', a 2nd century pagan, mention of a great solar eclipse and earthquake in Bithynia in Oly. 202, year 4 which they took as a reference to the darkness and quake at the Passion. However, others after Ussher have concluded Phlegon was, at best, referring to an eclipse in year 1 of Oly. 202 (AD 30).

As the Jews regulated the beginning of their months by the new moon, the time of our Lord's crucifixion was virtually mid-month – at the full moon phase – when a solar eclipse is impossible. Further, 7 minutes and 40 seconds is the maximum duration of a solar eclipse. Yet the Scriptures record that, beginning at noon, the sky was black for 3 hours (Mat. 27:45; Mark 15:33; Luke 23:44–45).

Being clearly of a supernatural origin, these phenomena associated with the crucifixion were dramatically different from those of an ordinary eclipse of the sun, and Phlegon should have noted these extraordinary differences. His failure to comment on any of these miraculous particulars greatly damages his credibility. Reference to the month and day of the event, essential details one would expect to accompany the statement, are also conspicuously absent. This is a most serious circumstance and further diminishes our estimation of his testimony. Indeed, there was only one significant eclipse visible in western Asia in Oly. 202: 29 Nov. AD 29 (Browne, *Ordo Saeclorum, op. cit.*, p. 76.).

Eusebius and Ussher also cited Thallus. Supposedly about the middle of the 1st century AD, Thallus argued that the abnormal darkness alleged to have accompanied the death of Christ was a purely natural phenomenon [Will Durant, *The Story of Civilization, Caesar and Christ*, vol. 3, (New York: Simon and Schuster, 1944), p. 555.]. Thallus speaks "of a darkness over all the world, and an earthquake which threw down many houses in Judea and in other parts of the earth."

The above failings plus other grounds which apply to Phlegon and generally to Thallus may be found in: McClintock and Strong, *Cyclopedia, op. cit.* p. 146, and Dr. Adam Clarke, *Clarke's Commentary*, vol. V, *op. cit.*, p. 276 [Matthew 27:45 comments].

Africanus (c.200–245 AD) also dismissed Phlegon and Thallus (Syncellus, *Historia Chronographia, op. cit.*, page 391). All this convinced the current author to disregard the testimonies of these two heathen.

Bul [Marchesvan] (29 days)

1= 11-12
2= 12-13
3= 13-14
4= 14-15
5= 15-16
6= 16-17
7= 17-18
8= 18-19
9= 19-20
10= 20-21
11= 21-22
12= 22-23
13= 23-24
14= 24-25
15= 25-26
16= 26-27
17= 27-28
18= 28-29
19= 29-30
20= 30-31
21= 31- 1
22= 1- 2
23= 2- 3
24= 3- 4
25= 4- 5
26= 5- 6
27= 6- 7
28= 7- 8
29= 8- 9

October 6 BC (31 days)

November 6 BC (30 days)

Chisleu [Kislev] (30 days)

1= 9-10
2= 10-11
3= 11-12
4= 12-13
5= 13-14
6= 14-15
7= 15-16
8= 16-17
9= 17-18
10= 18-19
11= 19-20
12= 20-21
13= 21-22
14= 22-23
15= 23-24
16= 24-25
17= 25-26
18= 26-27
19= 27-28
20= 28-29
21= 29-30
22= 30-31
23= 31- 1
24= 1- 2
25= 2- 3
26= 3- 4
27= 4- 5
28= 5- 6
29= 6- 7
30= 7- 8

December 6 BC (31 days)

Tebeth (29 days)

1= 9-10
2= 10-11
3= 11-12
4= 12-13
5= 13-14
6= 14-15
7= 15-16
8= 16-17
9= 17-18
10= 18-19
11= 19-20
12= 20-21
13= 21-22
14= 22-23
15= 23-24
16= 24-25
17= 25-26
18= 26-27
19= 27-28
20= 28-29
21= 29-30
22= 30-31
23= 31- 1
24= 1- 2
25= 2- 3
26= 3- 4
27= 4- 5
28= 5- 6
29= 6- 7

January 5 BC (31 days)

Shebat (30 days)

1= 7- 8
2= 8- 9
3= 9-10
4= 10-11
5= 11-12
6= 12-13
7= 13-14
8= 14-15
9= 15-16
10= 16-17
11= 17-18

Adar (30 days)
usually 29 days except when followed by a Veadar *Ency Judaica* Vol. 5, p. 43.

Veadar (29 days)

Nisan [Abib] (30 days)

12= 18-19
13= 19-20
14= 20-21
15= 21-22
16= 22-23
17= 23-24
18= 24-25
19= 25-26
20= 26-27
21= 27-28
22= 28-29
23= 29-30
24= 30-31
25= 31- 1
26= 1- 2
27= 2- 3
28= 3- 4
29= 4- 5
30= 5- 6
1= 6- 7
2= 7- 8
3= 8- 9
4= 9-10
5= 10-11
6= 11-12
7= 12-13
8= 13-14
9= 14-15
10= 15-16
11= 16-17
12= 17-18
13= 18-19
14= 19-20
15= 20-21
16= 21-22
17= 22-23
18= 23-24
19= 24-25
20= 25-26
21= 26-27
22= 27-28
23= 28- 1
24= 1- 2
25= 2- 3
26= 3- 4
27= 4- 5
28= 5- 6
29= 6- 7
30= 7- 8
1= 8- 9
2= 9-10
3= 10-11
4= 11-12
5= 12-13
6= 13-14
7= 14-15
8= 15-16
9= 16-17
10= 17-18
11= 18-19
12= 19-20
13= 20-21
14= 21-22
15= 22-23
16= 23-24
17= 24-25
18= 25-26
19= 26-27
20= 27-28
21= 28-29
22= 29-30
23= 30-31
24= 31- 1
25= 1- 2
26= 2- 3
27= 3- 4
28= 4- 5
29= 5- 6
1= 6- 7
2= 7- 8
3= 8- 9
4= 9-10
5= 10-11
6= 11-12
7= 12-13
8= 13-14
9= 14-15
10= 15-16
11= 16-17
12= 17-18
13= 18-19
14= 19-20
15= 20-21
16= 21-22
17= 22-23
18= 23-24
19= 24-25
20= 25-26
21= 26-27

February (28 days)

March (31 days)

April, 5 BC (30 days)

Iyyar [Zif] (29 days)

22= 27-28
23= 28-29
24= 29-30
25= 30- 1
26= 1- 2
27= 2- 3
28= 3- 4
29= 4- 5
30= 5- 6
1= 6- 7
2= 7- 8
3= 8- 9
4= 9-10
5= 10-11
6= 11-12
7= 12-13
8= 13-14
9= 14-15
10= 15-16
11= 16-17
12= 17-18
13= 18-19
14= 19-20
15= 20-21
16= 21-22
17= 22-23
18= 23-24
19= 24-25
20= 25-26
21= 26-27
22= 27-28
23= 28-29
24= 29-30
25= 30-31
26= 31- 1
27= 1- 2
28= 2- 3
29= 3- 4

May (31 days)

Sivan (30 days)

1= 4- 5
2= 5- 6
3= 6- 7
4= 7- 8
5= 8- 9
6= 9-10
7= 10-11
8= 11-12
9= 12-13
10= 13-14
11= 14-15
12= 15-16
13= 16-17
14= 17-18
15= 18-19
16= 19-20
17= 20-21
18= 21-22
19= 22-23
20= 23-24
21= 24-25
22= 25-26
23= 26-27
24= 27-28
25= 28-29
26= 29-30
27= 30- 1
28= 1- 2
29= 2- 3
30= 3- 4

June 5 BC (30 days)

Tammuz (29 days)

1= 4- 5
2= 5- 6
3= 6- 7
4= 7- 8
5= 8- 9
6= 9-10
7= 10-11
8= 11-12
9= 12-13
10= 13-14
11= 14-15
12= 15-16
13= 16-17
14= 17-18
15= 18-19
16= 19-20
17= 20-21
18= 21-22
19= 22-23
20= 23-24
21= 24-25
22= 25-26
23= 26-27
24= 27-28
25= 28-29
26= 29-30
27= 30-31
28= 31- 1
29= 1- 2

July 5 BC (31 days)

Ab (30 days)

1= 2- 3
2= 3- 4

August (31 days)

3= 4- 5
4= 5- 6
5= 6- 7
6= 7- 8
7= 8- 9
8= 9-10
9= 10-11
10= 11-12
11= 12-13
12= 13-14
13= 14-15
14= 15-16
15= 16-17
16= 17-18
17= 18-19
18= 19-20
19= 20-21
20= 21-22
21= 22-23
22= 23-24
23= 24-25
24= 25-26
25= 26-27
26= 27-28
27= 28-29
28= 29-30
29= 30-31
30= 31- 1

Elul (29 days)

September (30 days)

1= 1- 2
2= 2- 3
3= 3- 4
4= 4- 5
5= 5- 6
6= 6- 7
7= 7- 8
8= 8- 9
9= 9-10
10= 10-11
11= 11-12
12= 12-13
13= 13-14
14= 14-15
15= 15-16
16= 16-17
17= 17-18
18= 18-19
19= 19-20
20= 20-21
21= 21-22
22= 22-23
23= 23-24
24= 24-25
25= 25-26
26= 26-27
27= 27-28
28= 28-29
29= 29-30
30= 30-31

Tishri [Ethanim] (30 days)

October 5 BC (31 days)

1= 30-31
2= 31- 1
3= 1- 2
4= 2- 3
5= 3- 4
6= 4- 5
7= 5- 6
8= 6- 7
9= 7- 8
10= 8- 9
11= 9-10
12= 10-11

Bul [Marchesvan] (29 days)

November 5 BC (30 days)

222

Hebrew month	Day	Date	Civil month
	13=	11-12	
	14=	12-13	
	15=	13-14	
	16=	14-15	
	17=	15-16	
	18=	16-17	
	19=	17-18	
	20=	18-19	
	21=	19-20	
	22=	20-21	
	23=	21-22	
	24=	22-23	
	25=	23-24	
	26=	24-25	
	27=	25-26	
	28=	26-27	
	29=	27-28	
Chisleu [Kislev] (30 days)	1=	28-29	
	2=	29-30	
	3=	30- 1	
	4=	1- 2	December 5 BC (31 days)
	5=	2- 3	
	6=	3- 4	
	7=	4- 5	
	8=	5- 6	
	9=	6- 7	
	10=	7- 8	
	11=	8- 9	
	12=	9-10	
	13=	10-11	
	14=	11-12	
	15=	12-13	
	16=	13-14	
	17=	14-15	
	18=	15-16	
	19=	16-17	
	20=	17-18	
	21=	18-19	
	22=	19-20	
	23=	20-21	
	24=	21-22	
	25=	22-23	
	26=	23-24	
	27=	24-25	
	28=	25-26	
	29=	26-27	
	30=	27-28	
Tebeth (29 days)	1=	28-29	
	2=	29-30	
	3=	30-31	
	4=	31- 1	
	5=	1- 2	January 4 BC (31 days)
	6=	2- 3	
	7=	3- 4	
	8=	4- 5	
	9=	5- 6	
	10=	6- 7	
	11=	7- 8	
	12=	8- 9	
	13=	9-10	
	14=	10-11	
	15=	11-12	
	16=	12-13	
	17=	13-14	
	18=	14-15	
	19=	15-16	
	20=	16-17	
	21=	17-18	
	22=	18-19	
	23=	19-20	
	24=	20-21	
	25=	21-22	
	26=	22-23	
	27=	23-24	
	28=	24-25	
	29=	25-26	
Shebat (30 days)	1=	26-27	
	2=	27-28	
	3=	28-29	
	4=	29-30	
	5=	30-31	
	6=	31- 1	
	7=	1- 2	February (29 days) Leap Year
	8=	2- 3	
	9=	3- 4	
	10=	4- 5	
	11=	5- 6	
	12=	6- 7	
	13=	7- 8	
	14=	8- 9	
	15=	9-10	
	16=	10-11	
	17=	11-12	
	18=	12-13	
	19=	13-14	
	20=	14-15	
	21=	15-16	
	22=	16-17	
	23=	17-18	

Hebrew month	Day	Date	Civil month
	24=	18-19	
	25=	19-20	
	26=	20-21	
	27=	21-22	
	28=	22-23	
	29=	23-24	
	30=	24-25	
Adar (29 days)	1=	25-26	
	2=	26-27	
	3=	27-28	
	4=	28-29	
	5=	29- 1	
	6=	1- 2	March (31 days)
	7=	2- 3	
	8=	3- 4	
	9=	4- 5	
	10=	5- 6	
	11=	6- 7	
	12=	7- 8	
	13=	8- 9	
	14=	9-10	
	15=	10-11	
	16=	11-12	
	17=	12-13	
	18=	13-14	
	19=	14-15	
	20=	15-16	
	21=	16-17	
	22=	17-18	
	23=	18-19	
	24=	19-20	
	25=	20-21	
	26=	21-22	
	27=	22-23	
	28=	23-24	
	29=	24-25	
Nisan [Abib] (30 days)	1=	25-26	
	2=	26-27	
	3=	27-28	
	4=	28-29	
	5=	29-30	
	6=	30-31	
	7=	31- 1	
	8=	1- 2	April 4 BC (30 days)
	9=	2- 3	
	10=	3- 4	
	11=	4- 5	
	12=	5- 6	
	13=	6- 7	
	14=	7- 8	
	15=	8- 9	
	16=	9-10	
	17=	10-11	
	18=	11-12	
	19=	12-13	
	20=	13-14	
	21=	14-15	
	22=	15-16	
	23=	16-17	
	24=	17-18	
	25=	18-19	
	26=	19-20	
	27=	20-21	
	28=	21-22	
	29=	22-23	
	30=	23-24	
Iyyar [Zif] (29 days)	1=	24-25	
	2=	25-26	
	3=	26-27	
	4=	27-28	
	5=	28-29	
	6=	29-30	
	7=	30- 1	
	8=	1- 2	May (31 days)
	9=	2- 3	
	10=	3- 4	
	11=	4- 5	
	12=	5- 6	
	13=	6- 7	
	14=	7- 8	
	15=	8- 9	
	16=	9-10	
	17=	10-11	
	18=	11-12	
	19=	12-13	
	20=	13-14	
	21=	14-15	
	22=	15-16	
	23=	16-17	
	24=	17-18	
	25=	18-19	
	26=	19-20	
	27=	20-21	
	28=	21-22	
	29=	22-23	
Sivan (30 days)	1=	23-24	
	2=	24-25	
	3=	25-26	
	4=	26-27	

Hebrew month	Day	Date	Civil month
	5=	27-28	
	6=	28-29	
	7=	29-30	
	8=	30-31	
	9=	31- 1	
	10=	1- 2	June (30 days)
	11=	2- 3	
	12=	3- 4	
	13=	4- 5	
	14=	5- 6	
	15=	6- 7	
	16=	7- 8	
	17=	8- 9	
	18=	9-10	
	19=	10-11	
	20=	11-12	
	21=	12-13	
	22=	13-14	
	23=	14-15	
	24=	15-16	
	25=	16-17	
	26=	17-18	
	27=	18-19	
	28=	19-20	
	29=	20-21	
	30=	21-22	
Tammuz (29 days)	1=	22-23	
	2=	23-24	
	3=	24-25	
	4=	25-26	
	5=	26-27	
	6=	27-28	
	7=	28-29	
	8=	29-30	
	9=	30- 1	
	10=	1- 2	July (31 days)
	11=	2- 3	
	12=	3- 4	
	13=	4- 5	
	14=	5- 6	
	15=	6- 7	
	16=	7- 8	
	17=	8- 9	
	18=	9-10	
	19=	10-11	
	20=	11-12	
	21=	12-13	
	22=	13-14	
	23=	14-15	
	24=	15-16	
	25=	16-17	
	26=	17-18	
	27=	18-19	
	28=	19-20	
	29=	20-21	
Ab (30 days)	1=	21-22	
	2=	22-23	
	3=	23-24	
	4=	24-25	
	5=	25-26	
	6=	26-27	
	7=	27-28	
	8=	28-29	
	9=	29-30	
	10=	30-31	
	11=	31- 1	
	12=	1- 2	August (31 days)
	13=	2- 3	
	14=	3- 4	
	15=	4- 5	
	16=	5- 6	
	17=	6- 7	
	18=	7- 8	
	19=	8- 9	
	20=	9-10	
	21=	10-11	
	22=	11-12	
	23=	12-13	
	24=	13-14	
	25=	14-15	
	26=	15-16	
	27=	16-17	
	28=	17-18	
	29=	18-19	
	30=	19-20	
Elul (29 days)	1=	20-21	
	2=	21-22	
	3=	22-23	
	4=	23-24	
	5=	24-25	
	6=	25-26	
	7=	26-27	
	8=	27-28	
	9=	28-29	
	10=	29-30	
	11=	30-31	
	12=	31- 1	
	13=	1- 2	September (30 days)
	14=	2- 3	

Hebrew month	Day	Date	Civil month
	15=	3- 4	
	16=	4- 5	
	17=	5- 6	
	18=	6- 7	
	19=	7- 8	
	20=	8- 9	
	21=	9-10	
	22=	10-11	
	23=	11-12	
	24=	12-13	
	25=	13-14	
	26=	14-15	
	27=	15-16	
	28=	16-17	
	29=	17-18	
Tishri [Ethanim] (30 days)	1=	18-19	
	2=	19-20	
	3=	20-21	
	4=	21-22	
	5=	22-23	
	6=	23-24	
	7=	24-25	
	8=	25-26	
	9=	26-27	
	10=	27-28	
	11=	28-29	
	12=	29-30	
	13=	30- 1	
	14=	1- 2	October 4 BC (31 days)
	15=	2- 3	
	16=	3- 4	
	17=	4- 5	
	18=	5- 6	
	19=	6- 7	
	20=	7- 8	
	21=	8- 9	
	22=	9-10	
	23=	10-11	
	24=	11-12	
	25=	12-13	
	26=	13-14	
	27=	14-15	
	28=	15-16	
	29=	16-17	
	30=	17-18	
Bul [Marchesvan] (29 days)	1=	18-19	
	2=	19-20	
	3=	20-21	
	4=	21-22	
	5=	22-23	
	6=	23-24	
	7=	24-25	
	8=	25-26	
	9=	26-27	
	10=	27-28	
	11=	28-29	
	12=	29-30	
	13=	30-31	
	14=	31- 1	
	15=	1- 2	November 4 BC

P. THE IDENTIFICATION AND DATE OF ARTAXERXES

Of course several suppositions have been made which could alter the apparent precision in all of this. Perhaps the 15th year of Tiberius in reality should be taken as AD 14 as many well argue. Although all the preceding reasoning for four Passovers has been logical and valid, it still may be wrong. Indeed, perhaps all the Passovers were never intended to be mentioned over the course of the Lord's ministry, hence selecting them as a criteria in judging the length of his ministry may be wholly without merit. Regardless, the real point before us is that although 483 years (or 483 + 3 ½ years or 483 + 7 as some insist) from 445 BC takes the chronologist to AD 39, the general period of Christ Jesus' life; yet every detail of secular history cannot be worked out to perfectly fit that date.

Again, because it fully agreed with the time frame of the Daniel 9:25–27 prophecy, Sir Isaac Newton, Dr. Prideaux, and Klassen were led to settle on the 458 BC decree issued in the seventh year of Artaxerxes as being the correct edict. Despite this, the *context* still best fits that of the decree which was given in the 20th year of Artaxerxes, and this led Sir Robert Anderson to reexamine the entire matter in the late 1800's.

1. SIR ROBERT ANDERSON'S SOLUTION

The fact that the decree given in Artaxerxes' 20th year so tantalizingly nearly fit the time of Jesus (Anderson rejected AD 39 as being too late) became an annoyance to the Presbyterian scholar and former Head of the Criminal Investigation Division of Scotland Yard. Himself a biblicist, Anderson was confident that Daniel 9:25–27 had to have been precisely fulfilled else such failure would have given the Hebrews of Jesus' day just cause to reject His claim as Messiah, the rightful heir to David's throne. Indeed, never would He have been able to attract so many followers if His antagonists, themselves expert in the Law, could have so easily dismissed Christ by pointing out such a lack of fulfillment.

Anderson began his research with another preconception. Namely, that he would "accept without reserve not only the language of Scripture but the standard dates of history" as established by the best chronologists of his day.[1] The subtle danger in this latter commitment is that it elevates the secular data, which is subject to refinement and change, to the level of that which is God-breathed. It carries with it the potential of mixing the sweet with that which may be bitter and thus, so believes this author, Anderson unwittingly laid a snare for himself.

From Scripture (Gen. 7:11, 24; 8:3–4; Rev. 12:6, 13–14; 13:4–7), Anderson deduced that the Daniel 9:25 prophecy should be based upon "prophetic" years of 360 days rather than the solar year. Thus, Dan. 9:25's 483 years x 360 = 173,880 days. This reduced the 483 to about 476 "normal" years ($173,880 \div 365 = 476.3836$). He then engaged the services of the Royal Astronomer and concluded that the 14 Nisan full moon at the Passover of our Lord's crucifixion occurred in AD 32[2]. His famous calculation is:[3]

Nisan 1 in the 20th year of Artaxerxes Longimanus was March 14, 445 BC.

Nisan 10 whereupon Christ entered Jerusalem on the donkey was Sunday April 6, AD 32.

The intervening period was 476 years (plus the 24 days from 14 March to 6th April), thus:

476 x 365 = ... 173,740 days
Add 14 March to 6th April, inclusive............ 24 days
Add for leap years.................................... 116 days

173,880 days

As this total represents the entire number of days from the issuing forth of the decree in the 20th year of Artaxerxes (assumes Neh. 2:1 is 1Nisan) unto the crucifixion, all that now need be done was to divide 173,880 by 360 and obtain precisely 483 "prophetic" years with no remainder. Daniel 9:25–27 was apparently fulfilled to the very day.

---

[1] Anderson, *The Coming Prince, op. cit.*, preface to the tenth edition, p. ii.

[2] Anderson used the Julian calendar (*Coming Prince, op. cit.*, pages 127, 128 fn.): 476 may also be obtained by subtracting AD 32 from 445 BC (the 20th year of Artaxerxes) = 477 – 1 as the Julian calendar has no year zero. One BC to AD 1 is one year.

[3] *Ibid.*, pp. 121–128.

For Anderson, and nearly all conservatives since the 1882 publishing of his findings, this resolved the matter. Today, over a century above the release of his celebrated computation, others such as Dr. Harold Hoehner, using slightly different dates for Artaxerxes' 20th year, have applied his logic and principles to their own private interpretations.[1] By so doing, they have "refined" Anderson's values while obtaining similar results.[2]

The great weakness in this reasoning is that the material in Daniel must be compared to that of Genesis and Revelation in order to so calculate. The Hebrews were given this prophecy in order that they could know the time of Messiah's visitation, but as the Book of Revelation was not written until AD 90–98 it would not have been at their disposal. Thus, it is not probable that the Jews would have understood to use a 360-day year in order to make a calculation like Anderson's.[3] Indeed, as they had never experienced such a year they never would have so done, for from long before Abraham they had only known solar years of c. 365.2422 days.

This is true because the data in Genesis does indicate that the original creation years were 360 days long (Gen. 7:11,24; 8:3–4). Furthermore, the Book of Revelation indicates that the 360-day year will be restored during Christ Jesus' 1,000-year millennial reign on the earth (Rev.12:6, 13–14; 13:4–7). However, at the time of the Flood, the spin rate was altered and has been fixed near 365.2422 days per year until our day.[4] The 360-day "prophetic year" always was, and still is, an artificial contrivance. The 360-day years were *never* "prophetic." They were, and shall again be, real years.

Moreover, the precision achieved by Anderson and more recently by Dr. Harold Hoehner, which has won them many supporters, is not as exact as they purported. Each particular calendar is defined by its own set of rules. Both Anderson and Hoehner unwittingly violated the internal Julian calendar mathematics.

Anderson did this when he calculated that 119 leap years would occur in his 476-year prophetic period (476 ÷ 4 = 119) but then removed three and obtained 116 leap year days (his p. 128, see my page 224). He subtracted these because the last three of the 4 century-years (400, 300, 200, and 100 BC) between 445 BC and AD 32 were not divisible by 400 and thus not leap years. Removing these 3 century-years yielded 116.

---

[1] An exception to this entire assessment is E.W. Faulstich's interpretation. Taking 551 BC as being Cyrus' first year (rather than 536 BC, 2 Chron. 36:22–23; Ezra 1:1–4) and the *terminus a quo* for the Daniel 9:24–27 prophecy, Faulstich incredibly rejects that Christ Jesus is the object of these verses. Instead, he makes Nehemiah the "anointed one," the prince who comes to Jerusalem with permission to rebuild the walls after 49 years (seven sevens, Dan. 9:25a) bringing the 20th year of "Artaxerxes" (Faulstich's Darius I) to 502 BC (551 – 49 = 502).

Fulfilling the 434-year (62 sevens) part of the Daniel prophecy in 68 BC is Faulstich's second "anointed" individual, Hyrcanus the high priest who also functioned as a king (502 – 434 = 68). For Faulstich, when Hyrcanus' brother, Aristobulus, replaced him by mutual consent in that position in order to stop the civil war between them, Hyrcanus fulfilled Daniel 9:26a (i.e., "cut off" but not of his own doing). Then when 3½ years later (64 BC) Aristobulus stopped Pompey, the Roman general from sacrificing, he fulfilled Daniel 9:27b (causing the sacrifice to cease in the "midst of the week").

Faulstich concludes that the *terminus ad quem* of the 490 years (70 sevens, vs. 25) is 61 BC with Julius Caesar's taking control of the Jews (551 – 490 = 61). For Faulstich, Julius is the prince of verse 26, and "the people" of that prince who are to destroy Jerusalem are the Romans under Titus in AD 70. Thus, Faulstich presents the 490 years of Daniel 9:25 as the span from the time Cyrus issued the edict and restored the Jewish government in 551 BC until the Romans took their government in 61 BC (Faulstich, *History, Harmony and Daniel, op. cit.*, pp. 105–110.).

[2] Harold W. Hoehner, *Chronological Aspects of the Life of Christ*, (Grand Rapids, MI: Zondervan Pub., 1977), pp.134–139. Dr. Hoehner (Ph.D. Cambridge) of Dallas Theological Seminary is one of the better known who might be cited. He favors 444 BC as Artaxerxes' 20th and AD 33 as the crucifixion year.

[3] The feast in Esther 1:1–5 which lasted 180 days – exactly six months of a 360-day-year – was Persian and thus has no bearing.

[4] It is this author's contention that the yearly rotation sped up at the time of the Flood and has remained at or very near that rate ever since. At that time, the invisible water vapor canopy indicated by Genesis 1:7 which surrounded the earth at the top of our atmosphere condensed and fell to earth over a 40-day and 40-night period (Gen. 7:12). The dropping of this vast amount of water would have caused the rotation to increase much as when an ice skater increases the spin speed when they lower their center of gravity by pulling their outstretched arms into the body.

Of course, vast volumes of water also burst forth from the subterranean "fountains of the deep" (Gen. 7:11, this implies accompanying worldwide volcanic activity).

But "years ending in '00' that cannot be divided by 400 are not leap years" is a Gregorian calendar rule (see my page 287) and can not be used in a Julian-to-Julian calculation where one simply divides by four. The two systems cannot be mixed; 119 was the correct value all along.

Anderson compounded this three-day error when he said 10 Nisan AD 32 was Sunday April 6[1] (Julian[1]). It was *Wednesday* April 9. This would result in Christ dying on *Sunday*, yet Scripture teaches that was the day He arose from the dead. This means that Anderson's *year* is wrong! Dr. Hoehner also used Julian years and caught this latter Anderson mistake (his page 137). However, instead of using the Julian defined year of 365.25 days, he multiplied the 476 years by the 365.242199-day solar year (his page 138, cp. page 134). This is a violation of 4 days, 6 hours, 43 minutes, and the 6 hours, 43 minutes places him into day five.[2]

Finally, it must be seen as somewhat incongruous that from Creation to the 20th year of Artaxerxes only "normal" 365¼ (approx.) day years were utilized by Anderson and all others, yet suddenly at this point one is supposed to resort to 360-day "prophetic" years in order to complete the Old Testament chronology. Furthermore, Anderson and those who subscribe to his system do not then continue using such years throughout New Testament chronology. Hence, the entire line of reasoning seems to be little more than an expedient.

Anderson's acceptance that Longimanus was the biblical "Artaxerxes" followed by his presupposition to accept without reservation secular history's standard dates for that monarch must be seen as the critical factors in his searching for and deriving this expedience. In point of fact, other relevant historic data was known to Anderson, but his total commitment to Ptolemy's Canon brought him to reject its testimony. It is this almost forgotten data that must now be addressed.

---

[1] Anderson, *Coming Prince, op. cit.,* p. 127

[2] We are indebted to Pete Moore of Houston, TX (Director: Tubular Standards Development at Grant Prideco LP & Chairman of the American Petroleum Institute SC5 Manufacturers Advisory Group) who brought these violations to my attention. To my knowledge, he is the first to have detected them.

2. DATING ARTAXERXES LONGIMANUS WITH ANCIENT HISTORICAL DATA

As twentieth century scholars have uniformly accepted Ptolemy's Canon, it may come as a surprise for many to learn that there is significant ancient historic data that opposes (or modifies) it with regard to the dates of the Persian monarch Artaxerxes I Longimanus. This is possibly even more true of most biblical intellectuals who are familiar with the "Ussher" dates appearing in the Bibles published during the first half of the 20th century, for the years assigned to the "Artaxerxes" in question in those Texts are the same as Ptolemy's (i.e., *circa* 465–424 BC), leaving them with the impression that the matter is certain and without question or doubt. However, such is not the actual situation.

Whereas it is true that the marginal dates in the earlier Authorized Bibles (King James) represented in the main Archbishop Ussher's chronology, the reader is asked to recall that when Lloyd, the Bishop of Worchester, was entrusted with the task of editing the Bible that he chose to add those dates for the first time. Lloyd adopted Ussher's dates but made a few alterations in this edition which came to be popularly known as "Lloyd's Bible."

The foremost of these changes were the dates concerning Jacob's marriages, the birth of his children, and the departure from Laban by about seven years as well as changes to the Book of Nehemiah. The alterations were explained by Lloyd in his Tables at the end of the 1701 edition and in his *Chronological Tables* (printed but never published and now resides in the British Museum). In addition, several private papers of Lloyd's were published in 1913 by his chaplain, Benjamin Marshall, in Marshall's own *Chronological Tables* (see his appendix to Table 3 and the whole of Table 4).

For reasons which shall be detailed subsequently, Ussher had set aside Ptolemy's 465 BC date for the commencement of the reign of Artaxerxes Longimanus in favor of 473 BC (AM 3531). This latter year was based on much older historic data which Ussher considered more reliable than that of the Canon. It places the 20th year of Artaxerxes at 454 BC and brings the 483 years to an auspicious AD 30 fulfillment. However in 1701, 51 years after

Ussher had published, Lloyd set aside Ussher's chronology and inserted Ptolemy's date in its place. Let us now examine this ancient historical data and its effect on the 483 years of the Daniel 9 prophecy.

a. Ussher and the Ancient Records

At the onset, it must be noted that a truly serious period of time is not in question in the issue before us. Of all the many works which this author has examined, not one differs more than ten years from the other. Indeed, all chronologists to our knowledge agree that Xerxes ascended to the throne of Persia c. 486 BC and that his son, Artaxerxes Longimanus, died c. 424 BC. Thus it cannot be overstressed that the only matter in dispute before us here concerns the year that Artaxerxes Longimanus ascended the throne.

Ussher's objections to the "received" chronology (the Canon) largely depended on the testimony of Thucydides. He states that Longimanus had just come to the throne when Themistocles (having fled from the false charge of being in league with Pausanias' treason with Persia against Sparta and the punishment of ostracism [a ten-year public banishment] by his fellow Athenians) arrived at the Persian Court.[1]

Thucydides places the flight and coming of Themistocles to Artaxerxes' court between two notable historic events, the siege of Naxos[2] (c. 474/473 BC) and the famous victory over the Persians by the Athenian general, Cimon, at the mouth of the river Eurymedon. This river is located in Pamphylia of Asia Minor, some 125 miles from Cyprus).[3]

Moreover, Thucydides relates that during his passage from Athens to Asia Minor, Themistocles was driven by a storm into the midst of the Athenian fleet which was blockading Naxos. This is most significant for although he does not date the event, Thucydides places this siege of Naxos *before* the great victory of Cimon on the Eurymedon which

Diodorus Siculus (a Greek historian c. 80–20 BC) places in the year 470 BC.[4]

Further, Plutarch (AD 45–120) decidedly connected the death of Themistocles with the expedition of Cimon.[5] He adds that, like Thucydides, Charon of Lampsacus (one of three cities the Persian king gave to Themistocles), a contemporary of Themistocles (flourished back in Olympiad 69 or 504 BC, according to Suidas), related that Xerxes was dead and that his son Artaxerxes was the king who received the fleeing Athenian.[6]

Plutarch continued in the following sentences stating that Ephorus, Dinon, Clitarchus, Heracleides, and others maintained that Xerxes was alive at the time Themistocles came to the Persian court and that it was he with whom the interview was conducted rather than Artaxerxes. Notwithstanding, Plutarch continued in saying that though not securely established, the chronological data seemed to him to favor Thucydides over the opinions of these latter writers.

Although he believes Xerxes to still be king, Diodorus Siculus dates the arrival of Themistocles at the Persian court as being the year after the 77th Olympiad when Praxiergus was archon in Athens.[7] As the 77th Olympiad took place in 472 BC, Diodorus sets 471 as the year in which Themistocles sought refuge in Persia from his fellow Athenians. Cicero gives the year of the flight as 472[8] and Eusebius records the flight in the 4th year of the 76th Olympiad or 473 BC.[9]

---

[1] Thucydides, *History of Peloponnesian War*, vol. I, *op. cit.*, Bk. I, Ch. 137.

[2] *Ibid.*, Ch. 98, cp. 137. Naxos is a Greek island in the southern Aegean Sea. It is also the name of the most important town on the island.

[3] *Ibid.*, Ch. 98–100.

[4] Diodorus Siculus, *The Library of History, op. cit.*, Book XI, 60–61. Diodorus flourished c.AD 8.

[5] Plutarch, *Plutarch's Lives*: "Themistocles," vol. II, Loeb Classical Library, (Cambridge, MA: Harvard UP, 1967), Book II, 31.

[6] *Ibid.*, Book II, 27.

[7] Diodorus Siculus, *The Library of History, op. cit.*, Book XI, 53–57.

[8] Cicero, *Laelius de Amicitia*, vol. XX, Loeb Classical Library, trans. by W.A. Falconer, (Cambridge, MA: Harvard University Press, 1923) Ch. 12.

[9] Eusebius, *Chronicon*, Schone, ed., trans. by Petermann and Rodiger, (Berlin: n.p., 1866). See Ussher, *Annals, op. cit.*, p. 147 (1658 ed., p. 132).

It must not be overlooked that with regard to the varying ancient testimonies of the flight of Themistocles to Artaxerxes Longimanus rather than Xerxes, the resolution unquestionably favors the authority of Thucydides and Charon of Lampsacus. Unlike all other voices, they were writing as contemporaries to the facts.

The "prince" of Greek historians, Thucydides was contemporary with Artaxerxes I Longimanus and was born around the time of Themistocles' flight. Moreover, he relates that the reason for his digressing to give a brief summary of the events between the Persian and Peloponnesian War was that all his predecessors had omitted this period in their works except Hellanicus who had only treated it "briefly, and with inaccuracy as regards his chronology."[1] From this statement, it should be evident that the accounts of the period as found in the later authors cannot be certain because they can have no credible contemporary source from which to glean as such would surely have been known by Thucydides.

Indeed, Charon's witness must be given the highest regard for he was a writer of history and living in Lampsacus in Asia near the Hellespont (modern = Dardanelles) at the very time of the arrival of Themistocles. Remember, this was the same Lampsacus which was given to Themistocles – an event Charon could hardly have not noticed. On the other hand, the oldest witnesses for the opposite position lived more than a century after the event. Ephorus outlived the passing of Alexander the Great (323 BC); Clitarchus accompanied Alexander, and Dinon was his father.

Thus with the testimony of these and other witnesses, Ussher first raised a doubt on the matter while lecturing on "Daniel's Seventies" at Trinity College, Dublin in 1613.[2] He eventually wrote the argument in his *Annals of the World*, placing the date of Artaxerxes' first year as 473 BC.[3] This date was later adopted

by Campegius Vitringa. Nearly a century later Kruger, working independently, obtained the same result with many of the same arguments.[4]

In 1830, Kruger released a Latin translation of Clinton's "Tables BC 560–278" which included pages 2–207 of the second volume of *Fasti Hellenici*. Within the work, Kruger inserted some comments and observations in which he stated his views with regard to the first year of Artaxerxes as differing with the received Ptolemaic dates and agreeing with Ussher's previous findings. Still for over a century, it has been Ernest Wilhelm Hengstenberg who has been recognized as the champion of this position, and his treatise sets forth the view as thoroughly as has yet been done.[5]

Before continuing to give an evaluation and decision on this matter, it seems proper to first review the Canon of Ptolemy. In the following, we shall come to find just what it is, what it is not, and how it came to be.

b. An Examination of Ptolemy and the Canon

Claudius Ptolemaeus, or more commonly "Ptolemy," was born at Pelusium in Egypt about AD 70 and flourished during the reigns of Hadrian and Antoninus Pius, surviving the latter who died in AD 161. Ptolemy was an astronomer, astrologer and geographer. He recorded astronomical observations at Alexandria from AD 127 to 151, compiling the results into a system in which he placed the earth at rest at the center of the universe. He envisioned the planets and other heavenly bodies as encircling the earth in fixed orbits on a daily rotation about a celestial axis.

In AD 827, the 13 books bearing the title *Mathematike Syntaxis* (Mathematical System) which reflected all Ptolemy's astronomical observations, calculations, and solar system theory were translated by the Arabians into their language, coming to eventually be known among them as the *Al Magest* (The Great Work). From them, its contents were made known to Europe as the *Great System* (Ptolemaic System, The Great Construction or

1 Thucydides, *History of Peloponnesian War*, vol. I, *op. cit.*, Book I, Ch. 97.

2 James Ussher, *The Whole Works of the Most Rev. James Ussher*, C.R. Elrington and James Henthorn Todd, eds., (Dublin Ireland: Hodges & Smith Pub., 1864), vol. XV, p. 108. Petavius

3 Ussher, *Annals, op. cit.*, pp. 146–149 (1658 ed., 131–134).

4 Ernest W. Hengstenberg, *Christology of the Old Testament*, trans. by T.K. Arnold, (Grand Rapids, MI: Kregel, 1835), pp. 459–460.

5 *Ibid.*, pp. 459–470.

in Greek as *Megala Suntaxis* and in Latin as *Magna Constructio*).

Although believed erroneous by modern science, his system represented the phenomena of the heavens as they actually appear to a spectator on the earth. This enabled observers to have a practical workable procedure with regard to the motions of the sun and moon, as well as the ability to calculate and thus predict eclipses. Ptolemy welded the phenomena of the heavens into a system so comprehensive that it maintained its hold on European thought for 14 centuries.

It was not superseded until well after the AD 1543 publication of Nicolas Copernicus' (1473–1543) epoch-making *De Revolutionibus Orbium Coelestium* (Concerning the Revolutions of the Celestial Spheres) which contained the essence of the modern heliocentric system. This accomplishment is all the more amazing when one considers that Copernican astronomy, which places the sun at the center of the solar system, was taught in its essentials by Pythagoras (582–*circa* 500 BC) in his *Harmony of the Spheres* in which he explained the motions of the heavenly bodies some six centuries before Ptolemy saw the light of day (the basis of Pythagoras' decision was that the sun should be the center because it was the most magnificent of the gods).

The Royal or Ptolemy's Canon is merely a list of kings with the number of years of their reigns. It is not accompanied by any explanatory text.[1] Each king's year of accession is given as the last year of his predecessor. For example, Cyrus died and Cambyses began to reign in 530 BC, but the Canon gives the whole year to Cyrus and reckons it as his *last* year. Ptolemy does not address Cambyses' year of accession but would place 529 as his first year. Further, Ptolemy made no allowance or notice for reigns of less than a year. Those kings were completely omitted and their months were included in the last year of the preceding or the first year of the following monarch.

Significantly, Ptolemy made no indication or allowance for any co-regencies. The Canon

terminates with the Roman Emperor Antoninus Pius. Ptolemy's beginning point was the new moon on the first day of the first month (Thoth, 26 February) of the first year of the Era of Nabonassar (that Era being founded in Egyptian years of 365 days) or 747 BC.[2]

THE CANON OF PTOLEMY*

Monarch	Years of rule	Anno Nabonassar
BABYLONIAN KINGS		
Nabonassar	14	14
Nadius	2	16
Chinzer and Poros	5	21
Iloulanius	5	26
Mardokempad	12	38
Arkean	5	43
First Interregnum	2	45
Bilib	3	48
Aparanad	6	54
Rhegebel	1	55
Mesesimordak	4	59
Second Interregnum	8	67
Asaridin	13	80
Saosdouchin	20	100
Kinelanadan	22	122
Nabopolassar	21	143
Nabokolassar	43	186
Iloaroudam	2	188
Nerigasolassar	3	192
Nabonadius	17	209
PERSIAN KINGS		
Cyrus the Great	9	218
Cambyses I	8	226
Darius I	36	262
Xerxes I	21	283
Artaxerxes I	41	324
Darius II	19	342
Artaxerxes II	46	389
Ochus	21	410
Arogus	2	412
Darius III	4	416
Alexander of Macedo	8	424
partial listing		

---

[1] Ptolemy, "The Almagest," *Great Books of The Western World, op. cit.*, Appendix A, p. 466.

[2] Newton, *The Chronology of Ancient Kingdoms Amended, op. cit.*, pp. 35, 80–81.

As Anno Nabonassar 1 is 747 BC, the "running" Anno Nabonassar years seen on the preceding abridged Canon may be converted to BC dates by subtracting them from 747. Since the year after Nabonassar (the first name appearing on the Canon) is "14" (his total length of reign) all the Anno Nabonassarian years (the second column of numbers on the preceding chart) must be seen to represent the first year of the succeeding king. Hence, subtracting the 218 after Cyrus' name from 747 yields 529 BC, the first *official* year in which Cambyses came to the throne.

Although this "received" chronology is universally accepted, during the past century its reliability has been occasionally challenged. These challengers have underscored weaknesses in this work and many of them are, to some extent, valid. After all, Ptolemy was neither an eyewitness nor a contemporary historian. Yet despite the fact that he is merely a late second century compiler writing nearly a hundred years after Christ Jesus, he is our only authority for no other system bridges the gulf from 747 BC to AD 137. His Canon, or list of reigns, is the only thread connecting the reign of the biblical Darius I Hystaspis with Daniel's "notable" horned "he-goat" king of Greece who was to defeat the Medo-Persian empire (Dan. 8:5–8, 21–22; 11:2–4).

In producing the Canon, Ptolemy had access to the information written by the Chaldean priest Berosus (356–323 BC), the calculations of the astronomers Eratosthenes (276 BC, called the "Father of Chronology") and Apollodorus (2nd century BC), the writings of Diodorus Siculus[1] (c. 50 BC), and all the literature of ancient Greece and Rome at the Alexandrian library. However, it is the lunar eclipse data gleaned from the Chaldean records that accompanied portions of his king list that has given the Canon its high position of esteem in the realm of academia. As a result of these recorded lunar observations and calculations, it has always been regarded unsafe to depart from Ptolemy.

c. Challenges Against Ptolemy

Nevertheless, as Anstey, Ussher and others have pointed out, there are other voices more ancient than Ptolemy's which do not corroborate him. Early in this century, part of the Canon was questioned in the *Companion Bible* notes reflecting the work of Bullinger. Later Anstey, having been greatly influenced by Bullinger, enlarged upon his ideas compiling these ancient witnesses into a unified challenge against Ptolemy.[2]

The main point of contention is that from the 491 BC lunar eclipse in the 31st year of the reign of Darius, no other recorded eclipse data was available for Ptolemy to verify his king list over most of the later Persian period. It was this very portion of Ptolemy's chronology which Anstey (and Bullinger) felt contradicted the Hebrew Text as well as the other more ancient records whose testimony he amassed. As Anstey offers relevant material not discussed within the present work, it is recommended reading.

Much of the challenge against the Canon has been based upon statements by Sir Isaac Newton. Anstey especially based much of his thesis on Newton's observations and conclusions. Newton pointed out that all the nations of the distant past (particularly the Greeks, Egyptians, Latins and Assyrians), in order to assign credibility and status to themselves, greatly exaggerated the antiquity of their origins.

Over and over, Anstey emphasized Newton's statements regarding the Greek Antiquities, notably those relating to the deficiencies of Eratosthenes, and brought them to apply against Ptolemy.[3] As Ptolemy drew upon Eratosthenes, Anstey (and Bullinger) coupled that with other limitations with which Ptolemy was encumbered, and felt justified in concluding that the Canon was 82 years too

---

[1] Writing c. 200 years before Ptolemy and drawing heavily on Ctesias of Cnidus' *Persica* (*Library*, Bk. I, p. xxvi), Diodorus of Sicily described the Persian Empire from Xerxes to Alexander. His king list and dates are virtually those in the Canon.

[2] Anstey, *The Romance of Bible Chronology, op. cit.*, pp. 288–293. Although Anstey repeats many of Bullinger's arguments and various proofs against Ptolemy's Canon throughout his work, this portion is his final summation and a fair concise representation of his thesis.

[3] *Ibid.*, pp. 35–36, 58, 103–106, etc. Eratosthenes (born 276 BC) wrote about 100 years after Alexander the Great. His method of conjecture rather than testimony led him to greatly exaggerate the antiquity of the events of Greek history.

long in the later Persian period between the lunar eclipse in the 31st year of Darius I and Alexander the Great.[1]

Newton truly did maintain that all nations had, before they began to keep exact records of time, been prone to exaggerate their antiquities, saying:[2]

Some of the Greeks called the times before the reign of Ogyges, Unknown, because they had no history of them; those between his flood and the beginning of the Olympiads, Fabulous, because their history was much mixed with Poetical fables: and those after the beginning of the Olympiads, Historical, because their history was free from such fables.

As Anstey reported, Newton (in demonstrating that mankind was not older than that represented in Scripture) did say the "Greek Antiquities" were full of poetic fictions before the time of Cyrus. Newton related that they did not reckon events or kings' reigns by numbers of years or dateable events such as the Olympiads, but rather set reigns equivalent to a generation with about three generations to a hundred or a hundred and twenty years. From this, Newton argued that this resulted in the antiquities of Greece as being three to four hundred years older than the truth.[3]

He proceeded to point out that even the famous Arundelian Marble, composed 60 years after the death of Alexander the Great, made no mention of the Olympiads. Sir Isaac added that it was not until the following 129th Olympiad (260 BC) that Timaeus Siculus (circa 352 – circa 256 BC) published a history which utilized Olympiads to date historical people and events.

With regard to the late Persian period, Anstey noted that the only kings of Persia mentioned on the Arundelian Marble[4] after Xerxes were

the brother of Cyrus the younger (Artaxerxes Mnemon) and his son Artaxerxes III Ochus. Anstey further added that Newton proclaimed Eratosthenes, writing about a hundred years after Alexander, had produced a completely artificial chronology. Newton maintained that Apollodorus had followed Eratosthenes and that they had been followed by the chronologers who succeeded them.

Newton demonstrated the uncertainty of their chronology by showing that Plutarch quoted Aristotle who used the Olympic Disc which bore the name of Lycurgus making him contemporary with the first Olympiad in 776 BC, yet Eratosthenes and Apollodorus made him 100 years older. Newton added that Plutarch related the historic interview of Solon with Croesus (ruled Lydia 560–546 BC) whereas Eratosthenes and Apollodorus had placed Solon's death many years before the date of his visit to that Lydian monarch.[5]

Anstey forcibly maintained that when compared to the history of this latter Persian period as recorded in Josephus as well as the Jewish and Persian chronological traditions, all these weaknesses and the witness of the Marble testified that the chronology from Xerxes to Alexander had been exaggerated by Ptolemy.

Anstey reasoned from these witnesses that the six Persian kings listed on the Canon as filling this span were probably in reality only two or three who had been "multiplied" into more in order to fill the gap which he felt had been made by the artificial enlargement of the chronology by at least 82 years.

Writing in the eighteen hundreds concerning the Canon of Ptolemy, Philip Mauro said: "Ptolemy does not even pretend to have had any facts as to the length of the Persian period (that is to say, from Darius and Cyrus down to Alexander the Great)"; his dates are based on

---

1 Anstey, *The Romance of Bible Chronology, op. cit.*, pp. 20, 286, 292–293, etc.

2 Newton, *The Chronology of Ancient Kingdoms Amended, op. cit.*, pp. 44–45. Here Newton is quoting, at least in part, from Varro and Censorinus; see Ussher, *Annals, op. cit.*, p. 75 (1658 ed., p. 56).

3 *Ibid.*, pp. 1–4.

4 Martin Anstey, *The Romance of Bible Chronology, op. cit.*, pp. 289–290. Found on the island of Paros, Anstey relates that this Parian (Arundelian) marble became the

property of Thomas, Earl of Arundel in AD 1624. Being 5 inches thick and 3 feet 7 inches by 2 feet 7 inches, the marble slab displays the principal events of Greek history from its legendary beginnings down to Anno 4 of the 128th Olympiad (264 BC), the year in which it was engraved.

Among other events, it dates the reign of Cyrus, Darius I of Marathon, and Xerxes of Thermopylae.

5 Newton, *The Chronology of Ancient Kingdoms Amended, op. cit.*, pp. 3–4, 96.

"calculations or guesses made by Eratosthenes, and on certain vague floating traditions."[1] Mauro complains that despite this, Ptolemy's dates are often quoted as though they had special authority.

Indeed, biblicists such as Anstey, Bullinger, and Mauro are not the only challengers against Ptolemy. In 1977 a well-published astronomer, Dr. Robert R. Newton, issued forth a work entitled *The Crime of Claudius Ptolemy*. In it Newton charged, described, and demonstrated that Ptolemy was guilty of a betrayal against his fellow scientists. Robert Newton declared that Ptolemy had deliberately fabricated astronomical observations and that he may have also invented part of his king list, although he acknowledged that the latter part of the list concerning Cambyses and Darius I was verifiably correct.

Newton concluded that Babylonian chronology needed to be completely reviewed in order to remove any dependence upon Ptolemy's king list, stating that astronomically speaking, it was unlikely any serious error was present after "– 603, but errors before that year can have any size."[2] Professor Newton continued:[3]

> ... no statement made by Ptolemy can be accepted unless it is confirmed by writers who are totally independent of Ptolemy on the matters in question. All research in either history or astronomy that has been based upon the Syntaxis must now be done again. ... He [Ptolemy] is the most successful fraud in the history of science. (author's bracket)

In March 1979, *The Scientific American* published a repudiation of a previous article by Newton entitled "Claudius Ptolemy Fraud" (Oct. 1977, pp. 79–81) in which the above mentioned charges were detailed. The 1979 article, "The Acquittal of Ptolemy," listed several noted astronomers who, having reviewed Newton's charges of fraud, concluded they were groundless stating that such was "based on faulty statistical analysis and a disregard of the methods of early astronomy."[4]

It is significant to note that Newton's article in *The Scientific American* was but three pages, hence it hardly gave him full opportunity to document his case as he was able to do in his book. The present author admits that he has neither the time, disposition, nor skill to fully resolve this dispute. For the purpose at hand, it is sufficient to merely observe that the matter concerning the Canon of Ptolemy continues to produce much smoke and is an ongoing one, not having been completely resolved 350 years after Ussher. This again underscores my earlier position with regard to the improbability of ever attaining an "absolute" chronology.

Indeed, Ussher, Anstey, and Hengstenberg must be seen as correct when they insist that where the Canon has no astronomical observations, especially lunar eclipses, upon which to depend, Ptolemy had to rely on the same materials as other chronologists. In such places, his Canon stands on the same ground as all other historical sources such that when other substantial authorities oppose its testimony, it is not of itself sufficient to outweigh them. As Anstey himself remarked, this is not said to fault Ptolemy the man. It is only intended to call attention to his limited materials.

Nevertheless, after using Sir Isaac Newton at length in making the point that: (1) much of Eratosthenes' chronology was based upon conjecture and certain vague floating traditions; (2) the Greek chronology was much too long; and (3) Ptolemy consulted this data for his king list, Anstey continues arguing that the period which Ptolemy assigned to the Persian empire was 82 years too long in such a way as to give the impression that Isaac Newton concurred (Bullinger makes it 110, *Companion*, Appen. 86, p. 124). Whether intentional or not, Anstey and Bullinger are guilty of referencing a man of great stature to add credence to their position yet that man would never have agreed with

---

[1] Philip Mauro, *The Seventy Weeks and the Great Tribulation*, (Boston, MA: Scripture Truth Depot, 1923), pp. 22, 24.

[2] Robert R. Newton, *The Crime of Claudius Ptolemy*, (Baltimore, MD: John Hopkins Uni. Press, 1977), pp. xiii, 371–379. Professor Newton died in 1991.

[3] *Ibid.*, p. 379.

[4] *The Scientific American*, (March 1979), pp. 91–92.

their final conclusion. The *Companion Bible* best states their view:[1]

> If Newton was right, then it follows that the Canon of Ptolemy, upon which the faith of modern chronologers is so implicitly – almost pathetically – pinned, must have been built upon unreliable foundations. Grecian chronology is the basis of "Ptolemy's Canon"; and, if his foundations are "suspect," and this is certainly the case, then the elaborate superstructure reared upon them must necessarily be regarded with suspicion likewise.

Sir Isaac Newton did accuse the aforementioned chronologers of exaggerating the antiquity of Greek history, antedating its earlier events by 300–400 years. Furthermore, he did say:[2]

> The Europeans had no chronology before the times of the Persian Empire: and whatsoever chronology they now have of *ancienter* times, hath been framed since, by reasoning and conjecture. (author's emphasis)

Yet whereas it is true that Sir Isaac Newton took issue with the length of Greek chronology as passed along by Eratosthenes, he fully *endorsed* the Canon for the period that Anstey questioned. This may be established beyond any doubt for Newton used those dates and lengths of reigns of the Persian kings in his "Short Chronicle."[3] Therefore, as the italicized "ancienter" in the foregoing quote makes evident, it was the older dates beyond the 776 BC Olympiad, not the younger, that Newton rejected. This may also be seen in that whereas he normally references events and reigns by Anno Nabonassarian years, he also occasionally referenced by the Canon (*Chron. Amended*, pp. 302–303, esp. 358) as well as the Olympiads (*Chron. Amended*, pp. 353–355).

Moreover, Anstey pressed the fact that Newton noted the Arundelian Marble (also called the "Parian" Marble) made no mention of the Olympiads, and that it was not until the 129th

Olympiad (260 BC) that Timaeus Siculus first dated historical people and events utilizing them. From these two facts, Anstey declared that the 776 BC date for the Olympiad of Coraebus, long held as the first date in Grecian history which could be firmly established upon accurate authoritative evidence,[4] must be taken as untrustworthy.[5] Hence according to Anstey and the *Companion Bible*,[6] all events whose dates are referenced to the Olympiads before 260 BC are suspect or wrong.

Yet, as has been shown, these were not Newton's conclusions. Thus these men, who otherwise contributed much good work, have themselves erected chronologies based upon Newton's statements but, by the witness of Newton's own work, they have taken him out of context. Unfortunately, Newton's works are not easy to obtain in order to check his views against Anstey, etc. Thus, many who have read their work were not able to so discern and have followed them, not realizing that Newton did not agree with the final opinions concerning the reliability of the later Greek chronology as expressed by these men.

For that matter, neither did Clinton whom they also often cite sometimes favorably, other times negatively. While acknowledging that Eratosthenes date for the fall of Troy had been founded upon conjecture, Clinton stated that the 776 Olympiad of Coraebus was "the first date in Grecian chronology which can be fixed upon authentic evidence."[7]

As shall be shown, the real problem here is not at all that of the Greek records from the 776 Olympiads to the time of Christ or even with the Canon. Being a true biblicist and firmly believing these to be the problem, Anstey was drawn to conclude: "We have to choose between the Heathen Astrologer and the Hebrew Prophet. ... Here I stand. ... The received Chronology is false. The chronology of the Old

[1] Bullinger, *The Companion Bible, op. cit.*, p. 122; Anstey acknowledged following *The Companion Bible* (pp. 54, 139, 169).

[2] Newton, *The Chronology of Ancient Kingdoms Amended, op. cit.*, p. 45.

[3] *Ibid.*, pp. 40–42, 358. Indeed, Newton clearly endorses the value of the Canon of Ptolemy, especially with reference to the Persian Empire and its application to the books of Ezra and Nehemiah.

[4] Clinton, *Fasti Hellenici, op. cit.*, vol. I, p. 123.

[5] Anstey, *The Romance of Bible Chronology, op. cit.*, pages 31–32, 291, etc.

[6] Bullinger, *The Companion Bible, op. cit.*, p. 122; Martin Anstey, *The Romance of Bible Chronology, op. cit.*, p. 25.

[7] Clinton, *Fasti Hellenici, op. cit.*, vol. I, p. 123.

Testament is true."[1] Whereas this author entirely agrees with the intent and commitment inherent in such an affirmation, the actual case of the matter is not at all as Anstey perceived.

The real problem bringing about this apparent impasse between the secular data and the biblical record has nothing to do with a difficulty or mistake in the Canon. In wrongly deciding upon the decree of Cyrus as being the fulfillment of the Daniel 9:25 prophecy,[2] Anstey himself actually created the problem between Ptolemy and the Scriptures (as did *Companion Bible* in a similar vein). However when the decree in the 20th year of Artaxerxes is seen to be the only one of the four edicts which meets the requirements of the prophecy, the drastic and radical removal of 82 years (or 110, *Companion Bible*) of history is not at all necessary (again, see Appendix M, pp. 300-308).

Thus, the difficulty arose from well-intending biblicists having made faulty judgments with regard to Scripture and then forcing that error on the Canon, the very opposite of the practice of the Assyrian Academy. Both sides, the secular and the biblicist, therefore must be seen as being guilty of such practices from time to time and strong responsibilities toward one another's data must be better faced if the ultimate goal of reconstructing the truth is ever to be obtained.

Nevertheless, with the exception of this mistaken final conclusion, the present writer holds Anstey and the main of his work in the highest esteem. He has been selected, not for ridicule, but because of his deep commitment and the fact that he so well serves to illustrate how easy it is for even the most honest well-intended researcher to miss the mark and having done so, take the created mistake and use it to "correct" the efforts of others.

Having hopefully learned from such and trusting that this author is not guilty of the same error, let us return from this necessary digression to where we left off with a similar problem, yet of a much smaller magnitude. Namely, that the c. 445 BC date for the 20th

year of Artaxerxes, although coming into very close proximity, probably does not precisely bring the 483-year Daniel 9:25 prophecy into the lifetime of Christ Jesus. It is now time to see if a discrepancy, regardless of how small it may be, is demanded between the Canon and the Hebrew Text.

3. THE RESOLUTION OF PTOLEMY AND THE ANCIENT HISTORIANS

Being contemporaries of Artaxerxes I Longimanus and Themistocles, the testimonies of Thucydides and Charon of Lampsacus concerning the date in which that Persian monarch came to the throne must not continue being ignored by nearly all scholarship. Indeed, we have seen that Ussher and Anstey had an impressive array of ancient data, most of which was far older than that of Ptolemy, upon which to formulate conclusions which differed a few years from the Canon.

Having related that Eratosthenes, the astronomer-chronologer from whom Ptolemy not infrequently referred, and Apollodorus framed a chronology within which they made all the known facts of past history to fit as best they could, many credible former researchers have been called to testify that much of this was founded on conjecture, guesses, and "certain vague floating traditions." Besides, Eratosthenes flourished (c. 275–194 BC) and wrote many years after the time of Artaxerxes Longimanus and was thus not an eyewitness nor even in the immediate proximity to the event under examination. He, Apollodorus, and Ptolemy are all late compilers of this history.

Another allegation often repeated by Anstey and others is that Ptolemy is not corroborated in this period of Persian history, that his witness stands alone against many who contradict it.[3] To this Anderson has argued that Julius Africanus, writing around AD 240, independently confirmed Ptolemy's dates for Artaxerxes Longimanus in his *Chronographies*.[4] In it, Africanus does define that king's 20th year as the 115th year of the Persian Empire (reckoned from Cyrus at 559 BC) and the 4th

[1] Anstey, *The Romance of Bible Chronology, op. cit.*, pp. 20, 284.

[2] *Ibid.*, pp. 275–284.

[3] *Ibid.*, pp. 19–20, etc.

[4] Anderson, *The Coming Prince,. op. cit.*, p. 254.

year of the 83rd Olympiad (445 BC).[1] Of course it may equally be contended that as Ptolemy preceded Africanus by about a century, the latter's statement is not truly independent but rather derived from consulting the Canon.

Regardless, Ptolemy cannot rightly be as easily dismissed as Bullinger, Anstey, Mauro, etc. would have us believe, especially with respect to the magnitude of error which they have ascribed to him. After all, no less authority than Sir Isaac Newton, himself a most capable astronomer, defended Ptolemy with regard to the years of Cambyses and Darius I stating that their years were "determined by three eclipses of the moon recorded by Ptolemy, so that they cannot be disputed."[2]

As to Xerxes' dates, Sir Isaac Newton continued (*Chron. Amended*, pp. 353–354) saying that his expedition against the Greeks took place at the time of the 75th Olympic Games (480 BC), adding the critical comment that all chronologers agreed on that date. Diodorus Siculus (c. 80–20 BC), writing nearly a century before Ptolemy, gives these same facts[3] with regard to Xerxes and is undoubtedly Newton's primary source for that information.

Newton added that the Battle of Salamis was fought in the autumn and that an eclipse[4] took place a short time later on October 2nd. Herodotus mentions this same solar eclipse[5] and Ussher, citing him, also dates the famous naval conflict at Salamis as 480 BC.[6] The point is that having mentioned the October 2nd eclipse, Newton uses it to set the first year of Xerxes' reign as 485 BC (Anno Nabonassar 263) adding

that he reigned "almost twenty one years by the consent of all writers."

The importance of this or any support certifying Ptolemy can hardly be overstressed. This is all the more true since Robert Newton has recently shown the extreme limitations of Ptolemy's king list. Robert Newton convincingly illustrated that any modern historian or chronologist using Ptolemy's lunar eclipse records, even if many or all of the aspects of these eclipses were fabricated as Newton charged, would seem to verify his king list. Moreover, he showed quite remarkably that any king list, regardless of its accuracy, would seem to be eclipse validated such that, taken alone, Ptolemy's king list is of little value.[7]

However, Robert Newton goes on to show that the later part of his king list has independent verification such that there is strong confirmation for its correctness for Nebuchadnezzar and reasonable affirmation for Cambyses. From this, Newton concluded that any error in Ptolemy's list could be no more than a few years for dates after −603 JP (604 BC Gregorian), but as there was no astronomical confirmation available for earlier dates, errors before that year could be of any size.[8]

Yet from the foregoing testimony by Ussher, Diodorus Siculus, Herodotus, and Sir Isaac Newton, it cannot be fairly said that Ptolemy is not on firm ground at this place in the Canon. The length of Artaxerxes Longimanus' reign and the date of Alexander the Great are also settled within very narrow bounds by ample ancient voices, all of which confirm Ptolemy. What then is to be done with the impasse between Ussher and his sources (Thucydides, Charon of Lampsacus, etc.) and Ptolemy? Amid so much conflicting evidence and doubt, can the truth be found?

Although from all that has now been said on the matter, we may not be unconditionally certain; still, it is believed that a heretofore unattained responsible resolution has been reached. It is offered that, in general terms, all of the

[1] Africanus, *Chronographies, Ante-Nicene Fathers, op. cit.*, vol. VI, p. 135.

[2] Newton, *The Chronology of Ancient Kingdoms Amended, op. cit.*, p. 353.

[3] Diodorus Siculus, *The Library of History, op. cit.*, Book XI, 53–57.

[4] Newton, *The Chronology of Ancient Kingdoms Amended, op. cit.*, p. 354. Although Newton calls it a lunar eclipse, it was solar as the current text indicates. Undoubtedly this was a lapse by the great genius, almost certainly having been written during his final illness at the advanced age of 85.

[5] Herodotus, *The Histories, op. cit.*, vol. IV, Bk. 9, 10.

[6] Ussher, *Annals, op. cit.*, pp. 136, 141 (1658 = 121, 126).

[7] Newton, R., *The Crime of Claudius Ptolemy, op. cit.*, pp. 372–376.

[8] *Ibid.*, pp. 375–376.

formerly cited witnesses (page 225 ff.) have told the truth and are basically correct!

The solution proposed by this author is that, as many writers have heretofore stated, following Xerxes' humiliations at the hands of the Greeks in battles such as Thermopylae, Salamis, etc., his spirit was crushed resulting in the giving of himself over to a life of indolent ease, drink, and the sensual enjoyment of the harem. Further, that after some time of this debauched living, his desire and/or abilities to govern were diminished or impaired to the extent that he placed Artaxerxes Longimanus on the throne as his pro-regent some years before his death in his 21st year of rule, leaving the affairs of state in his son's hands.

Thus when Themistocles' flight ended, he arrived with Artaxerxes I Longimanus' having just come to the throne as Thucydides and Charon of Lampsacus reported. Most scholars have assumed from their histories that with Artaxerxes in power, his father was dead. Yet in point of fact, at no place in his narrative does Thucydides make mention of Xerxes' actually being dead at this time![1] This allows the possibility that Ephorus, Dinon, Clitarchus, Heracleides, Diodorus Siculus and others were also correct in part in maintaining that Xerxes was alive at the time the fleeing Athenian arrived at the Persian court and was the monarch with whom the interview was conducted rather than Artaxerxes. Xerxes was alive, but it was Artaxerxes with whom Themistocles spoke.

This solution differs from Ussher, Vitringa, Kruger, and Hengstenberg who interpreted Thucydides, etc. as meaning that Themistocles arrived at the onset of the *sole* reign of Artaxerxes I; hence they rejected Ptolemy's giving 21 years for Xerxes' kingship, conceding only some 11 or 12 years to him. The above resolution completely maintains the integrity of the Canon.

Although, as previously stated, there is some discrepancy as to the exact date for this event with Diodorus Siculus setting the year as 471, Cicero placing it as 472, and Eusebius along with Ussher opting for 473 BC, it seems certain to this author that it should be placed somewhere between 473–470. Nor should it be thought that he is alone in this determination among today's scholars.

As recently as AD 1990, Doctor Edwin M. Yamauchi, internationally noted professor of history at Miami University of Ohio, has decided in favor of Thucydides and that it was Artaxerxes I Longimanus before whom Themistocles appeared, giving 471/470 BC as the date for the ostracism of Themistocles.[2] This is all the more significant when one considers that the foreword to Dr. Yamauchi's *Persia* was written by none other than Donald J. Wiseman, world renown Professor Emeritus of Assyriology at the University of London. While not meaning to imply that Professor Wiseman agrees with all of Dr. Yamauchi's determinations, he writes:[3]

> The author's writings on archaeology and the Bible always give a balanced presentation of the evidence, and he brings out clearly and fairly those controversial points where scholars differ in interpretation. For this Yamauchi has rightly earned a good international reputation.

Thus if, for example, we take 473 BC as the year in which Xerxes installed Artaxerxes I Longimanus as his pro-regent (see section taken from Chart 5 on the following page), the Jews would quite naturally begin to reference the dates associated with him from that year as that would have been the point from which they began to have dealings with him as their sovereign. Numbering from that date would place his 20th year over the Jews as 454 BC (or AM 3550 inclusive, exactly as Ussher)[4] and the 483 years of the Daniel 9:25 prophecy brings us to AD 30 for its fulfillment (454 BC + AD 30 = 484 less one for going from BC to AD = 483).

---

[1] Thucydides, *History of Peloponnesian War*, vol. I, *op. cit.*, Book I, Ch. 137–138.

[2] Edwin M. Yamauchi, *Persia and the Bible*, (Grand Rapids, MI: Baker Book House, 1990), pp. 225–226.

[3] *Ibid.*, Foreword, p. 9.

[4] Ussher, *Annals, op. cit.*, page 152 (1658 ed., page 137). Based on Thucydides and Charon, Dionysius Petavius (a French Jesuit historian and theologian) also dated the 20th of Artaxerxes as 454 BC (rather than 445 BC) in his *Opus de Doctrina Temporum* (2 Vols., 1627; see Anstey, *Romance, op. cit.*, p. 280).

AD 30   40'ʌ

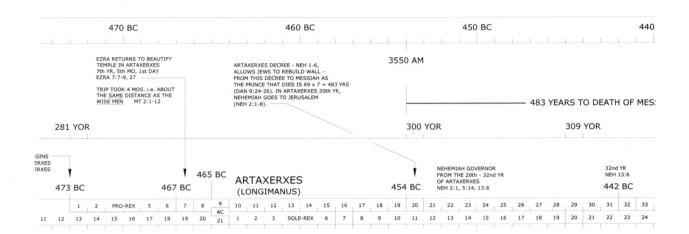

This date agrees with our previous determination. Going to the other extreme and taking 470 BC as the commencement year of Artaxerxes' pro-regency would result in 451 BC as being his twentieth and AD 33 would be the 483rd year from that point.

The above diagram is a section taken from Chart 5 which illustrates the newly author-modified Ussher-Thucydides solution to the Daniel 9:25 "483-year" prophecy. As explained in the preceding paragraph, Artaxerxes Longimanus became associated on the throne as pro-rex with Xerxes I around 473 BC.

Not only do both AD 30 and 33 fall during the accepted life time of Christ Jesus, the solution must be seen as a better alternative to Anderson's expediency as the chronology does not suddenly have to resort to inserting 360-day years instead of the solar year which was used over all the remainder of time from the Flood (see page 225). Moreover, the fact that not one historic event is known of Xerxes after his 11th year[1] should be viewed as a most significant circumstance in support of this resolution. To

the possible objection that Artaxerxes would have been too young at this time to assume the responsibilities of the government, it is replied that the Hebrew Text unmistakably places him of sufficient age in the seventh year of his dominion to have already fathered more than one son (Ezra 7:23).

We now remind our reader that beginning at page 220 and continuing to this point we have established AD 30 as best fitting the examined data in establishing the crucifixion year. Before closing this section, the following material is also presented toward forever fixing the correctness of this determination. Taken alone, these proofs are not of themselves deemed to be as significant as those already delineated but as a group, they must be seen as most substantial.

1. Whereas this author is absolutely not into numerology, it is nevertheless well-known that because of the frequency of the occurrence of the number "forty" and the uniformity of its association with a period of probation or testing, this number has long been recognized as significant within Scripture. Examples of "forties" abound: Israel in the wilderness, Israel under Philistine dominion (Judg. 13:1), Moses in Egypt, Moses in Midian, Moses on Mt. Sinai, Jonah's preaching of judgment on Nineveh, the span the 12 spies searched out Canaan, Elijah's fasting while fleeing from Jezebel, the span Goliath challenged Israel for a champion, the period of our Lord's being tempted by Satan, the length of days

---

[1] Sir Robert Anderson has taken exception with this by offering that the Book of Esther speaks of the 12th year of Ahasuerus and that the narrative carries into his 13th (*The Coming Prince, op. cit.,* pp. 256–257). This is true (Est.3:7, 12; 8:9; 9:1, 13–17); however, Anderson accepts that Ahasuerus is Xerxes and thus erroneously considers that these two years apply to Xerxes' reign. Of course, it has already been shown that this identification is false. Besides, the scenario being offered herein allows for Xerxes to still be alive over a full 21-year reign as Ptolemy listed.

He showed himself to the disciples after the resurrection, etc.

Thus, it is deemed reasonable that God gave Israel a 40-year period from the crucifixion to reconsider, repent, and receive the Lord Jesus as their long-awaited Messiah before bringing the judgment under Titus down upon them. Moreover, is it not logical to conclude that our Lord would forever end the efficaciousness of the animal sacrifice system by the willing sacrifice of himself 40 years prior to this historic event?

2. As Titus' destruction of the Temple is firmly fixed at AD 70, Eusebius places our Lord's death in AD 30 by writing: "For forty whole years it (i.e., God's Providence) suspended their (the Jews) destruction, after their crime against the Christ."[1]

3. Even the Jewish sages, who certainly have no reason to assist us in this determination, imply an AD 30 crucifixion. The Jerusalem (Yoma 43c) and Babylonian (Yoma 39b) Talmuds tell us that every night for 40 years before the destruction of the Temple the middle or chief light on the golden candlestick would simply go out and that the great brass Temple-gates which were closed each evening were seen to swing open every night of their own accord. Josephus tells us these doors were so massive that it took 20 men to close them (*Wars*, vi, 5, 3.).

4. The 40 years of Judah's iniquity and its association to a siege of Jerusalem in Ezek. 4:4–7 is herewith offered as a double reference prophecy with its second fulfillment being the span from the crucifixion to the ending of the sacrifice system by Titus' AD 70 destruction of the Temple and its altar (after all, the OT is about Christ, Luke 24:27, 44–45).

5. Moreover, Titus began the siege of Jerusalem on 14 Nisan AD 70.[2] Are we to actually believe it is a mere coincidence that this was 40 years to the very day from a 14 Nisan AD 30 crucifixion?

When these considerations are added to the detailed thesis already presented, the year AD 30 should be seen as the actual date of our Lord's crucifixion and thereby settle this issue.[3]

As to Ptolemy and the Royal Canon, we add that the formerly cited Adad-guppi inscription (page 194) gives all the reigns of the Neo-Babylonian kings from Nabopolassar to the ninth year of Nabonidus and the lengths of reign are in complete accordance with Ptolemy.[4] This is most significant as she was a contemporary and intimately associated with all these kings.

In addition to Adad-guppi's confirmation of these kings and their regnal spans, Nebuchadnezzar's 37th year has been absolutely fixed at 568/567 BC by an astronomical diary in the Berlin Museum designated as VAT 4956 which gives about 30 verified observations of the moon and the five then-known planets. Such a combination of astral positions is not duplicated again for several thousand years before or after this date. The tablet twice states that the observations were made in the 37th year of Nebuchadnezzar.[5]

Further, the Nabonidus No. 18 cylinder inscription gives a lunar eclipse which has been dated and confirmed as having occurred on September 20, 554 BC (Gregorian) during the second year of Nabonidus.[6] This, along with the data given by Adad-guppi and the VAT 4956 observations, gives strong, added validation to Ptolemy.

Finally, Nabonidus relates that the god Marduk instructed him to rebuild Ehulhul, the temple of the moon god Sin, in Haran which had been lying in ruin for 54 years due to its devastation by the Medes.[7] Adad-guppi dates this devas-

---

[1] Eusebius, *Ecclesiastical History, op. cit.*, vol. 1, III, vii, 9; parentheses mine.

[2] Josephus, *Wars of the Jews, op. cit.*, V, 13, 7.

[3] It is urged that the combined force of these 5 points far outweigh the uncertain statements of Phlegon and Thallus which Ussher relied on to establish AD 33 (fn. 1, p. 221).

[4] Pritchard, *ANET, op. cit.*, p. 561. She lists: Nabopolassar 21, Nebuchadnezzar 43, Evil Merodach 2, Neriglissar 4.

[5] Carl Olof Jonsson, *The Gentile Times Reconsidered*, 3rd edition, Rev. and Expanded, (Atlanta, GA: Commentary Press, 1998), pp. 158, 186.

[6] *Ibid.*, pp. 109–110. Charts 5 and 5c were completed years prior to my learning of this eclipse and the VAT 4956 observations. Both precisely confirm the dates that were already recorded on 5 and 5c.

[7] Pritchard, *ANET, op. cit.*, p. 311, (X).

tation as occurring in the 16th year of Nabopolassar[1] or 610 BC (see Chart 5c). Now the Nabonidus No. 18 cylinder eclipse just cited fixed the 2nd year of Nabonidus as 554 BC. Thus, his first year was 555, and Nabonidus is obviously reckoning the 54 years *from* the 16th of Nabopolassar to the beginning of his own reign. That is, it is 54 years *from* 610 to 555 (numbering exclusively) as shown on Chart 5c.

Ptolemy gives Nabopolassar a reign of 21 years, hence 5 remained from his 16th to his final year. If we take these five and add them to the 43 for Nebuchadnezzar, two for Evil Merodach, and four years for Neriglissar before Nabonidus ascended the throne we obtain 54 – which is the very number Nabonidus gives on his stele.

The sum of the evidence offered by this as well as the four preceding paragraphs is absolutely decisive. These, along with the cluster of lunar eclipse years recorded on page 194 (also Charts 5 and 5c), absolutely fix the years and reigns of the Neo-Babylonian kings listed by Ptolemy. True, a single eclipse calculation taken alone may prove faulty. In fact, many will never be seen as they transpire during the daylight hours, but the validity of such an array of astral observations presented here cannot be denied.

To the objection that too much emphasis has been placed on such astronomical observations, we remind our reader that God states in Genesis that one of the main purposes for His creating the sun, moon, and stars was that man could use them for telling time (i.e., seasons, days, and years — Genesis 1:14–19). Further, these astral observations have been confirmed by this author through the use of many scriptures relevant to the time-span in question.

In light of all the preceding, it should be clear that regardless of any challenges one may lay against the inherent weaknesses in the Persian chronology listed by Ptolemy, the Babylonian astronomical data absolutely fixes the number of years from the reigns of the Neo-Babylonian monarchs to the time of Christ. Thus, it is not possible that any years could have been added to history. Future discoveries could bring about some adjustments but in view of all that supports the Royal Canon, any such changes would be extremely minimal. Hence, the 82-

year discrepancy insisted upon by Anstey or the 110 years by the *Companion Bible* must be seen as totally unfounded and indefensible.

Accordingly, Ptolemy's dates and king list are acceptable as they stand within their heretofore stated known limitations such as his omissions of kings who reigned for less than a year. Examples of this practice are Artabanus who had a seven-month reign in 465 BC, and Xerxes II and Sogdianus who reigned 45 days and six months and 15 days respectively during 424 BC.[2] All this author's explanation does is merely add the pro-regency aspect to the relationship between Xerxes I and Artaxerxes I Longimanus which does no violation to Ptolemy for, as has been formerly stated, he makes no mention of such affinities.

Indeed, the fabric of the entire thesis concerning the biblical "Artaxerxes" as presented thusfar has been remarkably corroborated by an essay published in the 1863 *Journal of Sacred Literature and Biblical Record*. The article reports an Egyptian hieroglyphic inscription as having been found which stated that Artaxerxes Longimanus was associated with his father on the throne in the 12th year of Xerxes' reign:[3]

> It is satisfactory to know that the idea entertained by Archbishop Ussher of dating the commencement of Artaxerxes' reign nine years earlier than the canon of Ptolemy allows, grounded upon what Thucydides says of Themistocles' flight to Persia, has been confirmed by hieroglyphic inscriptions in Egypt, shewing that Artaxerxes was associated with his father in the twelfth year of

---

[1] Pritchard, *ANET, op. cit.*, p. 560.

[2] Clinton, *Fasti Hellenici, op. cit.*, vol. II, p. 378 and Thiele, *The Mysterious Numbers of the Hebrew Kings, op. cit.*, p. 228 (see: Internet–Sogdianus, Wikipedia encyclopedia).

[3] B.W. Savile, "Revelation and Science," *Journal of Sacred Literature and Biblical Record*, Series 4, (London: Williams and Norgate Pub., April, 1863), p. 156. This amazing documentation evidently confirms all that the author deduced from the available data before him at the time of the original writing. One cannot help wondering why in my many years of research, especially with regard to the Daniel 9:25 prophecy as related to the 483 years to the Messiah, this incredible find has never been detected in any written reference or in verbal discussions with contemporaries who are also knowledgeable concerning these matters. That notwithstanding, I am most grateful to have "happened" upon it so soon after having submitted the original paper.

Xerxes' reign, so that there ought to be no longer any doubt respecting that famous prophecy of Daniel, so far at least as regards the crucifixion.

Admittedly, this citation stunned the present author as it apparently confirms the preceding deduction given in this paper – yet the report is over a century old! The 1863 *Journal* was happened upon nearly six months after the completion of the previous research. This excerpt, taken from so prestigious a publication, is offered as being seemingly conclusive external evidence. Added to all the foregoing evidence given in this dissertation, it is submitted that the "Artaxerxes" problem is forever solved – his 20th year having been established as being 454 BC.

Remember, Anderson's solution did not provide a *direct* resolution. As formerly stated (page 224), it required the expediency of having to convert to the 360-day "prophetic year" in which the 483 years of the Daniel 9:25 prophecy are actually reduced to but 476.[1]

The solution given within the current paper must be seen as being far superior to such an artificial contrivance, especially as there is no stated scriptural basis for so computing. Conversely, the secular testimonies of Thucydides, Charon of Lampsacus, and this "new" hieroglyphic evidence combine forming a powerful, threefold witness (Ecclesiastes 4:12b) as to the correct historical date for Artaxerxes which agrees straightforwardly with the biblical data and confirms the AD 30 crucifixion year of our Lord.

One may continue clinging to the Anderson explanation only by setting these three independent witnesses at naught, but with what justification? It has been clearly shown that 32 AD is impossible for the year of our Lord's death (page 225 ff.) and that 445 BC for the 20th year of Artaxerxes should be 454 BC. Accordingly, it is submitted that the actual history has been reconstructed in the body of this work and is portrayed on Chart 5c as well as by the solid line upper solution on Chart 5.

---

[1] Indeed, Anderson's idea was not completely original. Bishop Lloyd had already (1701) adopted such a ploy by proposing that the 483 years were Chaldean years, rather than Anderson's "prophetic" years, of 360 days each; thereby obtaining the same results as did Sir Robert in 1882.

In view of all the foregoing regarding the Daniel 9 prophecy, the people of Jesus' day should have been aware its fulfillment was at hand and known "the time" of their Messiah's "visitation" (Luke 1:68, 78, and 19:44).

4. THE EZRA-NEHEMIAH PREDICAMENT AND ARTAXERXES' IDENTIFICATION

Nevertheless, a persisting problem remains. The unresolved matter is a serious one which places all previous solutions squarely on the horns of a dilemma.

It has long been recognized that the books of Ezra and Nehemiah exhibit a built-in yet distasteful quandary. The Book of Ezra begins in the 1st year of Cyrus, about 536 BC (Ezra 1:1), and the Book of Nehemiah ends around the 32nd year of a Persian king designated as "Artaxerxes" (Neh. 2:1; 13:6). As nearly all scholars identify this monarch as being Artaxerxes Longimanus, the Book of Nehemiah is seen to close near 434 BC (his 32nd year).

Thereby these two books apparently span nearly 102 years (536 – 434 = 102). Within them, the names "Ezra" (Neh. 12:1, cp. Ezra 1:1–2:2) and "Nehemiah" (Ezra 2:2) are found throughout beginning from the first year of Cyrus, at which time the men bearing these names are listed among the leaders returning from the Babylonian captivity with Zerubbabel, unto the end (or very nearly so, Neh. 12:36, etc.).

The "unpleasantness" produced by this is that although the context of the narrative seems to depict them as being the same two men, their ages become uncomfortably large. Being portrayed as leaders demands a minimal age of 30 in the first year of Cyrus, and when the 102-year span is added to this, Nehemiah would have been at least 132 and Ezra, who is last mentioned in the 20th year of "Artaxerxes" (c. 445?), a minimal of 121 years (536 – 445 = 91 + 30) by the story's end.

This is a problem for most as biblical life spans between these dates had shortened, coming in line with those of today (Psa. 90:10). The fact that the Books of Ezra and Nehemiah were originally only one volume makes this all the more troublesome.

Modern scholarship has resolved this perceived dilemma by deciding that there must surely be two Ezras and also two Nehemiahs, one pair at the first year of Cyrus who subsequently died and a second pair during the latter part of the narrative. This seems a simple and tidy solution; however the problem has not been resolved at all for there is much more to the enigma which few scholars seem to have noticed. This unresolved, "unnoticed" data is that which is at the heart of the matter.

The predicament arises from a comparison of the list of priests and Levites returning with Zerubbabel in the first year of Cyrus as sole rex of Persia and Babylonia (536 BC, Neh. 12:1–9) with the list of priests and Levites who sealed a covenant with Nehemiah (Neh. 10:1–10). The consensus of nearly all scholarship is that this latter event of sealing the covenant took place in the 20th year of "Artaxerxes" (445 BC?). The correlation reveals that at least 16 and possibly as many as 20 of those who returned with Zerubbabel in leadership positions over Israel (hence 30 years and older) were still alive in the 20th year of Artaxerxes, if indeed most scholars are correct in assigning the Nehemiah covenant to that date (see next page).

If this "Artaxerxes" were Longimanus, as is currently taught (and indeed is), then this generation of leaders would still have been alive 91 years (536 – 445 = 91) after they returned to Jerusalem![1] The youngest would then have been 121 (91 + 30 = 121) and others much older. Yet the Scriptures reveal that life spans were foreshortened such that for over 700 years only one man is recorded as having lived past age 100 (Jehoiada, 2 Chron. 24:15). It is thereby

inconceivable that an entire generation suddenly lived so long.

Therefore unless there is some resolution to this dilemma it would seem that the "Artaxerxes" of Nehemiah was another king of Persia *prior* to Longimanus, thereby reducing these men's ages. Thus the "creation" of a second Ezra and a second Nehemiah does nothing to resolve the problem. Not having noticed the problem inherent in comparing these two registers in relation to the dates they have assigned to them, nearly all scholars have failed to fathom the true extent and depth of the perplexity.

Probably because they failed to compare the two lists, few chronologers other than Anstey[2] and Faulstich[3] have addressed this awkward issue. Unless a solution is found, the time disparity between the Nehemiah 10 and 12 lists invalidates not only Sir Robert Anderson's solution and that formerly detailed and offered by this author in which Artaxerxes I is seen to function as his dissipated father's pro-regent beginning around 473–470 BC but all other accepted scenarios in use today as well. As a result of not having resolved this problem, *all* modern works dealing with the Books of Ezra and Nehemiah have chronologically misplaced all the material from Nehemiah 7:73b to 12:1–9.

Finally, the astronomical observations cited herein absolutely fix the 5th year of Nabopolassar (621 BC) to the 37th year (568/567) of his son Nebuchadnezzar. The 21-year reign of Nabopolassar recorded by Ptolemy has been confirmed by the Babylonian records and the Adad-guppi inscription. As the latter also confirms the 43 years Ptolemy assigned to the length of Nebuchadnezzar's reign, these dates are forever established.

Further, Jehoiakim's 4th regnal year is biblically fixed to Nebuchadnezzar's 1st and Zedekiah's 11th to his 19th. Thus, these dates are set at 605/604 and 586 respectively. Moreover, the eclipses in the reign of Darius fix his 6th year at 516 BC. As Scripture indicates this date is 70 years from the 586 destruction of Jerusalem, the secular and biblical data have been completely harmonized.

---

[1] The association of the biblical "Artaxerxes" with Artaxerxes I Longimanus resulted quite naturally as chronologers were understandably looking for the first "Artaxerxes" who reigned after Darius Hystaspis whose dominion extended for at least 32 years (Neh.5:14). The last parameter that had to be met was that his accession to the throne had to be at least 483 years from the time of Christ Jesus' first advent. Thus Longimanus was readily acknowledged as the correct choice.

However this determination potentially does much violence to Scripture, lengthening beyond reason the ages of the returning generation under Zerubbabel as seen by comparing the Nehemiah 10 and 12 rolls of returnees. The attempt by scholars to "fix" this gave rise to the "two Mordecai's," "two Ezra's," two Nehemiah's," etc. theory. The resulting disfigured chronology has thus far gone unchecked.

---

[2] Anstey, *The Romance of Bible Chronology, op. cit.*, p. 271.

[3] Faulstich, *History, Harmony, The Exile and Return*, (Spencer, IA: Chronology Books Inc., 1988), pp. 155–156.

Priests and Levites who returned
with Zerubbabel and Jeshua in the
1st yr of Cyrus, 536 BC, Neh. 12:1–9.

Priests and Levites who sealed a covenant
with Nehemiah in the 20th yr of Artaxerxes.
Traditional date is c. 445 BC, Neh. 10:1–13

I. PRIESTS

1. Seraiah	Seraiah
2. Jeremiah	Jeremiah
3. Ezra	(Azariah) ?
4. Amariah	Amariah
5. Malluch (Melicu)	(Malchijah) ?
6. Hattush	Hattush
7. Schechaniah (Shebaniah)	Shebaniah
8. Rehum (Harim)	Harim
9. Meremoth	Meremoth
10. Iddo	--
11. Ginnethon	Ginnethon
12. Abijah	Abijah
13. Miamin	Mijamin
14. Maadiah	(Maaziah) ?
15. Bilgah	Bilgai
16. Shemaiah	Shemaiah
17. Joiarib	--
18. Jedaiah	--
19. Sallu (Sallai)	--
20. Amok	--
21. Hilkiah	--
22. Jedaiah	--

Neh. 12:7 "These were chief of the
the priests and of their brethren
in the days of Jeshua."
(cp. spelling of these men
and their sons in Neh. 12:10–21)

Neh. 10:8 "These" (with Zidkijah,
Pashur, Malluch, Obadiah, Daniel,
Baruch and Meshullam) "were the
priests" who sealed with Nehemiah.

II. LEVITES

1. Jeshua	Jeshua, the son of Azaniah
2. Binnui (Bani, 8:7; 9:5?)	Binnui of the sons of Henadad
3. Kadmiel	Kadmiel
4. Sherebiah	Sherebiah
5. Judah	(Hodijah, cp.Ezra 2:40;3:9)
6. Mattaniah (over the choirs)	--
7. Bakbukiah	--
8. Hashabiah (12:24, cp.vv 8 and 9, 25, 11:17 and 19).	Hashabiah
9. Unni	-- (and 11 others)

Return from Babylon
Newton

a. Sir Isaac Newton's Solution

At least as far back as AD 1728 Sir Isaac Newton, the great scientific and mathematical genius as well as a remarkable Bible scholar, recognized that the Nehemiah 10 list of priests and Levites who sealed the covenant with Nehemiah were the same who had returned with Zerubbabel in the first year of Cyrus (Neh. 12; again, see diagram on the previous page). Newton noted that the Levites Jeshua, Kadmiel, and Hodaviah (or Judah, Ezra 3:9 or Hodevah, Neh. 7:43) were among the chief fathers returning with Zerubbabel in 536 BC (Ezra 2:40) and that they assisted:

(1) in laying the Temple foundation (Ezra 3:9),

(2) in the reading of the law (Neh. 8:7, along with Sherebiah, cp. Neh. 12:8 and possibly Binnui, Neh. 10:9; 12:8, cp. 8:7; 9:5), and

(3) in making and sealing the covenant (Neh. 9:5; 10:9–12).

Taking into account these overlaps between the Books of Ezra and Nehemiah, Sir Isaac Newton set forth the following chronology.

Beginning this segment of Jewish history at the return from their captivity in the first year of Cyrus (536 BC), Newton correctly depicted "Sheshbazzar, the prince of Judah" (Zerubbabel) leading nearly 50,000 returnees along with the holy vessels and a commission to rebuild the Temple (Ezra 1). The people came to Jerusalem and Judah, every one to his city, and dwelt in their ancestral cities until the seventh month (Tishri) at which time they gathered in Jerusalem.

Under the leadership of Zerubbabel and Jeshua the high priest, the altar was rebuilt, and on the first day of the seventh month they began offering the daily morning and evening burnt offerings (Ezra 2:1, 70, cp. Neh. 7:5–73; Ezra 3:1–3, 5–6). According to Newton, on that same day Ezra the priest read from the Book of the Law and then he, Nehemiah the Tirshatha, and the Levites taught the people (Neh. 7:73b–8:12).

Beginning on the 15th day of the 7th month, the people observed the Feast of Tabernacles (Ezra 3:4, cp. Neh. 8:13–18; Lev. 23:34). Then on the 24th day of the same month the children of Israel assembled for a solemn fast, read the Scriptures, confessed, worshiped the Lord, and sealed a covenant under Nehemiah the Tirshatha (Neh. 9:1–10:38). Thereafter, the rulers

dwelt at Jerusalem. The rest of the people cast lots to bring one out of every ten persons to Jerusalem in order to more fully repopulate it, leaving the remaining to dwell in the cities of Judah (Neh. 11).

After listing the priests and Levites returning with Zerubbabel in the first year of Cyrus and their genealogies, etc. (Neh. 12:1–26), Newton then resumes the chronology at Ezra 3:8 during the second month of the second year of their return at which time the work began on the house of the Lord. After completing the foundation of the Temple (Ezra 3:9–13), the adversaries of Judah troubled their building efforts and hired counselors against them all the days of Cyrus (*circa* 6 more years) until the reign of Darius I Hystaspis (Ezra 4:1–5). From there, Newton continues sequentially through Ezra chapter six with Darius' decree unto the completion of the Temple in the month of Adar (12th) of the sixth year of that Persian monarch ending with its dedication, the Passover and Feast of Unleavened Bread.

Again, taking into account the aforementioned overlaps between the Books of Ezra and Nehemiah, Sir Isaac Newton concluded that the Nehemiah 10 covenant was drawn up and sealed in the first year of Cyrus (536 BC). Although he does not say it as clearly as one would like, a careful reading of page 361 in his *Chronology of Ancient Kingdoms Amended* will reveal his resolution to the problem.

Like all others, he recognized that Nehemiah 7:4 leaves off in the 20th year of Artaxerxes with the insertion of data previously recorded in the second chapter of the Book of Ezra which applies to the return of Zerubbabel in the first year of Cyrus. However, whereas nearly all scholars regard the repeated insertion to end where "all Israel in their cities" of Ezra 2:70 corresponds to "all Israel, dwelt in their cities" in Nehemiah 7:73, Newton continued connecting the "seventh month" portion of Nehemiah 7:73 to the "seventh month" of the next verse – Nehemiah 8:2 (as does the Jewish chronology).[1]

Finding no contextual break in the narrative, he placed everything from Nehemiah 7:5 to 12:9 together as occurring in the first year of Cyrus. By inference, Newton then had Nehemiah 7:4

---

[1] *Seder Olam*, Heinrich Guggenheimer ed. (2005), p. 257.

resume with the wall of Jerusalem having just been completed (Neh. 6:15) to Nehemiah 12:27, at which point the wall was being dedicated. In general, Newton's chronology is:[1]

1. Ezra 1:1–11 followed by

2. Ezra 2:1–6 being overlapped by Nehemiah 7:5–73a with

3. Nehemiah 7:73b–12:9 following as an inserted unit after which comes

4. the remainder of the Book of Ezra (i.e., 3:8–10:44), then

5. Nehemiah 1:1 to 7:4 with the story of the completed walls of Jerusalem picking up again at

6. their dedication at Nehemiah 12:27 and thence in normal sequence to 13:31.

Thus Newton's solution is that just as the Nehemiah 12 register represents men who returned in the first year of Cyrus (536 BC), the making and sealing of the covenant with Nehemiah (the Tirshatha) also transpired in that same year and not in the 20th year of Artaxerxes. Consequently, according to Isaac Newton's chronology, no 91-year gap existed between the two chapters, thereby resolving the predicament (see diagram on following page).

He envisioned Zerubbabel as the governor and Nehemiah as his Tirshatha or second in command; thus for Newton every Scripture using that title signifies Nehemiah (Ezra 2:2, 63; Neh. 7:65, 70; 8:9; 10:1).[2] In this scenario, it was not until after Zerubbabel's death that Nehemiah was promoted and referred to by the higher appellation of governor, a position which he held for twelve years (Neh. 5:14).

Before appraising all of the foregoing, it should be remembered that the Hebrew manuscripts containing Scripture and the early printed editions of the Hebrew Text always treated Ezra and Nehemiah as *one* book. Moreover, the notes which the Masoretes placed at the end of each book appear at the end of Nehemiah; *none* are given at the end of Ezra.

Ezra primarily confined his narrative to events connected with the Temple whereas Nehemiah mainly addressed events connected with the wall and city of Jerusalem. As the Temple is morally and spiritually more important than the wall, the Book of Ezra logically comes first in the canonical order.

An assessment of Sir Isaac's treatise reveals both positive and, unfortunately, negative consequences inherent in his answer. In the first place, most modern scholars insist that Nehemiah 7:73b is a connecting statement logically belonging with chapter 8.[3]

---

[1] A precise Scripture summary of Newton's chronology for Ezra and Nehemiah is: Ezra 1:1–3:7 (Ezra 2:1,70, cp. Neh.7:5–73); Neh.7:73b–8:12; Neh.8:13–18 (cp. Ezra 3:4); Neh.9:1–12:26 (Believing that Darius the Persian was Darius II Nothus [423–405 BC, as did Newton, see p. 363 in his *Chronology of Ancient Kingdoms Amended, op. cit.*], this author acknowledges that the genealogy from 12:10–26 could have been prophetic or a later inserted addition.); Ezra 3:8–Neh.7:4; Neh. 12:27–13:31. Again, Newton places everything from Nehemiah 7:5 to 12:9 together as occurring in the first year of Cyrus (*Chronology of Ancient Kingdoms Amended, op. cit.*, p. 358). (See diagram on the following page.)

Newton also considered the naming of Cyrus, *, Darius, Ahasuerus, and Artaxerxes in Ezra 4 as their being given in order of succession such that these names represent Cyrus, *, Darius Hystaspis, Xerxes I (of Thermopylae), and Artaxerxes I Longimanus (*Chronology of Ancient Kingdoms Amended, op. cit.*, pp. 368–370).

The asterisk must surely represent Cambyses whom Newton acknowledges as having reigned (pp. 347 and 353) but believes he is passed over by the Scriptures. *The New Scofield Reference Bible, op. cit.*, makes the same identifications in the Ezra 4 footnotes and center reference, pp. 536–537. At first glance this perhaps somehow seems flawed in that opposition is portrayed as having taken place after the Temple project was completed for the Temple was completed on the 3rd day of the 12th month (Adar) in the sixth year of Darius I Hystaspis (Ezra 4:23–24, cp. 6:15), years before the reign of Xerxes I.

Yet the above apparently envisions Ezra 4:6–23 as applying to the opposition related to the building of the wall and City of Jerusalem which transpired after the Temple was finished. It may well be argued that the context bears this out, for never within these verses is the Temple actually mentioned by direct reference, but the wall and city are (vv. Ezra 4:12–13, 16, 21). This interpretation considers Ezra 4:6–23 as a parenthetic insertion with verse 24 again picking up the narrative which had left off at 4:5. It bears due consideration.

Newton makes no mention of the Book of Esther and its "Ahasuerus" but on page 370 he states that he takes "the Book of Esdras to be the best interpreter of the Book of Ezra," and 1 Esdras 3:1–2 makes the Ahasuerus of Esther Darius I Hystaspis.

---

[2] Newton, *The Chronology of Ancient Kingdoms Amended, op. cit.*, p. 368.

[3] Merrill F. Unger, *Unger's Commentary on the Old Testament*, vol. I, (Chicago, IL: Moody Press, 1981), p. 646. In this opinion, Unger is representative of the majority of modern scholarship.

Chronology of EZRA-NEHEMIAH

A Scripture summary of Newton's chronology for Ezra and Nehemiah is Ezr.1:1-3:7 (Ezr.2:1,70, cp. Neh.7:5-73); Neh.7:73b-8:12; Neh.8:13-18 (cp. Ezr.3:4); Neh.9:1-12:26 (believing that Darius the Persian was Darius II Nothus [B.C. 423-404, as did Newton, see p. 363 in his Chronology of Ancient Kingdoms Amended], this author acknowledges that the genealogy from 12:10-26 could have been prophetic or a later inserted addition.); Ezr.3:8-Neh.7:4; Neh.12:27-13:31. Again, Newton places everything from Nehemiah 7:5 to 12:9 together as occurring in the first year of Cyrus (Chronology of Ancient Kingdoms Amended, p. 358).

Newton also considered the naming of Cyrus, *, Darius, Ahasuerus, and Artaxerxes in Ezra 4 as their being given in order of succession such that these names represent Cyrus, *, Darius Hystapis, Xerxes I (of Marathon), and Artaxerxes I Longimanus (Chronology of Ancient Kingdoms Amended, p. 368-370).

Newton makes no mention of the Book of Esther and its "Ahasuerus" but states on page 370 that he takes "the book of Esdras to be the best interpreter of the book of Ezra" and I Esdras 3:1-2 makes the Ahasuerus of Esther Darius I Hystaspis.

Note: Nehemiah 12:10-26 is:

1. A list of high Priests beginning with Jeshua, who returned with Zerubbabel in 536 BC, down to Johanan & Jaddua, High Priests who served in the days of "Darius the Persian" (vv.10, 22 & 23; c.423-405 BC) who is Darius II Nothus, and

2. A list of the Chief Priests under Jeshua's son Joiakim (c.500-468 BC) during the days of Nehemiah and Ezra (vv.12 & 26) along with a few of the chief Levites.

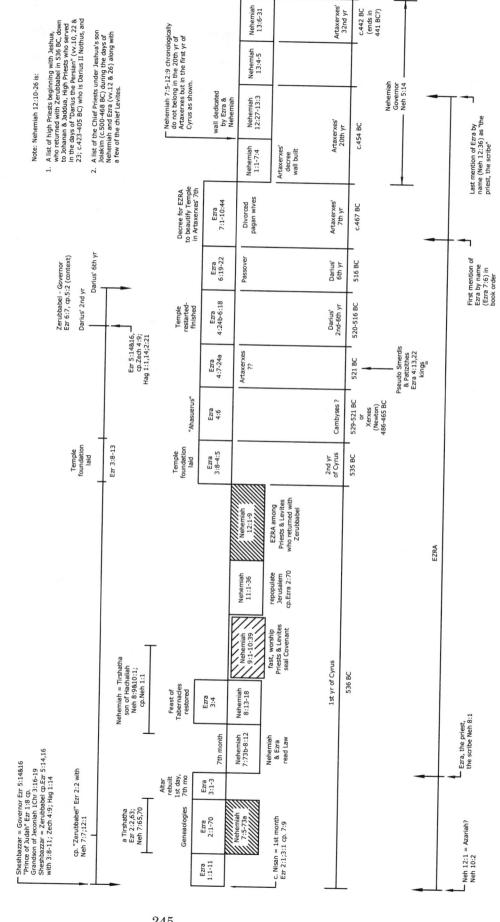

Thus to these scholars, the "seventh month" statements are connected to each other as Newton believed, but they are separated in context and time from Nehemiah 7:5–73a. Of course as this is interpretative and not conclusive, it cannot set aside Newton's proposition without strong additional support.

Moreover, this determination is not based upon the contextual flow of the scriptural narrative but upon the fragile deduction that the events in the eighth chapter of Nehemiah must transpire in approximately the 20th year of Artaxerxes Longimanus. This author stands with Newton here – as does Jewish chronology.[1]

Further, on the positive side, Newton's removal of the 91-year gap between chapters 10 and 12 of Nehemiah solved the ridiculous anomaly whereby an entire generation was suddenly presumed to have lived to and far beyond 120 years. After all, not since the time of Moses, almost 1,100 years hence, had an entire generation reached such an advanced age. However, in placing Nehemiah 10 in the first year of Cyrus (536 BC), Newton knowingly forced a great age on Nehemiah and subsequently Ezra.[2]

As the Nehemiah in 10:1 and Nehemiah in 1:1 of the book that bears his name both identify a Nehemiah "the son of Hachaliah" they must be one and the same man. Since Nehemiah 1:1 is in the 20th year of Artaxerxes (cp. Neh. 2:1) and as Newton correctly takes this Persian monarch to be Longimanus, Nehemiah's life is seen to reach from 536 BC, at which time he must be at least 30 years of age, to at least the year 434 BC (Artaxerxes' 32nd year of *sole* reign; Chart 5, 5c and Ptolemy, cp. Neh. 13:6). Using the Canon's dates for Artaxerxes, the "wall builder" would have been at least 132 years old in the 32nd year of "Artaxerxes" (536 − 434 = 102 + 30).

Having identified "Darius the Persian" as being Darius II Nothus, Newton actually considered that Nehemiah wrote the entire narrative and that 12:10–26 was not a later addition. Thereby Nehemiah would had to have lived unto at least 423 BC, the first year of Nothus' reign. This would make the wall builder no less

than 143 years old at the time of his death (536 − 423 = 113 + 30). As Newton's chronology also places Ezra in the first year of Cyrus (Neh. 8:1–2, cp. 12:26, 36 [the priest, the scribe]), he would have attained at least 121 years using the traditional date for Artaxerxes' 20th year (536 − 445 = 91 + 30).

However, these ages may be somewhat reduced by using the adjusted dates based on the pro-regency arrangement for Artaxerxes Longimanus and Xerxes I as required by the testimonies of Thucydides and Charon of Lampsacus. The reader will recall from page 228 that their witness was subsequently accepted and followed by Ussher, Vitringa, Kruger, Hengstenberg and in 1627, Petavius (also my refinement as formerly explained).

If, for example, one takes 473 BC as the "first year" of Artaxerxes Longimanus' joint reign, Nehemiah's age would have been as little as 124 years in the 32nd year of that king's reign (536 − 442 = 94 + 30). Having last been mentioned at the wall dedication during that same Persian monarch's 20th year, Ezra's life span could have been no more than 112 years (536 − 454 = 82 + 30). Although these are great ages, they are not excessive to the extreme as even today a few live to so advanced an age.

The conventional way around these two extended ages is to assume that there are two Ezras and two Nehemiahs who followed in successive generations, all in positions of leadership and bearing the same general positions of authority (an unlikely circumstance). However Newton's arrangement simply does not allow for this, especially not for Nehemiah.

From the context, Newton was convinced that the Ezra and Nehemiah found in the Book of Ezra were the same men by those names who were mentioned in the Book of Nehemiah. Besides, the fact that they originally had been only one book argues strongly in behalf of this thesis.

This author is persuaded that were it not for the extended ages of these two men, Sir Isaac's system would have long ago been accepted by conservative scholars. Yet strangely, they have instead adopted a chronology in which an entire generation lived to anomalous life spans. This latter is the great unresolved flaw inherent not

---

[1] *Seder Olam, op. cit.*, p. 257.

[2] Newton, *The Chronology of Ancient Kingdoms Amended, op. cit.*, pp. 368, 373.

only in Anderson's solution, but with all others who have not resolved the registers of priests and Levites in Nehemiah 10 and 12. Accordingly, Newton must be seen as a significant improvement.

That learned chronologer envisioned the Lord as granting long life to these two men in order that they might fulfill His desires with regard to the Temple, the wall, and city of Jerusalem similarly to that which He had done in imparting the unusual span of 130 years to Jehoiada the priest nearly four centuries earlier (2 Chron. 24:15). It is urged that aged men with such vigor would have been seen as unique agents of God by their far younger contemporaries; thus their advanced ages would have greatly added to their stature. Significantly, Josephus states that Ezra "died an old man"[1] and says Nehemiah died at a "great age."[2]

If, therefore, "Artaxerxes" were Longimanus as this author and nearly all other researchers hold, Sir Isaac Newton was correct for the chronology must then place both the 10th and 12th chapters of Nehemiah in the first year of Cyrus (as will be demonstrated below). By the context, no other way is seen at this time to keep the two registers from being separated by about 91 years. Consequently, Isaac Newton's system, used in concert with the pro-regency dates for Artaxerxes Longimanus as required by Thucydides and Charon of Lampsacus (Ussher et al., Charts 5 and 5c), is taken as the correct refinement and is believed by this author to reflect the actual history.[3]

Let us now apply this and consider the logic involved in establishing the correct chronology for the Books of Ezra and Nehemiah as depicted on page 245. The problem revolves around the proper chronological placement of the six rectangular blocks containing the Nehemiah passages 7:5–12:9 (left side). First, we observe that chapters of Ezra are placed above those of

Nehemiah on the diagram and that the block containing Ezra 2:1–3:3, 5 and 6 has been arranged directly above Nehemiah 7:5–73a in the first year of Cyrus. To this all scholars agree, as the context unmistakably demands it. The same may be said for the Nehemiah 12:1–9 block. All agree that the context also places these passages in the first year of Cyrus. These two Nehemiah blocks have been crosshatched alike to so designate this agreement in placement.

The problem is that modern workers have uniformly placed Nehemiah 7:73b–11:36 on the far right between the Neh. 1:1–7:4 and Neh. 12:27–13:3 blocks (the down arrow location) in accordance with their natural sequence in the Book of Nehemiah. However, such is not the correct chronological position.

Our study has established that many of the priests and Levites who returned with Zerubbabel in the first year of Cyrus as listed in Neh. 12:1–9 are the same as many of those listed within the contextually consistent Neh. 9:1–10:39 block (pages 245–246). Therefore, the Neh. 9:1–10:39 block (flagged by wider spaced crosshatches in the opposite direction of the former two mentioned crosshatched blocks) must be kept between the first two previously mentioned crosshatched blocks. This fixes the Neh. 9:1–10:39 passages of Scripture as also being in the first year of Cyrus (536 BC) and establishes the true chronological positioning of all three hatched blocks.

With these in place, note that the Nehemiah 11:1–36 narrative sequentially as well as contextually fits as placed between the Neh. 9:1–10:39 and Neh. 12:1–9 blocks. Next, we observe that Ezra 3:4 and Neh. 8:13–18 both speak of a Feast of Tabernacles (also Neh. 7:73b–8:12 speaks of a seventh month). The positioning of the various blocks thus far makes the conclusion that these are one and the same most compelling.

Now it may be clearly seen that the verses are not speaking of two different seventh months which transpire in different years, as nearly all modern scholarship would have us believe. They are the same Feast in the same year. This deduction is confirmed by Neh. 8:17: "And all the congregation of them who were come again out of the captivity made booths ..." Such

---

[1] Josephus, *Antiquities*, op. cit., XI, 5, 5.

[2] *Ibid.*, XI, 5, 8.

[3] Of course, the extended ages for Ezra and Nehemiah necessitated by Newton's (and now Jones') explanation does remain bothersome for some as it places us back where the problem began which tempts most to again ignore context and return to the "two Ezras, two Nehemiahs" scenario. Another possible solution is given in Appendix A, page 267 ff.

would be meaningless if 91 years had elapsed since Ezra 3:4 as nearly all of the returnees would surely have died during the interim. Seeing this avoids the unlikely placing of Neh. 7:73a around 91 years before 7:73b – which was always a most awkward handling of the 73rd verse.

Finally, the Neh. 7:73b–8:12 block contextually fits between the Neh. 7:5–73a and the Neh. 8:13–18 blocks. Now we find that the entire Neh. 7:5–12:9 section, not merely the first and sixth blocks, chronologically moves as a unit to the first year of Cyrus. Blocks 2–5 are not located many years later in the 20th year of Artaxerxes (445 BC by Anderson's reckoning or c. 454 by this study) as all modern scholarship holds. The reason for this is clear. Had all the data been given in chronological order, the historical narrative in the Book of Ezra would have been obscured.

As placed, the story is allowed to freely flow and is not lost amid all the lengthy lists, etc. contained in the six Nehemiah blocks – which have been placed out of sequence for the sake of continuity. Nehemiah 7 repeats Ezra 2:1–70 to enable us to chronologically position Nehemiah 7:5–12:9. Decisively, we observe that Nehemiah 6:15–7:4 ends the first block of the Nehemiah data (1:1–7:4) at the completion of the city wall and the chronology of the Nehemiah 12:27–13:3 block follows with the account of the dedication of that very wall!

b. Summation of the Ezra-Nehemiah Predicament

The chronology of the Books of Ezra and Nehemiah in use today by nearly all scholars, Christian or secular, is not tenable. The presence of an Ezra and a Nehemiah at the beginning and end of these books has long created a problem as the history spans from the first year of Cyrus (536 BC) to at least the 32nd year of a Persian monarch designated as "Artaxerxes." Although his identification was long held in debate, for the past several centuries he has commonly been identified as Artaxerxes I Longimanus, placing the 20th year of his rule at c. 445 BC and his 32nd as 433.

As Ezra and Nehemiah are specified to be among the leaders who returned from the Babylonian captivity in 536 BC with Zerubbabel,

their minimal ages would have exceeded 120 by even Artaxerxes' 20th year (536 − 445 = 91 + 30). Yet the biblical record reveals that by this time men's normal life spans were that of today (Psa. 90:10). Although Walter Williams, the last Confederate survivor of the American Civil War,[1] died in 1959 at 117, Carey White in 1991 at 115, a Japanese woman in 1986 at 120,[2] and nearly 5,000 individuals in the Caucasus Mountain region of Russia were documented as attaining 100 years with some becoming 110 to 141 years along with equal and even greater claims for Indians in the mountains of Ecuador,[3] most scholars have not been able to accept such extended life spans for Ezra and Nehemiah.

The result is that, in the main, the predicament has been managed by assuming that there must be two different Ezras and Nehemiahs, despite the fact that the context seems to indicate that they are one and the same. Inasmuch as it has been undeniably demonstrated that there are not merely two men involved in the problem, these scholars have wrongly assumed that two Ezras and Nehemiahs solves the dilemma.

Comparing the lists of the leaders of the priests and Levites in Nehemiah 10 and 12 which are supposedly separated by 91 years leaves the traditional modern solution, dealing as it does with only Ezra and Nehemiah, totally inadequate. Unless one chooses to believe the preposterous alternative that in two successive generations the leaders of a nation just happen to have the same names and titles, they must now deal with the fact that although they have removed the great age problem by "creating" two Ezras and Nehemiahs, they have not at all

---

[1] George Gipe, *Last Time When*, (New York: World Almanac Pub., 1981), p. 272. Walter Williams age was disputed by William Marvel in the February 1991 *Blue & Gray* magazine. Albert Woolson, a Union drummer boy, died 2 August, 1956 at 109. Jones Morgan, probably the last survivor of the Spanish American War (1898), died August 29, 1993 at age 110. He joined the army just before his 16th birthday and was given the duties of cook as well as tending the Roughriders' horses.

[2] *The 1992 Guiness Book of Records*, Donald McFarlan, et°al. eds., (NY: Bantam Books.). The Japanese woman, Shigechiyo Izumi, is given as 120 years and 237 days old.

[3] Leaf, Alex. M.D., "Every Day is a Gift When You Are Over 100," *National Geographic*, vol. 143, no.1, Jan. 1973, pp. 93–119.

noticed or dealt with the excessive age question concerning this entire generation of leaders (and population in general). The difficulty is much larger than just that of Nehemiah and Ezra.

As Sir Robert Anderson did not take this matter into account, those who utilize his solution for the 483 (490) year Daniel 9:25 prophecy simply fail to unravel the issue (see page 225 ff.) and secure the proper chronology. Although Sir Isaac Newton recognized the full extent of the conundrum and formulated a solution with regard to the Books of Ezra and Nehemiah which reduced the ages of the priests and Levites on the Nehemiah 10 and 12 registers to conform to the normal range thereby constructing an improvement over the traditional scheme, he knowingly left Ezra and Nehemiah as having attained ages 120 and older.[1]

Because of this, the vast majority of today's scholars find Newton's solution unsatisfactory. However, this author deems it as not only an acceptable answer[2] but a most meritorious piece of insight and revelation. Indeed, it appears that Azariah (IV), son of Hilkiah and Grandfather of Ezra, lived to the age of around 114, possibly older.[3]

---

[1] Of course, the proposal given in Appendix A whereupon the biblical "Artaxerxes" were a Persian king reigning before Longimanus resolves all these excessive age problems regardless of whose system is used with relation to the 483-year prophecy. Moreover, the fifth chart displays both solutions for comparison. The upper solution is the newly author modified Ussher-Thucydides explanation whereby Artaxerxes Longimanus entered into a pro-regency with Xerxes of Marathon around 473 BC (also see page 237). The lower dashed alternative scenario depicts Xerxes I as "Artaxerxes" acting in concert on the throne with Darius (see Appendix A, page 267, Anderson's is portrayed as the upper possibility on Chart 6 for comparison).

[2] A recent challenge was issued to Newton's resolution. Comparing the 38 wall-builders named in Nehemiah 3:1–32 with the 84 covenant-signers in Nehemiah 10:1–27, the scholar taking issue concluded that "some sixteen of the wall-builders were also covenant-signers." As Newton placed Nehemiah 10 in 536 BC and Nehemiah 3 in 445 (454 by my study), a "fatal blow" to the Newton-Jones solution was perceived as the matching groups would again be separated by 91 years (continued p. 251).

[3] Azariah's high priesthood must have begun c. 610 BC and terminated not long before the 586 BC exile or c. 594 BC for Seraiah, his son and Ezra's father, was the chief priest whom Nebuchadnezzar slew at Riblah when he took Jerusalem (1 Chron. 6:13–14; 2 Kings 25:18–22; Jer.

c. Closing Remarks Relevant to Chart 5

Chart 5a is merely Chart 5 with all documentation removed to yield a shorter, simplified version. Displaying the Nisan year positioning as well as the vast number of control points for "hands-on" study, Chart 5c is the most detailed, yet uncluttered, presentation of the divided monarchy period.

We close this segment by noting that when the calculations of Sir Robert Anderson and Dr. Hoehner are corrected to the *solar* year by simply multiplying the 483 solar years of the Daniel 9:25 prophecy by 365.242199 (the days in a solar year), we obtain a 176,412-day span rather than their 173,880 duration. If we take the 9:25 fulfillment as being when our Lord entered Jerusalem on 10 Nisan (March 31, AD 30 Gregorian, see calendar on page 273) riding on the donkey's colt,[4] as did both Anderson and Hoehner, and number back 176,412 days we come to 14 Nisan (Passover day) 454 BC – the day Artaxerxes issued the famous decree.[5]

Finally, a graphic summation outlining the Daniel 9:25 prophecy of 483 years from the 20th year of Artaxerxes Longimanus unto Messiah, the Prince, is submitted on pages 253–255. The illustration on page 258 depicts the complex family relationships between the Persians, Medes, Babylonians, and Assyrians. Its synthesis and production was a natural consequence of the Persian study required while documenting and analyzing the relevant data regarding the chronological synchronization of much of the period covered on the fifth chart.

52:24–27; Ezra 7:1–6). Yet Azariah is recorded as still alive 74 years later and "ruler of the house of God" (cp. 2 Kings 25:18, "2nd priest") at the return in 536 BC when Jeshua his great grandson is the high priest (Ezra 3:2, cp. Hag. 1:1). Were he 30 years old in 610, he would be c.104 at the return (610–536 = 74 + 30) and c.114 had he been 40 upon attaining his high priesthood – 124 if when 50. Remember, Josephus described Ezra as dying "an old man" (*Antiq.* XI, 5, 5) and Nehemiah as having lived to a "great age" (*Antiq.* XI, 5, 8).

[4] This was Christ's final official offer of himself as King and Messiah in fulfillment of Zech. 9:9 (compare Luke 19:35–38).

[5] Nehemiah 2:1 reads simply "in the month Nisan" which has been assumed by all as 1 Nisan. The uncertainty of this date has now been solved. Thus, the edict was given on 14 Nisan 454 BC, fulfilled 483 solar years later on 10 Nisan AD 30 and Christ died 14 Nisan AD 30.

(Herod's lunar eclipse in 1 BC, continued from page 209) Grant R. Jeffrey, for example, has recently argued this position [*Armageddon: Appointment With Destiny,* (Toronto, Ontario: Frontier Research Pub., 1988), pp. 225–227]. Based upon Eusebius the historian's appeal to the then (AD 315) still extant Roman governmental records which he used to prove that Jesus was born in Bethlehem at the time of the Luke 2:1–6 census and Justin Martyr's statement that the census records were available in his day (c. AD 155) which could verify the truth of Christ's prophesied birth in that same city [*The First Apology, Ante-Nicene Fathers,* Roberts and Donaldson, eds., (Grand Rapids, MI: Eerdmans Pub. Co., 1985]), ch. xxxiv, p. 174.], Jeffrey holds that Dionysius probably had access to records which allowed him to determine that Christ was born the year before AD 1 (i.e., 1 BC as there is no year "zero").

Jeffrey noted that one of the major reasons scholars had adjusted the date of Christ's Nativity back to at least 4 BC was their belief that Cyrenius (Quirinius) had ruled as governor of Syria from 7–4 BC (or 10–7, Ramsay). Citing Augustus Zumpt (1854, Anderson, *The Coming Prince, op. cit.,* pp. 92–93), Jeffrey maintained that Cyrenius (the administrator of the taxing registration in Luke 2:1–3) was governor of Syria twice. Others who likewise support the 1 BC date for the lunar eclipse concur. Many of these further cite Sir William Ramsay who, on the basis of inscriptional evidence, also determined that Cyrenius was twice governor of Syria [*The Bearing of Recent Discoveries on the Trustworthiness of the New Testament,* (London: Hodder and Stoughton, 1915), pp. 275–300].

In particular, Dr. Zumpt determined that Cyrenius' first term of office was from the close of 4 BC to 1 BC (*Das Geburtsjahr Christi,* Leipzig: 1869), and Sir Robert Anderson noted that Merivale unreservedly adopted those findings in his Roman history [Charles Merivale, *History of the Romans under the Empire,* 7 Vols., (New York: D. Appleman & Co., 1896)]. If this is correct, no contradiction exists between the time of Cyrenius' first governorship (4 BC to 1 BC) and the census of Luke 2:1–3 as having occurred during 1 BC as calculated by Dionysius.

Interestingly, after 11 pages of detailed discussion, Hoehner concluded that the exact date of the census could not be determined with precision but that it was probably taken sometime between 6 and 4 BC (*Chronological Aspects of the Life of Christ, op. cit.,* pages 13–23). Regardless, in order to uphold their position, champions from both sides invariably must appeal to other data (especially Josephus).

Moreover after considerable investigation into this matter, this author acknowledges that although the data seems to best testify as to a 4 BC birth year for the Lord Jesus, almost as strong a case could be made for the 1 BC date. Moreover, much can be said in its favor such that if somehow we were to come to "know" that the latter were indeed the actual birth year, there are enough conflicting and/or contradicting statements recorded in Josephus and other secular sources that the correcting adjustments could readily be made and accepted. It is precisely this circumstance that served as one of the major factors in leading me to conclude that an "absolute" chronology and/or harmony of the Gospels was unobtainable. Nevertheless, a very reliable "standard" of either is achievable.

* * * * * * * * * * * * *

(Andrews defends 25 December birth date for Christ, continued from page 210) Taking Luke's 1:5 statement that Zacharias "was of the course of Abijah" coupled with the fact, as we shall explain later within this study, that the priests were divided into 24 courses each of which officiated in its turn for a week at the Temple twice during the year (1 Chron. 24:1–19; Josephus, *Antiquities,* 7, 14, 7), Andrews states: "We need therefore only to know a definite time at which any one of the courses was officiating to be able to trace the succession. Such a datum we find in the Talmudical statements, supported by Josephus (*Wars,* 6, 4, 5), that at the destruction of the Temple by Titus on the 4th August, 823 (AUC or YOR, i.e., AD 70 on the 10th day of Ab, the 5th Jewish month, FNJ), the first class had just entered on its course. Its period of service was from the evening of the 4th August, which was the Sabbath, to the evening of the following Sabbath, on the 11th August. We can now easily compute backward, and ascertain as what time in any given year each class was officiating."

Andrews then took the year 749 (AUC or YOR) as the year of Christ's birth and 748 as the year of the appearance of the angel to Zacharias at which time he announced John's conception. The two periods of service for the course of Abijah for 748 were computed by him [and others such as Henry Browne, *Ordo Saeclorum, op. cit.,* p. 35 and Edward Greswell, *Dissertations upon the Principles and Arrangement of a Harmony of the Gospels,* 3 Vols., (Oxford, Eng: 1837), Vol. 1, p. 434] to be the week 17–23 of April and again from 3–9 October.

After a well documented defense in which he concluded that the Luke 2:8 passage did not preclude the possibility of the shepherds being in the field "keeping watch over their flocks by night" in the month of December (pages 16–18, also Hoehner p. 26), Andrews went on to show that if the 2nd course of 748 were the correct one, as it well may have been, and one counted forward 15 months from 3–9 October it would place the Lord's birth between the middle of December, 749 and the middle of January, 750. As a more definite result could not be obtained, Andrews went on to justify the acceptance of 25 December as the date of the Lord's birth based mainly on the "voice of tradition" [pages 18–22, also Finegan, *Handbook of Biblical Chronology, op. cit.,* p. 259].

As a priest and Pharisee who fought in the AD 70 war in which the Temple was destroyed, Josephus' date for that event should not be doubted. However, my research (which has not been inconsiderable) leaves me totally unable to verify and/or accept the Talmudic statement [Andrews does not give the reference; it is Mishna iii, 298, 3, see Browne, *Ordo Saeclorum, op. cit.,* p. 33] that the first course could have had either of its administrations begin 10 Ab (see page 211, fn. 4, paragraph 2). Thus, the above seems flawed at the onset.

* * * * * * * * * * * * *

(Hislop on Nimrod and the Tower of Babel, continued from page 211) Apparently when Nimrod (a black) died, Semiramis became pregnant out of wedlock. The child, like its father, was white.

Semiramis acting to save the moment declared that Nimrod's spirit had become one with the sun (incarnated with the sun) and that he had come to her in the night so that she had miraculously conceived a god-son. As the first mortal to be so deified, Nimrod thus became the actual "father of the gods." Semiramis presented the infant to the people and hailed him as the promised "seed of the woman" — the deliverer. Thus was introduced the "mystery" of the mother and the child, a form of idolatry that is older than any other known to man. The rites were secret. Only the initiated were permitted to know its mysteries, and it (along with all of its "offspring" cults) became known as various "mystery" religions. The whole system of the secret Mysteries of Babylon was intended to glorify a dead man while Semiramis gained glory from her dead husband's "deification." The people did not want to retain God in their knowledge, but preferred some visible object of worship. Wherever the Negro aspect of Nimrod became an obstacle to his worship it was taught that Nimrod had reappeared in the person of his fair-complected, supernaturally conceived son (Hislop, p. 69; Chaldeans believed in transmigration and reincarnation); thus the father and son were one. It was Satan's attempt to delude mankind with a counterfeit imitation that was so much like the truth that man would not know the real Seed of the woman when He came in the fullness of time.

Eventually this mystery religion spread from Babylon to all the surrounding nations. Everywhere the symbols were the same. The image of "the queen of heaven" (Semiramis, Jer. 44:19, 25; compare Isa. 47:5 where she is referred to as "the" or "our lady" — notre dame in French) with the babe in her arms was seen everywhere. It became the mystery religion of the seafaring Phoenicians and they carried it to the ends of the earth. It was known as Baal (Nimrod, the sun-god) worship in Phoenicia where the mother was known as Astoreth and the child as Tammuz (Tammuz Adonis). In Egypt the cult was known as that of Osiris, Isis and Horus. The mother and child were worshiped as Aphrodite and Eros in Greece, Venus and Cupid in Italy (in Rome the child was formerly called Jupiter). The Chinese called the mother goddess Shingmoo or the "Holy Mother." She is pictured with child in arms and rays of glory around her head (Hislop, p. 21). Among the Druids, the "Virgo-Paritura" was worshiped as the "Mother of God." In India, she was known as Indrani. In and near India, the mother and child were known as Devaki and Krishna; in Asia they were Cybele and Deoius. They were known by many other names in other parts of the world, but regardless of her name and place, she was the wife of Baal, the virgin mother (Hebrew = alma mater), the queen of heaven who bore a child although she supposedly never conceived. The mother and child were called by different names, due to the dividing of the languages at Babel. Over time, some of the rites and parts of the doctrine and story varied from place to place and cult to cult, but the essentials always remained the same.

Allied with this central mystery were countless lesser mysteries such as the teachings of purgatorial purification after death, salvation by countless sacraments such as sprinkling with holy water, priestly absolution, the offering of round (sun disks) cakes to the queen of heaven (Jer. 7:16–18; 44:15–30), the dedication of virgins to the gods, and weeping for Tammuz for a period of 40 days prior to the festival of Ishtar (Easter) to commemorate Ishtar's (another name for Semiramis) having received her son back from the dead. Tammuz was said to have been slain by a wild boar (the traditional Christmas pig) and afterward brought back to life. The egg became a sacred symbol depicting the mystery of his "resurrection." The evergreen tree became the symbol of his never ending life and birth at the winter solstice, when a boar's head was eaten (ham on New Year's day) in memory of his conflict. The burning of a Yule log always accompanied this winter celebration. The ankh, a distinctive cross, was the sacred symbol of Tammuz. The first letter of his name, it signified the life-giving principle (Ezek. 8, weeping for Tammuz). This ancient pagan symbol did not originate with Christianity as most suppose.

The mystery religion of Babylon, which had begun under Nimrod's direction until its dispersal at the Tower of Babel (Gen. 10 and 11; Isa. 47), continued over the centuries to flourish in the "land of Shinar." When the city of Babylon fell in 539 BC, the high priest fled with a group of initiates and their sacred vessels and images to Pergamos (Rev. 2:12–17; see J.D. Pentecost, pp. 365–367, where he cites H.A. Ironside). There, the symbol of the serpent was set up as the emblem of the hidden wisdom. From there, many of them crossed the sea and settled in the Poe Valley of northeast Italy where the Etruscans lived. When Rome conquered the Etruscans, the Etruscans brought their Babylonian cult religion to Rome where the child was known as Mithras (the mediator). Thus, when Christianity came to Rome, the whorish cult, the counterfeit, was waiting to join in an unholy union with it. These mystery cult teachings eventually invaded the Catholic church which is still full of its traditions, the roots of which lie deep in paganism. Every Roman emperor belonged to this cult. Everyone of means (the upper class) was an initiate. It was the "country club" to which to belong, much as is Freemasonry in many parts of the world today (The Lodge drew its basic teachings from various "denominations" within this mystery religion. The major writers within Freemasonry freely confess this, but almost no one reads these works to so learn.).

* * * * * * * * * * * * *

(A recent challenge to Newton-Jones solution, continued from page 249) Were these indeed the same men, the challenger would be correct in his assessment. However, as these distinguished men bear Hebrew names that were especially common for the period in question, repetitions should be expected.

Moreover, as Neh. 10:1–27 and Neh. 12:1–26 show (see comparison, page 242), the Scriptures are peculiarly consistent in ascribing the titles of "priest" and "Levite" to the men found therein. Thus, the norm is that these titles accompany the name in each different narrative, at least at the initial identification. If the designation is not given, it is almost always because it is not appropriate. As Neh. 3 precedes Neh. 10, the general absence of titles in chapter 3 strongly implies that such do not pertain to these men – hence they are not the titled men in Neh. 10. Applying these observations to the following chart, we note:

(1) Out of 22 possible correlations, eight are impossible (i.e., 6, 13, 14, 15, 16, 20, and either 9 or 10 as well as 21

or 22 for both cannot be the Hashub and Hananiah of Neh. 10:23), and #'s 11 and 12 are nearly so [The Hanuns in #'s 11 and 12 are not the same as any of the Hanans in Neh. 10:10, 22, 26. The spelling is also different in the Hebrew (חנון vs. חנן), and the Hanans are either Chiefs or a Levite] [#16, Bavai is not Bebai the Chief; their names are also spelled differently in the Hebrew]. Furthermore, 1, 3, 7, 8, 17, and 18 are doubtful or uncertain matches — thus 16 do not conclusively equate.

(2) Five others could be the same men but cannot be confirmed to equate; thereby they cannot be said to resolve the matter with certainty [i.e., 4, 5, 19, and (again) either 9 or 10 and 21 or 22 but not both. Binnui (#19), the son of Henadad (and brother of Bavai, 3:18), is not conclusively Binnui the Levite "of the sons of Henadad." Indeed, "The son of Henadad" and "of the sons of Henadad" are not equivalent terms.].

(3) Meremoth (number 2 on the chart) the wall builder in Artaxerxes' 20th year and son of Urijah, the son of Koz (priest family without genealogy; Ezra 2:61, Neh. 7:63) is almost certainly Meremoth, son of Uriah (Hebrew spelling the same as Urijah) the priest who came to Jerusalem with Ezra in Artaxerxes' 7th year (Ezra 8:33). He also could be Meremoth the priest of Neh. 10:5.

However likely this may appear, such cannot be said to be an undeniable identification. Moreover, as none of the other comparisons can be substantiated with certainty, the likelihood of their being the same man must be seen as greatly diminished. Hence, there is no compelling reason to conclude that they are not different men separated in time by a generation or more. Accordingly, the fabric of the Newton-Jones solution remains intact.

Wall Builders in Artaxerxes 20th Year Neh. 3:1–32					Covenant-Signers Neh. 10:1–27		
1	Zaccur	3:2	Son of Imri		Zaccur	10:12	Levite
2	Meremoth	3:4,21	Son of Urijah, of Koz-Ezr8:33	Priest	Meremoth	10:5	Priest
3	Meshullam	3:4, 3:30	Son of Berechiah, son of Meshezabeel, cp. Neh. 10:21 - Chief Meshezabeel		Meshullam	10:7	Priest
4	Meshullam	3:6	Son of Besodeiah – old gate		Meshullam	10:20	Chiefs
5	Zadok	3:4	Son of Baana		Zadok	10:21	Chiefs
6	Zadok	3:29	Son of Immer	Priest			
7	Hattush	3:10	Son of Hashabniah		Hattush	10:4	Priest
8	Malchijah	3:11	Son of Harim		Malchijah	10:3	Priest
9	Hashub	3:11	Son of Pahathmoab		Hashub	10:23	Chiefs
10	Hashub	3:23					
11	Hanun	3:13	repaired Valley Gate		Hanan (8:7)	10:10	Levite
12	Hanun	3:30	6th Son of Zalaph		Hanan	10:22	Chiefs
13					Hanan	10:26	Chiefs
14	Rehum	3:17	Son of Bani	Levite	Rehum	10:25	Chiefs
15	Hashabiah	3:17	Ruler of half of Keilah		Hashabiah	10:11	Levite
16	Bavai	3:18	Son of Henadad, " " "		Bebai	10:15	Chiefs
17	Baruch	3:20	Son of Zabbai		Baruch	10:6	Priest
18	Azariah	3:23	Son of Maaseiah, cp Neh 8:7	Levite?	Azariah	10:2	Priest
19	Binnui	3:24	Son of Henadad, brother of Bavai (#16)		Binnui	10:9	Levite, of the sons of Henadad
20	Shemaiah	3:29	Son of Shechaniah, keeper of the east gate	Levite	Shemaiah	10:8	Priest
21	Hananiah	3:8	Son of one of the apothecaries		Hananiah	10:23	Chiefs
22	Hananiah	3:30	Son of Shelemiah				

Finding The 20th Year of Artaxerxes – Neh. 2:1
The Beginning of the Commandment for the
69 Weeks of Daniel – Dan 9:25

BC

486	(AC)	Xerxes became king of Persia, his year of <u>accession</u>
485	(1)	
484	(2)	
483	(3)	
482	(4)	
481	(5)	
480	(6)	
479	(7)	
478	(8)	
477	(9)	
476	(10)	
475	(11)	
474	(12)	Xerxes 12th year – Artaxerxes made pro-rex – (his accession year)
473	(1)	Artaxerxes first official year over the Jews* (*begin* 20-year count here)
472	(2)	
471	(3)	
470	(4)	
469	(5)	
468	(6)	
467	(7)	
466	(8)	
465	(9)	Xerxes dies in the 21st official year of his reign
464	(10)	First official year of Artaxerxes sole reign (see Chart 5c)
463	(11)	
462	(12)	
461	(13)	
460	(14)	
459	(15)	
458	(16)	
457	(17)	
456	(18)	
455	(19)	

454	(20)	In 20th year of Artaxerxes – decree to Nehemiah to rebuild Jerusalem. Neh 2:1, 2:3, 2:8

453
452
451
450
449
448
447
446
445 *445 BC is commonly taken as the 20th year by wrongly starting
the count at 464. For Daniel's 69 weeks, it is imperative to know
that 454 BC was the true 20th year of Artaxerxes reign over the Jews.

Daniel 9:25 – 69 Weeks

Neh 2:1, 2:3, 2:8 – The commandment to rebuild Jerusalem
was given to Nehemiah by Artaxerxes in the year 454 BC.
(See Chart 5 proving 20th year of Artaxerxes)

Note – The Jews had:
Weeks of days = 7 days
Weeks of weeks = 7 weeks
Weeks of years = 7 years

Daniel 9:25 refers to weeks of years
Three score and two weeks = 62 weeks
7 weeks + 62 weeks = 69 weeks (weeks of years)
69 weeks of years means 69 "7's" or 483 years
Daniel 9:25 says –
It would be 483 years from the commandment to rebuild
the city of Jerusalem to Messiah the Prince.

Counting 483 years from 454 BC puts us in 30 AD

454 BC			
453 BC	(1)		
452 BC	(2)		
451 BC	(3)		
↓	↓		
1 BC	(453)		
1 AD	(454)	16 AD	(469)
2 AD	(455)	17 AD	(470)
3 AD	(456)	18 AD	(471)
4 AD	(457)	19 AD	(472)
5 AD	(458)	20 AD	(473)
6 AD	(459)	21 AD	(474)
7 AD	(460)	22 AD	(475)
8 AD	(461)	23 AD	(476)
9 AD	(462)	24 AD	(477)
10 AD	(463)	25 AD	(478)
11 AD	(464)	26 AD	(479)
12 AD	(465)	27 AD	(480)
13 AD	(466)	28 AD	(481)
14 AD	(467)	29 AD	(482)
15 AD	(468)	30 AD	(483)

[Simple check: 454 BC + AD 30 – 1 (no year zero) = 483 years]

Jesus came into the city to be declared Prince (or King) on the 10th
day of Nisan in the year AD 30. On the 14th of Nisan He was
crucified. On the 17th of Nisan He resurrected.

Daniel had prophesied the beginning and the end of a 483-year
period of time at least 80 years before it started!!

254

Finding The 15th Year of Tiberius –
The Year Jesus Began His Ministry – Luke 3:1, 23. (inclusive numbering)

AD
12	(1)	Tiberius became co-regent of Rome with Augustus = Emperor
13	(2)	
14	(3)	Tiberius' sole regency – wrong year 1 of Tiberius' reign*
15	(4)	
16	(5)	
17	(6)	
18	(7)	
19	(8)	
20	(9)	
22	(10)	
22	(11)	
23	(12)	
24	(13)	
25	(14)	

26	(15)	Jesus Baptized and tempted in preparation – "about" age 30 Luke 3:23

27	(16)	In 27 AD Jesus' *public* ministry began – age 30 Luke 3:23

28   *28 AD often mistaken as 15th year of Tiberius by starting 15-year count at 14 AD (puts Jesus starting ministry in 30 AD and therefore death/resurrection in 33 AD).

Finding Birth Year of Jesus Based On
Year of Public Ministry Beginning In 27 AD

AGE	YEAR	AGE	YEAR	AGE	YEAR	AGE	YEAR
30	27 AD	22	19 AD	14	11 AD	6	3 AD
29	26 AD	21	18 AD	13	10 AD	5	2 AD
28	25 AD	20	17 AD	12	9 AD	4	1 AD
27	24 AD	19	16 AD	11	8 AD	3	1 BC
26	23 AD	18	15 AD	10	7 AD	2	2 BC
25	22 AD	17	14 AD	9	6 AD	1	3 BC
24	21 AD	16	13 AD	8	5 AD		
23	20 AD	15	12 AD	7	4 AD	BIRTH	4 BC

Finding Death/Resurrection Year Of Jesus Based
On 3 ½ Year Ministry Beginning In 26/27 AD

26 AD	(¼)
27 AD	(1)
28 AD	(2)
29 AD	(3)

30 AD	(¼)	Death/Resurrection

COMPARATIVE DATINGS FOR THE TIMES OF CHRIST JESUS

AM	BC-AD	YEARS OF CHRIST		AUC (YOR)	YEARS OF AUGUSTUS	YEARS OF TIBERIUS
3960	44 BC			710	1	← Julius Caesar
1	43			11	2	slain March15.
2	42			12	3	Augustus (Octavian)
3	41			13	4	succeeds him for 57
4	40			714	5	← Herod made years & c. 6 mos. =
5	39			15	6	king in 714 AUC by / in year 58
6	38			16	7	Rome. According to / (Jos. War, ii, ix, 1;
7	37			17	8	Josephus, he died / Finegan, Handbook
8	36			18	9	37 years later / pp. 217, 226).
9	35			19	10	(Antiq. xvii, 8, 1).
3970	34			720	11	Josephus usually
1	33			21	12	reckoned years from
2	32			22	13	Nisan to Nisan thus
3	31	Battle of Actium		723	14	the death of Herod
4	30			24	15	would be 750 AUC / ← Augustus reigns
5	29			25	16	or 4 BC. / in Egypt upon death
6	28			26	17	of Antony/Cleopatra.
7	27			27	18	← 27 BC, the
8	26			28	19	Senate of Rome
9	25			29	20	voted Ocatvius the
3980	24			730	21	title "Augustus"
1	23			31	22	
2	22			32	23	
3	21			33	24	
4	20			34	25	
5	19			35	26	
6	18			36	27	
7	17			37	28	
8	16			38	29	
9	15			39	30	
3990	14			740	31	
1	13			41	32	
2	12			42	33	
3	11			43	34	
4	10			44	35	
5	9			45	36	
6	8			46	37	
7	7			47	38	
8	6			48	39	
9	5			49	40	
4000	4 BC	The Nativity-Lk.2:1-2 — The age	0 of our Lord	750	41	← Herod dies just / ← Birth of Jesus,
1	3		1	51	42	before Passover and / Irenaeus, Against
2	2		2	52	43	before an eclipse of / Heresies, iii, xxi, 3
3	1	BC	3	53	44	the moon (Jos., Ant. / (c. AD 180).
4004	1 AD	AD - no year zero	4	54	45	xvii, 9, 3; 6, 4). / ← AD reckoning
5	2		5	55	46	begins 4 years too
6	3		6	56	47	late due to error by
7	4		7	57	48	Tiberius adopted / Dionysius Exiguus
8	5		8	58	49	when he arranged
9	6		9	59	50	the calendar of the
4010	7		10	760	51	Christian Era in AD
1	8		11	61	52	532.
2	9	The boy Jesus	12 in the Temple	62	53	
3	10		13	63	54	
4	11		14	64	55	
5	12		15	765	56 the 1st yr. of Tiberius	1 co-rex of Augustus
6	13		16	66	57	2
7	14		17	67	58 19th August, Augustus dies	3 Tiberius sole rex
8	15		18	68		4
9	16		19	69		5
4020	17		20	770		6
1	18		21	71		7
2	19		22	72		8
3	20		23	73		9
4	21		24	74		10
5	22		25	75		11
6	23		26	76		12
7	24		27	77		13
8	25		28	78		14
9	26	John baptizes Jesus — & Satan tempts Him	29 in preparation for	79	His public ministry at the	15 of Tiberius
4030	27	Begin public ministry — the Lord Jesus being	30 years of age in yr.	780	end of the 15th year / beginning of the year	16 of Tiberius
1	28		31	81		17
2	29		32	82		18
4033	30	The Crucifixion year, — the Lord Jesus being	33 years of age in yr.	783	by Roman reckoning in the nineteenth year	19 of Tiberius

AM = *Anno Mundi* = in the year of the world; AUC = *Anno Urbis Conditae* = from the year in which the city of Rome was founded. Above chart adapted and corrected from E.W. Bullinger, *The Companion Bible*, (Grand Rapids, MI: Kregel Pub., 1990), Appendix 179. Remember, the Hebrew year begins around 1 April and thus differs from our calendar by about 3 months (1/4 year).

THE LISTS OF THE RETURNING EXILES IN EZRA 2 AND NEHEMIAH 7

Family Clans	Ezra 2:3–60	Nehemiah 7:8–62	Difference
Parosh	2,172	2,172	
Shephatiah	372	372	
Arah	775	652	−123
Pahath-Moab	2,812	2,818	+6
Elam	1,254	1,254	
Zattu	945	845	−100
Zaccai	760	760	
Bani (Binnui)*	642	648	+6
Bebai	623	628	+5
Azgad	1,222	2,322	+1,100
Adonikam	666	667	+1
Bigvai	2,056	2.067	−11
Adin	454	655	+201
Ater	98	98	
Bezai	323	324	+1
Jorah (Hariph)*	112	112	
Hashum	223	328	+105
Gibbar (Gibeon)*	95	95	
Inhabitants from Towns			
Bethlehem and Netophah	179	188	+9
Anathoth	128	128	
Azmaveth (Beth Azmaveth)*	42	42	
Kiriath-Jearim, Kephirah, and Beeroth	743	743	
Ramah and Geba	621	621	
Micmash	122	122	
Bethel and Ai	223	123	−100
Nebo	52	52	
Magbish **	156	—	−156
The other Elam	1,254	1,254	
Harim	320	320	
Lod, Hadid, and Ono	725	721	−4
Jericho	345	345	
Senaah	3,630	3,930	+300
Priests			
Jedaiah	973	973	
Immer	1,052	1,052	
Pashhur	1,247	1,247	
Harim	1,017	1,017	
Levites	74	74	
Asaph singers	128	148	+20
Gate keepers	139	138	−1
Nethinim and children of Solomon's servants	392	392	
Descendants of Delaiah, Tobiah, and Nekoda	652	642	−10
Totals	29,818	31,089	+1,271

The names in parentheses are the variant spellings in the Book of Nehemiah.

* None of the inhabitants of Magbish actually arrived in Jerusalem. They may have turned back or settled far north of the city.

Note: The list in Ezra 2 is probably that of the returnees taken *before* they departed from Babylon whereas the list found in Nehemiah 7 is that of those who *actually arrived* in Jerusalem. That is, some joined the returning exiles after their departure whereas others may have turned back. The main disparity is that of the Azgad clan. All or part of the 1,100 could also have been among the poor left in the land at the time of the deportation. Small changes could also be due to births/deaths en route.

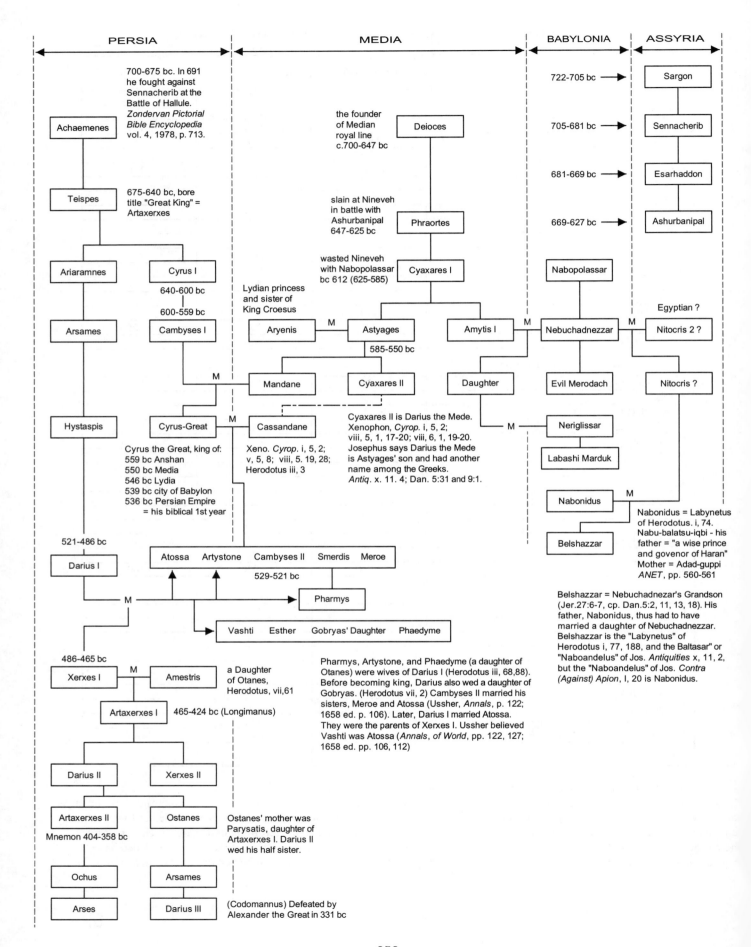

PERSIA	MEDIA	BABYLONIA	ASSYRIA

Achaemenes — 700-675 bc. In 691 he fought against Sennacherib at the Battle of Hallule. *Zondervan Pictorial Bible Encyclopedia* vol. 4, 1978, p. 713.

Teispes — 675-640 bc, bore title "Great King" = Artaxerxes

Ariaramnes

Cyrus I — 640-600 bc

Arsames

Cambyses I — 600-559 bc

Hystaspis

Cyrus-Great — Cyrus the Great, king of:
559 bc Anshan
550 bc Media
546 bc Lydia
539 bc city of Babylon
536 bc Persian Empire
= his biblical 1st year

Deioces — the founder of Median royal line c.700-647 bc

Phraortes — slain at Nineveh in battle with Ashurbanipal 647-625 bc

Cyaxares I — wasted Nineveh with Nabopolassar bc 612 (625-585)

Aryenis — Lydian princess and sister of King Croesus — M — **Astyages** 585-550 bc

Mandane — M — **Cyaxares II**

Cassandane — Xeno. *Cyrop.* i, 5, 2; v, 5, 8; viii, 5. 19, 28; Herodotus iii, 3

Cyaxares II is Darius the Mede. Xenophon, *Cyrop.* i, 5, 2; viii, 5, 1, 17-20; viii, 6, 1, 19-20. Josephus says Darius the Mede is Astyages' son and had another name among the Greeks. *Antiq.* x. 11. 4; Dan. 5:31 and 9:1.

Sargon — 722-705 bc
Sennacherib — 705-681 bc
Esarhaddon — 681-669 bc
Ashurbanipal — 669-627 bc

Nabopolassar

Amytis I — M — **Nebuchadnezzar** — M — **Nitocris 2 ?** Egyptian ?

Daughter — **Evil Merodach** — **Nitocris ?**

M — **Neriglissar**
Labashi Marduk

Nabonidus — M
Belshazzar

Nabonidus = Labynetus of Herodotus. i, 74. Nabu-balatsu-iqbi - his father = "a wise prince and govenor of Haran" Mother = Adad-guppi *ANET*, pp. 560-561

Belshazzar = Nebuchadnezar's Grandson (Jer.27:6-7, cp. Dan.5:2, 11, 13, 18). His father, Nabonidus, thus had to have married a daughter of Nebuchadnezzar. Belshazzar is the "Labynetus" of Herodotus i, 77, 188, and the "Baltasar" or "Naboandelus" of Jos. *Antiquities* x, 11, 2, but the "Naboandelus" of Jos. *Contra (Against) Apion*, I, 20 is Nabonidus.

Darius I — 521-486 bc

Atossa Artystone Cambyses II Smerdis Meroe — 529-521 bc

M — **Pharmys**

Vashti Esther Gobryas' Daughter Phaedyme

Pharmys, Artystone, and Phaedyme (a daughter of Otanes) were wives of Darius I (Herodotus iii, 68,88). Before becoming king, Darius also wed a daughter of Gobryas. (Herodotus vii, 2) Cambyses II married his sisters, Meroe and Atossa (Ussher, *Annals*, p. 122; 1658 ed. p. 106). Later, Darius I married Atossa. They were the parents of Xerxes I. Ussher believed Vashti was Atossa (*Annals, of World*, pp. 122, 127; 1658 ed. pp. 106, 112)

Xerxes I — 486-465 bc — M — **Amestris** — a Daughter of Otanes, Herodotus, vii,61

Artaxerxes I — 465-424 bc (Longimanus)

Darius II **Xerxes II**

Artaxerxes II Mnemon 404-358 bc   **Ostanes**

Ostanes' mother was Parysatis, daughter of Artaxerxes I. Darius II wed his half sister.

Ochus   **Arsames**

Arses   **Darius III** — (Codomannus) Defeated by Alexander the Great in 331 bc

258

CHART SIX

A. GENERAL CHART OVERVIEW

This display is a much embellished form of the first chart. The large print values found on the fourth line from the top represent significant biblical time segments. They are all derived on Chart 1 and explained in the second chapter of this dissertation. Chart 6 is a concise graphic overview of all that has been addressed on the other charts as well as the accompanying treatise. Of course, the entire object of all the time represented on Chart 6 is to go from the Creation and arrive at the small, nearly inconspicuous event in red on the right side – the life span of the Lord Jesus the Christ. In a very real sense, that which has transpired in between these two events has been vanity (Rom.8:20). Yet such is the wisdom of our Father and God in "bringing many sons unto glory" (Heb.2:10).

More specifically, the principal purpose of Chart 6 is to visually display the mathematical outline of Chart 1 by starting at the left side with 4004 BC (or 1 AM) as taken from the first chart (see derivation of Creation date, page 26 ff.). The extreme left side of the sixth chart gives all the scriptural documentation necessary to enable one to graph the patriarchs' lifelines beginning with Adam (life span = 930 years, Gen. 5:5) and displays those listed in Genesis 5 unto the year of the Flood (1656 BC).

Gleaned from the Scriptures on the left, these 1,656 years represent the time span from the birth, fathering, and death of each of the family patriarchs who lived from the Creation to the Flood. Thus the Word of God gives us a continuous uninterrupted genealogy of man's earliest record (defense on Chart 1; also pages 21–41 herein).

Next is depicted a 427-year period portraying the patriarchs' life spans from the Flood to the Covenant with Abraham as recorded in Genesis 10 and 11. This is followed by the 430-year interval from the covenant with Abraham to the Exodus, displaying the interval from 1921 BC to 1491 (Chart 1, see the encampments during the 40 years of wandering on page 262).

Then a 480-year segment (1 Kings 6:1) delineates the span from the Exodus to very early in Solomon's 4th year when he began to build the Temple, (1491 – 1012 BC). The remaining 36 (nearly 37) years of Solomon's 40-year reign beginning, not at the end of his 4th year but *during* the 4th (i.e., 3 years plus 1 month and 2 days, 1 Kings 6:1; 2 Chron. 3:1–2) is then added taking the history to 975 BC (AM 3029). This is the year of Solomon's death and the resulting disruption or schism of the kingdom into the two Kingdoms of Israel and Judah. These figures total 479 complete years, 1 month and 2 days, bringing us *into* the 480th year (pages 72–77).

Chart 6 then visually portrays this division of the kingdom and the 390-year period over which the Kingdom of Judah continued to exist as an entity (Ezek. 4:4–5, defended and explained pages 132–135), terminating about 586 BC. From that point, the 70-year segment of the "desolations," so called as throughout that interval there was no Temple in Jerusalem, brings the study forward to 516 BC, the sixth year of Darius I Hystaspis during which the new Temple was completed (Ezra 6:15).

Beginning at the 20th year of "Artaxerxes" to the time of Christ Jesus, three different interpretations of the Daniel 9:24–27 prophetic 483 (490) year span bring the chronology to its conclusion. The upper line represents the traditional interpretation by Sir Robert Anderson which has held sway among conservative scholars for the past century.

The lower line represents the author's secondary proposal whereby the biblical "Artaxerxes" is Xerxes I who is interpreted as having been installed around 505 BC as pro-regent by his father, Darius I (page 268 ff.). However, as already explained, the most logical and best solution is the author modified Ussher-Thucydides interpretation as portrayed by the middle line which continues directly from the 516 BC termination of the 70-year "desolation" segment to the Cross. (Note, all three honor Ptolemy's Canon.)

Finally, over the years detractors have observed the differing chronological solutions and concluded that the attempt to construct a reliable biblical framework was futile.

Event	Ussher – 1654 AD	Greswell – 1830 AD	F. N. Jones – 2004 AD
Creation	4004 BC	4004 BC	4004 BC
Deluge	2348 BC	2348 BC	2348 BC
Call of Abraham	1921 BC	2004 BC	1921 BC
Exodus	1491 BC	1560 BC	1491 BC
David's accession	1048 BC	1054 BC	1048 BC
Division of the kingdom	975 BC	974 BC	975 BC
Begin 70-year servitude	607 BC	606 BC	606 BC
Birth of Christ	4 BC	4 BC	4 BC
Baptism of Christ	AD 27	AD 27	AD 27
Crucifixion	AD 33	AD 30	AD 30

However, observe from the above chart how comparable the overall results with respect to major events are when varying chronologers working centuries apart approach the task with similar commitments and frames of reference.[1]

B. SPECIAL FEATURES

Several other items on this panoramic display are worthy of note which otherwise might pass unnoticed. First, the books of the Bible are placed near the top and immediately above the dates, events, and men's lives which transpired within their narratives so that it may be seen where they fit in relation and sequence to the unfolding history. In addition, the time span covered by each book has been carefully calculated, thus enabling one to place them at their precise proper location. The time of the writing of some of the books of the prophets is not known and, having been positioned as judiciously as possible, question marks designating their uncertain dates have been supplied.

The amount of time spanned by the events contained in the Book of Genesis is uncommonly conspicuous – that of 2,369 years! Being the "seedbed" for all the major doctrines of the New Testament, it is no small wonder that this book has been the special object of Satan's attacks concerning its validity and reliability over the centuries.

Second, as a result of the placement and length of time spanned by the various books, a peculiar result is that this becomes a visual aid to find-

---

[1] Namely, that God has providentially preserved the entire biblical text without error and that this deposit is found in the Hebrew Masoretic text as well as the Greek *Textus Receptus* New Testament (Ussher's commitment is well known, for Greswell's see: *Dissertation, op. cit.,* vol. I, p. 383 and vol. IV, p. 739 ff. for his dates).

ing where certain events occur in Scripture. For example, if one wishes to read about Saul (1095–1055 BC), he may look directly above Saul's name and learn that his life is recorded in 1 Samuel. Should we wish to study about David's reign as king, we would have to go to 2 Samuel, 1 Chronicles and, to a somewhat lesser degree, the Psalms.

If, however, one desires to read of David's life *before* he became king (i.e., when he slew Goliath or during his flights from Saul), he simply drops down to the lower line and locates the name "David." This represents the portion of David's 70-year lifeline from his birth unto the birth of his son and successor in the direct lineage to Messiah Jesus. Locating that portion of the line before David became king, one merely looks directly above to 1 Samuel.

Finally, the chart has been arranged such that if we begin at Adam and move to the right along his lifeline until he begets Seth (3874 BC), at which point one drops down following along Seth's lifeline to his son Enos. Again, drop down following Enos unto the birth of Cainan, drop down, etc. to Jacob – and we are following the direct family lineage to Messiah Jesus.

A divergence is seen to occur at Jacob. Here the principal direction of the biblical narrative continues through the lives of Joseph, Moses, Joshua, the judges, Saul, David, Solomon, the kings of Judah, etc. to the time of Christ. However, although Joseph received the *birth-right* (the double portion of the inheritance, etc.), Judah received the *blessing* (Gen. 49:8–12; cp. Psa.78:67) meaning that through his lineage would come the Messiah.

Hence, to continue following the Messiah's genealogy, one must drop from Jacob to the

lower line at the year of Judah's birth (1755 BC, Chart 3d) arriving at Judah's lifeline. Then we proceed following the blood line through the births of Perez (Pharez, c. 1721 BC), Hezron (c. 1706 BC), etc. unto Mary and her husband Joseph. Finally, we arrive at the birth and life of Christ Jesus – Creator, Lord, and Savior.

C. ESTABLISHING AND MANAGING CHART LIMITATIONS

Often data is not sufficient to allow for precise computation and positioning of the detailed events associated with the lives of the individuals displayed on the chart. However many times enough information has been recorded such that the estimates, although not precise, are made to conform to very narrow restrictions by other related evidence and hence represent reasonable approximations to the actual dates. For example, Perez's (Pharez) and Hezron's dates are approximate, yet there is much restraining pertinent data available allowing one to set their births within minimal boundaries of inexactness (see Chart 3f).

Still others such as Ram and Amminadab have no recorded controlling parameters from which to draw and Nahshon, Salmon, Boaz, Obed, and Jesse have but little more. Nevertheless, as Nahshon was the prince or leader of the tribe of Judah at the time of the Exodus (Num. 1:4–7, 16, cp. Exo. 6:23; Mat. 1:4) and as Salmon married Rahab, the converted former harlot (Mat. 1:5), reasonably near the fixed year of the entry, some control is available for their positioning (Chart 4a).

Having established the date of the disruption of the monarchy upon the death of Solomon as being 390 years from Nebuchadnezzar's destruction of Jerusalem, David's birth as well as many other events in his life may be determined or very closely approximated (see Chart 4 and pages 99–100). The mathematical restrictions placed on Judah's lineage from Salmon to Boaz, Obed, and Jesse unto the reliable fixed dates associated with David enable one to assign plausible estimates so that approximate birth dates may be assigned carrying the lineage on toward the Cross by filling in the gap over to David. (See Chart 4a where beginning with the 1451 date of the entry and David's birth set at 1085, the years were equally distributed between Salmon, Boaz, Obed and Jesse[1] across that period.)

Scripture records many details concerning the lives of nearly all of the kings of Judah as to when they began to rule relevant to some fixed event or person, the lengths of their reigns and often their ages upon ascending to the throne (Chart 5). This made it possible to compute most of their birth dates allowing for the construction of a secure bridge from Solomon to Jeconiah (Jehoiachin) as displayed at the bottom of Chart 6. In this manner, uncertain birth dates for Abijah and Asa present no real problem for they are confined to a very small time zone and surrounded by the "absolute" dates associated with Rehoboam (see boxed diagram on the right side of Chart 4) and Jehoshaphat.

Zerubbabel, prince of Judah and a direct descendant to Messiah Jesus through the kingly lineage (1 Chron. 3:17–18; cp. Matthew 1:12–16), was appointed governor of Judah in the first year of Cyrus (536 BC, Ezra 1:1, 8; 2:2; 5:2; etc.) and was still so functioning during the sixth year of Darius I (516 BC, Ezra 6:15, cp. Zech. 4:9) at which time the second Temple was completed. Placing him accordingly (Chart 5) also has the effect of restricting Shealtiel to within narrow limits. Finally, all the remaining descendants for whom no further information is known other than their being in Jesus' royal genealogy as given in the first chapter of Matthew were listed and equally distributed, thereby completing the family lineage connection from Adam unto the birth of Christ Jesus.

---

[1] Deeming the Hebrew text flawed, Dr. Hales supposes some names of ancestors to have been lost and would add four between Obed and Jesse: *A New Analysis of Chronology, op. cit.*, vol. III, p. 46.

THE 40 YEAR WILDERNESS ENCAMPMENTS
From Egypt to Sinai – 1491 BC

	Exodus 12-19	Numbers 33
1	Depart from Rameses (Exo. 12:37)	Depart from Rameses – after midnite Abib 15 (Num. 33:3, Exo. 12:29)
2	Succoth (Exo. 12:37)	Arrive at Succoth – Abib 15 (Num. 33:5)
3	Etham (Exo. 13:20)	Etham – Abib 16 (Num. 33:6)
4	Pi-hahiroth (Exo. 14:2)	Pi-hahiroth – Abib 17 (Num. 33:7)
5	Pass through the Red Sea (Exo. 14:22)	Pass through the Red Sea – Abib 17 (Num. 33:8)
6	3 day march into wilderness of Shur to Marah (Exo. 15:22-23)	3 day march into wilderness of Etham to Marah (Num. 33:8)
7	Elim (Exo. 15:27)	Elim (Num. 33:9)
8		Encampment by the Red Sea (Num. 33:10)
9	Wilderness of Sin (Exo. 16:1)	Wilderness of Sin (Num. 33:11)
10		Dophkah (Num. 33:12)
11		Alush (Num. 33:13)
12	Rephidim (Exo. 17:1)	Rephidim (Num. 33:14)
13	Wilderness of Sinai (Exo. 19:1; arrive 3rd day, 3rd month)	Sinai (Num. 33:15) depart 1 yr 1 mo + 20 days after the Exodus (Num. 10:11)

From Sinai to Kadesh the First time – 1490 BC

	Numbers 10-20	Numbers 33
14	Kibroth-hattaavah (Num. 11:34). Taberah = the name of the outermost edge of the camp (10:12, 11:3, Deut. 9:22), hence the omission of Taberah in Num. 33. Note: nothing is said about removing from Taberah to Kibroth-hattaavah	Kibroth-hattaavah (Num. 33:16)
15	Hazeroth (Num. 11:35)	
16	Wilderness of Paran (Num. 12:16; Deut. 1:1-2)	Terrible Wilderness near the Mt of the Amorites (Deut. 1:19)
17	**Kadesh** in Wilderness of Paran, arrive c. mo 5 (Num. 12:16, 13:20-26) from which they wander for 38 years (Num. 14:25 ff; Deut. 1:46, 2:1)	**Rithmah** (Num. 33:18) = the name of the encampment on the south side outskirt of the town of Kadesh (Keil) – rebelled in mo 6.
18		Rimmon-parez (Num. 33:19)
19		Libnah (Num. 33:20)
20		Rissah (Num. 33:21)
21		Kehelathah (Num. 33:22)
22		Mt Shapher (Num. 33:23)
23		Haradah (Num. 33:24)
24	The trail of 17 encampments	Makheloth (Num. 33:25)
25	between the first and second	Tahath (Num. 33:26)
26	encampments at Kadesh ──────────────────▶	Tarah (Num. 33:27)
27		Mithcah (Num. 33:28)
28		Hashmonah (Num. 33:29)
29		Moseroth (Num. 33:30)
30		Bene-Jaakan (Num. 33:31)
31		Hor-hagidgad (Num. 33:32)
32		Jotbathah (Num. 33:33)
33		Ebronath (Num. 33:34)
34		Ezion-geber (Num. 33:35)

Return to Kadesh Abib 1452 BC and thence to the Jordan River – Crossed Abib 10, 1451 BC

	Numbers 20, 21; Deut 1, 2, 10	Numbers 33
35	Return to Kadesh – in the Wilderness of Zin in the month of Abib, Miriam dies (Num. 20:1) by the way of Mt Seir (Deut. 2:1)	Return to Kadesh – in the Wilderness of Zin (Num. 33:36)
36	Beeroth Bene-Jaakan (Deut. 10:6) = wells of the sons of Jaakan	
37	Mt Hor, Aaron died & is mourned 30 days (Num. 20:29) – Mosera is the encampment at the foot of Mt Hor (Num. 20:22-29; Deut. 10:6)	Mt Hor (Num. 33:37), Aaron died 1st day 5th mo 1452 BC (Num. 33:38). Must go around the land of Edom & Moab (Num. 21:4; Deut. 2:8)
38	Gudgodah (Deut. 10:7)	
39	Jotbath – a land of rivers of waters (Deut. 10:7))	
40		Zalmonah (Num. 33:41)
41		Punon (Num. 33:42)
42	Oboth (Num. 21:10)	Oboth (Num. 33:43)
43	Elath & Ezion-geber – From Mt Hor by the way of the Red Sea to go around the land of Edom and Moab (Num. 21:4; Deut. 2:8)	
44	Brook Zered (Num. 14:45, 21:11-12; 33:44; Deut. 2:14)	◀── **From 1st arrival at Kadesh to Brook Zered = 38 years**
45	Ije-abarim (Num. 21:11; see Judg. 11:17-18)	Ije-abarim = Iim (Num. 33:44-45)
46	Brook Arnon crossed (Num. 21:13; Deut. 2:24)	
47		Dibon-gad (Num. 33:45)
48		Almon-diblathaim (Num. 33:46)
49	Beer (well, Num. 21:16-18)	
50	Mattanah (Num. 21:18)	
51	Nahaliel (Num. 21:19)	
52	Bamoth in the valley (Num. 21:19)	
53	Pisgah – a peak on or near Mt Nebo of the Abarim mountain range located near the NE end of the Dead Sea (Num. 21:20)	Nebo – a Mt in the Abarim mountain range opposite Jericho (Num. 33:47; cp. Deut. 32:49, 34:1)
54		Base camp – Beth-jesimoth to Abel-shittim (Num. 33:49) on the Plains of Moab by the Jordan River near Jericho (Num. 33:48) and Beth-peor (Deut. 3:29)
55	Amorite King Sihon of Heshbon refuses to let Israel pass through his land. Israel defeats him at Jahaz (Num. 21:21-26; Deut. 2:24-37)	
56	The Amorite city of Jaazer & villages fall to Israel (Num. 21:32)	
57	Og the Amorite of Bashan routed at Edrei (Num. 21:33-35; Deut. 3)	
58	Base camp at Shittim – Moses died on his 120 birthday and was mourned 30 days unto Abib 7 (Deut. 1:3, 31:2, 34:7-8; Josh. 1:11, 3:2, 4:19) Then Joshua and Israel removed to the Jordan for 3 days and crossed the river on Abib 10 (Josh. 2:1, 3:1-2, 4:19).	

CONCLUSION

In concluding this study, two quotes from long recognized authorities representing the two distinct world views will help bring into focus the issues encountered in this treatise. First, Henry Fynes Clinton, himself a biblical conservative, well wrote in 1834:[1]

> The history contained in the Hebrew Scriptures presents a remarkable and pleasing contrast to the early accounts of the Greeks. In the latter we trace with difficulty a few obscure facts preserved to us by the poets, who transmitted with all the embellishments of poetry and fable what they had received from oral tradition. In the annals of the Hebrew nation we have authentic narratives written by contemporaries, and these writing under the guidance of inspiration. ... For these reasons the history of the Hebrews cannot be treated like the history of any other nation; and he who should attempt to write their history, divesting it of its miraculous character, would find himself without materials. ...

On the following page Clinton continued:[2]

> From this spirit of the Scripture history, the writers not designing to give a full account of all transactions, but only to dwell on that portion in which the divine character was marked, many things which we might desire to know are omitted, and on many occasions a mere outline of the history is preserved.

Yet with regard to scriptural chronology, Clinton remarkably concluded:[3]

> It is mortifying to our curiosity that a precise date of many remarkable facts cannot be obtained. The destruction of the temple is determined by concurrent sacred and profane testimony to July B.C. 587. From this point we ascend to the birth of Abraham. But between these two epochs, the birth of Abraham and the destruction of the temple, two breaks occur in the series of Scripture dates, which make it impossible to fix the actual year of the birth of Abraham; and this date being unknown, and assigned only upon conjecture, all the preceding epochs are necessarily unknown also.

Although Clinton begins well, for the biblicist this last appraisal is truly distressing. This is all the more especially true as Clinton has long been acknowledged as "one of us" and for many years has rightfully held his earned reputation as a scholar and chronologer of the first rank. This last compromising conclusion, having actually been brought about by imperfect scriptural insight, has with the passing of time only worsened matters, bringing confidence in the trustworthiness of Scripture to even far lower proportions.

Representing the second world view formerly outlined and speaking for the Assyrian Academy, Professor A.H. Sayce concluded in a special head note to his article "The Bible and the Monuments" (appearing in *The Variorum Aids to Bible Students*) that the dates he gave throughout were "necessitated" by the Assyrian Canon.[4] As has been documented time and again in this paper, the testimony of the Assyrian data is accepted by academia in preference to the scriptural record, and is often used to impugn the statements and chronology of the biblical record. The result is exactly as given by Professor Sayce; today almost every date in the Old Testament has been re-dated because we have been assured that this is "necessitated" by the Assyrian Canon, etc.

Thus for quite some time the biblical witness has, in ever widening circles by outstanding scholars from both camps, been placed under the shadow of and even eclipsed by doubts. These doubts have arisen from both a misunderstanding of the Hebrew Text itself as well as the reliability of that account as compared to the historical records of neighboring nations. Yet throughout the past centuries a hardy band of scholars has persisted who, though not always agreeing precisely with one another, found the Hebrew Text totally trustworthy and

---

[1] Clinton, *Fasti Hellenici, op. cit.,* vol. 1, pp. 283–284.

[2] *Ibid.,* p. 285.

[3] *Ibid.*

[4] Archibald Henry Sayce, "The Bible and the Monuments," *The Variorum Aids to Bible Students,* page 78. An Assyriologist, Professor Sayce (1845–1933) was the son of a vicar of the Church of England and educated at Queens College, Oxford. Ordained and unmarried, he became deputy professor of comparative philology in 1876 and first professor of Assyriology at Oxford from 1891 until his retirement in 1919. Although he was a staunch opponent of rampant higher criticism, he was not a biblical literalist. He was a member of the Old Testament revision committee which produced the corrupt 1881 Revised Standard Version.

has so proclaimed. As stated at the onset, the two world views have led to the emergence of two distinct schools of biblical chronologists, with many compromising factions co-existing along the fringes. Obviously Professor A.H. Sayce is representative of the Assyrian Academy's position and procedures. Clinton's remarks typify the compromise within the ranks of the evangelical, conservative Christian quarters resulting from the ongoing relentless pressure exerted by the Academy. Nevertheless, "Let God be true, but every man a liar" (Rom.3:4).

The purpose of this dissertation has been not only to produce a faithful chronology of the Old Testament but to also examine the many claims, presuppositions, methodologies, of both schools and come to final conclusions. Toward that end and having made clear that this author was of the biblicist persuasion, a commitment was nevertheless made that the conflict between the two would be reported such that a comparison would be forthcoming exposing the vindication and/or deficiencies of both schools' methodologies. To facilitate this, the world views of both sides were outlined (pages 1–9) bringing all inquirers to the point of equal footing in understanding that which lay at the heart of the conflict.

The proposition was initially advanced that the chronology of the biblical record could be academically demonstrated solely from internal formulae within the text independent of religious overtones and further, that this internal structure had been preserved in a particular definable rendering of the biblical record specified as being the Hebrew Masoretic Text. The latter proposal has been documented (pages 9–17). The extant version of the LXX was demonstrated to be, at best, a highly corrupted unreliable remnant of the original thereby rendering it useless for analytical and/or chronological studies. Conversely, data illustrating the faithfulness of the Hebrew Text was provided, not only for the sake of imparting information but to encourage earnest contemplation (pages 16–17).

In order to maintain intellectual integrity in producing a biblical chronology which at all times would honor the internal Hebrew historical record as it had come down to this day yet remain independent of religious overtones, the implementation and maintenance of certain safeguards were established and observed. This was accomplished by first candidly setting forth my own philosophic world view, religious convictions, and frames of reference so that the reader could better ascertain whether the conclusions reached were justified from the data at hand or merely opinion-oriented. Placing these views in writing had the added effect of serving as a stimulus, goading the author to examine the motives and objectives regarding each decision along the way in order to be true to the goal.

Furthermore the data, having been taken and applied to the preparation of this continuously unfolding chronology, was at all times treated as a forthright factual historical account whose information and testimony relevant to the chronicle of the Hebrew people was to be respected and heeded, exactly as one would do with that of any other nation. In so doing, the data has been allowed to speak and testify on its own behalf thereby allowing a significant measure of scientific detachment to be attained. To further assist in achieving this ideal, concerted effort was made to observe and respect both the immediate and remote *context* of the applicable data under investigation.

Nevertheless, it must be conceded that on the basis of both its unrivaled antiquity as well as its unprecedented unbroken continuous narrative, a natural predilection in favor of the Hebrew Text apart from philosophic views must be seen as intellectually justifiable. Despite all assessments to the contrary, the undeniable fact is that it is simply by far the best, most complete record available to the extent that all other records of antiquity, mutilated and fragmented as they often are, fall far below it in analytical worth.

Indeed, the making of such a determination should not be esteemed as unusual or irresponsible as all fields of scholarly pursuit and discipline encounter the necessity of discriminating with respect to the weighing of various testimony, especially where discrepancies occur. The charge is repeated that an obvious prejudice exists in academia in general against this Hebrew witness which is unprecedented, not being evidenced concerning the historical account of any other people.

Thus, beginning on the 21st page, a methodical process was initiated in which a sustained series of examples following one after another was given. Using the accompanying charts and relevant text, these demonstrated that this Hebrew record contained internal data having the inherent capacity of being arranged into a flowing, self-correcting, systematized historical mosaic without necessitating any emendations or corrections in the Received Text. Consisting primarily of unadorned mathematical statements, this data readily submits to rigid non-emotional analysis.

This practice was continued, climaxing when the author's "triangulation" formula was introduced, explained, applied and illustrated in resolving the numerous chronological problems attendant in synchronizing the period of the disruption of the Hebrew monarchy (pages 135–137). Moreover, it was shown that mathematically embedded within the biblical text are the principles and concepts of accession/non-accession reckoning. Not only did this discovery resolve most of the difficulties by elevating the study of this interval to a scientific level of approach, it verified and substantiated our former contention that the dates obtainable and preserved in the King James Bible are demonstrably reliable. This having been done, and as the Masoretic Text is the underlying foundation upon which the King James is founded, the author should be regarded as having vindicated his decision in having returned exclusively to the Hebrew Masoretic Text as the only standard necessary for establishing the Old Testament chronology.

Moreover, the author's original allegation that the highly touted Assyrian records have time and again been misunderstood, misreported, misrepresented, misapplied and/or unjustified liberties have often been taken in the emendations and restorations by their translators (page iv) has been extensively demonstrated with explicit documented examples at all the principal areas of synchronization difficulty (pages 114–188). In point of fact, by these unscholarly practices the Assyrian Academy, whether deliberate or not, has been found guilty of having created problems with and thus greatly undermined the integrity of the Hebrew Text. Indeed, it has been shown that this has been the direct cause of nearly all the conflict

reported to exist between the Hebrew Text and that of the Assyrian Annals, etc., not the imagined "scribal errors" and other supposed "problems" in the biblical text. Hence the author's calling into question many of the "Assyrian Academy's" methods, especially its sometimes irresponsible reporting whereby the limitations imposed upon the data due to its mutilated condition is withheld from most articles intended for the consumption of pastors and the general public, has been justified.

Having utilized the Assyrian data in such a manner as to again and again violate the clear Hebrew history, Dr. Edwin R. Thiele, long recognized as the leading authority in the field of biblical chronology for the interval of the schism, came under the focus of this study. In order to establish and sustain his own findings, the author was forced to redress many of Dr. Thiele's widely published claims. As pledged in the abstract, all these which violated Scripture were systematically and thoroughly refuted with copious documentation.

Notwithstanding, it is important to distinguish that this study is not faulting the actual raw Assyrian data itself, only much of its application where it relates to the Hebrew record. Indeed, the same was found to be true with the other main secular reference, the Canon of Ptolemy. Actually most laymen, pastors, and seminary professors would be surprised at the amount of "restoration," private interpretation, and disparity existing between the opinions of individual Assyriologists as may be seen in both their accompanying footnotes and differing translations of these records.

The author's pledge to produce a less subjective, more technically stringent and exacting solution to the judges segment of Bible chronology was kept (pages 71–88, Chart 4). Being convinced that, at least for the literalist, most of the problems have now been resolved insofar as the internal biblical data will permit, it is nevertheless recognized that some refinements may be forthcoming. If biblically sound, the author will welcome them and looks forward to the day when they shall supersede that which he has advanced.

Likewise the author modified Ussher-Thucydides resolution of the "483-year – 20th year of Artaxerxes" question along with the

resurrected Newton chronology for the Book(s) of Ezra-Nehemiah should be seen as rendering this chronology as a unique contribution in theology as well as the field of education (pages 205–207, 220–249 and Chart 5). This is all the more so in view of the confirming cited article published in the 1863 *Journal of Sacred Literature and Biblical Record* which reported an Egyptian hieroglyphic inscription as having been found which stated that Artaxerxes was associated on the throne with Xerxes in the 12th year of his father's reign (page 239). As matters stand, due to the failure to recognize and/or resolve the two registers of priests and Levites recorded in Nehemiah chapters 10 and 12, not one Bible commentary, dictionary, encyclopedia, etc. available in the marketplace today has the correct chronology for these two books.

Finally, verification for all the preceding has been provided within this treatise in detailed documented form consisting of text, diagrams and detailed line drawings – without once compromising the context of a single Scripture. Indeed, it has been repeatedly shown from the abundant hard evidence and logic presented herein that, irrespective of religious beliefs, there is academic mathematical justification for a chronology based solely upon the internal formula contained in Scripture. Moreover, other frames of reference and world views have been challenged at the grass roots. The author therefore submits this dissertation "that ye might believe that Jesus is the Christ, the Son of God; and that believing ye might have life through his name" (John 20:31).

SOLI DEO GLORIA

DARIUS - the RESTRAINER
XERXES - Shah (king)
AHASUERUS - the mighty king or Ruffer...
prefix ARTA - the great or king of
ARTAXERXES - the great king or king of kings

CAESAR - KAISER & CZAR

Appendices

A. An Alternative Solution to Artaxerxes Longimanus

As we have seen by Newton's solution, the Nehemiah 12 register is firmly fixed in time to the first year of Cyrus in 536 BC (Neh. 12:1, cp. Ezra 1:1–2:2); hence the only possible way of reducing the apparent 91-year gap is to significantly increase the 445 BC date assigned to Nehemiah 10. Newton accomplished this by chronologically contextually connecting Nehemiah 7:73b to Ezra 3:1 and Nehemiah 8:2 (i.e. the "seventh month"), the result of which placed Nehemiah 10 as having also transpired in the first year of Cyrus but left Ezra and Nehemiah aged. However, an entirely different approach remains to resolving the dilemma so that all the men's ages are reduced by substantially increasing the Nehemiah 10 date. This solution revolves around the possibility that the "Artaxerxes" in question is not Artaxerxes Longimanus, but rather some Persian king ruling *before* him and therefore closer to the time of Cyrus. This would reduce the span of the problem gap.

This concept is easier to accept as a viable alternative when one discovers that "Darius," "Xerxes" and "Artaxerxes" are not personal names but appellatives or titles such as "pharaoh," "sultan" or "caesar" (from whence comes "kaiser" or "czar"). For example: Darius means "the restrainer," Xerxes connotes "shah" (i.e., king), Ahasuerus signifies "the mighty king" (or "high father") and the prefix "arta" denotes "the great" or "king of." Hence, Artaxerxes could mean either "the great king" or "king of kings" (cp. Ezra 7:12).

Observe that all of these appellatives are used in Scripture with reference to Jehovah God. Persian monarchs often claimed more than one such title for themselves. Cyrus the Great even called himself "Artaxerxes."[1] Furthermore,

Xerxes of Thermopylae in one protracted sentence on his inscription at Persepolis calls himself the "son of Darius" and then assumes the titles "Darius" and "Xerxes the Arta."[2]

1. ANSTEY'S ANSWER — "ARTAXERXES" IS DARIUS I

The concept of resolving this difficulty by associating the "Artaxerxes" in question with a Persian monarch ruling after Cyrus but before Artaxerxes I Longimanus is not original with this work. Having perceived the problem inherent in the two Nehemiah registers at least as far back as AD 1913, Martin Anstey proposed that the "Artaxerxes" of Ezra 7 and the Book of Nehemiah was Darius I Hystaspis. Although offering seven proofs in support of this proposition, the identification was primarily based upon Ezra 6:14–15 where he retranslated the Hebrew ו (a "waw") in verse fourteen from "and" to "even."[3] In so doing, he altered the verse from: "... and according to the commandment of Cyrus, and Darius, *and* Artaxerxes king of Persia" to read "... and according to the commandment of Cyrus, and Darius, *even* Artaxerxes king of Persia" thereby making "Artaxerxes" the same man as Darius.

This determination by Anstey immediately reduces the apparent 91-year gap to only about 34 (536 – c. 502 [the 20th year of Darius] = 34), thereby at once resolving the age problem between the Nehemiah 10 and 12 lists. The solution also carries with it an attractive bonus as it causes the story to seemingly move directly from the sixth year of Darius in Ezra 6:15 into his seventh year in chapter 7 (Ezra 7:1,7) giving the appearance of a continuous flowing historical narrative rather than a 30-year gap in which the last years of Darius and all of Xerxes' reign are passed over.

In 1988, E.W. Faulstich joined Anstey in that assessment. Although expanding on and adding to Anstey's argument, Faulstich followed him in seizing upon retranslating the Hebrew ו

---

[1] Klassen, *The Chronology of the Bible, op. cit.*, p. 44. Along these same lines, the name "Cyrus" is "Kurash" in Persian. Its Greek equivalent is "Kurios" which is rendered "Lord" in English. Thus "Cyrus" is a play on words concerning the Messiah, and as such it must be seen as prophetic. Accordingly, all of the biblical passages citing Cyrus are also cryptic allusions to the Lord Jesus. This is especially borne out in Isaiah 45:1 where Cyrus is called the "Lord's Messiah" ("Anointed One").

[2] Anstey, *The Romance of Bible Chronology, op. cit.*, pp. 261–262.

[3] *Ibid.*, pp. 269–272.

in verse 14 of Ezra 6:14–15 from "and" to "even" and contended that this identification was the key to the correct understanding and unification of the Book(s) of Ezra-Nehemiah.[1] The main departure between Anstey's and Faulstich's solutions is over the identity of "Darius the Persian" (Neh. 12:22). Following Josephus, Anstey makes him Darius III Codomannus whereas Faulstich argues that he is Darius I Hystaspis resulting in the unlikely circumstance that all the high priests mentioned in Ezra-Nehemiah are contemporaries.[2]

In assessing the "and" to "even" novelty proposed by Anstey and supported by Faulstich, little justification has been found in its favor. Upon consulting a Hebraist, the author has been informed that such a construction, although not the more conventional choice, is admittedly possible. That notwithstanding, having pursued the matter further by consulting over twenty versions at Ezra 6:14, it is noted that not one translator or team of translators rendered the "waw" (ו, pronounced "vau") beginning the Hebrew word for Artaxerxes as "even" (וארתחששתא). The same may be said for the author's four Hebrew interlinear Old Testaments.

When so many independent translations all designating the Hebrew as "and," can there be any real doubt as to the correct interpretation and can such handling of the Hebrew herein described be any more than grasping at straws? Why not insist upon "even" Darius in the same verse as the "waw" is also present there (ודריוש)? It would seem, therefore, that if the identification of Darius as being the same king as Artaxerxes in Ezra 6:14 were the key to the correct understanding and unification of the Book(s) of Ezra-Nehemiah, the proof is found to be resting upon a very insecure foundation. Thus while regarding Anstey's concept as having considerable merit, this author holds that Ezra 6:14 in particular and the Book of Ezra in general read such that the biblical "Artaxerxes" is a Persian king following after Darius Hystaspis.

---

[1] Faulstich, *History Harmony, The Exile and Return, op. cit.*, pp. 142–164.

[2] *Ibid.*, pp. 162–164.

2. A NEW CONSIDERATION — IS "ARTAXERXES" XERXES?

Like Anstey, in resolving the "great age" problem in order to construct a correct chronology for the Ezra-Nehemiah period, this author considers a resolution in which the difficulty is ameliorated by associating the "Artaxerxes" in question with a Persian monarch ruling *after* Cyrus but *before* Artaxerxes I Longimanus as being possible. Accordingly, the matter may be untangled by simply letting the Bible speak for itself. All the previously mentioned excessive age problems may be resolved by the possibility that as the Persian king who followed Darius I Hystaspis is an "Artaxerxes," he may be the "Xerxes I" of secular history rather than Longimanus.

This possibility is suggested by the fact that a biblical monarch of Persia bearing the title "Artaxerxes" is uniformly mentioned in the Scriptures following Darius I Hystaspis (Ezra 6 and 7; Nehemiah 2). Therefore "Artaxerxes" conceivably could be identified as the king who succeeded Darius I in the Canon. That king is, of course, Xerxes I. Furthermore, as has formerly been proven, the Ahasuerus of Esther is actually Darius I Hystaspis and *not* Xerxes I of Thermopylae.

The statements contained in Daniel 11:1–4 support both of these identifications. Using only biblical data and comparing the Persian kings of Daniel 10:1 and 11:1–4 with the Book of Ezra (4:5–7, 24; 6:14–15; 7:1–13, 29), the conclusion may be drawn that the fourth king of Daniel 11:2 and the "Artaxerxes" of the Ezra passage are one and the same, specifically secular history's "Xerxes I."

If this were the actual identification, the ages of Ezra and Nehemiah as well as the priests and Levites in Nehemiah 10 and 12 would no longer appear so great as to apparently necessitate having to have different men in successive generations bearing the same names. For example, almost any recent Bible Dictionary will identify the Ezra of Nehemiah 12:1,7 as a chief priest and leader who returned with Zerubbabel in the first year of Cyrus, distinguishing him as being different from the one in the Book of Ezra who is also a priest (Ezra 7:1–12) and leader. Yet "both" men are clearly alive during the reign of the same

Persian monarch, "Artaxerxes" (cp. Ezra 7:1, 12, 21 with Neh. 2:1; 5:14; 8:1–4, 9; 12:1). *Both* Ezras are contemporaries of Zerubbabel and are associated with a Nehemiah who is a leader (Neh. 8:1–4,9), not to mention that a "Nehemiah" is associated with Zerubbabel (Neh. 7:7). It is equally dismaying to "learn" that the Nehemiah returning from Babylon as a leader with Zerubbabel (Ezra 2:2; Neh. 7:7) is not supposed to be the same man as in the Book of Nehemiah who succeeded Zerubbabel as governor under Artaxerxes.[1]

Notwithstanding, this author is constrained to agree with the conclusion of Sir Isaac Newton; the context argues for only one Nehemiah and one Ezra, not two. Is it not *incomprehensible* that the leaders in two successive generations would have exactly the same names – names that are rare in the biblical text yet occurring exclusively in the same time frame and in only the Books of Ezra and Nehemiah (with but one exception[2])? The fact is they are not different men. The apparent great ages of Ezra and Nehemiah (and Mordecai) do not teach that they are two successive generations by the same name.

It has been shown that the lists of priests and Levites in Nehemiah 10 and 12, apart from a solution similar to Newton's, mathematically demand that the traditional identification of the "Artaxerxes" of the Book of Nehemiah as being Longimanus is erroneous. Secular history adds a confirming voice to this thesis in stating that Xerxes I was the last Persian king to practice

the liberal religious tolerance depicted by the biblical Artaxerxes.[3]

This second solution to the paradox lies in taking the biblical kings of Persia as having been mismatched to the secular list. Again, the great ages attributed to the men of Nehemiah's generation infer that the biblical "Artaxerxes" in question is a Persian king who reigned *before* Artaxerxes Longimanus. This correction reduces the outlandish ages of these men to conform to the evidence of other Scripture.

Thus in order to honor the testimony of both the Hebrew Text, which has been shown again and again throughout this dissertation to be absolutely faithful, and the Canon of Ptolemy, which gives Xerxes a 21-year term as sole rex, the deduction is introduced that Xerxes apparently was placed in consort with his father as pro-rex. By this manner, his authority over the Jews would have extended over a span of at least 32 years, and not merely the 21 years of his unshared kingship (Nehemiah 5:14; 13:6, see Chart 5 and the lower dashed secondary solution).

Josephus concurs indirectly, in that he first identifies the successor to Darius the son of Hystaspis as being "Xerxes" and then specifies that he was the Persian king with whom Ezra and Nehemiah dealt.[4] He later mentions an event that occurred in Xerxes' *28th* year.[5]

Although alone he cannot be taken as authoritative, Firdusi's "historical" poetic rendering of the legendary national traditions of Persia recounts that Darius Hystaspis was followed by an "Artaxerxes."[6]

---

[1] A further check will almost certainly "uncover" that the Mordecai of the Book of Esther will not be seen as the leader that returned with Zerubbabel (Ezra 2.2; Neh.7:7). Apparently Nehemiah, Mordecai and possibly Ezra, as key Jewish leaders, were recalled to serve various Persian kings who followed Cyrus. The biblical narrative reveals the circumstances as to what became of them. Nehemiah and Ezra, undoubtedly young among the leaders in the days of Cyrus and Zerubbabel, were subsequently allowed to return in the wisdom of their latter years and be used by the LORD in Jerusalem. Contrariwise, God's purpose for Mordecai's remaining was for the good of His people back in Persia who had wrongly chosen not to return to their native homeland.

[2] 1 Chron. 4:17, cp. vs.1, an Ezra was in Judah's lineage. A different Nehemiah, the son of Azbuk is also found in Scripture. He supervised the building of a portion of the wall of Jerusalem (Neh.3:16) and thus was a contemporary and worked under the authority of "Governor" Nehemiah.

[3] Hayes and Hanscom, *Ancient Civilizations, op. cit.*, p. 182.

[4] Josephus, *Antiquities, op. cit.*, compare XI, 3, 1 with XI, 5, 1–6.

[5] *Ibid.*, XI, 5, 8.

[6] Firdusi (AD 931–1020), the Persian Epic Poet born at Khorassan wrote a "history" of Persia in verse from the earliest times down to AD 632. Written in 1010 AD, *The Shah Nama of Firdusi, The Book of the Persian Kings*, [James V. S. Wilkinson, (London: Oxford UP, 1931)] is neither chronology nor history. It is a poetic rendering of the legendary national traditions of Persia. The unique value of Firdusi's poem is that it gathers and preserves the Persian tradition of the chronology of the period

Again, the author is persuaded that the Word of God is its own commentary and thus contains within itself all data necessary for its complete chronology. Therefore, the following logic is proposed for filling the chasm between 516 BC, the 6th year of Darius I Hystaspis, and the 15th year of Tiberius (c. AD 26), the year in which he became associated on the throne with Augustus Caesar. Using only biblical data and having begun with Adam (AM 1), this chronology has moved forward establishing 3488 AM (516 BC) as the 6th year of Darius I.

Since the only Scripture bridging unto the time of Christ Jesus is the aforementioned 483-year Daniel 9:24–26 prophecy, an impasse as to the actual identity of the biblical "Artaxerxes" is encountered at this juncture. This is due, as formerly delineated, to using Longimanus and the date of his twentieth year resulting in excessive ages being imposed on Ezra and Nehemiah and/or the priests and Levites. Having already successfully confronted and solved several such chasms earlier, the simple, straightforward tactic utilized in resolving them is now applied to this difficulty. Leaping forward in time and thus hurdling the gulf, a new fixed point of reference is selected from which to work back in time to the 20th year of "Artaxerxes."

Recalling from a former discourse, the most certain accurate event from which to establish the dates of all others in the life of Christ is that of the 15th year of Tiberius (c. AD 26, Luke 3:1) at which time the Lord Jesus was baptized being about age 30 (Luke 3:23, or from His cleansing of the Temple [John 2:13–22, cp. Mal.3:1] at the April Passover of AD 27 in the 46th year of Herod's repair on the Temple). Counting back 30 years (inclusive) from AD 26 establishes the birth of Jesus at 4 BC. As the ministry of Jesus seems to have lasted approximately 3½ years, the crucifixion and resurrection would have occurred AD 30.

Having determined these dates, it should be noted that the life of Jesus as recorded in the four gospels reveals four distinct occurrences as far exceeding all others in significance. Therefore one of these should be authenticated as the point from which to measure backward in order to establish the twentieth year of "Artaxerxes." These four events were:

1. His birth (c. 4 BC),

2. His 12th year when, after coming to Jerusalem for the Passover, He presented himself at the Temple before the priests and elders as the "wunderkind" beginning to "be about His Father's business" (c. AD 9, Luke 2:40–52, this being a partial fulfillment of the double reference prophecy of Mal.3:1),

3. the 15th year of Tiberius (c. AD 26, Luke 3:1) at which time the Lord Jesus Christ was baptized being about 30 years of age (Luke 3:23), or

4. His crucifixion and/or resurrection (only 3 days apart) in AD 30.

Thus, if we begin at each of these events and measure back 483 years (Dan. 9:24–27), the results may be compared with either the aforementioned 91-year time span between the leaders who returned with Zerubbabel in 536 BC and the sealing of the covenant with Nehemiah in the 20th year of "Artaxerxes" which results from the traditional modern chronological interpretation or with the extended ages Newton's solution confers upon Ezra and Nehemiah. The application of logic and deductive reasoning to these comparisons should enable us to eliminate unreasonable possibilities and allow the establishing of the correct benchmark.

Thus, measuring back 483 years from Jesus' baptism in c. AD 26 brings us to 457 BC as a potential date for the 20th year of Artaxerxes. However that would leave a 79-year gap (536 less 457 = 79) between the Nehemiah 10 and 12 lists to which at least 30 more years must be added (minimal leadership age) bringing the minimum age of that entire generation of leaders to 109 years. This is far too old and is thus ruled out.

---

between Darius Hystaspis and Alexander the Great (486–331 BC).

The Persians themselves have no records of this period as the Greek and Mohammedan invasions swept them all away. The only Persian witness, other than a scant few rock inscriptions, is that of certain vague, floating national traditions cast into an epic poem by Firdusi, and from these we are given a succession of Persian monarchs in which an "Artaxerxes" followed Darius Hystaspis (see Martin Anstey, *The Romance of Bible Chronology, op. cit.*, pp. 18–19, 24).

If the year of the crucifixion and the resurrection (c. AD 30) is selected, the men's ages will obviously be about 3+ years greater. Measuring from AD 9 (Jesus at the Temple in His 12th year), we arrive at 474 BC with the result that the minimum age of that generation is 92.

Lastly, measuring back 483 years (solar) from the birth (c. 4 BC) takes us to 486 BC as the 20th year of "Artaxerxes." This scenario gives a 50-year gap from the 1st year of Cyrus to the 20th of Artaxerxes, yielding an 80-year minimum age for that generation (536 − 486 = 50 + 30). This, then, is the only solution providing reasonable ages for these men when compared to the ages of their biblical predecessors.

Counting back 20 years from 486 BC, the "first year" of "Artaxerxes" (Xerxes I) is found to be 505 BC. The remaining years (506–516 BC) which close the gap are left to Darius as being those of his unshared reign after his sixth.

The justification for the preceding deductions is that the sum of the previous biblical and secular evidence suggests the distinct possibility that, perhaps in anticipation of some military undertaking or possibly due to a severe or protracted illness, Xerxes became associated in the throne with his father, Darius Hystaspis. The plausibility of this is apparent because Persian Law "which alters not" (Dan. 6:12, 15) forbade a king to march with his army until he had named his successor.[1] This event, if it did in fact occur, would have taken place near or during the 16th year of Darius' sole reign (505 BC). Very likely it would have been at that time the title "King of Babylon" was conferred upon Xerxes (Neh. 13:6).[2]

---

[1] Herodotus, *The Histories*, op. cit., VII, 1.

[2] This seems to be the emphasis of The Book of Nehemiah in which the Daniel 9:24–26 decree is associated, for nowhere in the book is Artaxerxes given any specific title other than "King" and "King of Babylon." Yet Nehemiah 1:1 makes it clear that he is a Persian monarch, the palace being at Susa (Shushan) and not at Babylon. Further evidence of his Persian distinction is afforded by the Book of Ezra in which he is ever referenced as "King of Persia" (Ezra 6:14; 7:1). As it was the custom of kings to affix the appellations of conquered kings to themselves along with their own titles, "Artaxerxes" (Xerxes?) held this title over a span of nearly 40 years until his death in

Upon his installation as pro-rex, Xerxes ("Artaxerxes") would have become the suzerain over the Jews and moreover that Persian with whom they would have to have dealt. It would have been natural that they would have referenced their years with respect to his date of overlordship rather than his date of sole reign which began at the end of Darius' 36th year (486 BC). It should be seen as most significant that the concept being presented results, from the Hebrew standpoint, in the *20th* year of "Artaxerxes" (Xerxes I) as falling in his father's final year (Chart 5).

This happenstance would seem to indicate that although Xerxes had been associated on the throne, he lacked sufficient authority to allow the Jews to rebuild the city and wall prior to the decease of his father, Darius. The implication being that though Darius had been persuaded from Cyrus' edict to allow the completion of the Temple (Ezra 5:16–17; 6:3,7,8,12), he had succumbed in part to the negative arguments presented by the counselors who had been hired by the enemies of the Jews (Ezra 4:4–24) and thus opposed further restoration which would result in Jerusalem's becoming a fortified city. Accordingly, Darius would have caused no problem when, in the seventh year of his viceroyship, Xerxes ("Artaxerxes") permitted Ezra to return to merely "beautify the house of the Lord which is in Jerusalem" (Ezra 7:11–28). Apparently then, the same year in which he gained full governmental power, Xerxes ("Artaxerxes") granted the decree for Nehemiah to return and rebuild the city and its wall.

Thus, if the "Artaxerxes" of the books of Ezra and Nehemiah (see Ezra 6:14; 7:1, 7, 12, 21; Neh. 2:1; 5:14, etc.) is Xerxes I as proposed, this would agree with Ptolemy's date of 486 BC as Xerxes' first year of sole reign and also leave his father Darius the 36 years of rule which Ptolemy's king list records. Hence as Ptolemy affirms, Xerxes may have ruled only 21 years as *sole* rex, but his total years associated on the throne over Israel would have been much more, around 40 years (505–465 BC). Moreover, no rejection of the Canon of Ptolemy is necessary,

---

465 BC (Nehemiah 2:1; 5:14; cp. 13:6!). Moreover, at the demise of Darius Hystaspis in 486 BC, "Artaxerxes" (Xerxes?) would have inherited the additional title "King of Persia."

merely a minor modification consisting of a pro-rex association. Recalling that Ptolemy does not acknowledge co-regencies, this resolution in no way conflicts with or alters his witness.[1] Again, when properly considered, both the biblical and secular data is found to be compatible such that a rejection of either is unwarranted.

3. CONCLUSION – ARTAXERXES IS LONGIMANUS

As simple and possible as this last solution may be, it is not deemed the best resolution.

We have now examined the relevant data as to whether Darius Hystaspis or Xerxes is the biblical Artaxerxes and are forced to conclude that neither is the true candidate. Hence, the previous discourse which resolved Ptolemy's Canon and the witness of the cited ancient historians (pages 226–240) whereby the biblical Artaxerxes was seen to be Longimanus is still regarded as the correct and historically best resolution.

---

[1] Ptolemy, the heathen astronomer-astrologer as a 2nd century AD worker, is a late compiler, not a contemporary historian or witness. Regarding the later Persian period, not only does the 73-year lifespan of Darius as preserved by Ctesias (page 200, footnote 4) go against him, arguing as it does for a 44-year reign rather than 36, but also the witness of his contemporary, Josephus, and that of the Arundelian Marble (page 231, fn. 4). Likewise, for this period his work is against the national traditions of Persia as preserved by Firdusi and that of the Jews as evidenced by conflicting data of well authenticated events, i.e., the flight of Themistocles to the Court of Artaxerxes Longimanus.

Although Ptolemy has been found reliable, he must not, in view of so many witnesses to the contrary, be taken as absolute truth. He should be used as a witness, or even as a guide to the facts of chronology, but he is not the judge. Indeed, as stated earlier, this author would not be astonished if subsequent archaeological finds caused slight insignificant modifications to his Canon.

That notwithstanding, when synchronizing Ptolemy's Persian King data to the Hebrew Text, the Royal Canon has proven a trustworthy guide such that if he is not exactly correct, he is very nearly so unto the 6th year of Darius. Moreover, in the matter of the length of the reign of Darius I, Ptolemy is supported by Herodotus who also gives him 36 years (Herodotus, *The Histories, op. cit.*, VII, 3).

Finally, as delineated on 238 and 239, the Royal Canon of Ptolemy is completely confirmed, as are the dates of its kings, over the span of the Neo-Babylonian Empire by the Adad-guppi stelae, the 30 astral observations from astronomical diary VAT 4956 in the Berlin Museum, the lunar eclipse in the 2nd year of Nabonidus as recorded on the Nabonidus No. 18 royal inscription cylinder, and the cluster of lunar eclipses cited on p. 194.

NISAN 1, AD 30
= Julian Period: March 24, AD 30 Julian Day = 1732097.75
= Gregorian: March 22, AD 30 – **Friday**
= Olympiad: 202, year 1

When new moon crescent is first **visible** and new month is **declared** at sunset in Jerusalem.

Month	Hebrew day of week	Sabbaths	Gregorian Astrological calculation of the Sun-Moon Conjunction Date and Time for New Moons					Julian Day Number
			Weekday	month	day	Year	Time	
01 - Nisan	Friday	02 – 09 – 16 – 23 – 30	Wed	Mar	20	AD 30	19:38	1732096
02 - Iyar	Sunday	07 – 14 – 21 – 28	Fri	Apr	19	AD 30	11:25	1732126
03 - Sivan	Tuesday	05 – 12 – 19 – 26	Sun	May	19	AD 30	02:56	1732156
04 - Tammuz	Wednes	04 – 11 – 18 – 25	Mon	Jun	17	AD 30	17:24	1732185
05 - Ab	Friday	02 – 09 – 16 – 23	Wed	Jul	17	AD 30	06:22	1732215
06 - Elul	Saturday	01 – 08 – 15 – 22 – 29	Thur	Aug	15	AD 30	17:56	1732244
07 - Tishri	Monday	06 – 13 – 20 – 27	Sat	Sep	14	AD 30	04:43	1732274
08 - Heshvan	Tuesday	05 – 12 – 19 – 26	Sun	Oct	01	AD 30	15:24	1732303
09 - Kislev	Thurs	03 – 10 – 17 – 24	Tue	Nov	12	AD 30	02:20	1732333
10 - Tebeth	Friday	02 – 09 – 16 – 23	Wed	Dec	11	AD 30	13:27	1732362
11 - Shebat	Sunday	07 – 14 – 21 – 28	Fri	Jan	10	AD 31	00:42	1732392
12 - Adar	Monday	06 – 13 – 20 – 27	Sat	Feb	08	AD 31	12:07	1732421

CALENDAR OF THE CRUCIFIXION MONTH
**Based on the above data which was taken from the
Calendar Conversion computer program designed by the
Harvard Center for Astrophysics.
The ephemeris generator for this software was developed from
Jean Meeus, *Astronomical Formulae for Calculators.*
It is the standard formula used by astronomers today.**

NISAN 30 AD						
SUN	MON	TUE	WED	THUR	FRI	SAT
					01	02
03	04	05	06	07	08	09
10	11	12	13	14	15	16
17	18	19	20	21	22	23
24	25	26	27	28	29	30

Note: 14 Nisan converts to Thursday, April 4th Gregorian calendar (6 April, JP); further, the actual first sighting of the new moon may be c. 15 to c. 25 hours after the astral conjunction calculation date and thus be as much as three days later.

Legend: N = night, D = day, p = pm, a = am

March / April	20	21	22	23	24	25	26	27	28	29	30	31	1	2	3	4	5	6	7
Western Time	Wed	Thur	Fri	Sat	Sun	Mon	Tue	Wed	Thur	Fri	Sat	Sun	Mon	Tue	Wed	Thur	Fri	Sat	Sun
(N 6p / D 6a)	N D	N D	N D	N D	N D	N D	N D	N D	N D	N D	N D	N D	N D	N D	N D	† D	N D	N D	N D
Jewish Time	Wed	Thur	Fri	Sat	Sun	Mon	Tue	Wed	Thur	Fri	Sat	Sun	Mon	Tue	Wed	Thur	Fri	Sat	Sun
Day of 1st Month (Nisan)			1	2	3	4	5	6	7	8	9	10	11	12	13	14	15	16	17

Western Time	Sunday		Monday		Tuesday		Wednesday		Thursday		Friday		Saturday		Sunday	
	Night 6pm	Daylite 6am	Night 6pm	Daylite 6am	Night 6pm	Daylite 6am	Night 6pm	Daylite 6am	Night 6pm	Daylite 6am	Night 6pm	Daylite 6am	Night 6pm	Daylite 6am	Night 6pm	Daylite 6am
									†	†						
									9	3						
Jewish Time	Sunday		Monday		Tuesday		Wednesday		Thursday		Friday		Saturday		Sunday	
Day of 1st Month (Nisan)	10		11		12		13		14		15		16		17	

Lunar months begin when the moon is situated on a direct line between the sun and earth (such alignments are called "conjunctions"). As a consequence, no sunlight can reflect to the earth from the side toward us. With its dark side toward us, the moon is nearly invisible. The moon travels about 12° each day, and it must be nearly a day old before it is far enough from the sun to reflect enough light to be seen. In AD 30, the Gregorian date and time of the conjunction of the sun and moon for the first of Nisan was Wednesday March 20th at 19:38 (7:38 PM Jerusalem time, the Julian Day = 1732096). As the Jewish day begins around 6:00 PM, this conjunction actually occurred on their Thursday. This would have resulted in their beginning 1 Nisan 24 hours later at 6:00 PM when the moon was 22 hours 22 minutes old (7:38 – 6:00 = 1:38 and 24 – 1:38 = 22 hrs. 22 min.). Further, as 6:00 PM began the Jewish day, 1 Nisan would have begun on their Friday. This would result in Nisan 2 falling on Saturday (a Sabbath).

The Jews regulated their months by direct observation of the new moon at the slim crescent phase, not at the 7:38 PM (19:38) Wednesday, March 20th conjunction which would have been in the less visible "dark moon" phase (see chart on page 273). The slim crescent begins to appear about 24 hours after the "dark moon." Indeed, a new moon rises at about the time the sun comes up. It is almost invisible during the daytime, but we can see it in the western sky for about an hour after sundown. Thus, the astronomically calculated date and time of the conjunction, which produces the dark new moon, is not the same as the observed date and time which may differ by as much as three days. Other factors such as hills, trees, and mountains may also result in delaying the date in which the crescent is actually seen by an observer at a given location. Moreover, many calculated cyclic events such as lunar or solar eclipses may elude accurate historic synchronization as clouds, rain, daytime occurrence, etc. may have hidden the phenomena from view. In such cases, synchronizing the actual observed event with the mathematical reckoning may be off by one or more cycles. Hence, astronomical calculations and their accompanying Julian Period years are useful as a guide, but they cannot be used exclusively in making final historical date determinations.

THE CRUCIFIXION WEEK

Western Time	Sunday (Night 6pm / Daylite 6am)	Monday (Night 6pm / Daylite 6am)	Tuesday (Night 6pm / Daylite 6am)	Wednesday (Night 6pm / Daylite 6am)	Thursday (Night 6pm / Daylite 6am)	Friday (Night 6pm / Daylite 6am)	Saturday (Night 6pm / Daylite 6am)	Sunday (Night 6pm / Daylite 6am)	Night 6pm
Jewish Time	Sunday	Monday	Tuesday	Wednesday	Thursday († | † 9 3)	Friday	Saturday	Sunday	
Day of 1st Month	10	11	12	13	14	15	16	17	
	Day after the anointing by Mary of Bethany during supper at Simon the Leper's John 12:1,12 — Triumphal Entry – laments Jerusalem — Passover lamb chosen – tested for 4 days 10th–14th Exo. 12:3	Curses fig tree — Cleanses Temple for the second time	Fig tree dead — Jesus' Authority challenged — Lamb of God examined and found spotless Mat. 22:15–46 — Scribes, elders, and chief priest plot to kill Jesus. — Satan enters Judas	The "silent" day — Disciples make Passover preparations Mark 14:12–16 Luke 22:7–13	After sunset as the 14th begins Mark 14:12–16 Luke 22:7–13 Eat Passover and Last Supper, Judas' betrayal cp. Num 9:6–13 — The "preparation" Mat. 27:62 Mark 15:42 Luke 23:54 John 13:1–2, 18:28, 19:14, 31 — Jesus arrested, 6 illegal trials, found innocent — **Crucified** — Lamb without blemish slain Lev. 23:5 Exo. 12	**High Sabbath** A holy convocation John 19:31 — 1st day of the Feast of Unleavened Bread Lev. 23:6–8	Regular weekly Sabbath see Mat. 28:1 where "Sabbath" is plural in the Greek, i.e., "Sabbaths"	**Jesus the firstfruits of the Resurrection** I Cor.15:20–23 — Day of Firstfruits Lev. 23:9–14 — 17th of Nisan Noah (Gen. 8:4, cp. Exo. 12:2, 13:4) and Israel (Num. 33:3–8) emerged from the waters of death (Rom.6:3–4)	

For as Jonas was three days and three nights in the whale's belly;
so shall the Son of man be three days and three nights in the heart of the earth.

(Matthew 12:40; cp. Jonah 1:17, Esther 4:16, 1 Sam. 30:12)

THE FEAST OF PENTECOST – Leviticus 23

Month	Day 1 Sunday	Day 2 Monday	Day 3 Tuesday	Day 4 Wed.	Day 5 Thursday	Day 6 Friday	Day 7 Saturday	Week
	10	**11**	**12**	**13**	**14**	(**15**)	**16**	
	1 **17**	2 **18**	3 **19**	4 **20**	5 **21**	6 **22**	7 **23**	**1**
First Month	8 **24**	9 **25**	10 **26**	11 **27**	12 **28**	13 **29**	14 **30**	**2**
	15 **1**	16 **2**	17 **3**	18 **4**	19 **5**	20 **6**	21 **7**	**3**
	22 **8**	23 **9**	24 **10**	25 **11**	26 **12**	27 **13**	28 **14**	**4**
Second Month	29 **15**	30 **16**	31 **17**	32 **18**	33 **19**	34 **20**	35 **21**	**5**
	36 **22**	37 **23**	38 **24**	39 **25**	40 **26**	41 **27**	42 **28**	**6**
	43 **29**	44 **1**	45 **2**	46 (**3**)	47 **4**	48 **5**	49 **6**	**7**
Third Month	50 **7**							

The oral giving of the Law was on the seventh day* of the third month (Sivan), 1491 BC. Moses and the children of Israel came to Sinai in the third month, "the same day" (Exo. 19:1), which means the third day of the third month. Moses "went up" on Mt. Sinai "unto God" the following day, which was the 4th of Sivan (Exo. 19:3). The people were to come back to the Mount three days after this (Exo. 19:9–19 where verse 10 speaks of the fifth day of the third month, i.e. *today* and the sixth day, i.e. *tomorrow*). Thus, they came back on the seventh day of the third month, which is permanently fixed as a Sunday by Leviticus 23:4–22 as being the "Feasts of Weeks" or Pentecost. Therefore, the Law was first given on what later came to be observed as the Day of Pentecost once the Jews entered the Land of Promise (Abib 10, 1451 BC, cp. Josh. 4:19) and began to till the land (1444 BC, after a 7 year war). As the Amalekite attack was prior to this, Moses was 80 and Aaron 83 years old at the time (Exo. 7:7).

* The above drawing and conclusions have been adjusted in this 17th edition by one day because although the illustration previously correctly depicted Abib as having 30 days, it incorrectly had the second month (Zif) as also being 30 days instead of 29. The Jews state that the Law was given on the 6th of Sivan, declaring it to have been a Sabbath (*Seder Olam Rabbah*, 5, see Guggenheimer, 2005 ed., p. 68), but Leviticus 23:15-16 demands Pentecost to be a Sunday (see above). Abib 14 in AD 30 calculates as Thursday, April 4, and Pentecost of that year was Sivan 7 (May 26) – which was a Sunday!

HEBREW MONTHS

	Month and Bible Reference	Approximate Modern Equivalent (mid to mid mo.)	Main Crops	Climate	Special Days
1.	Abib - Exo. 23:15 (Nisan) - Neh 2:1	March-April	Barley harvest, lentils	Latter Rains	14 = Passover 15–21 = Unleavened Bread 17 = Firstfruits Sheaf
2.	Zif - I Ki 6:1 (Iyyar)	April-May	General harvest		
3.	Sivan - Est 8:9	May-June	Wheat harvest	D R Y	7 = Pentecost
4.	Tammuz	June-July	Vine tending	S E A S O N	
5.	Ab	July-August	First grapes, figs, olives		
6.	Elul - Neh 6:15	August-September	Grapes, dates		
7.	Tishri - I Ki 8:2 (Ethanim)	September-October	Vintage, plowing		1 = Feast of Trumpets 10 = Day of Atonement 15–21 = Tabernacles Feast
8.	Bul - I Ki 6:38 (Marchesvan)	October-November	Wheat, barley, seed sowing	Early Rains	
9.	Chisleu - Zec 7:1 (Kislev)	November-December	Cool and rainy	R A I N	25 = Feast of Dedication John 10:22
10.	Tebeth - Est 2:16	December-January	Cold and rainy	S E A S O N	
11.	Shebat - Zec 1:7	January-February	Winter figs, citrus harvest		
12.	Adar - Est 3:7 Ezra 6:15	February-March	Almonds bloom, flax harvest		14–15 = Purim Est 9:20–28

LUNAR ECLIPSES – PTOLEMY

ASTRONOMICAL OR JULIAN PERIOD YEARS				GREGORIAN YEARS		
Year	Month/Day	King	Regnal Yr.	Year	Month/Day	Day of Week
- 620	22 April	Nabopolassar	5	621 BC	15 April	Saturday
- 522	16 July	Cambyses II	7	523 BC	10 July	Wednesday
- 501	19 Nov.	Darius I	20	502 BC	13 Nov.	Monday
- 490	25 April	Darius I	31	491 BC	20 April	Wednesday

Ptolemy records the following lunar eclipse data for Nabopolassar:[1]

For in the year 5 of Nabopolassar (which is the year 127 of Nabonassar, Egyptianwise Athyr 27–28 at the end of the eleventh hour) the moon began to be eclipsed in Babylon; ...

As Anno Nabonassar 1 is 747 BC, Nabonassarian years may be converted to astronomical years (Julian Period) by subtracting them from 747. Thus, 747 − 127 = −620 JP (see above). The month Athyr on the Egyptian sliding calendar falls in our March and April.

---

[1] Claudius Ptolemy, "The Almagest," *Great Books of The Western World*, R. M. Hutchins, ed., trans. by R. C. Taliaferro, (Chicago, IL: William Benton Publishers, 1952), Bk. 5, p. 172.

DATES FOR MAJOR BIBLICAL EVENTS

AM	BC	E V E N T
	4004	Creation – Adam and Eve – Universe
1	4003	Birth of Cain
129	3875	Cain slays Abel
130	3874	Birth of Seth
235	3769	Birth of Enos
325	3679	Birth of Cainan
395	3609	Birth of Mahalaleel
460	3544	Birth of Jared
622	3382	Birth of Enoch
687	3317	Birth of Methuselah
874	3130	Birth of Lamech
930	3074	Death of Adam
987	3017	Translation of Enoch
1042	2962	Death of Seth
1056	2948	Birth of Noah
1140	2864	Death of Enos
1235	2769	Death of Cainan
1290	2714	Death of Mahalaleel
1422	2582	Death of Jared
1556	2448	Birth of Japheth
1558	2446	Birth of Shem
1651	2353	Death of Lamech
1656	2348	Death of Methuselah
1656	2348	The Flood
1658	2346	Birth of Arphaxad
1693	2311	Birth of Salah
1723	2281	Birth of Eber
1757	2247	Birth of Peleg
1787	2217	Birth of Reu
1819	2185	Birth of Serug
1822	2182	Beginning of Nimrod's kingdom
1849	2155	Birth of Nahor
1878	2126	Birth of Terah
1996	2008	Death of Peleg
1997	2007	Death of Nahor
2006	1998	Death of Noah
2008	1996	Birth of Abraham
2018	1987	Birth of Sarah
2026	1978	Death of Reu
2049	1955	Death of Serug
2083	1921	Death of Terah
2083	1921	Abram leaves Haran, begins Sojourn
2094	1910	Birth of Ishmael
2096	1908	Death of Arphaxad
2107	1897	Circumcision instituted
2107	1897	Promise of Isaac
2108	1896	Birth of Isaac
2113	1891	Weaning of Isaac
2126	1878	Death of Salah
2141	1863	Abraham to offer up Isaac
2144	1860	Death of Sarah
2148	1856	Marriage of Isaac to Rebecca
2158	1846	Death of Shem
2168	1836	Birth of Jacob and Esau
2183	1821	Death of Abraham

AM	BC	E V E N T
2187	1817	Death of Eber
2208	1796	First marriage of Esau
2231	1773	Death of Ishmael
2245	1759	Flight of Jacob to Laban
2245	1759	Marriage of Jacob to Leah and Rachel
2246	1758	Birth of Reuben by Leah
2247	1757	Birth of Simeon by Leah
2248	1756	Birth of Levi by Leah
2249	1755	Birth of Judah by Leah
2249	1755	Rachel gives Bilhah to Jacob
2249	1755	Birth of Dan by Bilhah
2250	1754	Birth of Naphtali by Bilhah
2250	1754	Leah gives Zilpah to Jacob
2251	1753	Birth of Gad by Zilpah
2252	1752	Birth of Asher by Zilpah
2252	1752	Birth of Issachar by Leah
2253	1751	Birth of Zebulon by Leah
2254	1750	Birth of Dinah by Leah
2259	1745	Birth of Joseph by Rachel
2265	1739	Departure of Jacob from Laban
2265	1739	Rachel dies birthing Benjamin
2272	1732	Dinah raped
2276	1728	Joseph sold into slavery
2286	1718	Dreams of the Baker and Butler
2288	1716	Death of Isaac
2289	1715	Promotion of Joseph, age 30
2296	1708	7 years of plenty end
2297	1707	First journey of the patriarchs to Egypt
2298	1706	2 yrs of famine, Jacob and kin to Egypt
2315	1689	Death of Jacob
2369	1635	Death of Joseph
2433	1571	Birth of Moses
2473	1531	Flight of Moses into Midian
2475	1529	Birth of Caleb
2513	1491	Exodus of Israelites, Law given
2514	1490	Setting up of the tabernacle
2552	1452	Return of the Israelites to Kadesh
2552	1452	Death of Miriam and Aaron
2552	1452	Sihon King of Heshbon conquered
2552	1452	Death of Moses, Joshua the new leader
2553	1451	Israel crosses Jordan into Canaan
2559	1445	7-year war with Canaanites, etc. ends
2559	1445	Began dividing Canaan to the 12 Tribes
2560	1444	Tabernacle moved - Gilgal to Shiloh
2560	1444	Finish dividing Canaan to last 7 Tribes
2580	1424	Death of Joshua (approx.)
2599	1405	Micah's priest, tribe of Dan, Jud 17-18
2601	1403	The Levite's concubine, Jud 19–21
2604	1400	Subjugation by Chushan-Rishathaim
2612	1392	Deliverance by Othniel
2644	1360	Subjugation by Eglon
2662	1342	Deliverance by Ehud
2724	1280	Subjugation by Jabin
2744	1260	Judgeship of Shamgar
2744	1260	Deliverance by Barak And Deborah
2764	1240	Subjugation by the Midianites
2771	1233	Deliverance by Gideon
2804	1200	Usurpation by Abimelech

AM	BC	E V E N T
2807	1197	Judgeship of Tola
2830	1174	Judgeship of Jair
2834	1170	Subjugation by the Ammonites
2842	1162	Judgeship of Eli
2852	1152	Deliverance by Jephthah
2858	1146	Judgeship of Ibzan
2863	1141	Begin 40- yr Philistine Dominion
2865	1139	Judgeship of Elon
2875	1129	Judgeship of Abdon
2882	1122	Ark captured by Philistines – Eli dies
2883	1121	Judgeship of Samson
2883	1121	Ark at Kiriath-Jearim
2903	1101	Samson brings down Temple of Dagon
2903	1101	Samuel ends 40-yr Philistine Dominion
2909	1095	Accession of Saul
2909	1095	Defeat of the Ammonites by Saul
2911	1093	War of Saul with the Philistines
2919	1085	Birth of David
2934	1070	David is secretly anointed by Samuel
2937	1067	Combat of David with Goliath
2939	1065	Flight of David from Saul's Court
2939	1065	Refuge of David at Gath, etc.
2944	1060	Death of Samuel
2945	1059	David spares Saul the 2nd time
2946	1058	Residence of David at Ziklag
2948	1056	Death of Saul and Jonathan
2949	1055	David becomes king over Judah
2951	1053	Civil War – David and Ish-Bosheth
2956	1048	David made king over all the tribes
2956	1048	David takes Jerusalem from Jebusites
2957	1047	David defeats Philistines
2957	1047	Ark brought to Jerusalem
2964	1040	David restores Mephibosheth
2967	1037	Adultery of David with Bathsheba
2968	1036	Birth of Solomon
2969	1035	Incest of Amnon with Tamar
2977	1027	Rebellion of Absalom
2988	1016	Birth of Rehoboam
2989	1015	Usurpation of Adonijah
2989	1015	Solomon appointed pro-rex, then co-rex
2989	1015	David dies, Solomon becomes sole rex
2992	1012	Founding of Solomon's Temple
3000	1004	Dedication of Solomon's Temple
3029	975	Rehoboam becomes king over Judah
3029	975	Secession under Jeroboam I of Israel
3033	971	Shishak invades Judah
3046	958	Abijah becomes king over Judah
3048	956	Asa becomes king over Judah
3050	954	Nadab becomes king over Israel
3051	953	Baasha becomes king over Israel
3054	950	Birth of Jehoshaphat
3074	930	Elah becomes king over Israel
3075	929	Zimri reigns over Israel for 7 days
3075	929	Army makes Omri king over Israel
3075	929	Civil war – Tibni against Omri
3079	925	Birth of Jehoram of Judah
3079	925	Death of Tibni, Omri rules Israel alone
3086	918	Ahab becomes king over Israel

AM	BC	E V E N T
3087	917	Asa's feet diseased
3090	914	Jehoshaphat becomes king over Judah
3096	908	Birth of Ahaziah of Judah
3098	906	Elisha becomes Elijah's servant
3106	898	Jehoram made pro-rex of Judah
3107	897	Ahaziah becomes king over Israel
3107	897	Joram becomes king over Israel
3107	897	Elijah translated
3111	893	Jehoram made co-rex of Judah
3115	889	Jehoram becomes sole rex over Judah
3115	889	Elijah's prophetic letter to Jehoram
3117	887	Ahaziah made pro-rex over Judah
3118	886	Ahaziah becomes sole rex over Judah
3118	886	Jehu becomes king over Israel
3118	886	Usurpation of Athaliah over Judah
3125	879	Joash becomes king of Judah
3141	863	Birth of Amaziah of Judah
3147	857	Jehoahaz becomes king over Israel
3147	857	Temple not yet repaired, Joash's 23rd
3161	843	Jehoash made pro-rex over Israel
3164	840	Jehoash becomes sole rex over Israel
3165	839	Amaziah becomes king over Judah
3167	837	Jeroboam II made pro-rex over Israel
3177	827	Birth of Uzziah of Judah
3179	825	Jeroboam II becomes sole rex of Israel
3194	810	Uzziah becomes king over Judah
3218	786	The Great Earthquake, Amos 1:1
3220	784	Birth of Jotham of Judah
3220	784	Death of Jeroboam II of Israel
3220	784	Zachariah rules Israel or Interregnum
3232	772	Shallum rules Israel for 1-month
3232	772	Menahem becomes king over Israel
3241	763	Birth of Ahaz of Judah
3243	761	Pekahiah becomes king over Israel
3245	759	Pekah becomes king over Israel
3246	758	Jotham becomes sole rex over Judah
3252	752	Birth of Hezekiah of Judah
3262	742	Ahaz becomes king over Judah
3265	739	Pekah dies, Interregnum in Israel
3274	730	Hoshea becomes king over Israel
3278	726	Hezekiah becomes king over Judah
3281	723	Shalmaneser besieges Samaria
3283	721	Assyrian conquest of Israel
3291	713	Sennacherib's 1st invasion as Tartan
3291	713	Hezekiah ill, Life extended 15 years
3291	713	Sargon besieges Ashdod, Isa. 20:1
3292	712	Merodach-Baladan sends Embassy
3293	711	Ashdod falls to Sargon
3295	709	Sennacherib's 2nd invasion as co-rex
3295	709	Angel slays 185,000 Assyrians
3295	709	Birth of Manasseh of Judah
3295	709	15th Year of Jubilee begins, Isa 37:30
3307	697	Manasseh becomes king over Judah
3355	649	Birth of Josiah of Judah
3362	642	Amon becomes king over Judah
3364	640	Josiah becomes king over Judah
3370	634	Birth of Jehoiakim of Judah
3371	633	Conversion of Josiah

AM	BC	EVENT
3372	632	Birth of Jehoahaz of Judah
3375	629	Josiah's 1st reform – idols destroyed
3376	628	Jeremiah begins to prophesy
3381	623	Josiah repairs Temple – finds the Law
3386	618	Birth of Zedekiah of Judah
3388	616	Birth of Jeconiah (Jehoiachin) of Judah
3392	612	Nineveh falls to the Babylonians
3394	610	Haran falls to the Babylonians
3395	609	Josiah anoints Jeconiah as successor
3395	609	Pharaoh Neco slays Josiah
3395	609	Assyrian counter-attack fails
3395	609	Jehoahaz becomes king over Judah
3395	609	Jehoiakim becomes king over Judah
3398	606	Prince Nebuchadnezzar invades Judah
3398	606	1st Deportation to Babylon – Daniel 1
3399	605	Battle of Carchemish – Neco defeated
3399	605	Nebuchadnezzar's year of accession
3400	604	Nebuchad's 1st official yr as sole rex
3400	604	Daniel interprets Nebuchad's dream
3406	598	Minor deportation of captives 2 Ki 24:2
3406	598	Jeconiah becomes king over Judah
3407	597	2nd Deportation to Babylon
3407	597	Zedekiah becomes king over Judah
3411	593	Ezekiel begins to prophesy
3411	593	Zedekiah visits Babylon
3412	592	The glory departs from the Temple
3416	588	Final siege of Jerusalem begins
3416	588	Pharaoh approaches, siege briefly lifted
3418	586	Babylonians sack Jerusalem
3418	586	3rd Deportation to Babylon
3422	582	Minor deportation in Nebuchad's 23rd
3443	561	Release of Jeconiah by Evil-Merodach
3465	539	Babylon falls to Darius the Mede
3468	536	Cyrus' Decree for the Jews Return
3468	536	Return under Zerubbabel
3469	535	Foundation of the second Temple laid
3484	520	Darius' 2nd yr, begin rebuilding Temple
3485	519	Ahasuerus (Darius) divorces Vashti
3488	516	Completion of the second Temple
3489	515	Marriage of Esther to king Ahasuerus
3494	510	Haman initiates plot against the Jews
3495	509	Ahasuerus' insomnia
3495	509	Haman hanged on his own gallows
3495	509	Mordecai promoted to Prime Minister
3496	508	Mordecai and Esther deliver Jews
3537	467	Decree to beautify Temple in Arta's 7th
3537	467	Ezra arrives at Jerusalem
3537	467	Jews Divorce their Gentile wives
3549	455	Nehemiah learns of Jerusalem's status
3550	454	Artaxerxes Decree in his 20th year
3550	454	Begin Daniel's 70 Weeks to Messiah
3550	454	Nehemiah comes to Jerusalem
3550	454	Wall of Jerusalem built and dedicated
3562	442	Nehemiah returns to Persia
3563	441	Malachi, end of the O.T.
3673	331	Persian Empire falls to Alexander
3681	323	Alexander dies, Empire divided 4 ways
3833	171	Antiochus Epiphanes plunders Temple

AM	BC	EVENT
3836	168	Antiochus has sow offered on the altar
3836	168	Maccabean revolt against the Syrians
3839	165	Temple services renewed, 25th Kislev
3941	63	Jerusalem taken by Pompey
3964	40	Romans appoint Herod the Great king
3967	37	Herod takes Jerusalem by Storm
3984	20	Herod begins Temple renovation
4000	4	Death of Herod the Great
4000	4	Births of John the Baptist and CHRIST
4004	1	Beginning of the Christian Era
4012	9	12-year-old Jesus at the Temple
4015	12	1st year of Tiberius as co-rex
4017	14	Augustus dies, Tiberius sole rex
4029	26	Pontius Pilate Procurator of Judea
4029	26	John baptizes Jesus, 15th of Tiberius
4030	27	30 yrs old, Jesus begins public ministry
4032	29	Herod Antipas beheads John Baptist
4032	29	Transfiguration of Christ Jesus
4032	29	Feast of Tabernacles in John 7
4033	30	Crucifixion-Resurrection of our Lord
4033	30	Martyrdom of Stephen
4035	32	Conversion of Paul
4040	37	Caligula becomes Roman Emperor
4042	39	Herod Antipas banished to Gaul
4044	41	Claudius becomes Roman Emperor
4044	41	Conversion of Cornelius
4047	44	Martyrdom of James, Acts 12
4047	44	Death of Herod Agrippa I, Acts 12
4048	45	First Missionary Journey, Acts 13
4049	46	Paul stoned at Lystra, Acts 14
4053	50	Jerusalem Council on Circumcision
4055	52	Felix Procurator of Judea
4056	53	Second Missionary Journey, Acts 15
4057	54	Nero becomes Roman Emperor
4059	56	Third Missionary Journey, Acts 18
4062	59	Paul mobbed and arrested at the Temple
4062	59	Paul before Felix
4063	60	Festus Procurator of Judea
4064	61	Paul before Festus and Agrippa II
4065	62	Paul's First Arrival in Rome
4067	64	Paul released
4067	64	Nero begins persecution of Christians
4070	67	Martyrdom of Paul and Peter
4073	70	Titus destroys Jerusalem
4082	79	Titus becomes Roman Emperor
4084	81	Domitian becomes Roman Emperor
4099	96	John the Apostle banished to Patmos
4099	96	Nerva becomes Roman Emperor
4099	96	John released upon Nerva's accession
4101	98	Trajan, Roman Emperor until AD 117
?	?	John the Apostle dies in Trajan's reign

THE ASSYRIAN EPONYM AND KING LISTS

The following eponyms are based on the work of Daniel David Luckenbill, *Ancient Records Of Assyria And Babylonia*, Vol. II (London: Histories and Mysteries of Man Ltd., Pub., 1989) pp. 428–439. Our original research utilized Dr. Edwin R. Thiele's 1983 book, *The Mysterious Numbers of the Hebrew Kings*. As he accepted the shorter Assyrian chronology, the following depicts the same. Consequently, as in his work, Nabu-shar-user has been transferred from 784 to 786 where he occupies the same eponym year with Balatu (see F.N. Jones, page 146 ff.). This reduces each eponym beyond 786 by one year. The dates for the eponyms from 648 to 783 are the same. An asterisk * marks the eponymous year of each king of Assyria.

The words found in brackets in the translations have been supplied, often from parallel or similar passages. Broken brackets are employed where one or more characters of the word have been preserved. Where a number of words have been enclosed by a bracket and a broken bracket, the words up to, or after, the one carrying the broken bracket are conjectural. In parentheses are given literal or variant translations, and such additional words as are required by the difference of idiom to bring out the sense.

```
*1029    Shulmanu-asharidu, king          Shalmaneser I (II) 1030–1018 BC
 1028    Ilia-shangu-mushab[shi]
 1027    ... ash(?)-kuder)
 1026    ...........sa(?)-shum-usur
 1025    .............ku
 1024    .............lamur
 1023    ...........ash(?)ma (?)
 1022    ...........:............
 1021    ...................
 1020    Ni(?).......................
 1019    ...................
 1018    Siki-ilani(?) ............
            12 years
------------------------------------------------
*1017    Assur-nirari, [the king], who (reigned) after [Shalmaneser]
 1016    Assur-nirari
 1015    Assur-nirari
 1014    Assur-nirari
 1013    Assur-nirari
 1012    Assur-nirari
            6 years
------------------------------------------------
*1011    Assur-rabi
 1010    Assur-mushezib
 1009    Ittab[shi.....
 1008    Assur-etir[anni
 1007    Nabu-dan
 1006    Assur-ballit(?)
 1005    Kin- ...........
 1004    Ku.............
 1003    ...............
            (Break in the list)
  966    ................
 *965    Tukulti-apil-esharra
  964    Assur-bel-lamur
  963    again Assur-bel-lamur
  962    .........LAL RID
  961    ............RID
  960    .........mu......
  959    ......:............
  958    ......:............
  957    ......:............
  956    ......:............
  955    ......:............
  954    ....a..............
  953    .....tab(?)ilu(?)
  952    .....du
  951    Ishtar-dudu
  950    .....lika
  949    [Habil⌉-kinu
```

948   .....dinishe
947   Bau-shakin-mati
946–940 (*Break in the list*)
939   ....
938   Urta-...............
937   Assur-na- ....
936   Tukulti-apil- ....
935   Nadin-............
934   Bel-..............
933   Nannar-............
         33 years
*932   Assur-dan
931-893 ....
      (*Break in the list*)
892   ....shar.......
891   Urta-zarme
890   Tab-etir-Assur
889   Assur-la-Kinu
*888   Tukulti-Urta, the king
887   Tak-lak-ana-bel-ia
886   Abi-ili-a-a
885   Ilu-milki
884   Iari
883   Assur-shezibani
*882   Assur-nasir-apli, the king
881   Assur-iddin
880   Shumutti-adur
879   Sha-ilima-damka
878   Dagan-bel-nasir
877   Urta-pia-usur
876   Urta-bel-usur
875   Shangu-Assur-lilbur
874   Shamash-upahir (var. ub-la)
873   Nergal-bel-kumma
872   Kurdi-Assur
871   Assur-li'
870   Assur-natkil
869   Bel-mudammik
868   Daian-Urta
867   Ishtar-emukaia
866   Shamash-nuri
865   Mannu-dan-ana-ili
864   Shamash-bel-usur
863   Urta-iliai
862   Urta-etiranni
861   Urta (var. Assur,) -iliai
860   Nergal-iska-danin

859	Tab-Bel	when Shulman asharidu (Shalmaneser) son of Assurnasirpal [took his seat on the throne]	
858	Sharru-baltu-nishe		⌜against Hamanu⌝
*857	Shulman asharid (Shalmaneser)	king of Assur	⌜against Bit-Adini⌝
856	Assur-bel-ukin	field-marshal	[against Bit-Adini]
855	Assur-bunaia-usur	chief cup-bearer	[against Bit-Adini]
854	Abu-ina-ekalli-lil-bur	high chamberlain	....
853	Daian-Assur	field-marshal	[against Hatte]
852	Shamash-abua	governor of Nasibna	[against Til-Abni]
851	Shamash-bel-usur	(governor) of Calah	[against Babylonia]
850	Bel-bunaia	high chamberlain	[against Babylonia]
849	Hadi-lipushu	(governor) of	[against Carchemish]
848	Nergal-alik-pani	(governor) of	[against Hatte]
847	Bir-Ramana	[(governor) of	against Pakarhubuna]
846	Urta-mukin-nishe	[(governor) of	against Iaeti]
845	Urta-nadin-shum	[(governor) of	against Hatte]
844	Assur-bunua	[(governor) of	against Nairi]
843	Tab-Urta	[(governor) of	against Namri]
842	Taklak-ana-sharri (var. -Assur)	[(governor) of	against Hamanu]
841	Adad-rimani	[(governor) of	against Damascus⌝
840	Bel-abua (var., Shamash-)	[(governor) of Ahi-[Suhina]	⌜against Kue⌝
839	Shulmu-bel-lumur	(governor) of Rasappa	against ⌜Kumuhi⌝

Year	Eponym	Title	Campaign
838	Urta-kibsi-usur	(governor) of Ahi-Suhina	against Danabi
837	Urta-ilia	(governor) of Salmat	against Tabali
836	Kurdi-Assur	(governor) of ⌈Kirruri⌉	against Melidi
835	Shepa-sharri	(governor) of Nineveh	against Namri
834	Nergal-mudammik	the abarakku	against Kue
833	Iahalu	(governor) of ⌈Kakzi⌉	against Kue. The great god went out from Der.
		against Kue	
832	Ululaia	(governor) of ⌈Nasibina⌉	against Urartu (Armenia)
831	Nishpati-Bel	(governor) of ⌈Calah⌉	against Unki
830	Nergal-ilia	(governor) of Arrapha	against Ulluba
829	Hubaia	(governor) of [Mazamua⌉	against Mannai
828	Ilu-mukin-ahi	(governor) of	revolt
*827	Shulman-asharidu (Shalmaneser)	king of Assyria	revolt
826	Daian-Assur	[field-marshal]	revolt
825	Assur-bunaia-usur	[chief cup-bearer]	revolt
824	Iahallu	[abarakku]	revolt
823	Bel-bunaia	[high chamberlain]	revolt
*822	Shamshi-Adad	king of ⌈Assyria	against Sikris⌉
821	Iahalu	[field marshal	against Madai⌉
820	Bel-daian	high chamberlain	against.....shumme
819	Urta-upahhir	[abarakku	against Karne⌉
818	Shamash-ilia	[abarakku	against Karne⌉
817	Nergal-ilia	[(governor) of Arrapha	against Tille⌉
816	Assur-bana-usur	[chief cup-bearer	against Tille⌉
815	Nishpati-Bel	(governor) of ⌈Nasibina⌉	against Zarate
814	Bel-balat	(governor) of ⌈Calah⌉ against Der	The great god went to Der.
813	Mushiknish	(governor) of ⌈Kirruri⌉	against Ahsana
812	Urta-asharid	(governor) of [Salmat⌉	against Chaldea
811	Shamash-kimua	(governor) of Arrapha	against Babylonia
810	Bel-kata-sabat	(governor) of Mazamua	in the land
*809	Adad-nirari	[king] of Assyria	against Madai
808	Nergal-ilia	field-marshal	against Guzana
807	Bel-daian	high chamberlain	against Mannai
806	Sil-bel	chief cup-bearer	against Mannai
805	Assur-taklak	abarakku	against Arpadda
804	⌈Shamash-ilia⌉	abarakku	against Hazazi
803	Nergal-eresh	(governor) of Rasappa	against Bali
802	Assur-baltu-nishe	(governor) of Arrapha	against the seacoast. A plague.
801	Urta-ilia	(governor) of Ahi-Suhina	against Hubushkia
800	Shepa-Ishtar	(governor) of Nasibina	against Madai
799	Marduk-ishme-ani(?)	(governor) of Amedi	against Madai
798	Mutakkil-Marduk	Rab-shake	against Lusia
797	Bel-tarsi-iluma	(governor) of Calah	against Namri
796	Assur-bel-usur	(governor) of Kirruri	against Mansuate
795	Marduk-shaddua	(governor) of Salmat	against Der
794	Kin-abua	(governor) of Tushhan	against Der
793	Mannu-ki-Assur	(governor) of Guzana	against Madai
792	Mushallim-Urta	(governor) of Tille	against Madai
791	Bel-ikishani	(governor) of Mehi-nish(?)	against Hubushkia
790	Shepa-Shamash	(governor) of Isana	against Itu'a
789	Urta-mukin-ahi	(governor) of Nineveh	against Madai
788	Adad-Mushammir	(governor) of Kakzi	against Madai
787	Sil-Ishtar	(governor) of [Arba-ilu?]	The foundation of the temple of Nabu in Nineveh was torn up (for repairs)
786	Balatu	(governor) of [Shiba-niba?]	Against Madai. Nabu entered the new temple.
785	Adad-uballit	(governor) of ⌈Rimusi⌉	against ⌈Kiski⌉
784	Marduk-shar-usur	(governor) of	against Hubushkia. The great god went to Der.
783	Urta-nasir	(governor) of Mazamua	against Itu'
782	Nabu-li'	(governor) of Nasibina	against Itu'
(Var.,	786 Nabu-shar-usur		
	785 Adad-uballit		
	784 Marduk-shar-usur		
	783 Marduk-nasir		
	782 Ilima-li'-)		
*781	Shalman-asharid	king of Assyria	against Urarti

	(Shalmaneser)		
780	Shamshi-ilu	field-marshal	against Urarti
779	Marduk-rimani	chief cup-bearer	against Urarti
778	Bel-lishir	high chamberlain	against Urarti
777	Nabu-ishid-ukin	abarakku	against Itu'
	(var., Shamash-ishidia-ukin)		
776	Pan-Assur-lamur	shaknu	against Urarti
775	Nergal-eresh	(governor) of Rasappa	against Erini
774	Ishtar-duri	(governor) of Nasibina	against Urati (and) Namri
773	Mannu-ki-Adad	(governor) of Salmat	against Damascus
772	Assur-bel-usur	(governor) of Calah	against Hatarika
*771	Assur-dan	king of Assyria	against Gananati
770	Shamshi-ilu	field-marshal	against Marrat
769	Bel-ilia	(governor) of Arrapha	against Itu'
768	Aplia	(governor) of Mazamua	in the land
767	Kurdi-Assur	(governor) of Ahi-Suhina	against Gananati
766	Mushallim-Urta	(governor) of Tille	against Madai
765	Urta-mukin-nishe	(governor) of Kirruri.	against Hatarika. A plague.
764	Sidki-ilu	(governor) of Tushhan	in the land
763	Bur(Ishdi)-Sagale	(governor) of Guzana	revolt in city of Assur. In the month of *Simanu* an eclipse of the sun took place.
762	Tab-Bel	(governor) of Amedi	revolt in the city of Assur.
761	Nabu-mukin-ahi	(governor) of Nineveh	revolt in the city of Arrapha
760	Lakipu	(governor) of Kakzi	revolt in the city of Arrapha
759	Pan-Assur-lamur	(governor) of Arbailu	revolt in the city of Guzana. A plague.
758	Bel-taklak	(governor) of Isana	against Guzana. Peace in the land.
757	Urta-iddina	(governor) of Kurban	in the land
756	Bel-shadua	(governor) of Parnunna	in the land
755	Ikishu (var., Kisu)	(governor) of Mehi-nish(?)	against Hatarika
754	Urta-shezibani	(governor) of Rimusi	against Arpadda. Return from the city of Assur.
*753	Assur-nirari	king of Assyria	in the land
752	Shamshi-ilu	field-marshal	in the land
751	Marduk-shallimani	high chamberlain	in the land
750	Bel-dan	chief cup-bearer	in the land
749	Shamash-ken-dugul	abarakku	against Namri
748	Adad-bel-ukin	shaknu	against Namri
747	Sin-shallimani	(governor) of Rasappa	in the land
746	Nergal-nasir	(governor) of Nasibina	revolt in the city of Calah
745	Nabu-bel-usur	(governor) of Arrapha	On the thirteenth day of the month *Airu* Tiglath-pileser took his seat on the throne. In the month of *Tashritu* he marched to the territory between the rivers.
744	Bel-dan	(governor) of Calah	against Namri
*743	Tukulti-apal-esharra	king of Assyria	in the city of Arpadda. A massacre took place in the land of Urartu (Armenia).
	(Tiglath-pileser)		
742	Nabu-daninani	field-marshal	against Arpadda
741	Bel-harran-bel-usur	high chamberlain	against Arpadda. After three years it was conquered.
740	Nabu-etirani	chief cup-bearer	against Arpadda
739	Sin-taklak	abarakku	against Ulluba. The fortress was taken.
738	Adad-bel-ukin	shaknu	Kullani was captured.
737	Bel-emurani	(governor) of Rasappa	against Madai
736	Urta-ilia	(governor) of Nasibina	To the foot of Mount Nal
735	Assur-shallimani	(governor) of Arrapha	against Urarti
734	Bel-dan	(governor) of Calah	against Philistia
733	Assur-daninani	(governor) of Mazamua	against the land of Damascus
732	Nabu-bel-usur	(governor) of Si'me	against the land of Damascus
731	Nergal-uballit	(governor) of Ahi-Suhina	against Sapia
730	Bel-ludari	(governor) of Tile	in the land

Year	Name	Title	Event
729	Naphar-ilu	(governor) of Kirruri	The king took the hand
728	Dur-Assur	(governor) of Tushhan	The king took the hand of Bel
727	Bel-harran-bel-usur	(governor) of Guzana	against Damascus
			Shalmaneser took his seat on the throne
726	Marduk-bel-usur	(governor) of Amedi	in the land
725	Mahde	(governor) of Nineveh	against [Samaria]
724	Assur-ishmeani	(governor) of ⌜Kakzi⌝	against [Samaria]
*723	Shalmaneser	king of Assyria	against [Samaria]
722	Urta-ilia	⌜field-marshal⌝	[the foundation of the temple of Nabu was torn up (for repairs)⌝.
721	Nabu-taris	[high chamberlain]	[Nabu entered the new temple⌝.
720	Assur-iska-danin	[field-marshal	against Tabala⌝
*719	Sargon	King of ⌜Assyria⌝	the foundation of the [temple of Nergal⌝ was torn up (for repairs).
718	Zer-ibni	(governor) of Ra......	against Mannai
717	Tab-shar-Assur	⌜abarakku⌝	....provinces were established
716	Tab-sil-esharra	(governor) of Assur	....Musasir of Haldia.
715	Taklak-ana-bel	(governor) of Nazibina	great....in Ellipa
714	Ishtar-duri	(governor) of Arrapha	Nergal entered the new temple
713	Assur-bani	(governor) of Calah	against Musasir.
712	Sharru-emurani	(governor) of Zamua	in the land.
711	Urta-alik-pani	(governor) of Si'me	against Markasa.
710	Shamash-bel-usur	(governor) of ⌜Arzuhina⌝	against Bet-zernaid,
709	Manu-ki-Assur-li'	(governor) of Tille	the king in Kish.... Sargon took the hand of Bel.
708	Shamash-upahhir	(governor) of Kirruri	Kumuha was captured. A governor was appointed.
707	Sha-Assur-dubbi	(governor) of Tushhan	The king returned from Babylon.
706	Mutakkil-Assur	(governor) of Guzana	...from the city of Dur-Iakin brought out.
705	Nashir-Bel	(governor) of Amedi	the city of Dur-Iakin was destroyed.
704	Nabu-din-epush	(governor) of Nineveh	the gods entered into their temples.
703	Kannunnai	(governor) of Kakzi	[the nobles⌝ were in Karalli.
702	Nabu-li'	(governor) of Abailu	
701	Hananai	(governor) of ....bi	
700	Metunu	(governor) of Isana	
699	Bel-sharani	(governor) of [Kurban]	
698	Shulmu-shar	(governor) of	
697	Nabu-dur-usur	(governor) of	
696	Shulmu-bel	(governor) of Rimusa	
695	Assur-bel-usur	(governor) of	
694	Ilu-ittia	(governor) of Damascus	
693	Nadin-ahe	(governor) of	
692	Zazai	(governor) of Arpadda	
691	Bel-emurani	(governor) of Carchemish	
690	Nabu-mukin-ahi (var., Nabu-bel-usur)	(governor) of Samaria	
689	Gihilu	(governor) of Hatarika	
688	Nadin-ahe	(governor) of ⌜Simirra⌝	
*687	Sennacherib	king of Assyria	
686	Bel-emuranni	(governor) of Calah	
685	Assur-daninanni	(governor) of .....ub	
684	Mannu-zirni (var., Man-zirne)	(governor) of Kullania	
683	Mannu-ki-Adad	(governor) of Supite	
682	Nabu-shar-usur	(governor) of Markasi	
681	Nabu-ah-eresh	(governor) of Samalli	
680	Dananu	(governor) of ⌜Mansua⌝	
679	Itti-Adad-aninu	(governor) of Magidunu	
678	Nergal-shar-usur	chief-cup-bearer	
677	Abi-rama	high minister	

676	Banba	second minister
675	Nabu-ahi-iddina	chief governor
674	Sharru-nuri	(governor) of Barhalzi
673	Atar-ilu	(governor) of Lahiri
672	Nabu-bel-usur	(governor) of Dur-Sharrukin
671	Kanunai	SAR-TINU-official
670	Shulmu-bel-lashme	(governor) of Der
669	Shamash-kashid-aibi	(governor) of Ashdod
668	Mar-larim	field-marshal
667	Gabbar	(governor) of ....
666	Kanunai	(governor) of Bit-eshshi
665	Mannu-ki-sharri	perfect of the land
664	Sharru-ludari	(governor) of Dur-Sharrukin
663	Bel-naid	field-marshal
662	Tab-shar-Sin	(governor) of Rasappa
661	Arbailai	
660	Gir-zapuna	
659	Silim-Assur	
658	Sha-Nabu-shu	
657	Labasi	
656	Milki-ramu	
655	Amianu	
654	Assur-nasir	
653	Assur-ilai	
652	Assur-dur-usur	
651	Sagabbu	
650	Bel-harran-shadua	
649	Ahu-ilai	
648	Belshunu	

ASSYRIAN ACADEMY'S PARTIAL KING LIST

Shalmaneser I (II)	1030–1018 BC
Assur-nirari IV	1018–1012 BC
Assur-rabi II	1012–971 BC
Assur-resh-ishi II	971–966 BC
Tiglath-pileser II	966–934 BC
Assur-dan II	934–911 BC
Adad-nirari II	911–890 BC
Tukulti-Urta II	890–884 BC
Assur-nasir-pal II	884–859 BC
Shalmaneser II (III)	859–824 BC
Shamshi-Adad V	824–811 BC
Adad-nirari III	*811–783 BC
Shalmaneser III (IV)	783–773 BC
Assur-dan III (III)	773–754 BC
Assur-nirari V	754–745 BC
Tiglath-pileser (III)	745–727 BC
Shalmaneser IV (V)	727–722 BC
Sargon (II)	722–705 BC
Sennacherib	705–681 BC
Esar-haddon	681–669 BC
Assur-banipal	669–627 BC
Assur-etil-ilani	627–622 BC
Sin-shar-ishkun	621–612 BC
Assur-uballit II	612–609 BC

*If Ahab and Jehu were contemporaries with Shalmaneser II (III), a gap of c. 45 years is missing here in the Assyrian records. In such case, beginning at 783 BC, 45 would have to be added to all older dates (e.g., Adad nirari III = 856–828 BC).

CALENDARS

JULIAN CALENDAR: Julius Caesar abolished the use of the lunar year as well as the intercalary month and regulated the year using only the sun. He decreed that from 45 BC (709 YOR) there should be three years of 365 days each and then one year of 366 days in perpetual cycle. This became known as the Julian calendar. It is exactly 365.25 days per solar year (365 x 3 + 366 ÷ 4). It began the custom we still observe today of adding one day to February every fourth year (i.e., years divisible by 4 = leap years). Whereas the year had begun March 1, it now became January 1. To realign the calendar with the seasons, 46 BC was made 445 days long (called "the year of confusion" by the Romans).

Even though the Julian calendar was an enormous improvement over all previous systems, it still was not completely accurate. Since there are approximately 365¼ days in a solar year, the Julian calendar was reasonably satisfactory for many years – but there are not exactly 365¼ (365.25) days in a year. The mean solar year (often called the "tropical year") consists of 365 days, 5 hours, 48 minutes, 45.975 seconds (365.24219879 days). The difference is eleven minutes fourteen seconds, which results in a one day error every 128 years. Although small, this becomes appreciable over the course of centuries; hence, the Julian calendar needed adjusting.

GREGORIAN CALENDAR: In 1582 Pope Gregory XIII made another calendar correction. The Gregorian calendar is the one we use today. The mean Gregorian year has 365.2425 days. To make up for all the days that had accumulated since the beginning of the Julian calendar, Gregory XIII decreed the elimination of 10 days from the year 1582. The result was that in many countries the day after October 4, 1582 became October 15, 1582.[1]

Pope Gregory XIII kept the Leap Year rule whereby, normally, every year evenly divisible by four with no remainder would be a leap year. However, the Gregorian Leap Year rule adds the exception that every year ending in "00" whose number cannot be divided by 400 will not be a leap year. Thus, the years 1700, 1800, and 1900 were not leap years and had only 28 days in February. Being divisible by 400, February 2000 had 29 days. This system will serve us for more than a thousand years hence. The Gregorian year is 26 seconds longer than the

solar-tropical year; this is less than one day every 3000 years. Thus, although the Gregorian calendar is a great improvement over the Julian calendar, it still is not 100% accurate.

ADOPTION OF THE GREGORIAN CALENDAR: Although the initial adoption of the Gregorian calendar was in 1582, its use was by no means universal. The first countries to adopt the new calendar were primarily Roman Catholic nations. Most Protestant countries did not make the change until later. The American Colonies made the switch in 1752, the year in which the whole British Empire changed over. September 2, 1752 was followed by September 14, 1752.

Note that an eleven-day adjustment was now needed, the Julian calendar having added another day between 1582 and 1752. Dates preceding the change are sometimes designated OS for Old Style. Thus, George Washington's birthday was originally February 11, 1732 (OS), and only after the change to the Gregorian calendar was his birthday established as February 22, 1732. Most dates in American history have been converted to New Style (NS) or Gregorian. Other countries have been even slower in adopting the new calendar: Japan, 1873, China, 1912, Greece, 1924, Turkey, 1927.

CONVERSION: To make the conversion from Julian dates to Gregorian dates, add 10 days to the Julian date from October 5, 1582 through February 28, 1700. Then, add 11 days to Julian dates from March 1, 1700 through February 28, 1800; add 12 days to Julian dates from March 1, 1800 through February 28, 1900; add 13 days to Julian dates from March 1, 1900 through February 28, 2000; etc.

ASTRONOMICAL OR JULIAN PERIOD DATING: Today, the world as a whole uses the Gregorian calendar. As this calendar has no year "zero," when counting years from BC to AD we must subtract one year from the total. The same is true of the Julian calendar. Thus, the next year after 1 BC is AD 1, not zero; 1 BC to AD 1 is only one year.

This is not so with astronomical years. Astronomical or Julian Period years (not the same as the Julian calendar above) are the same as Gregorian years after AD 1; but as this calendar does have a year "zero," all BC dates will be one year less. Because astronomical years are frequently given a BC designation, they are often confused as being Gregorian. To avoid this, it is more prudent to display them as −620 and not 620 BC.

Astronomers normally give ancient dates and events such as eclipses Julian Period (JP) dates; but as most are not aware of this and since nearly all dates in American history have been converted to Gregorian, my work uses Gregorian dates.

---

[1] The days of the week, the weekly cycle, were not changed – nor have they ever. Dr. J.B. Dimbleby, astronomer and premier chronologist to the British Chronological and Astronomical Association, asserts: "If men refused to observe weeks and the line of time was forgotten, the day of the week could be recovered by observing when the transits of the planets or eclipses of the sun and moon occurred. These great sentinels of the sky keep seven days with scientific accuracy, thundering out the seven days inscribed on the inspired page" (*All Past Time*, c.1900, p. 10).

The Jubilee Cycle

Jubilee									

BC Years	711	710	709	708	707	706	705	704	703	702
	4	5	6	7	8	9				
Nisan (Abib) Years	46	47	48	49 (7th Sabbatic Year)	1	2	3	4	5	6	7

50th
Year
Jubilee

10th day of the 7th month

Whereas the Year of Jubilee is regarded as the 50th year (Lev. 25:10), there are only 49 years from one Jubilee to the next. Leviticus 25:8–10 explains that rather than the 50th year following at the end of the 49th, it begins midway in the 49th year on the Day of Atonement (10th day of the 7th month) and extends to the Day of Atonement in the 1st year of the next cycle. Thus the Jubilee year overlaps the 49th and 1st years as shown above. Otherwise, Jubilee would be every 50th year rather than every 49 years *on* the 50th year. Also note that most of the Jubilee year falls in 708 BC as Tishri (September/October) of 709 is near the end of that year. The next Jubilee would be 660/659 BC (709 – 49 = 660).

Many chronologers have given the subject of Jubilees and Sabbatical year cycles great prominence in their works,[1] but our study has not found them or the priestly cycles of much value with respect to establishing the chronology. One notable exception was the Jubilee of 709/708 BC which began in Tishri of the 18th year of Hezekiah (2 Kings 19:29; Isa. 37:30, cp. 2 Kings 18:13; Isa. 36:1). Terminating in Tishri of his 19th year, most of this Jubilee took place in AD 708 (pages 165–167). As Thiele and the Assyrian Academy remove at least 45 years from the period of the Hebrew kings and date Hezekiah's 14th year as 701 BC, they fail to honor this biblical Jubilee. Hence, this Jubilee completely exposes their historical reconstruction as flawed and invalid.

The only other of value in establishing the chronology was that beginning in the fall of AD 27 when our Lord read from Isaiah 61:1–2a at the synagogue in Nazareth at the beginning of His first tour of Galilee. This study understands His proclaiming "liberty to the captives" and "the acceptable year of the Lord" as a clear allusion to Jubilee, thereby fixing the date of this reading as occurring in a Jubilee year.

---

[1] Indeed, Faulstich maintains over and over that his entire chronology is largely based upon his computer's making use of these cyclic events (including the weekly Sabbath; e.g., *History, Harmony and the Hebrew Kings, op. cit.*, pp. 28–41, 175–191).

Jubilee Years

1451 BC Moses dies – Joshua crosses the Jordan River on the 10th day of Abib (Nisan = 1st month = Thursday April 2, 1451 Gregorian, Josh. 3:15, 4:19) and enters the Promised Land.

1445 BC Following 7 years of conflict with the Canaanites (c. April 1451 to near the end of 1445 = 7 years by inclusive reckoning: *Seder Olam Rabbah* agrees, page 116; see my Appendix L, page 295) during which Israel's base camp was at Gilgal, the wars ended at the close of 1445 BC. Joshua then began to divide the land on the west side of the Jordan by giving the tribes of Judah and Joseph (Ephraim and the half tribe of Manasseh) their portions.

1444 BC Early this year, the Tabernacle was moved to Shiloh. The rest of the land west of the Jordan was then divided among the remaining 7 tribes (Josh. 11:23, ch. 15–17), and the men from the 2½ tribes east of the Jordan returned home. Before this, Israel had lived off the crops planted by the Canaanites, volunteer crops, and supplies from the 2½ eastern tribes (Josh. 5:12, 24:13, 4:12–13; cp. Num. 26:7, 18, and 34). This was the beginning of their tillage; hence, from this year are reckoned the Sabbatic and Jubilee years (1444 – 49 = 1395 BC, the first Jubilee year; see below and Lev. 25:3, "six years thou shalt … gather in the fruit thereof").

Jubilee #	Floyd N. Jones	Ussher	W. Whiston (in Josephus)	Jubilee #	Floyd N. Jones
01	1395/4 BC	1396/5 BC	1395/4 BC	37	AD 370/1
02	1346/5 BC	1347/6 BC	1346/5 BC	38	AD 419/0
03	1297/6 BC	1298/7 BC	1297/6 BC	39	AD 468/9
04	1248/7 BC	1249/8 BC	1248/7 BC	40	AD 517/8
05	1199/8 BC	1200/9 BC	1199/8 BC	41	AD 566/7
06	1150/9 BC	1151/0 BC	1150/9 BC	42	AD 615/6
07	1101/0 BC	1102/1 BC	1101/0 BC	43	AD 664/5
08	1052/1 BC	1053/2 BC	1052/1 BC	44	AD 713/4
09	1003/2 BC	1004/3 BC	1003/2 BC	45	AD 762/3
10	954/3 BC	955/4 BC	954/3 BC	46	AD 811/2
11	905/4 BC	906/5 BC	905/4 BC	47	AD 860/1
12	856/5 BC	857/6 BC	856/5 BC	48	AD 909/0
13	807/6 BC	808/7 BC	807/6 BC	49	AD 958/9
14	758/7 BC	759/8 BC	758/7 BC	50	AD 1007/8
15	709/8 BC	710/9 BC	709/8 BC	51	AD 1056/7
16	660/9 BC	661/0 BC	660/9 BC	52	AD 1105/6
17	611/0 BC	612/1 BC	611/0 BC	53	AD 1154/5
18	562/1 BC	563/2 BC	562/1 BC	54	AD 1203/4
19	513/2 BC	514/3 BC	513/2 BC	55	AD 1252/3
20	464/3 BC	465/4 BC	464/3 BC	56	AD 1301/2
21	415/4 BC	416/5 BC	415/4 BC	57	AD 1350/1
22	366/5 BC	367/6 BC	366/5 BC	58	AD 1399/0
23	317/6 BC	318/7 BC	317/6 BC	59	AD 1448/9
24	268/7 BC	269/8 BC	268/7 BC	60	AD 1497/8
25	219/8 BC	220/9 BC	219/8 BC	61	AD 1546/7
26	170/9 BC	171/0 BC	170/9 BC	62	AD 1595/6
27	121/0 BC	122/1 BC	121/0 BC	63	AD 1644/5
28	72/1 BC	73/2 BC	72/1 BC	64	AD 1693/4
29	23/2 BC	24/3 BC	23/2 BC	65	AD 1742/3
30	AD 27/8	AD 26/7	AD 27/8	66	AD 1791/2
31	AD 76/7			67	AD 1840/1
32	AD 125/6			68	AD 1889/0
33	AD 174/5			69	AD 1938/9
34	AD 223/4			70	AD 1987/8
35	AD 272/3			71	AD 2036/7
36	AD 321/2			72	AD 2085/6

The Jubilee Cycle Begins

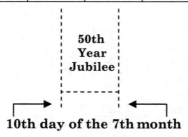

BC Years	1397	1396	1395	1394	1393	1392	1391	1390	1389	1388
	4	**5**	**6**	**7**	**8**	**9**				
Nisan (Abib) Years	46	47	48	49 7th Sabbatic Year	1	2	3	4	5	6	7

50th Year Jubilee

10th day of the 7th month

The Sabbatical Year

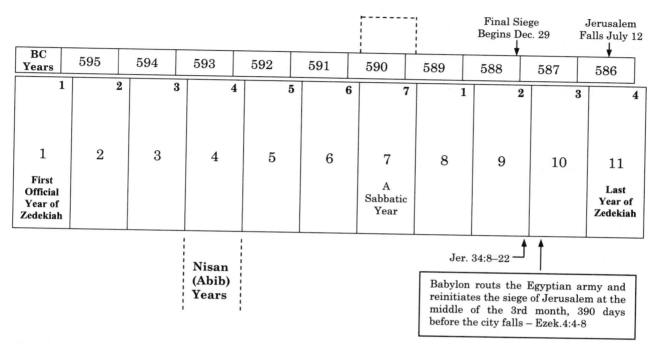

BC Years	595	594	593	592	591	590	589	588	587	586
	1	2	3	4	5	6	7	1	2	3	4
	1 First Official Year of Zedekiah	2	3	4	5	6	7 A Sabbatic Year	8	9	10	11 Last Year of Zedekiah

Final Siege Begins Dec. 29

Jerusalem Falls July 12

Nisan (Abib) Years

Jer. 34:8–22

Babylon routs the Egyptian army and reinitiates the siege of Jerusalem at the middle of the 3rd month, 390 days before the city falls – Ezek.4:4-8

As there are several well-attested historically recorded Sabbatical years, their cycles may readily be determined.[1] The non-inspired, non-canonical book of 1 Maccabees (yet a historical work of great value) records a Sabbatical year in the 150th year of the Seleucid era (= 163 BC, see 1 Mac. 6:20, 49, and 53). Another is recorded by Josephus as having occurred shortly after the death of Simon, the father and predecessor of John Hyrcanus, and soon after the accession of John (Antiquities, xiii, 8, 1). Simon was assassinated in the month of Shebat in the 177th year of the Seleucid era (1 Mac. xvi, 14). That would have been around the first of

February, 135 BC. A third is 37 BC, when Herod and Sosius took Jerusalem by force. Josephus states that the Jews were distressed by famine and the absence of necessities which was aggravated by the circumstance that it was a Sabbatical year (Antiquities, xiv, 16, 2). Fourth, there is a well-attested tradition that AD 70, the year Titus of Rome took Jerusalem, was part of a Sabbatical year (i.e., AD 69/70).[2]

If we select one of these historical Sabbatic years, say 163 BC, and calculate from it, the year 709/708 in Hezekiah's reign will be found to be Sabbatical (163 + [7 x 78] = 163 + 546 = 709) as well as being the years involving the 15th Jubilee.[3] We may now confirm the year of our initial 7th Sabbatical year and first Jubilee: 163 + (7 x 176) = 163 + 1232 = 1395 BC. Had we selected the historical Sabbatic year of 37 BC, the last calculation would be: 37 + (7 x 194) = 37 + 1358 = 1395 BC.

---

[1] That is, within one year. For example, some (Nicholas Toinard [1707], Dean Humphrey Prideaux [1716], William Whiston [1721], Henry Browne [1844], Ben Zion Wacholder [1973], Floyd Nolen Jones [2001], etc.) take the Sabbatic year of 37 BC to fall in the years 37/36 while others (Ussher [1658], B. Zuckerman [1856], Donald Blosser [1979], etc.) place it in the years 38/37. Regardless of which is selected, the year 37 BC is part of the Sabbatic year in question; hence, the time discrepancy is minimal. Most take the Sabbatic year to begin and end in Tishri, as do the Jubilees, rather than Nisan-to-Nisan but without firm biblical justification. They propose that Deut. 31:10–11 infers a Sabbatic-Tishri connection. Whereas this possibility is freely conceded, careful consideration will reveal that the reading of the Law during the Feast of Tabernacles in the 7th year does not actually demand that the "year of release" begin there.

[2] Browne, Ordo Saeclorum, op. cit., page 291; also: The Babylonian Talmud, Mishna Tract, Arakin 11b.

[3] Of the many works we have examined, all but Faulstich determine the year 709 as Sabbatical. He derives 708/707 BC. His next is 715 which is also his Jubilee (this Jubilee should be around 710 to 708, see page 289). Beginning at AD 70, he calculated backward (History, Harmony and the Hebrew Kings, op. cit., pp. 178, 211).

With reference to Sabbatic years, our final point has to do with Jeremiah chapter 34. Many take the freeing of the Hebrew servants recorded therein as demanding that these events take place in a Sabbatical year. As Nebuchadnezzar initiated the final siege of Jerusalem in the ninth year of Zedekiah, they now perform a quick Sabbatic calculation [for example, the fixed 163 + (7 x 61) = 163 + 427], obtain 590 BC, and assign it as Zedekiah's date and that of Jeremiah 34. With Zedekiah's 9th year now fixed as 590 and as the city fell in the 11th year of Zedekiah, the forced conclusion is that Jerusalem was captured in 588 BC.

However, it is a mistake to suppose that the manumission of the Hebrew slaves was appointed to take place in the Sabbatical year. The instructions for the Sabbatic year in Leviticus 25:1–7 speaks only of rest for the land, nothing more. There is no mention of the release of slaves. When the Sabbatical year is enlarged upon in Deuteronomy 15:1–11 under the designation "the year of release," only the subject of the suspension of the Hebrew servants debts are added (see also Neh. 10:31).

The freeing of Hebrew slaves had to do with the seventh year from the time when they were purchased – the seventh year of their servitude (Exo. 21:2; Deut. 15:12–15). These passages uniformly refer merely to a "seventh" year without using the term "Sabbatical" and thus should not be confused as though they are addressing the Sabbatical year.[1] The only other mention of a Hebrew servant regaining their freedom was every 50th year during Jubilee (Lev. 25:8–24).

The proper understanding of the above clarifies what should have previously been an enigma. Were the Hebrew servants released every Sabbatical year, after the seventh Sabbatic year who would have been set free in the Jubilee that immediately followed? All the Hebrews would already have been freed the prior year.

Such would greatly diminish the anticipation and significance attendant with the Jubilee. Thus resolved, the apparent inconsistency of the two laws ceases.

Accordingly, it is with the Hebrew servants' freedom after six years' service as given in Exodus 21:2 and Deuteronomy 15:12 that Jeremiah chapter 34 has to do and *not* with a Sabbatical year. Consequently, Jeremiah 34 does not have to be synchronized with the Sabbatical year 590 BC and that Sabbatical year does not have to correspond with the 9th year of Zedekiah.

Jerusalem's final siege began on the 10th day of the 10th month of Zedekiah's ninth year (2 Kings 25:1; Jer. 39:1, 52:4; cp. Ezek. 24:1–2), 28 December 588 (Gregorian). The Egyptian army broke the Babylonian siege in early 587 (Zedekiah's 10th and Nebuchadnezzar's 18th, probably in the spring) during which time Jeremiah was falsely accused and imprisoned (Jer. 32:1–2, ch. 37). Having quickly repulsed Pharaoh, Nebuchadnezzar returned and re-established the siege 390 days before the city of Jerusalem fell (the immediate context of Ezek. 4:1–6).

With famine raging after an 18-month siege, the city's defenses were broken up and the king fled on the ninth day of the fourth month of the 11th year of Zedekiah (2 Kings 25:2–4; Jer. 39:2, 52:5–7), 12 July 586. From the seventh to the tenth day of the fifth month (9–12 August 586) the city was burned (2 Kings 25:8–10; cp. Jer. 52:12–14) and its walls broken down. This was the 19th year of Nebuchadnezzar (2 Kings 25:8; Jer. 52:12).

About 5 months later, on the fifth day of the tenth month of the 12th year of the "Captivity" (31 December 586 BC), an escapee brought word of the fall of Jerusalem to Ezekiel and the exiles in Babylon.[2] Upon hearing this news, Ezekiel's speech returned (Ezek. 33:21–22; cp. 24:24–27).

---

[1] Although championing 588 BC for the year of the fall of Jerusalem, Browne also perceived this distinction (*Ordo Saeclorum, op. cit.*, p. 293) as did McClintock & Strong (*Cyclopedia, op. cit.*, vol. IX, pp. 200–201). Thus, the servant was normally to be given his freedom after six years' service. But if, for example, he had been bought 4 years before the Jubilee, he would not have waited until the seventh year. He would have been set free in the year of Jubilee. Also see, *King James Bible Commentary*, (Nashville, TN: Thomas Nelson Pub., 1999), p. 163 (Deu. 15).

[2] Ezra and his companions made a similar journey in 4 months (Ezra 7:9), thus confirming the general time necessary for the escapee's flight. In view of God's purpose in making Ezekiel a sign to Israel through the death of his wife and his loss of speech, any scenario that places the refugee's arrival around 17 months after the city's fall is seen as intolerably unreasonable. This latter circumstance will always occur if the year of Ezekiel's "captivity" is synchronized with Zedekiah's first official year.

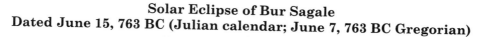

Solar Eclipse of Bur Sagale
Dated June 15, 763 BC (Julian calendar; June 7, 763 BC Gregorian)

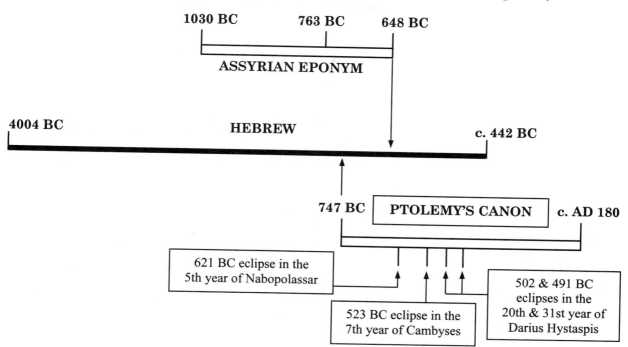

As the Assyrian Eponym List confirms the Assyrian part of the Canon of Ptolemy, most scholars hold that the validity of the rest of the Canon should be accepted with complete confidence. This may be true, but wherever the Assyrian list confirms the Assyrian part of the Canon, it also confirms the biblical record! Strangely, the world of scholarship seems unable to perceive this fact. Since the Canon of Ptolemy agrees with the Assyrian Eponym List in those places where the biblical record also agrees with it, why is this not seen as confirming proof of the authenticity of the Scriptures instead of assessing the situation as being that of having authenticated the Canon?

The Canon of Ptolemy's agreement with the Eponym List at the occasion where the Assyrian data is contiguous to the biblical record serves as positive external attestation to that account as being a verifiable and actual historical chronicle of the Hebrew people. Therefore, all religious overtones aside, due to its uninterrupted continuous record as compared to the mutilated records of all their neighbors, the Hebrew record deserves at least equal, if not preferred, esteem in establishing the chronology of the ancient world. Yet today's scholars proceed to "correct" the biblical record with the

Canon from 648 BC to the time of Christ during which there is no Assyrian record and by the Assyrian Eponym List prior to 747 BC where there is no record in the Canon of Ptolemy.

The biblical chronology is clear, uninterrupted, unambiguous, and precise. To displace it in favor of the Assyrian data demonstrates one's lacking not only scientific bearing with respect to approach and concept, but logic as well. Most have allowed their world view, bias and pre-suppositions against the Hebrew record as well as against all the Holy Writ to blind them, thereby rendering objective scientific investigation impossible. Yet these very scholars boldly assert that their methods and arguments represent the truly scientific approach void of "biblical" prejudices. Conversely, they contend biblicists are guilty of creating systems of Assyrian chronology that display preconceived biblical views and that all such work should be "disdained by the careful historian."

Obviously, if agreement with the Assyrian records authenticates Ptolemy's Canon, it must of necessity "authenticate" the biblical record as well. Furthermore, it should be noted that wherever these three witnesses overlap, they are in accord.

KING JOSIAH AND HIS SONS

[ ] – order in which they reigned
{ } – relative ages when Jeconiah ascended to the throne

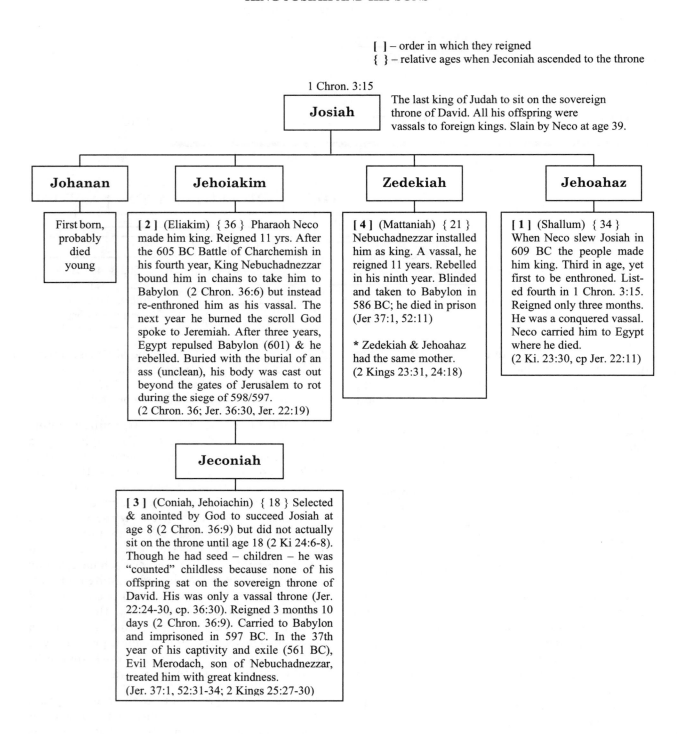

1 Chron. 3:15

Josiah

The last king of Judah to sit on the sovereign throne of David. All his offspring were vassals to foreign kings. Slain by Neco at age 39.

Johanan

First born, probably died young

Jehoiakim

[2] (Eliakim) { 36 } Pharaoh Neco made him king. Reigned 11 yrs. After the 605 BC Battle of Charchemish in his fourth year, King Nebuchadnezzar bound him in chains to take him to Babylon (2 Chron. 36:6) but instead re-enthroned him as his vassal. The next year he burned the scroll God spoke to Jeremiah. After three years, Egypt repulsed Babylon (601) & he rebelled. Buried with the burial of an ass (unclean), his body was cast out beyond the gates of Jerusalem to rot during the siege of 598/597.
(2 Chron. 36; Jer. 36:30, Jer. 22:19)

Zedekiah

[4] (Mattaniah) { 21 } Nebuchadnezzar installed him as king. A vassal, he reigned 11 years. Rebelled in his ninth year. Blinded and taken to Babylon in 586 BC; he died in prison (Jer 37:1, 52:11)

* Zedekiah & Jehoahaz had the same mother.
(2 Kings 23:31, 24:18)

Jehoahaz

[1] (Shallum) { 34 } When Neco slew Josiah in 609 BC the people made him king. Third in age, yet first to be enthroned. Listed fourth in 1 Chron. 3:15. Reigned only three months. He was a conquered vassal. Neco carried him to Egypt where he died.
(2 Ki. 23:30, cp Jer. 22:11)

Jeconiah

[3] (Coniah, Jehoiachin) { 18 } Selected & anointed by God to succeed Josiah at age 8 (2 Chron. 36:9) but did not actually sit on the throne until age 18 (2 Ki 24:6-8). Though he had seed – children – he was "counted" childless because none of his offspring sat on the sovereign throne of David. His was only a vassal throne (Jer. 22:24-30, cp. 36:30). Reigned 3 months 10 days (2 Chron. 36:9). Carried to Babylon and imprisoned in 597 BC. In the 37th year of his captivity and exile (561 BC), Evil Merodach, son of Nebuchadnezzar, treated him with great kindness.
(Jer. 37:1, 52:31-34; 2 Kings 25:27-30)

WHY JEWISH DATING IS DIFFERENT

THE SEDER OLAM RABBAH

The *Seder Olam Rabbah*[1] or the "Book of the Order of the World" was compiled by Rabbi Yose ben Halafta (died AD 160) and is to this day the traditional Jewish chronology.[2] From this ancient work, the Jewish people reckon the current year (AD 2001) as 5761 and understand it to be the number of years since the Creation.

At the time the *Seder Olam* was compiled, the Jews generally dated their years from 312 BC, the beginning of the Seleucid era. For the next few centuries, the *Seder Olam* was of interest exclusively to only students of the Talmud.[3] When the center of Jewish life moved from Babylonia to Europe during the 8th and 9th centuries AD, calculations from the Seleucid era became meaningless. Over those centuries, it was replaced by that of the *anno mundi* era (AM = "from the Creation of the world") of the *Seder Olam*. From the 11th century, *anno mundi* dating became dominant throughout most of the world's Jewish communities.[4]

As Old Testament Scripture is the basis for *Seder Olam* dating, we would suppose the Jewish chronology to be similar to that of Ussher's and thus expect them to place the Creation date around 6,000 years ago. Yet rather than 4004 BC, the *Seder Olam* places Creation at 3761. The question thus becomes: on what basis do the Jews number their years such that a 243-year shortfall occurs?

The Missing Years:[5]

1. From the Creation to the birth of Abraham

Ussher	2008 years	4004 – 1996 BC
Seder Olam	1948 years	3761 – 1811 BC
shortfall	60 years	

   Terah was 130 years old rather than 70 when Abraham was born (Gen. 11:26; but cp. 11:32 and 12:4 where 205 – 75 = 130). Thus the first deficit is c. 60 years.

2. From the birth of Abraham to the Exodus

Ussher	505 years	1996 – 1491 BC
Seder Olam	500 years	1811 – 1311 BC
shortfall	5 years	

   Abraham was 75 years old when the Covenant was made (Gen. 12:4); the Exodus was 430 years later (Gal.3:17; Exo. 12:40–41). Failing to see the significance of Isaac's weaning at age 5 when he was named the "seed" lineage and heir (my p. 58), *Seder Olam* reckons from his birth (pp. 8-9). Thus it concludes Abraham was 70 at the Covenant (70 + 430 = 500) – that he came to Haran, entered Canaan and *returned* to Haran all in his 70th year. Then 5 years later, he left and moved to Canaan. The shortfall is now 65.

3. From the Exodus to the laying of the Temple foundation (1 Kings 6:1)

Ussher	480 years	1491 – 1012 BC
Seder Olam	480 years	1311 – 831 BC
shortfall	0 years	

   As there is no difference, the total shortfall remains at 65 years.

4. From the foundation of the first Temple to the consecration of the second Temple

Ussher	497 years	1012 – 515 BC
Seder Olam	480 years	831 – 351 BC
shortfall	17 years	

---

[1] The *Seder Olam* is divided into three parts, each consisting of ten chapters (called tractates). Part 1 gives the dates of major events from the Creation to the crossing of the Jordan River under Joshua's command. Part 2 extends from the Jordan crossing to the murder of Zachariah, King of Israel (2 Kings 15:10). Chapters 21–27 of Part 3 extend to Nebuchadnezzar's destruction of the Temple, and chapter 28 to the conquest of Babylon by Cyrus. Chapter 29 and the first part of 30 cover the Persian period. The remainder of chapter 30 contains a summary of events from the conquest of Persia by Alexander to the AD 132 Bar Kokhba (also spelled "Cocheba") revolt during the reign of Hadrian (AD 76–138). *Encyclopedia Judaica*, (Jerusalem: Keter Publishing House, Ltd., 1971), vol. 14, "Seder Olam Rabbah," pp. 1091–1092.

[2] Jack Moorman, *Bible Chronology: The Two Great Divides* (Collingswood, NJ: Bible For Today Press, 1999), pages 10–15. Moorman's research was a primary source for this exposé.

[3] *Encyclopedia Judaica*, (Jerusalem, Israel: Keter Publishing House, Ltd., 1971), vol. 14, "Seder Olam Rabbah," p. 1092.

[4] *Ibid.*

---

[5] Not having access to *Seder Olam* for this exposé until my 16th edition, the numbers are those recorded by Moorman. As his source reckoned both exclusively and inclusively, so did he. Most Jewish dates may be confirmed in Finegan, *Handbook, op. cit.*, p. 130.

Differing decisions in placing the dates of the kings of Israel with respect to the kings of Judah during the period of the divided monarchy account for these 17 years.

Thus far, the *Seder Olam* reckons 82 (65 + 17) fewer years over a 3,489-year span (4004 – 515) from Creation to the consecration of the second Temple – of which the major part concerns the age of Terah at Abraham's birth.

5. From the consecration of the second Temple to its destruction by Titus of Rome

Ussher	584 years	515 BC – AD 70
Seder Olam	420 years	351 BC – AD 70
shortfall	164 years	

Here we see the main source of the discrepancy found in the *Seder Olam's* shorter chronology. Its 420 years are divided into spans of 34, 180, 103, and 103 years of successive foreign rule over Israel. As shown in that which follows, it is remarkable that the 164-year disparity is almost entirely from within (a; see below), the first or Persian period. The remaining three periods closely approximate that of the standard chronology.[1]

(a) 34 years (351–317 BC) for the remainder of the Persian rule over Israel: from the dedication of the second Temple to Ptolemy I Soter's invasion of Jerusalem (Ptolemy I was one of Alexander the Great's favorite generals, also called Soter or Savior, 367?–283 BC. After Alexander's death in 323, he seized Egypt as his share of the divided Greek empire and assumed the title "King of Egypt").

(b) 180 years ((317–137 BC) for the Grecian rule: from Ptolemy's invasion to the times when Simon the Maccabean became ruler in Israel and Rome recognized the independence of the Jewish state.

(c) 103 years (137–34 BC) for the rule of the Hasmonean (Maccabean) family in Israel: from Simon to the beginning of the reign of Herod the Great.

(d) 103 years (34 BC – AD 70) for the Herodian rule until the destruction of the Temple.

There is some discrepancy with the standard dates in the later three periods (b, c, and d). The standard date for Alexander's defeat of

Darius is 331 BC rather than the *Seder Olam's* 321. It gives Simon's rule as beginning in 142 BC (not 137) and Herod's in 37 BC (not 34).[2]

But what are we to understand from (a) where the *Seder Olam* allows only 34 years for the remainder of the Persian period? Indeed, by *Seder Olam* reckoning there are only 30 years from the dedication of the second Temple to Darius' defeat at the hands of Alexander in BC "321" and merely four years after that unto Jerusalem's capture by Ptolemy following Alexander's death.

Moreover, here the two systems exhibit a striking contrast. The Ptolemaic chronology lists eight Persian kings from Darius Hystaspis to Darius III Codomannus, the king whom Alexander overcame. However, the *Seder Olam* identifies the Darius who was reigning during the dedication of the second Temple as the same Darius that Alexander defeated.[3]

Recording only five Persian monarchs, the *Seder Olam* gives the following chronology for its 52/53-year depiction of Persian History:

1. Darius the Mede reigns 1 year   3389–3390 AM (374–373 BC)
   Babylon conquered
   Daniel in the lions den

2. Cyrus reigns 3 years   3390–3392 AM (373–371 BC)
   The Jews return
   Second Temple construction begins

3. Artaxerxes (Cambyses) reigns ½ yr   3393 AM (370 BC)
   Temple construction halted

4. Ahasuerus reigns 14 years   3393–3407 AM (370–356 BC)
   Esther chosen Queen
   Esther bears Darius the Persian

5. Darius the Persian reigns 35 years   3407–3442 AM (356–321 BC)
   Temple construction resumes   3408 AM (355 BC)
   Second Temple dedicated   3412 AM (355 BC)
   Ezra comes to Jerusalem   3413 AM (350 BC)
   Nehemiah comes to Jerusalem   3426 AM (337 BC)
   Darius defeated by Alexander   3442 AM (321 BC)

Thus the *Seder Olam* depicts the Kingdom of Persia as lasting a mere 53 years from 374 to 321 BC, rather than the 207 years Ptolemy gives (538–331 BC).[4]

---

[1] Moorman, *Bible Chronology, op. cit.,* p. 12.

[2] *Ibid.*

[3] Martin Anstey, *The Romance of Bible Chronology, op. cit.,* pp. 23–24.

[4] Moorman, *Bible Chronology, op. cit.,* p. 12.

Over the centuries, orthodox rabbis have differed somewhat in their listing of the Persian kings, but they generally have not departed from the 52/53-year parameter established within the *Seder Olam*.[1]

The result of this shorting of the span of the Persian Empire is that the paramount prophecy and major foundation block of chronology – the Daniel 9:25 seventy weeks of years – has become dislodged. Furthermore, this shorting as perpetuated within the *Seder Olam* is deliberate!

While not openly admitting this, present day Jewish scholars acknowledge that there is something enigmatic about the *Seder Olam's* dating. For example, after stating that the commonly received dates in the Ptolemaic chronology "can hardly be doubted," Rabbi Simon Schwab nevertheless goes on to uphold his own tradition:[2]

> It should have been possible that our Sages – for some unknown reason – had 'covered up' a certain historic period and *purposely eliminated and suppressed all records and other material pertaining thereto.* If so, what might have been their compelling reason for so unusual a procedure? Nothing short of a *Divine command* could have prompted ... those saintly 'men of truth' to leave out completely from our annals a period of 165 years and to correct all data and historic tables in such a fashion that the subsequent chronological gap could escape being noticed by countless generations, known to a few initiates only who were duty-bound to keep the secret to themselves (emphasis Schwab's).

This is an astonishing proposal! Schwab, along with other Jewish commentators, further suggests that the reason God directed the sages of the 2nd century AD to become involved in falsifying the data was to confuse anyone who might try to use the prophecies of Daniel to predict the time of the Messiah's coming.

This was supposedly done to honor Daniel 12:4: "shut up the words, and seal the book, even to the time of the end." He adds that the reason

the sages had adopted the non-Jewish Seleucid Era calendar was part of the scheme to do just that – to close up the words and seal the book of Daniel.[3] Schwab also states that if the 165 years were included it would reveal, "we are much closer to the end of the 6th Millennium than we had surmised"[4] (Schwab mentions this date as it is when many rabbis expect Messiah to come).

But can any sincere reader accept such a flimsy reason as justification for distorting history. It actually accuses God himself of perpetrating a dishonest deception.

Indeed, it is manifestly apparent that the real reasons for the deliberate altering of their own national chronology in the *Seder Olam* were:

(1) to conceal the fact that the Daniel 9:25 prophecy clearly pointed to Jesus of Nazareth as its fulfillment and therefore the long awaited Messiah, and

(2) to make that 70 weeks of years prophecy point instead to Simon Bar Kokhba!

Rabbis in the century immediately following Christ Jesus had a tremendous problem with so direct a prophecy as Daniel 9. This chapter speaks of Messiah's being cut off (slain) 69 "weeks" (i.e., 69 sevens) or 483 years after the going forth of a commandment to restore and to build Jerusalem. This 538 BC prophecy (Dan. 9:1) unmistakably points to Jesus Christ and His crucifixion.

Such must either be acknowledged and His person accepted or completely erased from Jewish consciousness. The latter could be accomplished if the 69 (or 70) weeks of years could somehow be made to apply to the century after the life of Christ. Then it would be possible for the rabbis to point to *another messiah* who, as circumstances would have it, was cut off in death some 100 years after the crucifixion of our Lord.[5]

---

[1] Moorman, *Bible Chronology, op. cit.,* p. 13.

[2] Simon Schwab, "Comparative Jewish Chronology," *Dr. Joseph Breuer Jubilee Volume,* (New York: Rabbi Samson Raphael Hirsch Publications Society, Philipp Felheim Inc., 1962), p. 188.

[3] Shimon Schwab, "Comparative Jewish Chronology," *Selected Speeches: A Collection of Addresses and Essays on Hashkafah, Contemporary Issues and Jewish History,* (Lakewood, NJ: CIS Pub.,1991), pp. 270–272.

[4] Schwab, "Comparative Jewish Chronology," *Dr. Joseph Breuer Jubilee Volume, op. cit.,* pp. 190–191.

[5] Of course no such admission by any of the Jewish sages can be cited, but the facts are obvious.

The ninth day of the month Ab (c. mid-July) is a great day of sorrow to Israel. On this day in 586 BC, the Babylonians destroyed Solomon's Temple. Further, the second Temple was laid waste by the Romans under Titus on the same day in AD 70. And on this very day in AD 135, at the conclusion of a 3½-year revolt, the Romans crushed the army of the "messianic" Simon Bar Kokhba (also spelled "Cocheba").

Bar Kokhba had been declared the long-awaited Messiah by the foremost Jewish scholar of that day, the highly venerated Rabbi Akiva (Akiba) ben Joseph. In 130 AD, Emperor Hadrian of Rome declared his intention to raise a shrine to Jupiter on the site of the Temple,[1] and in 131 he issued a decree forbidding circumcision as well as public instruction in the Jewish Law.[2] Having preached peace all his life, the 90-year-old Akiva gave his blessing to the revolution by proclaiming that Bar Kokhba was the "star out of Jacob" and the "scepter out of Israel" (Num. 24:17).[3]

In his 98th year Akiva was eventually imprisoned and condemned to death by the Romans.[4] Among the many accolades heaped upon Akiva, that which elevated him as a pre-eminent authority, was the acknowledging of him as "the father of the Mishnah."[5] Such prominence gave great weight to the messianic expectancy Akiva placed upon Bar Kokhba.

Akiva's students became some of the most prominent sages of the following generation. Among these was Yose (Josi) ben Halafta. Akiva's influence on Halafta is apparent from a statement made concerning his education; it was merely said that Rabbi Akiva had been his teacher.[6] As his mentor, Akiva's regard for Bar Kokhba would have been thoroughly imbedded in Yose.[7]

The preceding overview explains why the *Seder Olam* is held in such veneration and why the Jews still use it for their national dating. Yet the fact remains that it is a dishonest attempt to conceal the truth with regard to the Daniel 9 prophecy.

By removing the 164 (or 165) years from the duration of the Persian Empire, Rabbi Halafta was able to make the 483-year Daniel 9 prophecy fall reasonably close to the years prior to the AD 132 revolt during which Bar Kokhba rose to prominence as Israel's military and economic leader.[8] Then with Akiva proclaiming, "This is the King Messiah"[9] followed by "all the contemporary sages regarded him as the King Messiah,"[10] the Jewish populace united around this false hope.

Dio Cassius states that the whole of Judea was in revolt. To quell the rebellion, Hadrian dispatched Julius Severus, his ablest general, from Britain. The Romans destroyed 985 towns in Palestine and slew 580,000 men. A still larger number perished through starvation, disease, and fire. All Judah was laid waste, and

---

[1] Dio Cassius, *Roman History, op. cit.*, vol. VIII, Book 69, p. 447.

[2] Will Durant, *The Story of Civilization. Caesar and Christ*, Volume 3, (New York: Simon and Schuster, 1944), p. 548.

[3] *Encyclopedia Judaica, op. cit.*, vol. 2, "Akiva," p. 489.

[4] Durant, *The Story of Civilization. Caesar and Christ*, vol. 3, *op. cit.*, pp. 548–549.

[5] Akiva made a preliminary gathering and formulation of the material for the six orders (containing 63 chapters or tractates) of that religious code which was the heart of the Talmud. Near the end of the 2nd century, Judah ha-Nasi completed the work. Moorman, *Bible Chronology: The Two Great Divides, op. cit.*, p. 14.

[6] *Encyclopedia Judaica, op. cit.*, Volume 16, "Yose ben Halafta," p. 852.

[7] *Ibid.* p. 853. Yose ben Halafta's own influence may be seen in that some of his writings were included in Judah ha-Nasi's final editing of the Mishnah, and his name is mentioned in 59 of its 63 tractates. Though referred to in the Mishnah and Talmud, Halafta's *Seder Olam* is not a formal part of that work. Nevertheless, it is a work of Talmudic authority, and to openly contradict it would be unthinkable to orthodox Jews.

As Rabbi Schwab stated: "… our traditional chronology is based on *Seder Olam* because of the authority of its author. It is therefore quite inconceivable that any post-Talmudic teacher could possible 'reject' those chronological calculations which have been the subject of many a Talmudic discussion." (Schwab, *Dr. Joseph Breuer Jubilee Volume, op. cit.*, p. 186). Thus it is that the *Seder Olam* is held in such high esteem and is still used by the Jews for their national dating.

[8] *Encyclopedia Judaica, op. cit.*, vol. 4, "Bar Kokhba," p. 230.

[9] *Ibid.*

[10] *Ibid.*, p. 231.

Bar Kokhba himself fell while defending Bethar.[1]

Even more astonishing is that "even in later generations, despite the disappointment engendered by his defeat, his image persisted as the embodiment of messianic hopes."[2] Indeed, the consistent verdict of Jewish historians is: "The most important historical messianic figure was surely Bar Kokhba."[3]

Yose ben Halafta[4] and his fellow compilers of the *Seder Olam* sought to terminate the 69 "weeks of years" as close to the AD 132 revolt as possible, but they were limited as to where they could make the "cuts." As the chronology of the Seleucid era onward was firmly fixed among the Jews, years could not be pared from their history after 312 BC.

Since the Daniel 9 prophecy dealt with a decree that was biblically and historically issued by a Persian monarch, this left only the Persian period of history for them to exploit. The Persians had been so hated by the Greeks and later by the Moslems that these two conquerors destroyed nearly all of the Persian records. This has created great difficulty in recovering their sequence of kings, the length of their reigns, and thereby their chronology. Thus, the Persian period was readily vulnerable to manipulation.[5]

This author offers the conclusions given herein as the only reasonable, logical deductions that can be drawn from the historical and biblical facts. As indicated earlier, many of the orthodox rabbis are looking for Messiah to come in the year AM 6,000. Should they be correct in this assessment, the deception inherent within the *Seder Olam* would result in a great national tragedy for Israel. Their Messiah who "came unto His own, and His own received Him not" would not be coming to earth for the first time. Rather, He would be returning "as a thief in the night" about 243 years[6] before they would be expecting Him. O Israel, repent!

Regardless of the actual year of our Lord's return, He will come. At that time, He will fulfill all the many ancient biblical prophecies associated with that great event. He will save His own, slay all the wicked, and establish the promised thousand-year reign of righteousness. Even so, come quickly Lord Jesus.

---

[1] Dio Cassius, *Roman History*, vol. VIII, *op. cit.* Bk. 69, pp. 449–450; Durant, *The Story of Civilization. Caesar and Christ*, vol. 3, *op. cit.*, p. 548.

[2] *Encyclopedia Judaica*, *op. cit.*, vol. 4, "Bar Kokhba," p. 231.

[3] *Ibid*. vol. 11, "Messiah," p. 1410.

[4] Not only do the Jews venerate Jose because the *Seder Olam* had its origin in his school, he is regarded with a near superstitious reverence. This may be seen in that it was said: "that he was worthy of having the prophet Elijah reveal himself to him regularly in order to teach him" (*Encyclopedia Judaica*, *op. cit.*, vol. 16, "Yose ben Halafta," p. 853.).

[5] Yet despite all that has been said concerning the Jews veneration for Jose, the *Encyclopedia Judaica* forthrightly admits: "the most significant confusion in Jose's calculation is the compression of the Persian period, from the rebuilding of the Temple by Zerubbabel in 516 BC to the conquest of Persia by Alexander, to no more than 34 years" (*Encyclopedia Judaica*, *op. cit.*, vol. 14, "Seder Olam Rabbah," p. 1092).

[6] It should be noted that Anstey, Moorman, and others who reference the *Seder Olam's* chronology to reduce the length of the Persian Empire in order to sustain their interpretation of Acts 13:17–21 over the 1 Kings 6:1 480-year declaration (see my pages 72–77) always fail to mention that this same Jewish chronology accepts the 480 years in its scheme (see Finegan, *Handbook*, *op. cit.*, p. 128).

Isaiah To 308 Cyrus (handwritten)

The Decree of Cyrus

Inasmuch as Anstey and others insist that the Decree of Cyrus (2 Chron. 36:22–23; Ezra 1:1–4) was the fulfillment of the Daniel 9:24–27 prophecy rather than the decree issued by Artaxerxes Longimanus,[1] we will now briefly examine the former decree. After all, these men are brothers in Christ and many are diligent, capable students of Scripture. As such, their views deserve our careful consideration.

The ninth chapter of the Book of Daniel opens with Daniel and his people captives in Babylon. Their beloved city of Jerusalem and its Temple had been destroyed by the army of Nebuchadnezzar (2 Chron. 36:15–21). From the study of certain "books" which included Jeremiah's prophecy, Daniel came to understand that the captivity would last 70 years. After that, deliverance would come (Dan. 9:2).

As Daniel pondered these things and sought the Lord, the angel Gabriel came to him and spoke of another time period – seven times as long. This span would be 70 "weeks" of years or 70 sevens of years. Gabriel explained that the 70 weeks of years (69 of which would measure unto Messiah!), were to be counted from the going forth of "the commandment to restore and to build Jerusalem" (Dan. 9:25).[2]

> For thus saith the LORD, That after seventy years be accomplished at Babylon I will visit you, and perform my good word toward you, in causing you to return to this place (Jer. 29:10).

> And this whole land shall be a desolation, and an astonishment; and these nations shall serve the king of Babylon seventy years (Jer. 25:11).

The Book of Jeremiah explained that this servitude would last 70 years, and then they would be allowed to return to their homeland. Other details about this deliverance were given in the book of Isaiah, which may have been among the "books" Daniel had been reading. The Isaiah prophecy is especially significant, for it revealed the name of the man that would set

the captives free and cause Jerusalem to be built again. His name would be *Cyrus*.

> Thus saith the LORD to his anointed, to Cyrus, whose right hand I have holden, to subdue nations before him; and I will loose the loins of kings, to open before him the two leaved gates; and the gates shall not be shut; I will go before thee, and make the crooked places straight: I will break in pieces the gates of brass, and cut in sunder the bars of iron: And I will give thee the treasures of darkness, and hidden riches of secret places, that thou mayest know that I, the LORD, which call thee by thy name, am the God of Israel (Isaiah 45:1–3).

Various historians of antiquity have referred to Cyrus the Great. Herodotus says the Persians regarded him highly. Ammianus calls Cyrus "the amiable prince" of the Oriental world; Xenophon extolled the wisdom by which he governed; Plutarch declared that in wisdom and virtue he surpassed all kings.

Mentioned by name 23 times in the Bible, Cyrus was the monarch whose armies overthrew the Babylonian empire on the night the mysterious "handwriting on the wall" appeared during Belshazzar's great feast (Dan. 5). Concerning Cyrus, Isaiah 44:24, 28 and 45:1–4 adds:

> Thus saith the LORD ... of CYRUS, He is my shepherd, and shall perform all my pleasure: even saying to Jerusalem, Thou shalt be built; and to the temple, Thy foundation shall be laid. Thus saith the LORD to ... Cyrus ... I, the LORD, which call thee *by thy name*, am the God of Israel ... I have even called thee *by thy name*: I have surnamed thee, though thou hast not known me.

Called by name nearly 125 years prior to his birth,[3] Cyrus was thence commissioned by God

---

[1] Anstey, *The Romance of Bible Chronology, op. cit.*, pp. 277–293; also see my pages 206–207.

[2] Some erroneously interpret this to mean that the commandment which would end the 70 years captivity would also mark the beginning of the 70 weeks.

[3] Isaiah prophesied during the reign of Uzziah, Jotham, Ahaz, and Hezekiah (Isa. 1:1). The combined time that these men reigned is 113 years (2 Chron. 26–29). The kings that followed, reigned a total of over 110 years (2 Chron. 32–36). Then came the Babylonian captivity which lasted 70 years (2 Chron. 36:20,21). As we do not know exactly when during Isaiah's ministry that he prophesied about Cyrus, we cannot give an exact number of years. Nevertheless, basing our conclusions on what we do know from the Scriptures, we are safe in saying that the prophecy was given approximately 125 years before Cyrus was born and approximately 175 years or more before Babylon was overthrown.

to allow the captives to return and rebuild the Temple and the city of Jerusalem.

> That saith of Cyrus, He is my shepherd, and shall perform all my pleasure: even saying to Jerusalem, Thou shalt be built; and to the temple, Thy foundation shall be laid.
>
> ... I will direct all his ways: he shall build my city, and he shall let go my captives, not for price nor reward, saith the LORD of hosts (Isaiah 44:28; 45:13)

However before Cyrus could ever be in a position of authority in order to be able to fulfill this prophecy, Babylon – which held the Jews captive – would have to be *overthrown*. During the days of Cyrus, this seemed an almost impossible feat.

Ancient historians[1] tell us that the walls of Babylon were double; the outer was a square 56 miles in circumference and thus 14 miles along each face. Surrounded by a wide moat, this wall was c. 300 feet high, 87 feet thick with its top broad enough that four-horse chariots could pass each other and even turn around. There were 25 solid brass gates on each side protected by a total of 250 towers of 420' height. Also square but not as thick, the inner wall's perimeter was 42 miles. Gardens and crops were grown in the area between these walls, and the Babylonians boasted that their provisions could withstand a 20-year siege.

Flowing through the middle of the city from north to south, the Euphrates river had walls along both sides dividing the city into an eastern and western sector. On the bank of each side, between these walls and the river, was an 87' wide quay. A large bridge tied the two sections of the city together. Consequently, when Cyrus began to lay siege to Babylon, its citizens felt his efforts were useless. However, this overconfident attitude of security was the very source of their danger!

Learning that the Babylonians would be observing a great pagan festival, Cyrus planned a surprise attack. On the night of the festival – when the inhabitants and king would be

spending their time in revelry and drunkenness – he would divert the waters of the Euphrates (which ran beneath the city walls) into a vast 35 foot deep basin having a circumference of 48.3 miles. This "holding lake" had formerly been dug by the Babylonians to channel the river into so they could build the quay, the bridge, a tunnel at each end of the bridge that connected the two palaces on the banks of the river, and brick the banks to prevent erosion.

With the lowering of the water, the armies of Cyrus marched through the riverbed and beneath the two walls. With this in mind, we read the prophecy concerning Cyrus:

> Thus saith the LORD ... to the deep, Be dry, and I will dry up thy rivers: (Isaiah 44:24, 27)

However, after penetrating the main walls, the walls along the river front still prevented the army of Cyrus entrance into the city. Set in these walls, where streets crossed the river, were huge gates of brass which normally would have been closed and locked. However, caught up in the spell of the celebrations, the guards had neglected to secure these gates!

Now we can understand the true significance of the words:

> Thus saith the LORD to his anointed, to Cyrus, whose right hand I have holden, to subdue nations before him; and I will loose the loins of kings, to open before him the two leaved gates; and the gates shall not be shut; I will go before thee, and make the crooked places straight: I will break in pieces the gates of brass, and cut in sunder the bars of iron: ... (Isaiah 45:1, 2).

The way would be opened up for Cyrus. The problem posed by the two leaved gates and their iron bars would be completely removed as though "broken and cut in sunder"!

Daniel 5 records that which was happening at the same time inside the city. King Belshazzar had called 1,000 of the leaders of his kingdom unto a great feast at the palace. That night, they drank wine and praised their gods. Suddenly, the fingers of a man's hand appeared and wrote a mysterious message on the plaster of the palace wall! When this happened:

> Then the king's countenance was changed, and his thoughts troubled him, so that the

---

[1] Diodorus Siculus, *The Library of History, op. cit.*, vol. I, Book ii, 7–9; Herodotus, *The Histories, op. cit.*, vol. I, Book 1, 178–186; McClintock and Strong, *Cyclopedia of Biblical Theological and Ecclesiastical Lit., op. cit.*, vol. I, pp. 596–598 (Babylon).

joints of his loins were loosed, and his knees smote one against another (Dan. 5:6).

Such was exactly what God had revealed the king would do when He prepared the way for Cyrus:.

> Thus saith the LORD to ... Cyrus, ... I will loose the loins of kings, (Isaiah 45:1).

Although they could read the words, the wise men of Babylon could not interpret the meaning of the handwriting on the wall. Finally, Daniel was summoned. He explained that it was a message of doom for the king; moreover, his kingdom would be given over to the Medes and Persians. At that very moment, the armies of Cyrus were gaining entrance to the city to fulfill Daniel's words.

> In that night was Belshazzar the king of the Chaldeans slain. And Darius the Median took the kingdom, being about threescore and two years old (Dan. 5:30, 31).

Xenophon tells us that this Darius the Mede was the uncle of Cyrus and Prideaux adds: "Cyrus allowed him the title of all his conquests as long as he lived."[1] After consolidating the empire under his rule, Cyrus returned with his army and became sole ruler of the kingdom.[2]

In the prophecy to Cyrus, God said that he would "subdue nations before him" (Isa. 45:1). The list of 14 nations whom he conquered

---

[1] Xenophon, *Cyropaedia*, I, ii, 1. Darius the Mede, son of Ahasuerus (Dan.9:1), was Cyaxares II, son of Astyages (Jos. *Antiq*. x. 11. 4, note: Darius was "made" King, Dan. 9:1). See: Prideaux, *The Old and New Testament Connected in the History of the Jews*, op. cit., vol. 1, p. 137.

[2] In 559 BC Cyrus the Great became King of Anshan, a portion of Persia with Susa as its Capital. About 550, his maternal grandfather Astyages, King of Media, marched against Cyrus. Astyages was delivered by his own army over to Cyrus thus forging in one day the Empire of the Medes and Persians. About 546 he conquered Lydia, making a prisoner of Croesus, its king of fabled wealth.

At the end of the year 539 BC, he conquered Babylon, capital of the Babylonian Empire. Belshazzar, pro-regent for his father Nabonidus, was slain and Cyrus' uncle, Darius the Mede (same as Cyaxares II, Xenophon, *Cyropaedia*, I, 5, 2, the Son of Ahasuerus = Astyages) was "made king" over Babylon (Dan.9:1) by Cyrus who continued at the head of the army, annexing the remainder of the Empire.

In 536, Cyrus returned as sole rex over the expanded empire and as suzerain over the Jews. 536 BC is thus the date intended by Scripture as "the first year of Cyrus."

includes: the Cilicians, Syrians, Paphlagonians, Cappadocians, Phrygians, Lydians, Carians, Phoenicians, Arabians, Assyrians, Bactrians, Sacae, Maryandines, and the Babylonians.

Prophecy also revealed that God would cause Cyrus to receive the "treasures of darkness, and hidden riches of secret places" (Isaiah 45:3). It was the custom of the time for a conquering king to hide away the spoils taken in battle, and such were not used unless it became an absolute necessity. These were placed in the "treasure house" (cp. Dan. 1:2). This treasure house contained many valuables that had been taken from Egypt, Assyria, Judea, and other countries Babylon had conquered. Such hidden treasures of the kingdom – even as the prophecy had said – became the property of the conquering Cyrus! According to Pliny, Cyrus took in $353,427,200 dollars in silver and gold (by 1979 exchange rates) – along with various other jewels, vessels, and precious things.

These great victories of Cyrus' were an exact fulfillment of prophecy. In 536 BC, Cyrus came to be sole ruler in the kingdom. But for a worldly-minded sovereign – a battle-hardened warrior – to suddenly release thousands of his slaves "not for price nor reward" seemed unthinkable. Slaves meant wealth, fame, and prestige to any king. When Cyrus proclaimed that these slaves could return to their land, he had it put *in writing*.

> Now in the first year of Cyrus king of Persia, that the word of the LORD by the mouth of Jeremiah might be fulfilled, the LORD stirred up the spirit of Cyrus king of Persia, that he made a proclamation throughout all his kingdom, and *put it* also in writing, saying, Thus saith Cyrus king of Persia, The LORD God of heaven hath given me all the kingdoms of the earth; and he hath charged me to build him an house at Jerusalem, which is in Judah (note: this was in the prophecy of Isaiah 44:28). Who *is there* among you of all his people? his God be with him, and let him go up to Jerusalem, which is in Judah, and build the house of the LORD God of Israel, (he is the God,) which *is* in Jerusalem (Ezra 1:1–3; also see 2 Chron. 36:22, 23).

It is very likely that Cyrus had been shown the Isaiah prophecies. If so, he must have been amazed when he saw that which had been written of him so many years beforehand. Such would have provoked him to reflect and come to

realize that the God of Israel must be the true God. Regardless, the LORD stirred up the spirit of Cyrus to decree that the people of this God should be allowed to return to rebuild their temple.

The 70 "weeks," however, were to begin with "the going forth of the commandment to restore and to build Jerusalem" – that is – the city along with its walls as Daniel foretold:

> Seventy weeks are determined upon thy people and upon thy holy city. . . . Know therefore and understand, that from the going forth of the commandment to restore and **to build Jerusalem** unto the Messiah the Prince shall be seven weeks, and threescore and two weeks: the street shall be built again, and the **wall**, even **in troublous times**. And after threescore and two weeks shall Messiah be cut off, but not for himself (Dan. 9:24–26, author's emphasis).

The decree granting these privileges was issued when letters were given to Nehemiah to go to Jerusalem in the 20th year of Artaxerxes Longimanus (Neh. 2:1–9). This event, not the 536 BC decree of Cyrus, is the starting point of the 70 weeks prophecy.[1] The proclamation of Cyrus had only to do with the rebuilding of the "house of God" (Ezra 1, 5, and 6), whereas the 70 weeks were to begin with the commandment to build the city as well as its walls. Consequently, it is a mistake to reckon these 70-year weeks from the time Cyrus gave permission for the people to return and to build the Temple as they were to begin with permission to restore and build the city itself.

The portion of the decree of Cyrus that is recorded in the first chapter of Ezra mentions only the rebuilding of the Temple and does not specifically mention the rebuilding of the city (houses, streets, wall, etc.). The Temple, which was eventually decorated with gold and silver as well as rare vessels, would be under the protection of the Empire itself prior to the rebuilding of the city walls.

The decree in Nehemiah in which the commandment was given to rebuild the city was issued about 82 years after the decree of Cyrus

(536 – 454 = 82).[2] The Jews returned from Babylon and rebuilt the Temple, but because the Persians feared a revolt (Ezra 4:12–16) it was not until 82 years later that the decree was given for the city and its walls to be built! During the interim, the people lived among the ruins in the few restored homes as Nehemiah 1:3 and 2:3 depict.

Still, according to Bible prophecy, Cyrus was to be the one that would speak the word which would cause the *city* of Jerusalem to be built, as well as the Temple.

> ... He (Cyrus) is my shepherd, and shall perform all my pleasure: even saying to Jerusalem, Thou shalt be built; and to the temple, Thy foundation shall be laid (Isa. 44:28).

> I have raised him up in righteousness, and I will direct all his ways: he shall build my city, and he shall let go my captives, not for price nor reward, saith the LORD of hosts (Isa. 45:13).

As a result of Cyrus' 536 BC decree, Darius I Hystaspis (Darius of Marathon) allowed the work to restart in 520 BC after the Persian monarchs who had reigned in the period between Cyrus and Darius Hystaspis had caused the cessation of the reconstruction (Ezra 4; cp. chs. 5 and 6).

Again, the actual commandment to build the city did not go forth until 82 years after the return from Babylon in the days of Nehemiah. This was 76 years after the 530 BC passing of Cyrus.

This forces us to address the question – was the prophecy of Isaiah wrong or was Anstey et al. right all along? Should we measure the 483 years of the Daniel 9:25 prophecy from the 536 BC decree of Cyrus after all? Where does the truth lie for here we have Scripture saying that it would be Cyrus who would speak the command to restore and build Jerusalem: "even saying to Jerusalem, Thou shalt be built." How can this be if the rebuilding of the city is said to actually have been carried out by Nehemiah acting under the authority of the decree given by Artaxerxes Longimanus in the 20th year of

---

[1] Anderson, *The Coming Prince, op. cit.,* p. 124, among many others.

[2] See pages 227–228, 235–240.

his reign (454 BC)? Moreover, according to Josephus, Cyrus wrote:[1]

> God almighty hath appointed me to be king of the habitable earth ... indeed he foretold my name by the prophets, and that I should build Him a house at Jerusalem which is in the country of Judea.

After Cyrus had supposedly read the remarkable prophecy in Isaiah, Josephus added[2]:

> He called for the most eminent Jews that were in Babylon, and said to them, that he gave them leave to go back to their own country, and to *rebuild their city Jerusalem*, and the temple of God.

A letter written by Cyrus to the governors in Syria [3] is reported to have read:

> King Cyrus to Sisinnes and Sathrabuzanes, sendeth greeting. I have given leave to as many of the Jews that dwell in my country as please to return to their own country, and to *rebuild their city*, and to build the temple of God at Jerusalem on the same place where it was before.

Thus, Josephus declares that Cyrus was instrumental in building not just the Temple, but the CITY as well. This, along with the Isaiah passages already presented, represents the strongest, most convincing evidence in favor of the Cyrus Decree.

Admittedly, it seems substantial. Can it be answered or has our former decision in favor of the Artaxerxes Decree been incorrect, and how does one begin?

As biblicists, we simply begin in faith. Knowing that all the relevant scriptures are true, there must be a way to reconstruct the history while honoring each passage. If the secular data, such as Josephus, can be made to accord, it is taken as accurate and utilized. If not, it is viewed as incorrect and ignored. Armed with this frame of reference and world view, we proceed.

First, the Book of Nehemiah unmistakably says that the wall and city were in *ruins* (Neh. 1:3; 2:3; 7:4). Hence, although permission was given by Cyrus, the rebuilding of Jerusalem and its wall was not *written* into his formal decree. This is why the people had not nearly completed the task. Chapter by chapter, Ezra gives us the account of the sequence of events that transpired upon the Jews return.

EZRA CHAPTER ONE: records the proclamation that was made by Cyrus in which he allowed the captives to return. This decree clearly only authorizes the rebuilding of the Temple (vv. 2–5). The vessels from Solomon's Temple, which had been removed by Nebuchadnezzar and placed in the temple of his pagan gods, were placed in the care of "Sheshbazzar" (Zerubbabel).[4]

EZRA CHAPTER TWO: gives a list of the 12 leaders (undoubtedly one from each of the tribes) that returned to rebuild the Temple under Zerubbabel's leadership (cp. Neh. 7:7) and the names of those that returned with them.

EZRA CHAPTER THREE: states that the "people gathered themselves together as one man to Jerusalem" during the seventh month (vs. 1). They built an altar, and made offerings and entreated God to protect them from their enemies whom they feared. "But the foundation of the temple of the Lord was not yet laid" (vs. 6). However, they began making arrangements for its building "according to the grant that they had of Cyrus" (vs. 7). Then, in the second month of the second year after their return, "all the people shouted with a great shout ... because the foundation of the house of the Lord was laid" (vv. 8–11).

During the months before they laid the Temple foundation, the people lived in the ruins (Neh. 1:3; 2:3). The few inhabitants undoubtedly repaired or rebuilt homes in which to live from among the rubble, but these verses reveal that the city itself was far from being restored.

EZRA CHAPTER FOUR: tells of a letter in which their adversaries wrote: ."..the Jews... are come unto Jerusalem, building the rebellious and the bad CITY, and have set up the WALLS thereof, and joined the foundations" (vv. 11–16).

---

[1] Josephus, *Antiquities, op. cit.*, XI, 1.

[2] *Ibid.*, XI, 2)

[3] *Ibid.*, XI, 3)

[4] Sheshbazzar was the Chaldee name for the Persian title "Governor." It was an appellative referring to Zerubbabel by title rather than by name.

The mention of the walls in verse 12 had to do with the walls of the Temple, not the city (context, cp. vs. 24 whereas vv. 13 and 16 are the city wall). Moreover, vv. 13 and 16 show by the qualifying word "if" that the walls and city were not complete at that time. As the decree issued by Cyrus had not included the restoration of these, this unauthorized attempt on the part of the people was that which their enemies used against them. The attempt caused the work to halt.

It cannot be overemphasized that the complaint lodged against the Jews said nothing about the Temple (see vv. 12–13). This is because their enemies knew that its construction had been approved by Cyrus' decree. Obviously they also knew that the rebuilding of the city and its walls were not part of that edict; hence, they knew their complaint to the king would stand a good chance to bring about the results which they desired. Indeed, as Cyrus was often away on military campaigns, even during his reign Temple construction was thwarted (4:4–5) for direct appeal to him was not possible.

The enemies' letter accomplished its purpose. Fearing a rebellion and the loss of tribute, the Artaxerxes of Ezra 4:6–24 sent back a commandment that the building of "this city" should cease (vs. 21). With this, discouragement and unbelief set in for we now read: "then ceased the work of the house of God ... unto the second year of the reign of Darius, king of Persia" (vs. 24). By beginning construction on the city and its walls, the Jews went beyond that which was granted by Cyrus' official decree and this action brought about the problem.

Yet even with the Ezra 4:21 commandment, had the people acted in faith this mandate should have been no deterrent to continuing the work on the Temple. Indeed, this order applied only to the building of the city, not the House of God. Furthermore, if their enemies attempted to apply this latter order to cause work on the Temple to stop, appeal could have been made at such time to the Decree of Cyrus. As Persian decrees could not be altered (Esther 1:19; Dan. 6:8), the Decree of Cyrus could not have been repealed by that of another. Nevertheless, when the second year of Darius came (520 BC), the people were stirred to action by God's two prophets, Haggai and Zechariah.

EZRA CHAPTER FIVE: "Then the prophets, HAGGAI ... and ZECHARIAH ... prophesied unto the Jews" and the people again began working "to build the house of God" (vv. 1, 2). The book of Haggai picks up the narrative at this point and fills in more details. "In the second year of Darius the king ... came the word of the Lord by Haggai ... saying, This people say, The time is not come, the time that the Lord's house should be built."

The returnees had occupied the few houses rebuilt for their shelter (cp. Hag. 1:3 and 9) but had put off further work on the house of God. Again, the reconstruction of individual homes here and there within the boundary of old Jerusalem is not the same as the restoration of a city and its walls. Moreover the Book of Nehemiah says that in the 20th year of Artaxerxes the walls were down and the gates still in disrepair from having been burned (Neh. 1:3). During those days, Zechariah was instructed by the Lord to take certain men and "go into the house of Josiah" (Zech. 6:9–10). This again documents that some houses had been rebuilt.

Concerning this time frame, the Book of Zechariah adds: "In the second year of Darius, came the word of the Lord unto Zechariah" (Zech. 1:1). Zechariah encouraged the people to believe that God would enable them to complete the task which He had given them: "The hands of Zerubbabel have laid the foundation of this house; his hand shall also finish it" (4:9).

Reference is made to the "wall" in the third verse, but a comparison of verses 2, 8, and 9 reveals that the context is that of the Temple walls. As already shown, the 12th verse of the fourth chapter confirms this (context, cp. vs. 4:24); hence, these are not allusions to the wall of the city. The city walls were not completed until the 25th day of Elul in the 20th year of Artaxerxes (September 7, 454 BC, Neh. 6:15), whereas the events in the fifth chapter of Ezra transpired 66 years earlier during the second year of Darius (520 BC).

EZRA CHAPTER SIX: When their right to rebuild was contested (Ezra 5:6–17), King Darius ordered a search of the "house of rolls {scrolls}" in the city of Babylon. Cyrus' edict was found 300 miles away at Achmetha (Ecbatana), his Median capital. Thus we see the providen-

tial hand of God at work in His leading Cyrus to have put the edict in writing!

As we read the Decree of Cyrus recorded in this chapter (vv. 3–5) and the following confirming decree of Darius Hystaspis (vv. 6–12), it is most significant to observe that there is not found a single word concerning the rebuilding of Jerusalem or its walls! Over and over, it is the building of the "house of God" and that alone that is before us (e.g., vv. 3, 5, 7, 8, 12). This substantiates our conclusion on chapter 5 that the walls referred to in verses 3, 8, and 9 were those of the Temple and not those of the city.

Thus, it must be seen that although Cyrus may have given permission for the rebuilding of Jerusalem (possibly in private to some of the Jewish leadership, but see "Conclusion," p. 308) as some surmise from Isa. 44:28 and 45:13, at no place in Scripture is it recorded that he so did in his official written decree. In point of fact, citations from this decree are given three times and no mention whatsoever is made in any of them concerning the building of the city or its walls.[1] Thus, his pleasure regarding the Holy City was, at best then, verbal only. It was not placed in writing.

On the basis of Cyrus' former writ, Darius issued a decree in which he confirmed the words of his illustrious predecessor.

> And the elders of the Jews builded ... and this house was finished on the third day of the month Adar, which was in the sixth year of the reign of Darius (Ezra 6:14–15).

The Temple was completed on the 3rd of Adar, the last month of the sixth year of the reign of Darius (14 February 516 BC). Thus, the people had been back in the land for nearly 21 years (536–516 BC) before concluding a task which required but 4 years, 5 months and 10 days (Hag. 1:16; cp. Ezra 6:15). The Temple was then dedicated *before* the Passover which was held on the 14th day of the following month (Nisan, 6:16–22 and thus still in 516 BC).

EZRA CHAPTER SEVEN: "Now after these things, in the ... seventh year of Artaxerxes the king" (vv. 1, 7), Ezra was given a letter authorizing him to go to Jerusalem "and to carry the silver and gold, which the king and his counselors freely offered unto the God of Israel" (vs. 15). Ezra rejoiced because God had put it in the king's heart "to beautify the house of the Lord" (vs. 27). This decree was not to build the house of the Lord, but merely to beautify it, the Temple itself having already been rebuilt in the sixth year of Darius. It said nothing of the city or its walls.

EZRA CHAPTER EIGHT: gives a list of those that went from Babylon with Ezra to Jerusalem, their prayer for God's protection on the journey, and their subsequent safe arrival.

EZRA CHAPTER NINE: Ezra learns of many mixed marriages between the people of Israel, priests and Levites included, and the heathen Gentiles. Ezra takes the matter before the LORD in prayer, confessing these acts as sin and justifies God in His having disciplined the people. In the prayer, Ezra mentioned that the Lord had given them "a reviving" and had allowed them "to set up the house of our God" and had given them "a wall in Judah and in Jerusalem" (vs. 9).

Some attempt to use this reference to a "wall" as proof that the city and its surrounding wall had already been completed prior to Artaxerxes as a direct result of Cyrus' decree. However such is of no force, for the *context* of the 9th verse is that God has given them a "wall of protection" by His providential oversight and the granting of favor to Israel with the reigning Persian overlord ("Desolation" in vs. 9 refers to the 70 years of having no temple, 586–516, Dan. 9:17–18, cp. Dan. 9:1–2 and Jer. 25:9 and 11).

EZRA CHAPTER TEN: Finally, we are told that the people were called to Jerusalem from throughout Judea "and all the people sat in the street of the house of God" (vs. 9). Again, some insist that the mention of this street indicates that the 70 weeks prophecy which said "the street shall be built again, and the wall, even in troublous times" (Daniel 9:25) must have formerly been fulfilled in the days of Cyrus. But by now it should be clear that the repair of this street had to do with the rebuilding of the Temple area. Thus this street is one that would have given access to that structure.

Moreover, the above citation from Daniel does not fit the given facts previously enumerated in the Book of Ezra as does the narrative given in

---

[1] Again, they are at Ezra 1:14, 6:3–5 and 2 Chronicles 36:22–23.

the Book of Nehemiah. The building of the wall "in troublous times" was unmistakably fulfilled under the hand of Nehemiah (Neh. 2:17–6:15). These cited verses carefully record in great detail the struggle involved throughout this entire undertaking.

Thus according to Isaiah's prophecy, Cyrus was to be the one that would speak the word which would cause Jerusalem to be rebuilt – both the city and Temple. However, the scriptural history we have given reveals that the returning captives under Zerubbabel built only the Temple and merely homes enough to meet their immediate needs. Yet even though they did not fully restore the city, that which they did must be seen as sufficient to fulfill Isaiah as he made no mention of the walls. Moreover, it *was* on the basis of Cyrus' decree that the later decrees were mandated; thus, it may rightly be held that Cyrus built "my city" and said to Jerusalem "Thou shalt be built."

Now let us notice the order of events. The Temple was completed in the sixth year of Darius (Ezra 6). It was after this – in the seventh year of Artaxerxes – that Ezra came to Jerusalem to beautify the house of God. Still later – in "the twentieth year of Artaxerxes the king" (Neh. 2:1) – Nehemiah came to Jerusalem. He found only the Temple to have been rebuilt (Neh. 2:8, "the house"), and the commandment to rebuild the city given to *Nehemiah* by Artaxerxes was then put into effect (Neh. 2:5, 8, 13, and 17).

As the decree given to Nehemiah by Artaxerxes is the only one which has to do with rebuilding the **city** and **walls** ("in troublous times"), it must be the same decree referred to by Gabriel as having to do with the **beginning** of the 70 weeks prophecy. Let us now examine the first three chapters of Nehemiah as we have done with the Book of Ezra.

NEHEMIAH CHAPTER ONE: Nehemiah's brother (cp. Neh. 7:2) and certain men came from Judah to Shushan to see Nehemiah who was then serving as the king's cupbearer. Nehemiah asked them about the remnant of the Jews of the captivity and Jerusalem. Their report was that the Jews were in "great affliction and reproach" and that "the wall of Jerusalem" was broken down and "the gates" burned with fire.

When Nehemiah heard these things, he "wept, and mourned certain days, and fasted, and prayed" (vv. 1–4). This news was disheartening to Nehemiah because, although 82 years had passed (536 – 454 = 82), the rebuilding initiated by Cyrus had not been completed. Having returned with Zerubbabel and taken part in the project at its inception (Ezra 2:2, see discussion pages 240–249 and the display on page 245), Nehemiah had hoped the enormous project was surely finished and that the returnees were dwelling in safety and dignity – prospering in the land. Such was not the case.

NEHEMIAH CHAPTER TWO: Nehemiah was so overcome by the report of the sorry state in which Jerusalem still lay, he could not hide his sorrow – not even when coming before the king. "Now I had not been beforetime sad in his presence. Wherefore the king said unto me, Why is thy countenance sad, seeing thou art not sick? This was sorrow of heart." Nehemiah explained and asked permission to go unto Judah, to "the city of my fathers' sepulchres, that I may built it" (vs. 5).

This is *not* referring to a second repairing of the walls and gates to repair damage due to a recent attack as some suppose. Were such the case, surely such an important event would have been clearly denoted. Moreover, would it not be strange indeed that no mention of this attack upon the Holy City was recorded and expounded elsewhere within the Holy Writ, Josephus, Philo, etc.?

The wording is unmistakable and clear. Due probably to lack of funds and despair (cp. 4:10), the city itself was – after nearly 82 years – still largely in a state of disrepair. This decree is no mere passport giving Nehemiah permission to simply go to Judah as some affirm. Permission was asked to build the city (vs. 5), gates, wall, and to rebuild the home that he would occupy (vs. 8). In verse 8, Nehemiah also requested:

> ... a letter unto Asaph the keeper of the king's forest, that he may give me timber to make beams for the GATES of the palace ... and for the **wall** of the city, and for the house that I shall enter into. (author's emphasis)

NEHEMIAH CHAPTER THREE: gives a list of those who rebuilt and repaired the various portions of the wall. Several incidental references show that some of the houses of the

city had already been built before Nehemiah came to work on the walls. For example, we read of "the house of Eliashib, the high priest." Further, Benjamin and Hashup repaired the wall "over against their house" and Azariah "by his house." There is mention of "the king's high house." The priests repaired "every one over against his house." Zadok repaired "over against his house." Other verses in Nehemiah also show that the people had houses (4:14; 5:11, 13; 8:16). Some had even mortgaged their houses (Neh. 5:3–4).

However, it should not astonish us that the few returnees had built homes for themselves. Indeed, after 82 years we naturally expect this and should have been greatly surprised to learn otherwise. However, we must again emphasize that sporadically spaced houses here and there does not constitute a restored city.

NEHEMIAH, THE REMAINDER: Due to their enemies numerous threats, with the wall completed Nehemiah next made regulations concerning the opening and shutting of its gates and appointed: "watches of the inhabitants of Jerusalem, every one in his watch, and every one to be over against his house" (Neh. 7:3). The unprotected condition that had so long prevailed had left the city greatly under populated. This contributed extensively to the cities' lying in a general state of ruin these many years. Nehemiah 7:4 affirms this: "Now the city was large and great; but **the people were few, and the houses were not built.**"

Numerous references have been cited as to the presence of houses in Jerusalem. Consequently, the fourth verse must mean that the people living in Jerusalem were few in comparison to the number that had formerly occupied the city and the number of homes still in disrepair was great in comparison to those that had been rebuilt due to lack of returnees, funds, and general discouragement. True, Haggai 1:4 and 9 indicates that some were even prospering and living in paneled homes, but this does not alter the overall condition. They had houses, some of which were splendid. Yet large undeveloped spaces existed in between where houses had not yet been rebuilt. So at these places, scattered within the city where there were houses, various men were appointed "everyone in his watch" and each one at "his house."

Moreover, in a desperate attempt to sufficiently repopulate the city of Jerusalem, lots were cast among those of Judah and Benjamin whereupon a tenth were removed from the provinces to the capital (Neh. 11:1–2). Those who did so voluntarily were blessed by the people. A list of those new inhabitants followed.

CONCLUSION: Isaiah 44:24–28 is a protracted sentence consisting of a series of participial clauses that recite mighty acts of God from Creation down to Cyrus. Verse 26 clearly states that God himself will rebuild Jerusalem. Thus, the subject of "even saying to Jerusalem" in verse 28, which many attribute to Cyrus, may well refer instead to God.[1] The LXX and the Latin Vulgate both read this as meaning God, not Cyrus. Further, Cyrus did not directly build the city and its walls – Nehemiah did. If one still insists it is Cyrus who said to rebuild Jerusalem, we reply that it is not so stated in his decree as recorded at Ezra 6:3–5. Accordingly, Isaiah 45:13 refers to Messiah far better than to Cyrus. All this casts serious doubt and greatly diminishes the case for these verses favoring Cyrus' decree over that of Artaxerxes.

Indeed, it must be seen that however long it may have taken the people to rebuild the city, this has *nothing* to do with the beginning of the 70 weeks prophecy. This prophecy was *not* to begin with the *completion* of the city but from the *going forth* of the commandment to restore and build Jerusalem along with its wall! Nehemiah's work was primarily with the wall and rebuilding the city. The entire work of repairing the walls (in spite of threats, hardships, and summer's heat) was completed in 52 days (Neh. 6:15)! The Temple, the streets nearby, the homes of the indwelling remnant, etc., had already been built years before.

Once again, we see that the 70 weeks are to be counted from the 20th year of Artaxerxes when Nehemiah went to Jerusalem to repair the walls and the restore the city! The 69 "weeks" (69 sevens) or 483 years from this point do measure unto the "cutting off" of Messiah. The original 536 BC decree of Cyrus simply does not fit the context nor extend to the days of Christ.

---

[1] That is, "I say to Jerusalem," Albert Barnes, *Barnes' Notes*, Heritage Edition, Isaiah vol. 2, (Grand Rapids, MI: Baker Book House, 1998), p. 142 (1851).

The Year Nebuchadnezzar Razed Jerusalem

Without the use of any resources other than the Authorized Bible, the date Nebuchadnezzar burned Jerusalem and the Temple was first derived in AD 1977 by simply utilizing all the Scriptures exactly as recorded in the Chronological Compendium on page xiii. As already documented in our second chapter, these few passages established the year of the fall of the Kingdom of Judah in the 11th year of Zedekiah as AM 3418. The relevant Scriptures relating to the reigns of the kings of Judah were then charted in terms of AM years. This resulted in fixing the year of "the Captivity" as AM 3407.

Inclusively numbering 37 years from this first year of Jeconiah's (Jehoiachin) Captivity brought me to 3443 AM, the first year of the reign of Evil-merodach, son and successor of Nebuchadnezzar (2 Kings 25:27, cp. 2 Kings 24:12, 15). Counting back from 3443 AM, 3418 was found to be the 19th year of Nebuchadnezzar – the very year the Scriptures say he razed Jerusalem (Jer. 52:12–15). We have just seen in the above paragraph that this destruction took place in the 11th year of Zedekiah (2 Kings 25:1–7), thus confirming the synchronization of Judah and Babylon in 3418.

Numbering from Nebuchadnezzar's 19th year set AM 3399 as the year he ascended the throne. The Bible tallied that date with the 4th year of Jehoiakim (Jer. 25:1, cp. 46:2). The reader will note that connecting these two kingdoms was accomplished using only Scripture. No secular data whatsoever was consulted; neither was any needed.[1]

With the kingdoms of Judah and Babylon thus firmly synchronized, all that remained was to convert the *Anno Mundi* years to BC. Of course, as "BC" is a secular designation, consulting such data will be necessary for this step.

The simplest, most accurate and most direct way to accomplish this is to begin with the year of Nebuchadnezzar's accession to the throne of Babylon. It is the most reliable point of contact between the secular kingdoms and that of the Hebrew for the chronologer to so convert. As stated earlier in this treatise, Nebuchadnezzar's accession year is fixed by the well-documented lunar eclipse recorded by Ptolemy. This eclipse took place during the fifth year of Nebuchadnezzar's father, Nabopolassar.[2] Again, it has been dated as 22 April, – 620 (Julian Period, the historical Gregorian date is April 15, 621 BC).[3]

The Canon of Ptolemy and the Babylonian Chronicles tell us that Nabopolassar, reigned twenty-one years.[4] Hence, if we take 621 BC as the fifth year of his reign, the year of his death and the accession of his son will be fixed at 605 BC. Again, Jeremiah 25:1 states that Nebuchadnezzar's first year was the fourth year of the reign of Jehoiakim and this determines the BC date for that Judaic sovereign. Jeremiah also records that the Temple was burned in the nineteenth year of Nebuchadnezzar (Jeremiah 52:12–14, also 2 Kings 25:8); thus, the date for that conflagration is established as 586 BC.

This author and Ussher differ by two years with regard to this date. His date is 588 BC whereas mine is 586. Why is this since, as outlined in the foregoing, we both followed the same path (see fn. 1 below)?

As all the kings of Judah preceding this time period had used the accession method of reckoning (see Chart 5c), this author so continued and arrived at AM 3418 or 586 BC. Indeed, why would one suddenly change, without any compelling reason, to the non-accession method? Such would seem completely illogical. Yet here, Ussher suddenly ceased using the Judaic reckoning and assigned the non-accession system to Jehoiakim and Zedekiah. It was this decision that caused our two-year disparity.

---

[1] Upon first reading Ussher in 1992 – nearly sixteen years after making the above determinations – this author was stunned, yet most gratified, to find that Ussher had followed the same line of reasoning as that given above.

[2] All sources known to this author use this eclipse data to convert biblical dates to BC years.

[3] Ptolemy, "The Almagest," *Great Books of The Western World, op. cit.*, Book 5, p. 172; cp. Ussher, *Annals, op. cit.*, p. 93 (1658 ed., p. 80).

[4] Grayson, *ABC, op. cit.*, p. 99, and see the Canon on my page 229.

When all the eclipse data, Ptolemy's king list, Adad-guppi's tombstone inscription, along with all the other relevant biblical statements such as several 70-year prophecies and the 2 Kings 25:27 passage concerning the 37th year of Jehoiachin's captivity with the 1st year of Evil-merodach, etc. were integrated with 586 BC – everything meshed perfectly. However, Ussher's system change forced him to conclude that Nebuchadnezzar co-reigned two years with his father, Nabopolassar. Yet strangely, he offers no reference, no older authority to substantiate this.

Now such is quite unusual. Having over 12,000 footnotes as well as more than 2,500 citations from the Bible and the Apocrypha,[1] Ussher's work is one of the most thoroughly documented works known. Yet, here at one of the most crucial places in his entire chronology, he offers no corroboration. Hence, we are forced to conclude there is none. Ussher himself is the source of the "co-regency," and he created it in order to resolve the dilemma he had produced. It was the only way he could find to so do without violating Scripture – and violating the Word of God was a sin James Ussher would never commit.

Regarding Nabopolassar's 19th and 21st years, the Babylonian data (which was not known to Ussher and is over 2,200 years more ancient than he) refers four times to Nebuchadnezzar as the "mar sarri" (crown prince or prince) and twice as the "mar-su rabu" (eldest son,).[2] He is not called a co-rex. A prince or even a crown prince is not and may well never be a king.

Further, these historical records do not mention Nebuchadnezzar at all with regard to the 20th year of Nabopolassar. Of course, here we argue from silence which is always a weak position. Still, it seems most strange that a happening as significant as the exaltation of a prince to that of a co-regent would not have been recorded.

However, the most telling circumstance is that these same documents refer to Nebuchadnezzar's "year of accession" (Grayson, p. 100 and Wiseman, p. 69). Having already been equal to his father, a co-rex does not reckon an accession year.

Thus, the oldest and most knowledgeable source possible – the Neo-Babylonians themselves – attests that for the years in question, Nebuchadnezzar was nothing more than the heir apparent. It is therefore submitted that here brother Ussher was both logically and historically mistaken.

Further, Ussher's 588 BC as the year in which Jerusalem fell and the Temple was razed does not align with the recently released astronomical diary in the Berlin Museum. Designated as VAT 4956, this astral data absolutely fixes Nebuchadnezzar's 37th year at 568/567 BC[3] (see page 238), not 570/569 as Ussher's data yields[4] (the same is true for all others who use 588). Neither does 588 mesh with all the relevant lunar eclipses; and therefore, it does not exactly fulfill all the aforementioned 70-year prophecies.

Moreover, the 130-year span from 621–491 BC as depicted on Charts 5 and 5c precisely honors six astral fixes (two of which were unknown to Ussher) as well as the numerical values in over 100 Scriptures across this time period. The preponderance of this must be seen as overwhelming. No other chronology to date has ever achieved such concordance.

Of course, as stated previously, the calculation of a reported single astral event as an eclipse could be off by by several cycles, but not a cluster such as we have here. Indeed, here the meshing of such a vast number of Scriptures with these astral recordings serves to verify the accuracy and validity of these observations.

---

[1] This data was obtained via personal telephone call with Larry Pierce who has recently retranslated and published Ussher's Latin Version into modern AD 2003 English.

[2] Grayson, *ABC, op. cit.,* Chronicles 4 and 5, pp. 97–100; Wiseman, *Chronicles of Chaldaean Kings op. cit.,* BM 22047, 21946 (Obverse), pp. 65–69.

[3] Jonsson, *The Gentile Times Reconsidered, op. cit.,* pp. 158, 186.

[4] Ussher, *Annals of the World,* revised by Larry & Marion Pierce, *op. cit.,* p. 908.

BIBLIOGRAPHY

Africanus, Julius. *Chronographies. Ante-Nicene Fathers.* Vol. VI. Grand Rapids, MI: Eerdmans. 1978 (1867).

Aharoni, Yohanan and Michael Avi-Yonah. *The Macmillan Bible Atlas.* New York: Macmillan. 1968.

Albright, William Foxwell. "The Chronology of the Divided Monarchy of Israel." *Bulletin of the American Schools of Oriental Research 100.* (1945): 16-22.

-------. "The Seal of Eliakim and the Latest Preëxilic History of Judah, With Some Observations on Ezekiel." *Journal of Biblical Literature* 51 (1932): 77-106.

-------. *The Old Testament and Modern Study.* Oxford: 1951.

Anderson, Sir Robert. *The Coming Prince.* Grand Rapids, MI: Kregel. 1882.

Andrews, Samuel J. *The Life of Our Lord upon the Earth.* 4th ed. New York: Charles Scribner & Co. 1867.

Anstey, Martin. *The Romance of Bible Chronology.* London: Marshall Bros. 1913.

Archer, Gleason. *A Survey of Old Testament Introduction.* rev. ed. Chicago: Moody Press. 1974.

-------. *Encyclopedia of Bible Difficulties.* Grand Rapids, MI: Zondervan. 1982.

Ardsma, Gerald E. *Radiocarbon and the Genesis Flood.* San Diego, CA: Master Books. 1991.

Barnes, Thomas G. *Origin and Destiny of the Earth's Magnetic Field.* San Diego, CA: Master Books. 1973.

Beecher, Willis J. *The Dated Events of the Old Testament.* Phil., PA: Sunday School Times. 1907.

Blosser, Oliver R. "Historical Reliability of Genesis 1-11." *It's About Time.* Spencer, Iowa: Chronology-History Research Inst. (April-July 1986): 8, 9.

-------. "The Synchronization of Jehu with Shalmaneser III." *It's About Time.* Spencer, Iowa: Chronology-History Research Inst. (March, 1986): 4.

Bowden, Malcom. *Ape-Men - Fact or Fallacy?* Kent, Eng: Sovereign. 1977.

Breasted, James H. *Ancient Records of Egypt.* Vol. IV. New York: Russell & Russell. 1962.

Bright, John. *A History of Israel.* Philadelphia, PA: The Westminster Press. 1959.

Browne, Henry. "Chronology of the Holy Scriptures". *Ordo Saeclorum.* London: John Parker Pub. 1844.

Budge, E. A. Wallis. *Annals of the Kings of Assyria.* London: BM. 1902.

Bullinger, E. W., (ed.). *Companion Bible, The.* Grand Rapids, MI: Kregel Pub. 1990.

Burgon, John. *The Revision Revised.* Paradise, PA: Conservative Classics. 1883.

Burns, Edward McNall. *Western Civilizations.* New York: W. W. Norton. 1963.

Cicero, Marcus Tullius. *Laelius de Amicitia.* Vol. XX. The Loeb Classical Library. trans. by W. A. Falconer. Cambridge, MA: Harvard UP. 1923.

Clement of Alexander. *Stromata.* Book I. *Ante-Nicene Fathers.* Vol. II. Roberts and Donaldson, eds. Grand Rapids, MI: Eerdmans Publishing Co. 1885.

Clinton, Henry Fynes. *Fasti Hellenici.* Oxford, England: Oxford University Press. 1834.

Crockett, William Day. *A Harmony of the Books of Samuel, Kings, and Chronicles.* Grand Rapids, MI: Baker Book House. 1979.

Davis, John. *Paradise to Prison: Studies in Genesis.* Grand Rapids, MI: Baker Book House. 1975.

Dio Cassius. *Roman History.* Vols. VI & VIII. The Loeb Classical Library. trans. by Earnest Cary. Cambridge, MA: Harvard UP. 2000.

Diodorus Siculus. *The Library of History*. Vol. IV. The Loeb Classical Library. trans. by C. H. Oldfather. Cambridge, MA: Harvard UP. 1968.

Dolen, Walter R. *The Chronology Papers*. San Jose, CA: The Becoming-One Church Pub. 1977.

Dunbar, Carl O. *Historical Geology*. New York: John Wiley and Sons. 1953.

Dundee, Charles Roger. *A Collation of The Sacred Scriptures*. n.p. 1847.

Durant, Will. *The Story of Civilization. Caesar and Christ*. Volume 3. New York: Simon and Schuster. 1944.

Eddy, John A. *Geotimes*. Vol. 23. (September, 1978): 18.

Edersheim, Dr. Alfred. *Old Testament Bible History*. Grand Rapids, MI: Eerdmans. 1890. rep. 1990.

Eusebius. *Chronicon*. Schone, ed. translated by Petermann and Rodiger. Berlin: n.p. 1866.

-------. *Ecclesiastical History*. Vol. I. *The Loeb Classical Library*. trans. by Kirsopp Lake. Cambridge, MA: Harvard UP. 1980.

Faulstich, Eugene W. *History, Harmony & The Hebrew Kings*. Spencer, IA: Chronology Books. 1986.

-------. *History, Harmony, The Exile and Return*. Spencer, IA: Chronology Books. 1988.

-------. *History Harmony & Daniel*. Spencer, IA: Chronology Books. 1988.

Finegan, Jack. *Handbook of Biblical Chronology: Principles of Time Reckoning In The Ancient World and Problems of Chronology In The Bible*. Princeton, NJ: UP. 1964.

-------. *Handbook of Biblical Chronology: Revised Edition*. Peabody, MA: Hendrickson Pub. 1998

Firdusi, The Shah Nama of: The Book of the Persian Kings. London: Oxford UP. 1931.

Free, J. P. *Archaeology and Bible History*. rev. ed. Wheaton, IL: Scripture Press Pub. 1969.

Fuller, D. O., ed. *Which Bible?* Grand Rapids, MI: International Pub. 1970.

Galloway, William Brown. *The Chain of Ages*. London, England: Rivington et al. Pub. 1881.

Gehman, Henry Snyder, (ed.). *Westminster Dictionary of the Bible, The New*. Phil., PA: The Westminster Press. 1970.

Gentry, Robert V. *Creation's Tiny Mystery*. San Diego, CA: Master Books. 1986.

Gipe, George. *Last Time When*. New York: World Almanac Pub. 1981

Gish, Duane T. *Evolution, the Fossils Say No!* San Diego, CA: Master Books. 1972.

Glueck, Nelson. *Rivers in the Desert*. New York: Farrar, Strauss & Cudahy. 1959

Goodspeed, G. S. *A History of the Babylonians and Assyrians*. Cambridge, MA: Harvard UP. 1902.

Grayson, Albert K. "Assyrian and Babylonian Chronicles." *Texts From Cuneiform Sources*. A. L. Oppenheim, et al., eds. Locust Valley, NY: J. Augustin. 1975.

-------. *Assyrian Royal Inscriptions*. Wiesbaden, Germany: Otto Harrassowitz. 1972.

Greswell, Edward. *Dissertations upon the Principles and Arrangement of a Harmony of the Gospels*. 4 Vols. Oxford, England: n.p. 1830.

Hales, William. *A New Analysis of Chronology*. 2nd ed. 4 Vols. London: 1830 (1st 1809).

Hareuveni, Nogah. *Nature in Our Biblical Heritage*. Israel: Neot Kedumim Ltd. 1980.

Hayes, Carlton J. and J. H. Hanscom. *Ancient Civilizations*. New York: Macmillan. 1968.

Hengstenberg, E. W. *Christology of the Old Testament*. trans. T. K. Arnold. Grand Rapids, MI: Kregel. 1835.

Herodotus of Halicarnassus. *The Histories of Herodotus.* 4 Vols. The Loeb Classical Library. translated by A. D. Godley. Cambridge, MA: Harvard UP. 1975.

Hills, Edward F. *The King James Version Defended.* 4th edition. Des Moines, IO: Christian Research Press. 1984.

-------. *Believing Bible Study.* 2nd edition. Des Moines, IO: 1977.

Hislop, Alexander. *The Two Babylons.* NJ: Loizeaux Bros. 1916.

Hoehner, Harold W. *Chronological Aspects of the Life of Christ.* Grand Rapids, MI: Zondervan. 1977.

Horn, S. H. and L. H. Wood. "The Fifth-Century Jewish Calendar at Elephantine." *Journal of Near Eastern Studies 13* (Jan. 1954).

Horne, Thomas Hartwell. *An Introduction to the Critical Study and Knowledge of the Holy Scriptures.* 9th ed. London: Spottiswoode and Shaw. 1846.

Idler, Christian Ludwig. *Abhdll. der Berliner Academie der Wissensch. fur histor. Klasse.* 1814.

Irenaeus. *Against Heresies. Anti-Nicene Fathers.* Volume I. Roberts and Donaldson, eds. Grand Rapids, MI: Eerdmans. 1885.

Jack, J. W. *The Date of the Exodus.* Edinburgh: 1925.

Jackson, John. *Chronological Antiquities.* London: 1752.

Jeffrey, Grant R. *Armageddon: Appointment With Destiny.* Toronto, Canada: Frontier Research. 1988.

Jones, Floyd Nolen. *Which Version is The Bible?* 17th ed., rev. & enlarged. The Woodlands, TX: KingsWord Press. 1999 (1993).

-------. *The Septuagint: A Critical Analysis.* 6th edition, revised and enlarged. The Woodlands, TX: KingsWord Press. 2000 (1989).

Jonsson, Carl Olof, *The Gentile Times Reconsidered.* 3rd Edition, Rev. & Expanded. Atlanta, GA: Commentary Press. 1998.

Josephus, Flavius. *Josephus Complete Works.* trans. by William Whiston. Grand Rapids, MI: Kregel. 1960.

-------. *Antiquities of the Jews.*

-------. *Wars of the Jews.*

-------. *Dissertation V.*

Justin Martyr. *The First Apology. Ante-Nicene Fathers.* Roberts and Donaldson, eds. Grand Rapids, MI: Eerdmans Publishing Co. 1985.

Keil, Carl Friedrich. *Commentary On The Old Testament.* trans. by James Martin. Grand Rapids, MI: Eerdmans. 1976.

-------. and F. Delitzsch. *Commentary on the Old Testament in Ten Volumes.* rpt. Grand Rapids, MI: Eerdmans. 1986.

Klassen, Frank R. *The Chronology of the Bible.* Nashville, TN: Regal. 1975.

Kleber, Albert M. "The Chronology of 3 and 4 Kings and 2 Paralipomenon." *Biblica 2.* (1921).

Klotz, John W. *Genes, Genesis, and Evolution.* St. Louis, MO: Concordia. 1970.

Layard, Austen Henry. *Nineveh and Its Remains.* 2 Vols. New York: n.p. 1850.

Leaf, Alex. "Every Day is a Gift When You Are Over 100". *National Geographic. 143* (Jan. 1973): 93-119.

Letis, Theodore P., ed. *The Majority Text.* Grand Rapids, MI: Institute for Biblical Textual Studies. 1987.

-------. *Edward Freer Hill's Contribution to the Revival of the Ecclesiastical Text.* unpub. M.T.S. Thesis. Emory U. 1987.

Leupold, Herbert Carl. *Exposition of Genesis.* Columbus, OH: Wartburg Press. 1942.

Luckenbill, Daniel David. *Ancient Records of Assyria and Babylonia.* New York: Greenwood Press. 1968.

-------. *Ancient Records Of Assyria And Babylonia*. Vol. II. London: Histories & Mysteries of Man Pub. 1989.

Martyr, Justin. *The First Apology. Ante-Nicene Fathers*. Roberts and Donaldson, eds. Grand Rapids, MI: Eerdmans Publishing Co. 1985.

Mauro, Philip. *The Seventy Weeks and the Great Tribulation*. Boston, MA: Scripture Truth Depot. 1923.

McClain, Alva J. *Daniel's Prophecy of the Seventy Weeks*. Grand Rapids, MI: Zondervan Publishing House. 1972 (orig. 1940).

Merivale, Charles. *History of the Romans under the Empire* 7 Vols. New York: D. Appleman & Co. 1896.

Metzger, Bruce M. *The Text of the New Testament*. 3rd ed., enl. NY: Oxford UP. 1992.

Moorman, Jack A. *Forever Settled*. Collingswood, NJ: Bible For Today Press. 1985.

-------. *When The KJV Departs From The "Majority" Text*. Collingswood, NJ: B. F. T. 1988.

-------. *Bible Chronology: The Two Great Divides*. Collingswood, NJ: B.F.T. 1999.

Morris, Henry M. *Scientific Creationism*. San Diego, CA: Master Books. 1974.

-------. *The Scientific Case for Creation*. San Diego, CA: Master Books. 1977.

Mowinckel, Sigmund. "Die Chronologie der israelitischen und judischen Konige." *Acta Orientalia 10* (1932).

Moyer, Elgin S. *Who Was Who in Church History*. Chicago, IL: Moody Press. 1962.

Munro, J. Iverach. *The Samaritan Pentateuch and Modern Criticism*. London, Eng: J. Nisbet & Co., Ltd. Publishers. 1911.

Newton, Sir Isaac. *Observations on Daniel and the Apocalypse of St. John*. London: 1733.

-------. *The Chronology of Ancient Kingdoms Amended*. London: 1728.

Newton, Robert R. *The Crime of Claudius Ptolemy*. Baltimore, MD: John Hopkins UP. 1977.

Nolan, Frederick. *An Inquiry into the Integrity of the Greek Vulgate or Received Text of the New Testament*. London: F.C. and J. Rivington Pub. 1815.

Olmstead, A. T. "Fall of Samaria." *American Journal of Semitic Languages and Literatures 21* (1904-05).

Oppert, Jules. *Chronologie des Assyriens et des Babyloniens*. n.p. 1857.

Owen, John. "Of the Integrity and Purity of the Hebrew and Greek Text of the Scriptures". *The Works of John Owen*. Vol. XVI. ed. William H. Goold. Edinburgh, Scotland: Banner of Truth. 1968 (1850-53).

Pache, Rene. *Inspiration and Authority of Scripture*. Chicago, Il: Moody Bible Institute. 1969.

Pentecost, J. Dwight. *Things To Come*. Grand Rapids, MI: Zondervan Pub. House. 1973 (1958).

Pickering, Wilbur N. *The Identity of the New Testament Text*. Nashville, TN: Thomas Nelson. 1977.

Pliny. *Natural History*. Volume II. The Loeb Classical Library. translated by H. Rackhman. Cambridge, MA: Harvard UP. 1942.

Plutarch. *Plutarch's Lives: Themistocles*. Vol. II. The Loeb Classical Library. trans. B. Perrin. Cambridge, MA: Harvard UP. 1967.

Polyaenus. *Stratagematum Book 7*. trans. by R. Shepherd. Chicago, IL: Ares Pub. 1974.

Price, Ira M. *Ancestry of Our English Bible*. 3rd ed., rev. NY: Harper & Bros. 1956, (1906).

Prideaux, Humphrey. *The Old and New Testament Connected in the History of the Jews*. 25th edition. 2 Vols. London: 1858.

Pritchard, James B. *The Ancient Near East Text Relating to the Old Testament*. 3rd edition. Princeton: UP. 1969.

Ptolemy, (Claudius Ptolemaeus). "The Almagest." R. M. Hutchins, ed. *Great Books of The Western World*. trans. by R. C. Taliaferro. Chicago, IL: William Benton. 1952.

Ramsay, Sir William. *Was Christ Born at Bethlehem?* 2nd ed. London: Hodder and Stoughton Publishers. 1898.

-------. *The Bearing of Recent Discoveries on the Trustworthiness of the New Testament*. London: Hodder and Stoughton Pub. 1915.

Ray, Jasper J. *God Wrote Only One Bible*. Junction City, OR: Eye Opener Pub. 1980.

Robertson, A. T. *A Harmony of the Gospels for Students of the Life of Christ*. NY: Harper & Row. 1922.

Robinson, Edward. *Harmony of the Gospels in English*. Boston, MA: Crocker & Brewster. 1846.

Savile, B. W. "Revelation and Science." *Journal of Sacred Literature & Biblical Record*. Series IV. London: Williams & Norgate Pub. (April, 1863): p. 156.

Sayce, Archibald Henry. "The Bible and the Monuments." *The Variorum Aids to Bible Students*. n.p. c.1895.

-------. *The Higher Criticism and the Verdict of the Monuments*. London: The Society for Promoting Christian Knowledge. 1895.

Scalinger, Joseph. *Opus Novum De Emendatione Temporum*. Paris, France: 1583.

Schwab, Simon. "Comparative Jewish Chronology". *Dr. Joseph Breuer Jubilee Volume*. New York: Rabbi Samson Raphael Hirsch Publications Society, Philipp Felheim Inc. 1962.

-------. "Comparative Jewish Chronology". *Selected Speeches: A Collection of Addresses and Essays on Hashkafah, Contemporary Issues and Jewish History*. Lakewood, New Jersey: CIS Pub. 1991.

Scofield, C. I. *What Do the Prophets Say?* Phil., PA: The Sunday School Times Co. 1918.

Seder Olam. Heinrich Guggenheimer, ed. NY: Rowman & Littlefield Pub. 2005.

Shenkel James D., *Chronology and Recensional Development in the Greek Text of Kings*. Cambridge, MA: Harvard University Press. 1968.

Siculus, Diodorus. *The Library of History*. Vol. IV. The Loeb Classical Library. trans. by C. H. Oldfather. Cambridge, MA: Harvard UP. 1968.

Slusher, Harold S. *Critique of Radiometric Dating*. San Diego, CA: Master Books. 1973.

-------. *The Origin of the Universe*. San Diego, CA: Master Books. 1978.

Smith, George. *The Assyrian Eponym Canon*. London, England: Oxford UP. 1875.

Sturz, Harry A. *The Byzantine Text-Type And New Testament Textual Criticism*. Nashville, TN: Thomas Nelson. 1972.

Swete, Henry B. *An Introduction to the Old Testament In Greek*. rev. Peabody, MA: Hendrickson Pub. 1914. rep. 1989.

Syncellus, Georgius. *Historia Chronographia*. Paris, France: c.800.

Tacitus, Cornelius. *Annals*. Book I. The Loeb Classical Library. trans. by John Jackson. Cambridge, MA: Harvard UP. 1931.

Tadmor, Hayim. "Chronology of the Last Kings of Judah." *Journal of Near Eastern Studies 15* (1956): 227.

Tertullian. *An Answer to the Jews,* Part I & *On Idolatry*. Ante-Nicene Fathers. Vol. III. Roberts and Donaldson, eds. Grand Rapids, MI: Eerdmans Publishing Co. 1985

Thiele, Edwin R. *The Mysterious Numbers of the Hebrew Kings*. rev. Grand Rapids, MI: Zondervan. 1983.

-------. *A Chronology of the Hebrew Kings.* Grand Rapids, MI: Zondervan. 1977.

Thucydides. *History of the Peloponnesian War.* Volume I. The Loeb Classical Library. trans. by C. F. Smith. Cambridge, MA: Harvard UP. 1980.

Unger, Merrill Frederick. *Introductory Guide To The Old Testament.* Grand Rapids, MI: Zondervan Publishing House. 1976.

Ussher, Archbishop James. *Annals of the World.* Revised by Larry & Marion Pierce. Green Forest, AK: Master Books. 2003 (London, 1658 AD).

-------. *The Whole Works of the Most Rev. James Ussher.* C.R. Elrington and James Henthorn Todd, eds. Dublin Ireland: Hodges & Smith Pub. 1864.

Van Bruggen, Jakob. *The Ancient Text of the New Testament.* Winnepeg, Canada: Premier Printing Ltd. 1976.

Vitringa, Campegius. *Hyptoyposis Historiae et Chronologiae Sacrae.* Leeuwarden, Netherlands: n.p. 1698.

Waite, Donald A. *ASV, NASV, & NIV Departures From Traditional Hebrew & Greek Texts* Collingswood, NJ: Bible For Today Press. #986. 1981.

-------. *Biblical Chronology.* Collingswood, NJ: Bible For Today Press. #986. 1973.

Wallace, F. E. *A Review of the New Versions.* Ft. Worth, TX: Noble Patterson. 1973.

Walton, John H. *Chronological And Background Charts of The Old Testament.* Grand Rapids, MI: Zondervan. 1978.

Westcott, B. F. and F. J. A. Hort. *Introduction to the New Testament in the Original Greek.* New York: Harper and Bros. 1882.

Whitcomb, John C., Jr. and Henry M. Morris. *The Genesis Flood.* San Diego, CA: Baker Book House. 1972.

-------. *Darius the Mede.* Grand Rapids, MI: Eerdmans. 1959.

Wilkinson, Benjamin C. *Our Authorized Bible Vindicated.* Washington, DC: 1930.

Wilkinson, James V. S., (ed.). *The Shah Nama of Firdusi, The Book of the Persian Kings.* London: Oxford University Press. 1931 (orig. 1010 AD).

Wilkinson, Sir J. Gardiner. *Manners and Customs of the Ancient Egyptians.* 6 Vols. London: 1837-1841.

Wiseman, Donald. J. *Nebuchadressar And Babylon.* England: Oxford UP. 1983.

-------. *Chronicles of Chaldaean Kings (626-556 B.C.) in the British Museum.* London: British Museum Pub. 1956.

Xenophon. *Cyropaedia.* Vol. I & II. The Loeb Classical Library. trans. by W. Miller. Cambridge, MA: Harvard UP. 1983.

-------. *Hellenica.* Vol. II. The Loeb Classical Library. trans. by C. L. Brownson. Cambridge, MA: Harvard UP. 1921.

Yamauchi, Edwin M. *Persia and the Bible.* Grand Rapids, MI: Baker Book House. 1990.

COMMENTARIES, ENCYCLOPEDIAS, AND OTHER REFERENCES

American Presbyterian Review. "The Kings of Israel and Judah." April 1880.

Ante-Nicene Fathers, The. Vol. VI. Alexander Roberts and James Donaldson, eds. Grand Rapids, MI: Eerdmans Publishing Co. 1885.

Apocrypha, The. London, England: Oxford UP. n.d.

Authorized Holy Bible (King James). Regal Reference Edition. Eyre and Spottiswoode: London. 1987.

Babylonian Talmud, The. Tract Rosh Hashana and Tract Arakin.

Barnes' Notes. Albert Barnes. Heritage Edition Vol. 6. Isaiah, Vol. 2. Grand Rapids, MI: Baker Book House. 1998 (1851).

Bible Knowledge Commentary, The. John F. Walvoord and Roy B. Zuck, eds. 2 Vols. Wheaton, IL: Victor Books. 1985.

Bible Commentary: Rev., The New. D. Guthrie, et al., eds. Grand Rapids, MI: Eerdmans. 1984.

Clarke's Commentary. Clarke, Adam. 6 Vols. Nashville, TN: Abingdon. 1830.

Collier's Encyclopedia. New York: Macmillan. 1981.

Companion Bible, The. Bullinger, E. W., ed. Grand Rapids, MI: Kregel Pub. 1990.

Cyclopedia of Biblical Theological and Ecclesiastical Literature. McClintock and Strong. Grand Rapids, MI: Baker Book House. 1867.

Dake's Annotated Reference Bible. Finis Jennings Dake. 8th printing. Lawrenceville, GA: Dake Bible Sales, Inc. Pub. 1974.

Encyclopedia Judaica. Jerusalem, Israel: Keter Publishing House, Ltd. 1971

Gesenius' Hebrew and Chaldee Lexicon to the Old Testament Scriptures. trans. by Samuel Prideaux Tregelles. Grand Rapids, MI: Baker Book House. 1979.

Guiness Book of Records. Donald McFarlan, et al., ed. NY: Bantam Books. 1992.

Instant Quotation Dictionary. D. O. Bolander, comp. "Napoleon Bonaparte." Mundelein, IL: Career Institute Inc. 1969.

Interlinear Hebrew/Greek English Bible, The. Jay Green, ed. and trans. 4 Volumes. Wilmington, DE: Associated Pub. and Authors. 1976.

Interlinear Literal Translation of the Greek New Testament, The. George Ricker Berry. Grand Rapids, MI: Zondervan. 1977.

International Standard Bible Encyclopedia. Geoffrey W. Bromiley, editor. Grand Rapids, MI: Eerdmans. 1979.

King James Bible Commentary. Nashville, TN: Thomas Nelson Pub. 1999.

Liberty Bible Commentary. Nashville, TN: Thomas Nelson. 1983.

New International Dictionary of Biblical Archaeology, The. Edward Blaiklock, ed. Grand Rapids, MI: Zondervan Publishing House. 1983.

Oxford Bible Atlas. H. G. May, ed. New York: 1970.

Reese Chronological Bible, The. Minneapolis., MN: Bethany Fellowship Inc. 1980.

Schaff-Herzog Encyclopedia of Religious Knowledge, The New. Grand Rapids, MI: Baker Book House Pub. 1949.

Scientific American. March 1979, pp. 91-92.

Sculptures and Inscriptions of Darius the Great on the Rock of Behistun, in Persia. London: British Museum. 1907.

Self-Interpreting Bible, The. The Authorized Bible with Explanatory Notes by The Reverend John Brown. London and Edinburgh: A. Fullarton Co. 1873.

Septuagint, The. Alfred Rahlfs, editor. 3rd ed. American Bible Society. New York: 1935. rep. 1949.

Septuagint Version of the Old Testament and Apocrypha With an English Translation, The. Charles Lee Brenton, ed. Grand Rapids, MI: Zondervan. 1978.

Unger's Commentary on the Old Testament. Merrill F. Unger. 2 Vols. Chicago, IL: Moody Press. 1981

-------. *Unger's Bible Dictionary.* Chicago, IL: Moody Press. 1966.

-------. *Unger's Bible Dictionary, The New.* Chicago, IL: Moody Press. 1988.

Veteran of Foreign Wars (VFW) Magazine. November, 1992.

Westminster Dictionary of the Bible, The New. Henry Snyder Gehman, ed. Phil., PA: The Westminster Press. 1970.

Zondervan Pictorial Encyclopedia of the Bible, The. Merrill C. Tenney, gen. ed. 5 Vols. Grand Rapids, MI: Zondervan. 1978.

SECONDARY SOURCES

Bengel, John, A. *Gnomon of the New Testament.* 5 Vols. 6th ed. trans by The Rev. William Fletcher, D.D. Edinburgh: T. & T. Clark Pub. 1866 (1742).

Boutflower, Charles. *In and Around the Book of Daniel.* London: Society for the Promotion of Christian Knowledge. 1923.

Breasted, James H. A *History of the Ancient Egyptians.* NewYork: Charles Scribner's Sons. 1908.

Cornfeld, Gaalyah. *Archaeology of the Bible: Book by Book.* David N. Freedman, consul. ed. Peabody, MA: Hendickson. 1989.

Jarvis, Samuel Farmar. *A Complete History of the Christian Church, Introduction.* An Unfinished Work n.p. 1844.

Johns, C. H. W. *Ancient Assyria.* n.p. 1912.

Olmstead, A. T. *History of Assyria.* Chicago, IL: Chicago University Press. 1951.

-------. *History of the Persian Empire.* Chicago, IL: Chicago University Press. 1951.

Pritchard, James B. *The Ancient Near East in Pictures: Relating to the Old Testament.* 2nd edition with supplement. Princeton: University Press. 1969.

Rawlinson, George. *Ezra and Nehemiah: Their Lives and Times.* New York: Anson D. Randolph. 1980.

-------. *The Five Great Monarchies of The Ancient Eastern World: The History, Geography, and Antiquities of Chaldea, Assyria, Babylon, Media, and Persia.* 3 Vols. NY: Dodd, Mead. 1870.

-------. *History of Herodotus.* 4 Vols. London: n.p. 1858.

Rowley, Harold. H. *Darius the Mede and the Four World Empires in the Book of Daniel; A Historical Study of Contemporary Theories.* Cardiff: University of Wales. 1959.

Tadmor, Hayim. "Azriyau of Yaudi." *Studies in the Bible, Scripta Hierosolymitana 8* (1961).

Yamauchi, Edwin M. *The Stones and the Scriptures.* Philadelphia: J. B. Lippincott Co. Pub. 1972.

INDEX

How to Obtain Full-Size Prints

of the Charts That Are on the CD

If you are interested in a set of full-size prints of the historical charts that appear on the enclosed CD, please contact the Digital Vault at *A&E – The Graphics Complex* in any of the following ways:

- Telephone: 713-579-1234
- Toll Free: 888-621-0022 (ask for the Digital Vault)
- Fax: 713-966-8525
- E-Mail: vault@aecomplex.com
- Mail: ATTN: DIGITAL VAULT
                  A & E - The Graphics Complex
                  P.O. Box 27286
                  Houston, Texas 77227

Include your name, shipping address, day and night contact numbers, and e-mail address on all orders and correspondence. Any inquiries not directed to the Digital Vault may be delayed or lost. Vault personnel will provide you with information on method of payment. Please reference Quote Number (Floyd Jones Charts) IQ9209 when ordering.

The price of the set of 12 charts is $39.95 (US) plus shipping charges and sales tax. Since price is subject to change, please check when ordering to determine current price. Each chart is printed on 11" wide, bright white 20# bond, folded at 8½" intervals so that each chart folds and stacks to a size no larger than 8½" x 11". All the charts are then stacked, shrink-wrapped together, boxed, and shipped by whichever method you request. Unfortunately, we cannot accept orders for an incomplete set of charts or an individual chart.

Please let us know if you have any questions or concerns.

Thank you,

Tony Zal
A & E – The Graphics Complex
713-579-2085
tzal@aecomplex.com

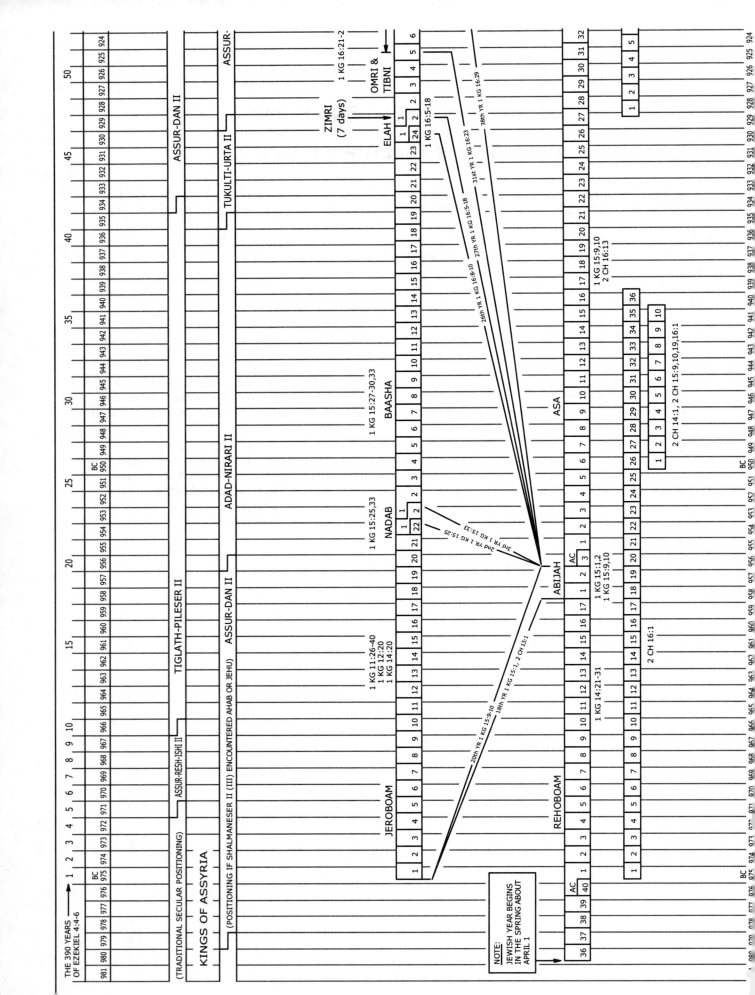

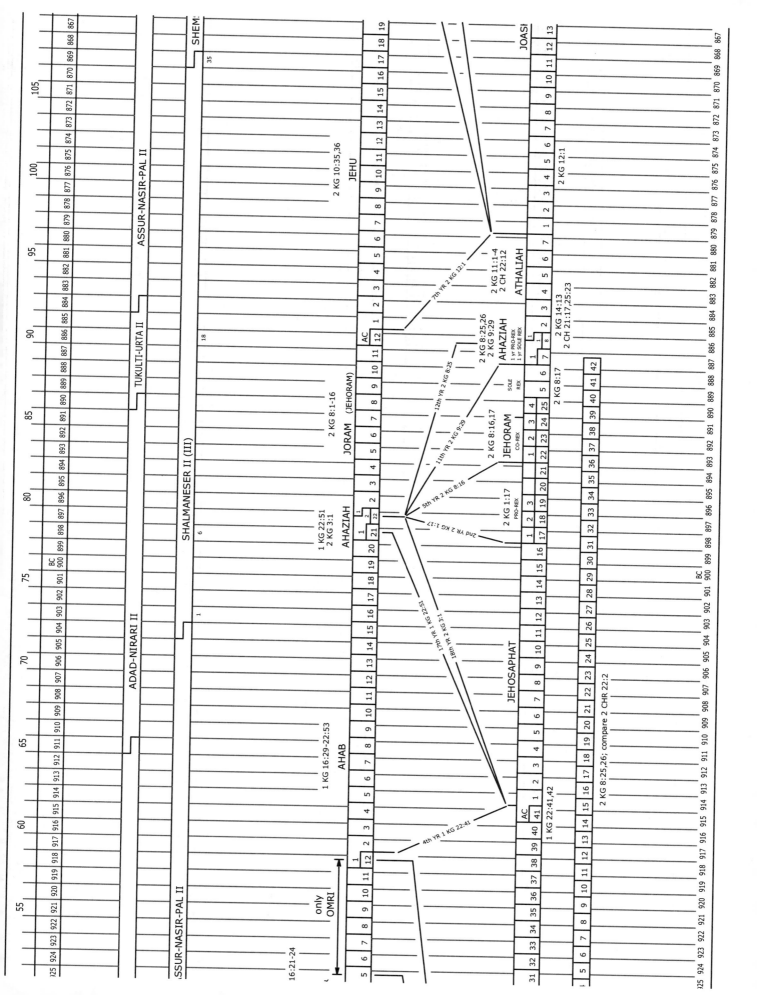

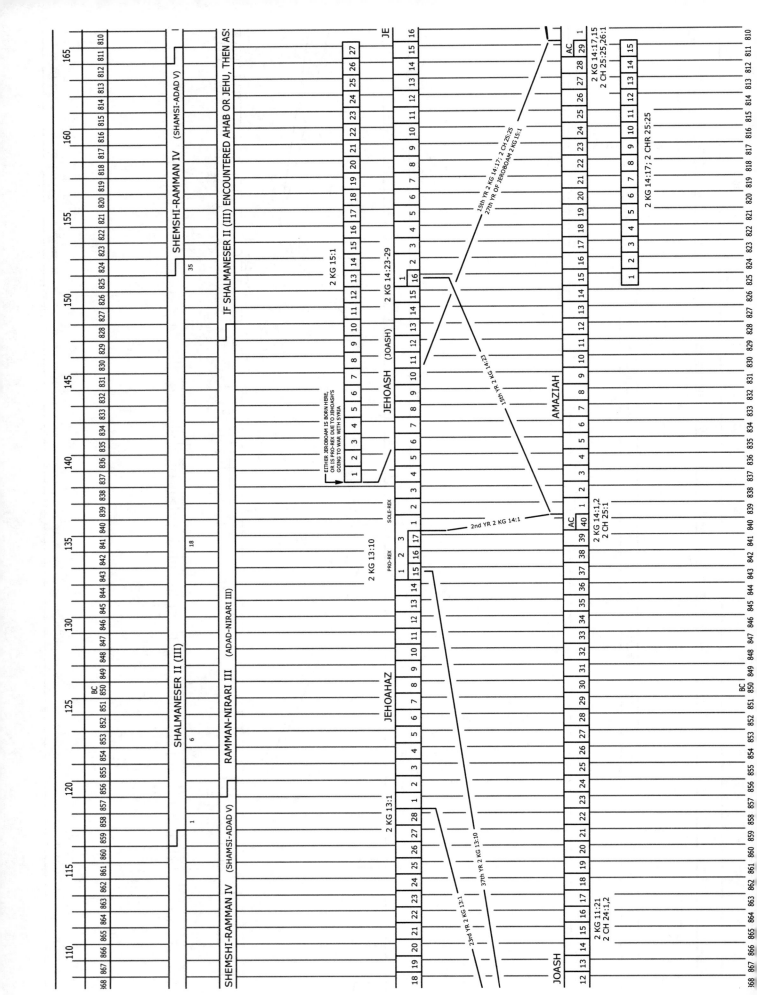

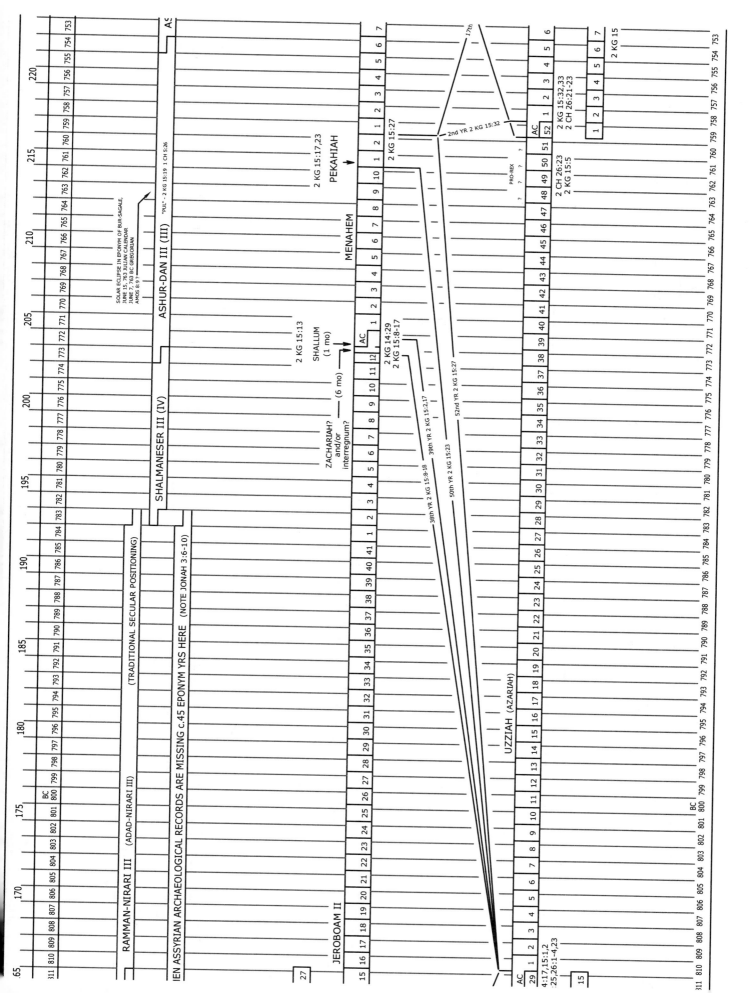

This chronological chart is a full-page illustration. Text labels visible within it include the following:

Top margin year markers (left to right across top): 220, 215, 210, 205, 200, 195, 190, 185, 180, 175, 170, .65

Eponym/BC year numbers run along top and bottom rows (753, 754, 755, 756, 757, 758, 759, 760, 761, 762, 763, 764, 765, 766, 767, 768, 769, 770, 771, 772, 773, 774, 775, 776, 777, 778, 779, 780, 781, 782, 783, 784, 785, 786, 787, 788, 789, 790, 791, 792, 793, 794, 795, 796, 797, 798, 799, 800, 801, 802, 803, 804, 805, 806, 807, 808, 809, 810, 811)

RAMMAN-NIRARI III   (ADAD-NIRARI III)   (TRADITIONAL SECULAR POSITIONING)

SHALMANESER III (IV)

ASHUR-DAN III (III)

SOLAR ECLIPSE IN EPONYM OF BUR-SAGALE, JUNE 15, 763 JULIAN CALENDAR JUNE 7, 763 B.C. GREGORIAN AMOS 8:9 ?

"PUL" - 2 KG 15:19 1 CH 5:26

...IEN ASSYRIAN ARCHAEOLOGICAL RECORDS ARE MISSING c.45 EPONYM YRS HERE   (NOTE JONAH 3:6-10)

JEROBOAM II

ZACHARIAH? and/or interregnum?

SHALLUM (1 mo)   (6 mo)   2 KG 15:13

2 KG 14:29   2 KG 15:8-17

MENAHEM

PEKAHIAH   2 KG 15:17,23

2 KG 15:27

38th YR 2 KG 15:8-18   39th YR 2 KG 15:2,17   50th YR 2 KG 15:23   52nd YR 2 KG 15:27

17th

2nd YR 2 KG 15:32

PRO-REX

UZZIAH (AZARIAH)

AC   2 CH 26:23   2 KG 15:5

2 KG 15:32,33   2 CH 26:21-23

AC   4:17,15:1,2   25,26:1-4,23

2 KG 15

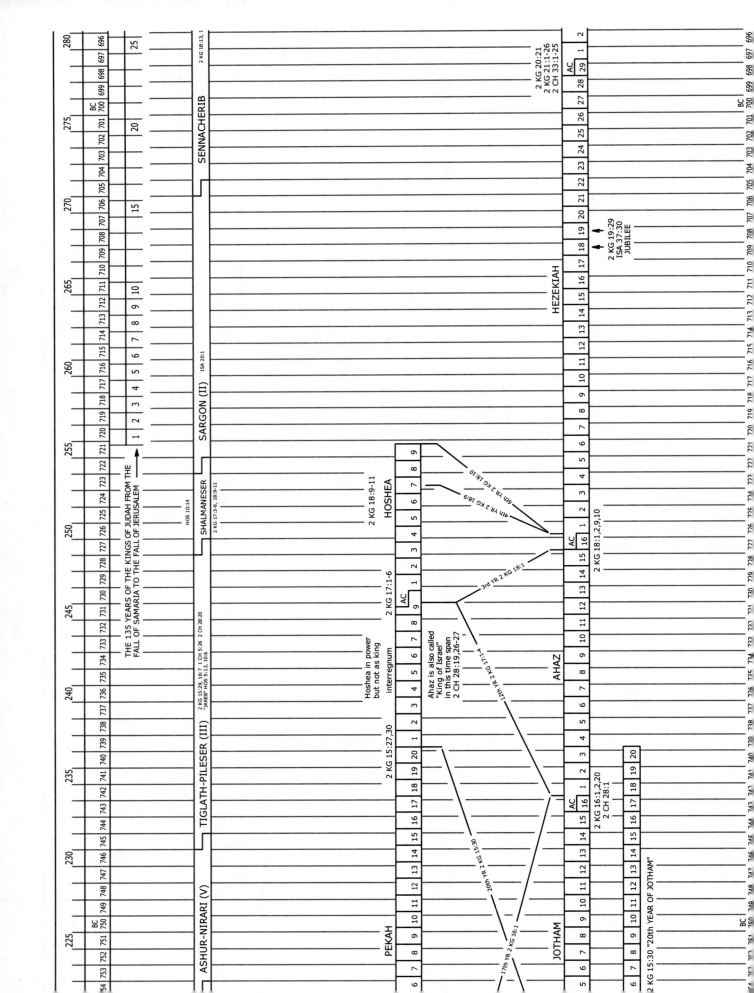

ASHUR-BANIPAL

ESAR-HADDON

AMON

MANASSEH

2 KG 21:18,19
2 CH 34:21

ADAD-GUPPI, THE MOTHER OF NABONIDUS KING OF BABYLON, RELATES ON A TOMB INSCRIPTION TAKEN FROM TWO STELE FOUND IN HARAN THAT SHE WAS BORN IN THE 20TH YEAR OF ASHURBANIPAL, KING OF ASSYRIA (650 BC). SHE FURTHER RECORDS THAT FROM HER BIRTH INTO THE FOURTH YEAR OF NERIGLISSAR WAS A SPAN OF 95 YEARS (650-556=95 YRS NUMBERED INCLUSIVELY). SHE RELATES THAT THE CITY OF HARAN FELL IN THE 16TH YEAR OF NABOPOLASSAR AND GIVES DATA ASSOCIATING HIS 1ST YEAR WITH ASHUR-ETIL-ILANI'S THIRD. SHE LIVED 104 YEARS AND DIED IN THE 9TH YR OF NABONIDUS.

AS ALL THE REIGNS OF THE NEO-BABYLONIAN KINGS FROM NABOPOLASSAR TO THE 9TH YEAR OF NABONIDUS ARE GIVEN ON THIS ROYAL INSCRIPTION, IT SERVES AS AN EYEWITNESS ACCOUNT FROM ONE INTIMATELY CONNECTED TO ALL THESE KINGS. SHE COMPLETELY CONFIRMS PTOLEMY'S ROYAL CANON AS TO THEIR LENGTHS OF REIGN.

"ASNAPPAR? EZR 4:10   SEE ANSTEY p. 219

KG 18:13, 19:16, 20, 36, 37   2 CH 32:1-2, 9-10, 22   ISA 36:1, 37:17, 21, 37-38

2 KG 19:37   EZR 4:2

PTOLEMY GIVES ESAR-HADDON 13 YRS BUT 3 TIMES THE "BABYLONIAN CHRONICLES" RECORDS 12.

:21
1-26
1-25

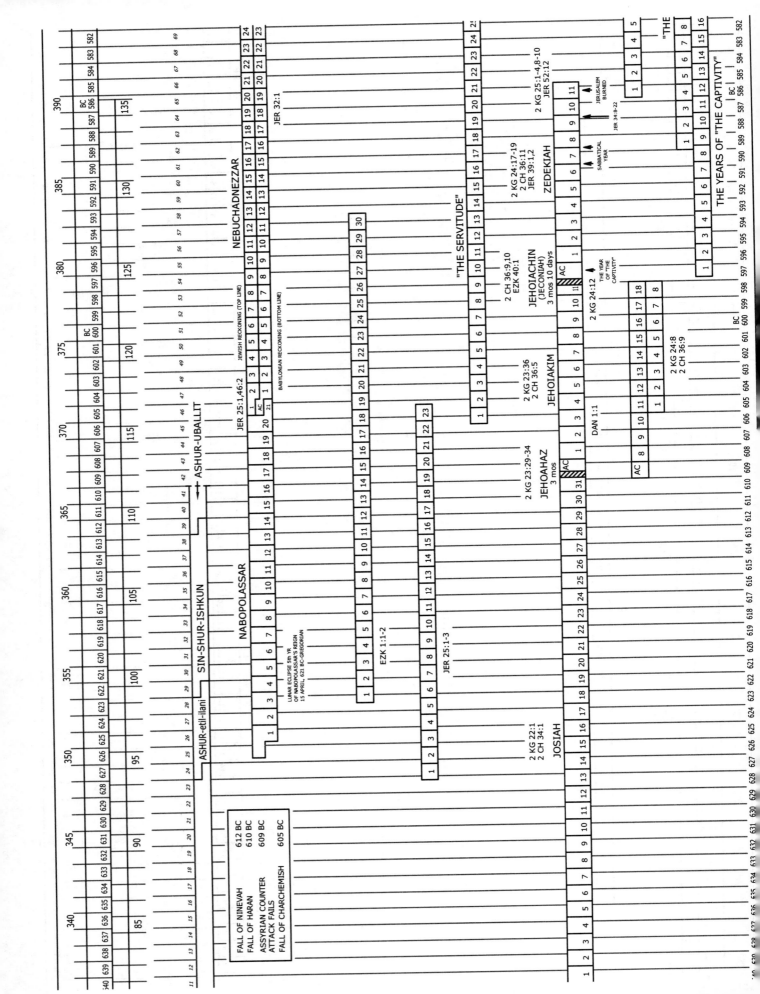

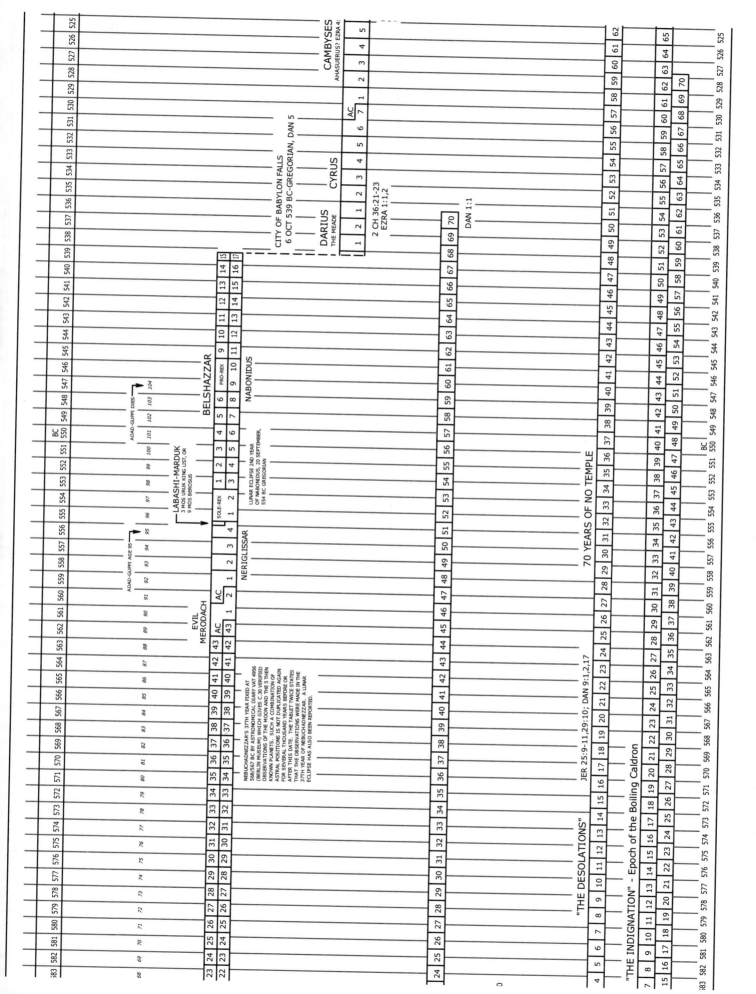

PRO-REX

6	5	4	3	2	1
18	17	16	15	14	13

12	11	10	9	8	7	6	5	4	3	2	1

XERXES I

AC
| 36 | 35 | 34 | 33 | 32 | 31 | 30 | 29 | 28 | 27 | 26 | 25 | 24 | 23 | 22 | 21 | 20 | 19 | 18 | 17 | 16 | 15 | 14 | 13 | 12 | 11 | 10 | 9 | 8 | 7 | 6 | 5 | 4 | 3 | 2 | 1 |

BC 500

DARIUS I (HYSTASPIS)

LUNAR ECLIPSE 31st YR
OF DARIUS' REIGN
491 BC-GREGORIAN

LUNAR ECLIPSE 20th YR
OF DARIUS' REIGN
502 BC-GREGORIAN

EZRA 6:7,14,15

DESOLATIONS END WITH COMPLETION OF 2ND TEMPLE
IN THE 6TH YEAR OF DARIUS, EZRA 6:15; ZECH 7:5 (CP. VS 1)

ALTHOUGH THE GREEKS AND MOSLEMS DESTROYED NEARLY ALL PERSIAN RECORDS,
THAT THE PERSIAN YEAR BEGAN C.OCTOBER 1. NEHEMIAH WAS AT THE PERSIAN PAL
SUSA) IN THE MONTH OF CHISLEU (KISLEV – THE HEBREW 9TH MONTH, NOVEMBER/
20TH YEAR OF ARTAXERXES. THE FOLLOWING NISAN (SPRING) WAS STILL IN THE S
THAT PERSIAN MONARCH. THEREFORE, HE IS REFERENCING BY FALL RECKONING BI
NISAN FOLLOWING CHISLEU OF THE 20TH YEAR WOULD HAVE BEEN IN THE 21ST YEAR
DOUBLE-DATED PAPYRI WRITTEN BY THE JEWS OF ELEPHANTINE DURING THE SAME
[S.H. HORN AND L.W. WOOD], THE FIFTH-CENTURY JEWISH CALENDAR AT ELEPHANT
NEAR EASTERN STUDIES, 13 (JAN., 1954), PP. 4, 20. ELEPHANTINE IS AN ISLAND AT
OF THE NILE OPPOSITE ASWAN.). ON THE PAPYRI, THE REIGNS OF THE PERSIAN KIN
THE TISHRI-TO-TISHRI (FALL) METHOD. NEVERTHELESS, IT WAS DECIDED TO DISPL
JANUARY-TO-JANUARY BC YEARS ON CHARTS 5 & 5C BECAUSE: (1) THIS DOES NOT
CHRONOLOGY OF SCRIPTURE, AND (2) NEARLY ALL HISTORY BOOKS AND REFERENCI
THEM IN THIS MANNER.

PSEUDO-SMERDIS
(GAUMATA) 7 MOS
ARTAXERXES? EZRA 4:7

	7 MOS
	8

LUNAR ECLIPSE 7th YR
OF CAMBYSES' REIGN
523 BC-GREGORIAN

THE EPOCH OF THE BOILING CALDRON EZK 24:1-14 BEGINS THE 70 YRS
OF GODS "INDIGNATION". THIS BEGAN WHEN ZEDEKIAH REBELLED. THE FINAL
SIEGE BEGAN 1 YR TO THE DAY FROM THIS PROPHESY AND LASTED c.18 MOS
i.e.: FROM 10-10-9th YR OF ZEDEKIAH JER 52:4, 39:1 AND 2 KG 25:1

THE EPOCH ENDED ON THE 24th DAY 9th MO 2nd YR DARIUS,
HAG 2:10, 15, 18-20 24th DAY 11th MO 2nd YR DARIUS, ZECH 1:7,12
"INDIGNATION" IS OVER.

61	62	63	64	65	66	67	68	69	70

54	65	66	67	68	69	70

BYSES

S? EZRA 4:6

5	6	7
4		

468 469 470 471 472 473 474 475 476 477 478 479 480 481 482 483 484 485 486 487 488 489 490 491 492 493 494 495 496 497 498 499 500 501 502 503 504 505 506 507 508 509 510 511 512 513 514 515 516 517 518 519 520 521 522 523 524 525 526

BC

DARIUS II (NOTHUS)

XERXES II (45 DAYS)
(SOGDIANUS, 6 MOS 15 DAYS)

483 YEARS TO
DEATH OF MESSIAH
DAN 9:24-27

ARTAXERXES
(LONGIMANUS)

SOLE-REX

BC

Top row (BC years): 469 468 467 466 465 464 463 462 461 460 459 458 457 456 455 454 453 452 451 450 449 448 447 446 445 444 443 442 441 440 439 438 437 436 435 434 433 432 431 430 429 428 427 426 425 424 423 422 421 420 419 418 417 416 415 414 413 412 411

Darius II regnal years: 1 2 3 4 5 6 7 8 9 10 11 12 13

Artaxerxes (Longimanus) regnal years:
5 6 7 8 9 10 11 12 13 14 15 16 17 18 19 20 21 22 23 24 25 26 27 28 29 30 31 32 33 34 35 36 37 38 39 40 41 42 43 44 45 46 47 48 49 50
17 18 19 20 AC 21 1 2 3 4 5 6 7 8 9 10 11 12 13 14 15 16 17 18 19 20 21 22 23 24 25 26 27 28 29 30 31 32 33 34 35 36 37 38 39 40 41

Bottom row (BC years): 469 468 467 466 465 464 463 462 461 460 459 458 457 456 455 454 453 452 451 450 449 448 447 446 445 444 443 442 441 440 439 438 437 436 435 434 433 432 431 430 429 428 427 426 425 424 423 422 421 420 419 418 417 416 415 414 413 412 411

THE 390 YEARS (

ARTAXERXES II (MNEMON)

AF

AC

(HUS)

BC	354	355	356	357	358	359	360	361	362	363	364	365	366	367	368	369	370	371	372	373	374	375	376	377	378	379	380	381	382	383	384	385	386	387	388	389	390	391	392	393	394	395	396	397	398	399	400	401	402	403	404	405	406	407	408	409	410	411	412
reign	5	4	3	2	1	46	45	44	43	42	41	40	39	38	37	36	35	34	33	32	31	30	29	28	27	26	25	24	23	22	21	20	19	18	17	16	15	14	13	12	11	10	9	8	7	6	5	4	3	2	1	19	18	17	16	15	14	13	2

THE TIME SPAN FROM DIVISION OF THE KINGDOM, TO THE TERMINATION OF THE KINGDOM OF JUDAH AT THE HAND OF NEBUCHADNEZZAR IN BC 586 WAS FIRST DETERMINED BY ADDING THE REIGNS OF JUDAH'S MONARCHS. THIS YIELDED 394 YEARS 6 MONTHS AND 10 DAYS. THIS MUST BE ADDED THE YEAR DESIGNATED AS "THE CAPTIVITY" (SEE CHART 5 OR 5C A 597). THE TOTAL NOW STANDS AT 395 YEARS 6 MONTHS AND 10 DAYS.

2 KI.8:16 STATES: "AND IN THE FIFTH YEAR OF JORAM THE SON OF AHAB KING OF ISRAEL, JEHOSHAPHAT BEING THEN KING OF JUDAH, JEHORAM THE SON OF JEHOSHAPHAT KING OF JUDAH BEGAN TO REIGN". THUS, JEHORAM ASCENDED THE THRONE WHILE JEHOSHAPHAT STILL REIGNING. 2 KI.3:1, 8:16, 8:25, & 9:29 SHOW THIS CO-REGENCY AS 4 YEARS (CHAR 8, 5C). SUBTRACTING THIS OVERLAP: 395 YRS. 6 MOS. 10 DAYS - 4 YRS. = 391 YRS. 6 MO 10 DAYS.

JEHORAM, ATHALIAH, & AHAZIAH ALL LAID CLAIM TO THE THRONE IN 886 BC (CHARTS 5 & THUS, THE OFFICIAL YEARS (3) BECOME 2 YEARS MORE THAN THE ACTUAL 1 YEAR SPAN. 3 YRS. 6 MOS. 10 DAYS - 2 YRS. YIELDS 389 YRS. 6 MOS. 10 DAYS, THE TRUE INTERVAL OF T DISRUPTED MONARCHY, AND THIS PLACES US "IN THE 390TH YEAR"!

THIS 390 YEAR TIME SPAN IS FIRST CONFIRMED BY EZEKIEL 4:4-8 WHERE THE PROPHET W TOLD TO LIE ON HIS SIDE EACH DAY FOR 390 DAYS IN SOLEMN PROTESTATION AGAINST T "INIQUITY" OF ISRAEL AS A SIGN UNTO THE PEOPLE SO THEY WOULD KNOW THAT THE FAL JERUSALEM WAS THE LORD'S WORK. EACH DAY REPRESENTED A YEAR ISRAEL HAD LIVED OPEN SIN AGAINST GOD UNTIL WHICH TIME HE WAS TO BRING JUDGMENT (OF COURSE, TH IMMEDIATE CONTEXT OF EZE 4:4-8 WAS THAT AFTER NEBUCHADNEZZAR ROUTED THE EGYPTIAN ARMY WHICH HAD COME TO AID ZEDEKIAH, HE WOULD RETURN AND RE-INITIAT THE SIEGE OF JERUSALEM 390 DAYS BEFORE THE CITY FELL (EQUALS THE MIDDLE OF THE THIRD MONTH OF ZEDEKIAH'S TENTH YEAR).), THIS PROPHECY WAS GIVEN JUST BEFORE 5 BC (EZK.1:1-2, CP. 8:1, SEE CHART 5 & 5C). THIS IS FURTHER CONFIRMED BY EZEKIEL 35:

"BECAUSE THOU (EDOM, CP. PSA.137:7) HAST HAD A PERPETUAL HATRED, AND HAST SHED THE BLOOD OF THE CHILDREN OF ISRAEL, BY THE FORCE OF THE SWORD IN THE TIME OF THEIR CALAMITY, IN THE TIME THAT THEIR INIQUITY HAD AN END".

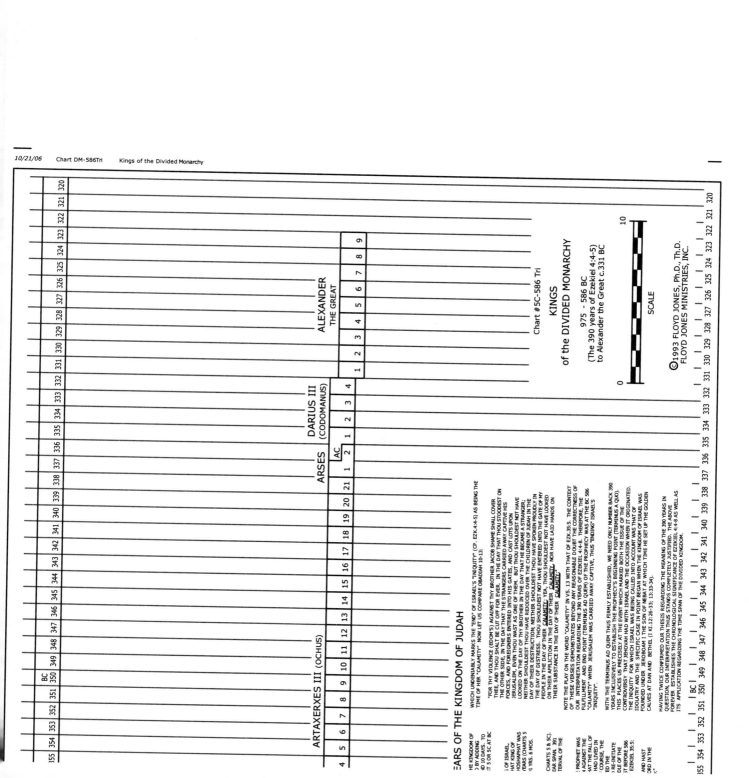

YEARS OF THE KINGDOM OF JUDAH

ARTAXERXES III (OCHUS)

ARSES

DARIUS III (CODOMANUS)

ALEXANDER THE GREAT

Chart #5C-586 Tri

KINGS
of the DIVIDED MONARCHY

975 - 586 BC

(The 390 years of Ezekiel 4:4-5)
to Alexander the Great c.331 BC

SCALE

©1993 FLOYD JONES, Ph.D., Th.D.
FLOYD JONES MINISTRIES, INC.

WHICH UNDENIABLY MARKS THE "END" OF ISRAEL'S "INIQUITY" (CP. EZK.4:4-5) AS BEING THE TIME OF HER "CALAMITY." NOW LET US COMPARE OBADIAH 10-13:

"FOR THY VIOLENCE (EDOM'S) AGAINST THY BROTHER JACOB SHAME SHALL COVER THEE, AND THOU SHALT BE CUT OFF FOR EVER. IN THE DAY THAT THOU STOODEST ON THE OTHER SIDE, IN THE DAY THAT THE STRANGERS CARRIED AWAY CAPTIVE HIS FORCES, AND FOREIGNERS ENTERED INTO HIS GATES, AND CAST LOTS UPON JERUSALEM, EVEN THOU WAST AS ONE OF THEM. BUT THOU SHOULDEST NOT HAVE LOOKED ON THE DAY OF THY BROTHER IN THE DAY THAT HE BECAME A STRANGER; NEITHER SHOULDEST THOU HAVE REJOICED OVER THE CHILDREN OF JUDAH IN THE DAY OF THEIR DESTRUCTION; NEITHER SHOULDEST THOU HAVE SPOKEN PROUDLY IN THE DAY OF DISTRESS. THOU SHOULDEST NOT HAVE ENTERED INTO THE GATE OF MY PEOPLE IN THE DAY OF THEIR CALAMITY; YEA, THOU SHOULDEST NOT HAVE LOOKED ON THEIR AFFLICTION IN THE DAY OF THEIR CALAMITY, NOR HAVE LAID HANDS ON THEIR SUBSTANCE IN THE DAY OF THEIR CALAMITY."

NOTE THE PLAY ON THE WORD "CALAMITY" IN VS. 13 WITH THAT OF EZK.35:5. THE CONTEXT OF THESE VERSES DEMONSTRATES BEYOND ANY REASONABLE DOUBT THE CORRECTNESS OF OUR INTERPRETATION REGARDING THE 390 YEARS OF EZEKIEL 4:4-8. THEREFORE, THE FULFILLMENT AND END POINT (TERMINUS AD QUEM) OF THE PROPHECY WAS AT THE BC 586 "CALAMITY" WHEN JERUSALEM WAS CARRIED AWAY CAPTIVE, THUS "ENDING" ISRAEL'S "INIQUITY".

WITH THE TERMINUS AD QUEM THUS FIRMLY ESTABLISHED, WE NEED ONLY NUMBER BACK 390 YEARS INCLUSIVELY TO ESTABLISH THE PROPHECY'S BEGINNING POINT (TERMINUS A QUO). THIS PLACES US PRECISELY AT THE EVENT WHICH MARKED BOTH THE ISSUE OF THE CONTROVERSY THAT JEHOVAH HAD WITH ISRAEL AND THE OCCASION WHEN IT ORIGINATED. THE INIQUITY FOR WHICH ISRAEL WAS BEING CALLED INTO ACCOUNT WAS THAT OF IDOLATRY AND THE SPECIFIC CASE IN POINT BEGAN WHEN THE KINGDOM OF ISRAEL WAS FOUNDED UNDER JEROBOAM I THE SON OF NEBAT AT WHICH TIME HE SET UP THE GOLDEN CALVES AT DAN AND BETHEL (1 KI.12:26-33; 13:33-34).

HAVING TWICE CONFIRMED OUR THESIS REGARDING THE MEANING OF THE 390 YEARS IN QUESTION, OUR INTERPRETATION THUS STANDS COMPLETELY JUSTIFIED. THE ABOVE FOREVER ESTABLISHES THE CHRONOLOGICAL SIGNIFICANCE OF EZEKIEL 4:4-8 AS WELL AS ITS APPLICATION REGARDING THE TIME SPAN OF THE DIVIDED KINGDOM.